Neurosymbolic AI

IEEE Press

445 Hoes Lane

Piscataway, NJ 08854

Neurosymbolic AI

Foundations and Applications

Edited by

Alvaro Velasquez
University of Colorado Boulder

Houbing Herbert Song
University of Maryland Baltimore

Pradeep Ravikumar
Carnegie Mellon University

S. Shankar Sastry
University of California Berkeley

Sandeep Neema
Vanderbilt University

IEEE*Press*
WILEY

Published by John Wiley & Sons, Inc., Hoboken, New Jersey.

Library of Congress Cataloging-in-Publication Data
Names: Velasquez, Alvaro (Of University of Colorado Boulder) editor | Sastry, Shankar editor | Ravikumar, Pradeep editor | Song, Houbing Herbert editor | Neema, Sandeep K. editor
Title: Neurosymbolic AI : foundations and applications / edited by Alvaro Velasquez, Shankar Sastry, Pradeep Ravikumar, Houbing Herbert Song, Sandeep Neema.
Description: Piscataway, NJ : IEEE Press : Wiley, [2026] | Includes bibliographical references.
Identifiers: LCCN 2025054246 | ISBN 9781394302376 hardback | ISBN 9781394302390 adobe pdf | ISBN 9781394302383 epub | ISBN 9781394302406 ebook
Subjects: LCSH: Artificial intelligence | Logic, Symbolic and mathematical–Data processing | Neural networks (Computer science)
Classification: LCC Q335 .N478 2026
LC record available at https://lccn.loc.gov/2025054246

Cover Design: Carlos A. Guzman Medina
Cover Image: © pongtap/stock.adobe.com (Generated with AI) - modified by Carlos A. Guzman Medina

To my parents, without whose sacrifice none of this would be possible.

Contents

List of Contributors

Kareem Ahmed
Department of Computer Science
University of California
Irvine, CA
USA

Ozgün Babur
University of Massachusetts Boston
Boston, MA
USA

Somil Bansal
Department of Aeronautics and Astronautics
Stanford University
Stanford, CA
USA

Neel P. Bhatt
Oden Institute of Computational Sciences and Engineering
The University of Texas at Austin
Austin, TX
USA

Nithin Chalapathi
EECS and Chemical Engineering
University of California
Berkeley, CA
USA

Kai-Wei Chang
Department of Computer Science
University of California
Los Angeles, CA
USA

Swarat Chaudhuri
Department of Computer Science
The University of Texas at Austin
Austin, TX
USA

Lekai Chen
Department of Computer Science
University of Colorado Boulder
Boulder, CO
USA

Yiran Chen
Duke University
Durham, NC
USA

Patrick Cooper
Department of Computer Science
University of Colorado Boulder
Boulder, CO
USA

Emek Demir
Oregon Health & Science University
Portland, OR
USA

Yiheng Du
EECS and Chemical Engineering
University of California
Berkeley, CA
USA

Abhishek Dubey
Institute for Software-Integrated Systems
Vanderbilt University
Nashville, TN
USA

Jaime F. Fisac
Department of Electrical and Computer Engineering
Princeton University
Princeton, NJ
USA

Artur d'Avila Garcez
Department of Computer Science
City St George's, University of London
London
UK

Manas Gaur
Department of Computer Science
University of Maryland, Baltimore Country (UMBC)
Baltimore, MD
USA

Gus Hahn-Powell
University of Arizona
Tucson, AZ
USA

Gwendolen Herongrove
RiverStone Resources
Manchester, NH
USA

X. Sharon Hu
University of Nortre Dame
Notre Dame, IN
USA

Susmit Jha
Neuro-Symbolic Computing and Intelligence
Information and Computing Sciences Division
SRI International
Menlo Park, CA
USA

Taylor T. Johnson
Institute for Software-Integrated Systems
Vanderbilt University
Nashville, TN
USA

Gabor Karsai
Institute for Software-Integrated Systems
Vanderbilt University
Nashville, TN
USA

Ramneet Kaur
Neuro-Symbolic Computing and Intelligence
Information and Computing Sciences Division
SRI International
Menlo Park, CA
USA

Chris H. Kim
University of Minnesota
Minneapolis, MN
USA

Xenofon Koutsoukos
Institute for Software-Integrated Systems
Vanderbilt University
Nashville, TN
USA

Aditi S. Krishnapriyan
EECS and Chemical Engineering
University of California
Berkeley, CA
USA

Hai "Helen" Li
Duke University
Durham, NC
USA

Diego Manzanas Lopez
Institute for Software-Integrated Systems
Vanderbilt University
Nashville, TN
USA

Baiting Luo
Institute for Software-Integrated Systems
Vanderbilt University
Nashville, TN
USA

Rajit Manohar
Yale University
New Haven, CT
USA

Miklos Maroti
Bolyai Institute
University of Szeged
Szeged
Hungary

Clayton T. Morrison
University of Arizona
Tucson, AZ
USA

Edjard Mota
Instituto de Computação,
Universidade Federal do Amazonas
Manaus
Brazil

Ayan Mukhopadhyay
Institute for Software-Integrated Systems
Vanderbilt University
Nashville, TN
USA

Sriraam Natarajan
Computer Science Department
The University of Texas at Dallas
Richardson, TX
USA

Enrique Noriega-Atala
University of Arizona
Tucson, AZ
USA

Ankur Padia
Department of Computer Science
University of Maryland
Baltimore, MD
USA

Miroslav Pajic
Duke University
Durham, NC
USA

Srinivasan Parthasarathy
Department of Computer Science
Ohio State University
Columbus, OH
USA

Nicholas Potteiger
Institute for Software-Integrated Systems
Vanderbilt University
Nashville, TN
USA

Sanjeev Raja
EECS and Chemical Engineering
University of California
Berkeley, CA
USA

Pradeep Ravikumar
Machine Learning Department
Carnegie Mellon University
Pittsburgh, PA
USA

Anirban Roy
Neuro-Symbolic Computing and Intelligence
Information and Computing Sciences Division
SRI International
Menlo Park, CA
USA

Yash Saxena
Department of Computer Science
University of Maryland
Baltimore, MD
USA

Serena Serbinowska
Institute for Software-Integrated Systems
Vanderbilt University
Nashville, TN
USA

Sahil Sidheekh
Computer Science Department
The University of Texas at Dallas
Richardson, TX
USA

Chandler Squires
Machine Learning Department
Carnegie Mellon University
Pittsburgh, PA
USA

Daniel Stojcsics
Institute for Software-Integrated Systems
Vanderbilt University
Nashville, TN
USA

Mihai Surdeanu
University of Arizona
Tucson, AZ
USA

Deepa Tilwani
Department of Computer Science
AI Institute
University of South Carolina
Columbia, SC
USA

Ufuk Topcu
Oden Institute of Computational Sciences and Engineering
The University of Texas at Austin
Austin, TX
USA

Son Tran
School of Information Technology
Deakin University
Melbourne
Victoria
Australia

Robert Vacareanu
University of Arizona
Tucson, AZ
USA

Marco A. Valenzuela-Escárcega
Lex Machina
Menlo Park, CA
USA

Guy Van den Broeck
Department of Computer Science
University of California
Los Angeles, CA
USA

Burak Varıcı
Machine Learning Department
Carnegie Mellon University
Pittsburgh, PA
USA

Alvaro Velasquez
Department of Computer Science
University of Colorado Boulder
Boulder, CO
USA

Zhangyang Wang
Oden Institute of Computational Sciences and Engineering
The University of Texas at Austin
Austin, TX
USA

Lucas White
Department of Computer Science
University of Colorado Boulder
Boulder, CO
USA

Xiaoxuan Yang
University of Virginia
Charlottesville, VA
USA

Shimeng Yu
Georgia Institute of Technology
Atlanta, GA
USA

Yunuo Zhang
Institute for Software-Integrated Systems
Vanderbilt University
Nashville, TN
USA

Antony Zhao
Department of Computer Science
University of Colorado Boulder
Boulder, CO
USA

About the Authors

Professor Alvaro Velasquez is affiliated with the University of Colorado Boulder and serves as CEO for his startup Neurosymbolic Intelligence Inc. His research focus is on developing data-efficient and generalizable foundation models through neurosymbolic AI. In his former position as program manager at the Defense Advanced Research Projects Agency (DARPA), Alvaro secured and led $200 million in programs on efficient neurosymbolic AI, robust autonomy, and foundation models for creative scientific discovery. He also served as the technical lead for AI at the Air Force Research Laboratory (AFRL). Alvaro's research has received best paper awards from the flagship conference of the Association for the Advancement of Artificial Intelligence (AAAI), the IEEE Computational Intelligence Society (CIS), and AFRL. He has published over 100 peer-reviewed papers, three patents, and his work has been featured in *Forbes* and *Washington Times*. Alvaro also serves as co-founder of the International Neuro-symbolic Systems (NeuS) conference and associate editor for the *IEEE Transactions on AI Journal*.

Houbing Herbert Song is a Professor in the Department of Information Systems and the Department of Computer Science and Electrical Engineering at the University of Maryland, Baltimore County, where he directs the Security and Optimization for Networked Globe Laboratory (SONG Lab). He is an IEEE Fellow, an ACM Distinguished Scientist, and serves as the Co-Editor-in-Chief (Co-EiC) of the *IEEE Transactions on Industrial Informatics*. He is the Founding Chair of the ACM Emerging Interest Group on Trustworthy and Responsible Systems (EIGTRUST), and the IEEE IoT Technical Community Trustworthy Internet of Things (TRUST-IoT) Working Group. He is an ACM Distinguished Speaker and a Distinguished Lecturer/Speaker across five IEEE societies (Computer Society, ComSoc, ITSS, VTS, Systems Council). His research interests include neurosymbolic AI, anomaly detection, artificial intelligence of things, autonomous and cyber-physical systems. He received his PhD degree in electrical engineering from the

University of Virginia in 2012. He has been named a Highly Cited Researcher by Clarivate since 2021. He received IEEE 2021 Harry Rowe Mimno Award, 2024 IEEE Computational Intelligence Society (CIS) Publication Spotlight, and 10+ Best Paper Awards from major international conferences. His other books include *AI for Cybersecurity: Research and Practice, Tiny Machine Learning: Design Principles and Applications, Security and Privacy in Cyber-Physical Systems: Foundations and Applications, and Smart Cities: Foundations, Principles, and Applications.*

Dr. Sandeep Neema is the Director of the Institute for Software Integrated Systems, Vanderbilt University and a Professor at the Department of Computer Science, Vanderbilt University. He served as a program manager at the Information Innovation Office of DARPA from 2016 to 2022, where he developed multiple large scale research programs at the intersection of artificial intelligence/machine learning and cyber physical systems. During this time Dr. Neema received the prestigious *Superior Public Service Medal* for his contributions to artificial intelligence and cyber physical systems. Dr. Neema's research portfolio includes cyber physical systems, artificial intelligence, model-based design methodologies, and secure distributed real-time embedded systems. He led numerous research projects in these areas funded by DARPA and NSF and published more than 150 peer-reviewed articles conference, journal publications, and book chapters.

Pradeep Ravikumar is a Professor in the Machine Learning Department, School of Computer Science at Carnegie Mellon University. He is a Sloan Fellow, a Siebel Scholar, a recipient of the NSF CAREER Award, and a co-editor-chief of *Journal of Machine Learning Research*. He was previously the Associate Editor-in-Chief for *IEEE Transactions on Pattern Analysis and Machine Intelligence* (TPAMI). His recent research interests are in neurosymbolic AI, combining statistical machine learning, and symbolic and causal learning.

S. Shankar Sastry is a professor at the University of California at Berkeley. He is also the former director of CITRIS (Center for Information Technology in the Interests of Society), an interdisciplinary center spanning UC Berkeley, Davis, Merced, and Santa Cruz. He served as Chairman, Department of Electrical Engineering and Computer Sciences, University of California, Berkeley and as Director of the Information Technology Office at DARPA. Dr. Sastry received his PhD degree in 1981 from University of California, Berkeley. He was on the faculty of MIT as Assistant Professor from 1980 to 82 and Harvard University as a chaired Gordon McKay professor in 1994. Dr. Sastry was elected into the National Academy of Engineering in 2001 "for pioneering contributions to the design of hybrid and embedded systems." He has supervised over 50 doctoral students to completion and over 50 MS students. His students now occupy leadership roles in several locations and on the faculties of many major universities in the United States and abroad.

Part I

Fundamentals

1

What Is Neurosymbolic AI? An Overview and Frontier Problems

Alvaro Velasquez, Lucas White, Patrick Cooper, Antony Zhao, and Lekai Chen*

Department of Computer Science, University of Colorado Boulder, Boulder, Colorado, USA

Corresponding Author: alvaro.velasquez@colorado.edu

1.1 Introduction

When the Turing test was originally proposed in 1950, it resulted from the admission that the question of whether machines can think was ill-posed, as the act of thinking lacked a formal definition. Instead, Turing proposed a so-called imitation game as a proxy for truly capable machines, whereby a human judge must determine whether the entity they are communicating with via text is human or not [1]. This Turing test has captured the imagination of computer scientists, statisticians, and mainstream audiences alike, with its achievement becoming a common trope in science fiction that acts as a precursor to dystopian or utopian realities. There is now a strong argument to be made that the advent of modern AI as characterized by large foundation models has passed the Turing test [2]. This turning point for the field has materialized in an abundance of applications, ranging from coding assistants [3] to scientific discovery [4]. Consequently, some of the classical challenges in AI have become more prominent than ever before. These challenges include the large amounts of data required to train AI models, the opacity of their responses due to their black-box nature, and their limited generalization in domains outside of classical vision and natural language problems.

In response to the foregoing, the field of neurosymbolic AI has received renewed interest. Whereas classical symbolic methods are performant for prescriptive problems in well-modeled environments, they are not capable of handling noise and

Neurosymbolic AI: Foundations and Applications, First Edition. Edited by Alvaro Velasquez et al.

generalizing to unknown environments. On the other hand, modern deep learning architectures leverage neural networks to achieve some level of generalization to domains that match the training distribution of data, but they lack the interpretability and verifiability of the symbolic methods. It is reasonable, then, to seek the integration of these two modalities of computation to achieve the best of both worlds. Said integration is not a new idea by any means and was explored by the symbolic and connectionist communities in the 1980s [5]. However, the landscape of challenges and opportunities facing this integration have changed significantly in that time.

The study of these dual processes, which we term neural and symbolic in the AI community, has roots in psychology and cognitive science, where two distinct modes of learning and decision-making are proposed. These modes are often referred to as subsymbolic vs. symbolic, implicit vs. explicit, parallel vs. sequential, or System 1 vs. System 2 [6]. The first mode – subsymbolic, implicit, and parallel – involves slow, trial-and-error learning. However, once skills are internalized, execution becomes rapid and automatic, integrating perception and motor responses seamlessly. The second mode – symbolic, explicit, and sequential – enables faster learning through deliberate reasoning, though its application tends to be slower and requires more effort. Thus, our cognitive systems face challenges similar to those encountered by AI. Developing expertise requires extensive time and experience, yet relying solely on trial-and-error is often inefficient and impractical. As an example, consider the problem of learning how to ride a bicycle, which entails learning and mastering a wide range of traffic rules, maneuvers, and specialized perceptual and sensorimotor skills. In generalizing from the biking experience obtained in one city, drivers must often adapt to new environments, such as rough terrain and different cities with unfamiliar traffic laws. Notably, that kind of adaptation to new environments does not require relearning from scratch. From an AI perspective, this represents a complex learning problem involving high-dimensional input, limited training data, delayed or sparse feedback, unpredictable distribution shifts, and the need for adaptation from few demonstrations.

1.2 Neurosymbolic Artificial Intelligence

The malleability of terms like *AI* preclude an all-encompassing definition of neurosymbolic AI, but broadly, we can define neurosymbolic AI as the integration of explicit symbolic representations, like logic, knowledge graphs, and physical dynamics, with neural networks, which are characterized by their ability to learn implicit representations of data in the form of features that can be extrapolated from during test time in order to generalize to new domains that share those features. The symbolic representations can be continuous or discrete; they may be given as domain knowledge by an expert; or they may be extracted from data, from neural network parameters, or from inference results. We briefly survey various directions of how neural networks can be integrated into symbolic methods and vice versa.

1.2.1 Explicit to Implicit: From Symbolic Representations to Neural Networks

A prominent example of the integration of symbolic human-derived knowledge and neural networks is the field of physics-informed machine learning. Here, methods such as physics-informed neural networks (PINNs), physics-informed neural operators (PINOs), and differentiable simulation incorporate prior knowledge encoded as partial differential equations (PDEs). These equations – thanks to their differentiability – can be directly embedded into model loss functions, enabling accurate predictions in complex domains like climate modeling and material deformation dynamics.

Beyond embedding PDEs into loss functions, another approach is to parameterize the terms in the equations with neural networks. This hybrid strategy maintains the structure provided by symbolic physics while allowing for flexibility and error correction through data-driven learning. An example is neural constitutive laws [7], which combine parameterized PDEs with differentiable simulations. These simulations define a visual loss function by comparing generated outputs with real video data, allowing the model to learn physical dynamics robustly. Remarkably, this neurosymbolic approach generalizes well to new geometries and boundary conditions, even when trained on minimal data – such as a single video sequence – something purely neural methods fail to achieve. Similarly, physics-informed enhancements to neural radiance fields (NeRFs), such as incorporating material point methods, ensure compliance with physical laws like conservation of momentum while also accelerating rendering speeds by up to two orders of magnitude over standard NeRF implementations [8]. A related line of work, known as generative physics engines, has similarly integrated physical models into generative AI to generate video and simulations that align with physical principles.

While the foregoing approaches integrate continuous symbolic representations, other growing trends in incorporating discrete symbolic representations are the use of differentiable logics that can be integrated into the loss functions of neural networks, e.g., differentiable Signal Temporal Logic (STL) for AI that satisfies STL traffic laws [9], as well as the use of knowledge graphs, which encode semantic relationships among entities. These graphs can improve model performance while reducing data requirements. For example, Amazon leverages a large-scale knowledge graph alongside its large language models (LLMs) in the COSMO system to extract knowledge from customer interactions. Recommendation systems can then exploit that extracted knowledge graph to better understand product relationships in terms of use cases or target audiences. Traditionally, such graphs were manually curated, but modern approaches like GraphRAG automate their extraction from large text corpora and incorporate them into retrieval-augmented generation (RAG) pipelines, enhancing text generation and improving the hallucination rates of models by incorporating retrieved relevant knowledge to the underlying query. Whereas the training of AI models typically entangles data, representation, and task into a single opaque model, knowledge graphs provide an avenue to modularize these components. This modularity means a graph built for one task can be reused across many others.

1.2.2 Implicit to Explicit: From Neural Networks to Symbolic Representations

Section 1.2.1 raises the question of how knowledge graphs and other discrete symbolic structures can be extracted from a given AI model. The problem of translating neural networks into some approximately equivalent symbolic representation is known as symbolic distillation [10]. Many of the methods in the field seek some form of quantized representation in the neural network, so that the activations of neurons are in some small discrete set that can be interpreted as the observation of semantically meaningful symbols in the deployed environment. For example, consider a learned neural network representation whose n weights or activations are binary. Each of these activations may denote the presence of, say, a red light or a pedestrian crossing the road. One can then interpret the 2^n possible quantized activation values as the variables in an explicit logical system, e.g., the activations in the preceding example could be used as input to a symbolic reasoning engine to determine whether an autonomous vehicle should or should not make a right turn. These logical variables resulting from the quantized neural network representation can also be used to extract symbolic graph representations, such as deterministic finite automata and knowledge graphs, using classical techniques like grammatical inference. See Carr et al. [11] for an example where an interpretable symbolic representation of the dynamics of a recurrent neural network is learned by introducing quantized layers during training. For additional information on popular forms of quantization and quantized models, we refer the reader to the literature on vector quantized variational auto-encoders (VQ-VAEs) [12, 13], vector quantized diffusion models [14], quantified bottleneck insertion [11, 15], and Quantized Low-Rank Adaptation (QLoRA) [16].

1.3 Frontiers Problems

At the time of this writing, there is an ongoing debate on whether agentic AI, or foundation models with the ability to use tools and take actions, will suffice to satisfy the vision of AI and its adoption across many sectors. Indeed, while it is broadly accepted that deep neural networks are not proficient at symbolic reasoning, a neural model can nevertheless be trained to invoke the relevant symbolic reasoning tools without having to actually learn what that reasoning entails. For example, a foundation model need not be capable of learning how to multiply arbitrarily large numbers if it can simply learn to invoke a calculator when such arithmetic problems arise in its prompting. Humans operate in a similar way when it comes to using tools, and a proper use of tools is seen as a hallmark of intelligence. In light of this debate, we present a trinity of open problems that we believe are particularly well-suited for neurosymbolic AI.

1.3.1 Neurosymbolic AI for Synthetic Biology

Artificial intelligence has recently begun reshaping how we understand and make predictions in the life sciences. Techniques that have propelled advances in natural language processing and computer vision are now being widely adapted across biotechnology, driving progress in areas such as drug development, therapeutic engineering, and the creation of novel biomaterials. Yet, a key limitation lies in the nature of the training data for these AI systems: it is heavily influenced by the inherent biases found in natural biology. Most biological datasets originate from observations and experiments within natural systems. As a result, AI models trained on this data tend to perform well only within the domain of biological sequences and structures that resemble those found in nature.

This presents a challenge when applying these models to synthetic biology, which can differ dramatically in sequence and structure from naturally occurring examples. The generalization capacity of current models often falls short when confronted with these synthetic variations. However, we propose that despite these differences, there exist deeper symbolic principles – such as the physical laws governing molecular interactions or formal language structures that define molecular representations – that are shared across both natural and synthetic biological systems.

To bridge this gap, we advocate for expanded research in neurosymbolic AI, which combines neural networks with symbolic reasoning. By embedding symbolic abstractions into biological AI models, we can better enable cross-domain generalization from natural to synthetic biology. This capability is crucial for advancing breakthroughs in several domains, including the design of therapeutics for previously untreatable conditions, the engineering of enzymes capable of degrading persistent plastics, the automation of cell fate manipulation, and the detection of engineered biological threats.

The dominant paradigm in bio-AI, which focuses on learning and generalizing from biological sequences and molecular structures, encounters major limitations when extended to synthetic biology. This is because synthetic biological systems often deviate considerably from natural ones in both sequence alignment (e.g., as measured by BLAST) and structural metrics (such as pLDDT scores or template matching), which are the primary signals most models are trained to optimize. Nonetheless, despite these surface-level differences, natural and synthetic biology are both governed by the same underlying physical laws and logical frameworks. These shared symbolic foundations – ranging from the principles of molecular motion to the rules of energy minimization – offer a more abstract, yet stable, basis for generalization. For example, tools from physics like stochastic differential equations in statistical mechanics [17], molecular dynamics force fields [18], and thermodynamic equilibrium models [19] provide rigorous, interpretable representations of molecular behavior. Recent studies are beginning to incorporate such symbolic elements into AI models, pointing to promising paths for more data-efficient and generalizable approaches across biological domains.

The role of logic in biological AI remains largely untapped, offering a compelling direction for the neurosymbolic AI field to explore. Many biological systems inherently exhibit symbolic and rule-based structures – for instance, the tree-like configurations of carbohydrate branching or the molecular graphs representing chemical compounds, both of which can be modeled using context-free languages [20, 21]. The context-free grammars provide a formal framework that defines valid molecular structures through well-defined logical rules, while the corresponding push-down automata can be used to evaluate whether a given molecular graph adheres to these constraints.

Similarly, RNA secondary structures can be described using more expressive formal systems. Their folding patterns correspond to context-sensitive languages [22], which can be characterized by context-sensitive grammars and recognized by linear bounded automata. Despite the biological richness of these symbolic representations, much of the bio-AI research to date has been narrowly focused on adapting LLMs and natural language methods to biological data. We argue that this focus overlooks a deeper, unifying structure: the formal languages that underpin both natural and synthetic molecular systems. Emphasizing these symbolic logics could provide a principled foundation for reasoning across a wider range of biological phenomena and is essential for pushing the boundaries of generalization in bio-AI.

The downstream benefits of integrating the foregoing symbolic representations into contemporary bio-AI models include improved correctness and generalization of the generated results, as well as improved data and training efficiency.

For improved correctness and generalization, the grammar of the formal language can be used in grammar-constrained decoding to enforce that the molecule generated by the algorithm satisfies the set of logical constraints in the grammar. For improved data and training efficiency, grammar-constrained decoding also significantly reduces the search space of generative models to outputs that satisfy the constraints or production rules of the grammar as opposed to broadly decoding the next most likely token. Such grammar-constrained decoding has been very effective in developing models for logically constrained text generation that are two orders of magnitude smaller than competing models while outperforming them by 30% based on human evaluation studies [23].

These logical formalisms can also be embedded directly into the training process of AI models, much like the approach taken by PINNs. In such models, physical laws – often expressed as PDEs – are integrated into the loss function to enforce scientific consistency, leading to dramatic improvements in data efficiency across various applications [24]. In a similar fashion, the automata structures derived from formal languages offer a powerful way to modularize learning. Instead of relying on a monolithic neural network, distinct neural components can be assigned to individual nodes within the automaton. These smaller, specialized models can then be composed to form the complete system. This decomposition not only improves interpretability and modularity but also reduces the overall data burden for training. Such architectures have already shown promise in reinforcement learning, particularly in complex game-playing scenarios, where they have enabled more scalable and efficient training [25].

With the progress made in physics-informed bio-AI and the growing use of AI to enhance molecular dynamics [26], ab initio simulations [27], and other computational models in biology [17], the stage is set for neurosymbolic bio-AI to take the next step. By incorporating both physical principles and formal logical representations into model architectures, we can unlock significant gains in data efficiency and cross-domain generalization. This fusion of symbolic reasoning with learning-based methods has the potential to drive breakthroughs in areas such as next-generation drug discovery, programmable cell engineering, and accurate prediction of molecular function, paving the way for a new era of biological innovation.

1.3.2 Neurosymbolic AI for Robust Autonomy

Consider the problem of transferring the autonomy learned in simulation to real-world environments under extreme data drifts, concept drifts, and distribution shifts. In this context, we use the term *autonomy* to refer to the systems that enable unaided operation in a target environment, including perception, planning, and control. We broadly call this space of problems abstract-to-real transfer to emphasize the fact that the underlying simulator is but a crude and noisy abstraction of a target environment that we do not know how to model very well. There is a need for such robustness to real-world uncertainty, and the lack thereof is a key reason why autonomy has been largely limited to domains where one can minimize the sim-to-real gap between simulation and reality, such as warehouse robotics and driving in geofenced locations, e.g., one cannot take an autonomous vehicle from San Francisco and operate it in New Delhi.

We argue that the main reason why the envisioned robust autonomy has not been possible is due to the conventional wisdom of employing a high-fidelity simulator and large datasets. This modus operandi results in two key limitations for the community. First, modeling and simulation using a high-fidelity simulator can lead to memorization or overfitting (e.g., agents can overfit to simulated physics) and also suffers from the problems of data drift, concept drift, and distribution shift, thereby reducing the efficacy of transferring autonomy across different environments and platforms. Second, the need for large datasets further precludes the adoption of conventional techniques in settings where such data is difficult to collect, such as underwater or space autonomy.

In contrast to the foregoing conventional wisdom, we argue that learning and transferring autonomy across diverse low-fidelity simulations in reference to their shared semantic abstractions (e.g., physics equations, knowledge graphs) will enable robust sim-to-real transfer. In particular, the diversity of simulations is conducive to improved adaptability to a variety of downstream platforms and domains, and the low-fidelity nature of the simulations will allow for greater speed of execution and data generation for faster learning and transfer. Moreover, the inherent imprecision and noise that characterize low-fidelity simulations can act as an impetus to greater generalization, analogous to the role that noise plays in improving the generalization of conventional machine learning models.

We begin by making the observation that even diverse and otherwise different-looking environments may nevertheless share some underlying semantics. Thus, even though there are large sim-to-real gaps, the semantic gap (or semantic similarity) in terms of some shared semantic abstraction is low. We believe that finding the level of abstraction where semantic similarity is high will provide the features along which robust generalization is possible. Indeed, classical assumptions on the effectiveness of machine learning rely on the fact that the underlying dataset shares some underlying features that can be learned and extrapolated from during test time. However, when transferring across different environments, e.g., from MiniGrid and Habitat to the real world, the conventional use of machine learning over raw visual and sensor data will fail, as the data generated by these environments are not likely to share features. We argue that more research is needed on how to extract and leverage the semantic abstractions that minimize the semantic gap between these environments as opposed to attempting to minimize the sim-to-real gap, which would be ineradicable in this case. These explicit symbolic representations can be used to define novel neurosymbolic AI model for robust autonomy by incorporating diverse environments and their shared semantic abstractions into the conventional pipeline of pretraining, fine-tuning, inferencing, and data generation.

1.3.3 Neurosymbolic AI for Creative Scientific Discovery

Imagine an AI whose capacity for creativity is so great that it can produce a body of work worthy of a Nobel Prize in chemistry, physiology, or medicine. One can view this type of transformational creativity as an extreme form of out-of-distribution generalization. Intuitively, the more creative the ideas are, the less likely they are to be reflected in the training distribution for the underlying AI. However, there is an additional challenge for such an AI in that transformational ideas often challenge or invalidate existing knowledge. A prominent example in biology was the discovery of intrinsically disordered proteins (IDPs), which are proteins that lack a fixed or ordered three-dimensional (3D) structure [28]. Imagine training a model for biology research before the discovery of IDPs, whereby the prevailing theory was that 3D structures of proteins must be fixed to accomplish their biological functions, and this conventional wisdom would make up the training data for the AI. It seems unlikely that such an AI would hypothesize the existence of IDPs given that such an output would disprove the existing domain knowledge in its training data.

The foregoing discussion raises the question of how a creative AI can become so effective at generalization that it can ultimately invalidate its own training data. Although it seems like a contradiction in terms, a related type of reasoning is often referred to as infeasible or non-monotonic reasoning, whereby reasoners can infer tentative conclusions and later retract them based on new knowledge. In contrast, most logics, including Linear Temporal Logic (LTL), have a monotonic entailment relation. This monotonicity implies that the addition of new information to the hypotheses does not prune the underlying set of conclusions. Therefore, the adoption of non-monotonic or defeasible reasoning is important for creativity, and it can be formalized in logic [29] and graphs [30], which provides an avenue for symbolic structures to be incorporated in the development of more creative neurosymbolic AI, which in turn would stand to benefit the enterprise of scientific discovery.

1.4 Conclusion

The recent successes in AI have materialized into a frenzy of applications in the public and private sectors that are set to augment or even revolutionize many industries. In light of this impact to society, it is more important than ever to consider how these AI systems can be made more trustworthy and efficient. Neurosymbolic AI has reemerged as a foundation for enabling these properties [31]. However, the integration of neural networks and symbolic computation introduces many technical challenges, some of which have been outlined in this chapter, and we believe a concerted research agenda will be necessary to realize the vision of neurosymbolic AI as means to achieve trustworthy and efficient models. To motivate this vision, we have proposed a trinity of frontier problems for the field in the hopes of spurring the community and driving impactful research outcomes that would be broadly useful to society.

References

1 Alan M Turing. *Computing Machinery and Intelligence*. Springer, 2009.

2 Melanie Mitchell. The turing test and our shifting conceptions of intelligence. *Science*, 385(6710):eadq9356, 2024.

3 Daye Nam, Andrew Macvean, Vincent Hellendoorn, Bogdan Vasilescu, and Brad Myers. Using an llm to help with code understanding. In *Proceedings of the IEEE/ACM 46th International Conference on Software Engineering*, pages 1–13, 2024.

4 Hanchen Wang, Tianfan Fu, Yuanqi Du, Wenhao Gao, Kexin Huang, Ziming Liu, Payal Chandak, Shengchao Liu, Peter Van Katwyk, Andreea Deac, et al. Scientific discovery in the age of artificial intelligence. *Nature*, 620(7972):47–60, 2023.

5 Fangju Wang. *Integrating Expert Vision Systems and Spatial Databases by Unifying Knowledge Representation Schemes: Development in Remote Sensing Image Analysis Expert Systems and Geographical Information Systems*. University of Waterloo, 1989.

6 Daniel Kahneman. *Thinking, Fast and Slow*. Farrar, Straus and Giroux, 2011.

7 Pingchuan Ma, Peter Yichen Chen, Bolei Deng, Joshua B Tenenbaum, Tao Du, Chuang Gan, and Wojciech Matusik. Learning neural constitutive laws from motion observations for generalizable pde dynamics. In *International Conference on Machine Learning*, pages 23279–23300, PMLR, 2023.

8 Xuan Li, Yi-Ling Qiao, Peter Yichen Chen, Krishna Murthy Jatavallabhula, Ming Lin, Chenfanfu Jiang, and Chuang Gan. Pac-nerf: Physics augmented continuum neural radiance fields for geometry-agnostic system identification. In *The Eleventh International Conference on Learning Representations*, 2023.

9 Ruijia Liu, Ancheng Hou, Xiao Yu, and Xiang Yin. Zero-shot trajectory planning for signal temporal logic tasks. *arXiv preprint arXiv:2501.13457*, 2025.

10 Kamal Acharya, Alvaro Velasquez, and Houbing Herbert Song. A survey on symbolic knowledge distillation of large language models. *IEEE Transactions on Artificial Intelligence*, 5(12):5928–5948, 2024.

11 Steven Carr, Nils Jansen, and Ufuk Topcu. Task-aware verifiable rnn-based policies for partially observable markov decision processes. *Journal of Artificial Intelligence Research*, 72:819–847, 2021.

12 Aaron Van Den Oord, Oriol Vinyals, and Koray Kavukcuoglu. Neural discrete representation learning. *Advances in Neural Information Processing Systems*, 30, 2017.

13 Ali Razavi, Aaron Van den Oord, and Oriol Vinyals. Generating diverse high-fidelity images with VQ-VAE-2. *Advances in Neural Information Processing Systems*, 32, 2019.

14 Shuyang Gu, Dong Chen, Jianmin Bao, Fang Wen, Bo Zhang, Dongdong Chen, Lu Yuan, and Baining Guo. Vector quantized diffusion model for text-to-image synthesis. In *Proceedings of the IEEE/CVF Conference on Computer Vision and Pattern Recognition*, pages 10696–10706, 2022.

15 Anurag Koul, Alan Fern, and Sam Greydanus. Learning finite state representations of recurrent policy networks. In *International Conference on Learning Representations*, 2019.

16 Tim Dettmers, Artidoro Pagnoni, Ari Holtzman, and Luke Zettlemoyer. Qlora: efficient finetuning of quantized llms. *Advances in Neural Information Processing Systems*, 36, 2024.

17 Lukas Herron, Kinjal Mondal, John S Schneekloth Jr, and Pratyush Tiwary. Inferring phase transitions and critical exponents from limited observations with thermodynamic maps. *Proceedings of the National Academy of Sciences of the United States of America*, 121(52):e2321971121, 2024.

18 Hugo AL Filipe and Luís MS Loura. Molecular dynamics simulations: advances and applications. *Molecules*, 27(7):2105, 2022.

19 Peter V Coveney and Shunzhou Wan. On the calculation of equilibrium thermodynamic properties from molecular dynamics. *Physical Chemistry Chemical Physics*, 18(44):30236–30240, 2016.

20 Mario Krenn, Qianxiang Ai, Senja Barthel, Nessa Carson, Angelo Frei, Nathan C Frey, Pascal Friederich, Théophile Gaudin, Alberto Alexander Gayle, Kevin Maik Jablonka, et al. Selfies and the future of molecular string representations. *Patterns*, 3(10):100588, 2022.

21 Nobuhisa Ueda, Kiyoko F Aoki-Kinoshita, Atsuko Yamaguchi, Tatsuya Akutsu, and Hiroshi Mamitsuka. A probabilistic model for mining labeled ordered trees: capturing patterns in carbohydrate sugar chains. *IEEE Transactions on Knowledge and Data Engineering*, 17(8):1051–1064, 2005.

22 Liming Cai, Russell L Malmberg, and Yunzhou Wu. Stochastic modeling of RNA pseudoknotted structures: a grammatical approach. *Bioinformatics*, 19(suppl_1):i66–i73, 2003.

23 Honghua Zhang, Po-Nien Kung, Masahiro Yoshida, Guy Van den Broeck, and Nanyun Peng. Adaptable logical control for large language models. *Advances in Neural Information Processing Systems*, 37:115563–115587, 2024.

24 Zhipeng Zhao, Bowen Li, Yi Du, Taimeng Fu, and Chen Wang. Physord: A neuro-symbolic approach for physics-infused motion prediction in off-road driving. In *2024 IEEE/RSJ International Conference on Intelligent Robots and Systems (IROS)*, pages 11670–11677, IEEE, 2024.

25 Mohammadhosein Hasanbeig, Natasha Yogananda Jeppu, Alessandro Abate, Tom Melham, and Daniel Kroening. Deepsynth: Automata synthesis for automatic task segmentation in deep reinforcement learning. In *Proceedings of the AAAI Conference on Artificial Intelligence*, volume 35, pages 7647–7656, 2021.

26 Sarah Lewis, Tim Hempel, José Jiménez-Luna, Michael Gastegger, Yu Xie, Andrew YK Foong, Victor García Satorras, Osama Abdin, Bastiaan S Veeling, Iryna Zaporozhets, et al. Scalable emulation of protein equilibrium ensembles with generative deep learning. *bioRxiv*, 2024. https://www.biorxiv.org/content/10.1101/2024.12.05.626885v1.

27 Tong Wang, Xinheng He, Mingyu Li, Yatao Li, Ran Bi, Yusong Wang, Chaoran Cheng, Xiangzhen Shen, Jiawei Meng, He Zhang, et al. Ab initio characterization of protein molecular dynamics with ai2bmd. *Nature*, 635(8040):1019–1027, 2024.

28 A Keith Dunker, J David Lawson, Celeste J Brown, Ryan M Williams, Pedro Romero, Jeong S Oh, Christopher J Oldfield, Andrew M Campen, Catherine M Ratliff, Kerry W Hipps, et al. Intrinsically disordered protein. *Journal of Molecular Graphics and Modelling*, 19(1):26–59, 2001.

29 Christian Straßer. *Adaptive Logics for Defeasible Reasoning*, volume 38. Springer, 2014.

30 Samuel Schapiro, Jonah Black, and Lav R Varshney. Transformational creativity in science: a graphical theory. *arXiv preprint arXiv:2504.18687*, 2025.

31 Alvaro Velasquez, Neel Bhatt, Ufuk Topcu, Zhangyang Wang, Katia Sycara, Simon Stepputtis, Sandeep Neema, and Gautam Vallabha. Neurosymbolic AI as an antithesis to scaling laws. *PNAS Nexus*, 4(5):pgaf117, 2025.

2

Reasoning in Neurosymbolic AI

*Son Tran,[1] Edjard Mota,[2] and Artur d'Avila Garcez[3]**

[1] *School of Information Technology, Deakin University, Melbourne, Victoria, Australia*
[2] *Instituto de Computação, Universidade Federal do Amazonas, Manaus, Brazil*
[3] *Department of Computer Science, City St George's, University of London, London, UK*

*Corresponding Author: a.garcez@city.ac.uk

2.1 What Is Reasoning in Neural Networks?

Increasing attention has been devoted in recent years to knowledge representation and reasoning in neural networks. The principled integration of reasoning and learning in neural networks is a main objective of the field of neurosymbolic Artificial Intelligence (AI) [1, 2]. In neurosymbolic AI, typically, an algorithm is provided that translates some form of symbolic knowledge representation into the architecture and initial set of parameters of a neural network. Ideally, a theorem then shows that the neural network can be used as a massively parallel model of computation capable of reasoning about such knowledge. Finally, when trained with data and knowledge, the network is expected to produce better performance, either a higher accuracy or faster learning, than when trained from data alone. Symbolic knowledge may be provided to a neural network in the form of general rules that are known to be true in a given domain or rules that are expected to be true across domains when performing transfer and continual learning. When rules are not available to start with, they can be extracted from a trained network. When rules are contradicted by data, they can be revised as part of the learning process. This has been shown to offer a flexible framework whereby knowledge and data, neural networks, and symbolic descriptions are combined, leading to a better understanding of complex network models with the interplay between learning and reasoning.

Neurosymbolic AI: Foundations and Applications, First Edition. Edited by Alvaro Velasquez et al.

This chapter includes a general discussion of how neurosymbolic AI can contribute to the goals of reasoning in neural networks and a specific illustration of a neurosymbolic system for reasoning in propositional logic with Restricted Boltzmann Machines (RBMs) [3]. We will describe a neurosymbolic system, called Logical Boltzmann Machines (LBMs), capable of (i) representing any propositional logic formula into a RBM, (ii) reasoning efficiently from such formula, and (iii) learning from such knowledge representation and data. LBM comes with an algorithm to translate any set of propositional logical formulae into a Boltzmann Machine (BM) and a proof of equivalence between the logical formulae and the energy-based connectionist model; in other words, a proof of soundness of the translation algorithm from logical formulae to neural networks. Specifically, the network is shown to assign minimum energy to the assignments of truth-values that satisfy the formulae. This provides a new way of performing reasoning in symmetrical neural networks by employing the network to search for the models of a logical theory, that is, to search for the assignments of truth-values that map the logical formulae to *true*.[1] If the number of variables is small, inference can be carried out analytically by sorting the free energy of all possible truth-value assignments. Otherwise, Gibbs sampling is applied in the search for logical models. We start, however, with a general discussion of reasoning in current AI including large language models (LLMs).

2.1.1 Reasoning in LLMs

Since the release of GPT4 by OpenAI in March 2023, a fierce debate developed around the risks of AI, Big Tech companies released various proprietary and open-source competitors to ChatGPT, and the European Union passed the regulatory AI Act in record time. Leading figures disagreed on what should be done about the risks of AI. Some claimed that Big Tech is best placed to take care of safety, others argued in favor of open source, and others still argued for regulation of AI and social media. As society contemplates the impact of AI on everyday life, the secrecy surrounding AI technology fueled fears of existential risk and even claims of an upcoming AI bubble burst. LLMs such as ChatGPT, Gemini, Claude, Mistral, and DeepSeek are a great engineering achievement, are impressive at text summarization and language translation, may improve productivity of those who are knowledgeable enough to spot the LLM's mistakes, but have great potential to deceive those who aren't.

There are various technical and nontechnical reasons why LLMs and current AI may not be deployed in practice: lack of trust or fairness, reliability issues, and public safety, as in the case of self-driving cars that use the same technology

1 We use the term *model* to refer to logical models and to neural network models. When the intended meaning is not clear from the context, we shall use the term *logical model*.

as LLMs. Fixing reliability issues case-by-case with Reinforcement Learning has proved to be too costly. A common risk mitigation strategy has been to adopt a *human-in-the-loop* approach: making sure that a human is ultimately responsible for decision-making. However, in the age of Agentic AI, where at least some decisions are made by the machine, simply apportioning blame or liability to a human does not address the problem. It is necessary to empower the user of AI, the data scientist, and the domain expert to be able to interpret, question, and, if necessary, intervene in the AI system. Neural networks that are accompanied by symbolic descriptions and sound reasoning capabilities will be an important tool in this process of empowering users of AI.

Consider LLMs' ability to produce code. If GPT4 was allowed to work, not as a stand-alone computer program, but in a loop whereby the code can be executed and data collected from execution to improve the code automatically, one can see how such self-improving LLM with autonomy may pose a serious risk to current computer systems. Recent experiments, however, indicated that the opposite, self-impairing, may also happen in practice, producing a degradation in performance. We will argue that the emerging field of neurosymbolic AI can address such failures and that there must be a better way, other than very costly post hoc model alignment, of achieving AI that can offer certain logical guarantees to network training.

LLMs have been considered to be general purpose because they will provide an answer to any question. They do that by doing only one thing: predicting the probability of the next word (token) in a sentence. Having made a choice of the next word, LLMs will apply the same calculations recursively to build larger sentences. They are called autoregressive machine learning models because they perform regression on the discrete tokens to learn such probabilities and apply recursively the learned function f to choose the word that comes at time $t+1$, given the words that are available at time t; that is, $x_{t+1} = f(x_t)$. Artificial General Intelligence (AGI), however, is best measured by the ability to adapt to novelty. It will require effective learning from fewer data, the ability to reason reliably about the knowledge that has been learned, the extraction of compact descriptions from trained networks, and the consolidation of knowledge learned from multiple tasks, using analogy to enable extrapolation to new situations at an adequate level of abstraction. It has been almost two years since GPT4 was released. The competition has caught up. Reliable data seem to have been exhausted. Performance increments obtained with increase in scale have not produced AGI. It is fair to say that the "scale is all you need" claim has not been confirmed. Notwithstanding, domain-specific AI systems that can exhibit intelligence at the level of humans or higher already exist. These systems exhibit intelligence in specialized tasks: targeted medical diagnoses, protein folding, and various closed-world two-player strategy games.

When LLMs make stuff up such as non-existing citations, they are said to hallucinate. AGI will require systems that never hallucinate (that is, reason reliably), that can form long-term plans and act on those plans to achieve a goal, and that can handle exceptions as they materialize, addressing shifts in data distribution not case-by-case, but requiring far less data labeling. This is very different from current LLMs that seem to have difficulty handling exceptions. For this reason, hallucinations are not going away, and the cost of post hoc model alignment has spiraled in the last two years.

As a case in point, take the o1 LLM system released by OpenAI in September 2024; o1 was claimed to "think before it answers" and to be capable of "truly general reasoning." Widely seen as a rebranding of the much anticipated GPT5, which was promised to be at AGI level, the little that we know about o1 is that it improved on reasoning and code generation benchmarks, and yet it can be stubbornly poor at simple tasks such as multiplication, formal reasoning, planning, or the formidable ARC-AGI-2 challenge (see https://arcprize.org/). Let us assume that OpenAI's o1 system is best described as "GPT-Go," a pretrained transformer to which a tree search is incorporated in the style of Google DeepMind's earlier Alpha-Go system. The tree search uses "Chain of Thought" (CoT) prompting: generation of synthetic data using the transformer neural network itself in a chain that breaks down a prompt into sub-prompts (subproblems to be solved in stages). o1's "thinking" time is presumably needed to build the tree for the CoT. And it's this breaking of the problem into subproblems that is expected to improve performance on reasoning tasks since this is how reasoning tasks are solved.

Leaving aside the practical question of how long users will be happy to wait for an answer, the main issue with o1 and successors is a lack of reliability of the synthetic data generation and combinatorial nature of CoT: CoT may solve one reasoning task well today only to fail at an analogous reasoning task tomorrow due to simple naming variations [4]. With synthetic data generation from GPT-like autoregressive models having been shown to impair model performance, the quality of the data decreases and the model continues to hallucinate [5].

What we are seeing in practice is that eliminating hallucinations is very difficult. And there is another concern: regurgitation. The New York Times (NYT) lawsuit against OpenAI argues that ChatGPT can basically reproduce (regurgitate) copyrighted NYT texts with minimal prompting. Whether regurgitation can be fixed remains to be seen. Efforts in this direction have been focused on a simple technique called Retrieval Augmented Generation (RAG) that fetches facts from external sources. What is clear is that further research is needed to make sense of how LLMs generalize to new situations and to find out whether performance depends on task familiarity or true generalization. In the meantime, there will be many relevant but domain-specific applications of LLMs in areas where the system has been deemed to have been controlled reasonably well or where controlling it isn't crucial.

In neurosymbolic AI, instead of adjusting the input to fix a misbehaving LLM as done with CoT, the idea is to control the architecture or the loss function of the system. Neurosymbolic AI integrates learning and reasoning to make model development parsimonious by following this recipe: (i) extract symbolic descriptions as learning progresses, (ii) reason formally about what has been learned, and (iii) compress the neural network as knowledge is instilled back into the network. Reasoning in neurosymbolic AI follows the tradition of knowledge representation in AI. It requires the definition of a semantics for deep learning, and it measures the capabilities of neural networks w.r.t. formally defined, sound, and approximate reasoning, providing a much-needed measure of the accumulation of errors in the AI system.

2.1.2 AI from a Neurosymbolic Perspective

It is paradoxical that computers have been invented to provide fast calculations and sound reasoning, and yet the latest AI may fail at calculations as simple as multiplication (even though a typical artificial neural network will rely on millions of correct multiplications as part of its internal computations). The first wave of AI in the 1980s was knowledge-based, well-founded, and inefficient if compared with deep learning. The second wave from the 2010s was data-driven, distributed, and efficient but unsound if compared with knowledge bases. It is clear that neural networks are here to stay, but the problems with deep learning have been stubbornly difficult to fix using neural networks alone. Next, we discuss how solving these problems will require the use of symbolic AI alongside neural networks. The third wave of AI, we argue, will be neurosymbolic [6].

In order to understand the achievements and limitations of AI, it is helpful to consider the *AGI debate*[2] with its focus on what is missing from current AI systems, i.e., the technological innovation that may bring about better AI or AGI. Simply put, such innovation may be described as the ability to apply knowledge learned from a task by a neural network to a novel task without requiring too much data.

As AI experts John Hopfield and Geoff Hinton are awarded the 2024 Nobel Prize for Physics, and AI expert Demis Hassabis is awarded the 2024 Nobel Prize for Chemistry (with David Baker and John Jumper), one can say that the era of computation as the language of science has begun. Hassabis led the team at Google DeepMind that created AlphaFold, an AI model capable of predicting with high accuracy the 3D structure of proteins given their amino acid sequence. AlphaFold is arguably the greatest achievement of AI to date, even though it is squarely an application-specific (or narrow) AI by comparison with LLMs. From

2 https://www.youtube.com/watch?v=JGiLz_Jx9uI.

particle physics to drug discovery, energy efficiency, and novel materials, AI is being adopted as the process by which scientific research is carried out. However, as noted earlier, the lack of a description or explanation capable of conveying a deeper sense of understanding of the solution being offered by AI is something that is very unsatisfactory. Computer scientists, in a great feat of engineering, will solve very challenging problems in science to a high degree of accuracy without necessarily improving their own understanding of the solutions provided by very large neural networks trained on vast amounts of data that are not humanly possible to inspect.

The risks of current AI together with this unsatisfactory lack of explainability confirm the need for neurosymbolic AI as an alternative approach. As mentioned, neurosymbolic AI uses the technology of knowledge extraction to interpret, ask *what-if* questions, and, if necessary, intervene in the AI system, controlling learning in ways that can offer correctness or fairness guarantees and, with this process, producing a more compact, data-efficient system. We start to see a shift toward such explainable neurosymbolic AI systems being deployed as part of a risk-based approach. As argued in Percy et al. [7], effective regulation goes hand in hand with accountability in AI, the definition of a risk mitigation strategy, and the use of technology itself such as explainable AI technology [8] to mitigate risks. We shall return to this discussion at the end of the chapter.

For more than 20 years, a small group of researchers has been advocating for neurosymbolic AI. Already around the turn of the twenty-first century, the importance of artificial neural networks as an efficient computational model for learning was clear to that group. But the value of symbol manipulation and abstract reasoning offered by symbolic logic was also obvious to them. Many before them have contributed to neurosymbolic AI. In fact, it could be argued that neurosymbolic AI starts together with connectionism itself, with the aptly titled 1943 paper by McCulloch and Pitts, *A Logical Calculus of the Ideas Immanent in Nervous Activity*, and with John Von Neumann's 1952 *Lectures on Probabilistic Logics and the Synthesis of Reliable Organisms from Unreliable Components*, indicating that the gap between distributed vector representations (embeddings) and localist symbolic representations in logic was not as big as some might imagine. Even Alan Turing's 1948 *Intelligent Machinery* introduced a type of neural network called a B-type machine. All of this, of course, before the term Artificial Intelligence was coined ahead of the now famous Dartmouth Workshop in 1956. Since then the field has separated into two: symbolic AI and connectionist AI (or neural networks). This has slowed progress as the two research communities went their separate ways with different conferences, journals, and associations. Following the temporary success of symbolic AI in the 1980s and the success of deep learning since 2015 with its now obvious limitations, the time is right for revisiting the approaches of the founding fathers of computer science and developing neurosymbolic AI that is fit for the twenty-first century. As a step in this direction, in what follows, we illustrate how a single bidirectional network layer in the form of a RBM can implement the full semantics of propositional logic, formally defined.

2.2 Background: Logic and RBMs

Differently from general-purpose LLMs, domain-specific AI, such as the protein-folding AlphaFold system, aims to develop systems for specific purposes, enabling human abilities to handle tasks that might otherwise take many years to solve. This goal of domain-specific AI is analogous to the invention of the Archimedean lever, which enhanced physical strength capabilities and has enabled humanity to make leaps in construction, mobility, and physical labor. AI can be a mental lever that enhances our ability to deal with problems requiring mental activity in volume or intensity that is difficult to accomplish in feasible time or with precision. Modeling such abstract human mental activity is a highly complex task, and we shall focus on representing two well-studied aspects: learning and reasoning.

A key step in this endeavor is to choose an appropriate language to represent the problem at hand. In the context of this chapter, such a choice will be deemed to be suitable if it allows the development of efficient algorithms to perform learning from data and reasoning about what was learned or if it allows one to identify patterns of solutions that will lead to adequate decisions. Traditional AI has separated the study of reasoning and learning with a focus on either knowledge elicitation by hand for the purpose of sound reasoning or statistical learning from large amounts of data. In neurosymbolic AI, this artificial separation is removed. The neurosymbolic cycle seeks to enable AI systems to *learn a little* and *reason a little* in integrated fashion. Learning takes place in the usual way within a neural network, but reasoning has to be formalized, whether taking place inside or outside the network. Instead of simply measuring *reasoning capabilities* of the networks using benchmarks, neurosymbolic AI networks seek to offer reasoning guarantees of correctness. It is crucial to pay attention to the many years of research in knowledge representation and reasoning within Computer Science logic. While learning may benefit from the use of natural language and other available multimodal data, sound reasoning requires a formal language. A choice of language adequate to the problem influences the system's ability to find a solution.

Formal logic, particularly Propositional Logic, is the most straightforward language for representing propositions about the problem domain. Propositional logic is the simplest formal language for representation, a branch of mathematics and logic that deals with simple declarative statements, called propositions, which can be *true* or *false*. As we shall see, in the context of neurosymbolic systems, statements are not purely *true* or *false* but are associated with confidence values, probability intervals, or *degrees of truth* denoting the intrinsic uncertainty of AI problems. It is therefore incorrect to assume that the use of logic is incompatible with uncertainty reasoning or limited to crisp, true or false statements. In its most general form, logic includes fuzzy and many-valued logics and various other forms of non-classical reasoning. We start, however, with propositional logic.

Think of propositions as the fundamental building blocks for reasoning. For instance, "it is raining" is a proposition because its truth can be determined by examining the current weather conditions. We typically use symbols such as P, Q, or R to represent these propositions.[3] To combine or modify these propositions, we use logical connectives or operators: AND ($\wedge$), OR ($\vee$), NOT ($\neg$), IMPLICATION ($\rightarrow$), and BICONDITIONAL ($\leftrightarrow$). For example, if P represents "it is raining" and Q represents "I have an umbrella," then $P \wedge Q$ means "it is raining AND I have an umbrella." The operators allow us to compose complex relationships among ideas in a precise way.

A syntactically correct expression in logic is said to be a Well-Formed Formula (WFF). A WFF in propositional logic is constructed according to the following rules:

1. Any atomic proposition (e.g., P, Q, R) is a WFF.
2. If A is a WFF, then $\neg A$ (the negation of A) is also a WFF.
3. If A and B are WFFs, then $(A \wedge B)$, $(A \vee B)$, $(A \rightarrow B)$, and $(A \leftrightarrow B)$ are also WFFs.
4. Nothing else is a WFF.

For example, the expression $(P \wedge Q) \rightarrow R$ is a WFF because it follows these rules: P, Q, and R are atomic propositions, $(P \wedge Q)$ is a valid combination using the AND operator, and the entire expression forms a valid implication. On the other hand, expressions like $P \wedge \vee Q$ are not WFFs because they violate the rules.

Propositional logic is also known as Boolean Logic, named after George Boole, a pioneer in the formalization of logical reasoning. Interestingly, George Boole is the great-great-grandfather of Geoffrey Hinton, a leading figure in the field of neural networks. Boole proposed his *Laws of Thought* using a simplified notation where 1 and 0 denote *true* and *false*, respectively. This binary representation aligns naturally with the semantic interpretation of neural networks and fits seamlessly into the reasoning method to be presented in this chapter.

By adhering to the rules of WFFs, we ensure that our logical expressions are unambiguous and well-structured (compositional), providing a solid foundation for further exploration of propositional logic and its applications. In the remainder of this chapter, unless otherwise specified, we shall use WFF to refer specifically to a subset of WFFs consisting only of formulas constructed using combinations

3 Any symbol, including indices, can be used as long as it is clear that they represent a specific proposition.

of negation (¬), conjunction (∧), and disjunction (∨). If other logical connectives, such as implication (→) or biconditional (↔), are included, we will explicitly clarify this deviation from the specific subset, noting that in Classical Logic $A \leftrightarrow B$ is equivalent to $(A \rightarrow B) \wedge (B \rightarrow A)$ and that $A \rightarrow B$ is equivalent to $\neg A \vee B$.

2.2.1 Illustrating Logical Reasoning with the Sudoku Puzzle

Sudoku is more than just a number puzzle (see Figure 2.1); it is a gateway to understanding the power of logical thinking. This globally beloved puzzle challenges us to impose order on apparent chaos, using nothing but numbers and logic. At its core, Sudoku is about solving constraints, ensuring that every row, column, and sub-grid (or block) adheres to a simple strict rule (containing one and only one of the elements of a given set). The same principle of constraint satisfaction is a cornerstone of AI and computational problem-solving. By learning how to express Sudoku's rules logically, we unlock the secrets of this captivating game and the tools to tackle more complex problem-solving. Let's explore how propositional logic can elegantly capture the rules of Sudoku as a way to illustrate structured reasoning.

For simplicity, we consider a smaller version of Sudoku, using a 4×4 grid instead of the standard 9×9. This simplified puzzle divides the board into four 2×2 blocks or sub-grids, each containing four positions (or cells). Blocks are counted from left to right and top to bottom: block 1 is on top of block 3, and block 2 is on top of block 4. Positions within each block are also counted from left to right and top to bottom. Each cell in the grid must contain a number from 1 to 4, with

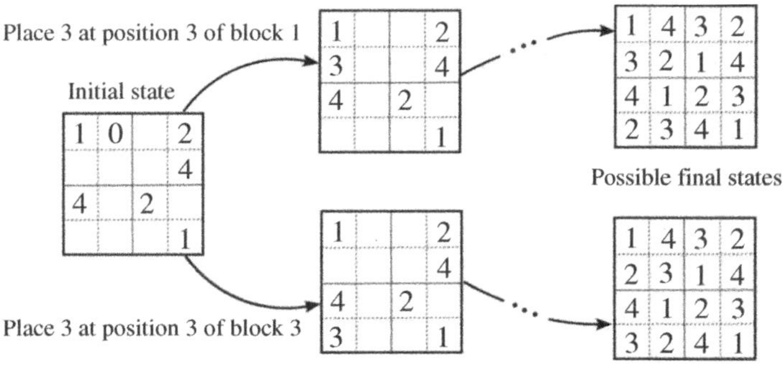

Figure 2.1 An initial Sudoku board and two branches generated by placing a 3 at position 3 of blocks 1 and 3, respectively, and corresponding final states satisfying the constraints of the game.

no repetition allowed in any row, column, or 2×2 block.[4] Figure 2.1 depicts an example of an initial setting for a Sudoku 4×4 board, followed by two possible transitions placing number 3 in two possible cells satisfying the constraints. Two possible final states are also shown, each derived from the above two states if every movement satisfies the constraints of the puzzle.

Solving Sudoku involves reasoning about these constraints, making it a good example for introducing logical notation. To model the problem using propositional logic, one can systematically represent the constraints in terms of propositional variables encoding the relationships between numbers, positions, rows, columns, and blocks. The rules dictate that every row, column, and block must include the numbers 1–4 exactly once. By encoding the problem in this way, one can use symbolic logical reasoning to systematically explore possible solutions while respecting all constraints. The rules are encoded as follows:

Logical Variables: Let the proposition $B_{i,j,k}$ denote that the block i at position j (that is, the cell (i, j)) contains the number k. Formally, $B_{i,j,k}$ is true if and only if $k \in \{1, 2, 3, 4\}$ is in position j of block i, $1 \leq i \leq 4$, $1 \leq j \leq 4$.

Logical Constraints: The constraints ensure that the numbers are placed correctly according to the rules of Sudoku. These constraints can be grouped into four categories:

1. Each cell must contain a number (cell (i, j) contains a 1 or a 2 or a 3 or a 4): $B_{i,j,1} \vee B_{i,j,2} \vee B_{i,j,3} \vee B_{i,j,4}$. When needed, we shall write:

$$\bigvee_{k=1}^{4} B_{i,j,k} \quad \text{as shorthand notation for } B_{i,j,1} \vee B_{i,j,2} \vee B_{i,j,3} \vee B_{i,j,4}.$$

There cannot be two or more numbers on the same cell[5] :

$$\neg(B_{i,j,k_1} \wedge B_{i,j,k_2}), \quad \text{for all } k_1 \neq k_2.$$

The above two rules can be written compactly as:

$$\left(\bigvee_{k=1}^{4} B_{i,j,k}\right) \wedge \left(\bigwedge_{k_1<k_2} \neg(B_{i,j,k_1} \wedge B_{i,j,k_2})\right),$$

where $\bigwedge_i x_i$ is shorthand for $x_1 \wedge x_2 \wedge \ldots$ and $k_1 < k_2$ is used to avoid repetition.[6]

---

4 In the real Sudoku puzzle, each block is 3×3 and the set of possible elements is $\{1, 2, \ldots, 9\}$ with the board having nine blocks in total.

5 Notice that $\neg(A \wedge B)$ implies $\neg(A \wedge B \wedge C)$.

6 Notice that $A \wedge B$ is logically equivalent to $B \wedge A$.

2. Each number appears exactly once per row. For each row across the entire board and each number k, exactly one position in that row must contain k. This is expressed as:

$$\bigvee_{j=1}^{4} B_{i,j,k}$$

along with the constraint that there cannot be two or more occurrences of the same number on the same row:

$$\neg(B_{i,j_1,k} \wedge B_{i,j_2,k}), \quad \text{for all } j_1 \neq j_2.$$

In compact form:

$$\left(\bigvee_{j=1}^{4} B_{i,j,k}\right) \wedge \left(\bigwedge_{j_1<j_2} \neg(B_{i,j_1,k} \wedge B_{i,j_2,k})\right).$$

3. Each number appears exactly once per column. In compact form (as above):

$$\left(\bigvee_{i=1}^{4} B_{i,j,k}\right) \wedge \left(\bigwedge_{i_1<i_2} \neg(B_{i_1,j,k} \wedge B_{i_2,j,k})\right).$$

4. Each number appears exactly once per block. For each 2×2 block and each number k, exactly one position within the block must contain k. For example, for the top-left block:

$$\bigvee_{(i,j)\in\{(1,1),(1,2),(2,1),(2,2)\}} B_{i,j,k},$$

along with the constraint:

$$\neg(B_{i_1,j_1,k} \wedge B_{i_2,j_2,k}), \text{ for all distinct pairs } (i_1, j_1) \neq (i_2, j_2).$$

In compact form:

$$\left(\bigvee_{(i,j)\in\text{block}} B_{i,j,k}\right) \wedge \left(\bigwedge_{(i_1,j_1)<(i_2,j_2)} \neg(B_{i_1,j_1,k} \wedge B_{i_2,j_2,k})\right).$$

The complete set of constraints for the 4×4 Sudoku puzzle is the conjunction of all the above conditions over all cells, rows, columns, and blocks. This logical formula guarantees that every number appears exactly once in each row, column, and block, satisfying the rules of Sudoku. It also provides a systematic framework for reasoning about the puzzle.

Example: For block 1, position 1, we have:

$B_{1,1,1} \vee B_{1,1,2} \vee B_{1,1,3} \vee B_{1,1,4}$
$\neg B_{1,1,1} \vee \neg B_{1,1,2}$
$\neg B_{1,1,1} \vee \neg B_{1,1,3}$
$\neg B_{1,1,1} \vee \neg B_{1,1,4}$
$\neg B_{1,1,2} \vee \neg B_{1,1,3}$
$\neg B_{1,1,2} \vee \neg B_{1,1,4}$
$\neg B_{1,1,3} \vee \neg B_{1,1,4}$

Some observations about this representation:

- This notation provides a framework whereby each possible combination of B with indices is assigned to *True* or *False*.
- Each rule above is called a *clause* (a disjunction of logic literals) and the complete set of clauses would be significantly larger to cover all rows, columns, and blocks.
- This representation can be used as input to a satisfiability (SAT) solver to find solutions to the Sudoku puzzle, that is, assignments of truth-values *True* or *False* to each literal that will provably satisfy the puzzle's constraints.

This Boolean logic representation allows us to express the Sudoku problem as a set of constraints that must be satisfied simultaneously. By finding a truth assignment to the variables that satisfy all the clauses, we determine a valid solution to the Sudoku puzzle.

2.2.2 Sudoku with Strategies of Sampling

1. Reasoning Strategy Based on Unused Numbers:
   To control which number to pick based on the bank of numbers not yet placed on the board, let us illustrate how additional constraints may be introduced that ensure unused numbers are considered first. A strategy such as this could be learned from observation of game plays as well as specified by hand.

   For each empty cell (i, j), define $U(i, j)$ as the set of numbers k such that k is not already used in the corresponding row, column, or block of cell (i, j).

   The constraint ensuring the selection of an unused number k can be expressed as:

   $$\bigvee_{k \in U(i,j)} B_{i,j,k},$$

   where $U(i, j)$ is defined as:

   $$U(i, j) = \{k \mid k \notin \{B_{i,j',k'} \mid j' \neq j\} \wedge k \notin \{B_{i',j,k'} \mid i' \neq i\}$$

   $$\wedge k \notin \{B_{i',j',k'} \mid (i', j') \in \text{block}(i, j)\}\}.$$

Here, block(i, j) denotes the set of positions in the same block as (i, j).

2. Priority Constraint for Unused Numbers:

   To prioritize the use of unused numbers, we can add a preference rule that assigns higher priority to considering numbers from $U(i, j)$ ahead of other possibilities.

   Formally, let $P(i, j, k)$ represent the priority of placing number k in cell (i, j). The priority can be defined as:

$$P(i, j, k) = \begin{cases} 1 & \text{if } k \in U(i, j) \\ 0 & \text{otherwise.} \end{cases}$$

   The constraint ensuring that the highest priority is given to unused numbers can be expressed as:

$$\bigvee_{k \in U(i,j)} (P(i, j, k) \wedge B_{i,j,k}).$$

The complete set of logical constraints for the 4×4 Sudoku puzzle now includes the original Sudoku constraints along with additional reasoning strategies that prioritize the use of unused numbers. These constraints ensure that every number appears exactly once in each row, column, and block while also guiding the generation of solutions (that is, the assignment of truth-values to the literals) by leveraging the bank of unused numbers. By incorporating these, the Sudoku-solving process becomes systematic and more efficient, as it should reduce the likelihood of the process getting stuck and having to backtrack when searching for a solution, or analogously in the case of a neural network getting stuck in local minima.

2.2.3 Restricted Boltzmann Machines

An RBM [3] is a two-layer neural network with bidirectional (symmetric) connections, which is characterized by a function called the energy of the RBM:

$$E(\mathbf{x}, \mathbf{h}) = -\sum_{i,j} w_{ij} x_i h_j - \sum_i a_i x_i - \sum_j b_j h_j, \tag{2.1}$$

where a_i and b_j are the biases of input unit x_i and hidden unit h_j, respectively, and w_{ij} is the connection weight between x_i and h_j. This RBM represents a joint probability distribution $p(\mathbf{x}, \mathbf{h}) = \frac{1}{Z} e^{-\frac{1}{\tau} E(\mathbf{x},\mathbf{h})}$, where $Z = \sum_{\mathbf{xh}} e^{-\frac{1}{\tau} E(\mathbf{x},\mathbf{h})}$ is the partition function and parameter τ is called the temperature of the RBM, $\mathbf{x} = \{x_i\}$ is the set of visible units, and $\mathbf{h} = \{h_j\}$ is the set of hidden units of the RBM.

Training RBMs normally makes use of the Contrastive Divergence learning algorithm [9], whereby each input vector from the training set is propagated to the hidden layer of the network and back to the input a number of times (n) using a probabilistic selection rule to decide at each time whether or not a neuron should be activated (with activation value in $\{0, 1\}$). The weight assigned to the connection between input neuron x_i and hidden neuron h_j is adjusted according to a simple update rule based on the difference between the value of $x_i h_j$ at time 1 and time n. More precisely, $\Delta W_{ij} = \eta((x_i h_j)_1 - (x_i h_j)_n)$, where η is a learning rate (a small positive real number).

2.3 Symbolic Reasoning with Energy-based Neural Networks

The content of this section is based on Tran and d'Avila Garcez [10].

Over the years, many neurosymbolic approaches have used a form of knowledge representation based on *if-then* rules [11–17], written $B \leftarrow A$ (make B $True$ if A is $True$) to distinguish from classical implication ($A \rightarrow B$). Under the convention that 1 represents $True$ and 0 represents $False$, given $B \leftarrow A$ and input 1 to neuron A, a neurosymbolic system would infer that neuron B should have activation value approximately 1. Given input 0 to neuron A, it would infer that B should have activation approximately 0.

LBMs allow for a richer representation than *if-then* rules using full propositional logic. Next, we review LBM's immediate related work, define a mapping from any logical formulae to LBMs, and describe how reasoning takes place by sampling and energy minimization. We also evaluate scalability of reasoning in LBM and learning by combining knowledge and data, evaluating results on benchmarks in comparison with a symbolic, another neurosymbolic and a neural network-based approach.

2.3.1 Related Work

One of the earliest works on the integration of neural networks and symbolic knowledge is known as Knowledge-based Artificial Neural Network (KBANN [11]), which encodes *if-then* rules into a hierarchical multilayer perceptron. In another early approach [18], a single-hidden-layer recurrent neural network is proposed to support logic programming rules. An extension of that approach to work with first-order logic programs, called Connectionist Inductive Logic Programming (CILP++) [12], uses the concept of *propositionalization* from Inductive Logic Programming (ILP), whereby first-order variables can be treated as propositional atoms in the neural network. Also based on first-order logic programs, Evans and Grefenstette [14] propose a differentiable ILP approach that can be implemented by neural networks, and Cohen et al. [19] map stochastic logic programs into a differentiable function also trainable by neural networks. These are all supervised learning approaches.

Early work in neurosymbolic AI has also shown a correspondence between propositional logic and symmetrical neural networks [20], in particular Hopfield networks, which nevertheless did not scale well with the number of variables. Among unsupervised learning approaches, Penalty Logic [21] was the first work to integrate nonmonotonic logic in the form of weighted if-then rules into symmetrical neural networks. However, Penalty Logic required the use of higher-order Hopfield networks, which can be difficult to construct[7] and inefficient to train with the learning algorithm for BMs. More recently, several attempts have been made to extract and encode symbolic knowledge into RBMs trained with the more efficient Contrastive Divergence learning algorithm [13, 22]. Such approaches explored the structural similarity between symmetric networks and logical rules with biconditional implication but do not have a proof of soundness. By contrast, and similarly to Penalty Logic, LBM is provably equivalent to the logic formulae encoded in the RBM. Differently from Penalty Logic, LBM does not require the use of higher-order networks.

Alongside the above approaches, which translate symbolic representations into neural networks (normally if-then rules translated into a feedforward or recurrent network), there are hybrid approaches that combine neural networks and symbolic AI systems as communicating modules of a neurosymbolic system. These include DeepProbLog [16] and Logic Tensor Networks (LTN) [23]. DeepProbLog adds a neural network module to probabilistic logic programming such that an atom of the logic program can be represented by a network module. LTN and various approaches derived from it use real-valued logic to constrain the loss function of the neural network given statements in first-order logic. Both DeepProbLog and LTNs use backpropagation, differently from the approach adopted here, which uses Contrastive Divergence.

Finally, approaches focused on reasoning include SAT solving using neural networks. In Hernandez et al. [24] and d'Anjou et al. [25], the maximum satisfiability (MaxSAT) problem is mapped onto BMs and higher-order BMs, which are used to solve the combinatorial optimization task in parallel, similarly to Pinkas [20]. In Wang et al. [26], the SAT problem is redefined as a soft (differentiable) task and solved approximately by deep networks with the objective of integrating logical reasoning and learning, as in the case of the approaches discussed earlier. This soft version of the SAT problem is therefore different from the satisfiability problem. A preliminary evaluation of our approach in comparison with symbolic SAT solvers shows that our approach allows the use of up to approximately 100 variables. This is well below the capability of symbolic SAT solvers. A way of improving the performance of neural SAT solvers may well be to consider approximate solutions as done by soft SAT solvers, including neuroSAT [27]. Although still not

7 Building such higher-order networks requires transforming the energy function into quadratic form by adding hidden variables not present in the original logic formulae.

beating SAT solvers, neuroSAT showed promise at addressing out-of-distribution learning after training on random SAT problems.

In our experiments on learning, the focus is on benchmark neurosymbolic AI tasks with available data and knowledge, obtained from França et al. [12]. We therefore compare LBM with a state-of-the-art ILP symbolic system Aleph [28], standard RBMs as a purely neural approach closest to LBM, and CILP++ as a neurosymbolic system. It is worth noting, however, that CILP++ is a neurosymbolic system for supervised learning while LBMs use unsupervised learning, and it is worth investigating approaches for semi-supervised learning and other combinations of such systems. Further comparisons and evaluations on both reasoning and learning are underway.

2.3.2 Knowledge Representation in RBMs

Before we present LBM, let's contrast the simple $B \leftarrow A$ example used earlier with classical logic. Given $A \rightarrow B$ as knowledge,[8] if neuron A is assigned input value 1 in the corresponding neurosymbolic network, we expect the network to converge to a stable state where neuron B has value approximately 1, similarly to the example seen earlier. This is because the truth-value of WFF $A \rightarrow B$ is *True*, given an assignment of truth-values *True* to its constituent literals A and B. Now, $A \rightarrow B$ is *False* when A is *True* and B is *False*. If neuron B is assigned input 0, we expect the network to converge to a stable state where A is approximately 0 ($A \rightarrow B$ is *True* when A is *False* and B is *False*). What if A is assigned input 0 (or B is assigned input 1)? In these cases, $A \rightarrow B$ is satisfied if B is either 1 or 0 (or if A is either 1 or 0). Differently from $B \leftarrow A$, the network will converge to one of the two options that satisfy the formulae.

From this point forward, unless stated otherwise, we will treat assignments of truth-values to logical literals and binary input vectors denoting the activation states of neurons indistinguishably.

Definition 2.1: Let $s_\varphi(\mathbf{x}) \in \{0, 1\}$ denote the truth-value of a WFF φ, given an assignment of truth-values $\mathbf{x}$ to the literals of φ, where truth-value *True* is mapped to 1 and truth-value *False* is mapped to 0. Let $E(\mathbf{x}, \mathbf{h})$ denote the energy function of an energy-based neural network $\mathcal{N}$ with visible units $\mathbf{x}$ and hidden units $\mathbf{h}$. φ is said to be *equivalent* to $\mathcal{N}$ if and only if for any assignment of values to $\mathbf{x}$ there exists a function ψ such that $s_\varphi(\mathbf{x}) = \psi(E(\mathbf{x}, \mathbf{h}))$.

Definition 2.1 is similar to that of Penalty Logic [21], where all assignments of truth-values satisfying a WFF φ are mapped to global minima of the energy function of network $\mathcal{N}$. In our case, by construction, assignments that do not satisfy

8 In classical logic, $A \rightarrow B$ is equivalent to $\neg A \vee B$, i.e., *True* if A is *False* regardless of the truth-value of B.

the WFF will, in addition, be mapped to maxima of the energy function. To see how this is the case, it will be useful to define strict and full DNFs, as follows.

Definition 2.2: A *strict DNF* (SDNF) is a DNF with at most one conjunctive clause (a conjunction of literals) that maps to *True* for any choice of assignment of truth-values **x**. A *full DNF* is a DNF where each propositional variable (a positive or negative literal) must appear at least once in every conjunctive clause (sometimes called a canonical DNF).

For example, to turn DNF $A \vee B$ into an equivalent full DNF, one needs to map it to $(A \wedge \neg B) \vee (\neg A \wedge B) \vee (A \wedge B)$, according to the truth-table for $A \vee B$. For any given assignment of truth-values to A and B, at most one of the above three conjunctive clauses will be *True*, by definition of the truth-table. Not every SDNF is also a full DNF; e.g., $(a \wedge b) \vee \neg b$ is a SDNF that is not a full DNF.

Lemma 2.1: *Let $\mathcal{S}_{T_j}$ denote the set of indices of the positive literals x_t in a conjunctive clause j. Let $\mathcal{S}_{K_j}$ denote the set of indices of the negative literals x_k in j. Any SDNF $\varphi \equiv \vee_j(\bigwedge_t \mathrm{x}_t \wedge \bigwedge_k \neg \mathrm{x}_k)$ can be mapped onto an energy function:*

$$E(\mathbf{x}) = -\sum_j \left(\prod_{t \in \mathcal{S}_{T_j}} x_t \prod_{k \in \mathcal{S}_{K_j}} (1 - x_k) \right).$$

Proof. Each conjunctive clause $\bigwedge_t \mathrm{x}_t \wedge \bigwedge_k \neg \mathrm{x}_k$ in φ corresponds to the product $\prod_t x_t \prod_k (1 - x_k)$, which maps to 1 if and only if x_t is *True* ($x_t = 1$) and x_k is *False* ($x_k = 0$) for all $t \in \mathcal{S}_{T_j}$ and $k \in \mathcal{S}_{K_j}$. Since φ is SDNF, φ is *True* if and only if one conjunctive clause is *True* and $\sum_j(\prod_{t \in \mathcal{S}_{T_j}} x_t \prod_{k \in \mathcal{S}_{K_j}} (1 - x_k)) = 1$. Hence, the neural network with energy function E is such that $s_\varphi(\mathbf{x}) = -E(\mathbf{x})$.

Theorem 2.1: *Any SDNF $\varphi \equiv \vee_j(\bigwedge_t \mathrm{x}_t \wedge \bigwedge_k \neg \mathrm{x}_k)$ can be mapped onto an RBM with energy function:*

$$E(\mathbf{x}, \mathbf{h}) = -\sum_j h_j \left(\sum_{t \in \mathcal{S}_{T_j}} x_t - \sum_{k \in \mathcal{S}_{K_j}} x_k - |\mathcal{S}_{T_j}| + \epsilon \right), \quad (2.2)$$

such that $s_\varphi(\mathbf{x}) = -E(\mathbf{x})$, where $0 < \epsilon < 1$ and $|\mathcal{S}_{T_j}|$ is the number of positive literals in conjunctive clause j of φ.

Proof. Lemma 2.1 states that any SDNF φ can be mapped onto energy function $E = -\sum_j(\prod_{t \in \mathcal{S}_{T_j}} x_t \prod_{k \in \mathcal{S}_{K_j}} (1 - x_k))$. For each expression $\tilde{e}_j(\mathbf{x}) = -\prod_{t \in \mathcal{S}_{T_j}} x_t \prod_{k \in \mathcal{S}_{K_j}} (1 - x_k)$, we define an energy expression associated with hidden unit h_j as $e_j(\mathbf{x}, h_j) = -h_j(\sum_{t \in \mathcal{S}_{T_j}} x_t - \sum_{k \in \mathcal{S}_{K_j}} x_k - |\mathcal{S}_{T_j}| + \epsilon)$. The term $e_j(\mathbf{x}, h_j)$ is minimized with value $-\epsilon$ when $h_j = 1$, written $min_{h_j}(e_j(\mathbf{x}, h_j)) = -\epsilon$.

This is because $-(\sum_{t\in\mathcal{S}_{T_j}} x_t - \sum_{k\in\mathcal{S}_{K_j}} x_k - |\mathcal{S}_{T_j}| + \epsilon) = -\epsilon$ if and only if $x_t = 1$ and $x_k = 0$ for all $t \in \mathcal{S}_{T_j}$ and $k \in \mathcal{S}_{K_j}$. Otherwise, $-(\sum_t x_{t\in\mathcal{S}_{T_j}} - \sum_{k\in\mathcal{S}_{K_j}} x_k - |\mathcal{S}_{T_j}| + \epsilon) > 0$ and $min_{h_j}(e_j(\mathbf{x}, h_j)) = 0$ with $h_j = 0$. By repeating this process for each $\tilde{e}_j(\mathbf{x})$, we obtain that the energy function $E(\mathbf{x}, \mathbf{h}) = -\sum_j h_j(\sum_{t\in\mathcal{S}_{T_j}} x_t - \sum_{k\in\mathcal{S}_{K_j}} x_k - |\mathcal{S}_{T_j}| + \epsilon)$ is such that $s_\varphi(\mathbf{x}) = -\frac{1}{\epsilon} min_{\mathbf{h}} E(\mathbf{x}, \mathbf{h})$.

It is well-known that any WFF φ can be converted into DNF. Then, if φ is not SDNF, by definition there is more than one conjunctive clause in φ that map to *True* when φ is satisfied. This group of conjunctive clauses can always be converted into a full DNF according to its truth-table. By definition, any such full DNF is also a SDNF. Therefore, any WFF can be converted into SDNF. From Theorem 2.1, it follows that any WFF can be represented by the energy function of an RBM. The conversion of WFFs into full DNF can be computationally expensive. Sometimes, the logic is provided already in canonical DNF form or in Conjunctive Normal Form (CNF), i.e., conjunctions of disjunctions. We will see later that any WFF expressed in CNF can be converted into an RBM's energy function efficiently without the need to convert into SDNF first. This covers the most common forms of propositional knowledge representation. Next, we describe a method for converting logical formulae into SDNF, which we use in the empirical evaluations that will follow. Consider a clause γ such that:

$$\gamma \equiv \bigvee_{t\in\mathcal{S}_T} \neg \mathrm{x}_t \vee \bigvee_{k\in\mathcal{S}_K} \mathrm{x}_k, \tag{2.3}$$

where $\mathcal{S}_T$ now denotes the set of indices of the negative literals, and $\mathcal{S}_K$ denotes the set of indices of the positive literals in the clause (dually to the conjunctive clause case). Clause γ can be rearranged into $\gamma \equiv \gamma' \vee \mathrm{x}'$, where γ' is obtained by removing x' from γ (x' can be either $\neg\mathrm{x}_t$ or x_k for any $t \in \mathcal{S}_T$ and $k \in \mathcal{S}_K$). We have:

$$\gamma \equiv (\neg\gamma' \wedge \mathrm{x}') \vee \gamma' \tag{2.4}$$

because $(\neg\gamma' \wedge \mathrm{x}') \vee \gamma' \equiv (\gamma' \vee \neg\gamma') \wedge (\gamma' \vee \mathrm{x}') \equiv True \wedge (\gamma' \vee \mathrm{x}')$. By De Morgan's law ($\neg(\mathrm{a} \vee \mathrm{b}) \equiv \neg\mathrm{a} \wedge \neg\mathrm{b}$), we can always convert $\neg\gamma'$ (and therefore $\neg\gamma' \wedge \mathrm{x}'$) into a conjunctive clause.

By applying Eq. (2.4) repeatedly, each time we eliminate a variable out of the clause by moving it into a new conjunctive clause. Given an assignment of truth-values, either the clause γ' will be *True* or the conjunctive clause $(\neg\gamma' \wedge \mathrm{x}')$ will be *True*, e.g., $a \vee b \equiv a \vee (\neg a \wedge b)$. Therefore, the SDNF for clause γ in Eq. (2.3) is:

$$\bigvee_{p\in\mathcal{S}_T\cup\mathcal{S}_K} \left(\bigwedge_{t\in\mathcal{S}_T\backslash p} \mathrm{x}_t \wedge \bigwedge_{k\in\mathcal{S}_K\backslash p} \neg\mathrm{x}_k \wedge \mathrm{x}'_p \right), \tag{2.5}$$

where $\mathcal{S} \setminus p$ denotes a set $\mathcal{S}$ from which element p has been removed. If $p \in \mathcal{S}_T$ then $\mathrm{x}'_p \equiv \neg\mathrm{x}_p$. Otherwise, $\mathrm{x}'_p \equiv \mathrm{x}_p$. As an example of the translation into SDNF, consider the translation of an *if-then* statement (logical implication) below.

Example 2.1: *Translation of if-then rules into SDNF. Consider the formula* $\gamma \equiv (x_1 \wedge x_2 \wedge \neg x_3) \rightarrow y$. *Using our notation:*

$$\gamma \equiv \left(\bigwedge_{t\in\{1,2\}} \mathrm{x}_t \wedge \bigwedge_{k\in\{3\}} \neg\mathrm{x}_k \right) \rightarrow \mathrm{y} \tag{2.6}$$

Converting to DNF:

$$\left(\mathrm{y} \wedge \bigwedge_{t\in\{1,2\}} \mathrm{x}_t \wedge \bigwedge_{k\in\{3\}} \neg\mathrm{x}_k \right) \vee \bigvee_{t\in\{1,2\}} \neg\mathrm{x}_t \vee \bigvee_{k\in\{3\}} \mathrm{x}_k. \tag{2.7}$$

Applying the variable elimination method to the clause $\neg\mathrm{x}_1 \vee \neg\mathrm{x}_2 \vee \mathrm{x}_3$, *we obtain the SDNF for* γ*:*

$$\left(\mathrm{y} \wedge \bigwedge_{t\in\mathcal{S}_T} \mathrm{x}_t \bigwedge_{k\in\mathcal{S}_K} \neg\mathrm{x}_k \right) \vee (\neg\mathrm{x}_1) \vee (\mathrm{x}_1 \wedge \neg\mathrm{x}_2) \vee (\mathrm{x}_1 \wedge \mathrm{x}_2 \wedge \mathrm{x}_3). \tag{2.8}$$

2.3.3 Reasoning in RBMs

We have seen how propositional logic formula can be mapped onto the energy functions of RBMs. In this section, we discuss the deployment of such RBMs for logical reasoning.

2.3.3.1 Reasoning as Sampling

There is a direct relationship between inference in RBMs and logical satisfiability, as follows.

Lemma 2.2: *Let $\mathcal{N}$ be an RBM with energy function E. Let φ be a WFF such that $s_\varphi(\mathbf{x}) = -E(\mathbf{x})$. Let $\mathcal{A}$ be a set of indices of variables in φ that have been assigned to either True or False. We use $\mathrm{x}_\mathcal{A}$ to denote the set $\{x_\alpha | \alpha \in \mathcal{A}\}$. Let $\mathcal{B}$ be a set of indices of variables that have not been assigned a truth-value in φ. We use $\mathbf{x}_\mathcal{B}$ to denote $\{x_\beta | \beta \in \mathcal{B}\}$. Performing Gibbs sampling on $\mathcal{N}$, given $\mathbf{x}_\mathcal{A}$, is equivalent to searching for an assignment of truth-values for $\mathbf{x}_\mathcal{B}$ that satisfies φ.*

Proof. Theorem 2.1 has shown that the assignments of truth-values to φ are partially ordered according to the RBM's energy function such that the models of φ (mapping φ to 1) correspond to minima of the energy function. We say that the satisfiability of φ is inversely proportional to the RBM's rank function.[9] A value of

9 When the satisfiability of φ is maximum ($s_\varphi(\mathbf{x}) = 1$), ranking the output of $-E(\mathbf{x})$ produces the highest rank.

$\mathbf{x}_{\mathcal{B}}$ that minimizes the energy function also maximizes satisfiability: $s_{\varphi}(\mathbf{x}_{\mathcal{B}}, \mathbf{x}_{\mathcal{A}}) \propto -min_{\mathbf{h}}E(\mathbf{x}_{\mathcal{B}}, \mathbf{x}_{\mathcal{A}}, \mathbf{h})$ because:

$$\mathbf{x}^*_{\mathcal{B}} = \arg\min_{\mathbf{x}_{\mathcal{B}_{\mathbf{h}}}} E(\mathbf{x}_{\mathcal{B}}, \mathbf{x}_{\mathcal{A}}, \mathbf{h}) = \arg\max_{\mathbf{x}_{\mathcal{B}}}(s_{\varphi}(\mathbf{x}_{\mathcal{B}}, \mathbf{x}_{\mathcal{A}})). \tag{2.9}$$

We can consider an iterative process to search for truth-values $\mathbf{x}^*_{\mathcal{B}}$ by minimizing an RBM's energy function. This can be done using gradient descent or contrastive divergence with Gibbs sampling. The goal is to update the values of $\mathbf{h}$ and then $\mathbf{x}_{\mathcal{B}}$ in parallel until convergence to minimize $E(\mathbf{x}_{\mathcal{B}}, \mathbf{x}_{\mathcal{A}}, \mathbf{h})$ while keeping the other variables ($\mathbf{x}_{\mathcal{A}}$) fixed. The gradients amount to:

$$\begin{aligned} \frac{\partial - E(\mathbf{x}_{\mathcal{B}}, \mathbf{x}_{\mathcal{A}}, \mathbf{h})}{\partial h_j} &= \sum_{i \in \mathcal{A} \cup \mathcal{B}} x_i w_{ij} + \theta_j, \\ \frac{\partial - E(\mathbf{x}_{\mathcal{B}}, \mathbf{x}_{\mathcal{A}}, \mathbf{h})}{\partial x_{\beta}} &= \sum_j h_j w_{\beta j} + theta_{\beta}. \end{aligned} \tag{2.10}$$

In the case of Gibbs sampling, given the assigned variables $\mathbf{x}_{\mathcal{A}}$, the process starts with a random initialization of $\mathbf{x}_{\mathcal{B}}$ and proceeds to infer values for the hidden units h_j and then the unassigned variables x_{β} in the visible layer of the RBM, using the conditional distributions $h_j \sim p(h_j|\mathbf{x})$ and $x_{\beta} \sim p(x_{\beta}|\mathbf{h})$, respectively, where $\mathbf{x} = \{\mathbf{x}_{\mathcal{A}}, \mathbf{x}_{\mathcal{B}}\}$ and:

$$\begin{aligned} p(h_j|\mathbf{x}) &= \frac{1}{1 + e^{-\frac{1}{\tau}\sum_i x_i w_{ij} + \theta_j}} = \frac{1}{1 + e^{-\frac{1}{\tau}\frac{\partial - E(\mathbf{x}_{\mathcal{B}}, \mathbf{x}_{\mathcal{A}}, \mathbf{h})}{\partial h_j}}}, \\ p(x_{\beta}|\mathbf{h}) &= \frac{1}{1 + e^{-\frac{1}{\tau}\sum_j h_j w_{\beta j} + \theta_{\beta}}} = \frac{1}{1 + e^{-\frac{1}{\tau}\frac{\partial - E(\mathbf{x}_{\mathcal{B}}, \mathbf{x}_{\mathcal{A}}, \mathbf{h})}{\partial x_{\beta}}}}. \end{aligned} \tag{2.11}$$

It can be seen from Eq. (2.11) that the distributions are monotonic functions of the negative energy's gradient over $\mathbf{h}$ and $\mathbf{x}_{\mathcal{B}}$. Therefore, performing Gibbs sampling on them can be seen as moving toward a local minimum that is equivalent to an assignment of truth-values that satisfies φ. Each step of Gibbs sampling, calculating $\mathbf{h}$ and then $\mathbf{x}$ to reduce the energy, should intuitively generate an assignment of truth-values that gets closer to satisfying the formula φ.

2.3.3.2 Reasoning as Lowering Free Energy

When the number of unassigned variables is not large, it should be possible to calculate the above probabilities directly. In this case, one can infer the assignments of $\mathbf{x}_{\mathcal{B}}$ using the conditional distribution:

$$P(\mathbf{x}_{\mathcal{B}}|\mathbf{x}_{\mathcal{A}}) = \frac{e^{-\mathcal{F}_{\mathcal{B}}(\mathbf{x}_{\mathcal{A}}, \mathbf{x}_{\mathcal{B}})}}{\sum_{\mathbf{x}'_{\mathcal{B}}} e^{\mathcal{F}_{\mathcal{B}}}(\mathbf{x}_{\mathcal{A}}, \mathbf{x}'_{\mathcal{B}})}, \tag{2.12}$$

where $\mathcal{F}_{\mathcal{B}} = -\sum_j(-\log(1 + e^{(c\sum_{i\in\mathcal{A}\cup\mathcal{B}} w_{ij}x_i+\theta_j)}))$ is known as the free energy; $\mathbf{x}'_{\mathcal{B}}$ denotes all the combinations of truth-value assignments to the literals in $\mathbf{x}_{\mathcal{B}}$; and c is a non-negative real number that we call a *confidence value*. The free energy term $-\log(1 + e^{(c\sum_{i\in\mathcal{A}\cup\mathcal{B}} w_{ij}x_i+\theta_j)})$ is a negative softplus function scaled by c, as shown in Figure 2.2. It returns a negative output for a positive input and a close-to-zero output for a negative input.

Each free energy term is associated with a conjunctive clause in the SDNF through the weighted sum $\sum_{i\in\mathcal{A}\cup\mathcal{B}} w_{ij}x_i + \theta_j$. Therefore, if a truth-value assignment of $\mathbf{x}_{\mathcal{B}}$ does not satisfy the formula φ, all energy terms will be close to zero. When φ is satisfied, one free energy term will be $-\log(1 + e^{c\epsilon})$, for a choice of $0 < \epsilon < 1$ from Theorem 2.1. Thus, the more likely that a truth assignment is to satisfying the formula, the lower the free energy. Formally:

$$s_\varphi(\mathbf{x}) = -\frac{1}{c\epsilon}\min_{\mathbf{h}} E(\mathbf{x}, \mathbf{h}) = \lim_{c\to\infty} -\frac{1}{c\epsilon}\mathcal{F}(\mathbf{x}). \tag{2.13}$$

Figure 2.3 shows the average values of the energy function and free energy for CNFs with 55 clauses as the number of satisfied clauses increases. The CNF is satisfied if and only if all 55 clauses are satisfied. As can be seen, the relationships

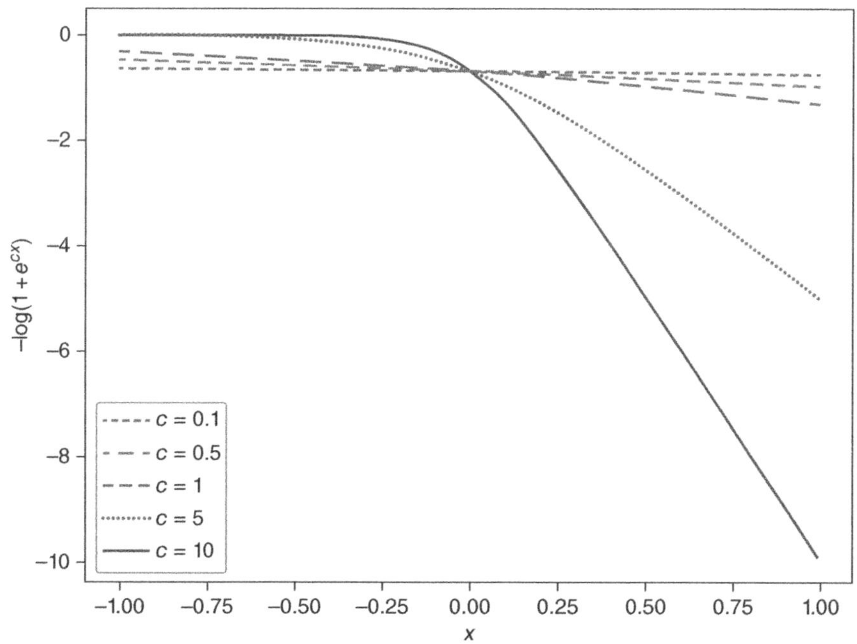

Figure 2.2 Free energy term $-\log(1 + e^{cx})$ for different confidence values c.

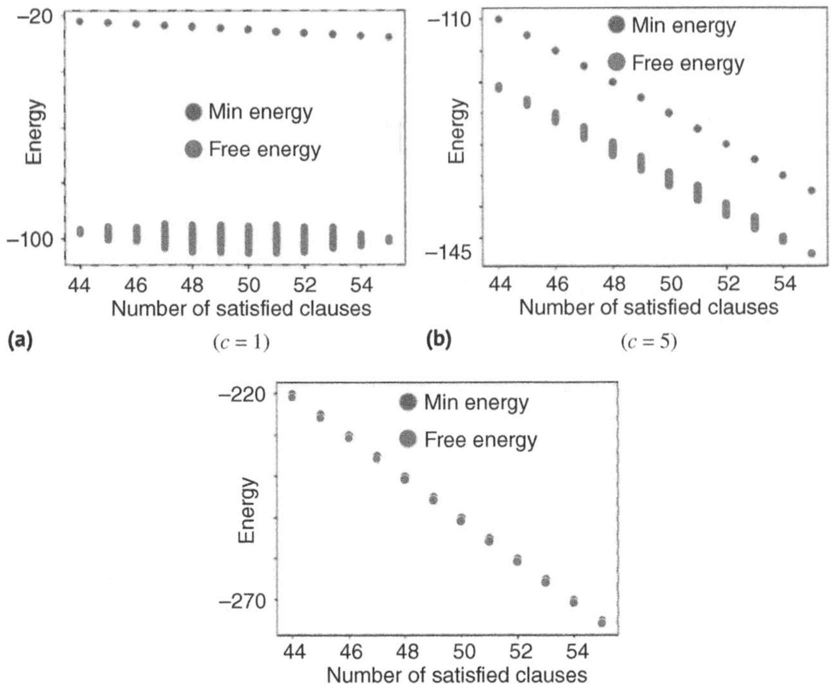

(a) $(c = 1)$ (b) $(c = 5)$ (c) $(c = 10)$

Figure 2.3 Linear correlation between satisfiability of a CNF and minimization of the free energy function for various confidence values c. *Source*: [10]/Association for the Advancement of Artificial Intelligence.

are linear. Minimum energy and free energy values converge with an increasing value of c.

2.3.4 Logical Boltzmann Machines

We are now in position to present a translation algorithm to build an RBM from logical formulae. The energy function of the RBM will be derived based on Theorem 2.1, given a formula in SDNF. The weights and biases of the RBM will be obtained from the energy function $E(\mathrm{x}, \mathrm{h}) = -(\sum_i \theta_i \mathrm{x}_i + \sum_j \theta_j \mathrm{h}_j + \sum_{ij} \mathrm{x}_i W_{ij} \mathrm{h}_j)$, where θ_i are the biases of the visible units, θ_j are the biases of the hidden units, and W_{ij} is the symmetric weight between a visible and a hidden unit. For each conjunctive clause in the formula of the form $\bigwedge_{t \in \mathcal{S}_T} \mathrm{x}_t \wedge \bigwedge_{k \in \mathcal{S}_K} \neg \mathrm{x}_k$, we create an energy term $-h_j(\sum_{t \in \mathcal{S}_T} x_t - \sum_{k \in \mathcal{S}_K} x_k - |\mathcal{S}_T| + \epsilon)$. The disjunctions in the SDNF are implemented in the RBM simply by creating a hidden neuron h_j for each disjunct in the SDNF.

Learning in LBM uses learning from data $\mathcal{D}$ combined with knowledge provided by the logical formulae. Learning with data and knowledge is expected to improve accuracy or training time. If the logical formula is empty, the weights and biases are initialized randomly, and one has a standard RBM. Learning in this case is an approximation of parameters Θ over a set of preferred models $\mathcal{D} = \{\mathbf{x}^{(n)} | n = 1, \dots, N\}$ of an unknown formula φ^*. Consider the case where the dataset $\mathcal{D}$ is complete, i.e., it contains all preferred models of an unknown φ^*. We will show that learning an RBM to represent the SDNF of φ^* is possible. Consider the gradient of the negative log-likelihood $(-\ell)$ of an RBM:

$$\frac{\partial - \ell}{\partial \Theta} = \mathbf{E}\left[\frac{\partial E(\mathbf{x}, \mathbf{h})}{\partial \Theta}\right]_{\mathbf{h}|\mathbf{x} \in \mathcal{D}} - \mathbf{E}\left[\frac{\partial E(\mathbf{x}, \mathbf{h})}{\partial \Theta}\right]_{\mathbf{h}, \mathbf{x},} \tag{2.14}$$

where $\mathbf{E}$ denotes the expected value. This function is not convex. Therefore, the RBM may not always converge to φ^*. Consider now the case where $\mathcal{D}$ is incomplete. At a local minimum, we have that $\frac{\partial\text{-}\ell}{\partial w_{ij}} = -\frac{1}{N} \sum_{\mathbf{x} \in \mathcal{D}} x_i p(h_j|\mathbf{x}) + \sum_{\mathbf{x}} x_i p(h_j|\mathbf{x}) p(\mathbf{x}) \approx 0$. A solution to this is $p(h_j|\mathbf{x}) p(\mathbf{x}) \approx \frac{p(h_j|\mathbf{x})}{N}$ if $\mathbf{x} \in \mathcal{D}$, and 0 otherwise. This can be achieved by either having $p(h_j|\mathbf{x}) \approx 0$ or $p(\mathbf{x}) \approx 0$ for all $\mathbf{x} \notin \mathcal{D}$ and $p(\mathbf{x}) \approx \frac{1}{N}$ for $\mathbf{x} \in \mathcal{D}$. Since $p(\mathbf{x}) = \frac{1}{Z} \sum_{\mathbf{h}} \exp(-E(\mathbf{x}, \mathbf{h}))$, then for a training example (preferred model) $\mathbf{x}$, we have $\sum_{\mathbf{x}} \sum_{\mathbf{h}} \exp(-E(\mathbf{x}, \mathbf{h})) \approx N \sum_{\mathbf{h}} \exp(-E(\mathbf{x}, \mathbf{h}))$. Hence, a solution is obtained if $\sum_{\mathbf{h}} \exp(-E(\mathbf{x}, \mathbf{h}))$ is equally large for all $x \in \mathcal{D}$, and much smaller otherwise. We can further factorize this sum to get $\sum_{\mathbf{h}} \exp(-E(\mathbf{x}, \mathbf{h})) \propto \prod_j (1 + \exp(\sum_i w_{ij} x_i + \theta_j))$. Now, suppose that an LBM with parameters $\Theta = (W^*, \theta^*)$ represents an unknown formula φ^*. Assuming that the LBM has large and equal confidence values c_∞ for its free-energy function (as discussed in Section 2.3.3.2), this LBM would allow only one hidden unit to be activated for a satisfying assignment $\mathbf{x}$. In the case of an unsatisfiable assignment, all hidden units would be deactivated. Therefore, one can choose c_∞ large enough to guarantee that a solution is found because $\prod_j (1 + \exp(\sum_i w^*_{ij} x_i + b^*_j)) \approx \exp(c_\infty \epsilon)$ if $\mathbf{x} \in \mathcal{D}$.

Example 2.2: *We use the symbol* $\oplus$ *to denote exclusive-or, that is* $\mathrm{x} \oplus \mathrm{y} \equiv ((\mathrm{x} \wedge \neg \mathrm{y}) \vee (\neg \mathrm{x} \wedge \mathrm{y}))$. *The formula* $\varphi \equiv (\mathrm{x} \oplus \mathrm{y}) \leftrightarrow \mathrm{z}$ *can be converted into the SDNF:*

$$\varphi \equiv (\neg \mathrm{x} \wedge \neg \mathrm{y} \wedge \neg \mathrm{z}) \vee (\neg \mathrm{x} \wedge \mathrm{y} \wedge \mathrm{z}) \vee (\mathrm{x} \wedge \neg \mathrm{y} \wedge \mathrm{z}) \vee (\mathrm{x} \wedge \mathrm{y} \wedge \neg \mathrm{z}).$$

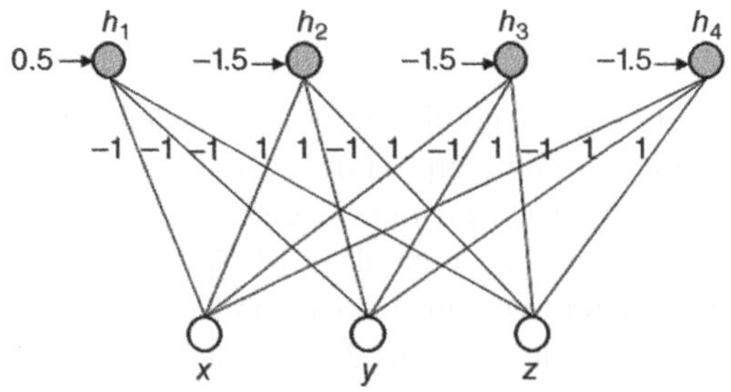

Figure 2.4 An RBM equivalent to the XOR formula $(x \oplus y) \leftrightarrow z$.

Table 2.1 Energy function and truth-table for the formula $((x \wedge \neg y) \vee (\neg x \wedge y)) \leftrightarrow z$.

x	y	z	$s_\varphi(x, y, z)$	$min_{\mathbf{h}} E(\mathbf{x}, \mathbf{h})$
0	0	0	*True*	−0.5
0	0	1	*False*	0
0	1	0	*False*	0
0	1	1	*True*	−0.5
1	0	0	*False*	0
1	0	1	*True*	−0.5
1	1	0	*True*	−0.5
1	1	1	*False*	0

For each conjunctive clause in φ, a corresponding term is added to the energy function. An RBM for the XOR formula φ can be built as shown in Figure 2.4 for a choice of $\epsilon = 0.5$ and zero bias for the visible units ($\theta_i = 0$). The energy function of this RBM is:

$$E = -h_1(-x - y - z + 0.5) - h_2(x + y - z - 1.5)$$

$$-h_3(x + y - z - 1.5) - h_4(-x + y + z - 1.5)$$

Table 2.1 shows the equivalence between $min_{\mathbf{h}} E(\mathbf{x}, \mathbf{h})$ and the truth-table for the XOR formula. The above example illustrates in a simple case the value of using SDNF, in that it produces a direct translation into an RBM, as also illustrated below.

Example 2.3: *We have seen that the SDNF of* $(\mathrm{x}_1 \wedge \mathrm{x}_2 \wedge \neg\mathrm{x}_3) \rightarrow \mathrm{y}$ *is* $(\mathrm{y} \wedge \mathrm{x}_1 \wedge \mathrm{x}_2 \wedge \neg\mathrm{x}_3) \vee (\mathrm{x}_1 \wedge \mathrm{x}_2 \wedge \mathrm{x}_3) \vee (\mathrm{x}_1 \wedge \neg\mathrm{x}_2) \vee \neg\mathrm{x}_1$. *We need an RBM with only 3 hidden units*[10] *to represent this SDNF. The energy function with* $\epsilon = 0.5$ *is:*

$$E = e_y + \sum_{i=1}^{3} e_i, \text{ where}$$

$$e_y = -h_y(y + x_1 + x_2 - x_3 - 2.5) \qquad (\mathrm{y} \wedge \mathrm{x}_1 \wedge \mathrm{x}_2 \wedge \neg\mathrm{x}_3)$$

$$e_3 = -h_3(x_1 + x_2 + x_3 - 2.5) \qquad (\mathrm{x}_1 \wedge \mathrm{x}_2 \wedge \mathrm{x}_3)$$

$$e_2 = -h_2(x_1 - x_2 - 0.5) \qquad (\mathrm{x}_1 \wedge \neg\mathrm{x}_2)$$

$$e_1 = 0.5x_1 \qquad (\neg\mathrm{x}_1)$$

The number of hidden units grows linearly with the number of disjuncts in the formula. The computationally expensive part is the translation from WFF to SDNF in case it is needed.

2.3.5 Experimental Results

2.3.5.1 Reasoning

We deployed LBM to search for satisfying truth assignments of variables in large formulae. Let us define a class of formulae as:

$$\varphi \equiv \bigwedge_{i=1}^{M} \mathrm{x}_i \wedge \left(\bigvee_{j=M+1}^{M+N} \mathrm{x}_j \right). \tag{2.15}$$

A formula in this class consists of 2^{M+N} possible truth assignments of the variables, with $2^N - 1$ of them mapping the formula to $true$ (call this the *satisfying set*). Converting to SDNF as done before but now for the class of formulae, we obtain:

$$\varphi \equiv \bigvee_{j=M+1}^{M+N} \left(\bigwedge_{i=1}^{M} \mathrm{x}_i \wedge \bigwedge_{j'=j+1}^{M+N} \neg\mathrm{x}_{j'} \wedge \mathrm{x}_j \right). \tag{2.16}$$

Applying Theorem 2.1 to construct an RBM from φ, we use Gibbs sampling to find the models of a formula given random initial truth assignments to all the variables. A sample is *accepted* as a satisfying assignment (a model) if its free energy is lower

10 In the case of $\neg x_1$, or any term of the energy function with a single variable, the term is implemented in the RBM via the bias of x_1. For a positive literal x, the energy term $-h(x - 1 + \epsilon)$ can be replaced by $-x\epsilon$. For a negative literal $\neg x$, the energy term $-h(-x + \epsilon)$ can be replaced by $-(1 - x)\epsilon$. This is possible because in order to minimize the energy, $h = 1$ if and only if $x = 0$ (in the case of $\neg x$); thus, $h = 1 - x$. Therefore, $-h(-x + \epsilon) = -(1 - x)(-x + \epsilon) = -(-x + \epsilon + x^2 - x\epsilon) = -(1 - x)\epsilon$, because $x = x^2$.

than or equal to $-\log(1 + \exp(c\epsilon)$ with $c = 5, \epsilon = 0.5$. We evaluate the *coverage* and *accuracy* of accepted samples. Coverage is measured as the proportion of the satisfying set that is accepted over time. In this experiment, this is the number of satisfying assignments in the set of accepted samples divided by $2^N - 1$. It can be seen as a measure of completeness. Accuracy is measured as the percentage of samples accepted by the RBM that do satisfy the logical formula.

We test different values of $M \in \{20, 25, 30\}$ and $N \in \{3, 4, 5, 6, 7, 8, 9, 10\}$. LBM achieves 100% accuracy in all cases, meaning that all accepted samples do satisfy the formula, as expected (given Theorem 2.1). Figure 2.5 shows the coverage as Gibbs sampling progresses (after each time that a number of random samples is collected). Four cases are considered: $M = 20$ and $N = 5$; $M = 20$ and $N = 10$; $M = 25$ and $N = 10$; $M = 30$ and $N = 10$.

In each case, we run the sampling process 100 times and report the average results with standard deviations. The satisfying set, and therefore the number of samples needed to achieve 100% coverage, is much lower than the number of possible assignments (2^{M+N}). For example, when $M = 20, N = 10$, all satisfying assignments are found after 7.5 million samples are collected, whereas the number of possible assignments is approximately 1 billion, producing a ratio of sample size to the search space size of just 0.75%. The ratio for $M = 30, N = 10$ is even lower at 0.37% w.r.t. 10^{12} possible assignments.

Figure 2.6 shows the time taken to collect all satisfying assignments for different N in $\{3, 4, 5, 6, 7, 8, 9, 10\}$ with $M = 20$. LBM needed around 10 seconds for $N \leq 8$, 25 seconds for $N = 9$, and 68 seconds for $N = 10$. As expected, the curve grows exponentially similarly to the search space size, but at a much smaller scale.

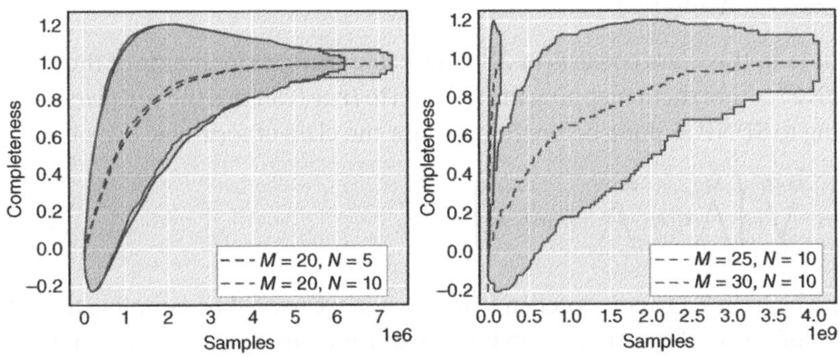

Figure 2.5 Percentage coverage as a measure of completeness as sampling progresses in the RBM. Coverage of 100% is achieved for the class of formulae with different values for M and N averaged over 100 runs. The number of samples needed to achieve 100% coverage is much lower than the number of possible assignments (2^{M+N}). For example, when $M = 20$ and $N = 10$, all satisfying assignments are found after approximately 7.5×10^6 samples are provided as input to the RBM, whereas the number of possible assignments is approximately 1 billion, a ratio of sample size to the search space of 0.75%. The ratio for $M = 30, N = 10$ is even lower at 0.37%. *Source*: [10]/Association for the Advancement of Artificial Intelligence.

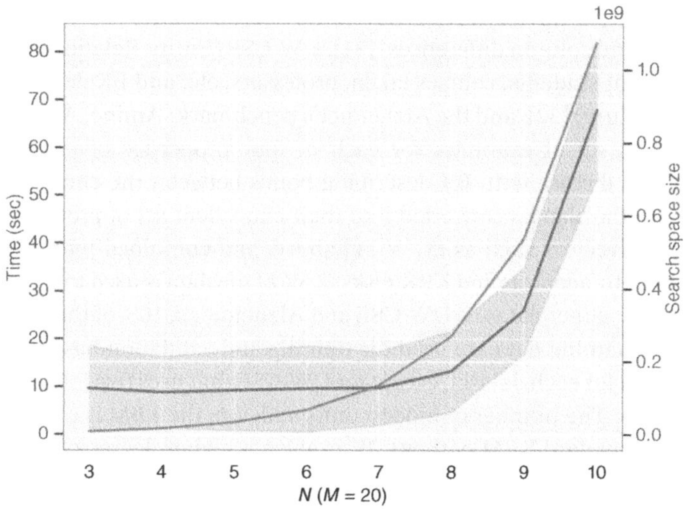

Figure 2.6 Time taken by LBM to collect all satisfying assignments compared with the size of the search space (i.e., the number of possible assignments up to 1 billion (1e9)) as N increases from 3 to 10 with fixed $M = 20$. LBM only needs around 10 seconds for $N \leq 8$, 25 seconds for $N = 9$, and 68 seconds for $N = 10$. The curve grows exponentially, similarly to the search space size, but at a much lower scale. *Source*: [10]/Association for the Advancement of Artificial Intelligence.

2.3.5.2 Learning from Data and Knowledge

We now evaluate LBM at learning the same ILP benchmark tasks used by neurosymbolic system CILP++ [12] in comparison with ILP state-of-the-art system Aleph [28]. As mentioned earlier, the systems Aleph, CILP++, and a fully connected standard RBM were chosen as the natural symbolic, neurosymbolic, and neural system, respectively, for comparison. An initial LBM is constructed from the clauses provided as background knowledge (BK). This process creates one hidden neuron per clause. Further hidden neurons are added using random weights for training and validation from data. Satisfying assignments can be selected from each clause as a training or validation example; for instance, given clause $x_1 \wedge \neg x_2 \rightarrow y$, assignment $x_1 = True, x_2 = False, y = True$ is converted into vector $[x_1, x_2, y] = (1, 0, 1)$ for training or validation. Both the LBM and the standard RBM are trained discriminatively using the conditional distribution $p(y|\mathbf{x})$ for inference as in Larochelle et al. [29]. In both cases, all network weights are free parameters for learning, with some weights having been initialized by the BK in the case of the LBM; that is, the BK can be revised during learning from data.

Seven datasets with available data and BK are used: Mutagenesis (examples of molecules tested for mutagenicity and BK provided in the form of rules describing relationships between atom bonds) [30], KRK (King-Rook versus King chess endgame with examples provided by the coordinates of the pieces on the board and BK in the form of row and column differences) [31], UW-CSE (Entity-Relationship diagram with data about students, courses taken, professors, etc. and BK describing the relational structure) [32], and the Alzheimer's benchmark: Amine, Acetyl, Memory, and Toxic (a set of examples for each of four properties of a drug design for Alzheimer's disease with BK describing bonds between the chemical structures) [33]. With the clauses converted into their equivalent set of preferred models in the form of vectors such as $[x_1, x_2, y]$ above, and combined with the available data, for the Mutagenesis and KRK tasks, 2.5% of the data is used to build the initial LBM. For the larger datasets UW-CSE and Alzheimer's, 10% of the data is used as BK. The remaining data are used for training and validation based on 10-fold cross-validation for each dataset, except for UW-CSE that uses five folds for the sake of comparison. The number of hidden units added to the LBM is chosen arbitrarily at 50. The standard RBM without BK is given a higher degree of freedom with 100 hidden units. Results are shown in Table 2.2.[11] It can be seen that LBM has the best performance in five out of seven datasets. Some of the results of the LBM and RBM are comparable when the BK can be learned from the examples, as in the case of the Alzheimer's amine dataset. In these cases, training the LBM is faster than the RBM. Aleph is better than all other models in the *alz-acetyl* dataset. This task must rely more heavily on the correctness of the BK than the data. CILP++, however, is considerably faster than Aleph, and it can achieve comparable results. Although direct comparisons of running times are not possible to make between CILP++ and LBM, LBM's running times look promising.

Table 2.2 Cross-validation performance of LBM against purely-symbolic system Aleph, neurosymbolic system CILP++ and a standard RBM on 7 benchmark data sets for neurosymbolic AI. We run cross-validation on RBM and LBM 100 times and report the average results with 95% confidence interval.

	Aleph	**CILP++**	**RBM**	**LBM**
Mutagenesis	80.85(±10.5)	91.70(±5.84)	95.55(±1.36)	**96.28**(±1.21)
KRK	99.60(±0.51)	98.42(±1.26)	99.70(±0.11)	**99.80**(±0.09)
UW-CSE	84.91(±7.32)	70.01(±2.2)	89.14(±0.46)	**89.43**(±0.42)
alz-amine	78.71(±5.25)	78.99(±4.46)	**79.13**(±1.14)	78.25(±1.07)
alz-acetyl	**69.46**(±3.6)	65.47(±2.43)	62.93(±0.31)	66.82(±0.28)
alz-memory	68.57(±5.7)	60.44(±4.11)	68.54(±0.97)	**71.84**(±0.88)
alz-toxic	80.50(±3.98)	81.73(±4.68)	82.71(±1.18)	**84.95**(±1.04)

Source: [10]/Association for the Advancement of Artificial Intelligence.

11 The results for Aleph and CILP++ are obtained from França et al. [12].

2.3.6 Extensions of LBMs

2.3.6.1 Translating CNF into RBMs

In the general case, translation to SDNF can be costly. When knowledge is provided in CNF form, it is useful to be able to translate the CNF directly into the RBM without the need for an intermediate step.

Every WFF can be converted into CNF. A CNF is a conjunction of clauses. Formally:

$$\varphi_{\mathrm{CNF}} \equiv \bigwedge_{m=1}^{M} \left(\bigvee_{t \in \mathcal{S}_T^m} x_t \vee \bigvee_{k \in \mathcal{S}_K^m} \neg x_k \right). \tag{2.17}$$

We will apply the same transformation process into SDNF to each conjunctive clause in the CNF. The result will be a conjunction of M SDNFs (itself not an SDNF), as follows:

$$\varphi_{\mathrm{CNF}} \equiv \bigwedge_{m=1}^{M} \left(\bigvee_{t \in \mathcal{S}_T^m} \neg \mathrm{x}_t \vee \bigvee_{k \in \mathcal{S}_K^m} \mathrm{x}_k \right) \equiv \bigwedge_{m=1}^{M} \left(\bigvee_{p \in \mathcal{S}_T^m \cup \mathcal{S}_K^m} \left(\bigwedge_{t \in \mathcal{S}_T^m \setminus p} \mathrm{x}_t \wedge \bigwedge_{k \in \mathcal{S}_K^m \setminus p} \neg \mathrm{x}_k \wedge \mathrm{x}'_p \right) \right), \tag{2.18}$$

where $\mathrm{x}'_p \equiv \neg \mathrm{x}_p$ if $p \in \mathcal{S}_T^m$; otherwise $\mathrm{x}'_p \equiv \mathrm{x}_p$.

This transformation would increase the space complexity from $\mathcal{O}(M \times N)$ to $\mathcal{O}(M \times N^2)$, where M is the number of clauses and N is the number of variables. This should not be a problem for current computing systems, especially when inference with RBMs can be highly parallelized.

Although the formula in Eq. (2.18) is not a SDNF, the equivalence between the CNF and the LBM still holds:

$$s_\varphi = \begin{cases} 1 & \text{when } -\dfrac{1}{\epsilon} min_{\mathbf{h}} E(\mathbf{x}, \mathbf{h}) = M \\ 0 & \text{otherwise.} \end{cases} \tag{2.19}$$

Eq. (2.19) holds because the CNF is satisfied if and only if all M SDNFs are satisfied. Under such circumstances, $min_{\mathbf{h}} E(\mathbf{x}, \mathbf{h}) = -M\epsilon$. Otherwise, $min_{\mathbf{h}} E(\mathbf{x}, \mathbf{h}) = -M'\epsilon$, where $M' < M$.

When a *confidence value* c is used, the number of satisfied clauses in CNF will be proportional to the minimized energy function, and to the free-energy function when c increases.

2.3.6.2 Toward Using LBM as a SAT Solver

The Boolean satisfiability (SAT) problem is a fundamental problem in Computer Science. It was the first problem that was proven to be non polynomial (NP) complete. A formula is satisfiable if and only if there exists an assignment of truth-values mapping the formula to True. In practice, formulae in SAT problems are represented as CNFs.

As discussed in Section 2.3.6.1, a formula in CNF can be converted into a LBM. The number of satisfied clauses in the CNF formula is proportional to the minimized energy function and the free-energy function of the LBM. This relationship allows us to solve SAT problems by transforming them into an optimization task: finding the minimum of the energy or free-energy function.

To make this approach computationally feasible, we focus on minimizing the free-energy function, as it is both easier to compute and differentiable. This transformation converts the discrete SAT problem into a continuous optimization problem. Instead of searching for solutions in a Boolean space (where variables x are either 0 or 1), we search in a continuous space for parameters θ, where each Boolean variable x is represented as a sigmoid function:

$$x = \sigma(\theta) = \frac{1}{1 + \exp(-\theta)}.$$

This mapping ensures that x smoothly transitions between 0 and 1 as θ changes, enabling gradient-based optimization techniques to be applied. To illustrate this process, consider a simple SAT problem with two variables:

$$(\neg x_1 \vee \neg x_2) \wedge (x_1 \vee \neg x_2) \wedge (\neg x_1 \vee x_2).$$

Figure 2.7 visualizes the landscape of the LBM's energy and free-energy functions for different values of θ_1 and θ_2, where $x_1 = \sigma(\theta_1)$ and $x_2 = \sigma(\theta_2)$. The plots reveal that when both θ_1 and θ_2 are more negative (corresponding to $x_1, x_2 \approx 0$), the functions approach their minima. This corresponds to a satisfying assignment of the CNF formula, illustrating how the optimization process identifies valid solutions.

We also analyze the impact of confidence values c on the landscapes of the energy and free-energy functions. Figures 2.7a–d show that confidence values do not significantly alter the landscape of the energy function. However, for the free-energy function (Figures 2.7e–h), smaller values of c result in smoother landscapes. While this smoothing effect can facilitate optimization by reducing sharp transitions, it also narrows the gap between local minima and the global minimum. Conversely, higher values of c increase the boundaries between optimal regions, making it more challenging to locate the global optimum. This trade-off highlights the importance of carefully selecting c based on the specific characteristics of the SAT problem being solved.

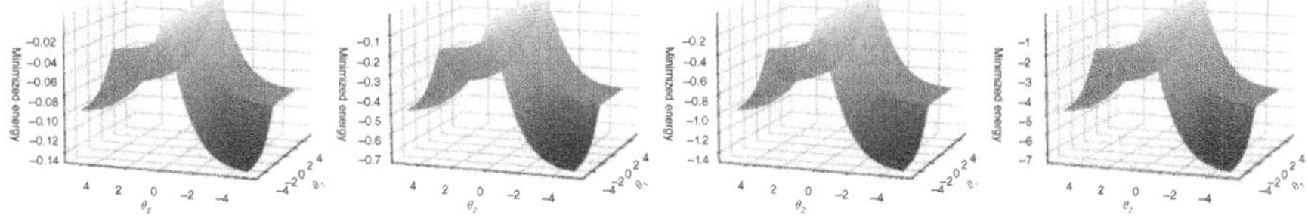

(a) $c = 0.1$ **(b)** $c = 0.5$ **(c)** $c = 1$ **(d)** $c = 5$

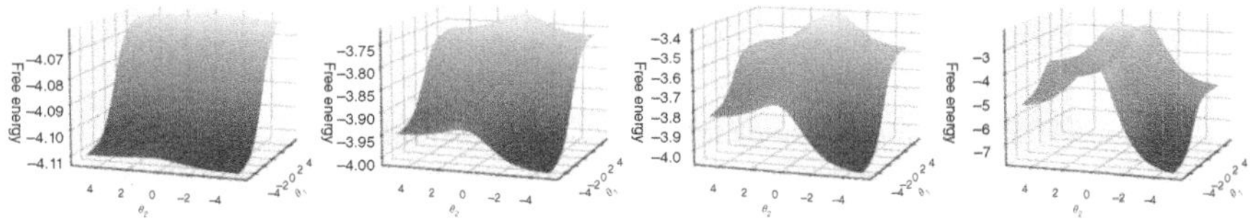

(e) $c = 0.1$ **(f)** $c = 0.5$ **(g)** $c = 1$ **(h)** $c = 5$

Figure 2.7 Energy function (top row) and free-energy function (bottom row) with different *confidence values*; c does not alter significantly the energy function landscape, while for the free-energy, smaller values of c result in smoother landscapes.

In summary, the LBM framework provides an approach to solving SAT problems by converting them into continuous optimization tasks. By leveraging the differentiability of the free-energy function and the flexibility of sigmoid mappings, this approach bridges logical reasoning and numerical optimization. Future work should explore adaptive strategies for adjusting confidence values to balance smoothness and optimality and consider ways to enhance performance in the case of specific classes of SAT problems.

2.3.6.2.1 Comparison to Other Approaches

Unlike recent neural network-based approaches for SAT solving [26, 27], which rely on large datasets generated by traditional SAT solvers for training, our method eliminates this dependency. Instead, we directly convert SAT problems (typically expressed in CNF) into LBM representations. This data-independent transformation should simplify the workflow by reducing the need for extensive preprocessing or model training. When compared with other SAT-solving methods that utilize BMs, such as those in Hernandez et al. [24] and d'Anjou et al. [25], our approach leverages the much simpler structure RBMs. These earlier methods often employ dense or higher-order structures, which are computationally complex and challenging to implement. By contrast, our use of RBMs maintains a streamlined architecture without requiring modifications to the network (e.g., adding configurations) to map SAT problems to BMs. Finally, while LBM is not yet competitive with state-of-the-art SAT solvers in terms of raw performance, it seems to open up a promising direction for further research. Unlike traditional SAT solvers, LBM is in essence a neural network. This should enable a seamless integration of reasoning and learning. Furthermore, LBM does not require prior knowledge of SAT problem structures or specific solving tactics such as backtracking or unit propagation. It is important to notice that our current implementation relies solely on off-the-shelf optimization methods, with room for significant improvements through parallelization optimization and the incorporation of advanced SAT-solving strategies.

2.3.6.2.2 SAT Solving Methodology and Initial Experimental Results

We used random SAT problems [34] as a case study. To solve SAT problems using LBM, we follow these steps:

- Convert a CNF into an RBM using the transformation described earlier.
- Apply various inference and optimization techniques to find satisfying assignments or determine unsatisfiability. Specifically:
  - Use Gibbs sampling to minimize the energy function and search for satisfying assignments.
  - Employ gradient-based methods from TensorFlow to optimize the differentiable free energy function.
  - Utilize stochastic optimization methods from the Scipy library, such as *dual_annealing* and *differential_evolution*.

Our experiments produced the following results:

- **Gibbs Sampling:**
  - Gibbs sampling can find satisfying assignments for CNFs with fewer than 40 variables. For larger formulae, Gibbs sampling often gets stuck in local minima, making it challenging to determine satisfiability. In such cases, if the free energy function does not decrease after 1000 steps of Gibbs sampling, we conclude that the formula is likely unsatisfiable.
- **Gradient-based Optimization (TensorFlow):**
  - Gradient-based methods are applied to minimize the differentiable free-energy function. However, these methods are prone to getting trapped in local minima, especially for SAT problems with more than 20 variables.
  - Attempts to smoothing the energy landscape by adjusting confidence values did not significantly improve performance, highlighting a difficulty in solving larger SAT instances with this approach.

- **Stochastic Optimization (Scipy):**
  - Among the stochastic optimization methods available in Scipy, *dual_annealing* and *differential_evolution* showed better scalability. These methods successfully solved SAT problems with up to 100 variables.
  - This suggests that stochastic global optimization techniques may offer a viable alternative for solving larger SAT instances with RBMs.

2.3.6.3 Implementing Penalty Logic in LBM

The closest work to LBM is Penalty Logic [21], which represents propositional formulae in Hopfield networks and BMs. In its first step, Penalty Logic creates *hidden variables* to reduce a formula φ to a conjunction of sub-formulae $\bigwedge_i \varphi_i$, each with at most three variables. This *naming* step makes conversion into an energy function easier, but some of the terms in the energy function may consist of hidden variables and therefore cannot be converted into an RBM. For example, a negative term $-h_1xy$ of a higher-order BM would be transformed into the quadratic term $-h_2h_1 - h_2x - h_2y + 5h_2$ with $-h_2h_1$ forming a connection between two hidden units, which is not allowed in RBMs. The three-variable term $-h_1xy$ is implemented in the higher-order network as a hypergraph. The variable h_2 is introduced to turn the hyper-edge into normal edges between each of the three variables and h_2 with an appropriate bias value for the new node h_2, in this example a value of 5.[12]

The LBM system converts any set of formulae $\Phi = \{\varphi_1, \ldots, \varphi_n\}$ into an RBM by applying Theorem 2.1 to each formula $\varphi_i \in \Phi$. In the case of Penalty Logic, formulae are weighted. Given a set of weighted formulae $\Phi = \{w_1 : \varphi_1, \ldots, w_n : \varphi_n\}$, one can also construct an equivalent RBM where each energy term generated from formula φ_i is multiplied by w_i. In both cases, the assignments that minimize the energy of the RBM are the assignments that maximize the satisfiability of Φ, i.e., the (weighted) sum of the truth-values of the formula.

Lemma 2.3: *Given a weighted knowledge-base $\Phi = \{w_1 : \varphi_1, \ldots, w_n : \varphi_n\}$, there exists an equivalent RBM $\mathcal{N}$ such that $s_\Phi(\mathbf{x}) = -\frac{1}{\epsilon} min_{\mathbf{h}} E(\mathbf{x}, \mathbf{h})$, where $s_\Phi(\mathbf{x})$ is the sum of the weights of the formulae in Φ that are satisfied by assignment* **x**.

12 Contrast the LBM for XOR in Figure 2.4 with the RBM for XOR built using Penalty Logic: first, one computes the higher-order energy function: $E^p = 4xyz - 2xy - 2xz - 2yz + x + y + z$, then transforms it to quadratic form by adding a hidden variable h_1 to obtain $E^p = 2xy - 2xz - 2yz - 8xh_1 - 8yh_1 + 8zh_1 + x + y + z + 12h_1$, which is not an energy function of an RBM, so one keeps adding hidden variables until the energy function of an RBM might be obtained, in this case: $E^p = -8xh_1 - 8yh_1 + 8zh_1 + 12h_1 - 4xh_2 + 4yh_2 + 2h_2 - 4yh_3 - 4zh_3 + 6h_3 - 4xh_4 - 4zh_4 + 6h_4 + 3x + y + z$.

A formula φ_i can be decomposed into a set of (weighted) conjunctive clauses from its SDNF. If there exist two conjunctive clauses such that one is subsumed by the other, then the subsumed clause is removed and the weight of the remaining clause is replaced by the sum of their weights. Identical conjunctive clauses are treated in the same way: one of them is removed, and the weights are added. From Theorem 2.1, we know that a conjunctive clause $\bigwedge_{t\in\mathcal{S}_{T_j}} \mathrm{x}_t \wedge \bigwedge_{k\in\mathcal{S}_{K_j}} \neg\mathrm{x}_k$ is equivalent to an energy term $e_j(\mathbf{x}, h_j) = -h_j(\sum_{t\in\mathcal{S}_{T_j}} x_t - \sum_{k\in\mathcal{S}_{K_j}} x_k - |\mathcal{S}_{T_j}| + \epsilon)$, where $0 < \epsilon < 1$. A weighted conjunctive clause $w' : \bigwedge_{t\in\mathcal{S}_{T_j}} \mathrm{x}_t \wedge \bigwedge_{k\in\mathcal{S}_{K_j}} \neg\mathrm{x}_k$, therefore, is equivalent to an energy term $w'e_j(\mathbf{x}, h_j)$. For each weighted conjunctive clause, we can add a hidden unit j to an RBM with connection weights $w_{tj} = w'$ for all $t \in \mathcal{S}_{T_j}$, and $w_{kj} = -w'$ for all $k \in \mathcal{S}_{K_j}$. The bias for this hidden unit will be $w'(-|\mathcal{S}_{T_j}| + \epsilon)$. The weighted knowledge-base and the RBM are equivalent because $s_\Phi(\mathbf{x}) \propto -\frac{1}{\epsilon} min_{\mathbf{h}} E(\mathbf{x}, \mathbf{h})$, where $s_\Phi(\mathbf{x})$ is the sum of the weights of the clauses that are satisfied by $\mathbf{x}$.

Example 2.4: *(Nixon diamond problem) Consider the following weighted knowledge-base from the original Penalty Logic paper [21] (the weights of 1000 and 10 are given and have been taken from the original paper):*

$1000 : \mathrm{n} \rightarrow \mathrm{r}$ *Nixon is a Republican.*

$1000 : \mathrm{n} \rightarrow \mathrm{q}$ *Nixon is also a Quaker.*

$10 : \mathrm{r} \rightarrow \neg\mathrm{p}$ *Republicans tend not to be Pacifists.*

$10 : \mathrm{q} \rightarrow \mathrm{p}$ *Quakers tend to be Pacifists.*

Converting all four weighted clauses above into SDNF produces eight conjunctive clauses. For example, weighted clause $1000 : \mathrm{n} \rightarrow \mathrm{r} \equiv 1000 : (\mathrm{n} \wedge \mathrm{r}) \vee (\neg\mathrm{n})$. *After adding the weights of clause* $(\neg\mathrm{n})$*, which appears twice, an RBM is created (Figure 2.8) representing the following unique conjunctive clauses with their corresponding confidence values:* $1000 : \mathrm{n} \wedge \mathrm{r}$, $2000 : \neg\mathrm{n}$, $1000 : \mathrm{n} \wedge \mathrm{q}$, $10 : \mathrm{r} \wedge \neg\mathrm{p}$, $10 : \neg\mathrm{r}$, $10 : \mathrm{q} \wedge \mathrm{p}$, $10 : \neg\mathrm{q}$.

With $\epsilon = 0.5$, *this RBM has energy function:* $E = -h_1(1000n + 1000r - 1500) - h_2(-2000n + 1000) - h_3(1000n + 1000q - 1500) - h_4(10r - 10p - 5) - h_5(-10r + 5) - h_6(10q + 10p - 15) - h_7(-10q + 5)$.

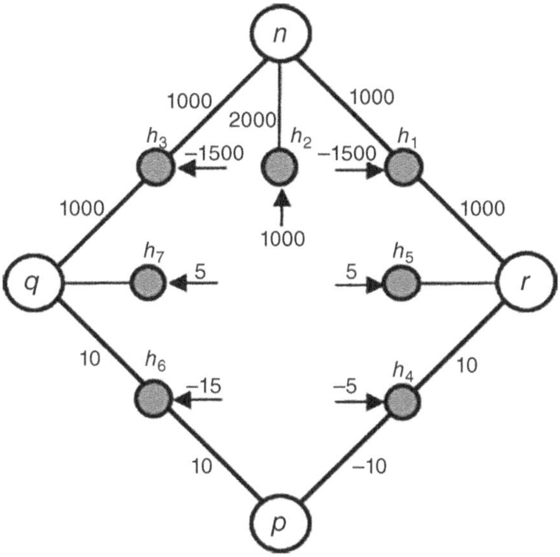

Figure 2.8 The RBM for the Nixon diamond problem has four input neurons $\{n, q, r, p\}$ and seven hidden neurons (shown in gray) as a result of the conversion into SDNF of the four weighted clauses shown in Example 2.4.

2.4 LBMs for MaxSAT

MaxSAT is a computational problem that extends the classical SAT problem. In MaxSAT, the goal is to find an assignment of truth values to the variables of a Boolean formula that maximizes the number of satisfied clauses. The formula is typically represented in CNF. We denote the number of satisfied clauses for a given assignment $\mathbf{x}$ as $\sum_m \mathbb{1}(\mathbf{x} \models \varphi_m)$. Here, $\mathbf{x} \models \varphi_m$ denotes that an assignment $\mathbf{x}$ satisfies the clause φ_m of the CNF, and $\mathbb{1}$ is an indicator function mapping a clause-satisfying assignment to 1, and everything else to 0. Differently from SAT, where the goal is to find any satisfying assignment, MaxSAT seeks the assignment that satisfies the maximum number of clauses, making it a combinatorial optimization problem:

$$\mathbf{x}^* = \arg\max_{\mathbf{x}} \sum_m \mathbb{1}(\mathbf{x} \models \varphi_m). \tag{2.20}$$

For example, consider the CNF formula:

$$\phi = (\neg x_1 \vee \neg x_2) \wedge (\neg x_1 \vee x_2) \wedge (x_1 \vee \neg x_2) \wedge (x_1 \vee x_2).$$

The goal is to find an assignment $x \in \{0, 1\}^n$ (where n is the number of variables; in this example, $n = 2$) that maximizes the number of satisfied clauses. We know that ϕ is unsatisfiable since each clause corresponds to exactly one assignment. An optimal solution will satisfy three out of the four clauses. This relaxation of the SAT task makes MaxSAT particularly suited for real-world optimization problems where constraints may need to be prioritized or relaxed to achieve the best overall solution. However, this flexibility comes at a cost: NP-Hardness, meaning that finding exact solutions becomes computationally infeasible as the number of variables grows. Many real-world applications, however, require approximate solutions to the MaxSAT problem, with the main challenge being how to balance accuracy and computation time.

Symbolic MaxSAT solvers have been the focus of intensive research for many years, gaining popularity among researchers and finding application in various domains from AI and computer-aided design to automated reasoning. Recent advancements in MaxSAT solvers have demonstrated significant improvements, with state-of-the-art solvers capable of scaling up to handling millions of variables and clauses.

MaxSAT has proven to be valuable in software analysis [35], hardware verification [36, 37], combinatorial optimization [38], bioinformatics [39], and data analysis [40]. Despite these achievements, the growing complexity of real-world problems has spurred interest in alternative approaches, such as leveraging the differentiable capabilities of Machine Learning to address MaxSAT by transforming the discrete problem into a continuous optimization task.

In recent years, there has been a growing interest in connectionist (differentiable) solvers. These solvers aim to represent MaxSAT problems using neural networks to benefit from the parallel computation and learning capabilities of such ML systems and from specialized neural network accelerators, such as GPUs and TPUs, to further enhance performance. Beyond providing an alternative approach to solving complex reasoning problems, connectionist MaxSAT solvers may promote the development of interpretable classification models [41], facilitating novel neurosymbolic learning and reasoning [10, 26] with the promise of offering more transparent decision-making in AI.

Deep learning-inspired MaxSAT solvers rely on real-valued weights often learned from example solutions [26]. In a related attempt, Liu et al. [42] seeks to train a Graph Neural Network for MaxSAT problem-solving. Unlike symbolic approaches, ML-based methods typically require a degree of supervision and may be criticized for their opacity. We take a different approach and use LBM along with a global optimization method called dual annealing, a modified version of a meta-heuristic method known as simulated annealing, to search for MaxSAT solutions. Using dual annealing, we will search the energy landscape of the RBM for a global minimum corresponding to a MaxSAT solution. The approach may be applicable to other classical optimization tasks that have also attracted considerable interest recently in connection with the use of differentiable approaches [43].

Research that has also focused on representing MaxSAT problems in connectionist networks without relying on explicit learning from examples includes Hernandez et al. [44], where the MaxSAT problem is mapped to a combinatorial optimization framework based on a high-order BM used to search for an approximate solution to SAT. However, the problems with efficiency of BMs are well-known. They have motivated the use of RBMs, first in Tran and d'Avila Garcez [10] and leading up to this work. In a more recent development also using RBMs, RBM-SAT was proposed to construct an RBM that represents the probability of an assignment w.r.t. the number of clauses that it satisfies [45]. The goal there is to conduct a heuristic search for solutions using block Gibbs samplings on neural network accelerators. Our goal, instead, is to make use of an interpretable RBM layer, as shown, e.g., in Figure 2.13, where each clause can be read off the LBM with binary weights.

Example 2.5: *An AND-gate* $\mathrm{x}_1 \wedge \neg \mathrm{x}_2$ *is represented by a free energy* $FE = -\log(1 + \exp(c \times (x_1 - x_2 - 0.5)))$. *Figure 2.9 illustrates the correspondence between the free energy and the truth-values for different values of c. Similarly, Figure 2.10 shows the free energy of an OR-gate (that is, a clause)* $\mathrm{x}_1 \vee \mathrm{x}_2$.

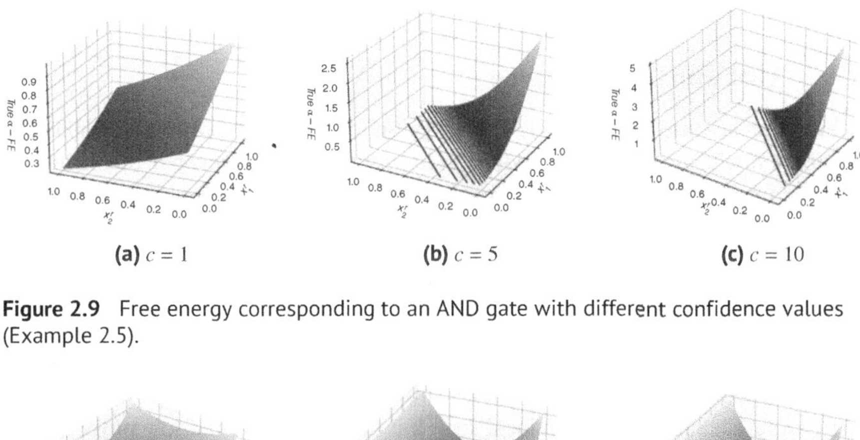

(a) $c = 1$ (b) $c = 5$ (c) $c = 10$

Figure 2.9 Free energy corresponding to an AND gate with different confidence values (Example 2.5).

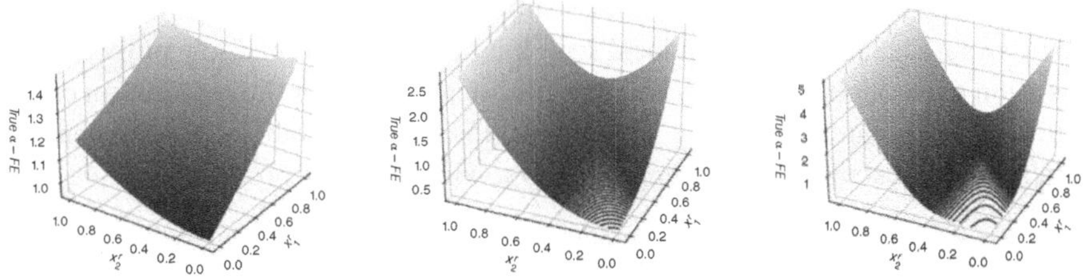

(a) $c = 1$ (b) $c = 5$ (c) $c = 10$

Figure 2.10 Free energy corresponding to an OR gate with different confidence values (Example 2.5).

This clause is transformed into SDNF $(\mathrm{x}_1 \wedge \neg \mathrm{x}_2) \vee \mathrm{x}_2$, *and the corresponding free energy is* $FE = -\log(1 + \exp(c \times (x_1 - x_2 - 0.5))) - \log(1 + \exp(c \times (x_2 - 0.5)))$. *As expected, the satisfying assignments are those that maximize the negative free energy.*

As we have seen already when using LBM as a SAT solver, a conjunctive clause φ_m can be represented in an RBM with the energy function $E_m = \sum_j e_j$, and, therefore, the energy function of a CNF will be:

$$E(\mathbf{x}) = \sum_m E_m. \tag{2.21}$$

The free energy of each clause corresponds to the truth values of the clause, i.e., $\mathbb{1}(\mathbf{x} \models \varphi_m) \propto FE_m(\mathbf{x})$. The free energy of the entire CNF $FE(\mathbf{x}) = \sum_m FE_m(\mathbf{x})$, therefore, corresponds to the number of satisfied conjunctive clauses, that is:

$$\sum_m \mathbb{1}(\mathbf{x} \models \varphi_m) \propto FE(\mathbf{x}). \tag{2.22}$$

An assignment that maximizes the number of satisfying clauses in a MaxSAT problem also minimizes the free energy of the LBM. Consequently, solving MaxSAT problems is equivalent to searching for a state of minimum free energy in the RBM.

2.4.1 LBM with Dual Annealing

When representing CNF in a RBM, one option for solving the MaxSAT problem is to utilize stochastic search methods like Gibbs sampling. However, in our scenario, Gibbs sampling exhibits slow convergence, necessitating potentially extensive computational resources to reach equilibrium. To mitigate this challenge, we have adopted simulated annealing, a meta-heuristic technique renowned for addressing global optimization problems [46]. Specifically, we employ dual annealing, which seamlessly integrates global and local search strategies to enhance efficiency [47].

In this approach, the search algorithm initially employs simulated annealing to identify a candidate region within the search space where global optima are likely to be situated. Subsequently, a local search is conducted to precisely pinpoint the location of the global optima. This hybrid strategy combines the exploration capabilities of simulated annealing with the exploitation capabilities of local search, offering a robust and efficient approach to solving MaxSAT problems.

2.4.2 Experimental Results of LBM for MaxSAT

As a preliminary evaluation, we compare the performance of LBM at solving MaxSAT problems with Loandra, a state-of-the-art MaxSAT solver. Loandra was chosen as benchmark solver due to its performance in the MaxSAT Evaluations

2023. Experiments were carried out on a set of challenging MaxSAT instances known as MaxCut, each containing 1260 clauses. Six distinct MaxCut problem instances were chosen from the MaxSAT 2016 benchmark. Both the LBM and Loandra solvers were run on each of the six instances with a timeout limit of 300 seconds for each run. The instances were chosen to represent diverse problem structures to evaluate the capabilities of the solvers without making assumptions about the CNF structure. All experiments were conducted on a standard desktop computer with a AMD Ryzen 7 5800X 8-core processor and 32 GB DDR4 RAM. The main evaluation metric was the number of satisfied clauses, indicating the solver's ability to maximize clause satisfaction within the given time constraints (Figure 2.11).

Loandra Satisfied Clauses Stats:

count	6.000000
mean	1089.000000
std	8.508819
min	1078.000000
25%	1083.500000
50%	1088.000000
75%	1095.500000
max	1100.000000

(a)

LBM Satisfied Clauses Stats:

count	6.000000
mean	1078.666667
std	3.502380
min	1075.000000
25%	1075.750000
50%	1078.500000
75%	1080.500000
max	1084.000000

(b)

Figure 2.11 Statistics for clause satisfaction for (a) Loandra (1089 clauses satisfied on average) and (b) LBM for MaxSAT (1078 clauses satisfied on average).

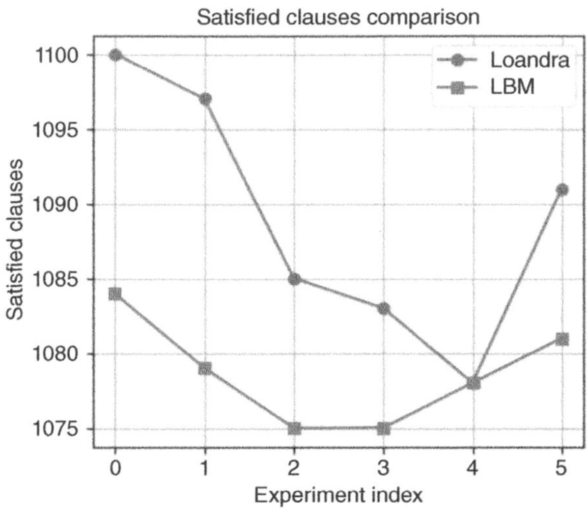

Figure 2.12 Performance of LBM and Loandra on six MaxCut experiments (0–5).

Figure 2.12 shows the number of clauses satisfied by the symbolic SAT solver Loandra and the LBM for MaxSAT approach in each of the six experiments. As a state-of-the-art solver, Loandra performed better than LBM in five out of six cases. However, the difference is relatively small, and further investigation is warranted, with numerous directions for future exploration. One possible direction involves investigating alternative global optimization methods such as evolutionary strategies. Another obvious direction is the implementation of parallel computation to improve scalability of LBM search, similar to the approach employed in RBMSAT. As future work, the task of *Image Sudoku* introduced in Stammer et al. [48] is an interesting extension to consider because of the interplay between object recognition and reasoning that is intrinsic to that task and aligned well with LBM's approach of integrating learning and reasoning, which we describe next.

2.5 Integrating Learning and Reasoning in LBMs

A key development in neurosymbolic AI will be the ability to add verified *modules* to existing networks. An RBM that can be shown to be provably equivalent to a given logical formula could act as one such module. A neurosymbolic module placed on top (at the output) of a larger network may serve to constrain that network's output to satisfy certain properties. In this process, the specification of a neurosymbolic module may benefit from the use of a logical language that is richer (more expressive) than propositional logic. In particular, the use of first-order logic may be required.

In first-order logic, instead of using propositions and connectives alone, logical *predicates* are used to represent relations among quantified variables. Statements such as $\forall X \exists Y.R(X, Y)$ are used to denote compactly a relation R between variables X and Y in a domain such that for all the values that variable X may admit, there is a value (an instance) of variable Y for which the relation R holds *True*.

As an example, if we were to rewrite into first-order logic the Boolean logical notation provided earlier for the Sudoku puzzle, we could use a ternary predicate $board(B, P, V)$, in which:

- B represents the block index (1–4),
- P represents the position index within the block (1–4), and
- V represents the value (1–4),

to make the problem description a lot more compact.

A first-order representation of the constraints of the Sudoku puzzle would include:

1. **Existence:** $\forall B, P, \exists V.board(B, P, V)$
   This ensures that every position in every block is filled with at least one value.
2. **Uniqueness:** $\forall B, P, V_1, V_2.(board(B, P, V_1) \wedge board(B, P, V_2)) \rightarrow V_1 = V_2$

This ensures that no position in the board can hold multiple values.

We will illustrate one way of integrating LBM as a logical layer on top of deep networks applied to a semantic image interpretation task. The task is to predict the relations between objects and their parts in an image. It requires the use of first-order logic. The knowledge base consists of symbolic facts expressing when an object type is normally part of another object type, e.g., $part$(Screen, TV), where Screen and TV are variables, denoting that TVs have screens. The knowledge base also includes a first-order rule connecting any two visual scenes (X_1 and X_2) with the symbols of the logic, as follows:

$$\begin{aligned}&\forall X_1, X_2, \exists T_1, T_2.((type(X_1, T_1) \wedge type(X_2, T_2)) \rightarrow \\ &\qquad (partOf(X_1, X_2) \leftrightarrow part(T_1, T_2))),\end{aligned} \tag{2.23}$$

where X_1, X_2 are real-valued variables representing visual features of objects (an embedding, pixel values, etc.), as done in Serafini and d'Avila Garcez [23], and T_1, T_2 are symbolic variables representing object types. Predicate $type$ is $True$ when an object, as defined by its visual features, is deemed to be of a given type (e.g., an object class). Given two visual scenes with their corresponding type classifications, $type(X_1, T_1)$ and $type(X_2, T_2)$, one visual scene will be part of the other, $partOf(X_1, X_2)$, if and only if the object type of the former is deemed to be part of the object type in the latter, $part(T_1, T_2)$.

In order to implement the above rule, we use Faster-RCNN to extract features from object images, from which we build two Neural Network Regressors (NNRs)[13] : $\mathcal{N}^{type}$ and $\mathcal{N}^{po}$, as learned functions for *type* and *partOf* respectively, as done in Donadello et al. [49]. Finally, we use an autoencoder $\mathcal{N}^{pt}$ to implement the relation $part(T_1, T_2)$ between the symbolic variables T_1 and T_2, following Tran [17]. Let $p^{po} = \mathcal{N}^{po}(X_1, X_2)$, $p^{pt} = \mathcal{N}^{pt}(T_1, T_2)$, $p^{t_1} = \mathcal{N}^{type}(X_1, T_1)$, and $p^{t_2} = \mathcal{N}^{type}(X_2, T_2)$, with $p^{po}, p^{pt}, p^{t_1}, p^{t_2} \in \{0, 1\}$, according to some choice of threshold. The first-order rule Eq. (2.23) can be converted to SDNF, as follows:

$$\begin{aligned}&(p^{t_1} \wedge p^{t_2}) \rightarrow (p^{po} \leftrightarrow p^{pt}) \equiv \\ &(p^{po} \wedge p^{pt} \wedge p^{t_1} \wedge p^{t_2}) \vee (\neg p^{po} \wedge \neg p^{pt} \wedge p^{t_1} \wedge p^{t_2}) \vee (\neg p^{t_1} \wedge p^{t_2}) \vee \neg p^{t_2}.\end{aligned}$$

From this SDNF, we build a LBM as the *logical layer* on top of the neural networks $\mathcal{N}^{type}$, $\mathcal{N}^{po}$, and $\mathcal{N}^{pt}$. Figure 2.13 shows the overall network architecture.

---

13 To represent first-order logic in LBM, we combine LBM with the Neural Network Regressors. Each NNR represents a predicate in the formulae and outputs a truth-value for that predicate. LBM takes as input the truth-values of the predicates coming from the outputs of the NNRs. In essence, LBM sits on top of the NNRs, connecting the predicates according to the connectives of the corresponding logic formulae.

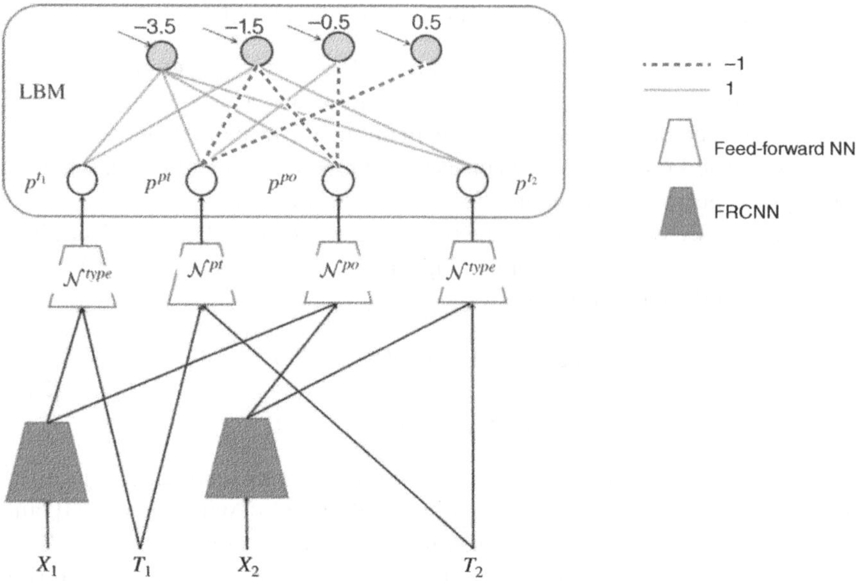

Figure 2.13 Learning and reasoning about the *partOf* relation in object images by grounding symbolic concepts into Convolutional Neural Networks and adding a logical layer in the form of a LBM module implementing the rule $(p^{t_1} \wedge p^{t_2}) \rightarrow (p^{po} \leftrightarrow p^{pt})$.

Reasoning in the LBM can inform learning in $\mathcal{N}$ by backpropagating inferred knowledge to update the weights of the CNN, regressor, or autoencoder. In particular, we train the entire system by minimizing the following loss function[14] :

$$||\mathcal{N}^{po}(x_1, x_2) - \text{LBM}(p^{po}|\mathcal{K}(x_1, x_2)||_2^2 +$$

$$||[\mathcal{N}^{type}(x_1, t_1), \mathcal{N}^{type}(x_2, t_2)] - \text{LBM}(p^{t_1}, p^{t_2}|\mathcal{K}(x_1, x_2))||_2^2,$$

where x_1, x_2 and $\mathcal{K}(x_1, x_2)$ are obtained from the training data; $\mathcal{K}$ denotes the knowledge pertaining to x_1, x_2, i.e., the type of x_1, type of x_2, and whether x_1 is part of x_2. We use $\text{LBM}(p^{po}|\mathcal{K}(x_1, x_2))$ and $\text{LBM}(p^{t_1}, p^{t_2}|\mathcal{K}(x_1, x_2))$ to denote the application of LBM to infer the value of p^{po} and of the pair $[p^{t_1}, p^{t_2}]$, respectively. For example, the LBM is used to infer p^{po}, which is used in turn to update $\mathcal{N}^{po}$.

Given, for instance, $x_1 =$  and $x_2 =$ , let's assume that we do not know whether x_1 is part of x_2. But, if the $\mathcal{N}^{type}$ networks tell us that $type(x_1, \text{Screen}) \equiv True$ and $type(x_2, \text{TV}) \equiv True$, and $\mathcal{K}(x_1, x_2)$ also includes $part(\text{Screen}, \text{TV})$, the LBM can infer that p^{po} should be $True$. Finally, this signal from the LBM's reasoning, obtained from the first term of the loss function, is used to update during

14 $[\mathcal{N}^{type}(x_1, t_1), \mathcal{N}^{type}(x_2, t_2)]$ denotes the concatenation of the outputs from the $\mathcal{N}^{type}$ networks; $||x||_2^2$ is the squared Euclidean norm.

Table 2.3 Comparison of neurosymbolic approaches; area under the curve (AUC) in the semantic image interpretation task.

	Object type (AUC)	**Part-of (AUC)**
DLN	0.791 ± 0.032	0.605 ± 0.024
CNLP	0.816 ± 0.004	**0.644 ± 0.015**
LTN	0.800	0.598
LBM	**0.828 ± 0.002**	**0.645 ± 0.027**

Source: [10]/Association for the Advancement of Artificial Intelligence.

learning the parameters of $\mathcal{N}^{po}$. Similarly, the second term of the loss function leverages information about the type of objects to update $\mathcal{N}^{type}$.

We compared the LBM-enhanced model with three other neurosymbolic systems: Deep Logic Networks (DLN) [13], LTN [49, 50], and Compositional Neural Logic Programming (CNLP) [17]. The task and dataset used were the same as in Donadello et al. [49], with the exception of the rule $(p^{t_1} \wedge p^{t_2}) \rightarrow (p^{po} \leftrightarrow p^{pt})$ only used by LBM. The *area under the curve* (AUC) results shown in Table 2.3 indicate that the use of this single first-order rule for reasoning with the LBM and training of the Faster-RCNN model, also used in Donadello et al. [49], produces a higher performance than LTN in the prediction of the part-of relation in images. LBM's performance is comparable to that of CNLP. For the object type prediction, the LBM model performs better than CNLP, DLN, and LTN.

2.6 Challenges for Neurosymbolic AI

We introduced an approach and neurosymbolic system to reason about symbolic knowledge in an energy-based neural network. Differently from most LLM approaches and CoT, where reasoning capabilities are expected to emerge and are measured post hoc using benchmarks, we use logic to provide a formal definition of reasoning. Only once a well-defined semantics is provided, one can show correspondence between networks and various forms of reasoning. We showed equivalence between propositional logic and RBMs. The finding led to a novel system, named LBMs integrating learning and reasoning in neural networks. Future work will focus on scaling up the application to SAT and learning from data and knowledge. Extensions include applications of weighted clauses, weighted SAT with parallel implementation, as well as evaluations on relational learning tasks.

Equipped with a proof and algorithm showing how RBMs can implement a category of required constraints, it is possible to imagine how an RBM may be added as a *module* to an existing network imposing such constraints on the network. This RBM module becomes a *verifiable component* of the system, implementing, for example, a fairness or safety requirement as argued for in Giunchiglia et al. [51].

Next, we discuss how this simple idea may open up directions for research addressing some of the biggest challenges for current AI: data efficiency, fairness, safety, and ultimately trust.

2.6.1 Nonmonotonic Logic

Consider the task of commonsense reasoning, the human-like ability to make sense of ordinary situations, such as making judgments about the nature of objects. It encompasses intuitive psychology (e.g., reasoning about intentions) and naive physics (a natural understanding of the physical world, including spatial and temporal reasoning). Commonsense reasoning requires an ability to jump to conclusions based on incomplete information and to retract or revise such conclusions when more information become available. There have been many attempts to formalize commonsense, not least the work of John McCarthy, who was responsible for coining the term Artificial Intelligence. Because it requires jumping to conclusions and therefore handling logical inconsistencies in a nonclassical way, commonsense reasoning is modeled by nonmonotonic logics, some of which are undecidable. LLMs have achieved much better results than logical formalizations of commonsense on reasoning benchmarks. It turns out that it is easier to learn commonsense from data than to formalize it logically. Yet, making sense of what has been learned by LLMs has been proven to be a daunting task. Making sense of what has been learned might help tremendously with the efforts to understand the limits of the formalization of commonsense in logic. As neural networks start to be deployed successfully in various fields of scientific discovery, achieving a true understanding of the processes at play will demand such an ability to explain the network's reasoning.

2.6.2 Planning

AGI will require the ability to plan toward a goal and the ability to ask questions in order to achieve that goal. Planning requires the ability to break down goals into sub-goals while reasoning with partial information over time. Having a goal, in turn, requires the provision of a description of the current state and the goal state and a mechanism that reduces the difference (e.g., some distance function) between the current state and the goal state by changing the current state in a reasonable way. If the mechanism isn't working, one may decide to change the goal or even change the mechanism itself.

Whether in Google's AlphaGo or Sudoku, the goal state is to win the game, and because it is a closed environment, simulation can be used to learn to minimize the distance function without the need for an explicit description. In open-ended situations, the problem becomes much harder. An explicit description is one that can be manipulated by asking questions: "What might happen if I were to make this or that change?" without making the change. An explicit description needs, therefore, to be amenable to symbolic manipulation. We argue that in open-ended scenarios, an explicit description needs, furthermore, to be abstracted from the situation given only a few examples. Reasoning in the form of symbol manipulation on that abstract description can then take place that will be of a different nature from reasoning carried out in terms of pattern matching with similarity and distance functions.

2.6.3 Learning from Its Mistakes

An AGI system should be able to learn from its mistakes, interact with users by asking questions, describe its understanding, and improve its performance in a controlled way toward a goal, even if changing the goal and the mechanism for performance improvement. Controlled at the level of its symbolic description, the system can be made safe. With reasoning taking place at both the pattern matching and the more abstract levels, as advocated by D. Kahneman's Thinking: Fast and Slow [52], the system will be able to adapt to novelty from only a few examples, check its understanding, multitask, and reuse knowledge from one task to another, thus improving data and energy efficiency in comparison with the demands of current AI systems.

Adapting to novelty (therefore solving the long-tail distribution problem and out-of-distribution problem in Machine Learning) requires creating compact representations (in the brain or the mind) but also being able to change that representation from time to time in order to obtain new insight. It is the change of representation that allows one to look at a problem from a new angle to obtain new insight. Think of the difference between two computer programs, both correct for their purpose, one so-called *spaghetti* code and the other an example of what programmers like to refer to as *beautiful* code. The former may be faster to run, but the latter needs to be neat, easy to understand, and useful to update and reuse. This is the core challenge of the latest research in neurosymbolic AI: extraction of relevant descriptions at the right level of abstraction from complex neural networks, sound application of reasoning and learning with various forms of representation – spatial, temporal, epistemic, normative, multimodal, nonmonotonic – and efficient knowledge and data reuse, and extrapolation to multiple tasks in different application domains.

Consider the kind of program learned by the latest GPT-based chatbots. Transformer neural networks work, in essence, by mapping sets to sets and not sequences to sequences (GPT-based chatbots require positional encoding to handle sequences). Interestingly, in neurosymbolic AI, the computation of the semantics of various logics by neural networks is also done by mapping sets to sets recursively [2]. A great innovation of deep learning was multiheaded attention, which is similar to representing binary relations in neurosymbolic networks. In certain domains of application, though, such as protein interaction, having the ability to represent not just binary but n-ary relations, such as *bond(Compound_Name, Bond_Type, Atom_1, Atom_2),* may be very useful. This is the case in the Mutagenesis task and dataset, where a chemical compound may have a bond of a certain type between any two atoms, and the goal is to identify mutagenic compounds given the atom bonds. Hypergraph neural networks have been used recently to represent and learn n-ary relations [53]. Finally, the neurosymbolic (NeSy) framework of fibring neural networks [54] has been shown recently to offer a common representational foundation for both graph neural networks and transformers via a proof of correspondence with propositional modal logic with self-fibring. These are some of the exciting recent developments in neurosymbolic AI (see the NeSy conference series for more [55]), contributing to both a better understanding of deep learning and the development of new formalisms for learning and reasoning.

2.7 Conclusion

Many influential leaders have been pointing out the risks of current AI and arguing for the adoption of regulation. While it is clear that worldwide regulation is not achievable in the current geopolitical climate [56], an alternative argument is that digital technology itself can offer, as part of an adequate accountability ecosystem, a new path to safer AI. In this new path, neural models can be validated symbolically by adopting the neurosymbolic cycle: train a little, reason a little, repeat. This is quite different from the current *scale-is-all-you-need* approach or what the EU AI Act has achieved. Regulation without accountability tends to increase weak competitiveness and may not decrease risks.

At first impression, the need for accountability in AI and the risks of current AI may seem to be quite disconnected from the technical contributions of this chapter. However, we argue that the kind of formalization offered here is key to accountability, fairness, and ultimately a safer AI. If neurosymbolic AI can show that compact network modules behave according to a given formal semantics, then these modules can be composed in ways that will offer guarantees to the overall system. Of course, this continues to be an important research challenge, but results such as the ones reported in this chapter point to an alternative to the current approach to AI, best illustrated by Figure 2.13, where a requirement (or a guardrail) can be implemented as a neurosymbolic network module on top of an existing complex network. For this reason, we conclude with a short summary and opinion on the need for accountability in AI.

The need for accountability in AI is now center stage, as indicated by the following quote from Imbrie et al. [57]: "A long-standing concern among analysts of AI development is the possibility of a race to the bottom in which multiple players feel pressure to neglect safety and security challenges in order to remain competitive. Perceptions - and therefore signals - are key variables in this scenario. Most actors would presumably prefer to have time to ensure their AI systems are reliable, but the desire to be first, the pressure to go to market, and the idea that competitors might be cutting corners can all push developers to be less cautious. Accordingly, signaling has an important role to play in mitigating race-to-the-bottom dynamics. Parties developing AI systems could emphasize their commitment to restraint, their focus on developing safe and trustworthy systems, or both. Ideally, credible signals on these points can reassure other parties that all sides are taking due care, mitigating pressure to race to the bottom." Percy et al. [7] goes further, arguing for an accountability in AI ecosystem. It proposes to map out the general principles of AI into industry-specific mechanisms, having stated as early as 2021: "at present the ecosystem is unbalanced, which can be seen in the failures of certain mechanisms that have been attempted by leading technology companies. By taking an ecosystem perspective, we can identify certain elements that need developing and bolstering in order for the system as a whole to function effectively. Corporate governance mechanisms such as standardized processes and internal audit frameworks, leading up to potential external accreditation, need to be made to work together in ways that go beyond regulatory requirements, especially in technologies' early period of evolution and deployment when regulation lags practice."

As part of a case study carried out with a global software provider operating primarily in the gambling sector with a focus on online gambling, Percy et al. [7] reports on the use of AI to help reduce harm from gambling. The application of AI in responsible gambling has been a relevant use case because of the high regulatory focus, divergent regulatory perspectives worldwide, and a longstanding debate over ethical dilemmas relating to an increase in gambling addiction. Results are drawn from the risk profiling of gambling behavior using neural networks and explainability. The neural network performs classification of problem gambling. Explainable AI evaluates indirect gender bias and the need for algorithmic fairness. Results are analyzed in connection with the proposed accountability ecosystem and its operationalization. The AI accountability ecosystem has as stakeholders: corporate actors, market counterparts, civil society and government, alongside mechanisms such as internal auditing, external accreditation, investigative journalism, risk-based regulation, and market shaping. Two key elements of the accountability ecosystem are discussed in detail in Percy et al. [7]: (i) interventions to reduce bias and (ii) increased transparency via model explainability. The benefits of having an industry-specific accountability process are illustrated in that it can be documented, reviewed, benchmarked, challenged, and improved upon, "both to build trust that the underlying ethical principle is being taken seriously and to identify specific areas to do more" [7]. The paper's conclusions support the importance of industry-specific approaches in the operationalization of accountability principles in AI, noting how different metrics, priorities, and accountability processes arise in online gambling compared to what might arise in other industries. Taken alongside relevant regulatory efforts on information security and privacy, accountability in AI is expected to reduce the risks of imbalances in regulation.

Widespread use of GPT-style chatbots is expected to increase productivity but also magnify errors, as humans become complacent in the use of the technology. When trying to distinguish genuine from malicious websites, people have learned over the years to look for grammatical errors, the quality of images, and other cues. Learning whether or not to trust the output of LLMs is much harder. At this unique juncture when AI leaves the research laboratory and enters everyday life, new ways of doing the things that we are used to and take for granted will need to be decided upon and implemented quickly, until a better way of doing AI comes that will offer safety guarantees to AI systems.

References

1 A. d'Avila Garcez, L. C. Lamb, and D. M. Gabbay. *Neural-Symbolic Cognitive Reasoning*. Springer, 2009.

2 Simon Odense and Artur d'Avila Garcez. A semantic framework for neurosymbolic computation. *Artificial Intelligence*, 340: 104273, 2025. https://doi.org/10.1016/J.ARTINT.2024.104273.

3 P. Smolensky. Constituent structure and explanation in an integrated connectionist/symbolic cognitive architecture. In *Connectionism: Debates on Psychological Explanation*, 1995.

4 Iman Mirzadeh, Keivan Alizadeh, Hooman Shahrokhi, Oncel Tuzel, Samy Bengio, and Mehrdad Farajtabar. GSM-symbolic: understanding the limitations of mathematical reasoning in large language models, 2024. https://arxiv.org/abs/2410.05229.

5 Ilia Shumailov, Zakhar Shumaylov, Yiren Zhao, Yarin Gal, Nicolas Papernot, and Ross, Anderson. The curse of recursion: Training on generated data makes models forget. *arXiv*, 2023. https://arxiv.org/abs/2305.17493

6 Artur d'Avila Garcez and Luís C. Lamb. Neurosymbolic AI: the 3rd wave. *Artificial Intelligence Review*, 56(11): 12387–12406, 2023. https://doi.org/10.1007/s10462-023-10448-w.

7 Chris Percy, Simo Dragicevic, Sanjoy Sarkar, and Artur d'Avila Garcez. Accountability in AI: from principles to industry-specific accreditation. *CoRR*, 2021. https://arxiv.org/abs/2110.09232.

8 Kwun Ho Ngan, James Phelan, Esma Mansouri-Benssassi, Joe Townsend, and Artur d'Avila Garcez. Closing the neural-symbolic cycle: Knowledge extraction, user intervention and distillation from convolutional neural networks. In Artur d'Avila Garcez, Tarek R. Besold, Marco Gori, and Ernesto Jiménez-Ruiz, editors, *Proceedings of the 17th International Workshop on Neural-Symbolic Learning and Reasoning, La Certosa di Pontignano, Siena, Italy, July 3-5, 2023, volume 3432 of CEUR Workshop Proceedings*, pages 19–43, CEUR-WS.org, 2023. https://ceur-ws.org/Vol-3432/paper3.pdf.

9 Geoffrey E. Hinton, Simon Osindero, and Yee-Whye Teh. A fast learning algorithm for deep belief nets. *Neural Computation*, 18(7): 1527–1554, 2006. http://dx.doi.org/10.1162/neco.2006.18.7.1527.

10 Son N. Tran and Artur d'Avila Garcez. Neurosymbolic reasoning and learning with restricted Boltzmann machines. *Proceedings of the AAAI Conference on Artificial Intelligence*, 37(5): 6558–6565, 2023. https://doi.org/10.1609/aaai.v37i5.25806.

11 G. Towell and J. Shavlik. Knowledge-based artificial neural networks. *Artificial Intelligence*, 70: 119–165, 1994.

12 M. França, G. Zaverucha, and A. d'Avila Garcez. Fast relational learning using bottom clause propositionalization with artificial neural networks. *Machine Learning*, 94(1): 81–104, 2014. http://dx.doi.org/10.1007/s10994-013-5392-1.

13 S. Tran and A. Garcez. Deep logic networks: Inserting and extracting knowledge from deep belief networks. *IEEE Transactions on Neural Networks and Learning Systems*, 29: 246–258, 2018. https://doi.org/10.1109/TNNLS.2016.2603784.

14 R. Evans and E. Grefenstette. Learning explanatory rules from noisy data. *Journal of Artificial Intelligence Research*, 61: 1–64, 2018.

15 Fan Yang, Zhilin Yang, and William W Cohen. Differentiable learning of logical rules for knowledge base reasoning. In I. Guyon, U. V. Luxburg, S. Bengio, H. Wallach, R. Fergus, S. Vishwanathan, and R. Garnett, editors, *Advances in Neural Information Processing Systems 30*, pages 2319–2328, Curran Associates, Inc., 2017. http://papers.nips.cc/paper/6826-differentiable-learning-of-logical-rules-for-knowledge-base-reasoning.pdf.

16 Robin Manhaeve, Sebastijan Dumancic, Angelika Kimmig, Thomas Demeester, and Luc De Raedt. DeepProbLog: Neural probabilistic logic programming. In S. Bengio, H. Wallach, H. Larochelle, K. Grauman, N. Cesa-Bianchi, and R. Garnett, editors, *Advances in Neural Information Processing Systems 31*, pages 3749–3759, Curran Associates, Inc., 2018. http://papers.nips.cc/paper/7632-deep problog-neural-probabilistic-logic-programming.pdf.

17 Son N. Tran. Compositional neural logic programming. In Zhi-Hua Zhou, editor, *Proceedings of the Thirtieth International Joint Conference on Artificial Intelligence, IJCAI-2021*, pages 3059–3066, International Joint Conferences on Artificial Intelligence Organization, 2021. https://doi.org/10.24963/ijcai.2021/421.

18 A. d'Avila Garcez, K. Broda, and D. Gabbay. Symbolic knowledge extraction from trained neural networks: a sound approach. *Artificial Intelligence*, 125(1–2):155–207, 2001.

19 William W. Cohen, Fan Yang, and Kathryn Mazaitis. Tensorlog: deep learning meets probabilistic dbs. *CoRR*, 2017.http://arxiv.org/abs/1707.05390.

20 Gadi Pinkas. Symmetric neural networks and propositional logic satisfiability. *Neural Computation*, 3(2): 282–291, 1991. http://dx.doi.org/10.1162/neco.1991.3.2.282.

21 G. Pinkas. Reasoning, nonmonotonicity and learning in connectionist networks that capture propositional knowledge. *Artificial Intelligence*, 77(2): 203–247, 1995. https://doi.org/10.1016/0004-3702(94)00032-V.

22 L. de Penning, A. d'Avila Garcez, L.C. Lamb, and J-J. Meyer. A neural-symbolic cognitive agent for online learning and reasoning. *Proceedings of the IJCAI-2011*, pages 1653–1658, 2011.

23 Luciano Serafini and Artur d'Avila Garcez. Learning and reasoning with logic tensor networks. In *AI*IA*, pages 334–348, 2016. https://doi.org/10.1007/978-3-319-49130-1_25.

24 C. Hernandez, F. Albizuri, A. DAnjou, M. Graña, and Francisco Torrealdea. Efficient solution of max-sat and sat via higher order Boltzmann. *Revista Investigación Operacional*, 22 (01) 2001.

25 A. d'Anjou, M. Graña, F. J. Torrealdea, and M. C. Hernandez. Solving satisfiability via Boltzmann machines. *IEEE Transactions on Pattern Analysis and Machine Intelligence*, 15(5): 514–521, 1993. https://doi.org/10.1109/34.211473.

26 Po-Wei Wang, Priya L. Donti, Bryan Wilder, and J. Zico Kolter. SATNet: Bridging deep learning and logical reasoning using a differentiable satisfiability solver. In Kamalika Chaudhuri and Ruslan Salakhutdinov, editors, *Proceedings of the 36th International Conference on Machine Learning, ICML 2019, 9-15 June 2019, Long* Beach, *California, USA, volume 97 of Proceedings of Machine Learning Research*, pages 6545–6554, PMLR, 2019. http://proceedings.mlr.press/v97/wang19e.html.

27 Daniel Selsam, Matthew Lamm, Benedikt Bünz, Percy Liang, Leonardo de Moura, and David L. Dill. Learning a SAT solver from single-bit supervision. In *International Conference on Learning Representations*, 2019. https://openreview.net/forum?id=HJMC_iA5tm.

28 A. Srinivasan. The Aleph manual. http://www.cs.ox.ac.uk/activities/machlearn/Aleph/aleph.html, 2007. [accessed: 2021-01-23].

29 Hugo Larochelle, Michael Mandel, Razvan Pascanu, and Yoshua Bengio. Learning algorithms for the classification restricted Boltzmann machine. *Journal of Machine Learning Research*, 13(1): 643–669, 2012.

30 A. Srinivasan, S. H. Muggleton, R.D. King, and M.J.E. Sternberg. Mutagenesis: Ilp experiments in a non-determinate biological domain. In *Proceedings of the 4th*

International Workshop on Inductive Logic Programming, volume 237 of GMD-Studien, pages 217–232, 1994.

31 Michael Bain and Stephen Muggleton. Learning optimal chess strategies. In K. Furukawa, D. Michie, and S. Muggleton, editors, *Machine Intelligence 13: Machine Intelligence and Inductive Learning*, pages 291–309, Oxford University Press, Inc., New York, NY, USA, 1994. http://dl.acm.org/citation.cfm?id=224230.224242.

32 Matthew Richardson and Pedro Domingos. Markov logic networks. *Machine Learning*, 62(1-2): 107–136, 2006. http://dx.doi.org/10.1007/s10994-006-5833-1.

33 Ross D. King, Michael J. E. Sternberg, and Ashwin Srinivasan. Relating chemical activity to structure: an examination of ILP successes. *New Generation Computing*, 13(3):411–433, 1995.

34 Saeed Amizadeh, Sergiy Matusevych, and Markus Weimer. Learning to solve circuit-SAT: An unsupervised differentiable approach. In *Proceedings of the ICLR-2019*, 2019.

35 Xujie Si, Xin Zhang, Radu Grigore, and Mayur Naik. Maximum satisfiability in software analysis: Applications and techniques. In Rupak Majumdar and Viktor Kuncak, editors, *Computer Aided Verification - 29th International Conference, CAV 2017*, Heidelberg, Germany, July 24-28, *2017, Proceedings, Part I, volume 10426 of Lecture Notes in Computer Science*, pages 68–94, Springer, 2017. https://doi.org/10.1007/978-3-319-63387-9_4.

36 Antonio Morgado, Mark Liffiton, and Joao Marques-Silva. MaxSAT-based MCS enumeration. In Armin Biere, Amir Nahir, and Tanja Vos, editors, *Hardware and Software: Verification and Testing*, pages 86–101, Springer, Berlin, Heidelberg, 2013.

37 Tiepelt Marcel Kevin and Singh Tilak Raj. Finding pre-production vehicle configurations using a MaxSAT framework. In *18th International Configuration Workshop*, pages 117–122, École des Mines d'Albi-Carmaux, 2016.

38 Mohit Kumar, Samuel Kolb, Stefano Teso, and Luc De Raedt. Learning maxsat from contextual examples for combinatorial optimisation. *Proceedings of the AAAI Conference on Artificial Intelligence*, 34(04): 4493–4500, 2020. https://doi.org/10.1609/aaai.v34i04.5877.

39 Volker Sperschneider. *Bioinformatics: Problem Solving Paradigms*. Springer Publishing Company, Incorporated, 2008.

40 Jeremias Berg, Antti Hyttinen, and Matti Jarvisalo. Applications of maxsat in data analysis. In Daniel Le Berre and Matti Jarvisalo, editors, *Proceedings of Pragmatics of SAT 2015 and 2018, volume 59 of EPiC Series in Computing*, pages 50–64, EasyChair, 2019. https://doi.org/10.29007/3qkh.

41 Dmitry Malioutov and Kuldeep S. Meel. MLIC: A MaxSAT-based framework for learning interpretable classification rules. August 2018. https://doi.org/10.48550/arXiv.1812.01843.

42 Minghao Liu, Pei Huang, Fuqi Jia, Fan Zhang, Yuchen Sun, Shaowei Cai, Feifei Ma, and Jian Zhang. Can graph neural networks learn to solve the maxsat problem? (student abstract). *Proceedings of the AAAI Conference on Artificial Intelligence*, 37(13): 16264–16265, 2023. https://doi.org/10.1609/aaai.v37i13.26992.

43 Ismail Alkhouri, Cedric Le Denmat, Yingjie Li, Cunxi Yu, Jia Liu, Rongrong Wang, and Alvaro Velasquez. Quadratic differentiable optimization for the maximum independent set problem. In *Proceedings of the ICML2025*, 2025. https://arxiv.org/abs/2406.19532.

44 M. C. Hernandez, F. X. Albizuri, A. d'Anjou, M. Graña, and F. J. Torrealdea. High-order Boltzmann machines for MAX-SAT and SAT. In Stan Gielen and Bert Kappen, editors, *ICANN-1993*, pages 479–479, Springer, London, 1993.

45 David Warde-Farley, Vinod Nair, Yujia Li, Ivan Lobov, Felix Gimeno, and Simon Osindero. Solving MaxSAT with matrix multiplication, 2023. https://doi.org/10.48550/arXiv.2311.02101.

46 S. Kirkpatrick, C. D. Gelatt, and M. P. Vecchi. Optimization by simulated annealing. *Science*, 220(4598): 671–680, 1983. https://doi.org/10.1126/science.220.4598.671.

47 Y Xiang, D.Y Sun, W Fan, and X.G Gong. Generalized simulated annealing algorithm and its application to the thomson model. *Physics Letters A*, 233(3): 216–220, 1997. https://doi.org/10.1016/S0375-9601(97)00474-X.

48 Wolfgang Stammer, Antonia Wüst, David Steinmann, and Kristian Kersting. Neural concept binder. *CoRR*, 2024. https://doi.org/10.48550/arXiv.2406.09949.

49 I. Donadello, L. Serafini, and A. S. d'Avila Garcez. Logic tensor networks for semantic image interpretation. In *Proceedings of the Twenty-Sixth International Joint Conference on Artificial Intelligence (IJCAI-17)*, pages 1596–1602, 2017.

50 Samy Badreddine, Artur d'Avila Garcez, Luciano Serafini, and Michael Spranger. Logic tensor networks. *Artificial Intelligence*, 303: 103649, 2022. https://doi.org/10.1016/j.artint.2021.103649.

51 Eleonora Giunchiglia, Alex Tatomir, Mihaela Cătălina Stoian, and Thomas Lukasiewicz. Ccn+: a neuro-symbolic framework for deep learning with requirements. *International Journal of Approximate Reasoning*, 171: 109124, 2024. https://doi.org/10.1016/j.ijar.2024.109124.

52 Daniel Kahneman. *Thinking, Fast and Slow*. Farrar, Straus and Giroux, New York, 2011.

53 João Pedro Gandarela de Souza, Gerson Zaverucha, and Artur d'Avila Garcez. Hypergraph neural networks with logic clauses. In *International Joint Conference on Neural Networks, IJCNN 2024*, Yokohama, Japan, *June 30 - July 5, 2024*, pages 1–8, IEEE, 2024. https://doi.org/10.1109/IJCNN60899.2024.10650412.

54 Artur d'Avila Garcez and Dov M. Gabbay. Fibring neural networks. In *Proceedings of the 19th National Conference on Artifical Intelligence*, AAAI'04, pages 342–347, AAAI Press, 2004.

55 Tarek R. Besold, Artur d'Avila Garcez, Ernesto Jiménez-Ruiz, Roberto Confalonieri, Pranava Madhyastha, and Benedikt Wagner, editors. *Neural-Symbolic Learning and Reasoning - 18th International Conference, NeSy 2024*, Barcelona, Spain, September 9-12, 2024, *Proceedings, Part I, volume 14979 of Lecture Notes in Computer Science*, Springer, 2024. https://doi.org/10.1007/978-3-031-71167-1.

56 Chris Miller. *Chip War: The Fight for the World's Most Critical Technology.* Scribner, New York, 2022.

57 Andrew Imbrie, Owen Daniels, and Helen Toner. Decoding intentions. https://cset.georgetown.edu/publication/decoding-intentions/, 2023. Center for Security and Emerging Technology [Online; accessed 20-Jan-2025].

3

Neurosymbolic Assurance Using Concept Probes in Foundation Models

*Ramneet Kaur, Anirban Roy, and Susmit Jha**

Neuro-Symbolic Computing and Intelligence, Information and Computing Sciences Division, SRI International, Menlo Park, California, USA

*Corresponding Author: susmit.jha@sri.com

3.1 Introduction

The integration of symbolic reasoning with neural machine learning models has introduced the paradigm of neurosymbolic AI, characterized by combining the logical rigor and human understandability of symbolic methods with the adaptability and scalability of deep learning. This synergy enables the development of systems that are interpretable while being capable of addressing complex, real-world problems. The rise of foundation models pretrained on diverse data modalities has further expanded the potential for neurosymbolic AI. In particular, it provides a promising avenue for ensuring the safety, interpretability, and reliability of deep neural networks (DNNs), especially in safety-critical applications.

A key challenge in neurosymbolic AI, particularly in the context of assurance, lies in obtaining the appropriate symbolic abstractions or "symbols" – that can be used to formally reason about and verify the behavior of DNNs. The abstraction process must align the latent representations within foundation models, such as large language models (LLMs) and vision-language models (VLMs), with human-understandable concepts. This alignment is critical for ensuring that the extracted symbols faithfully represent the underlying neural computations and provide a reliable basis for interpretability and safety assurance that we can understand as humans.

Neurosymbolic AI: Foundations and Applications, First Edition. Edited by Alvaro Velasquez et al.

One of the fundamental difficulties in this alignment stems from the observation that the symbolic abstractions used by humans may not necessarily align with those embedded in foundation models. Specifically, the multimodal language models such as VLMs are trained not just on autoregression over natural language but also on infilling in other modalities that can encourage alternative segmentation of observations that differ from human conceptual decomposition. Human concepts are shaped by cultural, linguistic, and contextual factors, while foundation models learn representations based on statistical patterns in training data. The language modality used in foundation models likely introduces this bias. Despite these differences, recent advancements in probing techniques suggest that it is possible to extract human-interpretable concepts from foundation models. The probing of these concepts involves identifying directions in the model's activation space that correspond to high-level semantic properties, making it feasible to bridge the gap between human reasoning and machine representations.

In neurosymbolic AI, the assurance of safety and interpretability can be achieved by extracting and analyzing the concepts that emerge in foundation models while processing an input query for generating its output. Concept probes over VLMs and logical specification frameworks have been employed to analyze, verify, and assure the behavior of neural systems. These frameworks provide mechanisms for integrating symbolic reasoning directly into the verification and assurance process of DNNs. By formally specifying high-level safety properties and logical constraints, these frameworks enable the decomposition of complex behaviors into interpretable unit concepts. This ensures that the outputs align with human-understandable reasoning and satisfy safety requirements. The consistency of logical relationships between concepts in the machine learning models with the expectation of humans can be an effective and scalable form of assurance of machine learning models.

Neurosymbolic approaches introduce a structured methodology for ensuring the compliance of neural networks with predefined specifications. It formalizes the concept of verifying neural behaviors against logical constraints and provides mechanisms to identify potential inconsistencies in feature representations. For example, using such frameworks, inconsistent relationships between concepts (due to systematic bias in learning or due to polysemantic representation of concepts) can be identified and analyzed for their impact on safety-critical applications. By grounding the assurance process in interpretable and validated symbolic abstractions, these approaches enhance the reliability of machine learning models and show the promise of neurosymbolic assurance methods in fields such as autonomous vehicles and medical diagnostics.

The verification of neural systems using concepts introduces a principled methodology to ensure consistency with high-level specifications. Concept-based verification not only addresses the challenges of disentangling overlapping features but also aligns neural representations with human-interpretable abstractions. By leveraging these tools, researchers can ensure that the symbolic abstractions extracted from foundation models are valid, interpretable, and aligned with safety objectives. This alignment establishes a pathway toward scalable, assured, and interpretable neurosymbolic AI systems capable of addressing real-world safety-critical challenges with enhanced trust and transparency.

3.2 Neural Features and Concept Probes

DNNs often represent features of the input as directions in activation space, offering a mechanism to align neural activations with human-understandable concepts. While this conceptualization reveals the potential for interpretability, the structure of these feature representations is not immediately evident and requires careful exploration. Additionally, ensuring the validity of these symbolic abstractions is central to providing guarantees about the behavior of the system. The "linear representation hypothesis" [1] provides a foundation for understanding how features are encoded in neural networks. It is characterized by two properties. First, the "decomposability" property claims that the neural representations can be broken down into independently understandable features. Second, the "linearity" property states that the features are represented as directions in the model's activation space. These properties are critical for reasoning about neural network behavior and ensuring that individual features can be identified and interpreted. For instance, word embeddings have been shown to exhibit linear semantic relationships, such as "king - man + woman = queen" [2], while VLMs capture high-level visual and textual concepts in shared embedding spaces.

Identifying feature directions is straightforward in some cases, such as when neurons correspond directly to specific features. For example, early layers of vision models like InceptionV1 contain neurons that detect simple features such as curves. However, challenges arise when features do not align directly with neurons, as seen with phenomena such as privileged bases and superposition [3]. Privileged bases correspond to the observation that only some representations would encourage alignment with basis directions corresponding to neurons. The application of nonlinear activation functions is more likely to encourage the neuron-aligned basis to be privileged. Superposition allows models to represent more features than available dimensions by overlapping feature representations. These phenomena complicate interpretability but enable more efficient use of neural resources. In particular, superposition allows compression beyond what a linear model can do with sparse features, but this leads to "interference" necessitating nonlinear filtering. It has also been recently observed that DNNs can compute over representations that use superposition. Consequently, there is a growing consensus that superposition in concepts inside DNNs can be viewed as a practical adaptation to available representation space to simulate larger, highly sparse networks that would have represented the same features without interference. Any n dimensional space can only have n orthogonal vectors, but it is possible to have $exp(n)$ many "almost orthogonal" (that is, $< \epsilon$ cosine similarity) vectors in high-dimensional spaces. The sparsity of features in most natural inputs minimizes the chances of interference, encouraging such superposition. The nonlinear activations can also mitigate some level of interference. This partly explains the debate on monosemanticity vs. polysemanticity of feature representations in deep learning models. While developing methods to disentangle concepts in the latent space of a model remains an important challenge, we focus more on exploiting existing concept probes for assurance of machine learning models.

Despite these challenges of superposition and privileged bases, several empirical observations support the role of foundation models in extracting meaningful concepts that can be used for neurosymbolic assurance. First, word embeddings have demonstrated that these capture semantic properties and enable interpretability and arithmetic-like operations. Second, interpretable directions in latent spaces have been shown to allow for controlled modifications, as seen in generative adversarial networks. Third, there have been several instances of finding interpretable neurons or sets of neurons that activate in response to understandable properties across different architectures. Recent empirical evaluations show that similar feature representations are consistently found across various models [4]. Concept probes, which align neural representations with human-understandable concepts, offer a framework for addressing these challenges. By extracting and validating emergent concepts within foundation models, safety and interpretability assurances can be provided for neurosymbolic AI systems. This approach facilitates bridging the gap between neural computation and symbolic reasoning, paving the way for more transparent and reliable AI systems.

3.3 Foundation Models as Specification Lens

Given the developing capability to probe concepts in large foundation models, these models, such as CLIP [5], can be viewed as a "lens" through which we can specify and reason about machine learning models. These models can process information in different modalities, and the joint embedding with text enables them to associate concepts in modalities such as vision with human-interpretable ontology. This offers an exciting and as-yet-only partially explored opportunity for the formal analysis of machine learning models.

Figure 3.1 illustrates an example architecture for using concept probes for specifying and verifying machine learning models based on our recent work [6]. The machine learning model under analysis is depicted on the left-hand side. In this case, it is a vision model that takes as input images and produces a label for the

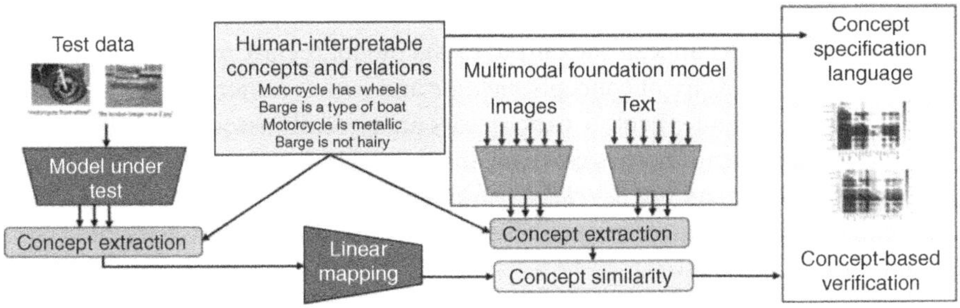

Figure 3.1 Leveraging multimodal models and concept probes for specification and assurance of machine learning models.

image. The DNN can be seen as the composition of an encoder responsible for translating low-level inputs (pixels composing images) into high-level representations with concepts represented in the feature space, and a head that makes predictions based on these representations. The VLM is depicted on the right-hand side. It consists of two encoders, one for each modality (text and image), that map inputs to a common representation space. We can extract concepts from both the model under test and the large multimodal foundation model that is expected to have generalized well and be useful as a specification lens. The universality of the feature representation of concepts encourages us to use a simple linear mapping trained using a small set of examples to align the latent space of the model under test and the multimodal foundation model. In practice, one could replace the linear mapping with a shallow DNN to learn a more accurate alignment, if needed. But it is crucial to keep the complexity of such auxiliary models low to ensure that these models do not start learning the associations using memorization capacity in their feedforward network weights on their own rather than merely translating the concepts. The similarity between the mapped concept and those extracted from the large foundation model can be measured using standard approaches such as the use of cosine metric. In the absence of superposition or when the conceptual features are sparse, this metric can accurately capture semantic similarity.

To reason about the vision model, we can formulate a logical specification language in terms of natural language, human-understandable concepts. For instance, for a vision model tasked with distinguishing between given classes like *cat, dog, bird, car,* and *truck*, relevant concepts could be *metallic, ears,* and *wheels.* Domain experts and model developers can then express DNN specifications using such concepts and relations. Given the quantitative notion of the occurrence of a concept (rather than a Boolean present/absent) in a DNN, a key ingredient of such a specification language is a strength predicate (denoted by >) defined between two concepts, which is meant to capture order relationships between concepts for a given class. For instance, if the output of the model is class *truck*, we expect the model to be more aware of concepts *metallic* and *wheels* rather than *ears*, written as metallic > ears and wheels > ears, as ears are typically associated with an animal. Informally, the properties can have the following flavor: *"if the input (image) has ears the output can not be (class) truck"* or conversely, *"if the output is (class) truck then the input (image) can not have ears"* (as *ears* are typically associated with an animal).

The formal definition of the specification language and its semantics can leverage recent work on concept representation analysis [7–9] that aims to extract meaningful concept representations, often in the form of directions (of vectors), from the latent spaces of neural networks, that are easy to understand and process. In practice, as previously noted in this chapter, there is a growing literature on probing for concepts in a DNN, and finding the direction corresponding to a concept requires data that is manually annotated with truth-values of concept predicates. Leveraging this progress, we argue for the use of foundational VLMs as tools for concept-based analysis of vision-based DNNs. As VLMs have been trained on a large body of images accompanied by their textual description, they are implicitly aware of high-level concepts describing the images. We leverage recent work by Moayeri et al. [10] to build an *affine map* between the image embedding space of the vision-based DNN and the corresponding image embedding space of the VLM. As a consequence, the image representation space of a VLM can serve as a proxy for the representation space of a separate vision-based DNN and can be used to check the specification over the common concepts. We recently demonstrated [6] how this can be leveraged to discover the natural-language predicates (or concepts) relevant to a task and can also be used to assign truth-values for the concept predicates as well as the queries, given an input image.

Checking that an image satisfies certain properties reduces to checking the similarity between the image representations and logical combinations of predicates encoded in the textual space. Importantly, the verification is performed in the common text/image representation space, and further, we showed that it can be simplified to solving linear constraints despite the fact that the similarity measure involves non-linear constraints, and it is thus scalable. The same techniques can be applied to the VLM itself to check the properties of image representations with respect to natural-language properties encoded in the textual representations. This approach can not only verify whether properties capturing relationships between concepts are consistent with the internal representation of a machine learning model, but it can also be used for fault localization to isolate the layer of the DNN where the concepts become inconsistent.

3.4 Symbolic Specification of ML Models Using Concept Probes

We briefly sketch a specification language that shows how concept probes can be used to specify requirements on any machine learning model. This language is based on the first-order specification language and is an extension of the language that we recently used to verify vision models [6]. The specification language can also be built using intuitionist logic to enable reasoning over exceptions. The key goal of this language is to make it convenient to provide human-interpretable semantic requirements on a machine-learning model that combines predicates representing concept probes using logical connectives. We also want this language to be amenable to automatic verification and generation of assurance arguments for the model under analysis.

Such a language needs to represent a set of inputs ($Vars$) and the associated set of concepts to these inputs. We can distinguish the feature concepts $Concepts$ obtained through probes from more high-level labels C available during supervision. A more general specification language can use complex ontologies available in the form of knowledge graphs. We assume that a domain expert defines such ontologies and relationships that are mapped using concept probes to verify machine learning models.

In the simple language with its syntax described in Figure 3.2 and semantics described in Figure 3.3, the predicate $>(x, con_1, con_2)$, called a strength predicate, to express concept-based specifications which will be true if x exhibits con_1 stronger than con_2, where con_1 and con_2 are constants from the set $Concepts$. This relative comparison avoids the need to empirically find thresholds for the strength of a concept activating for a given input. Instead, we rely on having a set of relevant concepts $Concepts$ such that comparison between them yields meaningful associations. Note that since con_1 and con_2 refer to constants, $>(x, con_1, con_2)$ is actually a template with a separate predicate defined for every valuation of the constants. $predict(x, c)$ constrains the output of a neural classifier to the class c for

$$\begin{aligned} &\text{(variables)} && x \in Vars \\ &\text{(concept names)} && con_1, con_2 \in Concepts \\ &\text{(classes)} && c \in C \end{aligned}$$

$$E ::= >(x, con_1, con_2) \mid predict(x, c) \mid \neg E \mid E \wedge E \mid E \vee E$$

Figure 3.2 Syntax of a simple language that represents a logical combination of presence and absence of concepts in an input.

$$
\begin{aligned}
\text{(expressions)} &\quad e \in E \\
\text{(classifiers)} &\quad f \in F := \mathbb{R}^d \rightarrow \mathbb{R}^{|C|} \\
\text{(inputs)} &\quad v \in X := \mathbb{R}^d \\
\text{(concept representation maps)} &\quad rep \in Rep := Concepts \rightarrow (\mathbb{R}^d \rightarrow \mathbb{R}) \\
\text{(semantics)} &\quad [\![e]\!] \in F \times X \times Rep \rightarrow \{\text{True}, \text{False}\}
\end{aligned}
$$

$$
\begin{aligned}
[\![>(x, con_1, con_2)]\!](f, v, rep) &:= rep(con_1)(v) > rep(con_2)(v) \\
[\![predict(x, c)]\!](f, v, rep) &:= c \in argmax(f(v)) \\
[\![\neg e]\!](f, v, rep) &:= \neg [\![e]\!](f, v, rep) \\
[\![e_1 \wedge e_2]\!](f, v, rep) &:= [\![e_1]\!](f, v, rep) \wedge [\![e_2]\!](f, v, rep) \\
[\![e_1 \vee e_2]\!](f, v, rep) &:= [\![e_1]\!](f, v, rep) \vee [\![e_2]\!](f, v, rep)
\end{aligned}
$$

Figure 3.3 Semantics of a specification language for vision models from our past work. *Source*: Adapted from [6].

an input x. We also find it useful to define the predicate $hasCon(x, con)$ to encode that input x contains the concept con most prominently, encoded as follows:

$$hasCon(x, con) := \bigwedge_{con_i \in Concepts \wedge con_i \neq con} >(x, con, con_i).$$

In practice, when defining $hasCon$, we typically restrict con_i to concepts that are not associated to x. This is motivated by the observation that even in the presence of superposition of concepts in the feature space and polysemanticity of the features, the sparseness of concepts often leads to a clearly identifiable concept (con) that is most prominently present for a specific input instance x and definitely more strongly present than irrelevant concepts.

We demonstrate the utility of this symbolic specification language using a simple example. Consider the five-way classifier over the classes of *cat, dog, bird, car,* and *truck*. We assume that a domain expert defines the set $Concepts$. In this example, we rely on RIVAL10 dataset [11] to provide the concepts and relationship of these concepts with the classes. $Concepts$ contains *metallic, ears,* and *wheels*; this does not necessarily encode all the possible concepts that are relevant to a task. With these concepts, we can next write down the specification $>(x, metallic, ears) \wedge >(x, wheels, ears) \Rightarrow (predict(x, truck) \vee predict(x, car))$. This states the expectation that an input image x with the output label as *truck* or *car* has concepts *metallic* and *wheels* stronger than concept *ears*, amongst the five classes. We can also state another specification $predict(x, truck) \Longrightarrow >(x, wheels, ears)$, which ensures that when the model predicts *truck* it ought to be the case that the concept *wheels* is more strongly present in the image than *ears*, i.e., the models predict *truck* for the "right" reasons. Thus, predicates of the form $>(x, wheels, ears)$ can be seen as formal explanations for the model decision on class *truck*.

Formal semantics of the specification can be provided as an interpretation over a triple, namely, the machine learning model $f \in \mathbb{R}^d \rightarrow \mathbb{R}^{|C|}$ under consideration, an input $v \in \mathbb{R}^d$, and a concept probe map $rep \in Concepts \rightarrow (\mathbb{R}^d \rightarrow \mathbb{R})$; rep maps each concept $con \in Concepts$ to a function of type $\mathbb{R}^d \rightarrow \mathbb{R}$ that takes in an input and returns a number indicating the *strength* at which concept *con* is contained in the input. There can be several possible implementations of rep, and we discuss a few examples in this chapter. But we emphasize that this interpretation of the symbolic concept itself could be a neural network [12]. The predicate $>(x, con_1, con_2)$ evaluates to **True** if, as per rep, the strength of concept con_1 in the input is greater than that of concept con_2. This is again one of several choices for comparing two concepts. If the concept probes can provide scaling factor or bias in the learned feature representation, we can scale the concept strengths before comparing the two concepts. The predicate *predict* encodes the final label predicted by the machine learning model under consideration on the given input. The semantics of the logical connectives are standard.

Given the semantics for the specification language, we can now define when a machine learning model $f : X \rightarrow Y$ is known to *satisfy* a specification e with respect to a concept representations map rep and an input scope B (where $B \subseteq X$). If e evaluates to **True** for all inputs in B, then f satisfies e. Here B could be the whole set X, or a *region* in X, or just a set of (in-distribution) test images. Ideally, we would like to show that a specification holds for all inputs $v \in X$, but such a requirement is too strong. The majority of the inputs in set X do not correspond to any meaningful image (i.e., are out-of-distribution), and attempting to verify model behavior at such inputs typically leads to verification failure without discovering any useful counterexamples. We therefore restrict to the scope B. An effective compromise is to verify the models on inputs that are in-distribution, i.e., in the support set of the distribution over X (denoted as *inDist*(X)) that characterizes the training data. While a sound and complete encoding of the *inDist* predicate (i.e., an encoding that evaluates to **True** if and only if a sample is in-distribution) is not feasible, we can utilize approximations of the same. Once again, the scope B itself might be represented as a neural network such as an autoencoder. To simplify the notation, we can drop the context and input from the notation as being implicit and simply write the predicate $>(x, con_1, con_2)$ as $con_1 > con_2$. Similarly, we can write $predict(c)$ instead of $predict(x, c)$. Even with these simplifications captured in Definition 3.1, we have recently demonstrated successful verification of vision models [6].

Definition 3.1 ***(Satisfaction of specification by model)*****:** Given a model $f : X \rightarrow Y$, a concept representations map rep, and an input scope $B \subseteq X$, (f, rep, B) satisfies a specification e (denoted as $(f, rep, B) \models e$) if,

$$\forall x \in B.\ [\![e]\!](f, x, rep) = \mathbf{True}.$$

3.5 Implementation and Evaluation

We briefly summarize our recent work that concretizes the specification language and its semantics presented earlier in this chapter and demonstrates how it can be used to verify vision language models [6]. We begin by providing a concrete implementation of rep before we can verify if a model satisfies a specification. The map rep needs to be semantically meaningful—ideally, the strength of a concept as defined by rep should be in congruence with the human understanding. For verification, it is also essential to ensure that rep can be encoded as efficiently verifiable constraints. We have demonstrated our approach using a performant and complex ResNet-based classifier trained on the RIVAL10 dataset [11]. RIVAL10 is a subset of ImageNet [13], restricted to 10 classes. Importantly, RIVAL10 images come with annotated attributes, which we leverage to define candidate properties to verify. In practice, we expect domain experts to provide these properties following the common practice in verification. We use the popular vision-language CLIP model as the VLM in our analysis.

To obtain a semantically meaningful concept representation map rep, we use large VLMs such as CLIP [5]. Using VLMs to implement rep is advantageous for several reasons. First, the manner in which VLMs such as CLIP are trained ensures that concepts are represented as directions in the common VLM representation space – the sparsity of concepts leads to minimum superposition. In particular, their training objective requires the pair of embeddings generated for an image-caption pair, by the image and text encoders of a VLM, to be aligned in the same direction as measured via cosine similarity. This supervision leads to language-expressed concepts being easily accessible in the latent space of the model. Second, since the image and language encoders in CLIP map to the same representation space, it allows the use of language for probing and reasoning about visual data. For instance, one can simply compute the embedding of a caption that references the relevant concept (say, *"Image of a wheel"* in case of our running example) to obtain the concept direction. This obviates the need for more advanced concept probes. Third, VLMs are typically treated as foundation models [14] that are well-trained on vast and diverse datasets. As a result, these models are exposed to a variety of concepts from multiple datasets and can therefore serve as a useful repository of concept representations. The richness of the VLM embedding space also opens up the opportunity to define aggregate concepts such as *"wheels and metallic*" where the logical connectives are not expressed externally, thereby simplifying the structure of the specification at the cost of more complex concepts.

Definition 3.2 describes the implementation that we use for the concept representation map *rep* that uses a VLM g [6]. This definition assumes that concepts are represented as probes or directions in the feature space. In this example implementation, we limit ourselves to concepts that were enforced by VLM's training objective. This objective requires the pair of embeddings generated for an image-caption pair, by the image and text encoders of a VLM, to be aligned in the same direction as measured via cosine similarity. While the definition still relies on the hypothesis that concepts are represented as directions, the direction corresponding to a concept *con* is easily extracted using the text encoder g_{enc}^{txt} of g. Following previous work [10], a vector $\overline{con}$ in the direction of concept is computed as the mean of text embeddings for a set of captions (denoted as $cap(con)$) that all refer to the concept *con* in different ways. We compute the mean since many semantically valid captions may be constructed for the same concept, and each caption leads to a slightly different embedding.

Definition 3.2 *(Linear rep via VLM)*: Given a VLM g with image encoder $g_{enc}^{img} : X \to Z$ and text encoder $g_{enc}^{txt} : T \to Z$ where $Z := \mathbb{R}^{d'}$ is the common feature space where the concepts are represented, the linear concept representation map, *rep*, via model g is defined as,

$$rep(con) := \lambda x.\ \cos(g_{enc}^{img}(x), \overline{con})$$

where $\overline{con} := \frac{\sum_{t \in cap(con)} g_{enc}^{txt}(t)}{|cap(con)|}$ and $cap(con)$ is a set of sentences or captions referring to concept *con*.

Definition 3.2 provides a simple implementation for *rep* which we empirically validate to check that it is semantically meaningful, according to human-understandable concepts. We can use *rep* to instantiate the semantics and reason about properties for the VLM (i.e., CLIP) itself. In principle, we can use the same implementation of *rep* to reason about the original vision model. However, this would introduce a significant scalability challenge in verifying a vision model *f*. We would not only need to reason about the whole model *f* but also about the complex image encoder g_{enc}^{img} of VLM g since g_{enc}^{img} is used to implement *rep*. We sidestep this challenge using the observed linearly transformable representation across models [10]. The representation spaces of vision DNN under test, and the VLMs such as CLIP can be linked to each other via an affine map. We can utilize this map to define an alternative implementation of *rep* that does not involve encoding the complex g_{enc}^{img}. Let $D_{\text{train}} \subset X$ denote an image dataset. Given the encoder $f_{enc} : X \to Z_f$ of a vision model f and the image encoder $g_{enc}^{img} : X \to Z_g$ of VLM g, we can learn a map $r_{map} : Z_f \to Z_g$ such that the representation spaces of the two models are *aligned* as much as possible, i.e., given an image $x \in X$, ideally $r_{map}(f_{enc}(x)) = g_{enc}^{img}(x)$ holds. Moayeri et al. [10] show that r_{map} can be restricted to the class of affine transformations, i.e., $r_{map}(z) := Mz + d$, where r_{map} is learned by solving the following optimization problem,

$$M, d = \arg\min_{M,d} \frac{1}{|D_{\text{train}}|} \sum_{x \in D_{\text{train}}} \left\| M f_{enc}(x) + d - g_{enc}^{img}(x) \right\|_2^2. \tag{3.1}$$

We use r_{map} to define rep as follows [6].

Definition 3.3 *(Linear rep via vision model, r_{map}, and VLM)*: Given a vision model $f : X \to Y$ with encoder $f_{enc} : X \to Z_f$, a VLM g with encoders $g_{enc}^{img} : X \to Z_g$ and $g_{enc}^{txt} : T \to Z_g$, and a linear map r_{map} as described above, then the concept representation map, rep, is defined as,

$$rep(con) := \lambda x.\ \cos(r_{map}(f_{enc}(x)), \overline{con})$$

where $\overline{con}$ is a vector in Z_g whose direction corresponds to concept con, i.e., $\overline{con} := \frac{\sum_{t \in cap(con)} g_{enc}^{txt}(t)}{|cap(con)|}$.

A key step is aligning the feature spaces of the two models for the extracted concepts to be comparable. We can formalize the notion of *faithful representation space alignment* (Definition 3.4 [6]). Intuitively, the alignment is faithful if no information is lost when using r_{map} to map between the two representation spaces.

Definition 3.4 *(Faithful representation alignment)*: Given an encoder $f_{enc} : X \to Z_f$ of a vision model and an image encoder $g_{enc}^{img} : X \to Z_g$ of a VLM g, the representation space of f_{enc} is faithfully aligned with the representation space of g_{enc}^{img} if there exists a map $r_{map} : Z_f \to Z_g$ such that,

$$\forall x \in X.\ r_{map}(f_{enc}(x)) = g_{enc}^{img}(x)$$

As long as the representation map, r_{map}, satisfies the condition of faithful alignment of features of the model under test and the VLM, then the implementations of rep according to Definitions 3.2 and 3.3 are consistent. Thus, we could implement rep using Definition 3.3 instead of Definition 3.2. However, it is possible that the representations spaces of a vision model and a VLM may not be always faithfully aligned; there may be cases such that for the r_{map} we learn, $r_{map}(f_{enc}(x)) = g_{enc}^{img}(x)$ does not hold for some images x. Thus, it is possible that the two implementations of rep as we defined (one via VLM and one via vision model and r_{map}) may yield different results for some inputs. Thus, it is important to note that the practical implementation of this conceptual verification method only provides statistical guarantees. Further, it may be the case that a $\overline{con}$ may not be an accurate representation of the corresponding human-understandable, natural-language concept due to, for example, inconsistent embedding in the VLM of the vision concept and its textual label. We address this problem by carefully validating our construction for rep against semantically meaningful strength predicates, as specified by human experts. We then focus the verification only on properties containing predicates with high statistical significance.

In general, we need efficient validation of conceptual probes efficacy over the large multimodal models before using them as specification lens to verify other machine learning models. Once we have an implementation of rep as per Definition 3.3, we can define a constraint-based verification procedure for the vision model f. This implementation of rep allows us to factor out the constraints corresponding to f_{enc} and g_{enc}^{img}, resulting in efficient verification. For example, we can exploit the decomposition of a vision model f into f_{enc} and f_{head} to define an efficient verification procedure for vision models with respect to a given specification. In particular, Theorem 3.1 in our prior work [6] shows that the verification of a model f with respect to a given specification e can be reduced to the verification of f_{head}, without involving g_{enc}^{img}. Without loss of generality, we assume that the machine learning model $f : X \to Y$ that can be decomposed into $f_{enc} : X \to Z$ and $f_{head} : Z \to Y$ where $Z := \mathbb{R}^{d'}$, a specification e, a linear concept representation map rep (as defined in Definition 3.3), and an input scope $B \subseteq X$. Intuitively, the encoder component of the model represents the embedding into the feature space where the concept probes were used, and the head corresponds to the model layers decoding the features to the output.

Theorem 3.1: *Given a vision model $f : X \to Y$ that can be decomposed into $f_{enc} : X \to Z$ and $f_{head} : Z \to Y$ where $Z := \mathbb{R}^{d'}$, a specification e, a linear concept representation map rep, as defined in Definition 3.3, and an input scope $B \subseteq X$,*

$$(f, rep, B) \models e \Leftrightarrow (f_{head}, \widehat{rep}, f_{enc}(B)) \models e$$

where $\widehat{rep}$ operates on embeddings instead of inputs and is obtained from rep by replacing f_{enc} with the identity function and $f_{enc}(B) := \{f_{enc}(x) \mid x \in B\}$.

We use the notation $\widehat{rep}$ for the function obtained from rep by replacing f_{enc} with the identity function, $f_{enc}(B) := \{f_{enc}(x) \mid x \in B\}$, and $f_{enc}^{-1}(v') := \{v \mid f_{enc}(v) = v'\}$ for the preimage under f_{enc} of a point v'. A general observation that holds given the definitions of rep (as per Definition 3.3) and $\widehat{rep}$ (all occurrences of f_{enc} in rep replaced by the identity function) is that,

$$\forall con \in Concepts. \forall v \in X.\ rep(con)(v) = \widehat{rep}(con)(f_{enc}(v)). \tag{3.2}$$

Using structural induction on the specification language, we can establish the following two lemmas [6].

Lemma 3.1:

$$\forall v \in B.\ [\![e]\!](f, rep, v) = [\![e]\!](f_{head}, \widehat{rep}, f_{enc}(v))$$

Lemma 3.2:

$$\forall v' \in f_{enc}(B). \forall v \in f_{enc}^{-1}(v').\ [\![e]\!](f_{head}, \widehat{rep}, v') = [\![e]\!]((f, rep, v)$$

The proof for Theorem 3.1 can be derived from these two lemmas and the detailed proof is presented in Mangal et al. [6]. We can also state a theorem similar to Theorem. 3.1 for the VLM model g.

Theorem 3.2: *Given a VLM g with encoders $g_{enc}^{img} : X \to Z$ and $g_{enc}^{txt} : T \to Z$ and head $g_{head} : Z \to Y$ where $Z := \mathbb{R}^{d'}$, a specification e, a linear concept representation map rep (as defined in Definition 3.2), and an input scope $B \subseteq X$,*

$$((g_{head} \circ g_{enc}^{img}), rep, B) \models e \Leftrightarrow (f_{head}, \widehat{rep}, g_{enc}(B)) \models e$$

where $\widehat{rep}$ is obtained from rep by replacing g_{enc}^{img} with the identity function

In our recent work Mangal et al. [6], we evaluated this approach using a ResNet18 vision model [15, 11] as the model under test, and CLIP [5] as the multimodal foundation model. We use the RIVAL10 (**RI**ch **V**isu**AL** Attributions) [11] dataset consisting of 26k images drawn from ImageNet [13]. The dataset is partitioned into a train set with 21k images and a test set with 5k images. The dataset is organized into 10 classes matching those of CIFAR10: *truck*, *car*, *plane*, *ship*, *cat*, *dog*, *equine*, *deer*, *frog*, and *bird* (which we use to define the set C of classes). The dataset contains manually annotated instance-wise labels for 18 attributes (which we use to define set $Concepts$) as well as the respective segmentation masks for these attributes on the images. The 18 attributes are *beak*, *colored-eyes*, *ears*, *floppy-ears*, *tail*, *horns*, *long-snout*, *mane*,*wings*, *wheels*, *tall*, *long*, *rectangular*, *hairy*, *metallic*, *wet*, *text*, and *patterned*. These annotations can be used to extract the concepts relevant to each class. We also elicit strength predicates for each of the concepts. For each class *c*, we compute the percentage of inputs (from the train set) that have ground truth *c* and are annotated with concept *con*. If this is greater than a threshold (70%), we consider that concept as *relevant*.

Figure 3.4 shows the relevant concepts that are computed for each class; on the y-axis we list the classes, on the x axis we list the concepts; dark boxes mark the relevant concepts. For instance, for class *truck*, concepts *wheels, tall, long, rectangular, metallic,* and *text* are all considered relevant, whereas the other concepts (e.g., *tail* and *wings*) are irrelevant. The information in Figure 3.4 can also be used to elicit strength predicates relevant for each class *c*—for each pair of

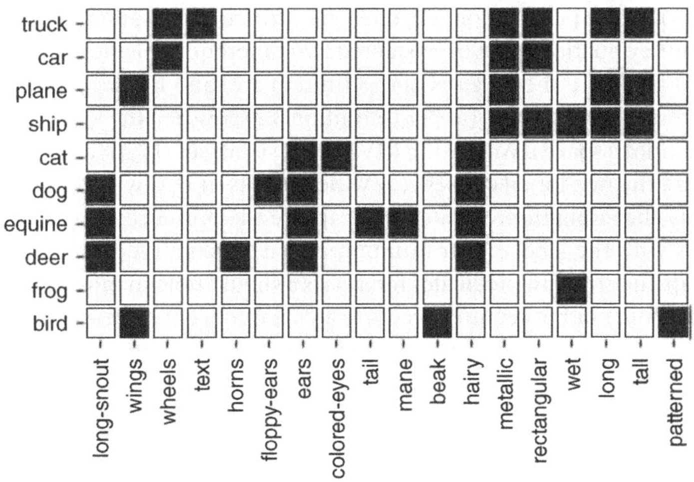

Figure 3.4 Relevance of concepts for different classes in the RIVAL10 dataset.

relevant (con_r) and irrelevant (con_{ir}) concepts. As explained earlier, we define a predicate $con_r > con_{ir}$ that should hold on all inputs of class c.

Given a model trained on the RIVAL10 dataset, as part of our evaluation, we aim to formulate specifications that require the model to not only make correct decisions but also make those for the "right" reasons. To this end, we use our language to encode specifications of the form, $predict(x, class, \delta) \Longrightarrow >(x, con_1, con_2, \epsilon)$, which states that if a model classifies an input image x to a certain class with some confidence threshold, then the image has a stronger presence of a relevant concept (con_1) than an irrelevant concept (con_2). We exhaustively enlist such specifications for each class in RIVAL10 (c_i, i ranging from 0 to 9), comparing each relevant concept for c_i with every corresponding irrelevant concept. Formally, for each class c_i, we enlist specifications $predict(x, c_i, \delta) \Longrightarrow >(x, con_r, con_{ir}, \epsilon)$, where $con_r \in R_i$, $con_{ir} \notin R_i$, R_i is the set of concepts identified as being relevant to c_i. For instance, for class *truck*, we formulate a total of 72 predicates, corresponding to all the possible combinations of relevant and irrelevant concepts; e.g., we elicit $wheels > wings$ and $metallic > tail$, as $wheels$ and $metallic$ are relevant concepts, whereas $wings$ and $tail$ are not. Overall, we formulate a total of 522 such predicates for the model. In practice, we expect human domain experts to directly provide the concepts and strength predicates relevant to the task. Since we only use the concept annotations to elicit the strength predicates, there is no need to manually annotate each image if these predicates are given.

The semantics of the specification depends on the representation of the concepts *rep*. In our evaluation [6], we considered two different implementations of *rep* – the first using CLIP model g (as per Definition 3.2) and the second one implemented via the affine map r_{map} (as per Definition 3.3) between the ResNet18 f and g's representations spaces. We use the RIVAL10 test dataset D_{test} in our evaluation and measure the rate for all classes c, at which inputs in D_{test} with ground-truth label c satisfy the strength predicates that capture the presence of relevant concepts in inputs with the label c. Our intuition is that, given an ideal concept representation map, the strength predicates for a class c should hold in most cases. Note that this procedure neither requires access to an ideal concept representation map nor data with manually annotated concept labels if the strength predicates are given.

The results for *rep* implemented only using CLIP model g (as in Definition 3.2) are shown in Figure 3.5. Concepts on the Y-axis represent cor_r and on the X-axis represent con_{ir} in the evaluated strength predicates. We see that for class *truck*,

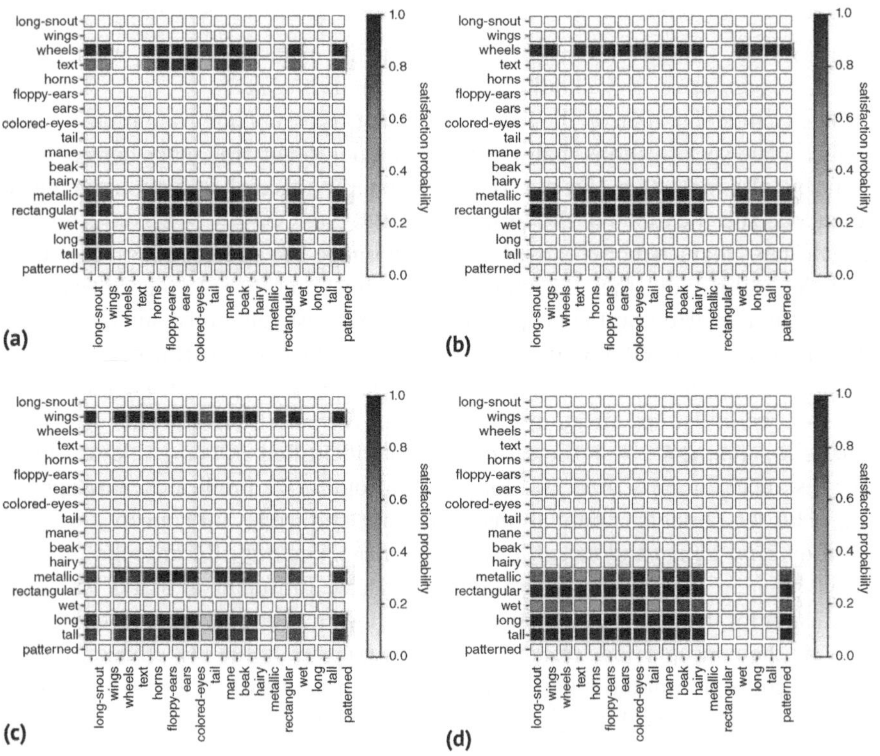

Figure 3.5 Satisfaction probabilities for *rep* implemented only using CLIP model g: (a) strength predicates for *truck*; (b) strength predicates for *car*; (c) strength predicates for *plane*; (d) and strength predicates for *ship*.

except for strength predicates involving concept *text*, the satisfaction probabilities of the presence of relevant concepts are consistently high. Similar results are observed for all the other classes. This provides strong evidence for our hypothesis that concept probes from the large foundation model (CLIP) can be used to verify machine learning models.

The results for *rep* implemented using the ResNet18 model f and CLIP model g via the affine map (as per Definition 3.3) are summarized in Figure 3.6. The trends are similar to those observed for *rep* implemented only using g. These results provide further evidence that the representation space of f_{enc} is well aligned with the representation space of g_{enc}^{img} via our learned affine map and can be used to relate the representation of concepts across different models.

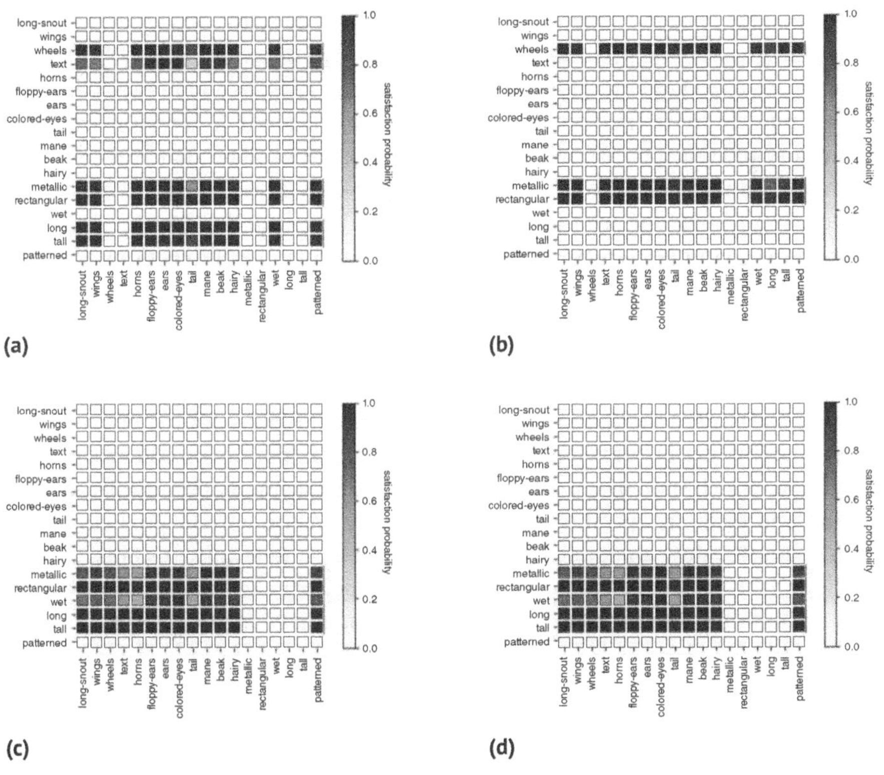

Figure 3.6 Satisfaction probabilities for *rep* implemented using ResNet18 model f and CLIP model g: (a) strength predicates for *truck*; (b) strength predicates for *car*; (c) strength predicates for *plane*; (d) and strength predicates for *ship*.

3.6 Conclusion and Open Challenges

The evolution of neurosymbolic AI assurance methods, driven by foundation models and concept-based verification techniques, holds immense promise for improving the safety, interpretability, and reliability of AI systems. By grounding assurance processes in human-interpretable symbolic abstractions, these approaches provide a structured and scalable method for verifying and analyzing the behavior of DNNs. Through concept probes, it becomes feasible to align the latent representations of complex models with meaningful human-understandable features, bridging machine learning and symbolic reasoning.

Despite these advancements, significant challenges remain. Aligning human concepts with the statistical representations of neural networks continues to be nontrivial, particularly in the presence of phenomena such as superposition and polysemantic neurons. Our verification is sound only with respect to the interpretation given to the predicates by the concept representation map (rep). In this chapter, we use a larger foundation model (such as VLMs) to obtain rep. The foundation models are trained on massive amounts of data and, as a result, are a rich repository of concepts. We use statistical analysis to validate that rep conforms with human understanding, that is, it is semantically meaningful. Note also that Theorem 3.1 holds for arbitrary decompositions of f into the decoder f_{head} and encoder f_{enc}. In practice, we may need to try multiple decompositions to find a layer where the representations of concepts in the latent space are well-aligned with human interpretation.

The implementation of neurosymbolic assurance frameworks has shown considerable promise in recent evaluations. For instance, leveraging multimodal models like CLIP, a semantically meaningful concept representation map was created to verify neural behaviors against logical constraints. Using datasets such as RIVAL10, which includes annotated attributes and segmentation masks, we can define and evaluate specifications that not only ensure correct predictions but also guarantee they are made for the "right" reasons. Relevant concepts, such as "wheels" for trucks or "metallic" for cars, can be extracted and used to formulate strength predicates, enabling a deeper evaluation of model performance. By linking the representation spaces of models under test with those of robust foundation models, effective verification approaches can be developed for semantic properties. The integration of neurosymbolic methods with the capability to probe concepts learned in the state-of-the-art foundation models is poised to redefine assurance methodologies in AI. Neurosymbolic AI can establish a foundation for developing trustworthy and reliable AI systems by fostering transparency and enabling rigorous verification.

References

1 Rishi Bommasani, Drew A. Hudson, Ehsan Adeli, Russ Altman, Simran Arora, Sydney von Arx, Michael S. Bernstein, Jeannette Bohg, Antoine Bosselut, Emma Brunskill, et al. On the opportunities and risks of foundation models. *arXiv*, 2021. https://crfm.stanford.edu/assets/report.pdf.

2 Trenton Bricken, Adly Templeton, Joshua Batson, Brian Chen, Adam Jermyn, Tom Conerly, Nick Turner, Cem Anil, Carson Denison, Amanda Askell, et al. Towards monosemanticity: decomposing language models with dictionary learning. *Transformer Circuits Thread*, 2023. See in particular the section "Phenomenology: Universality". https://transformer-circuits.pub/2023/monosemantic-features/index.html#phenomenology-universality.

3 Jia Deng, Wei Dong, Richard Socher, Li-Jia Li, Kai Li, and Li Fei-Fei. Imagenet: a large-scale hierarchical image database. In *2009 IEEE Conference on Computer Vision and Pattern Recognition*, pages 248–255, 2009. https://doi.org/10.1109/CVPR.2009.5206848.

4 Kaiming He, Xiangyu Zhang, Shaoqing Ren, and Jian Sun. Deep residual learning for image recognition. In *Proceedings of the IEEE Conference on Computer Vision and Pattern Recognition*, pages 770–778, 2016.

5 Been Kim, Martin Wattenberg, Justin Gilmer, Carrie Cai, James Wexler, Fernanda Viegas, and Rory sayres. Interpretability beyond feature attribution: quantitative testing with concept activation vectors (TCAV). In Jennifer Dy and Andreas Krause, editors, *Proceedings of the 35th International Conference on Machine Learning, volume 80 of Proceedings of Machine Learning Research*, pages 2668–2677. PMLR, 2018. https://proceedings.mlr.press/v80/kim18d.html.

6 Ravi Mangal, Nina Narodytska, Divya Gopinath, Boyue Caroline Hu, Anirban Roy, Susmit Jha, and Corina S Păsăreanu. Concept-based analysis of neural networks via vision-language models. In *International Symposium on AI Verification*, pages 49–77. Springer, 2024.

7 Tomáš Mikolov, Wen-tau Yih, and Geoffrey Zweig. Linguistic regularities in continuous space word representations. In *Proceedings of the 2013 Conference of the North American Chapter of the Association for Computational Linguistics: Human Language Technologies*, pages 746–751, 2013.

8 Mazda Moayeri, Phillip Pope, Yogesh Balaji, and Soheil Feizi. A comprehensive study of image classification model sensitivity to foregrounds, backgrounds, and visual attributes. In *Proceedings of the IEEE/CVF Conference on Computer Vision and Pattern Recognition*, pages 19087–19097, 2022.

9 Mazda Moayeri, Keivan Rezaei, Maziar Sanjabi, and Soheil Feizi. Text-to-concept (and back) via cross-model alignment. In *International Conference on Machine Learning*, pages 25037–25060. PMLR, 2023.

10 Catherine Olsson, Nelson Elhage, Neel Nanda, Nicholas Joseph, Rohin DasSarma, Tom Henighan, Ben Mann, Amanda Askell, Yuntao Bai, Anna Chen, et al. Toy models of superposition. *arXiv preprint arXiv:2209.10652*, 2022.

11 Kiho Park, Yo Joong Choe, and Victor Veitch. The linear representation hypothesis and the geometry of large language models. In *Causal Representation Learning Workshop at NeurIPS 2023*, 2023.

12 Alec Radford, Jong Wook Kim, Chris Hallacy, Aditya Ramesh, Gabriel Goh, Sandhini Agarwal, Girish Sastry, Amanda Askell, Pamela Mishkin, Jack Clark, et al. Learning transferable visual models from natural language supervision. In Marina Meila and Tong Zhang, editors, *Proceedings of the 38th International Conference on Machine Learning, volume 139 of Proceedings of Machine Learning Research*, pages 8748–8763. PMLR, 2021. https://proceedings.mlr.press/v139/radford21a.html.

13 Felipe Toledo, David Shriver, Sebastian Elbaum, and Matthew B. Dwyer. Deeper notions of correctness in image-based dnns: lifting properties from pixel to entities. In *Proceedings of the 31st ACM Joint European Software Engineering Conference and Symposium on the Foundations of Software Engineering*, pages 2122–2126, 2023.

14 Chih-Kuan Yeh, Been Kim, and Pradeep Ravikumar. Human-centered concept explanations for neural networks. In Pascal Hitzler and Md. Kamruzzaman Sarker, editors, *Neuro-Symbolic Artificial Intelligence: The State of the Art, volume 342 of Frontiers in Artificial Intelligence and Applications*, pages 337–352. IOS Press, 2021. https://doi.org/10.3233/FAIA210362.

15 Bolei Zhou, Yiyou Sun, David Bau, and Antonio Torralba. Interpretable basis decomposition for visual explanation. In *Proceedings of the European Conference on Computer Vision (ECCV)*, 2018.

4

Toward Assured Autonomy Using Neurosymbolic Components and Systems

Abhishek Dubey,[1] Taylor T. Johnson,[1] Xenofon Koutsoukos,[1] Baiting Luo,[1] Diego Manzanas Lopez,[1] Miklos Maroti,[2] Ayan Mukhopadhyay,[1] Nicholas Potteiger,[1] Serena Serbinowska,[1] Daniel Stojcsics,[1] Yunuo Zhang,[1] and Gabor Karsai[1]*

[1] *Institute for Software-Integrated Systems, Vanderbilt University, Nashville, Tennessee, USA*
[2] *Bolyai Institute, University of Szeged, Szeged, Hungary*

*Corresponding Author: gabor.karsai@vanderbilt.edu

4.1 Introduction

Neurosymbolic technology is expected to deliver better performance and novel capabilities in engineered systems that operate in a physical environment. Given a Neurosymbolic component, the "symbolic," i.e., the explicitly designed and algorithmic part can operate more efficiently and reliably, while the "neural," i.e., the data-driven and training based part can provide capabilities that are hard to implement algorithmically. Beyond this complementary view, a more symbiotic view is projected, where the two parts work together, in a cooperative way.

There are several research questions about how to design, implement, and verify such Neurosymbolic components for a larger system. Starting with the identification of the functional requirements, the designer has to decide how to map the desired functions into the symbolic and neural parts – or – into the symbiotically operating combination of the two. The actual implementation leads to challenges in the coding of the symbolic and the training of the neural part, and these cannot be performed independently from each other. Finally, the assurance of the Neurosymbolic component necessitates holistic methods that can verify the integrated component. This last step is especially challenging because traditional testing may be impractical for the neural part, and hence the integrated component.

Neurosymbolic AI: Foundations and Applications, First Edition. Edited by Alvaro Velasquez et al.

In the following sections, we introduce a notional cyber-physical system; an Unmanned Aerial Vehicle (UAV) that can perform specific missions, e.g., locating objects of interest with specific characteristics in an urban environment. We will use the autonomy software stack for such a vehicle to illustrate how Neurosymbolic technology can be applied to implement specific functions and present our approaches and results. The specific components include a probabilistic world model, a planner, and a trajectory controller. Having shown how these components can be implemented, we will present techniques for the verification of one specific type of Neurosymbolic component: the trajectory planner.

4.2 Problem Formulation and Challenges: Maneuver Control for Autonomous Vehicles

UAV, aka "drones," are widely used in industrial, military, and civilian applications. The evolution of such vehicles is moving in the direction of increasing autonomy, where the vehicle is capable of executing a complete mission, with minimum or no human involvement. Specifically, the vehicle is "instructed" about mission parameters, objectives, and constraints, and then the vehicle performs the mission, without a human operator. The vehicle is equipped with an "autonomy software layer" that interprets the mission instructions and performs all mission level control functions. This layer relies on low-level controllers that maintain vehicle stability and control that actual movement of the vehicle, as well as sensors that provide odometry, visual, and other data needed for the autonomy functions.

There are several examples for autonomous UAV missions; in this chapter, we will use one running example: finding a car of interest in a suburban environment. In this mission type, the UAV is given instructions as follows: (i) map of the geographical area to be searched, including a map of know obstacles (buildings, etc.) the UAV must not crash into, (ii) areas of interest on the map where the target car is expected to be found with some probability, (iii) areas that the UAV must not fly into (due to privacy concerns, for example), (iv) symbolic description of the target to be found (possibly accompanied by sample images of similar cars that could be used to train a perception system), and (v) other mission constraints (e.g., maximum flight time). Given this description, the autonomy software flies the vehicle from takeoff to landing with the goal of finding the target, within the constraints of the mission.

The autonomy software has two distinct components a perception component and a maneuvering component. The perception is responsible for detecting and recognizing the target, while the maneuvering component determines the flight path of the vehicle and issues commands to the low-level controllers. These two components work in close interaction with each other, but in the discussion below, we assume a simplified case where the perception component only feeds the maneuver component and information is not flowing in the opposite direction. Hence, we assume that the perception informs the maneuver whether the target has or has not been found. The maneuvering component takes these messages and issues the appropriate commands for the flight control system about where to fly, with what speed, and how to orient the vehicle (for maximum visibility of the target).

There are several interesting challenges for the maneuver component for mission type at hand. The maneuvering component has to (i) "understand" the mission description, (ii) construct and continuously update an internal representation of what the vehicle "believes" about its environment, (iii) plan the vehicle path on large scale (at coarse resolution), (iv) generate the flight trajectory on the small scale (at fine resolution), and (v) generate commands for the low-level controller to fly along that trajectory. In the subsequent discussion, we present how these functions can be designed and implemented with the help of Neurosymbolic techniques.

An autonomous UAV has to undergo a certification process before wide-scale deployment. The certification involves collecting supporting evidence for the safety of the vehicle, and some of this evidence may qualify individual components of the vehicle. In industrial terms, assurance arguments are necessary that justify why specific claims hold for the components. Hence, a further challenge is the assurance of the components, as well as the entire system.

4.3 Software Architecture: Components and Interactions

In the notional architecture of an UAV autonomy software stack, the maneuver component is responsible for high-level decision-making, including planning and trajectory control for the flight the vehicle, in a specific mission-specific way. This component is interfaced with other components in the larger software architecture of the system, and itself can be decomposed into function-specific components as shown on Figure 4.1.

The architecture is formulated as two layers: one layer representing the "Vehicle Platform" and encapsulating software and hardware components that produce sensor data streams and consume control commands to be executed by a low-level controller, and another layer including the "Perception" and "Maneuver" components. The "Perception" component receives sensor data streams and performs several functions, including image segmentation, object detection, recognition, and tracking. The outputs of the "Perception" component include segmented images and messages indicating that objects of interest have been detected, recognized, and tracked. Because the work described in this chapter focused on the "Maneuver" component, the "Perception" will be considered as black box and will not be discussed further.

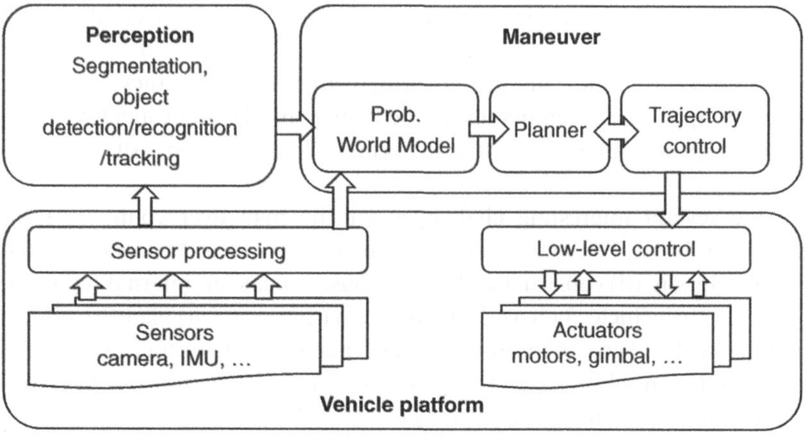

Figure 4.1 Architecture for the UAV software stack.

The "Maneuver" component can be decomposed into three distinct components, each with a specific function, as follows.

Probabilistic World Model (PWM): The PWM maintains a data structure representing what the UAV "believes" about its operating environment. This model includes knowledge about overall area, obstacles to be avoided, and possible locations for objects of interest. As the UAV keeps flying, the model is continuously updated based on observations made by the "Perception" component and other instrumentation data (e.g. odometry). Whenever the model is updated, it informs the downstream "Planner" component about it.

Planner: The Planner is tasked with determining the next waypoint the vehicle should navigate to. The planning algorithm should take into consideration of the current state of the PWM, overall mission objectives, and whether an object of interest has been found or not.

Trajectory Controller: A waypoint is relatively far from the current position, and there could obstacles on the straight path to the waypoint. Hence, the vehicle may have to fly a complex trajectory that avoids the obstacles while approaching the next waypoint. The "Trajectory controller" is responsible for computing and re-computing this trajectory, dynamically, as needed. The output here is a sequence of trajectory commands that can be executed by the low-level controller.

The above three components operate mainly in a pipelined manner: (i) the PWM updates the internal data structure based on inputs from the "Perception," (ii) using the latest world model, the "Planner" computes a new waypoint when the vehicle is about to reach the previous waypoint, and (iii) the "Trajectory controller" computes a fine-grain trajectory command sequence that is sent to the low-level controller for execution. One situation when this scheme does not work is if the "Trajectory controller" cannot find a feasible path to the next waypoint due to, e.g., obstacles where the trajectory would violate some safety constraint. In this case, the "Planner" is asked for new waypoint for which the trajectory is then computed. This iterative process continues up to a time limit when the missions is declared as unfeasible.

Notional Mission: Target Localization: The main mission type considered was locating an object of interest (a "target") in an urban neighborhood environment. The map of limited area neighborhood is assumed known, including the Three-dimensional (3D) shapes of obstacles to be avoided. Some obstacles may be missing from the map (e.g., trees), so the UAV has to detect and avoid them as well, while flying. Additionally, the map includes "no-go" zones (where the UAV cannot fly) and areas of interest that are marked with some probability indicating the likelihood that the target can be found there. A typical target is a car with a specific shape and color – this information is expressed symbolically and provided to the "Perception" component. The mission has constraints including the maximum flight time and the vehicle is subject to physical constraints (e.g., kinematics, camera viewing angles, and orientation, etc.).

The following sections describe how each of the above components implement their functions using Neurosymbolic techniques. The conclusion presents how these components can be verified in order to support assurance claims about them.

4.4 Probabilistic World Model

For an autonomous drone to successfully complete its intended missions, it must understand both its surrounding environment and its location within that environment. By a *world model*, we refer to any representation of the physical space where the drone operates. This includes, but is not limited to, the following: (i) the locations of observed obstacles and landmarks, (ii) objects of interest, whether stationary or movable, (iii) any prior information about these objects of interest, (iv) other movable objects, such as pedestrians, and (v) the drone itself, along with the predicted evolution of this environment over time. It is crucial that this information be represented in a fixed 3D world coordinate system, rather than one relative to the drone itself. This approach ensures the retention of previously discovered information. Given that all sensory inputs have uncertainties, the environment evolves unpredictably, and even prior knowledge about objects is uncertain, the world model must capture this knowledge probabilistically. This probabilistic representation is what we refer to as the PWM.

The main objective of the PWM is to bridge the perception AI component, interpret the mission specification, and provide actionable and accurate probability maps for planning and navigation. The PWM takes the following as inputs: (i) the mission specification, which can change over time and (ii) odometry and perception data, and produces the following outputs, (iii) an obstacle map in the world coordinate system for navigation, and (iv) a reward map for the planner component. The mission specification can define an initial map of the area and no-fly zones and describe objects of interest, including attributes such as type, color, potential location relative to other objects, speed, and probable initial location areas with assigned probabilities. While this specification could be generated by a large language model, the current implementation uses a domain-specific language, which is interpreted symbolically by the PWM. Odometry information provides the drone's location and orientation, as well as that of its camera. Perception data includes depth maps and segmented images categorized according to the mission specification. Since all sensory inputs have inherent uncertainties, one key goal of the PWM is to characterize and reduce these uncertainties as more data becomes available. The output obstacle map represents a likelihood function over the world coordinate system that describes the probability of obstacles at any given location. The output reward map is a Bayesian information gain function, which quantifies the expected reduction in uncertainty about the likely locations of targets of interest [1]. In the current implementation, all probability maps are stored as large matrices with a resolution of 1 m. An ongoing research objective is to explore how to compress this information into a more compact representation while maintaining efficient computational performance.

4.4.1 Obstacle Map Calculation

Part of the work done by the PWM is Simultaneous Localization and Mapping (SLAM), but in a much more limited capacity. SLAM for drone navigation involves complex challenges due to the dynamic and resource-constrained nature of drone platforms. The key challenges include limited onboard resources on real platforms, sensor noise and accuracy, dynamic and unstructured environment, and scalability of map management. SLAM is an extensively studied problem with several robust solutions, such as FastSLAM [2]. In this work, we have avoided the extra complexity of a full-fledged SLAM solution and replaced it with a custom probabilistic update based solution to focus on the symbolic computation and representation part of the problem. In the AirSim simulation environment that was used in the research, the localization is modeled with a precise GPS, and the image depth calculation from the camera to the scene can be considered ground truth, so the real error sources are time-synchronization inaccuracy and segmentation inaccuracy, see Figure 4.2.

The obstacle map is updated from each time we have a pair of depth and segmentation image obtained from the perception module. First, each pixel is mapped to a real-world 3D coordinate using an estimate of the drone location and its orientation and the camera parameters. For each 1 m grid cell, we maintain the probability of each object category, but for the obstacle map calculation, only the occupied (any object) or unoccupied (air) categories are used. Special care had to be taken to detect and discard whether artifacts, such as falling snow or leaves, based on subsequent rays going from the camera to far away objects but passing through previously occupied leaf cells. Other than this, the obstacle map calculation is straightforward. The obstacle map is continuously updated and periodically published during the mission Figure 4.3.

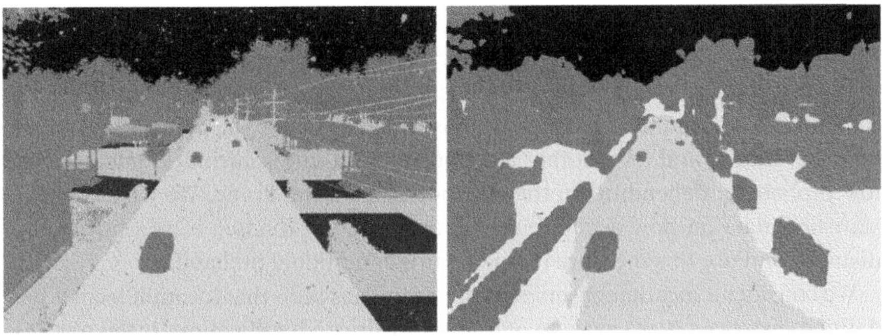

Figure 4.2 Ground truth vs. perception segmentation.

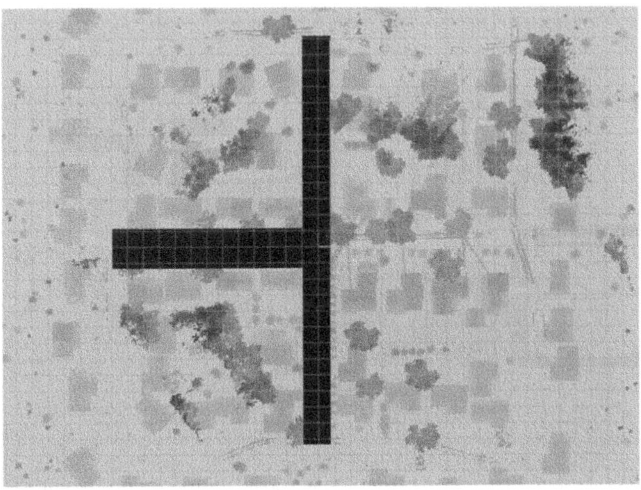

Figure 4.3 Obstacle map showing no-fly zones, houses, trees, and power lines.

4.4.2 Reward Map Calculation

The expected information gain calculation is much more involved than that of the target map. First, for each object of interest, we may have initial belief on its location and relations to other object types. There is a rich symbolic language describing these relationships, such as one object is "next to," "in front of," or "on top of" other objects, and other facts can be encode in this language such as "cars are not on top of buildings," or "cars are more likely on top of roads than on grass," etc. Based on these relationships, initial belief map, and updated obstacle map categories, we evaluate the probability of each target of interest to be present at any given location, see Figure 4.4.

The other piece of the puzzle is the part of the area that the drone has discovered and what we have seen there. Here, we are relying on the perception module to correctly identify the target of interest in images and present the 3D bounding box coordinates for the detection. What we actually need is the conditional probability of the target object being at any given location assuming that it is there. This map we can update from the object detections for areas where the perception module reported values, and for all other locations present in the current frame, we have low probability depending on the distance of from the drone. We have collected statistical data on how accurate the object detection module is as a function of distance and use this measure to update this conditional probability.

We consider a location observed if the drone has seen that location from a predefined distance (30 m) away to guarantee positive identification. If the object is further away, and the probability of the target being there is high (as calculated

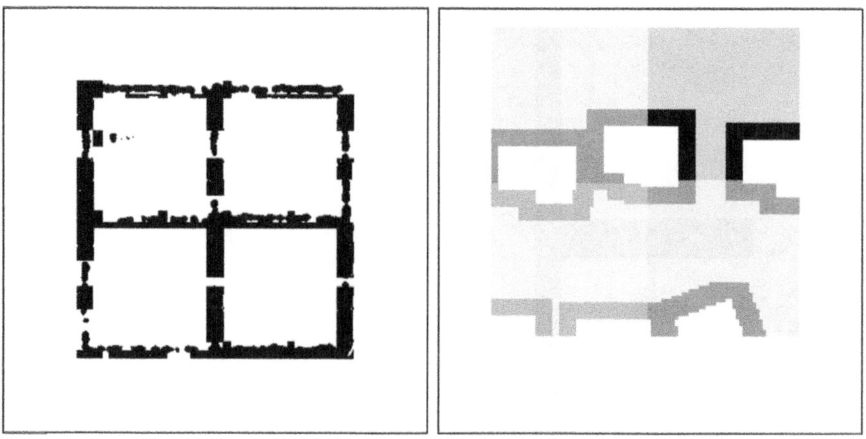

Figure 4.4 Road obstacles, probability map of target "near house" with prior probabilities.

Figure 4.5 Reward map describing all information gain of flying to a certain location.

from the prior and conditional probabilities calculated before), then the information gain by flying there is high. This information gain map is calculated for each individual target of interest, combined into a single reward map, and published periodically for the navigation component Figure 4.5.

4.5 Planner

In this section, we discuss how to make sequential decisions under environmental uncertainty for UAVs in a search and rescue setting. Naturally, in such a scenario, the target's position is often unknown, and as a result, an autonomous agent (i.e., the UAV) must make decisions under partial observability. Partially observable Markov decision processes (POMDPs) frameworks provide a principled mathematical framework for decision-making under exogenous uncertainty and partial observability [3]. By capturing unknown states, imperfect observations, and complex decision interdependencies, these frameworks excel at modeling the inherent challenges of time-critical missions, including limited visibility, dynamic weather conditions, and incomplete target information. Here, the primary challenge lies in the computational complexity of large-scale POMDP problems, where exponential growth in state space, observation space, and planning horizon makes exact solutions intractable for real-time applications. This has driven the development of online POMDP solutions that combine planning and execution through efficient sampling-based techniques.

This section presents a comprehensive POMDP framework for UAV search and rescue that optimizes real-time performance through several key innovations. We describe the POMDP model and then present a novel Monte-Carlo algorithm for efficient online planning. Specifically, we build on prior work by Silver and Veness [4] for efficient exploration of non-sparse regions with potential integration of Neurosymbolic adaptive belief distributions and a two-tiered granularity system for scalable state space management. We demonstrate our framework's effectiveness through comparative analysis against existing methods.

4.5.1 Formalization

The POMDP framework for UAV search and rescue is formulated as follows: The state space S encompasses the UAV position and target locations, represented as a $(3 + 2M)$-dimensional vector $s_t = [x_q, y_q, z_q, x_1, y_1, \dots, x_M, y_M]$, where $(x_q, y_q) \in \mathbb{R}^2$ is the UAV's horizontal position, $z_q \in \mathbb{R}^+$ is its altitude, and $(x_i, y_i) \in \mathbb{R}^2$ represents the i-th target location. The action space A consists of four cardinal directions $A = \{\text{West, South, East, North}\}$, with actual waypoints determined by $w_{t+1} = \arg\min_{w \in V(i',j')} \| w - x_t \|$. The observation space O provides partial state information through a tuple (γ_t, B_t), where $\gamma_t = (x_q, y_q, z_q) \in \mathbb{R}^3$ represents the exact UAV position and B_t is the belief state mapping grid cells to probabilities $B_t(i, j) \in [0, 1]$. The reward function combines target capture and exploration:

$$R = R_{\text{target}} + \alpha \cdot R_{\text{token}}$$

where R_{target} is binary (1 for target capture, 0 otherwise) and $R_{\text{token}} = \sum_i 1(i) \cdot P_i$ incentivizes exploration weighted by normalized cell probabilities. Decision epochs are triggered when the UAV reaches its waypoint or encounters an unreachable path.

4.5.2 Online Planning Through Monte Carlo Search

In a POMDP, the agent maintains a belief state $b(s)$, which is a probability distribution over all possible states. The belief state is updated after each action and observation using Bayes' rule. Solving a POMDP involves finding an optimal policy π^* that maximizes the expected cumulative reward through approximate methods, as exact solutions are computationally intractable. One such method is Partially Observable Monte Carlo Planning (POMCP) [4], which extends Monte Carlo Tree Search (MCTS) to POMDPs.

MCTS is a heuristic search algorithm for decision processes that is particularly effective in large state spaces. MCTS operates through four key phases: selection, expansion, simulation, and backpropagation. Selection uses UCT (Upper Confidence Bounds for Trees) as the child selection policy, given by $UCT = \overline{X_j} + C\sqrt{\frac{2\ln n}{n_j}}$, where $\overline{X_j}$ is the average reward from node j, n is the parent node visit count, n_j is child j visit count, and C is an exploration constant. Starting from the root, this selection policy recursively descends until reaching a leaf node, which is then expanded if possible. A simulation is run from the new node according to the default policy, and finally, the simulation result is backed up through the selected nodes to update their statistics.

In POMCP, goal sampling oscillation occurs when the algorithm repeatedly switches between different potential goal states during planning, as it struggles to maintain consistent belief updates across multiple tree searches, leading to inefficient exploration and suboptimal policy computation. The shrinking approach introduced in Zhang et al. [3] mitigates such issues by focusing on actions that lead to non-sparse regions.

The shrinking MCTS approach enhances the standard MCTS algorithm by determining *longer* action sequences rather than single actions at each step (as illustrated in Figure 4.6). Each belief node in the tree maintains both the UAV's position $\gamma(s) = (x_q, y_q)$ and its normalized probability $P(s)$, with nodes classified as non-sparse if the probability exceeds a threshold $P(b) > P_\varepsilon$, where P_ε is a predefined sparsity threshold. Note that the agent's focus on non-sparse regions during planning denotes the broader paradigm of using domain knowledge, potentially represented in a symbolic form. We argue that such inclusion is critical for two reasons: first, it leverages the structure of the problem for scalability, and second, given the stochastic nature of the environment, the inclusion of such information condenses the probability mass to plausible trajectories. In our use-case, the algorithm constructs action sequences $\{a_1, a_2, \dots, a_k\}$ by selecting actions $a_i = \arg\max_a Q(b_i, a)$, where $Q(b_i, a)$ represents the action-value function for belief state b_i and action a. These actions lead to updated beliefs $b_{i+1} = \tau(b_i, a_i, o_i)$, where τ is the belief update function given action a_i and observation o_i, until either reaching a non-sparse region $(P(b_{k+1}) > P_\varepsilon)$ or hitting the maximum depth (k = max_level), where max_level is a predefined search depth limit. This shrinking approach significantly reduces computational time by guiding the agent directly toward non-sparse regions, which is particularly crucial for real-world applications like "Search and Rescue" missions, where efficient exploration of high-probability areas is essential.

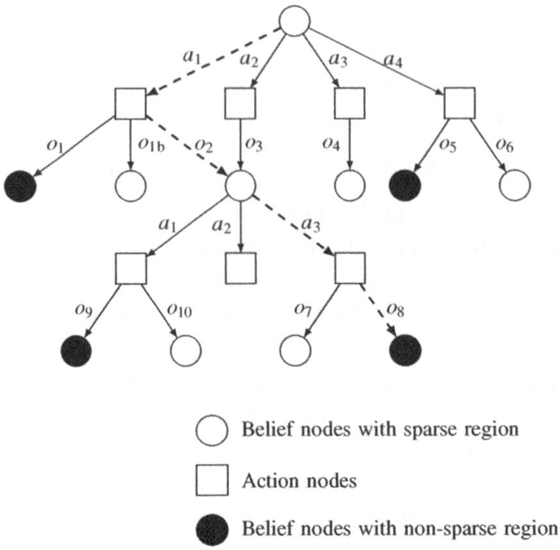

Figure 4.6 A belief tree constructed by the Shrinking POMCP approach. The dashed lines show the action sequence $\{a_1, a_2, \ldots, a_k\}$ decided by the agent, where each $a_i = arg\ max_a Q(b_i, a)$. This sequence terminates upon reaching either a non-sparse region (black node) or the maximum depth max level. Unlike standard MCTS, this approach efficiently guides the agent towards high-probability areas, thus avoiding goal sampling oscillation.

4.5.3 Scalability Through Hierarchical Planning

Our approach employs a hierarchical strategy to effectively scale the planning problem by representing positional information at two distinct levels of granularity. At the coarse level, we discretize the operational area into an $N \times N$ grid (with $N = 20$ in our implementation), where each cell represents a region of dimension $(L/N) \times (L/N)$ within the original map of side length L. This coarser discretization enables efficient MCTS simulation by reducing the state space complexity. At the fine-grained level, we maintain the exact position on a high-resolution $L \times L$ map, which is crucial for precise navigation and obstacle avoidance.

The interaction between these two granularity levels is particularly evident in the rollout process. When determining the next position given a current state and action, we first identify the target cell in the discretized grid. We then employ a sampling-based approach to find valid positions within that target cell, using a sampling function $S(\gamma_t)$ to select positions from the set of possible positions γ_t in the target cell. The next exact position γ_{next} is determined by minimizing the Euclidean distance from the current position among all valid sampled positions. This hierarchical representation allows us to balance computational efficiency with precise navigation capabilities. This rollout process can also be replaced by a neural component, which could potentially speed up the planning process.

4.5.4 Evaluation and Analysis

We performed an evaluation of our approach against other methods in AirSim, an open-source simulator for autonomous vehicles that provides a realistic physics-based environment. As described in the Introduction, while our UAV system comprises multiple Neurosymbolic components working together in a cooperative way, this evaluation specifically focuses on assessing the planner's ability to generate efficient search strategies. The evaluation framework consists of several key components: No-Fly-Zones define spatial and temporal constraints where the UAV must not enter, represented by geometric boundaries like cubes and cylinders with specified time windows; Entities of Interest are specific targets (e.g., red sedans) that the UAV must identify; and Evaluation Scenarios comprise mission configurations with various environmental factors. The performance metrics include (COP) Common Operating Picture Completeness measuring the percentage of correctly reported target information, COP Accuracy indicating the ratio of correctly reported targets, and COP Latency measuring the response time between target detection and reporting.

The experimental results (illustrated in Figure 4.7) demonstrate the superior performance of our Shrinking POMCP framework compared to the SOTA baseline (lawnmower pattern for trajectory with YOLO v8 as the perception component). Our approach achieved significantly better results across all three metrics: higher COP Completeness with a more concentrated distribution indicating consistent coverage; superior COP Accuracy with a median of 1.0 and average of 0.81 compared to the baseline's 0.57; and lower COP Latency with reduced variance suggesting more consistent response times. These improvements stem from our framework's ability to make efficient decisions by prioritizing high-probability areas and maintaining a focused search strategy, ultimately leading to more reliable and faster target identification in search and rescue operations.

4.5.5 Neurosymbolic Extensions for Planning Under Partial Observability

Planning in partially observable stochastic environments presents the challenge of approximating complex and multimodal posterior distributions $P(s'|s, a, o)$ that reflect the inherent uncertainty in state transitions given actions and observations in partially observable environments. In our case, the Planner integrates information gain and reward maps from the PWM, combining them with the UAV's position to estimate the posterior distribution. This distribution is updated as the

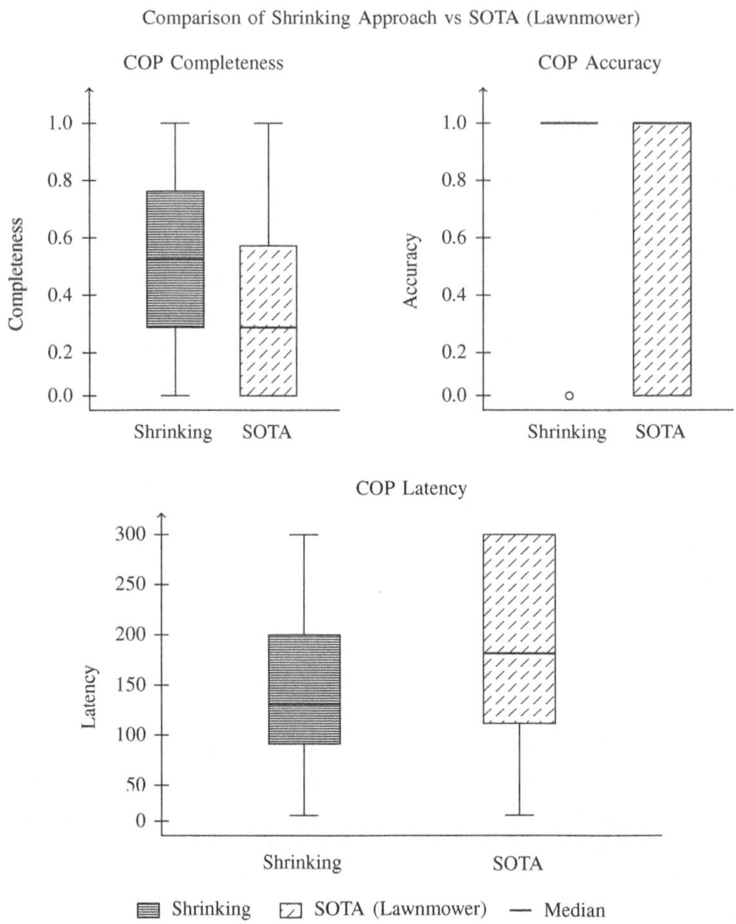

Figure 4.7 Performance comparison between the Shrinking POMCP approach and SOTA (Lawnmower) method. The box plots show the distribution of COP Completeness, COP Accuracy, and COP Latency across multiple runs. The Shrinking approach (horizontal lines pattern) consistently outperforms the SOTA method (diagonal lines pattern) across all metrics, with higher completeness and accuracy, and lower latency. Median values are indicated by thick horizontal lines.

UAV moves and uncovers new information. Note that the integration is particularly challenging as the observations (information gain) can be noisy and may not fully reflect the true state information, leading to inherently multimodal and complex posterior distributions. For instance, multiple regions might show similar probability patterns for the target's presence, or environmental factors could create ambiguous sensor readings, necessitating a sophisticated belief update mechanism.

The Shrinking POMCP approach introduced earlier benefits significantly from this adaptive belief distribution framework. While the Shrinking POMCP efficiently guides the search toward non-sparse regions, the adaptive belief distribution ensures accurate maintenance of uncertainty in these promising areas. This synergy is crucial because it combines the computational efficiency of symbolic guidance (through Shrinking POMCP's focused exploration) with robust uncertainty handling (through adaptive belief updates), which is particularly important when processing potentially noisy information gain signals from the PWM.

Traditional approaches to handling such complex distributions include Markov Chain Monte Carlo (MCMC) methods, which capture multimodality through posterior sampling, and Variational Inference, which approximates the posterior with simpler distributions. To enhance these approaches, neural samplers can be particularly effective in approximating complex multimodal distributions in high-dimensional state spaces. For example, as demonstrated in Uppal et al. [5], neural samplers can specify implicit distributions that better capture the true complexity of the belief space. This combination of symbolic guidance from Shrinking POMCP and neural approximation leads to more efficient and accurate belief updates in complex POMDP environments, balancing the strengths of rule-based decision-making with neural networks' flexibility and learning capabilities. Additionally, as we point out, the integration of symbolic rules for guiding search and neural components for estimating the value of rollouts could result in significant reduction in computation time for planning.

4.6 Trajectory Control with Evolving Behavior Trees (EBTs)

4.6.1 Safe Autonomous UAV Navigation

Autonomous agents designed for long-term objectives must execute multiple subtasks over time while simultaneously adhering to safety constraints. Subtasks can be arranged into task hierarchies, which can be coordinated to achieve the agent's main task. This structuring of subtasks should explicitly include safety considerations to ensure transparency regarding the role of safety within the hierarchical policy. Well-defined subtasks can incorporate LECs using Reinforcement Learning (RL) to adapt to the uncertainties and variations of real-world environments. The safety components should seamlessly align with the optimization process of the LECs to maintain desired properties during exploration and deployment. Finally, the policy may need to be deployed in various environments. Learning all components for each new environment may be computationally inefficient. Therefore, it is necessary to identify and update only relevant components, while preserving safety properties.

In the face of these challenges, the objective of this section is to design a trusted neurosymbolic autonomous agent for safe autonomous navigation. The agent design should: (i) capture the hierarchical structure and reactivity between subtasks with safety requirements, (ii) accommodate for optimization and deployment of LECs while ensuring collision avoidance, and (iii) allow for efficiently and reliably transferring agents to new environments. In particular, for optimization, we employ hierarchical reinforcement learning (HRL) with a dedicated safety layer.

4.6.1.1 Behavior Trees

The neurosymbolic agent we construct is a behavior tree (BT). BTs have the ability to model complex policies for, which has made them appealing for applications in Cyber-Physical Systems (CPS). Manually developing such BTs for complex systems is often tedious and sometimes infeasible. Therefore, recent work has focused on learning the structure of the BT [6–8] and optimizing behavior nodes using RL [9–11].

4.6.2 Safe EBTs for Navigation

Designing a trustworthy autonomous agent for complex, long-term navigation requires integrating safety, conventional, and learning-enabled components. We adopt EBTs to model the architecture and control flow. EBTs offer modularity, reactive switching between regular execution and safe control, and easy adaptability. We automate the integration of learned BT nodes into existing EBTs.

To achieve optimal EBT structures, we jointly optimize learning-enabled nodes under safety constraints tailored to the agent's dynamics. This approach ensures behaviors are transferable to novel environments.

In the following sections, we detail our method for designing EBTs: learning their structure, optimizing behavior nodes with LECs and safety components through HRL, and transferring EBTs to unknown environments.

4.6.2.1 Learning Structure

To learn the optimal structure of an EBT, we use a Genetic Programming (GP) algorithm combined with existing planned EBTs similar to Styrud et al. [12]. The inputs to the GP algorithm are pre-defined BT nodes and an existing baseline BT. The output is a BT that can achieve the main objective. This process uses an abstract environment that encapsulates the high-level knowledge to achieve the objective, which is autonomous navigation in our case. The BT structure can then be used without modification in a realistic environment after learning the node behaviors to account for the environment uncertainty. The final BT with modification with new behaviors for interaction with other components in the architecture is shown in Figure 4.8.

To navigate from an initial position p_0 to a goal position g requires a set of BT nodes. The main behaviors are for landmark selection, subgoal generation, and low-level control as presented in Potteiger and Koutsoukos [11]. Landmarks on a path to a goal g guide subgoals, which in turn direct low-level control actions.

Landmark selection includes the following nodes: *SetupLandmarkPath* and *UpdateLandmark*. *SetupLandmarkPath* generates a set of landmarks that can be used to construct a path where *UpdateLandmark* selects the next landmark on the path. Furthermore, subgoal generation is associated with *UpdateSubgoal*. Finally, the low-level control behavior is *CalculatePath*. Additional nodes need to be included to represent the conditions that define when transitions occur in the BT. The baseline BT used in the GP algorithm can generate subgoals and low-level control actions, but does not incorporate landmark selection or safety, and therefore corresponds to a BT that cannot fully navigate to the goal.

4.6.2.2 Landmark Planning

Landmarks are generated as a path of points given a voxel grid using a 2.5D Theta* algorithm implemented in the Rust programming language. The algorithm computes a path of landmarks using search actions and a cost function. The path with the optimal cost is then computed. There are 10 search actions from a particular grid cell: 8 directions for the current 2D plane and 2 actions for ascending or descending to a different altitude (z-plane). The cost of each path is defined using a distance-based heuristic that penalizes changes in altitude due to increased energy

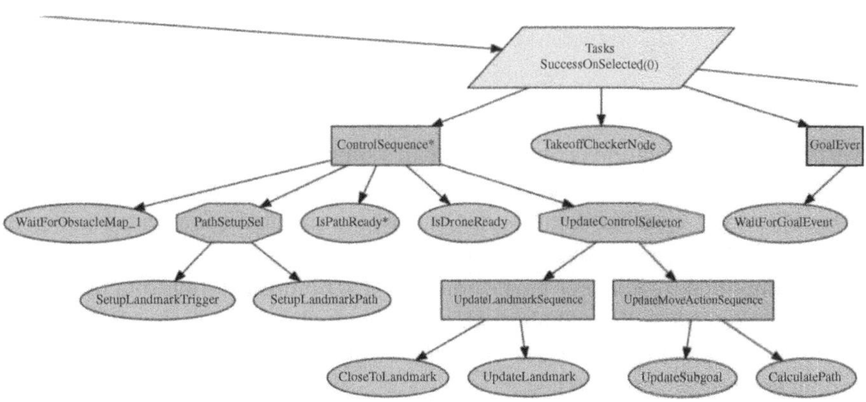

Figure 4.8 EBT Structure derived using genetic programming and manual expansion.

consumption. Furthermore, to incorporate safety the algorithm allows for adding a safety margin from obstacles to decrease the chance of collision. The algorithm is implemented in Rust for computational efficiency and memory safety.

4.6.2.3 Goal-conditioned RL for Motion Control

Goal-conditioned RL trains model parameters η to construct a goal-conditioned policy of the form $\pi_g := \pi(x; g, \eta)$ that inputs state x conditioned on a goal g and outputs control u to navigate a system with dynamics $\dot{x} = f(x, u)$ to goal g. The goal g is typically selected as an intermediate short-term goal, also known as a *subgoal*, helping to break down the long-term goal into adjacent subgoals. The reward is designed such that the policy computes actions that converge the system to g. The parameters η for motion control, where two-dimensional (2D) velocity are inputted as actions, in *CalculatePath* are optimized using the reward function:

$$r(p_t, a_t) = ||a_t - (g_t - p_t)||_2 - ||g_t - p_t||_2$$

that encourages velocity actions at time t, a_t, to be proportional to the distance from the current goal g_t to the position p_t.

4.6.2.4 Safe Subgoal Generation

In the component *GenerateSubgoal!*, a subgoal g_t is selected at each timestep t such that traveling to the subgoal will not lead to collision with obstacles. The subgoals are generated using an approach Model-Free Neural Lyapunov Control (MFNLC) from Xiong et al. [13] that jointly optimizes a neural Lyapunov function with a goal-conditioned RL policy. The neural Lyapunov function is used in reachability analysis to select a subgoal such that its set of reachable states does not intersect with obstacles. Ensuring this property is satisfied throughout control results in a safe trajectory.

4.6.3 Evaluation

We perform an evaluation of our approach in a simplified quadcopter environment to consider navigation and safety. We compare the MFNLC approach to selecting subgoals with a baseline, Landmark Only, where the goal-conditioned policy is only conditioned on the landmarks generated from Theta*.

The simplified quadcopter environment is a 3D representation of a neighborhood in Microsoft AirSim Shah et al. [14], where obstacles are voxels. The size of the environment is $[50, 50, 50]^3$ meters. The quadcopter is modeled with linear dynamics from Sabatino [15].

The first experiment evaluates the performance of Theta*. We compute 1000 landmark paths and record the success in finding a path and computation time. To add robustness to Theta*, if the path was not found at a particular safety margin, then the safety margin is decreased iteratively. The initial safety margin for this experiment is 3 m. The results in Table 4.1 demonstrate that our Theta* algorithm is able to generate landmark paths in minimal time on average (<0.2 seconds) with high success (>99%).

The second experiment evaluates our BT architecture for time to goal, timeouts, and collisions. We generate 1000 start positions p_0 and goal positions p_f with respective paths represented as sequences of landmarks computed using the Theta*, considering a safety margin of 1 m. An example path of landmarks is shown in Figure 4.9. The vehicle start location is p_0 as well as the initial landmark. The distance threshold to reach each landmark in the sequence is $\epsilon = 1.0$ m. A simulation is executed for 1000 timesteps for each pair, terminating if a collision occurs or the 1000 timesteps are reached (timeout). The results in Table 4.2 demonstrate that while the Landmark Only approach is more efficient at reaching the goal if a collision does not occur, MFNLC (ours) minimizes collisions to zero. Therefore, our approach minimizes collisions while still successful in navigating to the goal (minimizing timeouts).

Table 4.1 2.5D Theta* Experiment Results. Metrics are path success and path computation time (CT).

Path Success	Mean CT(s)	Std Dev CT(s)
0.996	0.07	0.01

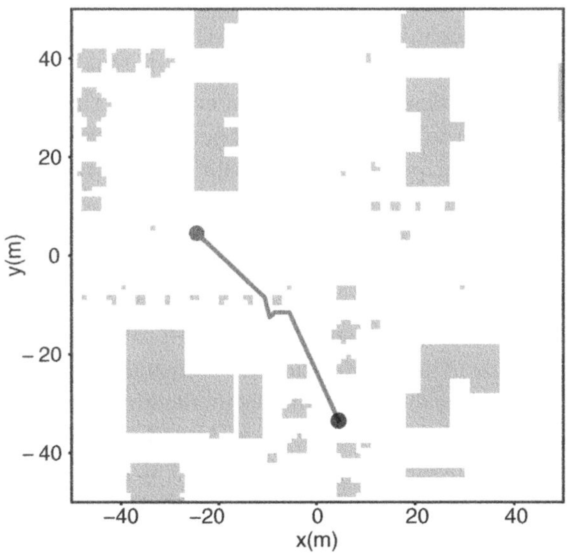

Figure 4.9 Example Theta* path in Microsoft AirSim Neighborhood environment.

Table 4.2 Neighborhood Experiment Results. Metrics are average TTG (time-to-goal), timeouts, and collisions. The best value for each metric is highlighted in bold.

Method	Mean TTG(s)	Timeouts	Collisions
Landmark Only	**13.537**	**4**	406
MFNLC (Ours)	31.677	**4**	**0**

4.7 Assurance for Neurosymbolic Systems

The increasing complexity of components used in autonomous systems has revolutionized the domain; however, their use in safety-critical systems has not reached its potential, as these typically cannot be analyzed using traditional V&V methods and may present unwanted outcomes, especially in the presence of neural network (NN) components. The opaque behavior of these components increases the complexity of analyzing them, which is crucial for the deployment of these systems, as neural networks are known to be susceptible to small adversarial perturbations.

To overcome this and provide guarantees on the behavior of these models, the formal methods community has been working on developing techniques to formally neural networks for over a decade. These can be based on abstract interpretation and reachability analysis such as CORA in Althoff [16], NNV in Tran et al. [17] and Lopez et al. [18], nnenum in Bak [19], and NeVer2 in Demarchi et al. [20], SAT-based methods such as Reluplex in Katz et al. [21] and Marabou in Katz et al. [22], and a combination of techniques such as α, β-CROWN in Xu et al. [23] and Wang et al. [24] using search methods in addition to reachability analysis, among others. For a more in-depth description of neural network verification methods and tools, we refer the reader to the verification of neural network competition in Brix et al. [25] and a survey paper on algorithms for NN verification in Liu et al. [26].

However, these approaches can only analyze the neural network components in isolation, which is insufficient for autonomous systems, as these require us to examine the interaction between them and other components of the system and environment. The neural network control system (NNCS) verification domain emerged to address these drawbacks. These techniques typically utilized hybrid system verification to model and analyze the plant dynamics of the system in combination with a NN verification technique such as CORA in Althoff [16], NNV in Lopez et al. [18] and Tran et al. [17], POLAR-Express in Wang et al. [27], Verisig in Ivanov et al. [28] and many others that can be found in Lopez et al. [29]. These methods can provide formal guarantees at design time under certain conditions, such as assuming a known and controlled environment. Despite the guarantees provided at design time, these are insufficient for autonomous systems, as they typically interact with an evolving and uncertain environment. Thus, runtime monitoring is necessary for providing further assurance to autonomous systems for unknown and uncertain conditions. Runtime assurance methods for autonomous systems include methods such as the simplex architecture using reachability analysis for safety monitoring such as refs. [30–32], which usually involves computing a projection of the state of the system into the future and examining if these will violate any of the specifications for the system. If it does, it switches the control action to avoid violating the specifications.

Another approach to overcoming the opaque behavior of neural network based systems is to provide reasoning components to them. Neurosymbolic systems have emerged to overcome these limitations, including the development of formal syntax to develop Neurosymbolic systems in a unified framework such as Scallop in Li et al. [33]. Despite some initial efforts, much work is still needed to provide efficient assurance and verification techniques for Neurosymbolic systems. In this work, we develop methods in a tool named BehaVerify to provide design time and runtime guarantees for assurance of Neurosymbolic systems.

4.7.1 Neurosymbolic Verification with BehaVerify

BehaVerify is a tool for the verification of BT [34–36]. The user provides input using a Domain Specific Language (DSL) developed for BehaVerify. The DSL allows the user to specify the structure of the BT, what each leaf node does, how the environment evolves, and safety and liveness properties. The safety and liveness properties are specified using Linear Temporal Logic (LTL), Computation Tree Logic (CTL), or invariants. BehaVerify then takes this input and can produce a Python implementation of the BT, a Haskell implementation of the BT, or a model for use with nuXmv [37], an existing model checker that can be used to verify LTL, CTL, and invariants.

As was discussed in Section 4.6, we are using a Behavior Tree to control the drone. Unfortunately, since the nuXmv, Python, and Haskell outputs of BehaVerify need to agree, there are some limitations on the inputs to BehaVerify. Since the EBT is a Neurosymbolic Behavior Tree (NSBT), the most obvious aspect of this is the need to handle neural networks. An NSBT is a Behavior Tree with at least one leaf node that uses a neural network; in the case of the EBT, the safe subgoal generation utilizes a neural network.

To accommodate neural networks in BehaVerify, we needed a way to represent neural networks in nuXmv. One possibility was to represent the neural networks directly; nuXmv allows for real-valued numbers to be represented. Provided the activation function could be represented in nuXmv (ReLU, notably, can easily be represented in nuXmv), this would allow us to encode a neural network in a nuXmv model by storing each weight and bias as a real and simply applying the necessary multiplications, additions, and activations. Unfortunately, the use of reals precludes the possibility of using finite model verification techniques in nuXmv. In particular, this means that we would no longer be able to prove LTL and CTL specifications and would need to use inductive invariants.

Another possibility was to represent the weights and biases of the network using finite integers. To do this, we considered three possible methods: converting the network to integer weights and biases (network quantization), using integers for a floating-point representation, and using integer for a fixed-point representation. While network quantization was interesting, we did not have good results trying to automate the process. This left two methods for representing reals using integers. In the floating-point case, we used a finite integer (word variable in nuXmv) to represent the "digits" of the real number, and a second finite integer to store where the decimal point was. The fixed-point case is identical, except there is no need for the second integer because the decimal point is always in the same place. In both cases, BehaVerify then creates a chain of "functions" (define variables in nuXmv) which perform forward propagation through the network. Each node in the network is represented by one of these functions. Consider the following illustrative example. We will store our values in integers of length 6 with 2 decimal points. Suppose we want to perform the operation $a * 3.4$. Here 3.4 may be a weight, while a may be an input. Suppose the value of a is 1.5. Then a would be stored as 000150, and 3.4 would be stored as 000340. We would then simply multiply these two values to get 051000. Now we bit shift by the number of decimal points (2 in this case) to get 000510. This represents 5.1, which is the result of $1.5 * 3.4$.

An immediate concern with this method is that it suffers from loss of precision. For instance, using the technique described above, $1.11 * 1.11$ would result in 1.23 instead of 1.2321. Our current solution to this is to require the user to carefully consider the network in question and set appropriate lengths for both the integer and decimal storage. Provided enough of an overflow buffer is present, the results will be correct. Finally, note that while these examples used base 10, our implementation uses base 2.

The final method we consider involves ignoring the internal mechanisms of the neural network. Since a neural network is a function, if it is presented with the same inputs, it will produce the same outputs. Thus, if there are a finite number of possible inputs, it is possible to store the output of each input in a look-up table and use this table as a function in place of the neural network. Crucially, this approach means we don't need to support specific types of activation functions or layers; we just need to be able to run the network.

4.7.2 Assurance on Grid Abstractions

We begin with a small scale example. Consider Figure 4.10. While the map is obviously much simpler, from the perspective of the drone, the objective is the same. The planner described in Section 4.5 provides a destination, which the drone needs to reach. The Behavior Tree controlling the drone then navigates toward the destination. Unlike the EBT described in Section 4.6, our NSBT's neural network has memorized the A* path algorithm. At each step, it takes as input the drone's current location (x_d, y_d) and the destination (x_g, y_g) and produces an output of north, south, east, west, or no action. A visualization of 20 iterations of this process can be seen in Figure 4.11. We are interested in the following specifications:

1. Safety (INVARIANT): $\phi_S = \forall(x_o, y_o) \in OBS, x_d \neq x_o \vee y_d \neq y_o$
2. Liveness (CTL): $\phi_L = AG((\exists(x_o, y_o) \in OBS, x_g = x_o \wedge y_g = y_o) \vee (AF\,(x_d = x_g \wedge y_d = y_g)))$

The first specification states that for each obstacle (OBS is the set of all obstacles), the location of the drone (x_d, y_d) is not inside that obstacle. The second specification states that always globally (AG), one of the following is true:

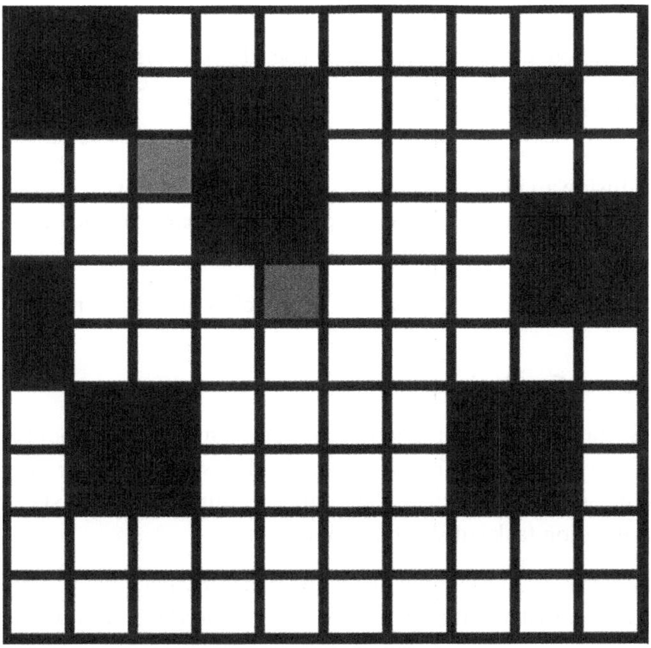

Figure 4.10 The drone (square 5 down and 5 right from top left corner) needs to reach the destination (square 3 down and 3 right from top left corner) while avoiding obstacles (black). The drone moves one square at a time. When the target is reached, a new destination is generated.

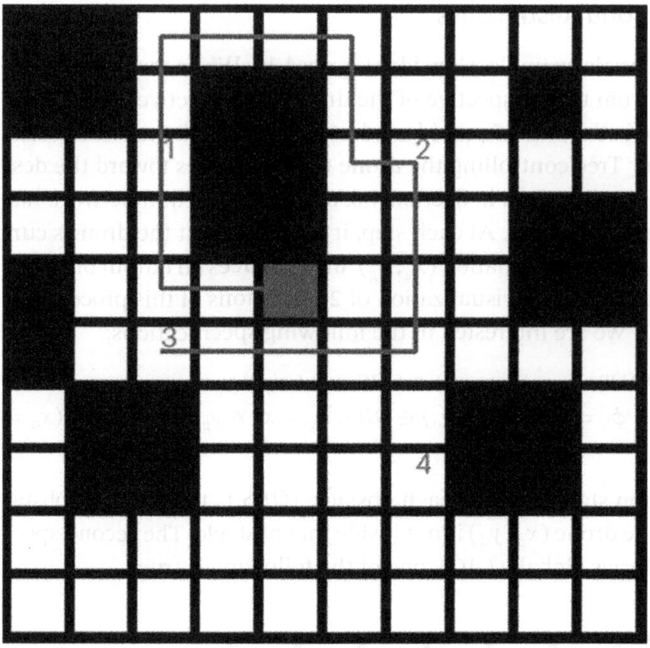

Figure 4.11 The drone traced out the path shown by the line. The numbers represent the order in which destinations were generated. The 4th destination was not reached because the simulation was terminated after 20 steps.

1. The destination is inside an obstacle (so there is no way to reach it).
2. Always finally (*AF*) the drone's location is eventually the same as the destination.

We will compare the performance of the various approaches on this example.

4.7.3 Timing Results and Conclusions

Table 4.3 demonstrates that the table approach clearly performs the best, though even it struggles on the larger scales.[1] The CTL specification scaling is far worse than the invariant scaling, which is expected. The temporal nature of the CTL specification makes the verification task substantially harder.

Neural A*: Our neural network in this specific example is fairly peculiar, in that it is not meant to generalize. Instead, it memorized A* *for a specific grid*. In point

1 These results may be recreated by visiting: https://github.com/verivital/behaverify/tree/main/REPRODUCIBILITY/2024_ANSR

Table 4.3 Each test ran with a 1-hour timeout on a modern laptop. Results are in seconds, with a - representing a timeout, and we compare the time to verify the safety and liveness specifications using the three different encodings of the neural network (Float: floating-point, Fixed: fixed-point, Table: look-up table). We consider two scenarios: on a small 10 by 10 grid, and a big 50 by 50 grid.

Specification	Grid Size	Float	Fixed	Table
ϕ_S	10×10	-	1068.09	0.36
ϕ_L	10×10	-	-	23.85
ϕ_S	50×50	-	-	41.869
ϕ_L	50×50	-	-	-

of fact, if we cut training off before 1.0 accuracy is achieved, it is possible for the specifications to be false. For instance, a .9993 accuracy network failed the invariant specification.

Scaling up: Finally, we did run our method on a scaled up test. We took the map the drone actually operates on and made each 8 m by 8 m square a single cell. Since the map was 400 m by 400 m, this gave us a 50 by 50 grid. As an additional precaution, we treated any unreachable locations as obstacles. We then tested if we were able to verify the specifications. We only did this for the table method, as the other methods were far too slow and would not scale up. We were able to verify the invariant specification in around 100 seconds, but we stopped the CTL attempt after 1 hour. An example trace can be seen in Figure 4.12. Finally, we generated a Python implementation using BehaVerify and hooked it into the ROS framework and confirmed the Python implementation could fly the drone.

4.7.4 Future Work

There are several avenues for advancing this work in the future. One is to improve our performance when using reals. Another is to utilize existing neural network verification tools, such as NNV, to generate guarantees about the network and utilize the guarantees in an assume-guarantee fashion, instead of encoding the network directly in different forms. Finally, we are interested in trying to train a neural network for this task that generalizes. It would be interesting to train a network to perform A* on arbitrary grids and verify that it functions as intended on specific grids.

Figure 4.12 The drone traced out the path shown by the gray line. The numbers represent the order in which destinations were generated. The 1st destination was placed in an obstacle and was therefore skipped.

4.8 Conclusions

We have presented how specific functions and components in the autonomy software stack of a UAV can be implemented using Neurosymbolic techniques, and how a component with a specific architecture can be verified. The components include (i) a PWM that manages a model representing what the UAV "believes" about is environment, (ii) a planner that incrementally computes waypoints the vehicle should fly to maximize missions success, and (iii) a trajectory controller that incrementally computes the fine-grain control commands for the vehicle's trajectory. The verification for the latter is based on an integrated model of the component, and advanced model checking techniques.

The results and the lessons learned indicate that the Neurosymbolic approach has potential, but the engineering of such components needs to be improved. Designers should develop an understanding for decomposing the problem into symbolic and neural parts, determining how they can be combined, and developing an interaction protocol between the two. Developing guidelines and methods for such engineering work could be a highly relevant research challenge.

Another research challenge is the development of assurance techniques. In Section 4.7.4, we have demonstrated one example, but it needs to be generalized or adapted to other Neurosymbolic architectures. Scaling the verification algorithms, possibly by introducing abstractions is another perennial issue that needs to be addressed before deploying such systems.

References

1 Alouette van Hove, Kristoffer Aalstad, and Norbert Pirk. Guiding drones by information gain. In *Northern Lights Deep Learning Conference*, pages 89–96. PMLR, 2024.

2 Michael Montemerlo. Fastslam: A factored solution to the simultaneous localization and mapping problem. *Proceedings of AAAI02*, 2002.

3 Yunuo Zhang, Baiting Luo, Ayan Mukhopadhyay, Daniel Stojcsics, Daniel Elenius, Anirban Roy, Susmit Jha, Miklos Maroti, Xenofon Koutsoukos, Gabor Karsai, et al. Shrinking POMCP: a framework for real-time uav search and rescue. In *2024 International Conference on Assured Autonomy (ICAA)*, pages 48–57, 2024. https://doi.org/10.1109/ICAA64256.2024.00016.

4 David Silver and Joel Veness. Monte-carlo planning in large pomdps. In J Lafferty, C Williams, J Shawe-Taylor, R Zemel, and A Culotta, editors, *Advances in Neural Information Processing Systems*, volume 23. Curran Associates, Inc., 2010. https://proceedings.neurips.cc/paper_files/paper/2010/file/edfbe1afcf9246bb0d40eb4d8027d90f-Paper.pdf.

5 Anshuk Uppal, Kristoffer Stensbo-Smidt, Wouter Boomsma, and Jes Frellsen. Implicit variational inference for high-dimensional posteriors. In *Proceedings of the 37th International Conference on Neural Information Processing Systems*, NIPS '23, Red Hook, NY, USA, 2024. Curran Associates Inc.

6 Matteo Iovino, Jonathan Styrud, Pietro Falco, and Christian Smith. Learning behavior trees with genetic programming in unpredictable environments. In *IEEE International Conference on Robotics and Automation (ICRA)*, pages 4591–4597, 2021. https://doi.org/10.1109/ICRA48506.2021.9562088.

7 Yue Cao and C S George Lee. Robot behavior-tree-based task generation with large language models. *arXiv preprint arXiv:2302.12927*, 2023.

8 Kevin French, Shiyu Wu, Tianyang Pan, Zheming Zhou, and Odest Chadwicke Jenkins. Learning behavior trees from demonstration. In *International Conference on Robotics and Automation (ICRA)*, pages 7791–7797, 2019. https://doi.org/10.1109/ICRA.2019.8794104.

9 Mart Kartasev. Integrating reinforcement learning into behavior trees by hierarchical composition. Master's thesis, KTH Royal Institute of Technology, 2019.

10 Frederik Lundberg. Evaluating behavior tree integration in the option critic framework in starcraft 2 mini-games with training restricted by consumer-level hardware. Master's thesis, KTH Royal Institute of Technology, 2022.

11 Nicholas Potteiger and Xenofon Koutsoukos. Safe explainable agents for autonomous navigation using evolving behavior trees. In *IEEE International Conference on Assured Autonomy (ICAA)*, volume 2, pages 44–52, 2023. https://doi.org/10.1109/ICAA58325.2023.00014.

12 Jonathan Styrud, Matteo Iovino, Mikael Norrlöf, Mårten Björkman, and Christian Smith. Combining planning and learning of behavior trees for robotic assembly. In *International Conference on Robotics and Automation (ICRA)*, pages 11511–11517, 2022. https://doi.org/10.1109/ICRA46639.2022.9812086.

13 Zikang Xiong, Joe Eappen, Ahmed H. Qureshi, and Suresh Jagannathan. Model-free neural lyapunov control for safe robot navigation. In *2022 IEEE/RSJ International Conference on Intelligent Robots and Systems (IROS)*, pages 5572–5579, Red Hook, NY, USA, 2022. Curran Associates Inc. https://doi.org/10.1109/IROS47612.2022.9981632.

14 Shital Shah, Debadeepta Dey, Chris Lovett, and Ashish Kapoor. Airsim: High-fidelity visual and physical simulation for autonomous vehicles. In *Field and Service Robotics*, volume 5, pages 621–635, Cham, Switzerland, 2017. Springer.

15 Francesco Sabatino. Quadrotor control: modeling, nonlinearcontrol design, and simulation. Master's thesis, KTH Royal Institute of Technology, 2015.

16 Matthias Althoff. An introduction to cora 2015. In *Proceedings of the Workshop on Applied Verification for Continuous and Hybrid Systems*, 2015.

17 Hoang-Dung Tran, Xiaodong Yang, Diego Manzanas Lopez, Patrick Musau, Luan Viet Nguyen, Weiming Xiang, Stanley Bak, and Taylor T Johnson. NNV: the neural network verification tool for deep neural networks and learning-enabled cyber-physical systems. In *32nd International Conference on Computer-Aided Verification (CAV)*, 2020.

18 Diego Manzanas Lopez, Sung Woo Choi, Hoang-Dung Tran, and Taylor T Johnson. Nnv 2.0: the neural network verification tool. In Constantin Enea and Akash Lal, editors, *Computer Aided Verification*, pages 397–412, Cham, 2023. Springer Nature Switzerland.

19 Stanley Bak. nnenum: Verification of relu neural networks with optimized abstraction refinement. In *NASA Formal Methods Symposium*. Springer, 2021.

20 Stefano Demarchi, Dario Guidotti, Luca Pulina, and Armando Tacchella. Never2: learning and verification of neural networks. *Soft Computing*, 28:11647–11665, 2024.

21 Guy Katz, Clark Barrett, David L Dill, Kyle Julian, and Mykel J Kochenderfer. Reluplex: an efficient smt solver for verifying deep neural networks. In *International Conference on Computer Aided Verification*, pages 97–117. Springer, 2017.

22 Guy Katz, Derek A Huang, Duligur Ibeling, Kyle Julian, Christopher Lazarus, Rachel Lim, Parth Shah, Shantanu Thakoor, Haoze Wu, Aleksandar Zeljić, et al. The marabou framework for verification and analysis of deep neural networks. In *International Conference on Computer Aided Verification*, pages 443–452. Springer, 2019.
23 Kaidi Xu, Huan Zhang, Shiqi Wang, Yihan Wang, Suman Jana, Xue Lin, and Cho-Jui Hsieh. Fast and complete: enabling complete neural network verification with rapid and massively parallel incomplete verifiers. In *International Conference on Learning Representations*, 2021. https://openreview.net/forum?id=nVZtXBI6LNn.
24 Shiqi Wang, Huan Zhang, Kaidi Xu, Xue Lin, Suman Jana, Cho-Jui Hsieh, and J Zico Kolter. Beta-CROWN: efficient bound propagation with per-neuron split constraints for complete and incomplete neural network verification. *Advances in Neural Information Processing Systems 34*, 2021.
25 Christopher Brix, Stanley Bak, Changliu Liu, and Taylor T Johnson. The fourth international verification of neural networks competition (vnn-comp 2023): summary and results. *arXiv*, 2023. https://arxiv.org/abs/2312.16760.
26 Changliu Liu, Tomer Arnon, Christopher Lazarus, Christopher Strong, Clark Barrett, and Mykel J. Kochenderfer. Algorithms for verifying deep neural networks. *Foundations and Trends in Optimization*, 4(3-4): 244–404, 2021. https://doi.org/10.1561/2400000035.
27 Yixuan Wang, Weichao Zhou, Jiameng Fan, Zhilu Wang, Jiajun Li, Xin Chen, Chao Huang, Wenchao Li, and Qi Zhu. Polar-express: efficient and precise formal reachability analysis of neural-network controlled systems. *Transactions on Computer-Aided Design of Integrated Circuits and Systems*, 43(3): 994–1007, 2023. https://doi.org/10.1109/TCAD.2023.3331215.
28 Radoslav Ivanov, James Weimer, Rajeev Alur, George J Pappas, and Insup Lee. Verisig: verifying safety properties of hybrid systems with neural network controllers. In *Proceedings of the 22Nd ACM International Conference on Hybrid Systems: Computation and Control*, HSCC '19, pages 169–178, New York, NY, USA, 2019. ACM.
29 Diego Manzanas Lopez, Matthias Althoff, Luis Benet, Clemens Blab, Marcelo Forets, Yuhao Jia, Taylor T Johnson, Manuel Kranzl, Tobias Ladner, Lukas Linauer, et al. Arch-comp24 category report: artificial intelligence and neural network control systems (ainncs) for continuous and hybrid systems plants. In Goran Frehse and Matthias Althoff, editors, *Proceedings of the 11th International Workshop on Applied Verification for Continuous and Hybrid Systems, volume 103 of EPiC Series in Computing*, pages 64–121. EasyChair, 2024. https://doi.org/10.29007/mxld.

30 Stanley Bak, Taylor T. Johnson, Marco Caccamo, and Lui Sha. Real-time reachability for verified simplex design. In *35th IEEE Real-Time Systems Symposium*, IEEE Computer Society, Rome, Italy, 2014.

31 Taylor T Johnson, Stanley Bak, Marco Caccamo, and Lui Sha. Real-time reachability for verified simplex design. *ACM Transactions on Embedded Computing Systems*, 15(2): 1–27, 2016. https://doi.org/10.1145/2723871.

32 Patrick Musau, Nathaniel Hamilton, Diego Manzanas Lopez, Preston Robinette, and Taylor T Johnson. On using real-time reachability for the safety assurance of machine learning controllers. In *2022 IEEE International Conference on Assured Autonomy (ICAA)*, pages 1–10, 2022. https://doi.org/10.1109/ICAA52185.2022.00010.

33 Ziyang Li, Jiani Huang, and Mayur Naik. Scallop: A language for neurosymbolic programming. *Proceedings of the ACM on Programming Languages*, 7(PLDI):1463–1487, 2023. https://doi.org/10.1145/3591280.

34 Serena S Serbinowska and Taylor T Johnson. Behaverify: Verifying temporal logic specifications for behavior trees. In *Software Engineering and Formal Methods: 20th International Conference, SEFM 2022*, Berlin, Germany, September 26-30, 2022, *Proceedings*, pages 307–323, Berlin, Heidelberg, 2022. Springer-Verlag. https://doi.org/10.1007/978-3-031-17108-6˙19.

35 Serena S Serbinowska, Nicholas Potteiger, Anne M Tumlin, and Taylor T Johnson. Verification of behavior trees with contingency monitors. In Matt Luckcuck and Mengwei Xu, editors, *Proceedings 6th International Workshop on Formal Methods for Autonomous Systems, Manchester, UK, 11th and 12th of November 2024, volume 411 of Electronic Proceedings in Theoretical Computer Science*, pages 56–72. Open Publishing Association, 2024a. https://doi.org/10.4204/EPTCS.411.4.

36 Serena S Serbinowska, Preston Robinette, Gabor Karsai, and Taylor T Johnson. Formalizing stateful behavior trees. In Matt Luckcuck and Mengwei Xu, editors, *Proceedings 6th International Workshop on Formal Methods for Autonomous Systems, Manchester, UK, 11th and 12th of November 2024, volume 411 ofElectronic Proceedings in Theoretical Computer Science*, pages 201–218. Open Publishing Association, 2024b. https://doi.org/10.4204/EPTCS.411.14.

37 Roberto Cavada, Alessandro Cimatti, Michele Dorigatti, Alberto Griggio, Alessandro Mariotti, Andrea Micheli, Sergio Mover, Marco Roveri, and Stefano Tonetta. The nuxmv symbolic model checker. In *CAV*, pages 334–342, Springer, 2014.

5

Safe Neurosymbolic Learning and Control

Somil Bansal[1]* *and Jaime F. Fisac*[2]*

[1] *Department of Aeronautics and Astronautics, Stanford University, Stanford, California, USA*
[2] *Department of Electrical and Computer Engineering, Princeton University, Princeton, New Jersey, USA*

*Both authors contributed equally
Corresponding Authors: Somil Bansal; somil@stanford.edu

After reading this chapter, you should be able to:

- Describe the fundamental concepts of safe learning and understand the role of neurosymbolic learning in designing safe controllers for autonomous systems.
- Explain how self-supervised and reinforcement learning approaches can be integrated with symbolic reasoning to learn safe controllers from data.
- Identify key techniques for providing formal safety assurances for learning-enabled controllers.

5.1 Problem Setup

Safe learning is the problem of enabling an autonomous system to explore candidate strategies and continually improve its operating performance under uncertain or changing conditions without ever suffering catastrophic failures. Systems in which such catastrophic failures would carry unacceptable consequences (typically due to harm to people or severe material damages) are called *safety-critical*, and have been historically unable to benefit from standard runtime learning

Neurosymbolic AI: Foundations and Applications, First Edition. Edited by Alvaro Velasquez et al.

schemes, whose lack of formal guarantees constitutes an untenable liability. Bridging this gap would require the system to carry out its learning in a safety-certified manner through one of two mechanisms:

1. A particular learning scheme that provides safety assurances.
2. A *safety filter* that modifies existing learning schemes rendering them certifiably safe.

Given that the specific learning objectives are often unknown at design time and that runtime learning is a rapidly evolving field (with particular algorithms frequently becoming deprecated), the second option is often deemed preferable. Indeed, safety filters have been the object of much interest in the past decade, since they tackle the problem of ensuring safe operation of an *arbitrary* control policy (or learning scheme) throughout a range of operating conditions. In the remainder of this section, we present the general *dynamical safety problem* that safety filters aim to address.

5.1.1 Dynamical Safety Problem

Consider an autonomous agent operating in an uncertain environment. We model the agent and its environment as a dynamical system whose state $x \in \mathbb{R}^n$ evolves over time influenced by a control input $u \in \mathcal{U} \subset \mathbb{R}^{n_u}$ and, possibly, a disturbance input $d \in \mathcal{D} \subset \mathbb{R}^{n_d}$. The disturbance might represent a exogenous physical input such as wind or, more generally, the environment uncertainty and modeling error the agent must safeguard against. We can model this evolution in either continuous or discrete time:

$$\dot{x}(t) = f\big(x(t), u(t), d(t)\big), \qquad t \in \mathbb{R}, \tag{5.1a}$$

$$x(t+1) = f\big(x(t), u(t), d(t)\big), \qquad t \in \mathbb{Z}. \tag{5.1b}$$

In either case, let $\mathbf{x}_{x,t}^{u,d}(\tau)$ denote the state reached at time τ from initial state x and initial time t, evolving under input signals $u(\cdot)$ and $d(\cdot)$ from t to τ.[1]

Since the system is safety-critical, there is a set of physically possible but practically unacceptable states that it must never enter, such as collisions, falls, or strictly forbidden configurations. We refer to the collection of all such states as the *failure set* $\mathcal{F} \subset \mathbb{R}^n$. Safety analysis aims to determine, for any initial state, *whether* and *how* the autonomous agent can prevent the state trajectory from ever entering the

1 Under mild assumptions on the continuity of f and the measurability of $u(\cdot)$ and $d(\cdot)$, the continuous-time trajectories are well defined in the Carathéodory sense [1, Chapter 2].

failure set for all possible realizations of the uncertainty. Formally, letting Π denote the collection of all control policies $\pi : \mathbb{R}^n \rightarrow \mathbb{R}^{n_u}$ that result in well-defined system trajectories for any measurable uncertainty realization $d(\cdot)$, a state $x \in \mathbb{R}^n$ is deemed *safe* with respect to $\mathcal{F}$ under uncertainty $\mathcal{D}$ if

$$\exists \pi \in \Pi : \forall d(\cdot), \forall \tau \geq t, \mathbf{x}_{x,t}^{\pi,d}(\tau) \notin \mathcal{F}, \tag{5.2}$$

with $\mathbf{x}_{x,t}^{\pi,d}(\cdot)$ denoting the unique system trajectory that solves (5.1a) or (5.1b) from initial conditions (x, t) and satisfies $u(\tau) = \pi(\mathbf{x}_{x,t}^{\pi,d}(\tau))$. This definition motivates the notion *unsafe set* of $\mathcal{F}$.

Safe and Unsafe Sets: The unsafe set for the system is defined as the collection of initial states from which the agent *cannot* prevent the state trajectory from entering the failure set $\mathcal{F}$ under worst-case disturbances. The finite-time unsafe set for a given time horizon $[t, T]$ is defined as

$$\mathcal{V}(t) := \{x : \forall \pi(\cdot), \exists d(\cdot), \exists \tau \in [t, T], \mathbf{x}_{x,t}^{\pi,d}(\tau) \in \mathcal{F}\}. \tag{5.3}$$

In many practical problems (e.g. all systems that can be controlled to a halt within a bounded radius), the dependence of $\mathcal{V}(\cdot)$ on the current time t vanishes as $T \rightarrow \infty$, and the all-time unsafe set is well defined as

$$\mathcal{V} := \{x : \forall \pi(\cdot), \exists d(\cdot), \exists \tau \geq t, \mathbf{x}_{x,t}^{\pi,d}(\tau) \in \mathcal{F}\}, \tag{5.4}$$

Thus, the unsafe set contains states that could *inevitably* lead to an eventual system failure and, therefore, should be avoided to maintain robust safety. Conversely, the safe set contains all states that are *robustly safe*:

$$\mathcal{S} := \{x : \exists \pi(\cdot), \forall d(\cdot), \forall \tau \geq t, \mathbf{x}_{x,t}^{\pi,d}(\tau) \notin \mathcal{F}\}. \tag{5.5}$$

By examining (5.4) and (5.5) under De Morgan's laws, we can see that these two sets are complementary, $\mathcal{S} = \mathcal{V}^c$, and therefore the state space can be exactly partitioned into safe and unsafe regions.

Safety Controller: While the safe/unsafe partition of the state space tells us *whether* the system can be kept failure-free from any state of interest, this descriptive characterization of safety is inseparably tied to a prescriptive one: *how* an agent can successfully prevent the system from entering the failure set. A key goal of safety analysis is finding an optimal safety controller π^* (also referred to as *safety policy* here on) that lets the agent enforce safety from all states where this is at all possible (i.e. safe states). That is, we seek a policy

$$\pi^* \in \Pi : \quad \forall x \in \mathcal{S}, \forall d(\cdot), \forall \tau \geq t, \mathbf{x}_{x,t}^{\pi^*,d}(\tau) \notin \mathcal{F}. \tag{5.6}$$

Safety Filtering: Once we obtain the unsafe set and the safety controller, they can also be used as a safety filter to monitor the safety of an existing learning scheme and render them certifiably safe. A simple example is the switched law

$$\pi^{\phi}(x) = \begin{cases} \hat{\pi}(x), & x \in \mathcal{S} \backslash \partial \mathcal{S}, \\ \pi^{*}(x), & \text{otherwise}, \end{cases} \tag{5.7}$$

where $\hat{\pi}$ is the nominal policy that we want to safeguard, possibly obtained from a learning scheme. Intuitively, the above filtering scheme minimally adjusts (i.e. "filters") a nominal policy to satisfy the safety constraint: as long as the nominal policy keeps the system in the interior of the safe set, it is allowed to operate unmodified; if it ever brings the system to the boundary, it is overridden by the safety policy, which (by definition) will keep the system from crossing over into the unsafe region. This *least-restrictive* intervention scheme guarantees safety while allowing the nominal policy to fully prioritize performance whenever safety is not imminently at risk [2–4].

This chapter gives an overview of state-of-the-art neurosymbolic methods to automatically compute the safe set and safety policy for general, nonlinear systems. We discuss computational algorithms for cases in which the system dynamics f are available in closed form, as well as for cases in which they are accessible only through direct experience or as a black box simulator. We begin by introducing a running example to ground the subsequent technical exposition.

5.1.2 Running Example: Air Collision Avoidance

We now introduce a collision avoidance problem between two aircraft, which we will use to illustrate the key ideas throughout the chapter (Figure 5.1). Here, the first aircraft – which we label the *evader* – is trying to avoid a collision with the second aircraft. If the intent of the second aircraft is completely unknown, the evader will need to safeguard against all of its possible behaviors to robustly enforce safety. We therefore model the second aircraft as an adversarial *pursuer* who – in the worst case – will actively attempt collide with the evader. The relative dynamics between the two aircraft are modeled as

$$\begin{aligned} \dot{x}_r &= -v_e + v_p cos\theta_r + \omega_e y_r, \\ \dot{y}_r &= v_p sin\theta_r - \omega_e x_r, \\ \dot{\theta}_r &= \omega_p - \omega_e; \quad \omega_e, \omega_p \in [-\bar{\omega}, \bar{\omega}], \end{aligned}$$

with $x := (x_r, y_r, \theta_r)$ the system state, where x_r and y_r represent the relative position between the aircraft, expressed in the evader's frame of reference, and θ_r represents their relative heading. The linear velocities of the evader and the pursuer,

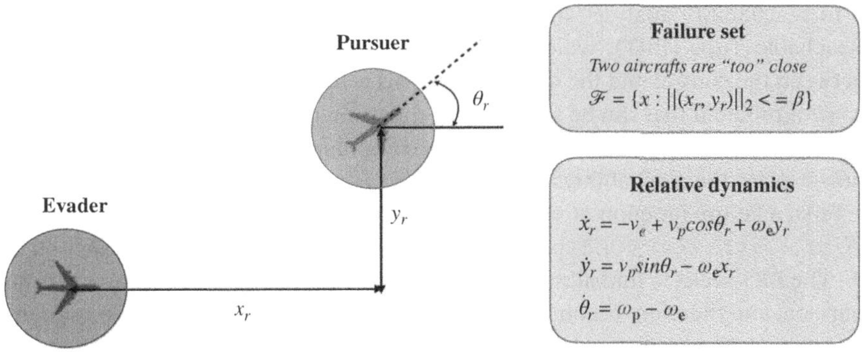

Figure 5.1 The two-aircraft collision avoidance example that we will use to highlight the key ideas throughout the chapter.

respectively v_e and v_p, are taken to remain constant throughout the encounter. Conversely, the two aircraft can instantaneously set their angular velocities ω_e and ω_p, within the bounded range $[-\bar{\omega}, \bar{\omega}]$, as the control and disturbance inputs to the system.

The failure set is given as $\mathcal{F} = \{x : \| (x_r, y_r) \| \leq \beta\}$, which corresponds to the set of all relative states where the evader and the pursuer are in close proximity (with $\beta > 0$ termed the capture or collision radius). Thus, the unsafe set contains all states from which the pursuer can drive the relative state into the collision set, despite the best efforts of the evader to avoid a collision. In this example, we choose the dynamics parameters $\beta = 0.25$ m, $v_e = v_p = 0.7$ m/s, $\bar{\omega} = 3$ rad/s, and consider a time horizon $T = 1$ s.

Even though only three-dimensional (3D), this problem is a popular benchmark in the dynamical safety literature. A key feature is the existence of a well-studied, (almost) analytic solution [5], against which others can be compared. Moreover, the unsafe set is known to be non-convex with a surface that is non-differentiable in places, making it challenging to compute.

5.2 Hamilton–Jacobi (HJ) Reachability

We now present a specific framework, Hamilton–Jacobi Reachability analysis, to compute the unsafe set and the safety controller. Hamilton–Jacobi (HJ) reachability analysis is a widely adopted verification tool to provide safety and performance guarantees for autonomous systems. Its advantages include compatibility with general nonlinear system dynamics, formal treatment of bounded disturbances, and the ability to deal with state and input constraints.

In reachability analysis, the unsafe set is often referred to as the Backward Reachable Tube (BRT), which is computed by formulating a zero-sum game between the control and the disturbance. This zero-sum game is a robust optimal control problem that can be solved using the principle of dynamic programming. The BRT (i.e. the unsafe set) can then be recovered from the obtained solution. We now explain the reachability framework in detail.

First, a failure function $\ell(x)$ is defined whose sub-zero level set is the failure set $\mathcal{F}$, i.e. $\mathcal{F} = \{x : \ell(x) \leq 0\}$. Typically, $\ell(x)$ is defined as a signed distance function to $\mathcal{F}$. The BRT seeks to find all states that could enter $\mathcal{F}$ at any point within the time horizon, and therefore become unsafe. This is computed by finding the minimum distance to $\mathcal{F}$ over time:

$$J(x, t, u(\cdot), d(\cdot)) = \min_{\tau \in [t,T]} \ell(\mathbf{x}_{x,t}^{u,d}(\tau)). \tag{5.8}$$

Our goal is to capture this minimum distance for *optimal trajectories* of the system. Thus, we compute the optimal control that maximizes this distance (and drives the system away from the failure set) and the worst-case disturbance signal that minimizes the distance.

Let $u(\cdot)$ and $d(\cdot)$ denote the control and disturbance functions over time. Since the control and disturbance are playing against each other (a differential game in this case), it is important to address what information they know about each other's decisions. We will assume that the disturbance only uses nonanticipative strategies, that is:

$$\begin{aligned} &\gamma \in \Gamma(t) \triangleq \{\vartheta : \mathcal{U}(t) \to \mathcal{D}(t) \mid u(r) = \hat{u}(r) \text{ for almost every } r \in [t, s] \\ &\implies \vartheta[u](r) = \vartheta[\hat{u}](r) \text{ for almost every } r \in [t, s]\}. \end{aligned}$$

Informally, this restriction means that if disturbance cannot distinguish between control signals $u(\cdot)$ and $\hat{u}(\cdot)$ until after time s, then it cannot respond differently to those signals until after time s. Under this setting, the disturbance still has an instantaneous advantage, as it can respond after observing the current control action. It turns out that under nonanticipative strategies, the BRT can be obtained using a value function that is the solution of certain Hamilton–Jacobi–Isaacs PDE [6]. For a more detailed discussion on non-anticipative strategies, we refer the interested readers to [6].

The value function corresponding to this robust optimal control problem is given by:

$$V(x, t) = \inf_{\gamma \in \Gamma(t)} \sup_{u(\cdot)} \{J(x, t, u(\cdot), \gamma[u](\cdot))\}. \tag{5.9}$$

The value function in (5.9) can be computed using the principle of dynamic programming, which results in the following final-value Hamilton–Jacobi–Isaacs Variational Inequality (HJI-VI):

$$\min \left\{ D_t V(x,t) + H(x,t), \ell(x) - V(x,t) \right\} = 0, \quad V(x,T) = \ell(x). \tag{5.10}$$

Here, D_t and ∇ represent the partial time and state derivatives, and H is the optimal Hamiltonian that encodes the effect of the dynamics on the evolution of the game's value under the optimal control and disturbance inputs:

$$H(x,t) = \max_u \min_d \langle \nabla V(x,t), f(x,u,d) \rangle . \tag{5.11}$$

Intuitively, (5.10) can be thought of as an analog of the Bellman equation in continuous time. The term $\ell(x) - V(x,t)$ in (5.10) restricts the system trajectories to enter and then leave the failure set, effectively enforcing that all trajectories that achieve negative distance at any time will continue to have negative distance for the rest of the time horizon.

Unsafe Set (or BRT): Once the value function is obtained, the BRT (or the unsafe set) is given as the sub-zero level set of the value function:

$$\mathcal{V}(t) = \{x : V(x,t) \leq 0\}. \tag{5.12}$$

Intuitively, the value function represents the closest the system will ever get to the failure set over the time horizon $[t, T]$. Thus, a negative value function implies that the system trajectory must have entered the failure set despite the best control effort. This is why the unsafe set is given by the sub-zero level set of the value function.

Safety Controller: The value function also provides a mechanism to obtain a safe controller for the system, given that the system starts outside the BRT:

$$\pi^*(x,t) = \arg\max_u \min_d \langle \nabla V(x,t), f(x,u,d) \rangle . \tag{5.13}$$

Intuitively, at any state, the optimal safety controller steers the system toward the highest value, i.e. toward safer states.

In fact, the reachability analysis provides a much broader class of safety controllers – the system can maintain safety by applying any control outside the BRT, as long as it applies the safety controller in (5.13) at the BRT boundary. This least-restrictive property of the reachability controller will be useful when we combine the safety controller with another nominal controller (e.g. a learning-based policy).

5.2.1 Methods to Solve HJI-VI and Compute Unsafe Set

An extensive body of research deals with scalable reachability analysis for dynamical systems:

Grid-based Methods: Methods that compute BRTs accurately up to numerical precision include level set methods [6–10]. Level set methods compute the value function by solving the HJI-VI on a grid representing a discretization of the state space [11–15]. Specifically, the time and spatial derivatives of the value function in (5.10) are approximated over the grid and the value function is numerically computed. These methods can easily deal with nonlinear dynamics and disturbances; however, using a grid representation results in an exponential scaling complexity both in computation and memory, limiting their direct use to up to 5D systems [10]. Recently, there have been attempts to scale these methods to 7D systems by using a very coarse discretization; however, the computed value function quickly accumulates numerical errors [16].

Set Representation-based Methods: Several approximate methods overcome these challenges by making tradeoffs in the class of dynamics they can consider; whether they can handle control inputs and/or disturbances in the system dynamics; and whether they compute an exact or an approximate BRT. For example, the methods presented in refs. [17–23] have had success in analyzing high-dimensional affine systems using sets of pre-specified shapes, such as polytopes, hyperplanes, ellipsoids, and zonotopes. However, these methods often rely on linearization for nonlinear dynamics [24] which might lead to an overly conservative BRT, especially in the presence of disturbances.

Leveraging Dynamics Structure: Other methods rely on specific dynamics, including that use sum-of-squares optimization [25, 26] and parallelotopes [27] for computing BRTs for polynomial dynamics [28]; leverage monotonicity of dynamics [29]; use decoupled or reduced order dynamics to decompose the BRT computation [30–32]; leverage the Hopf-Lax formula to compute BRTs for convex dynamics [33]; or deal with affine dynamics [34, 35]. However, general methods to compute unsafe sets for nonlinear dynamical systems are missing.

Control Barrier (and Lyapunov) Functions: Control barrier functions (CBFs) are also used to design safety controllers [36, 37]; however, finding feasible Lyapunov functions can be challenging, especially in the presence of control or disturbance bounds. Some recent constructive methods have been proposed using data-driven approaches and neural approximations [38–40], [41–44]. Since constructive methods have rarely been available for the CBF community, they often use hand-designed CBFs specific for their applications. These hand-designed CBFs may not be valid and therefore may lack safety. Another problem arises when the system has control input bounds: the CBF may be invalid under these bounds, causing the CBF-QP to become infeasible.

Data-driven Methods: Given recent advances in machine learning and AI, sampling and learning-based methods have been explored for computing reachable tubes [45], such as the methods that use scenario optimization for computing BRTs [46–48] or leverage adversarial sampling to compute a high-confidence convex hull of BRTs [49]. Other methods use Support Vector Machines [50] and DNNs [51–54] to approximate the value function and BRTs. These methods can leverage data to compute approximate BRTs for nonlinear systems and have shown promising results; however, they often struggle to compute accurate BRTs in the presence of adversarial disturbances and state constraints. Other methods require explicit supervision data for learning neural approximations of the safety value function, which is hard to generate for general high-dimensional systems.

Our focus in this chapter is to develop data-driven methods to compute BRTs and safety controllers for high-dimensional autonomous systems without requiring expensive and hard-to-collect data. To that end, we take a neurosymbolic perspective on this problem and use the HJ reachability conditions as symbolic guidance for training the neural network to predict the safety value function. We describe this approach in detail in Section 5.2.2. Before concluding this section, we showcase the unsafe set and the safety controller for the running example, computed using the grid-based reachability toolbox in ref. [11].

5.2.2 Running Example: Air Collision Avoidance

The margin function $\ell(x)$ for the running example is $\ell(x) :=\| (x_r, y_r) \| -\beta$. Note that $\ell \leq 0$ inside the failure set and positive outside. To solve the HJI-VI, we also need to compute the Hamiltonian. Since the dynamics are affine in control and disturbance inputs, the Hamiltonian can be computed analytically in this case, and it can be shown that [6]:

$$H(x,t) = p_1(-v_e + v_p \cos\theta_r) + p_2(v_p \sin\theta_r) - \bar{\omega}\,\|p_1 y_r - p_2 x_r - p_3\| + \bar{\omega} p_3, \tag{5.14}$$

where p_1, p_2, and p_3 are the three spatial derivative components of the value function with respect to x_r, y_r, and θ_r, respectively.

Remark 5.1: In general, the computation of the Hamiltonian in (5.11) requires solving an optimization problem; however, most mechanical systems are control and disturbance affine. For such systems, the Hamiltonian can be computed analytically in terms of value function gradients (e.g. see (5.14)).

The grid-based methods compute p_1, p_2, and p_3 numerically over a grid in the state space, which are then used to compute the Hamiltonian at all grid points using (5.14). The Hamiltonian is then used within the HJI-VI to propagate the value function one step backward, starting from the terminal time. This process is repeated until the value function converges or the initial time is reached. As an example, we use the state-of-the-art PDE solver, *Level Set Toolbox (LST)* [11] to numerically compute the value function for the two-aircraft collision-avoidance system. LST computes the value function over a discrete grid of size $101 \times 101 \times 101$. The corresponding value function and BRT slices are shown in Figure 5.2.

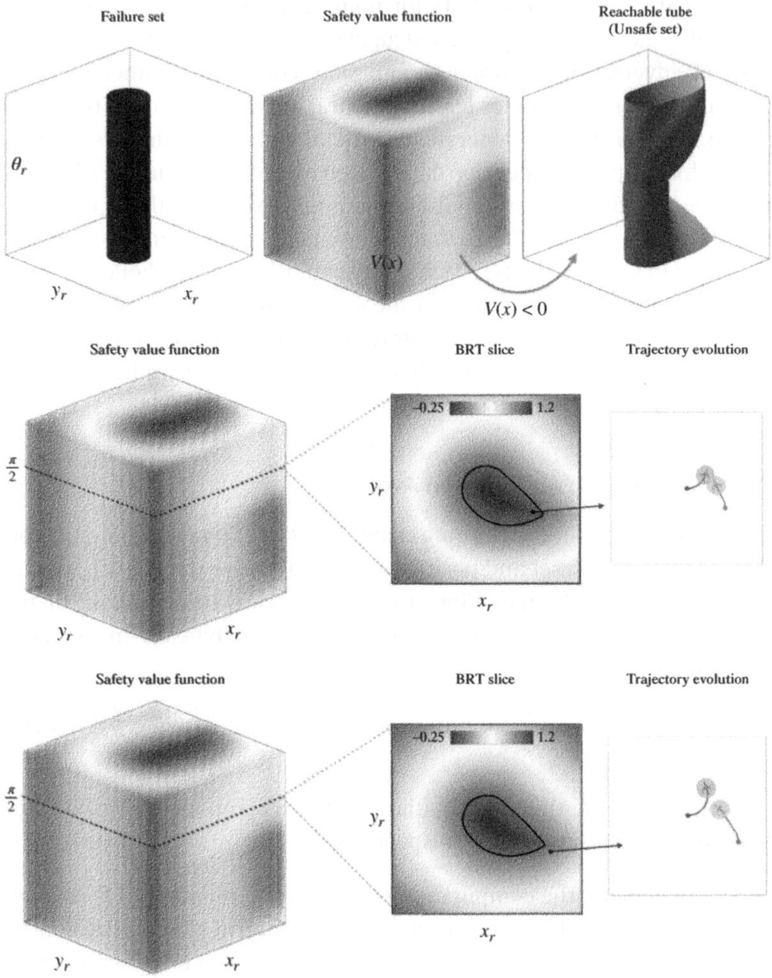

Figure 5.2 (Top) The failure set, the ground truth value function, and the BRT for the two-aircraft collision avoidance example. (Middle, Bottom) A slice of the value function corresponding to $\theta_r = \pi/2$ and the trajectory evolution starting from a state inside the BRT (middle) and outside the BRT (bottom). When the system starts inside the BRT, a collision cannot be avoided.

5.3 A Neurosymbolic Perspective on Learning Safe Controllers

5.3.1 Self-supervised Neurosymbolic Learning for Synthesizing Safe Controllers

Recent advances in Physics-Informed Machine Learning (PIML) [55] have shown promise in obtaining high-fidelity solutions to PDEs. The key motivation behind these approaches is that PDE captures the physical laws that govern the underlying phenomenon. Thus, using the PDE residual error as the optimization objective for training leads to a self-supervised and physically consistent learning of high-dimensional PDE solutions, without relying on computationally expensive numerical PDE solvers. PIML in this case can also be thought of as an instance of general neurosymbolic learning, wherein a *symbolic* loss function (residual PDE error in this case) is used to train a *neural* component to predict the PDE solution.

We can build upon the same insight to scalably learn safe sets and controllers for autonomous systems. In this case, the HJI-VI describes how the underlying physics, i.e. dynamics of the system and its control inputs, affect the system safety over time. Specifically, we discuss a deep learning-based approach to solving high-dimensional reachability problems, known in the literature as *DeepReach*. DeepReach leverages a deep neural network (DNN) to represent the value function in (5.10). The input to the DNN is a state vector x and a time point t, and its output is the corresponding value $V_\theta(x, t)$, where θ represents the parameters of the DNN. The key benefit of representing the value function through a DNN is that DNNs are agnostic to grid resolution, and the memory required generally scales with signal complexity, independent of spatial resolution. However, learning the parameters θ can be challenging in general, and might require supervision for $V(x, t)$, which itself is hard to generate for high-dimensional systems in the first place. Instead, we can use a self-supervision method inspired by PIML to learn the value function implicitly, using HJI-VI in (5.10) as the source of supervision. Given an input (x_i, t_i), the loss function $h(x_i, t_i; \theta)$ for training the DNN is given as:

$$\begin{aligned} h(x_i, t_i; \theta) &= h_1(x_i, t_i; \theta) + \lambda h_2(x_i, t_i; \theta), \\ h_1(x_i, t_i; \theta) &= \| V_\theta(x_i, t_i) - \ell(x_i) \| \, 1(t_i = T), \\ h_2(x_i, t_i; \theta) &= \| \min \left\{ D_t V_\theta(x_i, t_i) + H(x_i, t_i), \ell(x_i) - V_\theta(x_i, t_i) \right\} \|. \end{aligned} \tag{5.15}$$

Intuitively, h_2 incentivizes the DNN to learn a value function that is *consistent* with the HJI-VI without explicitly requiring the supervision for the value function. h_1 uses the ground truth value function (available only at the terminal time) to additionally force the DNN to learn the correct value function at the terminal time, thus avoiding learning any degenerate value functions (such as constant value functions, which will also satisfy the HJI-VI). λ trades-off the relative importance of the two loss functions. Together, the two loss functions encourage the DNN to learn a more and more accurate representation of the safety value function over time that satisfies the HJI-VI as well as the boundary condition. From the perspective of safe learning, DeepReach explicitly bakes in the safety requirements during the training process (via HJI-VI), allowing us to learn inherently safe controllers from data.

Choice of Activation Function: The loss function in (5.15) depends on the time and spatial gradients of the value function; thus, the DNN should not only represent the value function well but also its gradients. The gradients of the value function are also required at the inference time to obtain the optimal safe controller (see Eq. (5.11)). Unfortunately, widely popular, ReLU-based DNNs struggle to accurately represent the gradients of the value function, leading to a poor approximation of the value function. For example, ReLU-based DNNs can only represent piecewise constant spatial and time gradients and therefore struggle when encoding value function with fine details, as we demonstrate further in our case studies. To overcome these challenges, one can use a sinusoidal activation function instead, which has recently shown a lot of promise in representing not only the target signal but also its derivatives [56], along with the loss function in (5.15) to learn a high-quality approximation of the value function, without explicitly solving the HJ PDE. We next describe the training procedure to learn the value function using sinusoidal networks.

Training Procedure: To facilitate value function learning using sinusoidal networks, we first pre-train the DNN to learn the correct value function at the terminal time. λ is set to zero during this training phase. We then perform curriculum learning over the time interval – slowly decreasing the value of t linearly as training progresses, starting from T. This allows the terminal condition to slowly propagate to the earlier time points. At each training iteration, we sample N states from the state space uniformly randomly and optimize the DNN parameters to minimize the loss function h. We continue to do so until either the value function converges or a desired number of iterations are completed. The DeepReach framework is summarized in Figure 5.3 and in Algorithm 1.

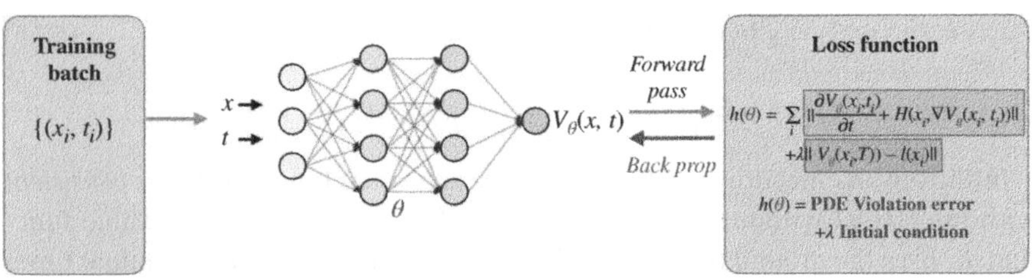

Figure 5.3 DeepReach relies on self-supervised neurosymbolic learning to compute scalable approximations of the reachability solutions.

Algorithm 1 DeepReach: A Self-supervised Learning Mechanism for Safe Controller Synthesis

for each epoch **do**
  $x_0 \sim P_0, t_0 \sim P_t$ ▷ Sample a batch of initial states and time for this epoch
  for each gradient step **do**
    $\theta \leftarrow \theta - \lambda_\theta \nabla_\theta h(\theta)$ ▷ Update value function (critic) parameters
$\pi^*_\theta(x, t) = \arg\max_u \min_d \langle \nabla V_\theta(x, t), f(x, u, d) \rangle$ ▷ Synthesize safety policy
$d^*_\theta(x, t) = \max_u \arg\min_d \langle \nabla V_\theta(x, t), f(x, u, d) \rangle$ ▷ Synthesize disturbance policy

5.3.1.1 Running Example: Air Collision Avoidance

We now apply DeepReach to the two vehicle collision avoidance example discussed in Section 5.1. We will first evaluate if DeepReach can approximate the value function and BRT well. We will additionally compare the learning performance for different activation functions. We first discuss some implementation details.

Data: The dataset is composed of randomly sampled 3D state coordinates, with $N = 65$k. During training, we scale all states to $[-1, 1]$ and time to $[0, 1]$, which we find improves convergence.

Architecture: For all experiments, DeepReach (and baselines) uses a 3-layer DNN, with a hidden layer size of 512. We use sine non-linearity for the neural network. We discuss the effect of different non-linearities later in this section.

Hyperparameters: We set λ in (5.15) to make each component of the loss approximately equal at the beginning of training. We pre-train the network for 10K iterations and then perform curriculum training for 100k iterations. We use the Adam optimizer with a learning rate of 10^{-4}.

Runtime: Training required approximately three hours to learn the value function using PyTorch with a single GPU worker.

Results: DeepReach approximates the BRT with high accuracy, achieving a small MSE of 1.9×10^{-4} with respect to the analytical solution (computed using [5]). However, the analytical solution only provides the boundary of the BRT; to analyze the quality of the learned value function, we also compare it against the Level Set Toolbox (LST) solution discussed in Section 5.2.2. A slice of the corresponding value functions for $x_3 = \pi/2$ is shown in Figure 5.4 (left and middle). DeepReach is able to recover a value function that closely mimics the LST value function and achieves an MSE of 1.01×10^{-4}.

We also compare the corresponding BRTs in Figure 5.4 (right), overlaid on top of each other. Even though there is a small error in the boundary of BRT obtained using DeepReach, the two boundaries closely mimic each other. We also compute the *BRT volume error* – the percentage volume of unsafe states that are marked safe (i.e. the set of states that should be in the BRT but are not, and vice-versa) – as

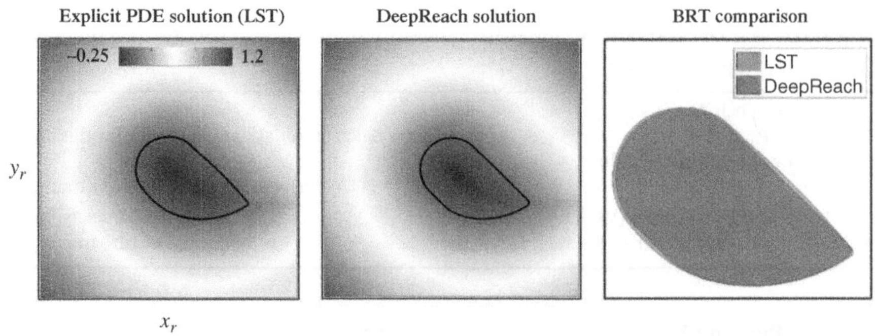

Figure 5.4 The slices of the value functions and BRTs for $\theta_r = \pi/2$. DeepReach recovers a value function (middle) that corresponds closely to the ground truth value function (left), computed using a principled HJI-VI solver [11]. The two BRTs also align closely (right) – they overlap in the dark gray region, and the light gray region is the error between the two BRTs.

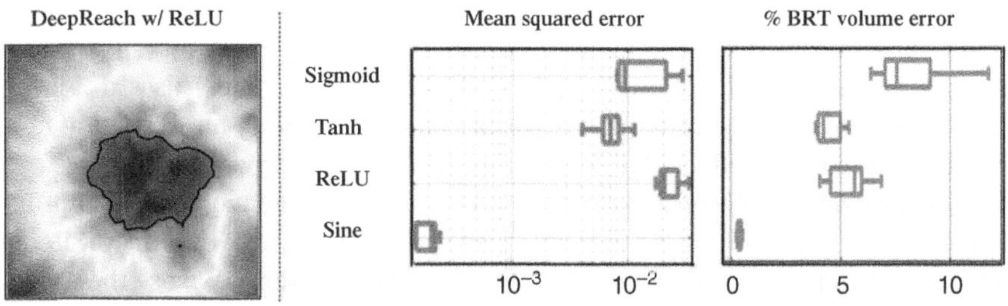

Figure 5.5 (Left) The slice of the value functions for $\theta_r = \pi/2$ corresponding to ReLU activation function. The ReLU architecture fails to learn the correct value function (compare with Figure 5.4). This is also evident from high MSE (middle) and % BRT volume error (right) metrics corresponding to other, non-periodic activation functions.

this percentage directly affects the quality of the safety controller. The BRT volume error for DeepReach is 0.43%, indicating the high quality of the obtained BRT.

Effect of Activation Function: To analyze the importance of using a periodic activation function in DeepReach, we replaced the sine activation function with ReLU, tanh, and sigmoid functions, and learned the value function using the training procedure outlined in Section 5.3.1. For each activation function, we initialized the learning process with 5 different seeds. The corresponding MSE (with respect to the analytical solution), as well as the BRT volume error, is reported in Figure 5.5. While DeepReach closely matches the analytical solution, the other architectures fail to find the correct solution, with an MSE that is an order of magnitude higher than DeepReach. This is because the PDE violation error depends on the value function gradients. Thus, to optimize the neural network parameters using violation error, we need to accurately represent the value function gradients as well. Unfortunately, the ReLU activation function is piecewise linear, thus the gradients are piecewise constant. Thus, the ReLU-based neural network fails to learn a good approximation of the value function, particularly in the regime where the value function gradient changes rapidly, as illustrated by Figure 5.5 (left). Other activation functions, such as Sigmoid and Tanh, suffer from saturating gradients, resulting in poor value function approximation.

5.3.1.2 Additional Case Study: Three-aircraft Collision Avoidance

We now introduce a high-dimensional, three-aircraft collision avoidance problem that highlights the importance of learning-based synthesis of the safety controller. The setup consists of two evader aircraft (e_1 and e_2) and one pursuer aircraft (p). The dynamics of the evaders and the pursuer aircrafts are given as:

$$\dot{x}_{1,i} = v_i \cos\left(x_{3,i}\right) \quad \dot{x}_{2,i} = v_i \sin\left(x_{3,i}\right) \quad \dot{x}_{3,i} = \omega_i, \tag{5.16}$$

leading to a 9D system overall in the joint state space of the evaders and the pursuer. The pursuer here represents an adversarial or uncertain agent that tries to steer evaders to collide either with the pursuer or with each other; evaders, on the other hand, try to avoid the collision. The failure set is $\mathcal{T} = \{x : d(e_1, e_2, p) \leq \beta\}$, where $d(e_1, e_2, p)$ is the minimum pairwise distance between the three vehicles. Intuitively, the failure set represents the set of states where any two aircraft are in close proximity of each other. The BRT corresponding to the above failure set thus represents the set of unsafe states for the evaders.

Given the high dimensionality of this problem, a direct computation of the BRT is not feasible in this case. To avoid the computational challenges, an approximation of the BRT is typically obtained by computing pairwise collision BRTs between all possible vehicle pairs, each of which is a lower dimensional reachability problem and can be solved in relative coordinates, for instance, using Section 5.2.2. The union of the pairwise BRTs is then used as an approximation for the BRT of the overall system [57]; however, as we demonstrate later in this section, this process often leads to an overly optimistic approximation of the unsafe states. In particular, an escape (safe) strategy for an evader in a pairwise pursuit-evasion game may no longer be safe in the presence of an additional evader, as it might lead to a collision with the other evader. Thus, the actual set of unsafe states (i.e. the BRT) is typically larger than the union of the pairwise BRTs. With DeepReach, we can directly compute the full 9D pursuit-evasion game and can capture these three-way interaction states, allowing us to reason about and safeguard against nuanced unsafe configurations of the system.

Given the higher dimensional system, we pre-train the network for 60k iterations, followed by training for 100k iterations, requiring a total of 3.5 hours to train the network. The other training hyperparameters are the same as Section 5.3.1.1.

In Figure 5.6 (left), we illustrate a slice of the obtained BRT (the shaded region) for a particular position and orientation of the two evaders (the dark gray and black aircraft) and a given heading of the pursuer (the direction of the dark gray aircraft located on the center-left). The shaded region represents the set of all starting positions of the pursuer for which a collision is unavoidable between at least one of the vehicle pairs. The inner gray region is the union of the pairwise BRTs, and the outer gray region is the set of additional states of the pursuer that are unsafe because of the three-way interaction between the vehicles. In Figure 5.6 (middle and right), we illustrate the vehicle trajectories when the pursuer starts at the solid dots marked positions, respectively, and when both the evaders and the pursuer uses the optimal controller (transparency is higher for the earlier time steps). In the inlets, we show the minimum across all pairwise distances between the vehicles when the full 9D value function is used (solid gray line) and when the pairwise value function is used (dashed gray line). The collision threshold β is shown in the bottom dashed line. When the pursuer starts inside the outer gray region, it is able to force the evaders to collide with each other, as indicated by the distance between the vehicles dropping below β (middle inlet). We show one such collision time in the trajectory plot below – the shaded circle region represents the set of states around the center vehicle that are considered to be in collision with

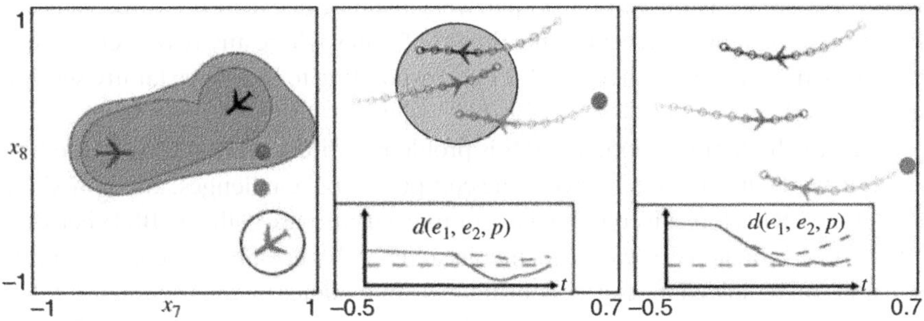

Figure 5.6 The slice of the BRT and example trajectories for the three-vehicle collision avoidance problem. (Left) The outer gray region represents the set of states that are unsafe because of the three-way interaction between vehicles and were hard to capture previously with low-dimensional, pairwise approximations (the inner gray region). We mark two starting positions of the pursuer (solid dots) and show the corresponding optimal trajectories for the three vehicles in the middle and the right panel, respectively. (Middle) When the pursuer starts inside the outer gray region, it is able to force the two evaders to collide with each other, despite their best efforts to avoid a collision. (Right) When the pursuer starts outside the outer gray region, the evaders are able to barely, but successfully, avoid a collision by applying the safety controller. (Inlets) Minimum pairwise distance between the vehicles under the optimal control when the full BRT is used (solid gray line) and the union of pairwise BRT is used (dashed gray line). The collision threshold β is shown in dashed line.

the center vehicle, and the black vehicle is in that region. On the other hand, if we simulate the trajectories of the two evaders using the pairwise BRT, no collision occurs between the vehicles (the dashed gray line is above the bottom dashed line at all times), indicating that these states are unsafe due to the three-way interaction between the vehicles. In contrast, when the pursuer starts just outside the outer gray region, the evaders have a strategy to avoid the collision despite the best efforts of the pursuer (Figure 5.6, right). This is also evident by the minimum distance between the vehicles being just above the bottom dashed line at all times. Overall, DeepReach is able to accurately capture the interactions between the vehicles to compute the set of joint unsafe states, which can subsequently be used to design more effective safety controllers.

5.3.2 Neurosymbolic Reinforcement Learning for Synthesizing Safe Controllers

Arguably the most widely successful data-driven approach to optimal control, reinforcement learning (RL) makes it possible to both quantify and improve the behavior of an autonomous agent through continual trial-and-error interactions with its environment. Unlike classical optimal control methods like Hamilton–Jacobi analysis, which require an explicit parametric representation of the system's dynamics, so-called "model-free" RL methods can compute a neural safety characterization with only empirical access to the system's behavior, whether through physical experimentation or as a black box simulator.

The standard RL formulation considers a learning agent whose goal is to accumulate the largest possible sum of rewards over time, typically with some preference for earlier rewards over later ones. This amounts to a time-additive (or Lagrange-type) optimal control objective:

$$J(x_0, u(\cdot)) = \sum_{t=0}^{\infty} \gamma^t r(x_t, u_t), \tag{5.17}$$

where $r : \mathcal{X} \times \mathcal{U} \to \mathbb{R}$ is the reward function of interest, t denotes the discrete time step, and $\gamma \in [0, 1)$ determines how strongly later rewards are discounted.

An attractive property of RL is that this agent (the learning algorithm in question) does not need to know – or even explicitly construct – a model of the system dynamics. Instead, so-called model-free RL algorithms can directly learn an effective control strategy (policy gradient methods), an approximation of the value function (value learning methods) or a combination of the two (actor–critic methods).[2] To do so, it is useful to work with the *state–action value function*, also known as *quality function* or simply *Q-function*, which encodes how well the

2 The term "model-free" should be understood with some nuance: while the algorithms themselves do not require an explicit model, their practical implementations are often trained in simulated environments, which are, by definition, models of the target deployment setting.

agent can do from an initial state after taking a given action. For problem (5.17), the discrete-time dynamic programming principle can be expressed through the Bellman equation

$$Q(x, u) = r(x, u) + \gamma \max_{u'} Q(x', u'), \tag{5.18}$$

with x' denoting the next state encountered by the agent, and u' the action it subsequently takes from this state. This Bellman equation underpins the general mechanism known as *temporal difference learning*, in which an agent continually bootstraps its value function estimate as it acquires more experience, comparing the predicted and observed outcome of each episode (x, u, x', r):

$$\hat{Q}^{k+1}(x, u) \leftarrow \hat{Q}^k(x, u) + \alpha_k \underbrace{\left[r + \gamma \max_{u' \in \mathcal{U}} \hat{Q}^k(x', u') - \hat{Q}^k(x, u)\right]}_{\text{temporal difference signal}}. \tag{5.19}$$

In the 1990s, the Q-learning scheme (5.19) was shown to converge to the quality function (whose maximization at each state yields optimal agent behavior) in decision problems with finite state and control spaces [58]. Modern deep RL methods perform remarkably well in continuous spaces beyond the computational reach of model-based optimal control tools, although without the global convergence properties of their discrete-space counterparts. We direct interested readers to a recent survey [59].

5.3.2.1 Learning Safety by Reinforcement

While RL has historically focused on reward accumulation, it is not fundamentally restricted to problems of this form. Indeed, the optimal control foundations of RL are highlighted by its pioneers Sutton et al. [60]. Viewing RL as a general data-driven optimal control methodology, enables us to apply its machinery to solve reachability-type problems. This idea was first articulated by Fisac et al. [61] and Akametalu et al. [62], who replaced the sum-of-rewards RL Bellman equation (5.18) with its minimum-safety-margin counterpart, suitably time-discounted to preserve the convergence of the learning process:

$$Q(x, u) = (1 - \gamma)g(x) + \gamma \min\left\{g(x),\ \max_{u'} Q(x', u')\right\}. \tag{5.20}$$

This *safety Bellman equation* induces a "safety Q-learning" scheme that converges under the same conditions as conventional Q-learning [61]. In problems with finite state and action spaces, the agent updates its tabular representation of the Q-function after each experienced episode (x, u, x', g), following a simple temporal-difference rule:

$$\hat{Q}^{k+1}(x, u) \leftarrow \hat{Q}^k(x, u) + \alpha_k \underbrace{\left[(1 - \gamma)g + \gamma \min\left\{g, \max_{u' \in \mathcal{U}} \hat{Q}^k(x', u')\right\} - \hat{Q}^k(x, u)\right]}_{\text{temporal difference signal}}, \tag{5.21}$$

The learning rate $\alpha_k \in [0, 1]$ should be scheduled to vanish asymptotically over time, with the only requirement that the series be squared-summable but not summable, i.e. $\sum_{k=0}^{\infty} \alpha_k^2 < \infty$ but $\sum_{k=0}^{\infty} \alpha_k = \infty$.

Much like in the case of self-supervised methods, the RL machinery for safety analysis truly shines in continuous-space problems, in which the safety Q-function is approximated by a neural network Q_θ (commonly called the *critic*). Rather than update the tabular entry for one state-action pair at a time as in (5.21), the neural critic's parameters $\theta \in \mathbb{R}^{n_\theta}$ are jointly updated by stochastic gradient descent on the aggregate temporal difference error or "Bellman loss". The contribution of each experienced episode (x, u, x', g) to this loss is the temporal difference

$$h(x, u, x', g; \theta) := \Big[(1-\gamma)g + \gamma \min\{\, g, Q_\theta(x', u')\} - Q_\theta(x, u)\Big]^2. \qquad (5.22)$$

In principle, learning from the correct temporal difference signal would require choosing the next control u' to maximize $Q_\theta(x', u')$. However, when the action space is continuous, it is common to concurrently train a (typically stochastic) neural control policy π_ω (referred to as the *actor*) to serve as a surrogate optimizer of $Q_\theta(x, \cdot)$ at each state x:

$$h_u(\omega) := \mathop{\mathbb{E}}_{x \sim \mathcal{B}}\Big[- Q_\theta(x, \tilde{u}) + \alpha_u \log \pi_\omega(\tilde{u} \mid x)\Big] \qquad (5.23)$$

The critic's per-episode training loss (5.22) is then bootstrapped by directly sampling $u' \sim \pi_\omega(\cdot \mid x)$, circumventing the need to solve a general nonlinear optimization problem at each experienced episode, as would be required in a strict Q-learning scheme (5.21). Many state-of-the-art RL algorithms are variants of this *actor–critic* methodology, and their extension to safety analysis problems usually requires a simple modification, replacing the additive temporal difference update based on (5.18) with its safety counterpart based on (5.20). Figure 5.7 shows color plots of the neural safety value function $V_\theta(x) := \max_u Q_\theta(x, u)$ learned by a deep Q network scheme for two commonly used benchmark problems: a double integrator (with position–velocity state) and a lunar lander (with 6D planar rigid body dynamics). Figure 5.8 illustrates various safety-seeking behaviors learned for an 18D half-cheetah system using the soft actor–critic (SAC) RL scheme with various control objectives: in this system, the safety Bellman equation allows the agent to reliably learn effective safety strategies, whereas the sum-of-rewards schemes often get stuck exploring ineffective behaviors that repeatedly violate the safety specification.

A key practical advantage the level-set safety objective in RL is that this minimum-margin-to-failure objective provides a dense training signal: While safe behavior can, in principle, be learned by a conventional RL agent that receives a negative reward whenever it enters a failure state [63, 64], in practice the process can be prohibitively slow and costly, since such an agent would only learn by repeatedly experiencing failures. In contrast, the safety Bellman Eq. (5.20) makes it possible to learn from near-misses and, more generally, from even small changes

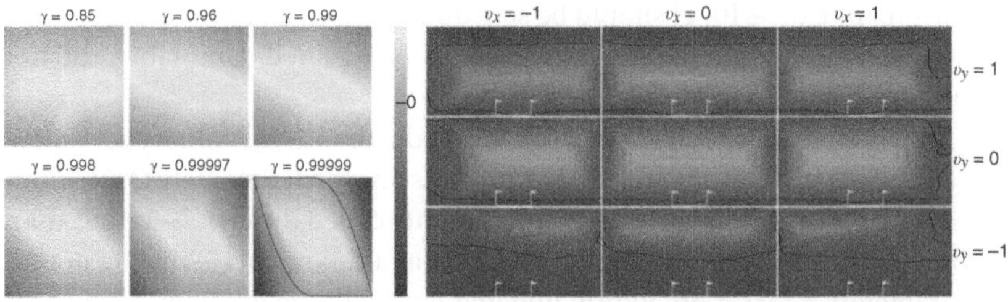

Figure 5.7 Value function learned by safety RL using the deep Q-network scheme. *Left:* value learned for a double integrator (linear point mass) required to remain in a bounded position interval. As the time discount factor γ is annealed toward 1, the learned zero level set converges to the analytical safety boundary (black contour). *Right:* $x-y$ slices (at different angles and velocities) of the 6D learned safety value for a lunar lander system required to remain in flight inside the rectangular frame. *Source:* [61]/IEEE.

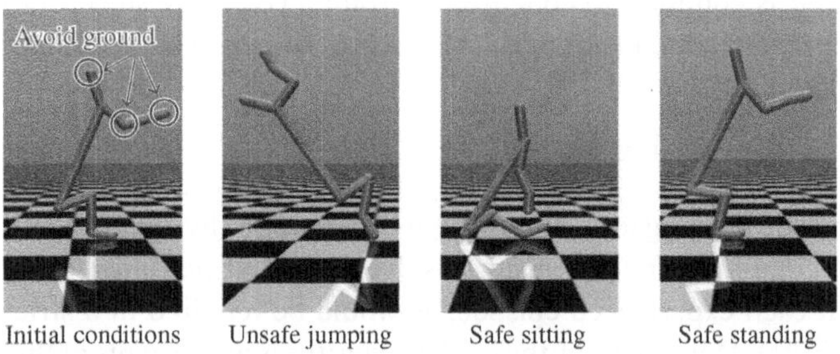

Figure 5.8 Safety problem setup and control strategies learned by soft actor–critic RL scheme for an 18D half-cheetah system required to keep the head and front leg off the ground. *Left to right:* typical configuration at the start of an episode, and visual depiction of the safety specification; an unsafe jumping policy learned using a sum of discounted rewards (heights of the critical points, or contact penalties) over time; a safe sitting policy learned using discounted safety or (less reliably) discounted sum of contact penalties; a safe standing policy learned using discounted safety. *Source:* [61]/IEEE.

in the closest approach to the failure set. An extensive comparative study by [65] showed that this dense learning signal enables substantially faster and more accurate learning of safe behavior relative to conventional RL alternatives (Figure 5.9).

5.3.2.2 Robust Safety by Gameplay Learning

The earlier safety RL formulation assumes that the uncertainty in system dynamics is negligible. We can extend it to the robust setting by reintroducing the disturbance input as an opposing player. The computation of an approximate solution to the zero-sum safety game can then be approached as a multi-agent reinforcement learning (MARL) problem, specifically as an instance of *adversarial reinforcement learning*.

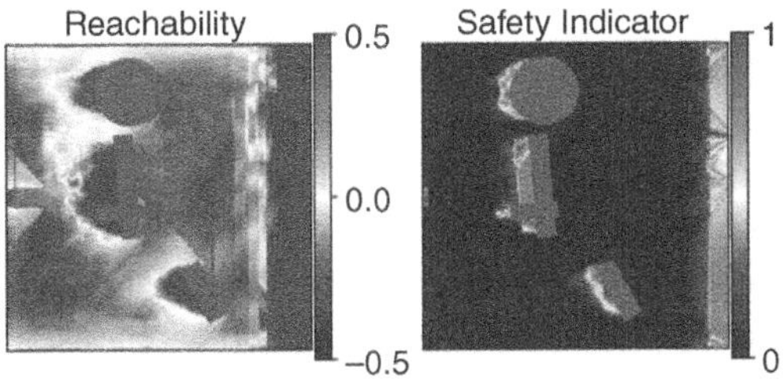

Figure 5.9 Comparison between the safety value functions learned with the safety Bellman Eq. (5.20) and the typical RL Bellman Eq. (5.18) in a robot navigation setting. The plots correspond to 2D slices of the learned value functions when the robot is facing to the right. The margin-based critic is trained using the observed distance to the nearest obstacle as the safety margin and aims to approximate the minimum future margin, while the reward-based critic is trained with a binary collision indicator as a negative reward (penalty) and aims to approximate the risk of a future collision. The margin-based critic learns a smooth value function that gradually decreases in the vicinity of obstacles, providing a continuous temporal difference signal. This contrasts with the abrupt change in the reward-based value function near the learned safety boundary, and near-constant value elsewhere. The smaller size of the unsafe regions learned by the reward-based critic suggests that the learning process has not properly converged, possibly due to the sparse temporal difference signal. *Source*: [65]/with permission of Elsevier.

Reinforcement learning has been used successfully to achieve superhuman performance in many well-known zero-sum games, including chess, shogi, and Go, and even some complex video games like StarCraft II [66, 67]. These successes are largely based on a training methodology known as *self-play*, whereby the policy is improved by repeatedly playing games against another instance of itself or, in some cases, a past or alternative version. In the case of safety analysis, the adversary cannot be realized by another instance of the control policy, because the safety game is generally asymmetrical: controller and disturbance typically have access to different physical variables, and they do not have analogous objectives (one seeks to precipitate an event, while the other aims to prevent it). This means that we need to co-train two distinct policies, one for each player.

The introduction of a second player in the RL process introduces greater technical challenges than may be apparent at first glance. The (stochastic) gradient-based learning dynamics that underpin deep RL ensure eventual convergence to a local optimum in the parametric representation of a single agent's behavior. Unfortunately, this is no longer the case when there exist multiple self-interested agents simultaneously pursuing local improvements in their respective objectives: the multiagent learning dynamics obtained by extending single-player schemes may fail to converge to a meaningful solution, such as a local Nash equilibrium, even in simple settings [68, 69].

A notable exception are zero-sum leader–follower games, wherein the players' gradient learning dynamics can be shown to converge to a local solution – a minimax equilibrium – whenever the ratio between their two learning rates, referred to as the *timescale separation*, is sufficiently large [70, 71]. This insight can be readily exploited in robust safety analysis to compute an approximate solution to the Hamilton–Jacobi–Isaacs (HJI) equation by adversarial RL, letting the disturbance act as the faster player ("follower") by increasing its learning rate relative to the controller ("leader").

The use of adversarial gameplay to learn robust safe sets and control policies was first explored in the Q-learning context [72], but its most popular and versatile form is the scheme known as iterative soft adversarial actor–critic for safety (ISAACS) [73]. This approach, which can be seen as a two-sided extension of soft actor–critic RL [74], trains a state–action value network in addition to two opposing policies:

$$h_Q(\theta) := \mathop{\mathbb{E}}_{(x,u,d,x',g)\sim\mathcal{B}}\Big[(1-\gamma)g + \gamma \min\{\, g, Q_\theta(x',u',d')\} - Q_\theta(x,u,d)\Big]^2 \tag{5.24a}$$

$$h_u(\omega) := \mathop{\mathbb{E}}_{(x,d)\sim\mathcal{B}}\Big[-Q_\theta(x,\tilde{u},d) + \alpha_u \log \pi_\omega(\tilde{u}\mid x)\Big] \tag{5.24b}$$

$$h_d(\psi) := \mathop{\mathbb{E}}_{(x,d)\sim\mathcal{B}}\Big[-Q_\theta(x,u,\tilde{d}) + \alpha_d \log \pi_\psi(\tilde{d}\mid x)\Big] \tag{5.24c}$$

where $\tilde{u} \sim \pi_\omega(\cdot \mid x)$, $\tilde{d} \sim \pi_\psi(\cdot \mid x)$, and α_u, α_d are hyperparameters incentivizing exploration (entropy in the stochastic policies), which decay gradually in magnitude through the training.

As seen in Algorithm 2, the disturbance policy is updated at a higher rate than the control policy (typically around one order of magnitude), allowing it to exploit any missteps taken by the controller during learning. Further analysis has shown that learning stability is improved by treating the critic as a third, non-adversarial player whose learning is in turn timescale-separated from the learning actors [75]. Investigations have focused on the critic acting as the slowest of all players, but recent evidence in the non-adversarial setting suggests that having the critic be the fastest to adapt may in fact be advantageous [76].

The ISAACS scheme has been used successfully across a variety of settings spanning robotics, multi-artificial intelligence (AI), and autonomous driving. The remainder of this section presents two relevant examples of varying complexity. The first one is an autonomous driving problem whose 5D dynamics make it possible to compare against the numerical HJI "oracle" solution. The second example, focused on legged locomotion, is far beyond the computational reach of numerical HJI tools. As we will see in later sections, the closer the learned approximate solution to the exact one, the less conservative the system will need to be in order to enforce safety.

5.3.2.3 Example: Road Collision Avoidance

To ground the workings of the ISAACS scheme in a concrete system, we consider an autonomous car with uncertain dynamics $\dot{x} = f(x, u, d)$ based on the 5D kinematic bicycle model, commonly used in autonomous driving:

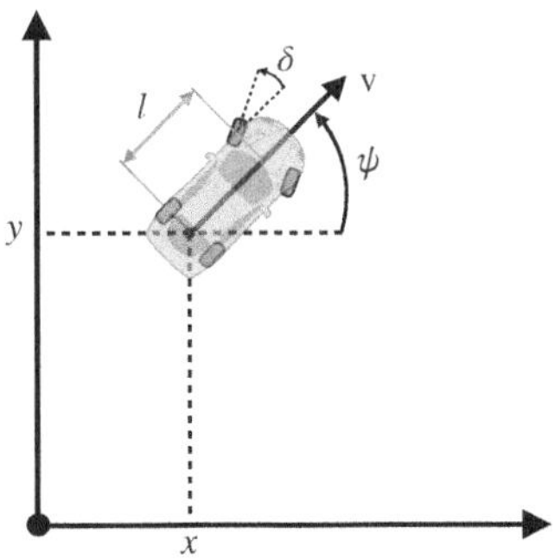

$$
\begin{aligned}
\dot{\mathrm{x}} &= \mathrm{v} \cos \psi + d_{\mathrm{x}} \\
\dot{\mathrm{y}} &= \mathrm{v} \sin \psi + d_{\mathrm{y}} \\
\dot{\mathrm{v}} &= a + d_{\mathrm{v}} \\
\dot{\psi} &= \frac{\mathrm{v}}{l} \tan \delta + d_{\psi} \\
\dot{\delta} &= \omega + d_{\delta}
\end{aligned} \tag{5.25}
$$

The car's state consists of the position (x, y) of its body frame, centered on the rear axle, its forward velocity v, its heading angle ψ and the front wheels' steering angle δ. The car's onboard controller has bounded control authority over acceleration and braking $a \in [\underline{a}, \overline{a}]$ as well as the steering rate $\omega \in [\underline{\omega}, \overline{\omega}]$. In turn, the disturbance is in control of the model uncertainty, which we bound within a box $d \in \mathcal{D} := \prod_{i \in I} [\underline{d}_i, \overline{d}_i]$, with $I = \{\mathrm{x}, \mathrm{y}, \mathrm{v}, \psi, \delta\}$. The modeled dynamics also depend on the wheelbase l between the front and rear axles, which we treat as a known constant parameter (manufacturing tolerances or measurement errors can be included in the steering uncertainty). To match the RL formulation, discrete-time dynamics can be obtained from (5.25) by fourth-order Runge–Kutta (RK4).

We consider the vehicle driving along a road, with safety constraints on heading angle, drivable surface, and obstacle clearance. The footprint of the car is represented by a box $B^b = [-b_r, l + b_f] \times [-\frac{w}{2}, \frac{w}{2}]$ in its body frame, with b_f and b_r the vehicle's front and rear overhang (axle-to-bumper distance). We define the safety margin function as

$$g(x) = \min \left\{ g_{\psi}(x),\ g_{\mathrm{road}}(x),\ g_{\mathrm{obs}}(x) \right\}, \tag{5.26}$$

where $g_{\psi}(x) := \frac{\pi}{2} - |\psi - \psi_{\mathrm{road}}(x)|$ is positive when the car faces forward along the direction of the road, $g_{\mathrm{road}}(x)$ is the signed distance between the car's footprint and the road boundary, and $g_{\mathrm{obs}}(x)$ is the signed distance between the car's footprint and the nearest obstacle. A safety control policy for the car $\pi_{\omega}(u \mid x)$ can be trained, jointly with an adversarial disturbance $\pi_{\psi}(d \mid x)$ and a safety critic $Q_{\theta} : (x, u, d) \to \mathbb{R}$, by repeatedly sampling initial conditions at random, simulating the gameplay between the two policies for a finite number of steps, and recording the safety margin achieved at each time step. In this example, taken from the original ISAACS paper [73], the length of each episode is 200 steps (20 seconds), and all neural networks consist of three fully-connected feedforward layers, with

256 neurons per layer for the actors and 128 for the critic. This amounts to 69,634 parameters or 284 KB of storage.

We can compare the learned ISAACS safe set and policies to an "oracle" solution based on a non-neurosymbolic solver. We can use resolution-complete finite-difference methods [12] to solve the HJI Eq. (5.10) numerically on a multi-dimensional grid. The value function is stored as a grid with about 91 million scalar values, taking 0.7 GB (over 2,500 times more). The comparison results, presented in Figure 5.10, indicate that the adversarial RL methodology can learn high-quality approximations to the safety problem solution, using a fraction of the computation and the memory. In the next section, we will discuss how to use these learned "untrusted" approximations (not guaranteed to be correct) to construct certifiable safety filters that can operate at runtime. We first conclude this section with a more complex example that emphasizes the scalability and generality of ISAACS.

5.3.2.4 Additional Case Study: Quadrupedal Robots

The adversarial RL approach especially shines when an explicit dynamical model is unavailable or too cumbersome to work with. Among the most significant demonstrations of ISAACS in recent years has been its use for quadrupedal robots with hybrid, nonlinear locomotion dynamics, involving more than 30 continuous state dimensions and tens of discrete contact configurations [77]. Since ISAACS

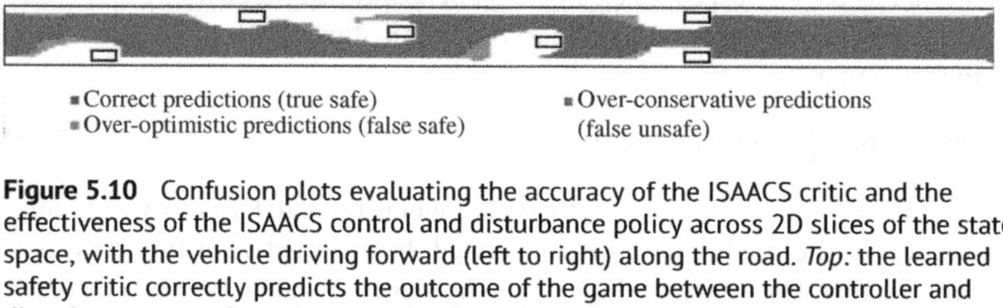

Figure 5.10 Confusion plots evaluating the accuracy of the ISAACS critic and the effectiveness of the ISAACS control and disturbance policy across 2D slices of the state space, with the vehicle driving forward (left to right) along the road. *Top:* the learned safety critic correctly predicts the outcome of the game between the controller and disturbance actors from the majority of starting states (true safe in dark gray, true unsafe in white), but can mispredict it in some cases near the estimated safe set boundary (false safe in light gray). *Middle:* the learned ISAACS safety policy achieves near-optimal success when pitted against the HJI disturbance, but is occasionally suboptimal—compared to the optimal "oracle" HJI controller—near the safe set boundary (evitable safety failures in gray). *Bottom:* the adversarial disturbance learned by ISAACS achieves equivalent outcomes against the optimal HJI safety policy as the true worst-case "oracle" HJI disturbance from the majority of starting states, but not all (missed failures in light gray); relying on direct rollouts of the learned disturbance can lead to over-optimistic safety assessments.

does not require an explicit model of the system dynamics, it can be trained using an off-the-shelf physics engine and a manufacturer-provided or otherwise acquired black box simulation model. The only additional requirement is a specification of safety. In the case of robot locomotion, we simply require that the robot prevent *falls*, i.e. any state in which some body part other than its feet is in contact with the terrain. The safety margin signal is then readily provided by the simulator at each state as the lowest height over the ground out of a designer-defined set of body key points (for example, all leg joints and the corners of the torso). Finally, the possible discrepancies between the nominal simulator model and the physical system (sim-to-real gap) can be encoded through bounded disturbances at each actuator joint or even as a simple external force acting on the robot's torso.

Once training has proceeded, the safety policy is deployed on the physical robot and stress-tested through various disruptions to the robot's operation, such as strong kicks (Figure 5.11). The robot's learned safety-seeking behavior includes highly dynamic strategies highly reminiscent of mammalian quadrupeds, such as extending its legs mid-air and, upon landing, adopting a crouching stance with a lowered center of gravity.

5.3.3 Connections Between Reinforcement and Self-supervised Neurosymbolic Learning

Reinforcement and self-supervised neurosymbolic learning approaches for obtaining safety value functions reveal two complementary perspectives on addressing the same fundamental dynamical safety problem. From one angle, both learning variants aim to approximate solutions to the same safety-related optimization problem in dynamical systems, but they employ distinct strategies. The RL-based approach combines a policy-driven exploration mechanism with supervised updates to the critic, effectively leveraging new data to refine the safety value function iteratively. DeepReach, in contrast, relies on structured, self-generated pseudo-labels derived from the symbolic abstraction of HJI-VI,

Figure 5.11 Experiments on the Spirit S40 quadruped robot demonstrate the ability of ISAACS to synthesize robust and effective safety strategies for a nonlinear system with 36 state dimensions and uncertain contact dynamics in mere hours of wall-clock time (compared to months of manual engineering design). This is the first instance of a full-state controller based on (approximate) Hamilton–Jacobi safety analysis being computed for a system with 30+ state dimensions and a simulation-trained legged robot controller achieving zero-shot safety when subject to significant perturbations such as kicks and tugs.

using them to approximate the same safety values without requiring explicit reward signals or exploration. From another angle, RL itself can be viewed as a specific form of self-supervised learning, where the exploration mechanism serves as the data generation process, and the critic performs supervised learning to align predictions with safety objectives. By presenting side-by-side comparisons of reinforcement and self-supervised learning algorithms, the nuanced differences become clear—while RL emphasizes reward-guided exploration and data collection (lines 4–7 in Algorithm 2), DeepReach relies on intrinsic, self-labeled data drawn from underlying domain structures. Both approaches, however, converge toward constructing robust safety value functions critical for ensuring safe behavior in dynamical systems. This synergy between the two approaches suggests opportunities for hybrid methods that combine the structured insights of self-supervised learning with the adaptive exploration strategies of RL to advance safety algorithms for autonomous systems.

Algorithm 2 ISAACS: Iterative Soft Adversarial Actor-critic for Safety (Offline Safety Synthesis)

1: **for** each tournament round **do**
2:     **for** each episode **do**
3:         $x_0 \sim P_0$ ▷ Sample initial state for this episode
4:         **for** each time step **do**
5:             $u_t \sim \pi_\omega(\cdot|x_t),\ d_t \sim \pi_\psi(\cdot|x_t)$ ▷ Sample control and disturbance from policies
6:             $x_{t+1} = f(x_t, u_t, d_t)$ ▷ Get transition from the environment
7:             $\mathcal{B} \leftarrow \mathcal{B} \cup \{(x_t, u_t, d_t, x_{t+1}, g_{t+1})\}$ ▷ Store the transition in the replay buffer
8:         **for** each gradient step **do**
9:             $\theta \leftarrow \theta - \lambda_\theta \nabla_\theta h(\theta)$ ▷ Update critic parameters
10:            $\psi \leftarrow \psi - \lambda_\psi \nabla_\psi L(\psi)$ ▷ Update disturbance policy parameters
11:            $\omega \leftarrow \omega - \frac{1}{\tau}\lambda_\omega \nabla_\omega L(\omega)$ ▷ Update safety policy parameters at a slower rate

5.4 Safety Assurances for Learned Controllers

Ideally, we might hope to construct a safety filter directly from the neural safety analysis performed through self-supervised or reinforcement learning. For example, we may propose a value-based safety filter using the learned value function as the safety monitor, such that

$$\pi_{\text{safe}}(x, t) = \begin{cases} \pi_{\text{nom}}(x, t), & V_\theta(x, t) > 0 \\ \pi_\theta^*(x, t), & V_\theta(x, t) \le 0, \end{cases} \tag{5.27}$$

where V_θ is the learned value function, π_θ is the safety controller corresponding to V_θ, which can be computed using Eq. (5.13), and π_{nom} is some nominal controller for the system. A similar filtering mechanism can be constructed using Q_θ, wherein instead of $V_\theta(x, t)$, we check the sign of $Q_\theta(x, \pi_{\text{nom}})$.

Unfortunately, due to the approximate nature of Q_θ and V_θ, this is only a *best-effort* safety filter: unlike (5.7), it comes with no invariance guarantees and it cannot generally prevent safety violations. In this section, we discuss how we can embed learned safety critics with safety assurances.

5.4.1 Probabilistic Safety Assurances Through Conformal Prediction

We first discuss how we can recover an approximation of the value function and the safe set with probabilistic guarantees. Specifically, we want to find an approximation of the safe set, $\hat{S}$, such that:

$$\mathop{\mathbb{P}}_{x \in \hat{S}} (x \in \mathcal{V}) \leq \epsilon \tag{5.28}$$

for some violation parameter $\epsilon \in (0, 1)$. Recall that $\mathcal{V}$ represents the true unsafe set of the system. Intuitively, Equation (5.28) bounds the rate of safety violation within the approximated safe set $\hat{S}$, thereby providing a high-confidence approximation of the safe set.

We now present a *conformal* probabilistic safety verification method to obtain $\hat{S}$ from the neural reachability methods discussed in Section 5.3. The method is a straightforward application of split conformal prediction, a widely used method in the machine learning community for uncertainty quantification [78].

Procedure: Consider the superlevel sets of the learned value function, $V_\theta(x, T)$, as candidates for $\hat{S}$. Ideally, any super-δ level set of $V_\theta(x, T)$ for $\delta > 0$ should be a valid safe set; however, due to learning errors, that might not be true in practice. In order to provide a probabilistic safety assurance for $\hat{S}$, we first sample N independent and identically distributed (i.i.d.) states $x_{1:N}$ from $\hat{S}$ according to some probability distribution $\mathbb{P}$ over $\hat{S}$. Since $\hat{S}$ is defined implicitly by $V_\theta(x, T)$, we use rejection sampling. We next compute the safety costs $J(x_i, 0)$ for $i = 1, 2, \ldots, N$ by rolling out the system trajectory starting from the state x_i under the induced safe policy $\pi^*_\theta(x, t)$. Here, the safety cost is given by (5.8), which essentially captures the closest distance between the system trajectory and the failure set.

Let k refer to the number of "outliers" - samples that are empirically unsafe, i.e. $J(x_i, 0) \leq 0$. Then the following theorem provides a probabilistic guarantee on the safety of the learned value function as well as the candidate safe set $\hat{S}$:

Theorem 5.1 *(Conformal Probabilistic Safety Verification)*: *Let the number of outliers k and the number of samples N be as defined in the procedures above. Then:*

$$\mathop{\mathbb{P}}_{x \in \hat{S}} (J(x, 0) > 0) \sim \text{Beta}(N - k, k + 1) \tag{5.29}$$

Proof. Theorem 5.1 can be established via a straightforward application of the split conformal prediction method detailed in Angelopoulos and Bates [78], where we set the conformal "input" $x = x$, "output" $y = -J(x, 0)$, "score function" $s(x, y) = y = -J(x, 0)$, "size of the calibration set" $n = N$, and "user-chosen error rate" $\alpha = \frac{k+1}{N+1}$. The conformal $\hat{q}$ is then computed as the $\frac{\lceil (N+1)(1-\alpha) \rceil}{N}$ quantile of the calibration scores $-J(x_{1:N}, 0)$. The quantile is $\frac{\lceil (N+1)(1-\alpha) \rceil}{N} = \frac{\lceil (N+1)(1-\frac{k+1}{N+1}) \rceil}{N} = \frac{\lceil (N+1)(\frac{N-k}{N+1}) \rceil}{N} = \frac{N-k}{N}$, where we have defined k as the number of scores $-J(x_i, 0) \geq 0$. Thus, this quantile corresponds precisely to the largest *negative* score, so we know that $\hat{q} < 0$. Theorem 1 in Angelopoulos and Bates [78] then yields:

$$\begin{aligned}
&\mathop{\mathbb{P}}_{(x_{1:N}, x) \in \hat{\mathcal{S}}} (-J(x,0) \leq \hat{q}) \geq 1 - \alpha \\
&\mathop{\mathbb{P}}_{(x_{1:N}, x) \in \hat{\mathcal{S}}} (J(x,0) \geq -\hat{q}) \geq 1 - \frac{k+1}{N+1} \\
&\mathop{\mathbb{P}}_{(x_{1:N}, x) \in \hat{\mathcal{S}}} (J(x,0) > 0) \geq \frac{N-k}{N+1}
\end{aligned} \tag{5.30}$$

where Eq. (5.30) follows from the line preceding it because if $J(x,0) \geq -\hat{q}$, then certainly $J(x,0) > 0$. This coverage property result is precisely the same as described in Remark 5.2. Furthermore, Section 3.2 in Angelopoulos and Bates [78] yields:

$$\begin{aligned}
&\mathop{\mathbb{P}}_{x \in \hat{\mathcal{S}}} (J(x,0) > 0) \sim \text{Beta}(N+1-l, l), \quad l = \lfloor (N+1)\alpha \rfloor \\
&\mathop{\mathbb{P}}_{x \in \hat{\mathcal{S}}} (J(x,0) > 0) \sim \text{Beta}(N-k, k+1)
\end{aligned} \tag{5.31}$$

which is precisely the result of Theorem 5.1. □

Theorem 5.1 states that the fraction of $\hat{\mathcal{S}}$ that is safe is distributed according to the Beta distribution with shape parameters $N-k$ and $k+1$. Intuitively, the mass in the distribution shifts toward 0 as k increases for a fixed N, implying that it is more likely that a smaller fraction of $\hat{\mathcal{S}}$ is safe, as expected. For a fixed ratio $N : k$, N controls how concentrated the mass is around the mean; i.e. for larger sample sizes N, we can more confidently determine the fraction of $\hat{\mathcal{S}}$ that is safe.

To better understand Theorem 5.1, we show in Figure 5.12 the Beta distribution of $\mathop{\mathbb{P}}_{x \in \hat{\mathcal{S}}} (J(x,0) > 0)$ for a solution learned by DeepReach on the multi-vehicle collision avoidance example introduced in Section 5.3.1.2, for which $k = 731$ outliers are found from $N = 3684118$ samples.

Remark 5.2: The mean of the Beta distribution in Eq. (5.29) is given as $\frac{N-k}{N+1}$, which is roughly the fraction of the empirically safe samples. One can immediately derive that the safety probability of $\hat{\mathcal{S}}$, marginalized over the sampled "calibration" states, is given as: $\mathop{\mathbb{P}}_{(x_{1:N}, x) \in \hat{\mathcal{S}}} (J(x,0) > 0) \geq \frac{N-k}{N+1}$, which precisely resembles the most commonly used **coverage property** of split conformal prediction.

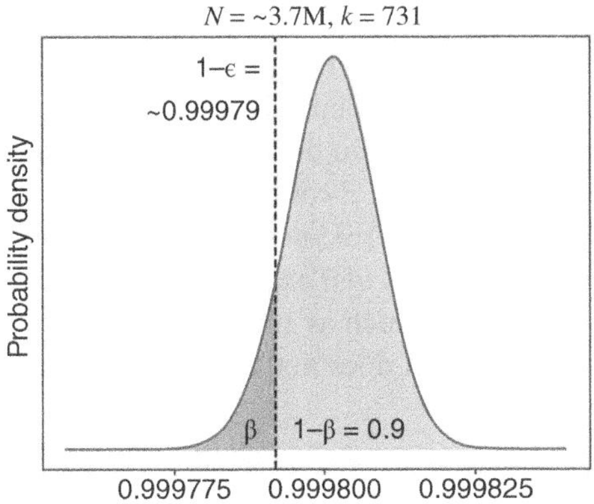

Figure 5.12 The Beta distribution of $\mathbb{P}_{x \in \hat{S}}(J(x, 0) > 0)$ when $k = 731$ outliers are found from $N = 3684118$ samples. (Dashed black line) For an example choice of confidence $1 - \beta = 0.9$ (shaded light gray), we can lower-bound the fraction of $\hat{S}$, which is safe with at least $1 - \epsilon = 0.99979$ (99.979%) confidence.

Even though Theorem 5.1 provides the distribution of the safety level, when we compute safety assurances in practice, it is often desirable to know a lower-bound on the safety level with at least some desired confidence. This corresponds to choosing a lower-bound whose accumulated probability mass is smaller than some confidence parameter β (shaded dark gray in Figure 5.12). The following lemma formalizes this by using the CDF of the Beta distribution in Theorem 5.1.

Lemma 5.1 ***(Conformal Probabilistic Safety Verification):*** *Select a safety violation parameter $\epsilon \in (0, 1)$ and a confidence parameter $\beta \in (0, 1)$ such that*

$$\sum_{i=0}^{k} \binom{N}{i} \epsilon^i (1 - \epsilon)^{N-i} \leq \beta \tag{5.32}$$

where k and N are as defined above. Then, with probability at least $1 - \beta$ over the draws of the samples, the following holds:

$$\mathbb{P}_{x \in \hat{S}}(V(x, 0) \leq 0) \leq \epsilon \tag{5.33}$$

Disregarding the confidence parameter β for a moment, Lemma 5.1 states that the fraction of $\hat{S}$ that is unsafe is bounded above by the violation parameter ϵ, where ϵ is computed empirically using Eq. (5.32) based on the outlier rate k encountered within N samples. ϵ is thus a reflection of the safety quality of $\hat{S}$, which degrades with the increase in the number of outliers k, as expected. Overall, Lemma 5.1 allows us to compute probabilistic safety guarantees for any neural set $\hat{S}$ based on a finite number of samples. Subsequently, this result can be used to find some $\hat{S}$ for which ϵ is smaller than a desired threshold.

To interpret β, note that k is a random variable that depends on the randomly sampled $x_{1:N}$. It may be the case that we just happen to draw an unrepresentative sample, in which case the ϵ bound does not hold. β controls the probability of this adverse event happening, which regards the correctness of the probabilistic safety guarantee in Eq. (5.33). Fortunately, β goes to 0 exponentially with N, so β can be chosen to be an extremely small value, such as 10^{-16}, when we sample large N. $1 - \beta$ will then be so close to 1 that it does not have any practical importance.

We apply this method to the three-vehicle collision avoidance problem introduced earlier as shown in Figure 5.13. We are interested in computing an approximation of the safe set that is safe with a probability of at least 0.999. Here, the innermost light gray region(s) is the learned unsafe set. The middle dark gray region represents the area that required correction as per the conformal prediction method. In this case, this causes a uniform correction of 0.1 (i.e. $\delta = 0.1$), ultimately giving us the certified safe set in light the outer light gray region. In this case, epsilon is 0.001; thus, if we sample any state inside the outer light gray region set, the probability of failure is less than 0.001. In other words, the outer light gray region is 99.9% safe.

5.4.2 Robust Safety Assurances Through Forward Reachability

Alternatively, we may seek robust assurances in the same *if–then* form provided by Hamilton–Jacobi–Isaacs analysis. For example, *as long as* the friction coefficient is bounded above a minimum value and the wind disturbance is no greater than a prescribed limit, a robot can be guaranteed to maintain safety. In other words, robust safety guarantees certify a system's safety across all conditions that fall under an operational design domain (ODD) (Figures 5.14 and 5.15).

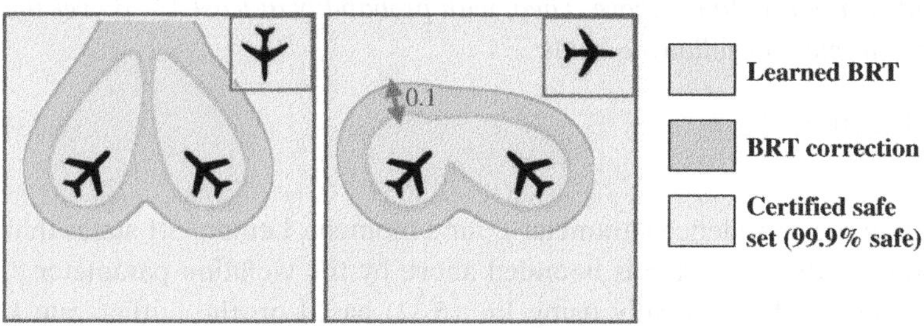

Figure 5.13 Conformal prediction-based verification method applied to the three-vehicle collision avoidance example.

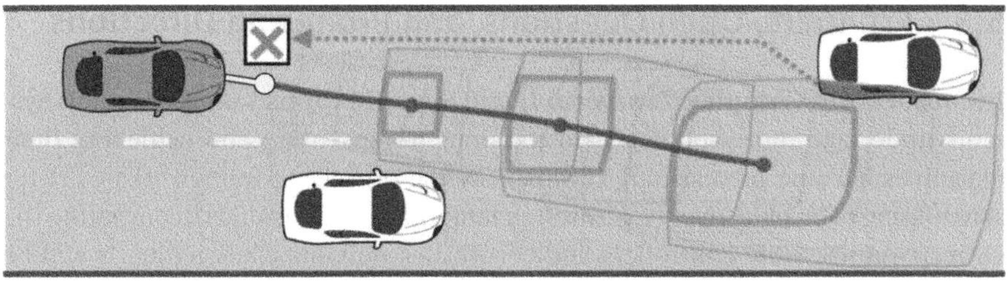

Figure 5.14 Runtime certification of the ISAACS learned safety policy for the 5D car example. The learned safety policy is rolled out under all disturbance realizations. Here, the forward-reachable sets (smaller inner squares with thick lines) are safe if their footprint-augmented counterparts (larger outer squares with thin lines) remain collision-free and within the road boundaries. This predictive monitoring scheme can readily be used in a *robust safety filter*, wherein control actions proposed by the nominal task policy (visualized in white line directly in from of the leftmost vehicle) are allowed if a subsequent safety policy rollout ("fallback," in longer line in front of that white line) is certified safe; otherwise, the (already certified) fallback tracking policy is used.

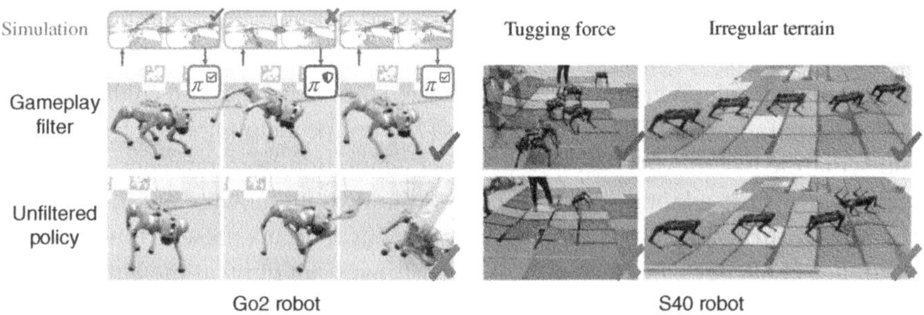

Figure 5.15 The game-theoretic predictive safety filter approach running on two different quadruped robots (S40 and Go2) equipped with safety-agnostic walking policies. The *gameplay filter* continually monitors the robot's safety by rapidly simulating worst-case futures invoked by a learned virtual adversary, and it preemptively disallows task-driven actions that would cause the robot to lose to it (violate safety). The gameplay-filtered robots exhibit rich and highly robust behaviors such as counterbalancing to fight persistent pulls and springing into a wide stance to break imminent falls.

How can we recover a strict robust guarantee despite relying on a possibly inexact neural safety analysis? The key idea is to separate the *prescriptive* and *predictive* components of this analysis.

Once trained, the neural safety policy can be used as the receding-horizon reference for a robust fallback control strategy, defining a compact forward-reachable set that can be checked for safety violations. This results in a recursive safety filter with an equivalent invariance property to the accurate but less scalable counterpart (5.7) enabled by numerical HJI methods.

5.5 Frontiers, Open Questions, and Promising Directions

Incorporating Complex Temporal Logic Specifications: As autonomous systems undertake more sophisticated missions, representing and achieving their objectives become increasingly complex. While promising frameworks exist for articulating such objectives (e.g. through temporal logic formulas), computing the corresponding safety controllers and certificates remains challenging. It will be interesting to investigate the extension of neural safety methodologies discussed in this chapter to accommodate complex and intricate safety specifications.

Online Adaptation of Safety Controllers: Conventional safety analysis relies on experts to define and construct safety constraints, which can be a challenge in complex and dynamic environments where such constraints might be dynamic, difficult to specify, or context-dependent (e.g. a T-bone collision is often worse than a side-swipe for an autonomous car). As we learn and update our understanding of safety constraints, system dynamics, or environmental factors, it's imperative that our safety assurances can adapt just as swiftly. Developing methods for online adaptation of safety assurances, especially when the changes are complex and cannot be parameterized easily, is an exciting future direction. There have been several exciting developments recently that address online adaptation challenges via offline preparation for parametric changes [79], online adaptation to physical [80] and semantic hazards [81], as well as direct adaptation from raw sensory inputs [82]; however, fast adaptation methods for "unknown unknowns" are still lacking.

Human Interaction: Systems that interact with humans present fundamental assurance challenges, because overall safety hinges not only on the autonomous agent's internal decision-making but also on the highly uncertain behavior of external human actors. For instance, an autonomous vehicle navigating a busy downtown area must contend with the complex and largely unobservable internal states of pedestrians, cyclists, and other drivers, whose interwoven decisions, partly in response to the autonomous agent's ongoing course of action, can be extremely difficult to predict. This human–automation coupling also means that traditional safe control algorithms, which have been designed to encapsulate automated policies, cannot be readily extended to work in a shared autonomy setting, where an intervention meant to preempt a potential future risk can instead create dangerous conditions by confusing or even alarming the human whose decisions are being overridden. Neurosymbolic approaches are likely to play a crucial role in incorporating rich, flexible data-driven predictions of interactive human behavior into the rigorous decision pipeline needed for safety assurance [83, 84].

Perception Uncertainty: Current safety frameworks typically presume perfect state measurement; however, real-world sensors are imprecise and result in incomplete, inaccurate, and intermittent sensor data [85, 86]. There is a promising opportunity to extend neural reachability analysis to learn safety controllers and safe sets directly from rich sensory inputs or language specifications, thus circumventing the need for explicit state estimation. In parallel, we should advance Hamilton–Jacobi (HJ) reachability theory to account for potential state and output uncertainty during the reachable set and safety controller computations [87]. This dual approach can be particularly beneficial in situations where explicit state estimation is preferred but is subject to variability and noise.

Co-optimization of Safety and Performance: Performance and safety are two crucial factors we must consider when designing algorithms for autonomous systems. Clearly, we would like the systems to be effective in performing useful tasks. At the same time, the systems must satisfy safety requirements. As a result, these two factors must be considered simultaneously when we are designing control algorithms. Unfortunately, performance and safety can sometimes be competing objectives, which renders the co-optimization between them difficult. One popular family of methods is safety filtering [23, 78, 12, 29], which provides safety-preserving interventions when necessary in runtime. They generally lead to myopic and suboptimal behaviors as, by design, the safety requirement is often not considered during the performance controller synthesis. Joint synthesis of performance and safety controllers has shown promise in robotic settings [65] but remains a largely underexplored direction.

References

1 Earl A Coddington and Norman Levinson. *Theory of Ordinary Differential Equations*. International Series in Pure and Applied Mathematics. McGraw-Hill, New York, 1955.

2 Kim P Wabersich, Andrew J Taylor, Jason J Choi, Koushil Sreenath, Claire J Tomlin, Aaron D Ames, and Melanie N Zeilinger. Data-driven safety filters: Hamilton–Jacobi reachability, control barrier functions, and predictive methods for uncertain systems. *IEEE Control Systems Magazine*, 43(5): 137–177, 2023.

3 Kai-Chieh Hsu, Haimin Hu, and Jaime F Fisac. The safety filter: a unified view of safety-critical control in autonomous systems. *Annual Review of Control, Robotics, and Autonomous Systems*, 7:47–72, 2023a.

4 Javier Borquez, Kaustav Chakraborty, Hao Wang, and Somil Bansal. On safety and liveness filtering using hamilton-jacobi reachability analysis. *IEEE Transactions on Robotics*, 2024.

5 Ian Mitchell. A robust controlled backward reach tube with (almost) analytic solution for two dubins cars. *EPiC Series in Computing*, 74: 242–258, 2020.

6 Ian M Mitchell, Alexandre M Bayen, and Claire J Tomlin. A time-dependent hamilton-jacobi formulation of reachable sets for continuous dynamic games. *IEEE TAC*, 50(7): 947–957, 2005.

7 John Lygeros. On reachability and minimum cost optimal control. *Automatica*, 40(6): 917–927, 2004.

8 K. Margellos and J. Lygeros. Hamilton-Jacobi formulation for reach–avoid differential games. *IEEE Transactions on Automatic Control*, 56(8): 1849–1861, 2011.

9 Jaime F Fisac, Mo Chen, Claire J Tomlin, and S Shankar Sastry. Reach-avoid problems with time-varying dynamics, targets and constraints. In *International Conference on Hybrid Systems: Computation and Control*. ACM, 2015.

10 S. Bansal, M. Chen, S. Herbert, and C. J. Tomlin. Hamilton-Jacobi reachability: a brief overview and recent advances. In *CDC*, 2017.

11 Ian M Mitchell. A toolbox of level set methods, 2004. http://www.cs.ubc.ca/mitchell/ToolboxLS/toolboxLS.pdf.

12 Minh Bui, George Giovanis, Mo Chen, and Arrvindh Shriraman. Optimizeddp: an efficient, user-friendly library for optimal control and dynamic programming. *arXiv preprint arXiv:2204.05520*, 2022.

13 Edward Schmerling. hj_reachability: Hamilton–Jacobi reachability analysis in JAX. https://github.com/StanfordASL/hj_reachability.

14 Ken Tanabe, Mo Chen, Somil Bansal. BEACLS: Berkeley efficient API in C++ for level set methods. https://hjreachability.github.io/beacls/.

15 helperOC Team. helperOC library, 2019. https://github.com/HJReachability/helperOC.

16 Karen Leung, Edward Schmerling, Mengxuan Zhang, Mo Chen, John Talbot, J Christian Gerdes, and Marco Pavone. On infusing reachability-based safety assurance within planning frameworks for human–robot vehicle interactions. *The International Journal of Robotics Research*, 39(10-11): 1326–1345, 2020.

17 Mark R Greenstreet. Integrating projections Mark R. Greenstreet department of computer science. In *Hybrid Systems: Computation and Control: First International Workshop, HSCC'98*, Berkeley, California, USA, April 13-15, 1998, *Proceedings*, page 159. Springer, 1998.

18 G. Frehse, C. Le Guernic, A. Donzé, S. Cotton, R. Ray, O. Lebeltel, R. Ripado, A. Girard, T. Dang, and O. Maler. SpaceEx: Scalable verification of hybrid systems. In *Proceedings International Conference. Computer Aided Verification*, 2011.

19 Alexander B Kurzhanski and Pravin Varaiya. Ellipsoidal techniques for reachability analysis: internal approximation. *Systems & Control Letters*, 41(3):201–211, 2000.

20 Alexander B Kurzhanski and Pravin Varaiya. On ellipsoidal techniques for reachability analysis. Part II: Internal approximations box-valued constraints. *Optimization Methods and Software*, 17(2):207–237, 2002.

21 John N Maidens, Shahab Kaynama, Ian M Mitchell, Meeko MK Oishi, and Guy A Dumont. Lagrangian methods for approximating the viability kernel in high-dimensional systems. *Automatica*, 49(7):2017–2029, 2013.

22 Antoine Girard. Reachability of uncertain linear systems using zonotopes. In *International Workshop on Hybrid Systems: Computation and Control*, pages 291–305. Springer, 2005.

23 Matthias Althoff, Olaf Stursberg, and Martin Buss. Computing reachable sets of hybrid systems using a combination of zonotopes and polytopes. *Nonlinear Analysis: Hybrid Systems*, 4(2): 233–249, 2010.

24 Bastian Schürmann and Matthias Althoff. Guaranteeing constraints of disturbed nonlinear systems using set-based optimal control in generator space. *IFAC-PapersOnLine*, 50(1): 11515–11522, 2017.

25 A. Majumdar, R. Vasudevan, M.M. Tobenkin, and R. Tedrake. Convex optimization of nonlinear feedback controllers via occupation measures. *The International Journal of Robotics Research*, 33(9):1209–1230, 2014.

26 A. Majumdar and R. Tedrake. Funnel libraries for real-time robust feedback motion planning. *The International Journal of Robotics Research*, 36(8): 947–982, 2017.

27 T. Dreossi, T. Dang, and C. Piazza. Parallelotope bundles for polynomial reachability. In *Proceedings of the ACM International Conference on Hybrid Systems: Computation and Control*, 2016.

28 D. Henrion and M. Korda. Convex computation of the region of attraction of polynomial control systems. *IEEE Transactions on Automatic Control*, 59(2): 297–312, 2014.

29 Samuel Coogan and Murat Arcak. Efficient finite abstraction of mixed monotone systems. In *Proceedings of the 18th International Conference on Hybrid Systems: Computation and Control*, pages 58–67, 2015.

30 M. Chen, S. Herbert, M. Vashishtha, S. Bansal, and C. J. Tomlin. Decomposition of reachable sets and tubes for a class of nonlinear systems. *IEEE Transactions on Automatic Control*, 2018.

31 Patrick Holmes, Shreyas Kousik, Bohao Zhang, Daphna Raz, Corina Barbalata, Matthew Johnson-Roberson, and Ram Vasudevan. Reachable sets for safe, real-time manipulator trajectory design. *arXiv preprint arXiv:2002.01591*, 2020.

32 Jinsun Liu, Pengcheng Zhao, Zhenyu Gan, Matthew Johnson-Roberson, and Ram Vasudevan. Leveraging the template and anchor framework for safe, online robotic gait design. In *2020 IEEE International Conference on Robotics and Automation (ICRA)*, pages 10869–10875. IEEE, 2020.

33 Yat Tin Chow, Jérôme Darbon, Stanley Osher, and Wotao Yin. Algorithm for overcoming the curse of dimensionality for time-dependent non-convex hamilton–jacobi equations arising from optimal control and differential games problems. *Journal of Scientific Computing*, 73(2–3): 617–643, 2017.

34 Stanley Bak, Hoang-Dung Tran, and Taylor T Johnson. Numerical verification of affine systems with up to a billion dimensions. In *Proceedings of the 22nd ACM*

International Conference on Hybrid Systems: Computation and Control, pages 23–32, 2019.

35 Petter Nilsson and Necmiye Ozay. Synthesis of separable controlled invariant sets for modular local control design. In *2016 American Control Conference (ACC)*, pages 5656–5663. IEEE, 2016.

36 Aaron D Ames, Xiangru Xu, Jessy W Grizzle, and Paulo Tabuada. Control barrier function based quadratic programs for safety critical systems. *IEEE Transactions on Automatic Control*, 62(8): 3861–3876, 2016.

37 Aaron D Ames, Samuel Coogan, Magnus Egerstedt, Gennaro Notomista, Koushil Sreenath, and Paulo Tabuada. Control barrier functions: theory and applications. In *2019 18th European Control Conference (ECC)*, pages 3420–3431. IEEE, 2019.

38 Alexander Robey, Haimin Hu, Lars Lindemann, Hanwen Zhang, Dimos V Dimarogonas, Stephen Tu, and Nikolai Matni. Learning control barrier functions from expert demonstrations. In *59th IEEE Conference on Decision and Control (CDC)*, pages 3717–3724. IEEE, 2020.

39 Chuanzheng Wang, Yinan Li, Yiming Meng, Stephen L Smith, and Jun Liu. Learning control barrier functions with high relative degree for safety-critical control. *arXiv preprint arXiv:2011.10721*, 2020.

40 Andrew Taylor, Andrew Singletary, Yisong Yue, and Aaron Ames. Learning for safety-critical control with control barrier functions. In *Learning for Dynamics and Control*, pages 708–717. PMLR, 2020.

41 Mohit Srinivasan, Amogh Dabholkar, Samuel Coogan, and Patricio A Vela. Synthesis of control barrier functions using a supervised machine learning approach. In *IEEE/RSJ International Conference on Intelligent Robots and Systems (IROS)*, pages 7139–7145. IEEE, 2020.

42 Charles Dawson, Zengyi Qin, Sicun Gao, and Chuchu Fan. Safe nonlinear control using robust neural Lyapunov-barrier functions. *arXiv preprint arXiv:2109.06697*, 2021.

43 Simin Liu, Changliu Liu, and John Dolan. Safe control under input limits with neural control barrier functions. In *Conference on Robot Learning*, pages 1970–1980. PMLR, 2023.

44 Charles Dawson, Zengyi Qin, Sicun Gao, and Chuchu Fan. Safe nonlinear control using robust neural lyapunov-barrier functions. In Aleksandra Faust, David Hsu, and Gerhard Neumann, editors, *Proceedings of the 5th Conference on Robot Learning, volume 164 of Proceedings of Machine Learning Research*, pages 1724–1735. PMLR, 2022.

45 Lucas Liebenwein, Cenk Baykal, Igor Gilitschenski, Sertac Karaman, and Daniela Rus. Sampling-based approximation algorithms for reachability analysis with provable guarantees. In *RSS*, 2018.

46 Tobias Sutter, Angeliki Kamoutsi, Peyman Mohajerin Esfahani, and John Lygeros. Data-driven approximate dynamic programming: a linear programming approach. In *2017 IEEE 56th Annual Conference on Decision and Control (CDC)*, pages 5174–5179. IEEE, 2017.

47 Devonport, Alex, and Murat Arcak. “Estimating reachable sets with scenario optimization.” In Learning for dynamics and control, pp. 75–84. PMLR, 2020.

48 Shromona Ghosh, Somil Bansal, Alberto Sangiovanni-Vincentelli, Sanjit A Seshia, and Claire Tomlin. A new simulation metric to determine safe environments and controllers for systems with unknown dynamics. In *Proceedings of the 22nd ACM International Conference on Hybrid Systems: Computation and Control*, pages 185–196, 2019.

49 Thomas Lew and Marco Pavone. Sampling-based reachability analysis: a random set theory approach with adversarial sampling. *arXiv preprint arXiv:2008.10180*, 2020.

50 Ross E Allen, Ashley A Clark, Joseph A Starek, and Marco Pavone. A machine learning approach for real-time reachability analysis. In *2014 IEEE/RSJ International Conference on Intelligent Robots and Systems*, pages 2202–2208. IEEE, 2014.

51 Vicenç Rubies-Royo, David Fridovich-Keil, Sylvia Herbert, and Claire J Tomlin. A classification-based approach for approximate reachability. In *2019 International Conference on Robotics and Automation (ICRA)*, pages 7697–7704. IEEE, 2019.

52 Jerome Darbon, Gabriel P Langlois, and Tingwei Meng. Overcoming the curse of dimensionality for some Hamilton–Jacobi partial differential equations via neural network architectures. *Research in the Mathematical Sciences*, 7(3): 1–50, 2020.

53 KN Niarchos and John Lygeros. A neural approximation to continuous time reachability computations. In *Proceedings of the 45th IEEE Conference on Decision and Control*, pages 6313–6318. IEEE, 2006.

54 Badis Djeridane and John Lygeros. Neural approximation of pde solutions: an application to reachability computations. In *Proceedings of the 45th IEEE Conference on Decision and Control*, pages 3034–3039. IEEE, 2006.

55 George Em Karniadakis, Ioannis G Kevrekidis, Lu Lu, Paris Perdikaris, Sifan Wang, and Liu Yang. Physics-informed machine learning. *Nature Reviews Physics*, 3(6): 422–440, 2021.

56 Vincent Sitzmann, Julien NP Martel, Alexander W Bergman, David B Lindell, and Gordon Wetzstein. Implicit neural representations with periodic activation functions. *arXiv preprint arXiv:2006.09661*, 2020.

57 Aparna Dhinakaran, Mo Chen, Glen Chou, Jennifer C Shih, and Claire J Tomlin. A hybrid framework for multi-vehicle collision avoidance. In 2017 IEEE 56th Annual Conference on Decision and Control (CDC), pages 2979–2984. IEEE, 2017.

58 John N Tsitsiklis. Asynchronous stochastic approximation and Q-learning. *Machine Learning*, 16(3): 185–202, 1994. https://doi.org/10.1007/BF00993306.

59 Xu Wang, Sen Wang, Xingxing Liang, Dawei Zhao, Jincai Huang, Xin Xu, Bin Dai, and Qiguang Miao. Deep reinforcement learning: a survey. *IEEE Transactions on Neural Networks and Learning Systems*, 35(4): 5064–5078, 2024. https://doi.org/10.1109/TNNLS.2022.3207346.

60 Richard S Sutton, Andrew G Barto, and Ronald J Williams. Reinforcement learning is direct adaptive optimal control. *IEEE Control Systems Magazine*, 12(2): 19–22, 1992. https://doi.org/10.1109/37.126844.

61 Jaime F Fisac, Neil F Lugovoy, Vicenç Rubies-Royo, Shromona Ghosh, and Claire J Tomlin. Bridging Hamilton–Jacobi safety analysis and reinforcement learning. In *2019 International Conference on Robotics and Automation (ICRA)*, pages 8550–8556. IEEE, 2019.

62 Anayo K. Akametalu, Shromona Ghosh, Jaime F. Fisac, Vicenc Rubies-Royo, and Claire J. Tomlin. A minimum discounted reward Hamilton–Jacobi formulation for computing reachable sets. *IEEE Transactions on Automatic Control*, 69(2): 1097–1103, 2024. https://doi.org/10.1109/TAC.2023.3327159.

63 Homanga Bharadhwaj, Aviral Kumar, Nicholas Rhinehart, Sergey Levine, Florian Shkurti, and Animesh Garg. Conservative safety critics for exploration. In *International Conference on Learning Representations*, 2020.

64 Brijen Thananjeyan, Ashwin Balakrishna, Suraj Nair, Michael Luo, Krishnan Srinivasan, Minho Hwang, Joseph E Gonzalez, Julian Ibarz, Chelsea Finn, and Ken Goldberg. Recovery RL: safe reinforcement learning with learned recovery zones. *IEEE Robotics and Automation Letters*, 6(3): 4915–4922, 2021. https://doi.org/10.1109/LRA.2021.3070252.

65 Kai-Chieh Hsu, Allen Z Ren, Duy P Nguyen, Anirudha Majumdar, and Jaime F Fisac. Sim-to-Lab-to-Real: safe reinforcement learning with shielding and generalization guarantees. *Artificial Intelligence*, 314(C):103811, 2023c. https://doi.org/10.1016/j.artint.2022.103811.

66 David Silver, Thomas Hubert, Julian Schrittwieser, Ioannis Antonoglou, Matthew Lai, Arthur Guez, Marc Lanctot, Laurent Sifre, Dharshan Kumaran, Thore Graepel, et al. A general reinforcement learning algorithm that masters chess, shogi, and Go through self-play. *Science*, 362(6419): 1140–1144, 2018. https://doi.org/10.1126/science.aar6404.

67 Oriol Vinyals, Igor Babuschkin, Wojciech M Czarnecki, Michaël Mathieu, Andrew Dudzik, Junyoung Chung, David H Choi, Richard Powell, Timo Ewalds, Petko Georgiev, et al. Grandmaster level in StarCraft II using multi-agent reinforcement learning. *Nature*, 575(7782): 350–354, 2019. https://doi.org/10.1038/s41586-019-1724-z.

68 Eric Mazumdar, Lillian J Ratliff, Michael I Jordan, and S Shankar Sastry. Policy-gradient algorithms have no guarantees of convergence in linear quadratic games. In *Proceedings of the 19th International Conference on Autonomous Agents and MultiAgent Systems*, AAMAS '20, pages 860–868, Richland, SC, 2020. International Foundation for Autonomous Agents and Multiagent Systems.

69 Benjamin Chasnov, Lillian Ratliff, Eric Mazumdar, and Samuel Burden. Convergence analysis of gradient-based learning in continuous games. In *Proceedings of the 35th Uncertainty in Artificial Intelligence Conference*, pages 935–944. PMLR, 2020.

70 Tanner Fiez and Lillian J Ratliff. Local convergence analysis of gradient descent ascent with finite timescale separation. In *Proceedings of the International Conference on Learning Representations*, 2021.

71 Tanner Fiez, Lillian Ratliff, Eric Mazumdar, Evan Faulkner, and Adhyyan Narang. Global convergence to local minmax equilibrium in classes of nonconvex zero-sum games. In *Advances in Neural Information Processing Systems (NeurIPS)*, volume 34, pages 29049–29063. Curran Associates, Inc., 2021.

72 Kai-Chieh Hsu, Vicenç Rubies-Royo, Claire J Tomlin, and Jaime F Fisac. Safety and liveness guarantees through reach-avoid reinforcement learning. In *Robotics: Science and Systems XVII*. Robotics: Science and Systems Foundation, 2021. https://doi.org/10.15607/RSS.2021.XVII.077.

73 Kai-Chieh Hsu, Duy Phuong Nguyen, and Jaime Fernàndez Fisac. ISAACS: Iterative soft adversarial actor-critic for safety. In *Proceedings of the 5th Annual Learning for Dynamics and Control Conference*, pages 90–103. PMLR, 2023b.

74 Tuomas Haarnoja, Aurick Zhou, Pieter Abbeel, and Sergey Levine. Soft actor-critic: off-policy maximum entropy deep reinforcement learning with a stochastic actor. In *International Conference on Machine Learning*, pages 1861–1870, 2018.

75 Justin Wang, Haimin Hu, Duy P Nguyen, and Jaime Fernández Fisac. MAGICS: Adversarial RL with minimax actors guided by implicit critic Stackelberg for convergent neural synthesis of robot safety. In *Workshop on the Algorithmic Foundations of Robotics (WAFR)*, 2024a.

76 Liyuan Zheng, Tanner Fiez, Zane Alumbaugh, Benjamin Chasnov, and Lillian J Ratliff. Stackelberg actor-critic: game-theoretic reinforcement learning algorithms. In *Proceedings of the AAAI Conference on Artificial Intelligence*, volume 36, pages 9217–9224, 2022.

77 Duy P Nguyen, Kai-Chieh Hsu, Wenhao Yu, Jie Tan, and Jaime F Fisac. Gameplay filters: robust zero-shot safety through adversarial imagination. Conference on Robot Learning (CoRL), 2024. https://doi.org/10.48550/arXiv.2405.00846.

78 Anastasios N Angelopoulos and Stephen Bates. Conformal prediction: a gentle introduction. *Foundations and Trends® in Machine Learning*, 16(4): 494–591, 2023. https://doi.org/10.1561/2200000101.

79 Javier Borquez, Kensuke Nakamura, and Somil Bansal. Parameter-conditioned reachable sets for updating safety assurances online. In *IEEE International Conference on Robotics and Automation (ICRA)*, 2023.

80 S. Herbert, M. Chen, S. Han, S. Bansal, J. Fisac, and C. J. Tomlin. Fastrack: a modular framework for fast and guaranteed safe motion planning. In *CDC*. IEEE, 2017.

81 Leonardo Santos, Zirui Li, Lasse Peters, Somil Bansal, and Andrea Bajcsy. Updating robot safety representations online from natural language feedback. IEEE International Conference on Robotics and Automation (ICRA), 2025.

82 Albert Lin, Shuang Peng, and Somil Bansal. One filter to deploy them all: robust safety for quadrupedal navigation in unknown environments. *arXiv preprint arXiv:2412.09989*, 2024.

83 Micah Carroll, Rohin Shah, Mark K. Ho, Tom Griffiths, Sanjit Seshia, Pieter Abbeel, and Anca Dragan. On the utility of learning about humans for human-AI coordination. *Advances in Neural Information Processing Systems 32*, 2019.

84 Bajcsy, Andrea, and Jaime F. Fisac. “Human-ai safety: A descendant of generative ai and control systems safety.” arXiv preprint arXiv:2405.09794 (2024).

85 Forrest Laine, Chih-Yuan Chiu, and Claire Tomlin. Eyes-closed safety kernels: Safety of autonomous systems under loss of observability. In *Robotics: Science and Systems XVI*. Robotics: Science and Systems Foundation, 2020. https://doi.org/10.15607/RSS.2020.XVI.096.

86 Zixu Zhang and Jaime F Fisac. Safe occlusion-aware autonomous driving via game-theoretic active perception. In *Robotics: Science and Systems XVII*. Robotics: Science and Systems Foundation, 2021. https://doi.org/10.15607/RSS.2021.XVII.066.

87 Haimin Hu, Zixu Zhang, Kensuke Nakamura, Andrea Bajcsy, and Jaime Fernández Fisac. Deception game: closing the safety-learning loop in interactive robot autonomy. In *Conference on Robot Learning (CoRL)*, 2023.

6

Controllable Generation via Locally Constrained Resampling

Kareem Ahmed,[1] Kai-Wei Chang,[2] and Guy Van den Broeck[2]*

[1] *Department of Computer Science, University of California, Irvine, California, USA*
[2] *Department of Computer Science, University of California, Los Angeles, California, USA*

*Corresponding Author: ahmedky@uci.edu

6.1 Introduction

The advent of large language models (LLMs) has brought about a paradigm shift toward generating sequences of tokens that jointly constitute the desired output. Such multi-token outputs exhibit an amount of structure to them: in free-form generation, the model is expected to generate coherent paragraphs; in question answering, it is expected to provide answers to the posed questions; and in summarization, it is expected to condense lengthy documents into concise summaries. And while current LLMs are remarkably apt at generating fluent sentences, there is a need for generations that go beyond that, exhibiting more intricate structure [1]. Such structure includes, e.g., API calls and code snippets [2], JSON schemas [3], logical puzzles [4, 5], all of which LLMs struggle with Sun et al. [6].

Consequently, several approaches to constraining LLMs were developed, all bolstering a similar underlying idea: at every generation step, *greedily* mask the LLM outputs that could lead to the constraint being violated. That is, the "defacto" recipe [7–10] for applying constraints to LLMs consists of the following:

1. Based on the current state of the constraint, build a mask of valid next tokens.
2. Mask out logits for invalid tokens, normalize, and sample.
3. Based on the sampled token, update the constraint state for the next time step.

Neurosymbolic AI: Foundations and Applications, First Edition. Edited by Alvaro Velasquez et al.

The above recipe is limited in a number of ways. First, the masking process is *myopic* [11], as the constraint is enforced *greedily* on a per-token basis rather than jointly across the entire generation. This is as opposed to *Bayesian* conditioning, where we consider the entire sequence. Second, the constraint specification language is typically regular expressions, which can be significantly more verbose than their target compilation forms, deterministic finite automata (DFAs) [10, 12, 13]. Lastly, there exists classes of constraints that can only be described by DFAs whose size grows exponentially w.r.t. the constraint.

In this work, we develop an approach that departs from the previously established recipe for constraining LLMs, tackling all the aforementioned shortcomings in the process. Our approach starts with the observation that *an LLM sample induces a local, factorized distribution* $\tilde{p}$. We use a tractable compilation form, *constraint circuits* [14], that subsume DFAs on bounded-length strings while being more expressive and efficient [15]. That is, there are classes of functions that we can represent using constraint circuits that we could not otherwise as efficiently represent using DFAs [16]. Such constraint circuits can be specified as Boolean python functions, alleviating the need for writing regular expressions or other domain specific languages. We show that we can leverage logical circuits to tractably condition $\tilde{p}$, drawing samples that are biased yet provably satisfy the constraint. Sampling from the LLM subject to a constraint α then entails conditioning $\tilde{p}$ on α, drawing biased samples from $\tilde{p}(\cdot \mid \alpha)$, which we debias by reweighing them proportionally to their probability under the LLM and resampling. The samples are distributed according to the conditional LLM distribution and satisfy the constraint. An overview of our approach can be seen in Figure 6.1.

We start our evaluation by testing our approach on the toy task of predicting shortest paths under an autoregressive model, and observe a significant improvement upon the baseline performance. Next, we evaluate our approach on the task of LLM detoxification where we show that, by virtue of its probabilistic nature, by simply disallowing a list of toxic expressions, our approach is able to steer the model away from toxic generations, outperforming previous approaches to detoxification. Lastly, we show our approach achieves a perfect accuracy on Sudoku compared to an almost 26% and 45% accuracy achieved by Gemini 1.5 Flash and GPT4-o models, respectively.

6.2 Background

6.2.1 Notation and Preliminaries

We write uppercase letters (X, Y) for Boolean variables and lowercase letters (x, y) for their instantiation ($Y = 0$ or $Y = 1$). Sets of variables are written in bold uppercase ($\mathbf{X}$, $\mathbf{Y}$), and their joint instantiation in bold lowercase ($\boldsymbol{x}$, $\boldsymbol{y}$). A literal is a

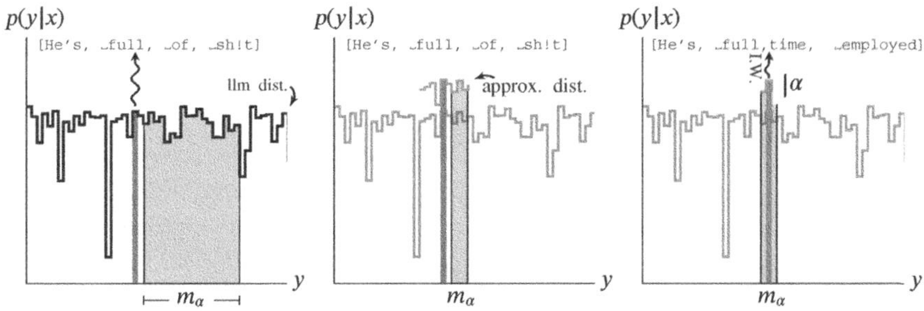

Figure 6.1 An illustration of our proposed approach. (left) An LLM induces a distribution over all possible sentences. Autoregressively sampling from the LLM distribution, we obtain a sentence (▇) $\tilde{y}$ = `[He's, _full, _of, _sh!t]`. This sentence $\tilde{y}$ violates a constraint α that disallows toxic words, including the word "`sh!t`". The subset of sentences that satisfy the constraint α (▇) are denoted by $\vdash m_\alpha \dashv$. (center) The sentence $\tilde{y}$ induces a local, tractable approximation of the true distribution centered around $\tilde{y}$. (right) We can efficiently condition this tractable approximation on the constraint α, trimming away portions of its support that do not satisfy the constraint. Sampling from the LLM distribution subject to the constraint α then corresponds to sampling from the conditional approximate distribution and adjusting the sample weights using importance weighting. This yields a sentence (▇) $\boldsymbol{y}$ = `[He's, _full, time, _employed]` that satisfies α.

variable (Y) or its negation ($\neg Y$). A logical sentence (α or β) is constructed from variables and logical connectives ($\wedge$, $\vee$, $\neg$, $\implies$) and is also called a (logical) formula or constraint. A state or world $\boldsymbol{y}$ is an instantiation to all variables $\mathbf{Y}$. A state $\boldsymbol{y}$ satisfies a constraint α, denoted $\boldsymbol{y} \models \alpha$, if the sentence evaluates to true in that world. A state $\boldsymbol{y}$ satisfying a constraint α is said to be a model of α. We denote by $m(\alpha)$ the set of α's models. Throughout this paper, in reference to DFAs, we limit our discussion to those defined on bounded-length inputs, which are equivalent to ordered binary decision diagrams, or OBDDs [17].

6.2.2 A Probability Distribution over Sentences

Let α be a logical constraint defined over Boolean variables $\mathbf{Y} = \{Y_{11}, \dots, Y_{nk}\}$, where n denotes the number of time steps in the sentence, and k denotes the size of the vocabulary, i.e., the number of possible tokens at each time step. An autoregressive model induces a probability distribution $p(\cdot)$ over all possible sentences $\boldsymbol{y}$. At every time step i, the autoregressive model ensures that exactly one token is predicted; i.e., exactly one Boolean variable $\{Y_{i1}, \dots, Y_{ik}\}$ can be set to true for each time step i. We will write $\boldsymbol{y}_i$ to denote that variable Y_{ij} is set to true in sentence $\boldsymbol{y}$. More precisely, we let $\boldsymbol{y}_i \in \{0, 1\}^k$ be the one-hot encoding of Y_{ij} being set to

1 among $\{Y_{i1}, \dots, Y_{ik}\}$. The probability assigned by the autoregressive model to a sentence $\boldsymbol{y}$ is then defined as

$$p(\boldsymbol{y}) = \prod_{i=1}^{n} p(\boldsymbol{y}_i \mid \boldsymbol{y}_{<i}), \tag{6.1}$$

where $\boldsymbol{y}_{<i}$ denotes the sentence prefix, $\boldsymbol{y}_1, \dots, \boldsymbol{y}_{i-1}$.

6.2.3 The State of Conditional Sampling

Sampling from an autoregressive distribution conditioned on a logical constraint α constitutes a major challenge: computing the *exact* conditional distribution $p(\boldsymbol{y} \mid \alpha) = \frac{p(\boldsymbol{y}, \alpha)}{p(\alpha)}$ is intractable even for the simplest constraints [18], e.g., asserting that the word "dog" appears at the end of the sentence. Intuitively, conditioning on α requires that we compute the marginal probability of the constraint $p(\alpha)$, in turn requiring that we enumerate all sentences ending with the word "dog."

The defacto approach has therefore been to *greedily* constrain the distribution, at every time step masking out logits that lead to generations that violate the constraint, followed by re-normalizing the conditional token distribution [7–10]. Let the conditioning of the constraint α on the prefix $\boldsymbol{y}_{<i}$, which we write as $\alpha_{|\boldsymbol{y}_{<i}}$, be a *subconstraint* defined on $\mathbf{Y}_{i:n}$ that results from setting the variables $\mathbf{Y}_{1:i-1}$ to their values in $\boldsymbol{y}_{<i}$. Semantically, $\alpha_{|\boldsymbol{y}_{<i}}$ denotes the set of $\boldsymbol{y}_{i:n}$ that, taken together with the prefix $\boldsymbol{y}_{<i}$, would satisfy the constraint. Moreover, let $\beta_i := \exists \boldsymbol{y}_{>i}\, \alpha_{|\boldsymbol{y}_{<i}}$ denote the set of tokens allowed at the ith position such that there exists some completion $\boldsymbol{y}_{>i}$ of the sentence that satisfies the constraint α, given the current prefix $\boldsymbol{y}_{<i}$. Then we can define the above greedy, or *myopic*, distribution as

$$p^{\text{myopic}}(\boldsymbol{y} \mid \alpha) \quad := \prod_{i=1}^{n} \frac{p(\boldsymbol{y}_i, \beta_i \mid \boldsymbol{y}_{<i})}{\sum_j p(y_{ij}, \beta_i \mid \boldsymbol{y}_{<i})} = \prod_{i=1}^{n} \frac{p(\boldsymbol{y}_i \mid \boldsymbol{y}_{<i}) [\![\boldsymbol{y}_i \models \beta_i]\!]}{\sum_j p(y_{ij} \mid \boldsymbol{y}_{<i}) [\![y_{ij} \models \beta_i]\!]},$$

Of note here is that since the approximate distribution is modeling the joint probability of the sentence and the constraint, in principle, the logical reasoning is sound, i.e., the constraint is guaranteed to hold. Rather, the shortcoming is in the way the *probabilistic reasoning* is performed: instead of normalizing the joint distribution by the marginal probability of the constraint, we are performing it token-wise steering us toward sampling sequences that are locally likely rather than globally likely. To see this, consider an LLM trained to output a uniform distribution over binary strings of length 4. We have $2^4 = 16$ possible generations, each with probability $1/16$. Assume we are given a constraint specifying that if a generation starts with 0, then all subsequent characters need to be 0. Conditioned on the constraint, the possible generations are $\{0000, 1000, 1001, 1010, 1011, 1100, 1101, 1110, 1111\}$, and the LLM is expected to generate each string with an equal probability of 1/9. Since the LLM generates each of the 16 possible strings with equal probability, it must generate a string starting with 0 or 1 with equal probability, and so greedy constrained decoding mistakenly generates the string 0000 50% of the time [19].

The second issue lies with the logical constraint along two different axes. First is the lack of conciseness of the constraint specification language. The most common language for specifying constraints is regular expressions, which can be significantly more verbose [10, 12, 13] compared to the equivalent logical form. This is due to the inability to reference and reuse sub-expressions without introducing additional features such as lookaround operations, which can cause an exponential blowup in the size of the target representations [20], or backreferences that allow us to describe non-regular languages at the expense of an exponential runtime due to backtracking. Second is the lack of succinctness of the target representation. All of the current approaches compile the specified regular expressions into DFAs. DFAs represent Boolean functions by recursively performing Shannon-decomposition on the function: disjointing the value of the sub-function with the value of the current variable chosen to be true and false, respectively. Consequently, for many constraints of interest, the size of DFA can grow prohibitively. It turns out that there exists another class of target representation that subsume DFAs on bounded-length strings: at every step in the function decomposition we can branch not only on the value of a single variable, but rather that of an *entire sentence* [14]. This class of target representations, which we shall henceforth denote as *constraint circuits* are not only more succinct than DFAs in practice but are provably exponentially more succinct: there are classes of functions with exponentially sized DFAs but polynomially sized constraint circuits [16].

6.3 Locally Constrained Resampling: A Tale of Two Distributions

We depart from the established recipe for conditional autoregressive sampling, providing a treatment of the problem from first principles that tackles all of the shortcomings detailed above. The crux of our approach is the idea that we can approximate the intractable autoregressive distribution $p(\boldsymbol{y})$ using a local, tractable distribution $\tilde{p}(\boldsymbol{y})$. The distribution $\tilde{p}(\boldsymbol{y})$ is amenable to exact and efficient probabilistic reasoning, allowing us to efficiently condition on the constraint α and draw samples from the distribution $\tilde{p}(\boldsymbol{y} \mid \alpha)$. We can transform the biased samples drawn from $\tilde{p}(\boldsymbol{y} \mid \alpha)$ into samples from $p(\boldsymbol{y} \mid \alpha)$ by considering the discrepancy between the probability of the sample under the true distribution and the approximate distribution. More formally, we wish to draw samples from

$$p(\boldsymbol{y} \mid \alpha) = \frac{p(\boldsymbol{y}, \alpha)}{p(\alpha)}, \tag{6.2}$$

which is intractable. Instead, we design a tractable proposal distribution q such that $q(\boldsymbol{y}) > 0$ whenever $p(\boldsymbol{y} \mid \alpha) > 0$. We associate with a *constrained sample* $\boldsymbol{y}$ an *unconstrained sample* $\tilde{\boldsymbol{y}}$, where $\boldsymbol{y}$ can be understood as a *projection* of $\tilde{\boldsymbol{y}}$ onto α s.t. $\boldsymbol{y} \models \alpha$. We define our proposal as

$$q(\boldsymbol{y}) = \sum_{\tilde{\boldsymbol{y}}} p(\tilde{\boldsymbol{y}}) \cdot p_{\tilde{\boldsymbol{y}}}(\boldsymbol{y} \mid \alpha), \tag{6.3}$$

where $p(\tilde{\boldsymbol{y}})$ is the autoregressive distribution, and $p_{\tilde{\boldsymbol{y}}}(\boldsymbol{y} \mid \alpha)$ is a distribution over projections $\boldsymbol{y}$ of the unconstrained $\tilde{\boldsymbol{y}}$ given the constraint α. The above definition outlines a two-step procedure for sampling a sentence $\boldsymbol{y}$ that satisfies a given constraint α. We sample a sentence $\tilde{\boldsymbol{y}}$ autoregressively from $p(\tilde{\boldsymbol{y}})$, followed by sampling $\boldsymbol{y}$ from the distribution conditioned on $\tilde{\boldsymbol{y}}$ and the constraint α, $p_{\tilde{\boldsymbol{y}}}(\boldsymbol{y} \mid \alpha)$. By incorporating the autoregressive distribution $p(\tilde{\boldsymbol{y}})$, we ensure that we can potentially generate any sentence. $p_{\tilde{\boldsymbol{y}}}(\boldsymbol{y} \mid \alpha)$ then refines $\tilde{\boldsymbol{y}}$ by *projecting* it to satisfy the constraint α. It is straightforward to sample from $p(\tilde{\boldsymbol{y}})$, but what exactly is $p_{\tilde{\boldsymbol{y}}}(\boldsymbol{y})$, and how do we condition it on α? Moreover, a proposal distribution typically implies biased samples; how do we correct for this bias?

6.3.1 Inducing a Local Tractable Distribution

Our goal is to design a probability distribution $p_{\tilde{\boldsymbol{y}}}(\boldsymbol{y} \mid \alpha)$ that is first, tractable for conditioning on the constraint α and likelihood evaluation, and second, assigns high probability mass to sentences that are close to the model sample y and low probability mass to sentences that are far away, thereby providing a sample-efficient approximation of the true distribution [21].

As noted earlier, the hardness of computing the conditional probability distribution in Eq. (6.2) is in large part due to the autoregressive nature of the LLM distribution. A logical constraint might have exponentially many solutions, yet lend itself to reusing of solutions to sub-problems, and therefore a tractable computation of the normalizing constant, the denominator in Eq. (6.2). An example being the n choose k constraint [22], where the conditional distribution can be computed in quadratic time under the fully factorized distribution, despite having combinatorially many solutions. Moving away from fully factorized distribution and toward autoregressive distributions, however, requires that we enumerate all sentences, even for very simple constraints.

To sidestep the hardness of the autoregressive distribution, we attempt to move toward the tractability of fully factorized distributions, while retaining as much of the contextual information. To that end, we consider the *pseudolikelihood* $\tilde{p}(\cdot)$ of a sentence $\tilde{\boldsymbol{y}}$ [23, 24], i.e.,

$$p(\tilde{\boldsymbol{y}}) \approx \tilde{p}(\tilde{\boldsymbol{y}}) := \prod_{i} p(\tilde{\boldsymbol{y}}_i \mid \tilde{\boldsymbol{y}}_{-i}), \tag{6.4}$$

where $\tilde{\boldsymbol{y}}_{-i}$ denotes $\tilde{\boldsymbol{y}}_1, \dots, \tilde{\boldsymbol{y}}_{i-1}, \tilde{\boldsymbol{y}}_{i+1}, \dots, \tilde{\boldsymbol{y}}_n$. Unfortunately, Eq. (6.4) would still not ensure the tractability of Eq. (6.2] since different solutions depend on different sets of conditionals. Instead, we define the pseudolikelihood of a sentence $\boldsymbol{y}$ *in the neighborhood of a sentence* $\tilde{\boldsymbol{y}}$

$$p_{\tilde{\boldsymbol{y}}}(\boldsymbol{y}) := \prod_i p(\boldsymbol{y}_i \mid \tilde{\boldsymbol{y}}_{-i}) \tag{6.5}$$

which can be understood as the *contextualized probability* of a sentence $\boldsymbol{y}$ given the context $\tilde{\boldsymbol{y}}$. We will next show how, given the structure of the contextualized pseudolikelihood distribution, we are able to efficiently condition it on a constraint α. Furthermore, [24] have shown the contextualized pseudolikelihood distribution to be a local, high-fidelity approximation of the LLM distribution. That is, the distribution has low entropy, considering only assignments centered around the model sample, while at the same time having low KL-divergence and is therefore faithful to the true distribution in the neighborhood of the model sample.

6.3.2 Tractable Operations via Compilation

We appeal to knowledge compilation, a class of methods that transform, or *compile*, a logical constraint into a tractable target form which represents functions as parameterized computational graphs, or *circuits*. Knowledge compilers allow us to programmatically specify constraints as Python [25] or PyTorch functions [26] from which they construct circuits. By enforcing certain structural properties on the compiled circuits, we can enable the tractable computation of corresponding classes of probabilistic queries over the encoded functions. As such, circuits provide a language for both constructing and reasoning about tractable representations. An example of a logical constraint specified as a PyTorch function, which gets compiled into a constraint circuit, is shown in the bottom left of Figure 6.2 with the corresponding circuit in Figure 6.2, right.

Formally, a *logical circuit* is a directed, acyclic computational graph representing a logical formula over variables $\mathbf{X}$. Each node n in the DAG encodes a logical subformula, denoted $[n]$. Each inner node in the graph is an AND or an OR gate, and each leaf node encodes a Boolean literal (Y or $\neg Y$). We denote by $\mathsf{in}(n)$ the set of a node n's children. We associate with every node n a *scope* function $\phi(\cdot)$ such that $\phi(n) \subseteq X$ evaluates to the subset of variables the subfunction at n is defined over.

A circuit is *decomposable* if inputs of every AND gate depend on disjoint sets of variables i.e., for $\alpha = \beta \wedge \gamma$, $\mathsf{vars}(\beta) \cap \mathsf{vars}(\gamma) = \emptyset$. A circuit is said to be *structured-decomposable* if every AND gate is decomposable, and any pair of AND gates sharing the same scope decompose in the same way. Intuitively, decomposable AND gates encode local factorizations over variables of the function. We assume that decomposable AND gates always have two inputs, a condition enforceable on any circuit for a polynomial size increase [27, 28].

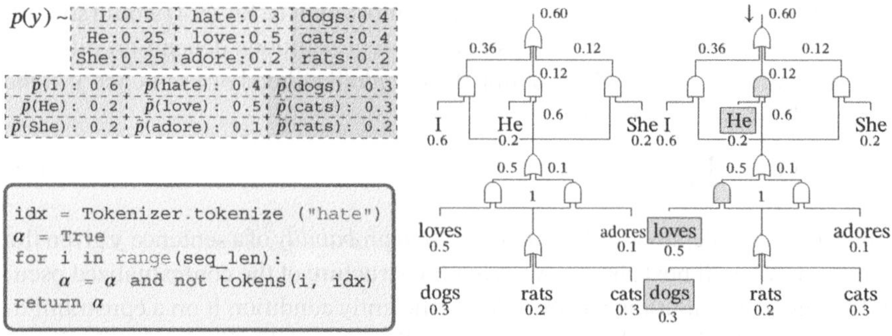

Figure 6.2 Constructing and sampling the proposal distribution. (Top left) We start by sampling a sentence $\tilde{\boldsymbol{y}}$ from the model p. Our goal is to compute the full conditional probability of every word in the vocab i.e., $\tilde{p}(\tilde{y}_{ij}) := p(\tilde{y}_{ij} \mid \tilde{\boldsymbol{y}}_{-i})$. We start by expanding the sampled sentence $\tilde{\boldsymbol{y}}$, including all sentences that are a Hamming distance of 1 away from the sample $\boldsymbol{y}$. We proceed by (batch) evaluating the samples through the model, obtaining the joint probability of each sample. We then normalize along each column, obtaining the conditionals $p(\tilde{y}_{ij})$. (Bottom left) We can easily specify a logical constraint that prevents the word "hate" from appearing as a simple python function that gets compiled in the constraint circuit on the right. (Center) A logical circuit encoding constraint ¬hates, with a simplified vocab is shown in the figure. To construct the distribution $p_{\tilde{\boldsymbol{y}}}(\boldsymbol{y} \mid \alpha)$, we feed the computed contextual probabilities at the corresponding literals. We push the probabilities upwards, taking products at AND nodes and sums at OR nodes. This induces a distribution $p_{\tilde{\boldsymbol{y}}}(\boldsymbol{y} \mid \alpha)$. (Right) To sample from this distribution, we start at the root of the circuit, sampling a child of every OR gate according to the logits of the distribution, and concatenating at every AND gate. We sample the sentence "He loves dogs" satisfying the constraint.

A second useful property is *smoothness*. A circuit is said to be *smooth* if the children of every OR gate depend on the same set of variables, i.e., for $\alpha = \bigvee_i \beta_i$, we have that $\text{vars}(\beta_i) = \text{vars}(\beta_j)\ \forall i, j$. Decomposability and smoothness are sufficient and necessary for tractable integration over arbitrary sets of variables in a single pass, as they allow larger integrals to decompose into smaller ones.

Further, a circuit is said to be *deterministic* if, for any input, at most one child of every OR node has a non-zero output, i.e., for $\alpha = \bigvee_i \beta_i$, we have that $\beta_i \wedge \beta_j = \bot$ for all $i \neq j$. Similar to decomposability, determinism induces a recursive partitioning of the function, but over the support of the function. We consider a stronger form of determinism, *strong determinism*. A circuit is said to be *strongly deterministic* if, for every OR node, $\alpha = \bigvee_i (\beta_i \wedge \gamma_i)$, the β_i's are mutually exclusive i.e., $\beta_i \wedge \beta_j = \bot$ for any $i \neq j$. Ensuring they are exhaustive i.e., $\bigvee_i \beta_i = \top$, with structured decomposability, we recover sentential decision diagrams [14], or *constraint circuits*.

Algorithm 1 Compute $p_y(\tilde{\boldsymbol{y}} \mid \alpha)$

Input: Constraint α, LLM distribution $p(\cdot)$
Output: $p_{\tilde{\boldsymbol{y}}}(\cdot \mid \alpha)$ defined in Eq. (6.5)
$\tilde{\boldsymbol{y}} \sim p(\cdot)$
$\triangleright$ Expand the batch to contain all perturbations
$\triangleright$ of $\boldsymbol{y}$ that are a Hamming distance of 1 away
$\tilde{\boldsymbol{y}} = \tilde{\boldsymbol{y}}$.`expand`(n, vocab)
$\tilde{\boldsymbol{y}}$[:, `range(n)`, :, `range(n)`] = `range(vocab)`
$\triangleright$ Evaluate expanded samples through model
$\log p = p(\tilde{\boldsymbol{y}})$.`log_softmax(dim = -1)`
$\triangleright$ Compute $\log \tilde{p}_\theta[i][j] = \log p_\theta(\boldsymbol{y}_j | \boldsymbol{y}_{-j})$
$\log \tilde{p} = \log p - \log p$. `logsumexp(dim = -1)`
$\triangleright$ A vector of conditional marginals $\tilde{p}_{\tilde{\boldsymbol{y}}}(y_{ij} \mid \alpha)$
`return` $p_{\tilde{\boldsymbol{y}}}(\cdot \mid \alpha)$

Algorithm 2 Locally Constrained Resampling

Input: Constraint α, LLM distribution $p(\cdot)$
Output: $\boldsymbol{y}$ drawn approximately from $p(\boldsymbol{y} \mid \alpha)$
$\triangleright$ Sample $\boldsymbol{y}$ and $\tilde{\boldsymbol{y}}$ from $p(\boldsymbol{y})$ and $p_y(\tilde{\boldsymbol{y}} \mid \alpha)$ resp.
$\tilde{\boldsymbol{y}} \sim p(\cdot)$
$\boldsymbol{y} \sim p_{\tilde{\boldsymbol{y}}}(\cdot \mid \alpha)$ $\triangleright$ From Algorithm 1
$\triangleright$ Compute importance weights
`q_w` $= p(\tilde{\boldsymbol{y}}) \cdot p_{\tilde{\boldsymbol{y}}}(\boldsymbol{y} \mid \alpha)$
`p_w` $= p(\boldsymbol{y}) \cdot [\![$`canonize`$(\boldsymbol{y}) \models \alpha]\!] \cdot p_y(\tilde{\boldsymbol{y}})$
`w = p_w/q_w`
$\triangleright$ Resample distribution according to weights
$p^* =$ `Categorical(weights = w)`
`return` p^*`.sample()`

Given a constraint circuit c_α that encodes a logical constraint α, we can compute the pseudolikelihood $\tilde{q}(\alpha)$ by feeding the probability of each literal at the corresponding leaf node and evaluating the circuit upwards, taking sums at OR gates and products at AND gates. This defines a distribution $p_y(\tilde{y} \mid \alpha)$. To sample from the distribution, starting from the root node, we trace the circuit top-down, sampling a child at every OR-gate encountered. Figure 6.2 (center) shows an example of computing such a distribution, and Figure 6.2 (right) demonstrates the process of sampling from it.

6.3.3 Intermezzo: Constraint Circuits and DFAs

Constraint circuits can implement decisions of the form

$$\bigvee_{i=1}^{m} \beta_i(\mathbf{X}) \wedge \gamma_i(\mathbf{Y}), \tag{6.6}$$

at OR gates, where **X** and **Y** are disjoint *sets* of variables, as opposed to DFAs that are restricted to Binary (or Shannon) decisions and therefore boil down to very special decisions of the form

$$(\neg x \wedge \gamma_1(\mathbf{Y})) \vee (x \wedge \gamma_2(\mathbf{Y}))$$

where the variable X is not in the variable set **Y**. Therefore, constraint circuits are exponentially more succinct than DFAs, i.e., there are families of functions can only be represented by a exponentially sized DFAs, but have a polynomially sized constraint circuit [16]. Barring such families of functions, constraint circuits are also empirically more succinct than DFAs [29]. In practice, this also allows us to construct shallower (i.e., less layers) and wider (i.e., units per layer) constraint circuits that are more amenable to GPU parallelization [30], therefore exhibit a much lower vectorized computational complexity [22].

6.3.4 Correcting Sample Bias: Importance Sampling... and Resampling

We have now sampled $\boldsymbol{y}$ from our proposal distribution $q(\boldsymbol{y})$, where $\boldsymbol{y}$ is a projection of some latent unconstrained sample $\tilde{\boldsymbol{y}}$, and satisfies the constraint α. However, our proposal distribution $q(\boldsymbol{y})$ might not align perfectly with our target distribution $p(\boldsymbol{y} \mid \alpha)$. We therefore need to account for the mismatch between the two distributions, which we can do by defining importance weights that are a function of the original $\boldsymbol{y}$ and its projection $\tilde{\boldsymbol{y}}$. We start by defining the true augmented distribution

$$p(\boldsymbol{y} \mid \alpha) \propto \sum_{\tilde{\boldsymbol{y}}} p(\boldsymbol{y}, \alpha) \cdot p_{\boldsymbol{y}}(\tilde{\boldsymbol{y}}). \tag{6.7}$$

This factorization reflects the process of first generating a constrained sentence $\boldsymbol{y}$, and marginalizing over all the unconstrained sentences $\tilde{\boldsymbol{y}}$ that could have given rise to $\boldsymbol{y}$ and can therefore be thought of as reversing the proposal distribution. We calculate the self-normalized importance weights

$$w = \frac{p(\boldsymbol{y}, \alpha) \cdot p_{\boldsymbol{y}}(\tilde{\boldsymbol{y}})}{p(\tilde{\boldsymbol{y}}) \cdot p_{\tilde{\boldsymbol{y}}}(\boldsymbol{y} \mid \alpha)} \tag{6.8}$$

These weights quantify the discrepancy between the proposal and target distributions, allowing us to correct for the biased sampling. Note, however, that the importance sampling does not generate samples from the target distribution $p(\boldsymbol{y} \mid \alpha)$, only a set of weighted particles. Rather, to transform our weighted particles into samples drawn from $p(\boldsymbol{y} \mid \alpha)$, we need to apply a resampling step according to the importance weights. That is, given particles $\boldsymbol{s}_i$ with their corresponding importance weights w_i, if we resample $\boldsymbol{s}_i$ with replacement from $\{\boldsymbol{s}_1, \ldots, \boldsymbol{s}_n\}$ with probabilities proportional to the importance weights i.e.,

$$p^*(\boldsymbol{s}_i) = \frac{w_i}{\sum_{j=1}^{n} w_j}$$

then $\boldsymbol{s}_i$ is drawn from the true distribution in the limit of a large sample size n. Our full algorithm is shown in Algorithm 2, and follows PyTorch syntax [31]. One thing to note is the use of the `canonize` function on line 6 in Algorithm 2, where `canonize` returns the *canonical* tokenization of an expression [32]. This ensures that, e.g., in the case of language detoxification, we are banning all the possible ways of generating a given expression.[1] We can now prove that Algorithm 2 is guaranteed to return samples that satisfy the constraint α. Our algorithm is implemented in log-space to preserve numerical stability.

Theorem 6.1: *Locally Constrained Resampling returns a sample $\boldsymbol{y} \models \alpha$.*

Proof. Let $\boldsymbol{y} = (y_1, \ldots, y_n)$ denote a string. Let vocabulary $\mathcal{V}$ denote a set of subwords, or *tokens*. A *tokenization* of a string $\boldsymbol{y}$ w.r.t. a vocabulary $\mathcal{V}$ is a sequence of tokens $\boldsymbol{v} = (v_1, \ldots, v_n)$, such that each $v_i \in \mathcal{V}$ and the concatenation of all tokens v_i constitutes the string $\boldsymbol{y}$, i.e., $v_1 \circ \ldots \circ v_n = \boldsymbol{y}$.

An autoregressive distribution $p(\cdot)$ defines a conditional probability distribution over tokens, *inducing a distribution over tokenizations of a string* $\boldsymbol{y}$ [32]

$$p(\boldsymbol{v}, \boldsymbol{y}) = \begin{cases} \prod_{i=1}^{|\boldsymbol{v}|} p\left(v_i | v_1, \ldots, v_{i-1}\right) & \text{if } \boldsymbol{v} \models \boldsymbol{y}, \\ 0 & \text{otherwise,} \end{cases}$$

where $\boldsymbol{v} \models \boldsymbol{y}$ denotes that $\boldsymbol{v}$ is a tokenization of $\boldsymbol{y}$.

We start by showing that, if the canonical tokenization of a string $\boldsymbol{y}$ does not satisfy α, then Algorithm 2 precludes any non-canonical tokenizations of the string $\boldsymbol{y}$. To see that, observe that a non-canonical tokenization of a sentence $\boldsymbol{y}$ generated by Algorithm 2 is subsequently cast into a canonical tokenization by invoking the `canonize` function. It is then assigned an importance weight of zero, and therefore zero probability in the resampling distribution on line 9 in Algorithm 2. During the resampling step, the set of candidate samples are only those sampled from $p_{\boldsymbol{y}}(\cdot \mid \alpha)$.

1 This issue has received an amount of attention in the past https://github.com/huggingface/transformers/issues/17504

We will now show that we can always construct $p_y(\cdot \mid \alpha)$ given a constraint α defined over variables $\{Y_{11}, \dots, Y_{nk}\}$ and a contextualized psuedolikelihood distribution $\tilde{p}_y(\cdot)$. Recall from Section 6.3.1 that the contextualized pseudolikelihood distribution is fully factorized. We can therefore construct a deterministic and decomposable circuit representing the contextualized pseudolikelihood distribution where with a slight abuse of notation, we use $\tilde{p}_y(\cdot)$ to refer to both the distribution as well as its circuit representation. Such a construction proceeds by introducing a Bernoulli distribution unit for each variable, and connecting them using a singular product node.

Given a constraint α, we can compile it into a constraint circuit c_α. The simplest construction is as follows. Order the variables lexicographically. Alternate OR and AND nodes. An OR node branches on the current variable being true or false, and has two children: a left (right) AND node whose children are the positive (negative) literal and the subtree corresponding to substituting the positive (negative) literal into the constraint. Repeat the above process till exhausting all the variables.

Given a constraint circuit c_α and a deterministic and omnicompatible circuit [33] $\tilde{p}_y(\cdot)$, we can compute their product $\tilde{p}_y(\cdot, \alpha)$ in time $\mathcal{O}(|p||c|)$ by Theorem 3.2 in Vergari et al. [33]. The resulting circuit $\tilde{p}_y(\cdot, \alpha)$ can be normalized in time $\mathcal{O}(|\tilde{p}|)$ to obtain $\tilde{p}_y(\cdot \mid \alpha)$ by Proposition 2.1 in Vergari et al. [33]. ■

6.4 Related Work

There has been a long line of work tackling constrained generation with LLMs. One of the earlier approaches was to use search-based decoding algorithms, such as NeuroLogic Decoding [34, 35]. While these methods explicitly search for high-probability sequences that satisfy the constraint, they face scalability issues due to the exponential growth of the search space as the sequence length increases. Another set of techniques that include GeDi [36], FUDGE [37], and NADO [38] employ auxiliary neural classifiers to approximate the intractable conditional distribution, but do not guarantee that the constraint is satisfied and require that a classifier be trained for every new constraint type. Approximate inference methods attempt to approximate the intractable conditional distributions [39–41] but suffer from high variance and do not guarantee constraint satisfaction.

Recently, Outlines [9] and Guidance [8], and along similar lines SGLang [42], were proposed, also guaranteeing that the constraint is satisfied. Outlines employs a precompilation step where constraints specified in regular expressions are compiled into DFAs that are "indexed" to create a token-based overlay. This overlay guides the decoding process, ensuring adherence to the constraints. Koo et al. [10] recently recast the entire process in an automata-theoretic framework. Similar to Outlines, Guidance utilizes a trie to efficiently store and search through valid token continuations based on the grammar. This allows for dynamic vocabulary matching at each decoding step, offering flexibility potentially at the cost of impacting efficiency. These approaches are considered the "defacto" approaches for constrained generation.

More recently, GeLaTo [43] and subsequently CTRL-G [44] have utilized Hidden Markov Models (HMMs) to guide the generation from LLMs toward constraint satisfaction, but require training a new HMM for every target model. The very recently proposed ASAp [19] aims to debias the greedy approach through repeated sampling and discovery of mass assigned to non-grammatical completions, reducing each overapproximation to make it more accurate. While similar in intention, our approach relies on a closed-form tractable approximation of the target distribution to correct for the bias, avoiding the need to oversample the LLM.

Finally, some other approaches no longer predictively mask logits, but instead sample unconstrained continuations and reject invalid ones post-hoc. For example, PICARD [45] converts the top-k tokens to text and performs various levels of validation. While such approaches are very simple in principle, and in fact perform exact Bayesian conditioning, the number of samples required can be prohibitive, especially when the constraint requires selecting very low probability tokens.

6.5 Experimental Evaluation

We evaluate our approach, GEN-C on several tasks spanning a number of domains. We start by evaluating on Warcraft shortest-path finding, where we are given an image of a Warcraft tilemap and are tasked with *autoregressively* generating one of the potentially many minimum-cost paths between two end points conditioned on the map, where the cost is determined by the *underlying* cost of the tiles spanned by the path. We move on to evaluating on the classic, yet challenging, task of solving a 9×9 Sudoku puzzle where an LLM is presented with an incomplete Sudoku puzzle and asked to provide the solved puzzle without extraneous text. We also evaluate on the task of LLM detoxification. In this task, we are interested in the generations produced by an LLM when presented with a prompt input by the user. More specifically, we are interested not only in how good these models are at the modeling aspect, but also how *toxic* their outputs might be, a measure that includes sexual explicitness, identity attacks, and profanity, among others. Our goal in this task is then to shift the model's distribution away from toxic generations, and toward nontoxic ones, all while maintaining its original ability to model text. We believe this to be a timely and important problem due to the prevalence and widespread usage of LLMs coupled with the fact that previous work [46] has found non-negligible amounts of toxic, harmful, and abusive text in the corpora used to train LLMs. Experimental details, hardware specifications, and training details are provided in the appendix. The implementation of our approach will be made publicly available.

Warcraft Shortest Path: For this task, we follow the experimental setting set forth by Pogančić, et al. [47], where our training set consists of 10,000 terrain maps curated using Warcraft II tileset. Each map encodes a 12×12 grid superimposed on a Warcraft terrain map, where each vertex is weighted according to the cost of the tile, which in turn depends on type of terrain it represents e.g., earth has lower cost than water. These costs are *not* presented to the network. The task is then to generate a minimum-cost path from the upper left to the lower right vertices, where the cost of a path is defined as the sum of costs of the vertices visited by the edges along the path, and the minimum-cost path is not unique, i.e., there exists many correct paths with the minimum cost.

We use a CNN-LSTM model, where, presented with an image of a terrain map, we use a ResNet18 [48] to obtain a 128 image embedding, which is then passed on to an LSTM with a single layer, a hidden dim of size 512, and at every time step predicts the next edge in the path conditioned on the image embedding and previous edges. The constraint used in this task is that the predicted edges form a valid simple path from the upper left vertex to the lower right corner of the map.

As has been established in previous work [49–51], the accuracy of predicting individual labels is often a poor indicator of the performance of the neural network in neurosymbolic settings, where we are rather more interested in the accuracy of our predicted structured object *exactly* matching the groundtruth label, e.g., *is the prediction a shortest path?*, a metric that we denote "Exact" in our experiments, as well as the accuracy of predicting objects that are *consistent* with the constraint, e.g., *is the prediction a valid path?*, a metric denoted "Consistent." Our results are shown in Table 6.1. We compare against two different baselines: the baseline model trained on the task and *oversampling*, whereby we draw many samples conditioned on the input image and then resample this distribution, a variant of our approach where the proposal distribution is the autoregressive model itself. We find that our approach improves the exact match from 62.00% and 69.10% to 78.13% while guaranteeing the sampled sequences of edges constitute valid paths.

Sudoku: Next, we consider the task of predicting a solution to a given Sudoku puzzle. Here the task is, given a 9×9 partially filled grid of numbers to fill in the remaining cells such that the entries in each row, column, and 3×3 square are unique, i.e., each number from 1 to 9 appears exactly once. We use the dataset provided by Wang et al. [52], consisting of 10K Sudoku puzzles, split into 9K training examples, and 1K test samples, all puzzles having 10 missing entries.

Each LLM is prompted with the string "Give me the solution of the following Sudoku without any extra text or quotes" followed by the Sudoku Puzzle. As baselines, we used Gemini 1.5 Flash and GPT-4o mini, and post-process the responses to remove any extraneous text returned by the LLM. We compare the baselines against Llama3-8B constrained using our approach GEN-C, with the constraint

Table 6.1 Results on Warcraft.

Test accuracy %	**Exact**	**Consistent**
CNN-LSTM	62.00	76.60
+ oversampling	69.10%	84.50%
+ GEN-C (Ours)	**78.13%**	**100%**

Table 6.2 Results on Sudoku across 3 runs.

Test accuracy %	**Exact**	**Consistent**
Gemini 1.5 Flash	31.00% ± 4.19	31.00% ± 4.19
GPT-4o mini	40.90% ± 7.90	40.90% ± 7.90
GEN-C (Ours)	**100%**	**100%**

that the elements of every row, column and 3×3 square are unique. Our results are shown in Table 6.2. We see that whereas Gemini and GPT4o are able solve only 26% and 45% of the Sudoku puzzles, our approach consistently manages to recover the correct Sudoku Puzzle solution.

LLM detoxification: Lastly, we consider the task of LLM detoxification. That is, we investigate the effectiveness of logical constraints, enforced using GEN-C, at steering the model away from toxic prompted-generations. We choose a *very* simple constraint to be enforced by GEN-C throughout this task, namely, we ban any of a list of "bad words," including profanity, slurs, and swear words[2] from appearing as part of the model's generations. Similar to previous work [46, 53], we evaluate on the REALTOXICITYPROMPTS, a dataset of almost 100k prompts ranging from nontoxic, assigned a toxicity score of 0, to very toxic, assigned a toxicity score of 1. We focus on LLAMA3-8B [54] as a base model for detoxification. As customary [46, 53], we use Perspective API, an API for toxic language and hate speech detection, to score the toxicity of our predictions. It returns scores in the range 0–1.0, corresponding to nontoxic on the one end, and extremely toxic on the other. The toxicity score can be interpreted as the likelihood of the text being perceived as toxic and was shown to strongly correlate with human evaluations [53, 55].

We compare LLAMA3-8B against WORD BANNING, which for this simple constraint functions very similarly to Outlines [9] and Guidance [8]. It keeps track of the words generated so far, and prevents the banned expression from appearing by setting its probability to 0. Word Banning could therefore be seen of as a greedy approximation of what we might hope to achieve using GEN-C: intuitively, it might

2 List downloaded from here.

not be able to recover from generating a sentence associated with a toxic intent as a result of making greedy decision at every step of the generation. We report the *Expected Maximum Toxicity* and the *Toxicity Probability*. The *Expected Maximum Toxicity* measures the worst-case toxicity by calculating the maximum toxicity over 25 generations under the same prompt with different random seeds, and averaging the maximum toxicity over all prompts. This metric can be seen as a measure of how intensely offensive a generation is. *Toxicity Probability* estimates the empirical probability of generating toxic language by evaluating the fraction of times a toxic continuation is generated at least once over 25 generations with different random seeds for all prompts. This metric can be seen as a measure of how likely the LLM is to be offensive. Both of the above metrics are computed for the full set of prompts, only the toxic subset of the prompts, and only the nontoxic subset of the prompts. To understand the impact of detoxification, we evaluate the quality of the LLM generations by measuring the perplexity of the generations according to LLAMA3-70B averaged across 5 different runs. Our results are seen in Table 6.3.

We can see that word banning lowers the toxicity of the generations produced by LLAMA3-8B at a negligible decrease in perplexity. More specifically, we observe that it reduces the average worst-case toxicity as well as the probability of producing a toxic generation when prompted with nontoxic prompts by a modest 1%, but when prompted with nontoxic prompts the reduction in toxicity is much higher at 3% and almost 6% for the expected maximum toxicity and toxicity probability, respectively. Moving on to constraining our LLAMA3-8B with our approach, GEN-C attains the same perplexity as using word banning, but greatly reduces the toxicity of LLAMA3-8B, especially on toxic prompts, where it results in almost twice as much the reduction in toxicity affected by word banning, both in terms of the expected maximum toxicity as well as the toxicity probability.

Table 6.3 Evaluation of LLM toxicity and quality across different detoxification methods on Llama3-8b. Model toxicity is evaluated on the RealToxicityPrompts benchmark through Perspective API. **Full**, **Toxic** and **Nontoxic** refer to the full, toxic and nontoxic subsets of the prompts, respectively. **PPL** refers to the perplexity of Llama3-70B on the model generations using five different seeds. In line with Gehman et al. [46], Wang et al. [53], we characterize toxicity using two metrics: the **Expected Maximum Toxicity** over five generations, and the **Toxicity Probability** of a completion at least once over five generations.

Models	How toxic is the model? (↓)		How often is it toxic? (↓)		PPL (↓)
	to toxic	to nontoxic	to toxic	to nontoxic	
LLAMA3-8B	0.43	0.20	38.30%	7.60%	14.45
+ Greedy Decoding	0.40	**0.19**	32.43%	6.93%	**14.50**
+ GEN-C *(ours)*	**0.37**	**0.19**	**28.00%**	**6.35%**	**14.50**

6.6 Conclusion and Future Work

We proposed a new approach for constraining LLMs, which we called GEN-C. Given a logical constraint, GEN-C guarantees that an autoregressive model's generations satisfy the constraint. GEN-C is probabilistically sound, while providing a concise constraint specification language as well as an exponentially more succinct compilation form compared to current defacto approaches to controlled generation. We have showed that GEN-C can be applied to autoregressive models such as LSTMs as well as large-scale LLMs, outperforming the baselines on the tasks of minimum-cost paths prediction, language as well as solving Sudoku puzzles, where we achieved a perfect accuracy, beating both GPT-4o and Gemini 1.5 by a large margin. We have also shown that by virtue of its probabilistic nature, GEN-C is able to outperform current approaches for constrained generation on LLM detoxification using only a list of toxic expressions as a constraint, relying on probabilistic inference.

We envision extending and building upon GEN-C in a multitude of ways. First, on the systems side, since GEN-C extensively uses the language of tractable circuits, we plan on a tight integration with circuit libraries, such as pyjuice [30] to greatly improve the efficiency of our approach, as well as open the door for many potentially interesting probabilistic queries. Second, we hope to explore more applications of constrained generation, with one alluring possibility being the use of constraints to improve the factual accuracy of current LLMs.

Appendix A Controllable Generation via Locally Constrained Resampling

A.1 Language Detoxification

The experiments were run on a server with an AMD EPYC 7313P 16-Core Processor @ 3.7GHz, 3 NVIDIA RTX A6000, and 252 GB RAM. Our LLM detoxification experiments utilized both GPUs using the Huggingface Accelerate [56] library.

In order to construct our constraint, we start with the list of bad words[3] and their space-prefixed variants.[4] We then tokenize this list of augment bad words, yielding 871 unique possibly bad tokens (some tokens are only bad when considered in context with other tokens), in addition to an extra catch-all good token to which remaining tokens map to. Our constraint then disallows all sentences containing any of the words on the augmented list, starting at any of the sentence locations 0 through len(sentence) - len(word).

3 List downloaded from here.

4 A word will be encoded differently whether it is space-prefixed or not.

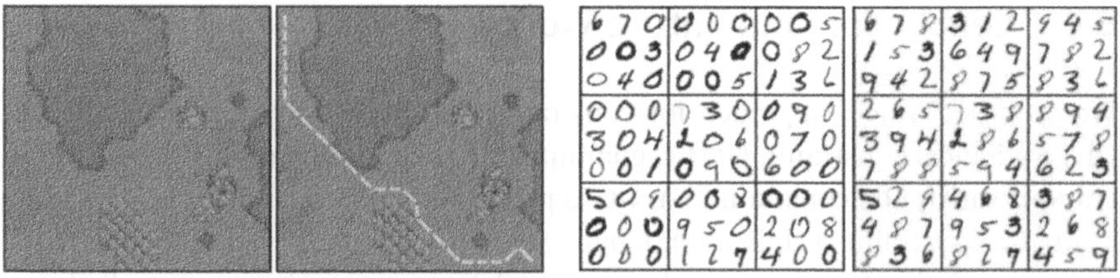

Figure A.1 Example inputs and groundtruth labels for two of the three tasks considered in our experimental evaluation. (Left) Example Warcraft terrain map and a possible (non-unique) minimum-cost shortest path. (Right) Example Sudoku puzzle and corresponding (unique) solution.

We use a batch size of 10 during generation, and only sample every sentence 5 times. The model sentence $\boldsymbol{y}$ was generated using nucleus sampling with $p = 0.9$ and a temperature of 1. We experimented with tempering the contextualized pseudo-likelihood distribution on a random set of prompts of size 1000 using $\tau = \{0.1, 0.3, 0.5, 0.7, 0.9, 1.0\}$. Our final results are reported on a random subset of the RealToxicityPrompts dataset of size 10k, average over 5 different runs using 5 different seeds. For this task, our implementation makes use of top-k to construct the pseudo-likelihood distribution (lines 7-12 in Algorithm 1) due to the lack of computational resources. Generations from all methods were limited to a maximum of 20 new tokens.

A.2 Sudoku

The experiments were run on a server with an AMD EPYC 7313P 16-Core Processor @ 3.7GHz, 2 NVIDIA RTX A6000, and 252 GB RAM. We use the dataset provided by Wang et al. 52, consisting of 10K Sudoku puzzles, split into 9K training examples, and 1K test samples, all puzzles having 10 missing entries. Our constraint disallows any solution in which the rows, columns and square are not unique. An example of an input Sudoku puzzle and it's corresponding solution is provided in Figure A.1 (right).

A.3 Warcraft Shortest Path

The experiments were run on a server with an AMD EPYC 7313P 16-Core Processor @ 3.7GHz, 2 NVIDIA RTX A6000, and 252 GB RAM. We used the best model trained by 24. The model uses a CNN-LSTM model for this task. Precisely, a ResNet-18 encodes the map to an embedding of dimension 128. An LSTM with 1 layer, and a hidden size of 512 then predicts the next edge in the shortest path conditioned on the input map and all previous edges. The constraint disallows any prediction not a valid path connecting upper left and lower right vertices. An example of an input Warcraft terrain map and a corresponding solution is provided in Figure A.1 (left).

A.4 Broader Impact

The work presented in this paper has a significant potential for positive societal impact. Neuro symbolic AI moves us closer to models whose behavior is trustworthy, explainable and fair. This extends to critical domains such as autonomous driving, medical diagnosis and financial planning to name a few. LLMs have recently seen an exponential increase in popularity, crossing the threshold of being mere research tools into products that are utilized by the general public. Unfortunately, the same expressivity that renders these models so powerful also makes it hard to reason about their behavior. We believe our proposed approach is a step in right direction: it expands the class of logical constraints we can tackle while account for and acknowledging the underlying probability distribution. And we have shown the merits of our approach when applied to LLM detoxification. We must, however, also be cognizant of the potential negative societal impacts: In very much the same way that our approach can be used to output non-toxic generations, it can be used to output toxic and harmful generations. Footnote

References

1 Michael Xieyang Liu, Frederick Liu, Alex Fiannaca, Terry Koo, Lucas Dixon, Michael Terry, and Carrie Cai. "We need structured output": Towards user-centered constraints on large language model output. *In Extended Abstracts of the CHI Conference on Human Factors in Computing Systems (CHI EA),* 2024.

2 Bailin Wang, Zi Wang, Xuezhi Wang, Yuan Cao, Rif A Saurous, and Yoon Kim. Grammar prompting for domain-specific language generation with large language models. In *Thirty-seventh Conference on Neural Information Processing Systems*, 2023.

3 OpenAI. Introducing structured outputs in the API, 2023. https://openai.com/index/introducing-structured-outputs-in-the-api/ [Accessed 2023-09-24].

4 Chinmay Mittal, Krishna Kartik, Mausam, and Parag Singla. Puzzlebench: Can llms solve challenging first-order combinatorial reasoning problems? *arXiv preprint arXiv:2402.02611*, 2024.

5 Liangming Pan, Alon Albalak, Xinyi Wang, and William Wang. Logic-LM: Empowering large language models with symbolic solvers for faithful logical

reasoning. In *Findings of the Association for Computational Linguistics: EMNLP 2023*, 2023.

6 Jiao Sun, Yufei Tian, Wangchunshu Zhou, Nan Xu, Qian Hu, Rahul Gupta, John Wieting, Nanyun Peng, and Xuezhe Ma. Evaluating large language models on controlled generation tasks. In *Proceedings of the 2023 Conference on Empirical Methods in Natural Language Processing*, 2023.

7 Daniel Deutsch, Shyam Upadhyay, and Dan Roth. A general-purpose algorithm for constrained sequential inference. In *Proceedings of the 23rd Conference on Computational Natural Language Learning (CoNLL)*, 2019.

8 Scott Lundberg, Marco Ribeiro, Richard Edgar, and Harsha-Nori. Guidance: a guidance language for controlling large language models, 2024.

9 Brandon T. Willard and Rémi Louf. Efficient guided generation for large language models. *arXiv preprint arXiv:2307.09702*, 2023.

10 Terry Koo, Frederick Liu, and Luheng He. Automata-based constraints for language model decoding. *arXiv preprint arXiv:2407.08103*, 2024.

11 Andy Shih, Dorsa Sadigh, and Stefano Ermon. Long horizon temperature scaling. In *Proceedings of the 40th International Conference on Machine Learning (ICML)*, 2023.

12 Hermann Gruber and Markus Holzer. Tight bounds on the descriptional complexity of regular expressions. In *Proceedings of the 13th International Conference on Developments in Language Theory*, DLT '09, pages 276–287, Berlin, Heidelberg, 2009. Springer-Verlag. https://doi.org/10.1007/978-3-642-02737-6_22.

13 Hermann Gruber and Markus Holzer. From finite automata to regular expressions and back–a summary on descriptional complexity. In *Proceedings of the 14th International Conference on Automata and Formal Languages*, 2014.

14 Adnan Darwiche. SDD: A new canonical representation of propositional knowledge bases. In *IJCAI*, 2011.

15 YooJung Choi, Antonio Vergari, and Guy Van den Broeck. Probabilistic circuits: a unifying framework for tractable probabilistic modeling. *In UCLA StarAI*, 2020.

16 Simone Bova. Sdds are exponentially more succinct than obdds. In *AAAI Conference on Artificial Intelligence*, 2016.

17 Randal E. Bryant. Symbolic Boolean manipulation with ordered binary-decision diagrams. *ACM Computing Surveys*, 24(3): 293–318, 1992.

18 Dan Roth. On the hardness of approximate reasoning. In *IJCAI*, pages 613–619. Morgan Kaufmann, 1993.

19 Kanghee Park, Jiayu Wang, Taylor Berg-Kirkpatrick, Nadia Polikarpova, and Loris D'Antoni. Grammar-aligned decoding. In *NeurIPS*, 2024.

20 Konstantinos Mamouras and Agnishom Chattopadhyay. Efficient matching of regular expressions with lookaround assertions. *In Proceedings of ACM Programming Languages (POPL)*, 2004.

21 Daphne Koller and Nir Friedman. *Probabilistic Graphical Models: Principles and Techniques*. MIT Press, 2009.

22 Kareem Ahmed, Zhe Zeng, Mathias Niepert, and Guy Van den Broeck. Simple: A gradient estimator for k-subset sampling. In *Proceedings of the International Conference on Learning Representations (ICLR)*, 2023.

23 Julian Besag. Statistical analysis of non-lattice data. *Journal of the Royal Statistical Society. Series D (The Statistician)*, pages 179–195, 1975.

24 Kareem Ahmed, Kai-Wei Chang, and Guy Van den Broeck. A pseudo-semantic loss for deep generative models with logical constraints. In *NeurIPS*, 2023.

25 Wannes Meert. PySDD. In *Recent Trends in Knowledge Compilation*, 2017.

26 Kareem Ahmed, Tao Li, Thy Ton, Quan Guo, Kai-Wei Chang, Parisa Kordjamshidi, Vivek Srikumar, Guy Van den Broeck, and Sameer Singh. Pylon: A pytorch framework for learning with constraints. In *Proceedings of the 36th AAAI Conference on Artificial Intelligence (Demo Track)*, 2022.

27 Antonio Vergari, Nicola Di Mauro, and Floriana Esposito. Simplifying, regularizing and strengthening sum-product network structure learning. In *Joint European Conference on Machine Learning and Knowledge Discovery in Databases*, pages 343–358. Springer, 2015.

28 Robert Peharz, Steven Lang, Antonio Vergari, Karl Stelzner, Alejandro Molina, Martin Trapp, Guy Van den Broeck, Kristian Kersting, and Zoubin Ghahramani. Einsum networks: fast and scalable learning of tractable probabilistic circuits. In *International Conference of Machine Learning*, 2020.

29 Yexiang Xue, Arthur Choi, and Adnan Darwiche. Basing decisions on sentences in decision diagrams. *Proceedings of the AAAI Conference on Artificial Intelligence*, 2012.

30 Anji Liu, Kareem Ahmed, and Guy Van den Broeck. Scaling tractable probabilistic circuits: a systems perspective. In *International Conference on Machine Learning (ICML)*, 2024.

31 Adam Paszke, Sam Gross, Francisco Massa, Adam Lerer, James Bradbury, Gregory Chanan, Trevor Killeen, Zeming Lin, Natalia Gimelshein, Luca Antiga, et al. Pytorch: An imperative style, high-performance deep learning library. In H. Wallach, H. Larochelle, A. Beygelzimer, F. d'Alché-Buc, E. Fox, and R. Garnett, editors, *Advances in Neural Information Processing Systems*, volume 32. Curran Associates, Inc., 2019.

32 Renato Lui Geh, Honghua Zhang, Kareem Ahmed, Benjie Wang, and Guy Van den Broeck. Where is the signal in tokenization space? In *Empirical Methods in Natural Language Processing 2024*, 2024.

33 Antonio Vergari, YooJung Choi, Anji Liu, Stefano Teso, and Guy Van den Broeck. A compositional atlas of tractable circuit operations for probabilistic inference. *Advances in Neural Information Processing Systems 34*, 2021.

34 Ximing Lu, Peter West, Rowan Zellers, Ronan Le Bras, Chandra Bhagavatula, and Yejin Choi. Neurologic decoding:(un) supervised neural text generation with predicate logic constraints. In *Proceedings of the 2021 Conference of the North American Chapter of the Association for Computational Linguistics: Human Language Technologies (NAACL)*, 2021.

35 Ximing Lu, Sean Welleck, Peter West, Liwei Jiang, Jungo Kasai, Daniel Khashabi, Ronan Le Bras, Lianhui Qin, Youngjae Yu, Rowan Zellers, et al. Neurologic a* esque decoding: constrained text generation with lookahead heuristics. In *Proceedings of the 2022 Conference of the North American Chapter of the Association for Computational Linguistics: Human Language Technologies*, pages 780–799, 2022.

36 Ben Krause, Akhilesh Deepak Gotmare, Bryan McCann, Nitish Shirish Keskar, Shafiq Joty, Richard Socher, and Nazneen Fatema Rajani. Gedi: Generative discriminator guided sequence generation. In *Findings of the Association for Computational Linguistics: EMNLP 2021*, pages 4929–4952. Association for Computational Linguistics, 2021.

37 Kevin Yang and Dan Klein. Fudge: Controlled text generation with future discriminators. In *Proceedings of the 2021 Conference of the North American Chapter of the Association for Computational Linguistics: Human Language Technologies (NAACL)*, 2021.

38 Tao Meng, Sidi Lu, Nanyun Peng, and Kai-Wei Chang. Controllable text generation with neurally-decomposed oracle. In *Advances in Neural Information Processing Systems 35 (NeurIPS)*, 2022.

39 Lianhui Qin, Sean Welleck, Daniel Khashabi, and Yejin Choi. Cold decoding: energy-based constrained text generation with langevin dynamics. *Advances in Neural Information Processing Systems*, 35: 9538–9551, 2022.

40 Edward J. Hu, Moksh Jain, Eric Elmoznino, Younesse Kaddar, Guillaume Lajoie, Yoshua Bengio, and Nikolay Malkin. Amortizing intractable inference in large language models. In *The 12th International Conference on Learning Representations*, 2023.

41 Alexander K. Lew, Tan Zhi-Xuan, Gabriel Grand, and Vikash K. Mansinghka. Sequential monte carlo steering of large language models using probabilistic programs. *arXiv preprint arXiv:2306.03081*, 2023.

42 Lianmin Zheng, Liangsheng Yin, Zhiqiang Xie, Chuyue Sun, Jeff Huang, Cody Hao Yu, Shiyi Cao, Christos Kozyrakis, Ion Stoica, Joseph E. Gonzalez, et al. SGLang: Efficient execution of structured language model programs. *NeurIPS 2024*, 2024.

43 Honghua Zhang, Meihua Dang, Nanyun Peng, and Guy Van den Broeck. Tractable control for autoregressive language generation. In *Proceedings of the 40th International Conference on Machine Learning (ICML)*, 2023.

44 Honghua Zhang, Po-Nien Kung, Masahiro Yoshida, Nanyun Peng, and Guy Van den Broeck. Adaptable logical control for large language models. In *NeurIPS*, 2024.

45 Torsten Scholak, Nathan Schucher, and Dzmitry Bahdanau. PICARD: Parsing incrementally for constrained auto-regressive decoding from language models. In *Proceedings of the 2021 Conference on Empirical Methods in Natural Language Processing*, 2021.

46 Samuel Gehman, Suchin Gururangan, Maarten Sap, Yejin Choi, and Noah A. Smith. Realtoxicityprompts: evaluating neural toxic degeneration in language models. *arXiv:2009.11462*, 2020.

47 Marin Vlastelica Pogančić, Anselm Paulus, Vit Musil, Georg Martius, and Michal Rolinek. Differentiation of blackbox combinatorial solvers. In *ICLR*, 2020.

48 Kaiming He, Xiangyu Zhang, Shaoqing Ren, and Jian Sun. Deep residual learning for image recognition. In *CVPR*, 2016.

49 Jingyi Xu, Zilu Zhang, Tal Friedman, Yitao Liang, and Guy Van den Broeck. A semantic loss function for deep learning with symbolic knowledge. In *International Conference on Machine Learning*, pages 5502–5511. PMLR, 2018.

50 Kareem Ahmed, Stefano Teso, Kai-Wei Chang, Guy Van den Broeck, and Antonio Vergari. Semantic probabilistic layers for neuro-symbolic learning. In *NeurIPS*, 2022.

51 Kareem Ahmed, Eric Wang, Kai-Wei Chang, and Guy Van den Broeck. Neuro-symbolic entropy regularization. In *The 38th Conference on Uncertainty in Artificial Intelligence*, 2022.

52 Po-Wei Wang, Priya L Donti, Bryan Wilder, and J Zico Kolter. Satnet: Bridging deep learning and logical reasoning using a differentiable satisfiability solver. In *ICML, volume 97 of Proceedings of Machine Learning Research*, pages 6545–6554. PMLR, 2019.

53 Boxin Wang, Wei Ping, Chaowei Xiao, Peng Xu, Mostofa Patwary, Mohammad Shoeybi, Bo Li, Anima Anandkumar, and Bryan Catanzaro. Exploring the limits of domain-adaptive training for detoxifying large-scale language models. In *Neurips*, 2022.

54 Alec Radford, Jeff Wu, Rewon Child, David Luan, Dario Amodei, and Ilya Sutskever. *Language Models Are Unsupervised Multitask Learners*. OpenAI, 2019.

55 Johannes Welbl, Amelia Glaese, Jonathan Uesato, Sumanth Dathathri, John F. J. Mellor, Lisa Anne Hendricks, Kirsty, Anderson, Pushmeet Kohli, Ben Coppin, and Po-Sen Huang. Challenges in detoxifying language models. *arXiv preprint arXiv:2109.07445*, 2021.

56 Sylvain Gugger, Lysandre Debut, Thomas Wolf, Philipp Schmid, Zachary Mueller, and Sourab Mangrulkar. Accelerate: *Training and Inference at Scale Made Simple, Efficient and Adaptable*. HuggingFace, 2022.

7

Tractable and Expressive Generative Modeling with Probabilistic Flow Circuits

Sahil Sidheekh and Sriraam Natarajan*

Computer Science Department, The University of Texas at Dallas, Richardson, Texas, USA

*Corresponding Author: sahil.sidheekh@utdallas.edu

7.1 Introduction

Probabilistic generative modeling plays a central role in machine learning and artificial intelligence, aiming to approximate the probability distribution that gave rise to the observed data. By capturing the uncertainty and variability in the data, probabilistic generative models facilitate principled decision-making, robust inference, and controlled generation of new data. Whether one considers decision-support systems, medical diagnosis, natural language understanding, computer vision, or autonomous control, the capacity to reason probabilistically about unseen scenarios, to estimate likelihoods of events, and to generate novel yet coherent samples is important.

However, as data grows increasingly complex and high-dimensional, the generative modeling problem becomes more challenging. On one hand, we desire **expressivity** – the ability to model complex, multi-modal distributions with intricate dependencies between variables. On the other hand, we also value **tractability** – the capability to answer various inference queries exactly and efficiently. These queries might include computing marginal probabilities, conditional probabilities given partial observations, or even more sophisticated operations like finding the most probable explanation or performing certain forms of probabilistic conditioning that can guide decision-making under uncertainty.

Historically, this trade-off between expressivity and tractability has driven research in two distinct directions. Some families of models, such as classic

Neurosymbolic AI: Foundations and Applications, First Edition. Edited by Alvaro Velasquez et al.

probabilistic graphical models [1], introduced explicit conditional independence assumptions to ensure efficient inference. The price paid was often reduced representational flexibility. In contrast, many contemporary deep generative models [2] – such as variational autoencoders (VAEs) [3], generative adversarial networks (GANs) [4], normalizing flows [5, 6], and diffusion models [7, 8] – emphasize on using flexible function approximators, typically neural networks, to capture highly complex data distributions. However, they often lack the exact tractability or interpretability of their more structured counterparts.

In recent years, *Probabilistic Circuits (PCs)* [9] have emerged as a powerful framework that unifies a variety of tractable probabilistic models, including sum-product networks (SPNs) [10], probabilistic sentential decision diagrams (PSDDs) [11], and ACs [12], among others. PCs are essentially directed acyclic computational graphs whose leaves represent simple distributions over subsets of variables and whose internal nodes are sums (mixtures) and products (factorizations) that combine these distributions in a hierarchical manner. By imposing certain structural constraints such as *smoothness*, *decomposability*, and *determinism*, PCs guarantee tractable exact inference for a broad class of queries. Thus, PCs lie at a crucial point in the generative modeling landscape: they are more expressive than simple factorized distributions or low-treewidth graphical models, yet still tractable enough to avoid the need for sampling-based or approximate inference techniques for many tasks.

Despite their appealing properties, classical PCs have limitations. While they outperform simpler tractable models, their representational capacity can still be insufficient for very complex real-world data. One might try to scale up PCs by adding more layers, more components, or more complex leaf distributions. However, scaling alone may not suffice. Indeed, it has been observed that merely increasing model size does not always yield significant improvements in model accuracy or fidelity [13, 14]. These insights motivate the search for more flexible parameterizations and functional forms to place at the leaves of a PC – distributions that can be smoothly adapted to data complexity without sacrificing tractability.

On the other side of the spectrum, *normalizing flows* [5, 6, 15] have risen to prominence as deep generative models that are both expressive and offer exact likelihood evaluation. A normalizing flow transforms a simple, tractable base distribution (e.g., an isotropic Gaussian) into a complex target distribution by applying a sequence of invertible, differentiable transformations. Each transformation layer is designed so that the Jacobian determinant can be computed efficiently, allowing exact probability density computation. Flows yield flexible densities capable of modeling complex multi-modal data, but, unlike PCs, they do not inherently guarantee tractable computation of more intricate inference tasks like marginalization or conditioning on arbitrary subsets of variables. While a flow can easily provide $p(\mathbf{x})$, performing integrals over subsets of variables or determining conditional probabilities often requires numerical approximations.

This motivates a natural question: *Can we combine the structural advantages of PCs, which facilitate tractable inference, with the expressive power of normalizing flows?* Such a combination would ideally produce a model that remains tractable for a range of inference queries, while simultaneously representing extremely flexible distributions at the leaves.

First attempts to integrate PCs and flows included placing invertible affine transformations inside PCs [16]. Intuitively, it can be understood as considering the distributions modeled by internal nodes in a PC as the base distribution for a flow. However, initial work in this direction revealed a subtle issue: integrating flows arbitrarily can break the crucial decomposability property of PCs. If a flow-based transform node acts over a set of variables in a way that mixes them nontrivially, it can introduce dependencies across previously independent components, rendering marginal and conditional inference intractable.

To address this, subsequent research [17] introduced a key refinement: the concept of *τ-decomposability*. This notion specifies conditions under which a transform node, representing an invertible flow, can be inserted into a PC without destroying its structural guarantees. In essence, τ-decomposability enforces that any invertible transformation applied at a product node must factorize along the same subspace partitions encoded by that product node. Consequently, this requirement ensures that the decomposability of the PC remains intact. By carefully restricting how we integrate flows into PCs, we can push all transformations down to the leaves, obtaining a new class of models known as *Probabilistic Flow Circuits (PFCs).*

PFCs represent a breakthrough: they maintain all the classical tractability guarantees of PCs but replace their simple leaf distributions with powerful normalizing flows. Thus, they strike a desirable balance. One can now model far more complex marginal distributions at the leaf level, capturing non-linear distortions and multi-modal behaviors that would be impossible with, say, simple Gaussians. Meanwhile, the circuit-level structure still ensures that various inference queries – like conditioning on observed variables, marginalizing out others, or even certain structured optimization queries – remain polynomial – time operations.

This chapter[1] offers a comprehensive exploration of this emerging paradigm.

(1) We begin by reviewing the fundamentals of tractable inference in PCs, including crucial structural properties and learning algorithms. We discuss parameter estimation for PCs via maximum likelihood and expectation-maximization

1 This chapter consolidates and expands the works originally presented in our UAI paper [17], that introduced Probabilistic Flow Circuits and our IJCAI survey paper [18], on building expressive and tractable generative models.

and outline known structure learning approaches. We also examine how these models relate to and differ from deep neural architectures, highlighting their probabilistic semantics and computational efficiency. We then turn to normalizing flows, describing their mechanism, the change-of-variables formula, invertible transformations, and their expressive capabilities. We stress the complementary strengths of PCs and flows: the exact tractability of the former for multiple inference queries and the representational richness of the latter.

(2) The main theoretical insight we present is the introduction of τ-decomposability. We show that this property is necessary to integrate flows into PCs without compromising their tractable nature. We prove that if a transform node violates this condition, it introduces scope overlap and breaks decomposability, making marginal or conditional queries intractable. We then leverage this insight to conclude that, after enforcing the τ-decomposability, the resulting architecture is equivalent to having normalizing flows only at the leaves, leading to the definition of Probabilistic Flow Circuits.

(3) We provide detailed derivations, theorems, and proofs to ensure that the reader is able to gain a detailed understanding of the mathematical nuances. This chapter also presents experimental results originally described in the technical paper that introduced PFCs [17], demonstrating the superior density estimation capabilities of PFCs compared to vanilla PCs and other baselines.

(4) We conclude the chapter with possible future directions. Hybrid models like PFCs represent just one step in bridging the gap between tractability and expressivity. We will raise open problems and envision new families of models that integrate even more sophisticated transformations, latent variable models, or neural parameterizations at different levels of a PC. We also touch on the potential for these models to support advanced tasks beyond density estimation, such as exact computation of certain information-theoretic measures or controlling the generative process conditioned on complex events, all leveraging the tractability inherited from PCs. In particular, tractability for marginal and conditional queries can serve as a critical building block in downstream applications where one needs fast and exact inference. In fields like healthcare (where partial observations are common), finance (where conditional scenario analysis is routine), or interactive machine learning (where we need to revise distributions as new evidence comes in), the ability to query complex distributions on-the-fly is invaluable. By coupling this ability with the flexible representational power of normalizing flows, PFCs hold substantial promise for practical, real-world deployment.

The structure of this chapter is as follows.

- **Section 7.2: Background on Tractable Probabilistic Modeling:** We begin by reviewing basic concepts in tractable inference, introducing key inference queries, and discussing their computational complexity. We will highlight the necessity of imposing structure on generative models to achieve tractability.

- **Section 7.3: Probabilistic Circuits:** We delve into the definition of PCs, their structural properties, and how these ensure exact polynomial time inference for various queries. We will briefly discuss parameter and structure learning techniques, as well as recent trends that have made PCs "deeper" and more parallelizable, bringing them closer to neural networks.
- **Section 7.4: Normalizing Flows and Their Capabilities:** We then introduce normalizing flows, explaining how these models allow exact likelihood estimation. We examine their strengths and limitations, focusing on the difficulty of performing tasks like marginalization.
- **Section 7.5: Integrating Normalizing Flows into PCs – Challenges and Theoretical Foundations:** Here we present the core theoretical results and explain why naïve insertion of invertible transformations can break decomposability. We define and explore the τ-decomposability property, proving that it is necessary for preserving tractability. We also show how all valid transform nodes can be equivalently "pushed down" to the leaves, culminating in the concept of PFC.
- **Section 7.6: Probabilistic Flow Circuits:** We formally define PFCs and explore their properties. We discuss how leaf-level normalizing flows (particularly linear rational splines) equip PCs with the ability to model highly flexible distributions at each variable. We then reason about how this impacts overall modeling power and what inference operations remain tractable.
- **Section 7.7: Empirical Evaluation and Experiments:** We present comprehensive experiments from the original technical paper. Starting with low-dimensional synthetic datasets, we show how PFCs significantly outperform PCs and other baselines in density estimation. We then scale to high-dimensional tabular data and image datasets, comparing PFCs to standard PCs, normalizing flows, and other deep models. These experiments clearly demonstrate that PFCs outperform PCs with simple distributions and even surpass certain normalizing flows and other DGMs in terms of likelihood scores, all while retaining the ability to perform exact inference queries.
- **Section 7.8: Discussion:** We finally conclude with a discussion on the significance of PFCs in the broader context of generative modeling. We also discuss potential extensions to PFCs and directions for future research.

By the end of this chapter, we hope the reader will have a deep understanding of why combining tractable probabilistic models (specifically PCs) with deep generative models (specifically normalizing flows) is challenging yet worthwhile, and why PFCs represent a promising direction for future research and application. This line of work emphasizes a trend in machine learning: we need not choose strictly between elegant tractable theory and empirical expressiveness. With careful design and theoretical insights, we can merge them into a single framework, better addressing the demands of modern machine learning and AI applications.

Notation: We use $\mathbf{X} = (X_1, X_2, \dots, X_d)$ to denote a set of $d-$ random variables and $\mathbf{x} = (x_1, x_2, \dots, x_d)$ denote an assignment of values to $\mathbf{X}$. We use $P_{\mathbf{X}}$ to denote the true probability distribution over $\mathbf{X}$ and P_θ to denote the distribution captured by a generative model parameterized by θ.

7.2 Tractable Probabilistic Modeling

In the field of probabilistic modeling, a primary interest lies in not only representing complex distributions over high-dimensional data but also in performing inference tasks efficiently. Given a learned probability distribution $P_\theta(\mathbf{X})$ over random variables $\mathbf{X} = (X_1, \dots, X_d)$, we often want to answer specific questions about the distribution. For example, how probable is a particular data point $\mathbf{x}$? What is the marginal probability of a subset of variables $\mathbf{X}_A$? What is the probability of some event given partial observations of other variables? Or which assignment of $\mathbf{X}_A$ maximizes a posterior distribution conditioned on $\mathbf{X}_B$? These questions, known as *inference queries*, typically translate into various forms of integrals, optimizations, or conditional computations over the joint probability distribution. While simple distributions – such as independent factorized models – make these queries easy, they are too inflexible for many real-world data distributions. Conversely, flexible and expressive models – like large graphical models with complicated dependency structures – can represent complex generative process well, but may require expensive approximate methods like Markov Chain Monte Carlo [19] or variational inference [20] to handle even relatively simple queries.

This dichotomy led researchers to focus on building *tractable* models, i.e., representations that can answer a broad class of inference queries in time polynomial in the size of the representation. Such tractability is not guaranteed for arbitrary distributions. Indeed, it is well known that certain inference problems – like exact marginalization or computing the MAP configuration in arbitrary graphical models – can be #P- or NP-hard [21]. This hardness implies that, without structural restrictions or special assumptions, we cannot hope to achieve exact and efficient inference for arbitrary distributions.

The core idea behind *tractable probabilistic modeling* is to impose certain constraints on the model's form. By engineering models whose structure encodes factorizations and mixtures in a well-controlled manner, we can ensure that certain classes of inference queries remain tractable. The main challenge is achieving a good balance between *expressivity* (the ability to model complex data distributions accurately) and *tractability* (the ability to perform inference efficiently and exactly). In this section, we will formalize the notion of tractability, describe the inference tasks commonly of interest, and highlight why imposing structure is often necessary. We will also provide a high-level taxonomy of inference queries and discuss their computational complexity, setting the stage for why frameworks like PC are appealing.

7.2.1 Inference Queries

To understand what makes probabilistic modeling challenging, let us start by enumerating some core inference tasks:

1. **Evidential Inference:** Given a model $P_\theta(\mathbf{X})$ and a full assignment $\mathbf{x}$ to all variables in $\mathbf{X}$, *evidential inference* asks us to compute $P_\theta(\mathbf{x})$. In other words, how likely is this particular point according to the learned distribution? This task underlies maximum likelihood training, as we often need to evaluate or maximize $P_\theta(\mathbf{x})$ over the model parameters θ. Models that can compute $P_\theta(\mathbf{x})$ efficiently are sometimes called *explicit density models*. However, evaluating the joint probability exactly is not always straightforward, especially if the model's structure is complex.
2. **Marginal Inference:** In marginal inference, we are interested in $P_\theta(\mathbf{X}_A)$ for some subset $A \subseteq \{1, \dots, d\}$. Computing this quantity involves integrating or summing over the other variables:

$$P_\theta(\mathbf{X}_A) = \int_{\mathbf{x}_B} P_\theta(\mathbf{X}_A, \mathbf{X}_B) d\mathbf{x}_B$$

   where $\mathbf{X} = \{\mathbf{X}_A, \mathbf{X}_B\}$. For discrete variables, the integral turns into a sum, and for continuous variables, it remains an integral. Without special structure, this integral or summation can be exponential in $|B|$ or require complex approximation schemes.
3. **Conditional Inference:** Conditional distributions of the form $P_\theta(\mathbf{X}_A | \mathbf{X}_B = \mathbf{x}_B)$ are critical when we have partial information about some variables and want to update our belief about others. For instance, given partial sensor readings (evidence), what is the distribution over the remaining unknown variables? Computing such a quantity directly involves:

$$P_\theta(\mathbf{X}_A | \mathbf{X}_B = \mathbf{x}_B) = \frac{P_\theta(\mathbf{X}_A, \mathbf{X}_B = \mathbf{x}_B)}{\int_{\mathbf{x}_A} P_\theta(\mathbf{X}_A, \mathbf{X}_B = \mathbf{x}_B) d\mathbf{x}_A}.$$

   Although this does not introduce additional complexity beyond marginalization, conditional inference requires the capacity to efficiently marginalize the joint distribution over arbitrary subsets of variables.

4. **MAP Inference (Most Probable Assignment):** The MAP problem seeks the assignment $\mathbf{x}_A$ that maximizes $P_\theta(\mathbf{X}_A|\mathbf{X}_B = \mathbf{x}_B)$ or equivalently $P_\theta(\mathbf{X}_A, \mathbf{X}_B = \mathbf{x}_B)$ when B is given. This is a combinatorial optimization problem:

$$\mathbf{x}_A^* = \arg\max_{\mathbf{x}_A} P_\theta(\mathbf{X}_A, \mathbf{X}_B = \mathbf{x}_B).$$

MAP inference is a challenging and an NP-hard problem even for unrestricted graphical models. Ensuring polynomial-time MAP inference again requires imposing special structural assumptions.
5. **More Complex Queries:** Beyond the standard tasks, one may be interested in computing moments, marginal MAP (where one subset of variables is marginalized while another is maximized), or even divergence measures between distributions. Such tasks build on marginal and conditional inferences, or optimizations defined over functions of the joint likelihood. Their tractability depends on the model's ability to handle integrals, products, ratios of distributions, and transformations of distributions efficiently.

Without additional structure, these queries are often computationally intractable for general distributions. Complexity results from graphical models indicate that inference tasks can quickly become NP-hard or #P-hard as we introduce dense interactions among variables.

7.2.2 The Expressivity-tractability Trade-off

A fundamental theme in probabilistic modeling is the *expressivity-tractability trade-off*. On one end of the spectrum, consider models that assume independence among all variables:

$$P_\theta(\mathbf{X}) = \prod_{i=1}^{d} P_\theta(X_i).$$

Such a model is trivially tractable. Evaluating a joint, marginal, or conditional query is straightforward, and MAP inference is trivial. However, this model is usually too simplistic, as real-world data rarely factorize into completely independent components. The representational power of such a model is limited, leading to poor performance. On the other end, consider a very flexible model like a large neural network that can approximate any distribution. This model might be extremely expressive but lacks explicit structure and factorization properties. Performing marginalization or conditional inference might require computationally expensive integrations. To build models that are both tractable and somewhat flexible, we need to carefully inject structural assumptions into the distribution. Classical approaches, like bounded-treewidth graphical models, attempt to ensure that certain inference routines remain polynomial time. However, imposing these restrictions often curtails expressivity.

One classical approach to ensure tractability is to limit the types of dependencies allowed in the model. For example, consider a graphical model with a low treewidth structure. Inference (marginalization) in such models can be done in time exponential in the treewidth, but if the treewidth is small and fixed, then inference is polynomial with respect to the size of the input graph. Yet, limiting treewidth often reduces the model's ability to represent complex dependencies.

Another approach is to represent complex distributions as *hierarchical mixtures* of factorized distributions. Mixture models, which sum over components each focusing on a subset of the data distribution, can approximate complex densities by blending simpler pieces. When those simpler pieces are themselves factorized or low-dimensional distributions, we can maintain tractability for queries that break down nicely along mixture and factorization boundaries.

For example, a mixture of factorized distributions:

$$P_\theta(\mathbf{X}) = \sum_{k=1}^{K} w_k \prod_{i=1}^{d} P_{\theta_k}(X_i)$$

retains tractability for all basic queries if it is easy to integrate out the factorized components. While more flexible than a purely factorized model, a naive mixture might require a large number of components K to achieve good approximations, and thus still not be efficient. Going one step further, we might build hierarchical structures: mixtures of products, and products of mixtures, recursively. Such hierarchical structures can represent exponentially large and complex distributions in a compact form, provided they share scopes and factorizations appropriately. This idea underlies the design of PCs.

7.3 Probabilistic Circuits

Having established the motivations and foundations of tractable probabilistic modeling, we now focus on *PCs* [9]. PCs provide a unified framework that encompasses a wide variety of tractable probabilistic models. They were introduced to present a coherent perspective that subsumes several previously proposed models, such as Arithmetic Circuits (ACs) [12], SPNs [10], Probabilistic Sentential Decision Diagrams (PSDDs) [11], and Cutset Networks [22], among others.

The key idea of a PC is to represent a probability distribution over a set of variables $\mathbf{X}$ using a computational graph composed of three node types: *leaf*, *sum*, and *product* nodes. By combining these nodes in carefully structured ways, we can encode complex probability distributions while retaining the ability to answer a variety of inference queries in polynomial time. The structural constraints placed on this graph ensure that integrals factorize nicely and that certain combinatorial explosions of complexity are avoided. In this section, we will delve deeply into the concept of PCs, discussing their definition, the structural properties critical for tractable inference, how these properties enable a broad class of inference queries, and how PCs can be learned from data. These insights lay the groundwork for understanding how PCs can serve as the backbone in which we integrate more powerful leaf distributions – like normalizing flows – while preserving tractability.

7.3.1 Defining a Probabilistic Circuit

A Probabilistic Circuit $\mathcal{C}$ is a rooted acyclic computational graph whose internal nodes represent either mixtures or factorizations of distributions, and whose leaves represent tractable univariate distributions over subsets of the variables. More formally, let $\mathbf{X} = (X_1, \dots, X_d)$ be a d-dimensional vector of random variables. A PC is a computational graph comprising:

- **Leaf nodes:** Each leaf node encodes a tractable univariate distribution over a single variable X_i. For example, it might represent a Gaussian $\mathcal{N}(X_i; \mu, \sigma^2)$, a Categorical distribution for discrete variables, or any distribution with a closed-form density or mass function that is easy to evaluate, differentiate, and integrate. Leaf nodes provide the building blocks – simple, tractable distributions that can be combined to form more complex models.
- **Sum nodes:** A sum node represents a mixture over its children distributions. If a sum node S has children $\{N_1, N_2, \dots, N_k\}$, each of which is a node (or subcircuit) encoding a distribution over the same subset of variables, then:

  $$S(\mathbf{x}) = \sum_{j=1}^{k} w_j N_j(\mathbf{x})$$

  where $w_j \geq 0$ and $\sum_j w_j = 1$. Thus, sum nodes form convex combinations of their children, representing a mixture model. The parameters w_j are part of the circuit's parameters.
- **Product nodes:** A product node represents a factorization. If a product node P has children $\{N_1, N_2, \dots, N_k\}$, each of which encodes a distribution over disjoint subsets of $\mathbf{X}$, say $\psi_{N_1}, \psi_{N_2}, \dots, \psi_{N_k}$, then:

  $$P(\mathbf{x}) = \prod_{j=1}^{k} N_j(\mathbf{x}_{\psi_{N_j}}).$$

  By structuring the children's scopes to be disjoint, product nodes encode conditional independence relations that allow factorizing the joint distribution into simpler distributions over smaller subsets of variables.

The overall probability distribution modeled by the PC is given by the value of its root node R evaluated at $\mathbf{x}$, i.e., $P_\theta(\mathbf{x}) = R(\mathbf{x})$. Thus, a PC is essentially a computational structure for generating and combining probability distributions. By feeding $\mathbf{x}$ into the leaves and propagating the values upwards through sums and products, we obtain $P_\theta(\mathbf{x})$.

7.3.2 Structural Properties

Not all arbitrary combinations of sum and product nodes yield a tractable model. In fact, ensuring tractability requires imposing certain structural constraints that guarantee polynomial-time inference for a broad class of queries. Three crucial properties include:

Smoothness: A PC is *smooth* if for every sum node, all of its children have the same scope. Recall that the scope of a node is the set of variables that node's distribution depends on. Smoothness ensures that the mixture operation outputs a well-defined distribution. Formally, for a sum node S with children $N_1, \dots, N_k$:

$$\text{Smoothness: } \forall j,\ \psi_{N_j} = \psi_S.$$

This ensures validity of the distribution and allows integrals to be pushed inside sums easily.

Decomposability: A PC is *decomposable* if each product node combines distributions over disjoint sets of variables. If a product node P has children $N_1, \dots, N_k$, then:

$$\text{Decomposability: } \forall j \neq l,\ \psi_{N_j} \cap \psi_{N_l} = \emptyset.$$

This implies that at a product node, the variables factor cleanly. As a result, when we perform marginalization, integrals factorize, and complex inference queries that require integration simplify to products of simpler integrals. Decomposability is central to maintaining polynomial-time inference complexity for tasks like marginalization and conditional probability computation.

Determinism: A PC is *deterministic* if for every sum node, at most one child can evaluate to a non-zero probability for any given input $\mathbf{x}$. Another way to phrase this is that sum nodes represent "hard" mixtures, where the data point effectively chooses one component rather than mixing continuously. Determinism is not necessary for basic inference tasks like evidential or marginal inference but is known to be essential (or at least highly beneficial) for MAP inference. Deterministic PCs, also known as "selective" circuits [23], allow tractable MAP computation, as the maximization over sum nodes reduces to a maximization over a single chosen component, rather than having to consider a combination of all components.

While smoothness and decomposability are typically considered the basic requirements for tractability of marginals and conditionals, determinism is often introduced to extend tractability to more complex inference queries like MAP. PCs that are smooth, decomposable, and deterministic are sometimes referred to as *complete and decomposable* [24].

7.3.3 Tractable Inference with PCs

With smoothness and decomposability, a PC enables polynomial-time exact computations of a variety of queries. Consider a smooth and decomposable PC

- **Evidential Inference:** Evaluating $P_\theta(\mathbf{x})$ for a fully observed $\mathbf{x}$ simply involves a bottom-up pass through the circuit. The time complexity is linear in the size of the circuit (i.e., the number of edges), as each node just performs a sum or a product of previously computed values.
- **Marginal Inference:** To compute $P_\theta(\mathbf{X}_A)$ for $A \subseteq \{1, \dots, d\}$, we must integrate out $\mathbf{X}_B$, where B is the complement of A. In a general model, this can be intractable. But for a smooth and decomposable PC, integrals pass through sum and product nodes straightforwardly. Sum nodes, by smoothness, ensure all children have the same scope, so integration is uniform. Product nodes, by decomposability, factor the integral over independent subsets. Thus, it reduces to a series of local operations at the leaves. Since the leaves are univariate distributions chosen for tractability (e.g., Gaussians), these integrals can be computed in closed form. The entire process remains polynomial, in fact linear, in the circuit size.
- **Conditional Inference:** Conditional probabilities $P_\theta(\mathbf{X}_A | \mathbf{X}_B = \mathbf{x}_B)$ can be derived from $P_\theta(\mathbf{X}_A, \mathbf{X}_B)$ and $P_\theta(\mathbf{X}_B)$, both of which are tractable to compute in a PC. This again takes polynomial time and requires no approximate inference.
- **MAP Inference:** Deterministic PCs allow MAP queries to be solved efficiently by performing a form of "max-product" inference. Instead of computing integrals, we seek $\arg\max_{\mathbf{x}_A} P_\theta(\mathbf{X}_A | \mathbf{X}_B = \mathbf{x}_B)$. In a deterministic PC, each sum node essentially "selects" one child that attains the maximum. This process can be done by substituting sums with max operations and descending the circuit to find the argmax solution. Thus, MAP inference is also polynomial-time for deterministic PCs.

This capability to handle a broad array of queries exactly and efficiently sets PCs apart from many other generative model classes that might require sampling or variational approximations.

7.3.4 Parameter Learning for PCs

One of the advantages of PCs is that they are differentiable computational graphs. The parameters θ of a PC include the mixture weights at sum nodes and the parameters of the leaf distributions (e.g., mean and variance of Gaussian leaves). Learning these parameters from data can be done using standard maximum likelihood estimation (MLE):

$$\theta^* = \arg\max_{\theta} \sum_{i=1}^{N} \log\ P_{\theta}(\mathbf{x}^{(i)}),$$

where $\{\mathbf{x}^{(i)}\}_{i=1}^{N}$ is the training dataset.

Because the circuit is a differentiable model, we can compute the gradient of the log-likelihood with respect to all parameters using backpropagation. Once we have these gradients, we can use gradient-based optimizers such as SGD, Adam, etc. This approach has been successfully used [17, 25] in practice and is straightforward to implement.

Expectation Maximization. An alternative optimization scheme proposed for PCs is expectation-maximization (EM), which is popularly used for maximum likelihood learning in the presence of missing data [26]. The crux of EM involves iterating between the following two steps until convergence after initializing from a random configuration – (1) the E-step, which involves computing the expected value of the missing variables given the observed variables, and (2) the M-step, which maximizes the likelihood given the complete expected assignment. As PCs are essentially hierarchical mixture models, their sum nodes can be viewed as marginalizing out an unobserved discrete latent variable. Peharz et al. [27] formalized this latent variable interpretation for PCs by explicitly introducing the unobserved latent variables in the computational graph to create an *augmented* circuit. As we do not know the assignments for these variables for the data points in hand, it becomes a learning with missing data problem and can be solved using expectation maximization. Compared to gradient ascent, EM has been observed to result in a larger boost in the data likelihood [25, 27, 28], especially in the early phase of learning.

7.3.5 Structure Learning for PCs

Choosing the correct structure (which variables to mix at sum nodes, how to factor at product nodes) is a non-trivial task, and several approaches have been proposed. Gens and Domingos [29], introduced a systematic greedy algorithm, often referred to as *LearnSPN*, to define scopes for sum and product nodes. Specifically, a product node is formed by applying statistical tests of independence to identify subsets of variables that are mutually independent, while a sum node is formed by running an EM-based clustering routine on data instances. The fractional membership of each cluster becomes the weight of the corresponding sum node edge. By iterating these two steps, one partitions columns (for product nodes) and rows (for sum nodes) of the data matrix until univariate leaves are reached. Subsequent work built on this idea. For instance, Rooshenas and Lowd [30], combined indirect interactions at higher latent levels with direct dependencies among observed variables by embedding tractable Markov networks at lower levels. Meanwhile, Adel et al. [31], proposed an SVD-based method that unifies row-wise and column-wise splitting from LearnSPN into a single rank-one submatrix extraction procedure. Other approaches have employed an information bottleneck criterion [32], or cutset-like conditioning that mimics decision-tree learning [22]. Despite these varied methods, they remain heuristic-based and lack firm theoretical underpinnings.

Bayesian Perspectives: A more principled approach to PC structure learning takes a Bayesian view. In this framework, one treats both the circuit structure $\mathcal{G}$ and the parameters θ as latent variables, writing $P_{\theta,\mathcal{G}}(\mathbf{x}) = P(\mathbf{x} \mid \theta, \mathcal{G})$. Defining a *Bayesian Structure Score* ($\mathcal{B}$) quantifies how the structure $\mathcal{G}$ contributes to the overall likelihood:

$$\mathcal{B}(\mathcal{G}) = P(\mathcal{D} \mid \mathcal{G}) = \int_{\theta} P(\mathcal{D} \mid \theta, \mathcal{G}) \, P(\theta \mid \mathcal{G}) \, d\theta,$$

where $P(\theta \mid \mathcal{G})$ is a prior over parameters and $\mathcal{D}$ is the dataset. Intuitively, marginalizing out θ yields a structure score reflecting how well $\mathcal{G}$ alone explains the data [33, 34]. However, computing this integral can be challenging in practice. Recently, Yang et al. [35], demonstrated that one can compute this score exactly and tractably for *deterministic* PCs, coupling it with a greedy cutset approach [22], and structural expectation maximization [36], to learn state-of-the-art PC structures. They also showed that for discrete data and a Dirichlet prior on sum-node parameters, the Bayesian structure score reduces to the Bayes-Dirichlet (BD) score [37], connecting it to classical Bayesian network scoring. While Bayesian methods offer theoretical rigor for exploring candidate structures, they can be computationally expensive, so many practical approaches continue to rely on heuristic or greedy structure-learning algorithms that, while lacking formal guarantees, perform well in empirical evaluations.

A complementary perspective suggests that *structure learning may be less critical when over-parameterization is possible.* Peharz et al. [28] demonstrated that a sufficiently large ensemble of random structures can yield results on par with learned structures. They extended earlier notions of Region Graphs [32, 38] to *Random Region Graphs*, which, by recursively and randomly partitioning the variables at each node, produce valid PCs. Unlike classical approaches, this random parameterization has reduced sparsity and is highly parallelizable on GPUs, enabling large-scale learning. Follow-up efforts have also considered randomized structures for deterministic PCs [39, 40]. Notably, Peharz et al. [25], built upon RAT-SPNs by introducing a tensorized "einsum" design that stacks sum-product operations in layers, reminiscent of deep neural networks, achieving significant speedups. More recently, Mari et al. [41], proposed a unifying framework encompassing multiple tensorized parameterizations for PCs, showing that *low-rank decompositions* can maintain expressivity while further boosting computational efficiency.

Taken together, these random or over-parameterized strategies shift emphasis away from carefully crafted structures, relying instead on random, parallelizable architectures that can scale to large datasets. They complement traditional structure learning approaches – both heuristic and Bayesian – by suggesting that a sufficiently large, well-parameterized PC may obviate the need for complex structure searches in many real-world settings.

The Section 7.4 is dedicated to normalizing flows. We will discuss their mathematical foundations, their advantages as generative models, their challenges in performing queries other than full-density evaluation, and how they might complement PCs. Equipped with this understanding, we will then proceed to the theoretical analysis of merging flows and PCs, culminating in the construction of PFCs.

7.4 Normalizing Flows: A Primer

Normalizing flows are a class of deep generative models that have emerged as a popular approach for learning probability distributions while retaining the ability to compute exact densities and perform stable maximum likelihood training. Their construction, based on composing invertible transformations, makes them a natural candidate for enriching PCs. In this section, we provide a comprehensive introduction to normalizing flows. We begin by recalling the change-of-variables formula, the central theoretical tool that allows exact likelihood computation for transformed random variables. We then describe the concept of invertible parameterized mappings, or "flow steps," each chosen to be both expressive and computationally tractable for density evaluation, and how flows are trained via maximum likelihood. This sets the stage for understanding how flows can be integrated into PCs to create Probabilistic Flow Circuits (PFCs).

From Simple Base Distributions to Complex Data Distributions: Many generative modeling approaches rely on starting with a simple base distribution – commonly an isotropic Gaussian – and then gradually "warping" or "transforming" it into a complex target distribution that better fits the observed data. Normalizing flows follow this principle but enforce that the transformations be *invertible* and *differentiable*, forming a diffeomorphism between the latent (or base) space and the data space.

Concretely, let $\mathbf{Z} = (Z_1, \dots, Z_d)$ be a random vector drawn from a simple base distribution $p_\mathbf{Z}(\mathbf{z})$. Typically, $p_\mathbf{Z}$ is chosen as a standard Gaussian, i.e., $p_\mathbf{Z}(\mathbf{z}) = \mathcal{N}(\mathbf{z}; \mathbf{0}, \mathbf{I})$. A normalizing flow defines an invertible function: $f : \mathbb{R}^d \to \mathbb{R}^d$ such that the target variable $\mathbf{X} = f(\mathbf{Z})$ now has a distribution $p_\mathbf{X}(\mathbf{x})$ that can be obtained via the change-of-variables formula. If f is invertible with inverse f^{-1} and Jacobian matrix $J_f(\mathbf{z}) = \frac{\partial f(\mathbf{z})}{\partial \mathbf{z}}$, we have:

$$p_\mathbf{X}(\mathbf{x}) = p_\mathbf{Z}(f^{-1}(\mathbf{x})) \left|\det(J_{f^{-1}}(\mathbf{x}))\right| .$$

Since $\det(J_{f^{-1}}(\mathbf{x})) = 1/\det(J_f(\mathbf{z}))$, we often write:

$$p_\mathbf{X}(\mathbf{x}) = p_\mathbf{Z}(\mathbf{z})\left|\det(J_f(\mathbf{z}))\right|^{-1},$$

where $\mathbf{z} = f^{-1}(\mathbf{x})$. Because we typically start from a simple $p_\mathbf{Z}$ where densities are easy to compute, and we can compute f and f^{-1} efficiently, evaluating $p_\mathbf{X}(\mathbf{x})$ becomes feasible. This is the crux of normalizing flows: flexible densities and exact likelihood evaluation.

Composing Multiple Invertible Transformations: A single invertible transformation f might not be sufficiently expressive. To achieve complex transformations, flows compose multiple transformations:

$$f = f_K \circ f_{K-1} \circ \cdots \circ f_1.$$

Each f_i is a simple invertible mapping with a tractable Jacobian determinant. The composition of invertible functions is also invertible, so f is invertible. To evaluate the probability density under $p_\mathbf{X}$, we must chain the Jacobians:

$$\log p_\mathbf{X}(\mathbf{x}) = \log p_\mathbf{Z}(f^{-1}(\mathbf{x})) - \sum_{i=1}^{K} \log |\det(J_{f_i}(\mathbf{z}_{i-1}))|,$$

where $\mathbf{z}_0 = \mathbf{z}$ and $\mathbf{z}_K = \mathbf{x}$. Different choices of f_i strike different balances between expressivity and computational complexity. This factorization into K simpler transformations (often called "flow steps" or "layers") allows normalizing flows to be constructed incrementally. Each step f_i can be chosen from a family of invertible functions that are easy to evaluate and differentiate.

Training Normalizing Flows: Normalizing flows are typically trained via maximum likelihood. Given a dataset $\{\mathbf{x}^{(i)}\}_{i=1}^{N}$, we aim to find parameters θ of the transformations that maximize:

$$\mathcal{L}(\theta) = \sum_{i=1}^{N} \log p_{\mathbf{X}_\theta}(\mathbf{x}^{(i)}).$$

Since $p_{\mathbf{X}_\theta}(\mathbf{x})$ is given by a known base distribution and a computable Jacobian determinant term, we can backpropagate through this objective easily. Gradient-based optimization (e.g., Adam) is used, and no approximations like variational inference or adversarial losses are needed. This stability and direct maximum likelihood training are major strengths of normalizing flows.

7.4.1 Sampling and Inference in Flows

Flows are designed so that sampling and density evaluation are both tractable:

- **Sampling:** To sample from $p_{\mathbf{X}}(\mathbf{x})$, we first sample $\mathbf{z}$ from the base distribution $p_{\mathbf{Z}}$. Since f is invertible, we apply f to $\mathbf{z}$ to get $\mathbf{x} = f(\mathbf{z})$. This process is exact and does not require rejection sampling or approximate methods. The complexity is linear in the number of transformations composed.
- **Density Evaluation:** Given $\mathbf{x}$, we invert through the flow to find $\mathbf{z} = f^{-1}(\mathbf{x})$ and compute the Jacobian determinants along the way. This yields $p_{\mathbf{X}}(\mathbf{x})$ exactly. Compared to other deep generative models like VAEs or GANs, normalizing flows do not require variational approximations or adversarial games to obtain the density.
- **Conditionals and Marginals:** Despite having exact densities and easy sampling, normalizing flows do not inherently provide easy marginalization or conditional computations over arbitrary subsets of variables. To compute $P(\mathbf{X}_A)$, one must integrate out $\mathbf{X}_B$ from $P_{\mathbf{X}}(\mathbf{X}_A, \mathbf{X}_B)$:

  $$P(\mathbf{X}_A) = \int P_{\mathbf{X}}(\mathbf{X}_A, \mathbf{X}_B) d\mathbf{X}_B.$$

  Performing this integral is generally as hard as in other high-dimensional models since no internal factorization is guaranteed. Similarly, conditional distributions are not straightforward unless special flow architectures are designed to factor the Jacobian in a way that isolates certain subsets of variables.

This last point is critical. While flows offer exact density evaluation and easy sampling, their lack of built-in structure for marginalization or conditioning on subsets of variables is a known limitation. This is where integrating flows with PCs becomes appealing. PCs, with their decomposability and smoothness, guarantee tractable marginal and conditional inference. If we can leverage the representational power of flows at the level of leaf distributions inside PCs, we can combine the strengths of both.

7.5 Integrating Normalizing Flows and PC

Having introduced PCs as tractable generative models and normalizing flows as flexible yet structured transformations, we now address the central question of how to unify these two paradigms. The goal is to combine the powerful inference capabilities of PCs – enabling efficient exact marginal, conditional, and even MAP inference – with the expressive representational power of flows, which can model highly complex, non-linear distributions at the leaves. At first glance, the integration seems natural: if the internal nodes of a PC, which previously modeled some probability distribution over a subset of variables, are augmented with a normalizing flow node that maps it to a more complex distribution, then the resulting model could approximate complicated distributions while retaining the PC's inference tractability. However, this naïve approach may fail if the introduction of flow transformations breaks the structural properties – particularly decomposability – that are essential for tractable inference.

This section presents the theoretical foundations for correctly integrating normalizing flows into PCs. We will introduce the notion of *τ-decomposability*, a key property that ensures transform nodes (representing flow transformations) do not violate the decomposability property of the circuit. We will show that without enforcing τ-decomposability, the introduction of invertible transformations can cause previously independent subsets of variables to become entangled, making marginal and conditional queries intractable.

We will then prove that if all transform nodes satisfy τ-decomposability, any arrangement of flows inside a PC can be "pushed down" to the leaves. This essentially reduces the problem of designing a hybrid model to simply equipping each leaf with a univariate normalizing flow, ensuring both tractability and expressivity. These results set the stage for defining *Probabilistic Flow Circuits (PFCs)* in the next section.

7.5.1 The Challenge

Recall that decomposability is a critical property for PCs: each product node must factor over disjoint subsets of variables. This ensures integrals factorize and complexity does not explode combinatorially. Now consider introducing a transform node – representing an invertible mapping $g : \mathbb{R}^n \to \mathbb{R}^n$ – somewhere above a product node in the circuit. If g mixes variables that were previously separated into disjoint subsets, it can destroy the neat factorization structure. For instance, suppose a product node P is defined over two sets of variables $(\mathbf{X}_1, \mathbf{X}_2)$ that are independent at that node. Before applying a transformation, we have:

$$P(\mathbf{x}) = N_1(\mathbf{x}_1) \cdot N_2(\mathbf{x}_2)$$

for children nodes N_1 and N_2, whose scopes are $\mathbf{X}_1$ and $\mathbf{X}_2$, respectively. If we apply a transformation g that mixes $\mathbf{x}_1$ and $\mathbf{x}_2$, the factorization might no longer hold. This leads to integrals over $\mathbf{x}_2$ that cannot be separated from $\mathbf{x}_1$, breaking tractability.

Transform Nodes and Their Impact on Decomposability: A *transform node* $\mathcal{T}$ in a sum-product-transform network (SPTN) [16], or a general PC+flow model applies an invertible transformation g to its child's distribution. Formally if $\mathcal{T}$ has one child node $\mathcal{N}$ with scope $\psi_{\mathcal{N}}$, and g is an invertible mapping on $\mathbb{R}^{|\psi_{\mathcal{N}}|}$, then:

$$\mathcal{T}(\mathbf{x}) = \mathcal{N}(g(\mathbf{x})) \left|\det(J_g(\mathbf{x}))\right|,$$

where J_g is the Jacobian of g. This equation reflects the change-of-variables formula. If this transform node is placed arbitrarily in the PC, the variable mixing caused by g could mean that previously factorized distributions no longer factor. The product of distributions over disjoint scopes becomes a product of distributions over entangled variables, losing the simplicity required for tractability.

7.5.2 τ-Decomposability

To prevent the violation of decomposability, we must restrict how transformations g operate at product nodes. The key idea is that if a product node divides variables into disjoint subsets, the transformation must respect this partitioning.

Definition 7.1(*τ-Decomposability*): A sum-product-transform network (or PC with transform nodes) is *τ-decomposable* if, for every product node $\mathcal{P}$ in the circuit, the invertible transformation g associated with any transform node above $\mathcal{P}$ decomposes with respect to the collection of disjoint subsets defined by the children of $\mathcal{P}$. In other words, g can be block-diagonalized so that it transforms each subset of variables independently, without mixing them across subsets.

Formally, let a product node $\mathcal{P}$ have children $N_1, \dots, N_k$ with scopes $\psi_{N_1}, \dots, \psi_{N_k}$ that form a partition of the scope of $\mathcal{P}$. A transform node $\mathcal{T}$ above $\mathcal{P}$ with transformation $g : \mathbb{R}^{|\psi_{\mathcal{P}}|} \to \mathbb{R}^{|\psi_{\mathcal{P}}|}$ is τ-decomposable if:

$$\forall i \neq j, \frac{\partial g(\mathbf{x})_{\psi_{N_i}}}{\partial \mathbf{x}_{\psi_{N_j}}} = 0.$$

This means g maps each subset of variables in the partition to itself without cross-dependencies.

If every transform node in the circuit is τ-decomposable, the decomposability property of the PC is preserved. Intuitively, this restricts how flows are applied: no mixing of variables belonging to different product components is allowed.

Necessity of τ-Decomposability: One can prove that τ-decomposability is not just a sufficient condition but also a necessary one for preserving tractability. Consider the contrapositive: if τ-decomposability does not hold, there exists at least one product node $\mathcal{P}$ and a transformation g that mixes variables across disjoint subsets. This mixing induces joint dependencies at a node that was meant to factorize distributions. As a result, integrals over these subsets cannot be pushed down to the leaves and computed independently.

Lemma 7.1: *If a PC with transform nodes is decomposable, then all transform nodes must be τ-decomposable.*

Proof. (Sketch) Assume there is a transform node $\mathcal{T}$ associated with g above a product node $\mathcal{P}$. If g is not τ-decomposable, it introduces cross-dependencies among subsets. This cross-dependency leads to a violation of decomposability at $\mathcal{P}$. Since decomposability is required for tractability, we have a contradiction. Hence, g must be τ-decomposable.

This shows that allowing arbitrary invertible transformations inside a PC is not an option if we want to maintain exact tractability for queries like marginalization and conditioning.

Expressivity Implications of τ–Decomposability: Another crucial theoretical result is that, given a τ-decomposable PC+flows, we can always "push down" the transformations towards the leaves. Essentially, any transform node placed above a sum node can distribute down to its children, and any transform node above a product node can be broken down into block-diagonal transformations that apply independently to each subset of variables.

Theorem 7.1: *Any τ-decomposable PC with transform nodes is equivalent to a PC where all the transforms are consolidated at the leaves, forming leaf-level normalizing flows over individual variables.*

Proof. Let $\mathcal{C}_{\mathcal{SPTN}}$ be τ-decomposable sum product transform network, and $\mathcal{S}, \mathcal{P}, \mathcal{T}, \mathcal{L} \in \mathcal{C}_{\mathcal{SPTN}}$ denote a sum node, product node, transform node, and leaf node, respectively. For any arbitrary node $\mathcal{N}$, we will show that defining transformations over $\mathcal{N}$ reduces to transformations over the children of $\mathcal{N}$.

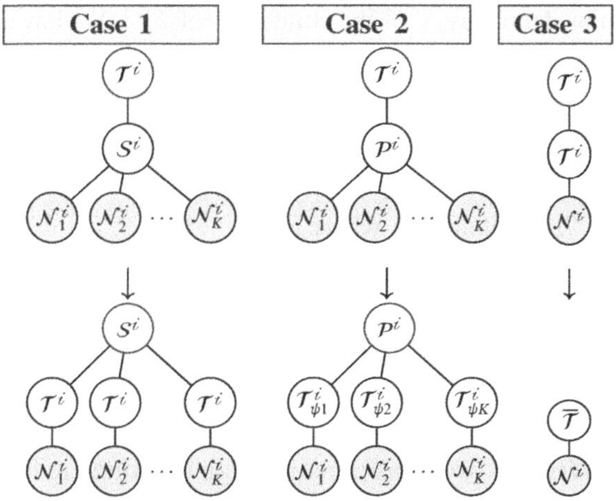

Case 1: When $\mathcal{N} = \mathcal{S}$, we have,

$$\begin{aligned}
\mathcal{T}(\mathcal{S}(\boldsymbol{x})) &= \mathcal{S}(\mathrm{g}(\boldsymbol{x}))|\det J_{\mathrm{g}}| \\
&= \sum_{\mathcal{N}_i \in ch(\mathcal{S})} w_i \mathcal{N}_i(\mathrm{g}(\boldsymbol{x}))|\det J_{\mathrm{g}}| \\
&= \sum_{\mathcal{N}_i \in ch(\mathcal{S})} w_i \mathcal{T}(\mathcal{N}_i(\boldsymbol{x}))
\end{aligned}$$

Case 2: When $\mathcal{N} = \mathcal{P}$, we have,

$$\begin{aligned}
\mathcal{T}(\mathcal{P}(\boldsymbol{x})) &= \mathcal{P}(\mathrm{g}(\boldsymbol{x}))|\det J_{\mathrm{g}}| \\
&= \left[\prod_{\mathcal{N}_i \in ch(\mathcal{P})} \mathcal{N}_i(\Pi_{\psi_{\mathcal{N}_i}}(\mathrm{g}(\boldsymbol{x})))\right] |\det J_{\mathrm{g}}| \\
&= \left[\prod_{\mathcal{N}_i \in ch(\mathcal{P})} \mathcal{N}_i(\mathrm{g}_{\psi_{\mathcal{N}_i}}(\boldsymbol{x}_{\psi_{\mathcal{N}_i}}))\right] |\det J_{\mathrm{g}}|
\end{aligned}$$

Since g is decomposable w.r.t the collection (Ω) of scopes of children of $\mathcal{P}$, the Jacobian of g is a block diagonal matrix, each block corresponding to the Jacobian of the independent transformations, $J_{\mathrm{g}_{\psi_i}}$ for $\psi_i \in \Omega$. Thus, $|\det J_{\mathrm{g}}| = \prod_{\mathcal{N}_i \in ch(\mathcal{P})} |\det J_{\mathrm{g}_{\psi_{\mathcal{N}_i}}}|$. Hence,

$$\begin{aligned}
\mathcal{T}(\mathcal{P}(\boldsymbol{x})) &= \prod_{\mathcal{N}_i \in ch(\mathcal{P})} \left[\mathcal{N}_i(\mathrm{g}_{\psi_{\mathcal{N}_i}}(\boldsymbol{x}_{\psi_{\mathcal{N}_i}}))|\det J_{\mathrm{g}_{\psi_{\mathcal{N}_i}}}|\right] \\
&= \prod_{\mathcal{N}_i \in ch(\mathcal{P})} \mathcal{T}_{\psi_{\mathcal{N}_i}}(\mathcal{N}_i(\boldsymbol{x}))
\end{aligned}$$

Case 3: When $\mathcal{N} = \mathcal{T}^{i-1}$, let us denote by $\mathcal{N}^{i-1}$ the child node of $\mathcal{T}^{i-1}$. We have,

$$\begin{aligned}\mathcal{T}^i(\mathcal{T}^{i-1}(\mathcal{N}^{i-1}(\boldsymbol{x}))) &= \mathcal{T}^i(\mathcal{N}^{i-1}(g^{i-1}(\boldsymbol{x}))|\det J_{g^{i-1}}| \\ &= \mathcal{N}^{i-1}(g^{i-1}(g^i(\boldsymbol{x})))|\det J_{g^{i-1}}||\det J_{g^i}| \\ &= \mathcal{N}^{i-1}(\overline{g}(\boldsymbol{x}))|\det J_{\overline{g}}|, \text{ where } \overline{g} = g^{i-1}\circ g^i \\ &= \overline{\mathcal{T}}(\mathcal{N}^{i-1}(\boldsymbol{x}))\end{aligned}$$

i.e., $\mathcal{T}^i$ with transformation g^i and $\mathcal{T}^{i-1}$ with transformation g^{i-1} can be combined into a single transform node $\overline{\mathcal{T}}$ with an associated transformation $\overline{g} = g^{i-1}\circ g^i$. This follows from the fact that compositions of invertible transformations are invertible and the Jacobian of composition of two transformations can be written as the product of the Jacobians of the individual transformations.

Thus, recursively pushing down transformations along the path from the root to each leaf node, we end up with compositions of transformations defined only over the leaf nodes. Let l_i be the number of transform nodes along the path from the root to the leaf $\mathcal{L}^i$ and let $\overline{\mathcal{T}}$ denote the composition $\mathcal{T}^1\circ\mathcal{T}^2 \dots \mathcal{T}^{l_i}$. $\mathcal{C}_{\mathcal{SPTN}}$ has now reduced to containing only sum nodes, product nodes and a transformed leaf node, where the new leaf node $\overline{\mathcal{L}}$ is defined as: $\overline{\mathcal{L}}(\boldsymbol{x}) = \overline{\mathcal{T}}(\mathcal{L}(\boldsymbol{x})) = \mathcal{L}(g^1\circ g^2\circ \dots \circ g^{l_i}(\boldsymbol{x}))\prod_{i=1}^{l} |\det J_{g^i}|$

Thus, each leaf node now becomes a normalizing flow. This theorem is significant. It states that no matter how we insert flow transformations into a τ-decomposable PC, we can equivalently represent the same distribution by simply enhancing the leaves with normalizing flows. Thus, the complicated problem of where and how to place flows inside the circuit reduces to a much simpler design: put a univariate flow at each leaf.

Ensuring Invertibility and Efficient Computation at the Leaves: Given that we must place flows at the leaves for simplicity, what is needed to maintain tractability? Each leaf now models a single variable X_i via a flow:

$$p_{X_i}(x_i) = p_{Z_i}(g_i^{-1}(x_i))|\det(J_{g_i}(x_i))|^{-1},$$

where g_i is a univariate invertible flow transformation and p_{Z_i} is a simple base distribution (e.g., Gaussian). For a univariate transformation, the Jacobian determinant is simply the absolute value of the derivative of g_i. Evaluating integrals over X_i remains tractable because integrating a univariate function with respect to a variable is straightforward, especially if we choose transformations with closed-form inverses and integrals (like linear rational splines [42]. Thus, τ-decomposability and pushing transforms to leaves ensure that we do not compromise the PC's ability to handle marginals and conditionals efficiently.

7.6 Probabilistic Flow Circuits

Having established the theoretical underpinnings of integrating normalizing flows into PCs, we now introduce *Probabilistic Flow Circuits (PFCs)*. PFCs are a new class of tractable probabilistic models that combine the structural advantages of PCs with the expressive power of normalizing flows at their leaves. They inherit from PCs the ability to perform exact inference tasks – such as evidential, marginal, conditional, and MAP inference – efficiently, while from flows, they gain the capacity to flexibly approximate complicated distributions that are challenging for simpler leaf families.

Definition of a PFC: A *PFC* is a computational graph representing a probability distribution over a set of variables $\mathbf{X} = (X_1, \dots, X_d)$, structured exactly like a probabilistic circuit, but with each leaf distribution replaced by a *univariate normalizing flow*. More formally:

- **Structure:** A PFC is a rooted directed acyclic graph composed of sum nodes and product nodes, as in a standard PC. Each sum node represents a mixture over its children, and each product node represents a factorization over disjoint subsets of variables.
- **Leaf Nodes:** Instead of a simple distribution like a Gaussian, each leaf node in a PFC encodes a one-dimensional normalizing flow. Specifically, for leaf L_i corresponding to variable X_i, we define:

  $$p_{X_i}(x_i) = p_{Z_i}(z_i) \left| \frac{dz_i}{dx_i} \right|,$$

  where $z_i = g_i^{-1}(x_i)$ and g_i is an invertible monotonic transformation parameterized by a set of parameters ϕ_i. The base distribution $p_{Z_i}(z_i)$ is typically chosen as a standard Gaussian or another simple distribution with closed-form density.
- **Parameters:** The parameters of a PFC include:
  1. The mixture weights at sum nodes, which must be non-negative and sum to one.
  2. The parameters of the univariate flows at the leaves (ϕ_i), describing the transformation g_i.
  3. Any parameters defining the base distributions at the leaves, if not fixed (although these are often fixed to a standard form).

By design, the internal structure of the PFC (the arrangement of sum and product nodes) remains the same as in a PC. The critical difference is that the leaves are now highly flexible distributions obtained by applying invertible transformations to simple base densities. Figure 7.1 shows

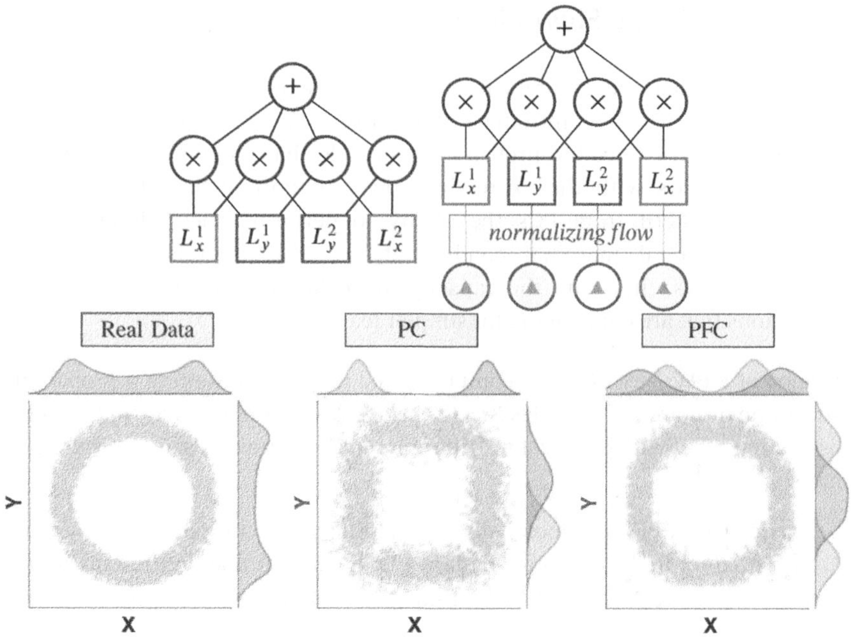

Figure 7.1 Modeling a 2D data distribution (bottom left) using a PC (top left) and a PFC (top right). The light gray and dark gray marginal plots indicate the respective leaf distributions L_x and L_y. While the PC struggles to capture the shape of the distribution, the PFC, with its multi-modal leaf flows, can better model the observed data.

an example of how a standard PC (left) may fail to capture a complex two-dimensional data distribution, whereas a PFC (right) better models the underlying structure by placing a flow transformation at each leaf. As illustrated, the PFC is able to learn multi-modal or skewed shapes at each univariate leaf, all while preserving the tractability of the overarching circuit structure. This balance of structure and flexibility is central to the design of PFCs and distinguishes them from both plain PCs and standalone flow-based generative models.

PFC via Linear Rational Splines: The requirement at the leaf node for a PFC is that it should enable tractable computation of probability densities. Any diffeomorphic transformation enables computing the exact density using the change of variables formula. Thus, any expressive normalizing flow architecture can, in principle, be used to implement a PFCs.

However, the nature of inference tasks that we need tractability for can demand additional characteristics that are desirable of the diffeomorphisms defined at the leaves. For example, in order to support MAP inference, deterministic PCs require that the argmax over the leaf density is easily computable. In PCs, since leaf distributions over continuous variables are typically parameterized as Gaussians, the argmax (or the mode of the distribution) corresponds to the mean. However, by defining distributions using normalizing flows, the leaf nodes in a PFC now model arbitrarily complex probability distributions. Since they are no longer restricted to be uni-modal, computing the argmax over this distribution becomes a challenging task. Thus, one design principle for PFCs could be defining diffeomorphisms that support easy computation of modes, without imposing significant limitations on its expressivity.

We propose to parameterize g using a family of invertible piecewise functions, known as *linear rational splines (LRS)*. Spline-based normalizing flows [42, 43], have attracted much research interest in recent years and are among the state-of-the-art. We will adapt the computationally efficient LRS transformations defined by Dolatabadi et al. [42], to define expressive leaf distributions with easily computable modes.

Definition 7.2: An invertible linear rational spline transformation is a piecewise function that divides the input space (X) into bins (or intervals) and defines a monotonic rational function of the form $y = \frac{a_1 x + b_1}{a_2 x + b_2}$ within each bin, such that they are knotted together at the boundaries so as to define a differentiable function. Formally, given a set of monotonically increasing points $\{(x^k, y^k)\}_{k=0}^{K}$ known as knots, derivatives $\{d^k > 0\}_{k=0}^{K}$ at the knots, and parameters $\{\lambda^k \in (0, 1)\}_{k=0}^{K}$, the LRS transformation within each bin, say for $x \in [x^k, x^{k+1}]$ is defined as:

$$y = g_{lrs}(\phi), \text{ where } \phi = \frac{(x - x^k)}{(x^{k+1} - x^k)}, \text{ and}$$

$$g_{lrs}(\phi) = \begin{cases} \dfrac{w^k y^k(\lambda^k - \phi) + w^m y^m \phi}{w^k(\lambda^k - \phi) + w^m \phi} & 0 \le \phi \le \lambda^k \\[2ex] \dfrac{w^m y^m(1 - \phi) + w^{k+1} y^{k+1}(\phi - \lambda^k)}{w^m(1 - \phi) + w^{k+1}(\phi - \lambda^k)} & \lambda^k \le \phi \le 1 \end{cases}$$

Given the knots and the derivatives, the parameters w^k, w^m, w^{k+1}, λ^k, and y^m are constructed in such a manner [42], that the overall function defined is differentiable everywhere. The width and height of each bin, the derivatives at the knots, and λ are defined as learnable parameters for an LRS flow. The form for the analytical inverse of g_{lrs} and its Jacobian are given in Dolatabadi et al. [42]. Defining a flow at the leaf also requires specifying a base distribution. While any distribution with an analytically computable density can be used, for theoretical purposes, we will use a Student's-t distribution with 3 degrees of freedom, as the form of its density function simplifies the analysis when used with g_{lrs}. We summarize the tractability of our model below before we present empirical results.

Lemma 7.2: *A PFC ($C_{\mathcal{F}}$) with leaf distributions defined using g_{lrs} transformations and a Student's-t distribution with $\nu = 3$ as the base distribution is a tractable model for (a) evidential inference if $C_{\mathcal{F}}$ is smooth, (b) Marginal and conditional inference if $C_{\mathcal{F}}$ is smooth and decomposable, and (c) MAP inference if $C_{\mathcal{F}}$ is smooth, decomposable, and deterministic.*

Proof. The tractability of evidential, marginal and conditional inference for $C_{\mathcal{F}}$ follows trivially from the fact that $C_{\mathcal{F}}$ is a probabilistic circuit and hence inherits the tractability offered by the circuit properties of a PC under the structural constraints of smoothness and decomposability. We elaborate on this further as follows:

a. **Evidential inference:** In order to tractably perform evidential inference, $C_{\mathcal{F}}$ requires that the leaf nodes compute a valid probability density over its scope. A normalizing flow supports exact density evaluation using the change of variables formula and hence enables tractable evidential inference. Smoothness of $C_{\mathcal{F}}$ further ensures that its sum nodes compute valid mixture densities. However, note that smoothness is not a necessary condition, as a non smooth PC can, in polynomial time, be converted to a smooth PC [9].
b. **Marginal and conditional inference:** For a smooth and decomposable $C_{\mathcal{F}}$, marginalizing out a variable X_i from its modeled density reduces to marginalizing out the corresponding leaf distribution. This is because marginalization of X_i involves integrating the model density over $\boldsymbol{val}(X_i)$, and as proved in Choi et al. [9], the integral over the circuit reduces to integrals over the leaf distributions having X_i in their scope, when the circuit is smooth and decomposable. Note that each leaf nodes in $C_{\mathcal{F}}$ represents a probability distribution over a single variable, and marginalizing it out is equivalent to setting the corresponding leaf density to 1. Thus, $C_{\mathcal{F}}$ supports tractable marginal inference. Also, the tractability of conditional inference naturally follows from the tractability of evidential and marginal inference.
c. **MAP inference:** Along the same lines, computation of MAP queries for $C_{\mathcal{F}}$ reduces to computing argmax over leaf densities if $C_{\mathcal{F}}$ is smooth, decomposable and deterministic [9]. Thus, if we can compute the mode of the distribution modeled by the leaf nodes, we can ensure tractability for MAP inference. For $x \in [x^i, x^{i+1}]$, let $\phi = \dfrac{(x - x^{i+1})}{x^{i+1} - x^i}$, and let g denote the linear rational spline transformation associated with the bin, which has the form $g(\phi) = \dfrac{q(\phi)}{r(\phi)} = \dfrac{a_1\phi + b_1}{a_2\phi + b_2}$. Let S_t denote a Student's-t distribution with 3 degrees of freedom. The pdf of a Student's-t distribution with ν degrees of freedom is given by:

$$p(x;\nu) = \frac{\Gamma\left(\frac{\nu+1}{2}\right)}{\sqrt{\nu\pi}\,\Gamma\left(\frac{\nu}{2}\right)}\left(1+\frac{x^2}{\nu}\right)^{-\left(\frac{\nu+1}{2}\right)}$$

Thus, we have the following form for the density modeled at the leaf distributions,

$$\begin{aligned} p(x) &= S_t(g(\phi)).|\frac{\partial g(\phi)}{\partial x}| \\ &= \frac{1}{(x^{i+1}-x^i)}S_t(g(\phi)).|\frac{\partial g(\phi)}{\partial \phi}| \\ &= C_1 S_t\left(\frac{q(\phi)}{r(\phi)}\right)(r(\phi))^{-2} \\ &= \frac{C_1\Gamma(2)}{\sqrt{3\pi}\Gamma\left(\frac{3}{2}\right)}\left[1+\frac{1}{3}\left(\frac{q(\phi)}{r(\phi)}\right)^2\right]^{-2}(r(\phi))^{-2} \\ &= C_2[3r(\phi)+q(\phi)g(\phi)]^{-2} \end{aligned}$$

where C_1, C_2 are constants. Thus, we have $\log p(x) = \log C_2 - 2\log(3r(\phi) + q(\phi)g(\phi))$. Now, $\log p(x)$ is maximized when $f(\phi) = 3r(\phi) + q(\phi)g(\phi)$ is minimized. Differentiating and equating to zero, we have,

$$3r'(\phi) + q'(\phi)g(\phi) + q(\phi)g'(\phi) = 0$$

$$\Rightarrow\ 3a_2 r(\phi)^2 + a_1 q(\phi)r(\phi) + (b_2a_1 - a_2b_1)q(\phi) = 0$$

Note that as $q(\phi), r(\phi)$ are linear in ϕ, the above equation is quadratic in ϕ. Thus, we can check if any of its real roots lie within the interval $[0, 1]$. If it does, then the maximum density within that bin is given by the density at the root. If not, then the maximum occurs at either of the interval boundaries. Thus, we can compute the maximum within each bin analytically. The maximum density across all the bins gives the mode of the distribution.

Note that the above analysis also extends to compositions of LRS transformations as a composition of linear rational functions is a linear rational function. i.e., for $g_1(\phi) = \dfrac{a_1\phi + b_1}{a_2\phi + b_2}$ and $g_2(\phi) = \dfrac{c_1\phi + d_1}{c_2\phi + d_2}$, we have,

$$\begin{aligned} g_2(g_1(\phi)) &= \frac{c_1\left(\frac{a_1\phi+b_1}{a_2\phi+b_2}\right)+d_1}{c_2\left(\frac{a_1\phi+b_1}{a_2\phi+b_2}\right)+d_2} \\ &= \frac{(c_1a_1+d_1a_2)\phi + c_1b_1 + d_1b_2}{(c_2a_1+d_2a_2)\phi + c_2b_1 + d_2b_2} \end{aligned}$$

is also a linear rational function.

Training a PFC: Training a PFC can be done by maximum likelihood just as with PCs or flows alone. Consider a dataset $\{\mathbf{x}^{(i)}\}_{i=1}^{N}$. The MLE objective is:

$$\theta^* = \arg\max_{\theta} \sum_{i=1}^{N} \log p_\theta(\mathbf{x}^{(i)}).$$

Since PFCs are differentiable computational graphs, we can compute the gradient of the log-likelihood w.r.t. all parameters, including:

- Sum node weights: updated similarly to PCs.
- Leaf flow parameters: updated by backpropagating through the inverse flow transformations and Jacobian computations. This is standard practice in normalizing flow training.

Complexity and Scalability: A PFC's computational complexity remains comparable to a PC of similar size, with an additional factor from evaluating leaf flows. Since each leaf flow evaluation is $O(K)$ for K segments in a spline, and there are d variables, the leaf evaluation adds a small overhead relative to the overall circuit size. Modern tensorized PC implementations leverage GPU acceleration for both the PC structure (via einsum operations) and the leaf flow computations. As a result, PFCs can scale to high-dimensional datasets. They also benefit from parallelization since each variable's flow is independent at evaluation time.

7.7 Experiments and Results

This section presents a comprehensive suite of experiments designed to answer critical questions about PFCs in practice, summarized as follows:

1. **Expressivity:** Can PFCs model complex distributions better than standard PCs with simple leaf distributions, and do they approach the representational flexibility of standalone normalizing flows?
2. **Inference Tractability:** Do PFCs retain the hallmark inference tasks – such as tractable marginalization and conditioning – efficiently on challenging datasets?
3. **Training Stability and Efficiency:** How do PFCs train compared to PCs and normalizing flows? Are there any stability or convergence issues?
4. **Sample Quality and Conditional Generation:** Can PFCs generate higher-quality samples and effectively handle conditional queries, improving over vanilla PCs?

We will first describe the experimental setup, including datasets and baselines. We then present a detailed account of the experiments from low-dimensional synthetic tasks to high-dimensional image and tabular datasets. Finally, we provide ablation studies and additional analyses to show how different design choices affect performance. The experiments and results presented here distill and expand upon those introduced in the original technical work on PFCs, preserving the key findings and their significance.

7.7.1 Modeling Complex 3D Manifolds

Datasets: We first evaluate on six synthetic 3D data distributions (shown in Figure 7.2), each with a challenging manifold structure: *Interlocked-Circles*, *Helix*, *Bent-Lissajous*, *Disjoint-Circles*, *Twisted-Eight*, and *Knotted*. These datasets, adapted from Sidheekh et al. [44], are both low-dimensional (so visualizations are straightforward) yet possess non-trivial geometric properties, making them suitable benchmarks for generative modeling. We compare three models:

1. **EinsumNet:** A tractable PC parameterized as an *einsum* network [25], with Gaussian leaves.
2. **EinsumNet + Affine:** A PFC variant where each leaf is augmented with an invertible affine transformation [16], implemented via SVD/householder parameterization.
3. **EinsumNet + LRS:** A PFC variant using a *Linear Rational Spline (LRS)* flow at each leaf, yielding a more expressive univariate transformation.

For each 3D dataset, we generate 20,000 points, splitting into 10,000 for training and 5,000 each for validation and testing. We train these models using the Adam optimizer (learning rate 10^{-3}) on the same circuit structure, varying only the leaf parameterization. Figure 7.3 shows validation log-likelihood curves for two of the 3D datasets, while Table 7.1 presents final test log-likelihoods.

From Figure 7.3 and Table 7.1, we see that EinsumNet + Affine gives only moderate gains over the baseline EinsumNet, likely because affine transformations of Gaussians remain Gaussians. By contrast, EinsumNet + LRS consistently shows

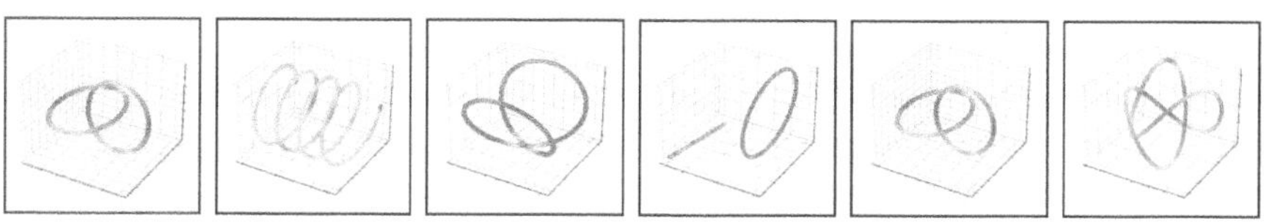

Figure 7.2 Visualizations of the six **3D data distributions** over complex manifolds used in our experiments.

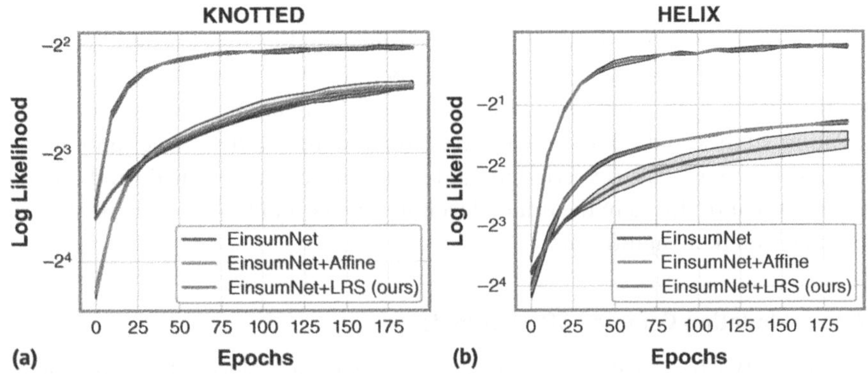

Figure 7.3 **Learning curves** on two of the 3D datasets. We compare: *EinsumNet*, *EinsumNet+Affine*, and *EinsumNet+LRS*. Shaded regions depict standard deviation over three trials.

substantial improvements in final likelihood and faster convergence, suggesting that more expressive leaf transformations are crucial for capturing these manifold distributions.

7.7.2 Scaling to High-dimensional Data

To test how PFCs scale to larger and more complex datasets, we train models on six high-dimensional datasets: four UCI tabular datasets (POWER, GAS, MINIBOONE, HEPMASS) and two image datasets (MNIST [45], and Fashion-MNIST [46]). We preprocess the tabular data following Papamakarios et al. [47]. Each model is trained for 100 epochs on the tabular datasets and 50 epochs on the image datasets. We compare:

- **EinsumNet:** The PC baseline with Gaussian leaves.
- **EinsumNet + LRS:** The proposed PFC version using linear rational spline flows at each leaf.
- We also provide additional references to the performance of *MADE* [48], *Real NVP* [15], and *MAF* [47], (from Papamakarios et al. [47], to indicate how standard deep generative models (without tractable conditional or marginal inference) perform on these datasets.

Table 7.2 shows mean test log-likelihoods. PFCs (EinsumNet + LRS) notably outperform the baseline EinsumNet across all six datasets. Interestingly, they can even match or surpass certain purely flow-based models in some cases (e.g., RealNVP on GAS and MADE on POWER), highlighting that introducing flows at the leaves of a tractable circuit can deliver competitive expressivity without sacrificing exact inference capabilities. While PFCs are not specifically tailored to specialized tasks such as high-resolution image modeling (like PixelCNN or advanced VAEs),

Table 7.1 Test log-likelihood (higher is better) on the 3D datasets.

	Helix	Knotted	Disjoint-Circles	Interlocked-Circles	Twisted-Eight	Bent-Lissajous
EinsumNet	-2.94 ± 0.24	-5.23 ± 0.07	-1.71 ± 0.19	-2.88 ± 0.07	-3.02 ± 0.24	-3.02 ± 0.06
+ Affine	-2.47 ± 0.09	-5.18 ± 0.11	-1.18 ± 0.06	-2.52 ± 0.05	-2.79 ± 0.07	-2.69 ± 0.05
+ LRS	-1.04 ± 0.02	-4.09 ± 0.03	-0.81 ± 0.03	-2.44 ± 0.02	-2.43 ± 0.01	-2.53 ± 0.02

Note: Values represent mean $\pm$ standard deviation over three trials.

Table 7.2 Test log-likelihood (higher is better) on tabular and image datasets.

	POWER	GAS	MINIBOONE	HEPMASS	MNIST	Fashion-MNIST
MADE	-3.08 ± 0.03	3.56 ± 0.04	-15.59 ± 0.50	-20.98 ± 0.02	-1380.8 ± 4.8	–
Real NVP	-0.02 ± 0.01	4.78 ± 1.80	-13.55 ± 0.49	-19.62 ± 0.02	-1323.2 ± 6.6	–
MAF	0.14 ± 0.01	9.07 ± 0.02	-11.75 ± 0.44	-17.70 ± 0.02	-1300.5 ± 1.7	–
EinsumNet	0.20 ± 0.01	3.57 ± 0.08	-35.93 ± 0.06	-22.79 ± 0.05	-1015.1 ± 0.9	649.1 ± 0.3
Einsum+LRS	0.36 ± 0.01	4.79 ± 0.04	-34.21 ± 0.01	-22.46 ± 0.01	-959.4 ± 1.4	655.6 ± 0.6

Values for MADE, RealNVP, and MAF are Adapted from Papamakarios et al. [47].

these results emphasize that an appropriately chosen univariate flow at each leaf can substantially boost the modeling power of PCs in higher dimensions.

7.7.3 Sample Generation and Inference

Figure 7.4 compares samples generated by EinsumNet (Gaussian leaves) and EinsumNet+LRS on MNIST. The flow-augmented leaves produce sharper, more diverse digit-like structures, indicating a better learned manifold. Leveraging the tractability of PCs, a PFC can condition on arbitrary subsets of variables and sample from the remaining ones exactly. Figure 7.5 illustrates this for (a) MNIST and (b) Fashion-MNIST with the top half of each image occluded. We also demonstrate (c) partial conditioning in a 3D *Helix* dataset by fixing certain coordinates to lie along a specific curve. These tasks are typically intractable for standard flows or GAN-based models, underscoring the advantage of PFCs' inherited structure.

7.7.4 Ablation: Influence of PC Complexity

To examine how a PFC's performance depends on the underlying PC, we vary the hyperparameters (k and r) that govern an einsum network's size. We train *EinsumNet* and *EinsumNet+LRS* on MNIST for $k, r \in \{1, 2, 4, 8, 16, 32\}$, and plot test log-likelihood in Figure 7.6. Even for very small PCs ($k = r = 1$) adding a spline flow to each leaf yields large gains. This suggests that leaf-level flow transformations provide a flexible modeling capability that is complementary to the global mixture-product structure, rather than purely dependent on it.

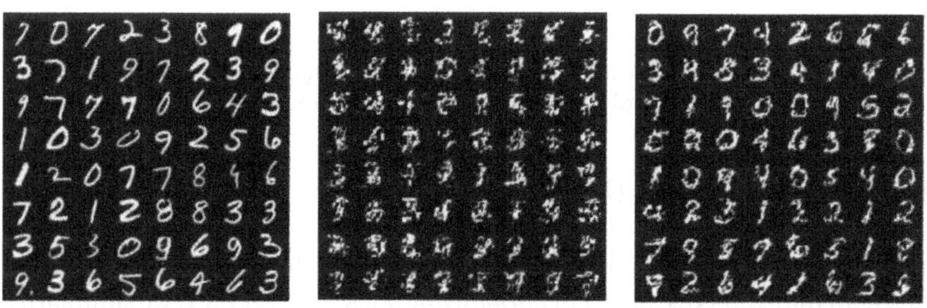

(a) Ground Truth **(b)** EinsumNet **(c)** Einsum + LRS

Figure 7.4 Unconditional Samples generated by EinsumNet and EinsumNet+LRS on MNIST. The flow-enhanced leaves yield noticeably sharper and more diverse digits.

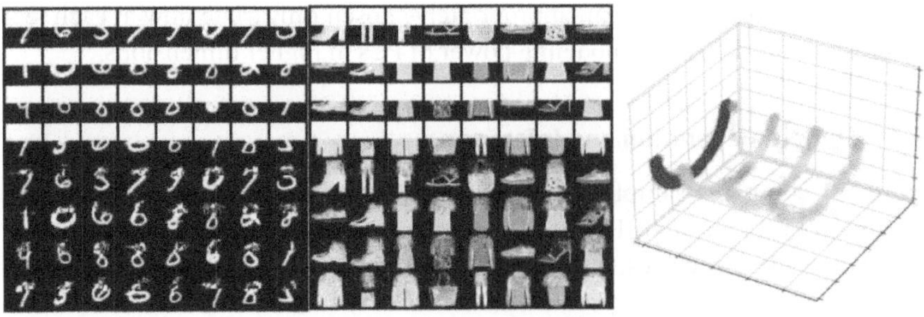

(a) MNIST **(b)** Fashion-MNIST **(c)** Helix

Figure 7.5 Conditional Generation with EinsumNet + LRS. (a) and (b): Inpainting half-occluded images. (c) Generating 3D Helix data points constrained to a certain arc.

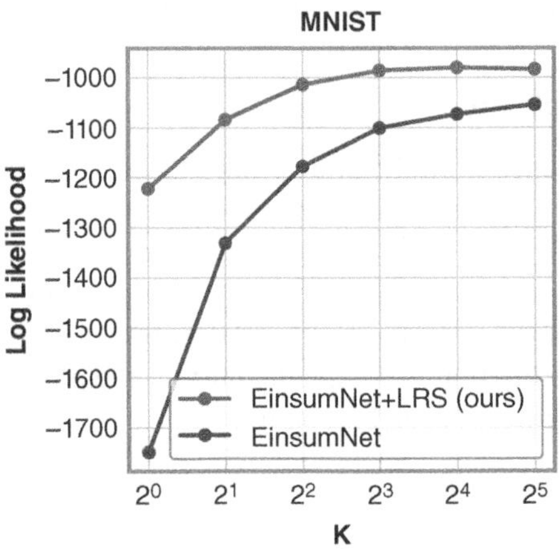

Figure 7.6 Ablation on MNIST: Test log-likelihood vs. PC size (k, r). EinsumNet+LRS outperforms the baseline at all sizes, indicating that flow augmentation at the leaves contributes substantially regardless of the PC's structural complexity.

7.8 Conclusion and Discussion

In this chapter, we introduced *PFCs* as a novel approach for uniting the tractability of *PCs* with the expressive power of *normalizing flows*. Section 7.8.1, we summarize our main findings, reflect on the strengths and limitations of the framework, and propose avenues for further investigation.

7.8.1 Key Takeaways

Bridging Tractability and Expressivity: A central motivation for PFCs was to remedy the relatively modest expressiveness of PCs while retaining their hallmark inference capabilities – namely tractable marginalization, conditioning, and (if deterministic) MAP inference. By incorporating univariate flow-based transformations at the leaf nodes, we saw that we can substantially expand the set of distributions PCs can model, including multi-modal, skewed, or otherwise intricate patterns that ordinary Gaussian leaves fail to capture.

Improvements over Standard PCs: Across numerous tasks – ranging from synthetic 2D/3D manifolds to high-dimensional tabular and image datasets – we saw that PFCs consistently outperformed baseline PCs with Gaussian leaves in log-likelihood and sample fidelity, validating the theoretical claim that adding flow transformations at the leaves significantly enhances modeling flexibility.

Competitiveness with Standard Flows: While specialized normalizing flow architectures sometimes have an edge on certain datasets, PFCs often rival or exceed them in performance, especially given that standard flows typically lack built-in support for tractable queries like marginal and conditional probabilities. Hence, PFCs offer a compelling alternative in situations where exact inference is desirable.

Stable and Efficient Training: Despite adding potentially complex univariate transformations at every leaf, PFCs remain straightforward to train using maximum likelihood. Neither specialized adversarial methods nor intricate variational schemes are required. As a result, practical deployment does not differ drastically from training a standard PC or normalizing flow alone, yet PFCs, being a hybrid model, gain benefits from both domains.

7.8.2 Limitations and Future Directions

We outline some existing challenges and opportunities for further improvement:

- **Univariate Leaves:** At present, each leaf focuses on a single variable, allowing us to preserve tractability when marginalizing distributions. Exploring *multivariate leaf flows* that remain integrable while capturing local dependencies is an intriguing but non-trivial future direction.
- **Structure Selection or Learning:** While random region graphs and large "over-parameterized" PCs often suffice to approximate many distributions, identifying or learning high-quality structures remains a significant research problem. Bayesian or heuristic structure-learning algorithms can help tailor PCs to specific, data scarce domains.

- **Restricted Transformations:** We have focused primarily on linear rational splines as flexible univariate transformations. Other invertible maps – potentially specialized to certain manifolds or domain knowledge – may improve the ability to capture sharp boundaries or complex latent geometries.
- **Partial Mixing in the Circuit:** Although pushing flows to the leaves ensures that variables do not get mixed in a way that breaks decomposability, some limited cross-variable transformations might be allowed without fully forfeiting tractability. Discovering precisely how to design such partial transforms (and where to place them) could further enhance expressivity.

Another interesting direction is to consider *conditional flows* at the leaves, wherein each leaf distribution adapts its parameters based on learned global features or latent variables within the circuit. Such an approach could bring the representational benefits of deep latent models into the PFC framework, possibly yielding powerful hybrid architectures.

To conclude, in proposing PFCs, we aimed to show that tractable inference need not come at the expense of expressive modeling. Empirically, we verified that adding robust, invertible transformations to the leaves of a PC significantly enlarges the class of representable distributions, all while retaining fast and exact solutions to key inference queries. These findings place PFCs as a valuable addition to the spectrum of generative models, one that marries the advantages of PCs and normalizing flows in a theoretically sound and practically effective manner. Continuing research in this direction will likely focus on refining leaf transformations, expanding the scope of tractable structures, and extending partial mixing to combine variables more flexibly. Ultimately, such progress may further advance the frontiers of probabilistic modeling, opening doors for real-world applications requiring both powerful representation and reliable uncertainty quantification.

Acknowledgements

This chapter consolidates and expands the work originally presented in our UAI paper [17], that introduced PFC and our IJCAI survey paper [18], on building expressive and tractable generative models. The authors gratefully acknowledge the generous support by the NIH grant R01HD101246, the AFOSR award FA9550-23-1-0239, the ARO award W911NF2010224, and the DARPA Assured Neuro Symbolic Learning and Reasoning (ANSR) award HR001122S0039.

References

1 Daphne Koller and Nir Friedman. *Probabilistic Graphical Models: Principles and Techniques.* MIT Press, 2009.

2 S. Bond-Taylor, A Leach, Y Long, and C G Willcocks. Deep generative modelling: a comparative review of VAEs, GANs, normalizing flows, energy-based and autoregressive models. *IEEE Transactions on Pattern Analysis and Machine Intelligence*, 44(11):7327–7347, 2022.

3 Diederik P. Kingma and Max Welling. Auto-encoding variational bayes. In Yoshua Bengio and Yann LeCun, editors, *Proceedings of ICLR*, 2014.

4 Ian J Goodfellow, Jean Pouget-Abadie, Mehdi Mirza, Bing Xu, David Warde-Farley, Sherjil Ozair, Aaron C Courville, and Yoshua Bengio. Generative adversarial nets. In *NeurIPS*, 2014.

5 Esteban G Tabak and Cristina V Turner. A family of nonparametric density estimation algorithms. *Communications on Pure and Applied Mathematics*, 66(2):145–164, 2013.

6 George Papamakarios, Eric T Nalisnick, Danilo Jimenez Rezende, Shakir Mohamed, and Balaji Lakshminarayanan. Normalizing flows for probabilistic modeling and inference. *Journal of Machine Learning Research*, 22(57):1–64, 2021.

7 Jascha Sohl-Dickstein, Eric Weiss, Niru Maheswaranathan, and Surya Ganguli. Deep unsupervised learning using nonequilibrium thermodynamics. In *International Conference on Machine Learning*, pages 2256–2265. PMLR, 2015.

8 Jonathan Ho, Ajay Jain, and Pieter Abbeel. Denoising diffusion probabilistic models. *Advances in Neural Information Processing Systems*, 33: 6840–6851, 2020.

9 YooJung Choi, Antonio Vergari, and Guy Van den Broeck. Probabilistic circuits: a unifying framework for tractable probabilistic models, 2020. http://starai.cs.ucla.edu/papers/ProbCirc20.pdf

10 Hoifung Poon and Pedro M Domingos. Sum-product networks: a new deep architecture. In *UAI*, 2011.

11 Doga Kisa, Guy Van den Broeck, Arthur Choi, and Adnan Darwiche. Probabilistic sentential decision diagrams. In *KR*, 2014.

12 Adnan Darwiche. A differential approach to inference in Bayesian networks. *Journal of the ACM*, 50(3):280–305, 2003.

13 Anji Liu, Honghua Zhang, and Guy Van den Broeck. Scaling up probabilistic circuits by latent variable distillation. In *ICLR*, 2023.

14 Xuejie Liu, Anji Liu, Guy Van den Broeck, and Yitao Liang. Understanding the distillation process from deep generative models to tractable probabilistic circuits. In *ICML*, 2023b.

15 Laurent Dinh, Jascha Sohl-Dickstein, and Samy Bengio. Density estimation using real NVP. In *Proceedings of ICLR*, 2017.

16 Tomáš Pevný, Václav Smídl, Martin Trapp, Ondřej Poláček, and Tomáš Oberhuber. Sum-product-transform networks: exploiting symmetries using invertible transformations. In *PGM*, 2020.

17 Sahil Sidheekh, Kristian Kersting, and Sriraam Natarajan. Probabilistic flow circuits: towards unified deep models for tractable probabilistic inference. In *UAI*, 2023.

18 Sahil Sidheekh and Sriraam Natarajan. Building expressive and tractable probabilistic generative models: a review. In Kate Larson, editor, *Proceedings of the 33rd International Joint Conference on Artificial Intelligence, IJCAI-24*, pages 8234–8243. International Joint Conferences on Artificial Intelligence Organization, 2024. https://doi.org/10.24963/ijcai.2024/910. Survey Track.

19 Walter R Gilks, Sylvia Richardson, and David Spiegelhalter. *Markov Chain Monte Carlo in Practice*. CRC Press, 1995.

20 David M Blei, Alp Kucukelbir, and Jon D McAuliffe. Variational inference: a review for statisticians. *Journal of the American Statistical Association*, 112(518): 859–877, 2017.

21 Solomon Eyal Shimony. Finding MAPs for belief networks is NP-hard. *Artificial Intelligence*, 68(2): 399–410, 1994.

22 Tahrima Rahman, Prasanna Kothalkar, and Vibhav Gogate. Cutset networks: a simple, tractable, and scalable approach for improving the accuracy of chow-liu trees. In *ECML PKDD*, 2014.

23 Robert Peharz, Robert Gens, and Pedro Domingos. Learning selective sum-product networks. In *LTPM Workshop, ICML*, 2014.

24 Raquel Sánchez-Cauce, Iago París, and Francisco Javier Díez. Sum-product networks: a survey. *IEEE Trans Pattern Anal Mach Intell*, 44(7):3821–3839, 2021.

25 Robert Peharz, Steven Lang, Antonio Vergari, Karl Stelzner, Alejandro Molina, Martin Trapp, Guy Van den Broeck, Kristian Kersting, and Zoubin Ghahramani. Einsum networks: fast and scalable learning of tractable probabilistic circuits. In *ICML*, 2020.

26 Arthur P Dempster, Nan M Laird, and Donald B Rubin. Maximum likelihood from incomplete data via the em algorithm. *Journal of the Royal Statistical Society: Series B (Methodological)*, 39(1):1–22, 1977.

27 Robert Peharz, Robert Gens, Franz Pernkopf, and Pedro Domingos. On the latent variable interpretation in sum-product networks. *IEEE Transactions on Pattern Analysis and Machine Intelligence*, 39(10):2030–2044, 2016.

28 Robert Peharz, Antonio Vergari, Karl Stelzner, Alejandro Molina, Xiaoting Shao, Martin Trapp, Kristian Kersting, and Zoubin Ghahramani. Random sum-product networks: a simple and effective approach to probabilistic deep learning. In *UAI*, 2020.

29 Robert Gens and Pedro M. Domingos. Learning the structure of sum-product networks. In *ICML*, 2013.

30 Amirmohammad Rooshenas and Daniel Lowd. Learning sum-product networks with direct and indirect variable interactions. In *ICML*, 2014.

31 Tameem Adel, David Balduzzi, and Ali Ghodsi. Learning the structure of sum-product networks via an svd-based algorithm. In *UAI*, 2015.

32 Robert Peharz, Bernhard C Geiger, and Franz Pernkopf. Greedy part-wise learning of sum-product networks. In *ECML PKDD*, 2013.

33 Nir Friedman and Daphne Koller. Being Bayesian about network structure. a Bayesian approach to structure discovery in Bayesian networks. *Machine learning*, 50:95–125, 2003.

34 Stuart J Russell. *Artificial Intelligence a Modern Approach, 4th ed.* Pearson,2020.

35 Yang Yang, Gennaro Gala, and Robert Peharz. Bayesian structure scores for probabilistic circuits. In *AISTATS*, 2023.

36 Nir Friedman. The Bayesian structural EM algorithm. In *UAI*, 1998.

37 David Heckerman, Dan Geiger, and David M Chickering. Learning Bayesian networks: the combination of knowledge and statistical data. *Machine Learning*, 20(3):197–243,1995.

38 Aaron W. Dennis and Dan Ventura. Learning the architecture of sum-product networks using clustering on variables. In *NeurIPS*, 2012.

39 Nicola Di Mauro, Antonio Vergari, Teresa M A Basile, and Floriana Esposito. Fast and accurate density estimation with extremely randomized cutset networks. In *ECML PKDD*, 2017.

40 Nicola Di Mauro, Gennaro Gala, Marco Iannotta, and Teresa M A Basile. Random probabilistic circuits. In *UAI*, 2021.

41 Antonio Mari, Gennaro Vessio, and Antonio Vergari. Unifying and understanding overparameterized circuit representations via low-rank tensor decompositions. In *The 6th Workshop on Tractable Probabilistic Modeling*, 2023. https://openreview.net/forum?id=1btutFdIya.

42 Hadi Mohaghegh Dolatabadi, Sarah M. Erfani, and Christopher Leckie. Invertible generative modeling using linear rational splines. In *AISTATS*, 2020.

43 Conor Durkan, Artur Bekasov, Iain Murray, and George Papamakarios. Neural spline flows. In *NeurIPS*, 2019.

44 Sahil Sidheekh, Chris B. Dock, Tushar Jain, Radu V. Balan, and Maneesh Kumar Singh. VQ-Flows Vector quantized local normalizing flows. In James Cussens and Kun Zhang, editors, *Uncertainty in Artificial Intelligence, Proceedings of the 38th Conference on Uncertainty in Artificial Intelligence, UAI 2022*, 1-5 August 2022, *Eindhoven, The Netherlands*, 2022.

45 Li Deng. The MNIST database of handwritten digit images for machine learning research. *IEEE Signal Processing Magazine*, 29(6):141–142, 2012.

46 Han Xiao, Kashif Rasul, and Roland Vollgraf. Fashion-MNIST: a novel image dataset for benchmarking machine learning algorithms. *arXiv preprint arXiv:1708.07747*, 2017.

47 George Papamakarios, Iain Murray, and Theo Pavlakou. Masked autoregressive flow for density estimation. In *NeurIPS*, 2017.

48 Mathieu Germain, Karol Gregor, Iain Murray, and Hugo Larochelle. MADE: masked autoencoder for distribution estimation. In Francis R Bach and David M Blei, editors, *ICML*, JMLR Workshop and Conference Proceedings, 2015.

8

Toward Verifiable and Scalable In-context Fine-tuning in Neurosymbolic AI

Neel P. Bhatt,[1] Alvaro Velasquez,[2] Zhangyang Wang,[1] and Ufuk Topcu[1]*

[1] *Oden Institute of Computational Sciences and Engineering, The University of Texas at Austin, Austin, Texas, USA*
[2] *Department of Computer Science, University of Colorado Boulder, Boulder, Colorado, USA*

*Corresponding Author: Neel P. Bhatt; npbhatt@utexas.edu

8.1 Introduction

Scaling laws have dominated the research space in artificial intelligence (AI) since the last decade. The argument made is rather simple: by increasing the amount of training data and compute availability, neural models can approximate any function, leading to better performance across a multitude of tasks. Purely neural approaches, driven by scaling laws, excel at capturing statistical correlations, however, the "bigger is better" philosophy will ultimately reach practical and theoretical limits. In a recent work by Zhang et al. [1], it was demonstrated that even when neural models achieve high in-distribution accuracy in logical reasoning tasks, they often fail to learn true reasoning capabilities and instead exploit statistical patterns in the data. This reinforces our argument that simply scaling up models is insufficient; we need approaches that can truly upend scaling laws. This realization prompts the search for more scalable, sustainable, and innovative solutions.

Specifically, we need to embrace methods that integrate domain knowledge, logical reasoning, and efficient problem-solving strategies and this is where neurosymbolic AI excels. Neurosymbolic AI is a growing area that promotes methodological heterogeneity and aims to push the frontiers of AI through the efficient use of structure and prior knowledge for scaling. Neurosymbolic AI leverages the raw pattern recognition power of neural networks and the structured and verifiable properties of symbolic representations (such as logic-based representations,

Neurosymbolic AI: Foundations and Applications, First Edition. Edited by Alvaro Velasquez et al.

knowledge graphs, and differential equations) posing the potential to break out of the cycle of diminishing returns by enabling smarter and more efficient systems.

The symbolic space itself is discrete, however, the mapping between neural and symbolic spaces can be understood through the lens of probabilistic reasoning. The mapping functions between the two spaces can be formalized as:

- **Neural → Symbolic:** A lifting operation that extracts discrete logical structures from continuous neural representations, similar to how probabilistic circuits can be used to derive most likely explanations.
- **Symbolic → Neural:** A projection operation that transforms logical constraints into differentiable loss terms that guide neural network training.

The theoretical justification for why the synergistic interleaving of neural and symbolic representations can reduce data and computational requirements comes from the complementary strengths of each representation. Specifically, neural representations excel at learning smooth manifolds in high-dimensional spaces, whereas symbolic representations enable exact reasoning over discrete structures. The interleaving allows each representation to handle the aspects of the problem for which it is best suited.

Neurosymbolic AI approaches may perform the lifting and projection operations within a feedback loop. Such a unified neurosymbolic approach generally performs the following sequence of steps:

- **Extract Neural Embeddings:** Using deep neural networks, learn high-dimensional embeddings that capture the complex, underlying structure of the data.
- **Identify Symbolic Variables:** Apply techniques such as symbolic regression, discovery, or geometric manifold learning to distill these embeddings into compact, interpretable state variables.
- **Lift to Symbolic Space:** Map the identified variables to symbolic representations, enabling logical reasoning and manipulation.
- **Project Back to Neural Space:** Integrate the symbolic reasoning results back into the neural learning process, creating a feedback loop that refines both the neural and symbolic components.

One of the unique strengths of neurosymbolic AI is its flexibility in applying symbolic reasoning across different stages of neural computation. While several neurosymbolic integration methodologies exist in the literature, these methodologies integrate symbolic reasoning via processing of the inputs, outputs, or intermediate representations of the neural models.

Both output reasoning and input prompting methods treat neural models as “black boxes,” however, they probe different aspects of the framework. Methods that perform output reasoning generally view neural models as powerful generators and probe their outputs, verifying them against several logical rules before task execution. Input prompting introduces structured information into the input space of neural models, which indirectly influences the resulting outputs. Intermediate representation engineering moves beyond simple input-output mappings and delves into the internal structure of neural models to uncover representations that can bridge the gap between neural and symbolic reasoning.

One area where neurosymbolic AI has already demonstrated its potential is in planning, a notoriously difficult problem for purely neural models. While LLMs excel at generating approximate plans based on vast textual data, they struggle with the logical consistency required for executable plans. Frameworks processing the outputs of LLMs with external symbolic verifiers address complex planning tasks by using LLMs as candidate plan generators while relying on external verifiers to ensure correctness and logical soundness. Specifically, LLMs offer versatility and generalization, while symbolic verifiers provide rigorous, structured reasoning. By combining these components, we can achieve robust, flexible planning solutions that neither approach can offer independently.

In this chapter, we present two **verifiable** and **scalable** neurosymbolic methodologies [2, 3] that perform output reasoning for planning in detail and briefly outline a hybrid framework for dynamic interleaving of neural and symbolic reasoning during model training.

8.2 Neurosymbolic Fine-tuning Using Automated Feedback from Formal Verification

8.2.1 Introduction

Foundation models, such as pre-trained language models, encode rich world knowledge useful for planning and control in sequential decision-making tasks from software development to robotics. The resulting policies yield high-level actions an agent should take to satisfy objectives specified via natural language prompts.

However, in safety-critical domains, pre-trained models may fail to generate consistent and appropriate decision-making policies as outlined in Ge et al. [4] and Wang et al. [5]. For instance, an autonomous driving system may require knowledge about traffic rules and conventions specific to a given country. Such rules and conventions may be beyond the knowledge encoded in the pre-trained model.

Recent works such as by Christiano et al. [6], Rafailov et al. [7] and Stiennon et al. [8] address this shortcoming by integrating human feedback to incorporate domain knowledge and fine-tune foundation models. Human feedback evaluates how much a foundation model's output aligns with the desired objectives. For example, a binary ranking of likes or dislikes for each model output can act as a feedback source. However, obtaining feedback from humans is labor-intensive and costly.

Some existing works, such as by Baral et al. [9], Sadoun et al. [10] and Ghosh et al. [11], convert natural language to formal language, which can be used for verification and subsequently for model fine-tuning. Recent works show that language models can be trained to convert natural language to formal language, with applications in representing mathematics, generating proofs, and creating assurance cases [12–15]. The approach presented below is to design input prompts that include task-specific information (e.g. definitions, response templates, and detailed examples) that enable a language model to divide a goal into individual steps and develop formal constraints on the system [15]. Other methods iteratively refine the input prompt to the language model based on counter-examples until the outputs pass formal verification [16, 17]. Although these works utilize formal methods, there are still humans in the loop, while the method presented below is fully automated and does not require any human intervention.

8.2.2 Preliminaries

Automaton-based System Model: A model encodes the static and dynamic information of a system or an environment in an abstract representation. We use a transition system to build such a model.

A transition system $\mathcal{M} := \langle \Gamma_{\mathcal{M}}, Q_{\mathcal{M}}, \delta_{\mathcal{M}}, \lambda_{\mathcal{M}} \rangle$ consists of a set of output symbols $\Gamma_{\mathcal{M}}$, a set of states $Q_{\mathcal{M}}$, a non-deterministic transition function $Q_{\mathcal{M}} \times Q_{\mathcal{M}} \rightarrow \{0, 1\}$, and a labeling function $\lambda_{\mathcal{M}} : Q_{\mathcal{M}} \rightarrow \Gamma_{\mathcal{M}}$.

We introduce a set of atomic proposition P such that $\Gamma_{\mathcal{M}} := 2^P$, i.e. a symbol $\sigma \in \Gamma_{\mathcal{M}}$ is the set of atomic propositions in P that evaluate to *True*. Each symbol σ captures the system or environment behavior. We present an example in Figure 8.1. We will leverage the fact that automaton-based structures are formally verifiable in the proposed method.

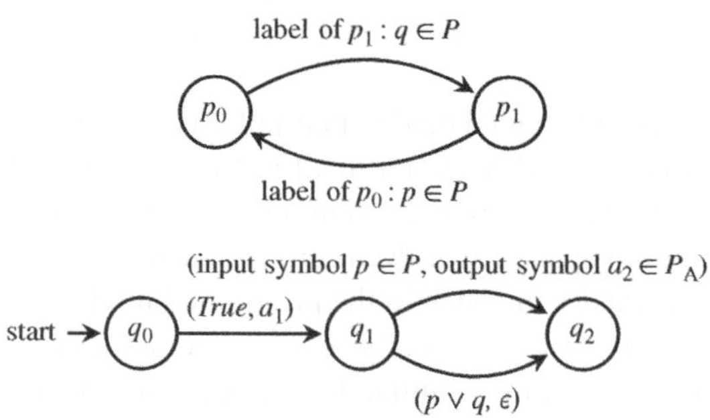

Figure 8.1 Examples of an automaton-based model (top) and a controller (bottom).

Automaton-based Controller: A controller is responsible for making decisions and taking actions based on the system's state. A controller can be mathematically represented as a mapping from the system's current state to an action, which is executable in the task environment. We use a *finite state automaton* (FSA) to build a controller for a sequential decision-making task.

A FSA is a tuple $\mathcal{A} = \langle \Sigma, A, Q, q_0, \delta \rangle$ where Σ and A are the sets of input and output symbols, $q_0 \in Q$ is the initial state, and $\delta : Q \times \Sigma \times A \times Q \rightarrow \{0, 1\}$ is a non-deterministic transition function. The transition function is a membership function – a transition exists when it evaluates to 1.

Each input symbol $\sigma \in \Sigma$ is composed of the atomic propositions from P, which is the set of atomic propositions we introduced for the model. We introduce another set of atomic propositions P_A for the output alphabets $A := 2^{P_A}$. We also allow for a "no operation/empty" symbol $\epsilon \in A$. Note that the input symbols comprise all possible dynamics of the environment or system in which the controller operates, and the output symbols comprise all the actions allowed by the controller. See Figure 8.1 for an example.

8.2.3 Methodology

We present a neurosymbolic output reasoning method for automated fine-tuning of pre-trained language models for planning tasks, named *direct preference optimization via automated feedback* (**DPO-AF**) as shown in Figure 8.2. The method first obtains human-provided information regarding the autonomous system. It then constructs a model that encodes the information about the system. Next, we query the pre-trained language model on a particular system control task and get multiple responses from the language model via sampling. We construct automata from the responses and apply verification methods to check how many user-provided specifications each automaton satisfies. We rank the responses by the number of satisfied specifications. Last, we send the prompt and ranked responses to the DPO algorithm to fine-tune the language model [7].

DPO-AF does not require repeated feedback from humans. Therefore, we can obtain an unlimited number of prompt-response pairs until the language model converges.

Autonomous System Modeling: DPO-AF first constructs an automaton-based model encoding the information about the autonomous system as shown in Figure 8.3. This system information is obtained from external sources such as human domain experts or system operation manuals. The information includes a set of propositions that describe the system's behaviors and a set of control signals

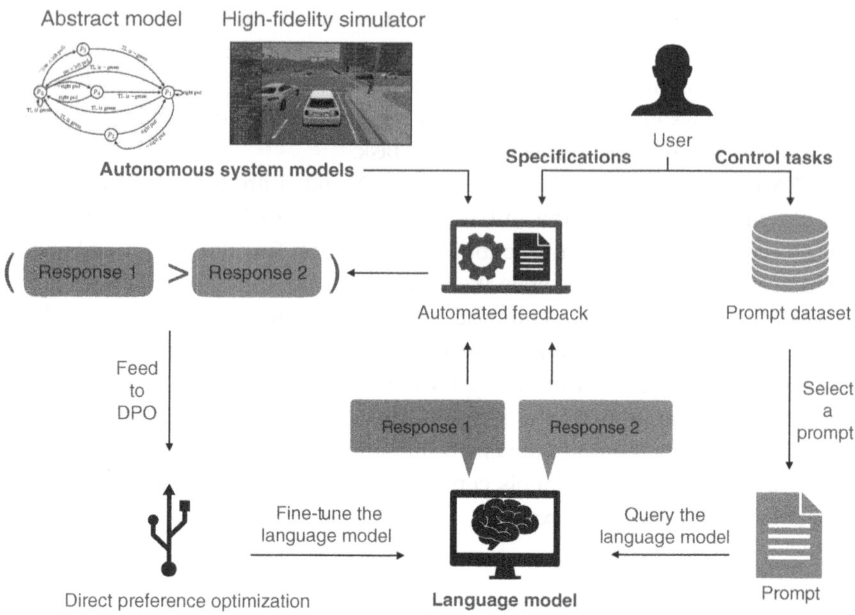

Figure 8.2 The overall pipeline of fine-tuning a language model for autonomous systems via automated feedback.

(actions) that can affect the system's states. We encode the set of behaviors in an atomic proposition set P and the set of actions in an atomic proposition set P_A.

Recall that a model consists of a set of states, a set of symbols, a transition function, and a label function. As we defined P and P_A, we build $2^{|P|}$ states whose label is $\sigma \in 2^P$ respectively. $|P|$ is the number of propositions in P. Next, for every two states p_i and p_j, we check whether the system supports the transition between the label of p_i and the label of p_j. If the system supports such a transition, we add it into the transition function.

Finally, we remove the states with no incoming and outgoing transitions. However, from a conservative perspective, we can build transitions for every pair of states and not remove any states. The conservative approach can avoid potential missing transitions but will significantly increase the computation cost for formal verification.

Task Prompt Engineering: Prior to fine-tuning the language model, we collect a prompt dataset. The prompt dataset consists of the queries on the control tasks that operate in the autonomous system.

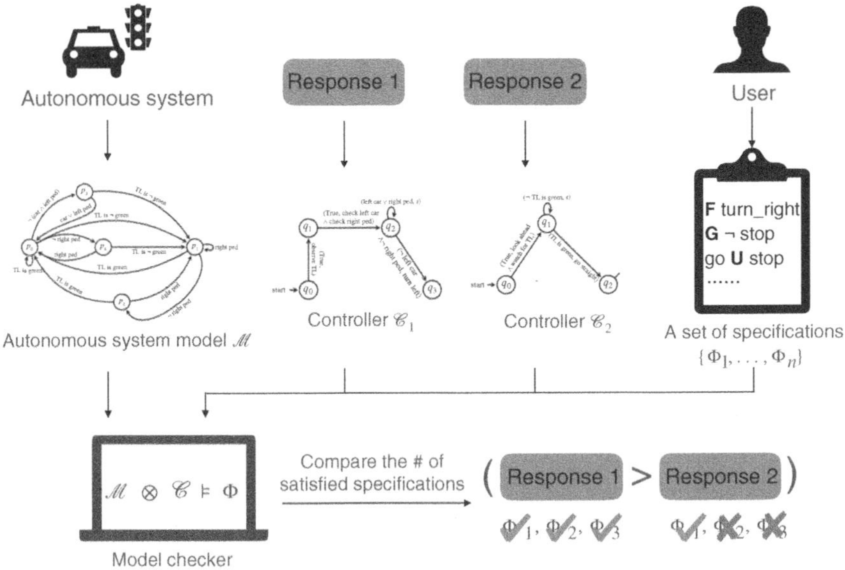

Figure 8.3 This diagram depicts the method of ranking responses by formal verification of the induced automata. We present the sample automata in Figures 8.4 and 8.6.

Algorithm 1 An Algorithm for System Modeling

Input Atomic Proposition Set P, System $\mathcal{S}$
Output $\Gamma_{\mathcal{M}}, Q_{\mathcal{M}}, \delta_{\mathcal{M}}, \lambda_{\mathcal{M}}$
$\Gamma_{\mathcal{M}} = 2^P$
for σ in $\Gamma_{\mathcal{M}}$
  $Q_{\mathcal{M}} = Q_{\mathcal{M}} + p_{new}$
  $\lambda_{\mathcal{M}}(p_{new}) = \sigma$
end for
for (p_i, p_j) in $Q_{\mathcal{M}}$
  if $p_i \rightarrow p_j$ is allowed by $\mathcal{S}$ $\{\mathcal{S}$ encodes a set of allowable transitions in a system$\}$
    $\delta_{\mathcal{M}}(p_i, p_j) = 1$
  end if
end for
$Q_{\mathcal{M}} = Q_{\mathcal{M}} \setminus \{p_i | \forall_j \delta_{\mathcal{M}}(p_i, p_j) = \delta_{\mathcal{M}}(p_j, p_i) = 0\}$

Then, we define a prompt engineering procedure to extract relative task knowledge from the language model. For each prompt in the prompt dataset, we first a prompt template to obtain the responses from the language model:

```
1 Define the steps for task description
2 1. description for step 1
3 2. description for step 2
4 ...
```

Line 1 and 2 onward depict the input prompt and the language model's responses, respectively. This format forces the outputs to be a list of step descriptions for the task described in the input prompt.

Once we get the responses, we query the language model again to map the step descriptions into the set of defined atomic propositions P.

We rephrase the step description so that the propositions and actions are consistent with the model. Therefore, we avoid failing the verification process due to language ambiguity, i.e. different phrases with the same meaning.

Note that DPO-AF also aims to fine-tune the language model to output steps that can be easily aligned to the propositions and actions. Therefore, the expected responses from the fine-tuned language model should have the following properties: (i) The language model can easily and correctly align the textual step descriptions to the given propositions and actions. (ii) The aligned step descriptions satisfy the user-provided specifications.

To check the second property, we need to construct an automaton-based controller from the textual step descriptions. Then, we implement the controller in the model and verify it against the specifications.

Controller Construction: We follow the method GLM2FSA introduced by Yang et al. [17] to construct an FSA-based controller to encode the textual step descriptions. Specifically, we start from the aligned textual step descriptions and apply semantic parsing to break the steps into a list of verb phrases. Recall that a controller consists of a set of states Q, an initial state q_0, input symbols Σ, output symbols A, and a transition function δ. We use the verb phrases to define the input and output symbols according to the grammar from GLM2FSA. Then, we build one state corresponding to each step, with the state corresponding to the first step as the initial state. Last, we follow the GLM2FSA algorithm to build the transition rules. We present a step-by-step illustrative example in Section 8.2.4.

Given a set of specifications, we provide two ways of checking whether the controllers constructed from the language model's outputs satisfy each specification. For each output, the method generates feedback consisting of the number or percentage of specifications being satisfied.

Formal Verification: Formal verification requires an automaton-based model, an automaton-based controller, and a set of logical specifications. So far, we have constructed the model and the controller. The specifications include the expectation of task achievement or safety requirements, represented in temporal logic (e.g. linear temporal logic [18]). The temporal logic specifications are logic formulas over propositions $P \cup P_A$. These specifications are either provided by the task designer or extracted from existing rule books.

In the verification procedure, we first implement the controller in the model. Mathematically, we define a product automaton $\mathfrak{P} = \mathcal{M} \otimes \mathcal{C}$ describing the interactions of the controller $\mathcal{C}$ with the model $\mathcal{M}$, i.e. how the controller's actions change the model's states and how the model's states affect the controller's decision-making on its next action. Note that the verification procedure implicitly assumes that all the actions can be successfully operated and hence lead to the corresponding states of the controller and the model.

We run a model checker (e.g. NuSMV [19]) to verify if the product automaton satisfies each specification,

$$\mathcal{M} \otimes \mathcal{C} \models \Phi. \tag{8.1}$$

We verify the product automaton against each specification for all the possible initial states. If the verification fails, the model checker returns a counter-example. The counter-example is a trace – a sequence of states – violates the specifications. The NuSMV model checker returns the sequence of states from the product automaton along with the output symbols. Mathematically, the traces are in a format of $(p_1, q_1, c_2 \cup a_1), (p_2, q_2, c_2 \cup a_2), \ldots$ where $p_i \in Q_{\mathcal{M}}, q_i \in Q$, $c_i = \lambda_{\mathcal{M}}(p_i)$, $a_i \in A$ such that $\delta(q_i, \lambda_{\mathcal{M}}(p_i), a_i, q_{i+1}) = 1$.

Empirical Evaluation: In some scenarios, obtaining models for autonomous systems may be hard. We propose using empirical evaluation to account for the scenarios where models are not present. Empirical evaluation requires an autonomous system $\mathcal{S}$, a constructed controller $\mathcal{C}$, an atomic proposition set P, a set of actions P_A, and a grounding method $\mathbf{G}$. Specifically, $\mathbf{G} : \mathcal{C} \times \mathcal{S} \to (2^P \times 2^{P_A})^N$ operates the controller directly in the system and returns a sequence of propositions and actions describing the operation. N is the max length of the sequence. The sequence is evaluated as follows:

$$\mathbf{G}(\mathcal{C}, \mathcal{S}) = (2^P \times 2^{P_A})^N \models \Phi. \tag{8.2}$$

After evaluating every sequence against the specifications, we get the percentage of sequences, $\mathbb{P}_\Phi$, which satisfy each specification:

$$\mathbb{P}_\Phi = \frac{\text{number of sequences satisfying } \Phi}{\text{total number of sequences}}.$$

Collection of the Language Model's Outputs: Once we select the autonomous system and obtain the model for the system, we can query the model for instructions on tasks that are operable in the system, following the format described in the previous section. Different responses for the same input task can be sampled from the language model. Then, we can rank these responses and fine-tune the language model to output the best response according to the system model.

Ranking Outputs and Model Fine-tuning: We apply the automated feedback method for every two responses from the language model associated with the same task prompt to rank the preferences of the two responses. As a result, we obtain a data point (x, y_w, y_l), where x is the input prompt, y_w is the preferred response and y_l is the unpreferred response. For a given set of specifications, we construct a controller from each response and verify it against each of the specifications. The response satisfying more specifications (or having a higher percentage $\mathbb{P}_\Phi$ of sequences satisfying the specifications) is preferred. If we have collected N tasks and m responses per task. Then, we will have a maximum number of $N \times C_2(m)$ data points, where $C_i(j)$ is the binomial coefficient meaning j choose i.

Then, we feed the pairs of responses, along with their prompt, to the DPO algorithm. The DPO algorithm fine-tunes the parameters of the language model accordingly. During fine-tuning, we use low-rank approximation to reduce computational complexity [20].

8.2.4 Experimental Results

To validate the proposed method, we apply DPO-AF on Llama2-7B for controlling an autonomous driving system. We first provide a demonstration of how we obtain the verification feedback. Then, we present quantitative results to show the effectiveness of DPO-AF at the mathematical level. Next, we use an autonomous driving simulator, Carla [21], to show Llama's performance enhancement at the operation level. Lastly, we provide evidence that the generated controller can be transferred to real-life, indicating the applicability of our approach.

System Modeling: To obtain formal verification feedback for the language model's outputs, we first construct automaton-based models that encode the information of the autonomous driving system. Such information includes the objects from the environment and potential environment dynamics that can be perceived by the autonomous vehicle. Note that the models are externally provided, either from human expertise or system manuals.

Figure 8.4 shows the automaton-based models encoding the information on a regular traffic light intersection (which we present in Figure 8.5). We construct one model for each scenario in the autonomous driving system. We integrate these models together to form a universal model representing the entire system. In this way, we can later implement the constructed controllers into the model for formal verification.

System Specifications: For verification purposes, we generate a set of traffic rules in the form of temporal logic. We denote the traffic rules as *specifications*. Some examples from the set of specifications in the temporal logic formula are presented below:

$\Phi_1 = \square(\text{pedestrian} \rightarrow (\lozenge\text{stop}))$,
$\Phi_2 = \square(\neg\text{turn left} \vee (\neg\text{opposite car} \vee \text{green left-turn light})$,
$\Phi_3 = \square(\neg\text{green traffic light} \rightarrow \neg\text{go straight})$,
$\Phi_4 = \square(\text{stop sign} \rightarrow \lozenge\text{stop})$,
$\Phi_5 = \square\neg\text{turn right} \vee \neg(\text{car from left} \vee \text{pedestrian at right})$,

From the provided models and specifications, we can extract a set of atomic propositions and a set of actions. We add the English vocabulary from the model's

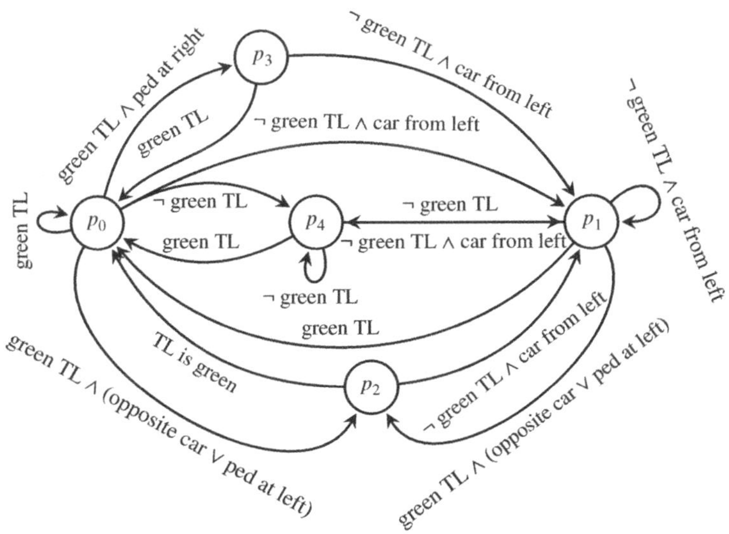

Figure 8.4 An automaton-based model represents a vehicle's environment dynamics at a regular traffic signal at an intersection. TL represents "traffic light," and ped represents "pedestrian."

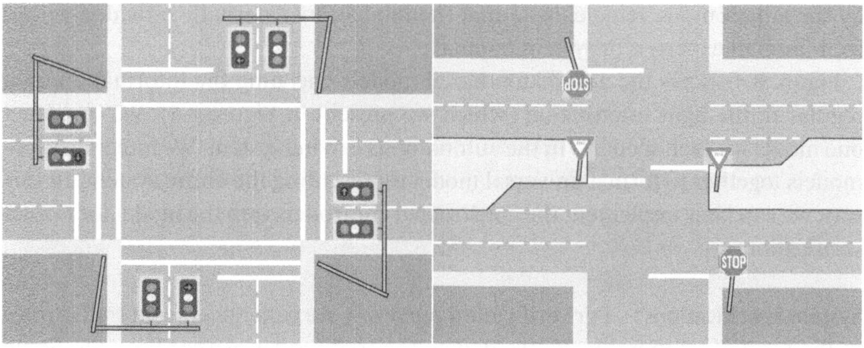

Figure 8.5 Illustration of two sample scenarios from the autonomous driving system. The left figure is an intersection with the traffic light. We encode this scenario in a model in Figure 8.4. The right figure is an intersection with a wide median.

input symbols to the set of atomic propositions. We add any vocabularies from the temporal logic formulas that are not already in the proposition set to the action set. Now, we have obtained a set of atomic propositions and allowable actions from the model and specifications. The propositions include { green traffic light, green left-turn light, flashing left-turn light, opposite car, car from left, car from right, pedestrian at left, pedestrian at right, pedestrian in front, stop sign }, and the actions are { stop, turn left, turn right, go straight }.

Once we have the models representing the autonomous system and a set of specifications, we can construct controllers for various tasks that can operate in the system and verify whether the controllers satisfy the specifications when operating in the system.

Example on Controller Construction: Right Turn: In this example, we use a simple task "turn right at the traffic light" to demonstrate the controller construction and verification. Then, we compare the controllers constructed using the language model prior to and after the fine-tuning stage. Hence, we can give a straightforward demonstration of how DPO-AF improves the language model.

We start by constructing a controller using the language model before fine-tuning it. First, we query the language model on the steps of turning right at the traffic light in the following format:

```
Steps for "turn right at traffic light"
1. Look straight ahead and watch for traffic light.
2. If the traffic light turns green, start moving forward.
3. As you approach the intersection, look to your left for
   oncoming traffic.
4. If there is no traffic coming from your left, check
   pedestrians on your right.
5. If it is safe, turn your vehicle right.
```

Next, we again query the language model to align the step instructions to the defined propositions and actions:

```
Rephrase the following steps to align the defined Boolean
    Propositions {green traffic light, car from left, ......}
    and Actions {stop, turn left, turn right, go straight}:
1. Look straight ahead and watch for traffic light.
......
5. If it is safe, turn your vehicle right.

1. Observe the state of the green traffic light.
2. If the green traffic light is on, execute the action go
    straight.
3. As you approach the intersection, observe the state of the
    car from left.
4. If the car from left is not present, check the state of the
    pedestrian at right.
5. If the pedestrian at right is not present, execute the action
     turn right.
```

By doing so, we have aligned the vocabularies from the initial responses to the defined propositions and actions. Note that such alignment may also introduce mistakes that violate more specifications, but reducing the probability of an alignment mistake is also a goal for DPO-AF.

Then, we apply semantic parsing to break the sentence into verb phrases and keywords (e.g., if) and then shorten the phrases for presentation purposes:

```
1. <observe traffic light>.
2. <if> <green traffic light>, <go straight>.
3. <observe car from left>.
4. <if> <no car from left>, <check pedestrian at right>.
5. <if> <no pedestrian at right>, <turn right>.
```

Last, we follow the algorithm GLM2FSA [17] to construct an FSA representing the steps of this task, as presented in the left of Figure 8.6.

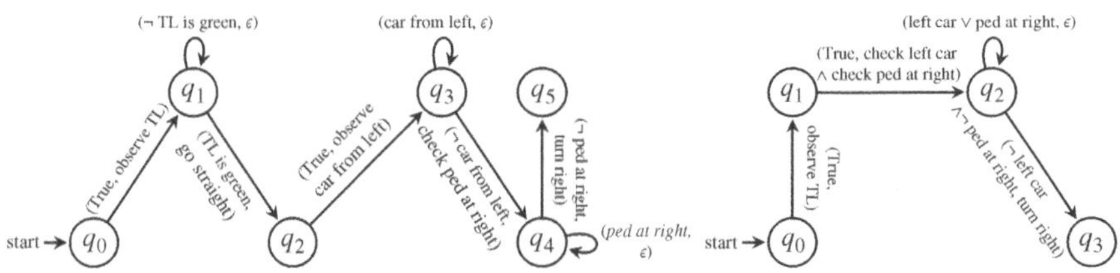

Figure 8.6 Automaton-based controllers for the task "turn right at the traffic light." The left controller is obtained before fine-tuning the language model, and the right controller is obtained after the fine-tuning. TL represents "traffic light."

```
Steps for "turn right at traffic light"
1. Observe the traffic light in front of you.
2. Check for the left approaching car and right side pedestrian.
3. If no car from the left is approaching and no pedestrian on
   the right, proceed to turn right.
```

Formal Verification: We first implement both controllers in the automaton-based model presented in Figure 8.4, i.e. construct a product automaton for each controller and the model.

Second, we verify both product automata against the set of provided specifications. During the verification step, the model checker finds that the controller obtained before fine-tuning fails the specification Φ_5. The model checker returns a counter-example on states $(p_0, q_3), (p_4, q_4), (p_1, q_5)$.

This counter-example captures an edge case: The traffic light turns back to red and a car is coming from the left immediately after the agent is checking or waiting for pedestrians. In this scenario, the agent does not check for the traffic light and cars from left again and directly turns right, which can lead to an accident. We argue that this edge case can hardly be caught by human inspection but can be found by the model checker. Hence we highlight this counter-example to indicate the necessity of formal verification.

In contrast, the controller obtained after fine-tuning satisfies all the specifications. Through this right-turn example, we observe the language model's enhancement through DPO-AF.

Fine-tuning via DPO: DPO fine-tunes a language model to output responses that match desired specifications. DPO requires a data set where each data point has the form (x, y_w, y_l), where x is a user input (i.e. "Steps for turn right at the traffic light"), y_w and y_l are the language model's text responses such that the user prefers y_w over y_l. In our experiments, the preferred response is the one whose FSA-based representation satisfies more of the specifications than the other response. We collect approximately 3000 data points to fine-tune the language model. After fine-tuning, the language model shows a preference for the responses as indicated in the training dataset.

We measure the DPO training performance via three metrics: DPO loss, accuracy, and marginal preference. Loss refers to the modified maximum likelihood loss function from the DPO algorithm, which is minimized via gradient descent. Accuracy measures how often the model prefers the correct response over the incorrect response. Accuracy is the mean over the dataset of $\mathbb{I}(P(y_w|x, \theta) > P(y_l|x, \theta))$, where $\mathbb{I}$ is the indicator function returning one if the input is true and zero otherwise, and θ is the current value of the model parameters.

Marginal preference measures how strongly the model prefers the correct output compared to the original reference model. Marginal preference is calculated as the mean over the dataset of $(log(P(y_w|x,\theta)) - log(P(y_w|x,\theta_{ref}))) - (log(P(y_l|x,\theta)) - log(P(y_l|x,\theta_{ref})))$. Zero indicates indifference, positive values indicate stronger preferences for the favored answer, and negative values indicate preference for the less preferred response.

We show the fine-tuning performance on the Llama2-7B model over the three metrics in Figure 8.7. Note that the variance between random seeds is relatively small because the model starts with the same parameters, and only the order of the data changes between seeds.

Evaluation via Formal Verification: TWe provide an additional metric to evaluate the proposed DPO-AF. During the fine-tuning procedure, we save a checkpoint language model for every 20 epochs. For each checkpoint language model, we query it for various autonomous driving tasks and obtain the task controllers. Then, we verify the controllers against 15 provided specifications following the formal verification method in Section 8.2.3. Thus, we obtain the number of specifications being satisfied for each controller.

Figure 8.8 shows the relationship between the number of satisfied specifications and the number of epochs of DPO training. Simultaneously, we divide the results into two categories – training and validation – depending on whether the task is included in the training dataset. Hence, we have shown the relationships between the numbers of satisfied specifications and epochs for both training data and validation data.

For both training and validation data, we observe an increase in the number of specifications satisfied as we fine-tune for more epochs. This result indicates that our approach can improve the language model's ability to satisfy critical requirements. Therefore, our approach can act as a starting point to guide the design process for real-world implementations of autonomous driving systems.

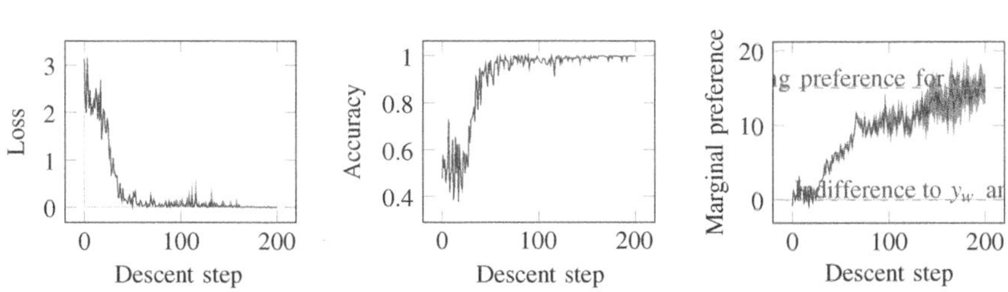

Figure 8.7 This figure shows fine-tuning statistics for Llama2-7B optimized for an autonomous driving system. All plots show the mean over five seeds. Shaded areas indicate maximum and minimum values. Plots from left to right show the DPO losses, accuracies, and marginal preferences over different epochs, respectively.

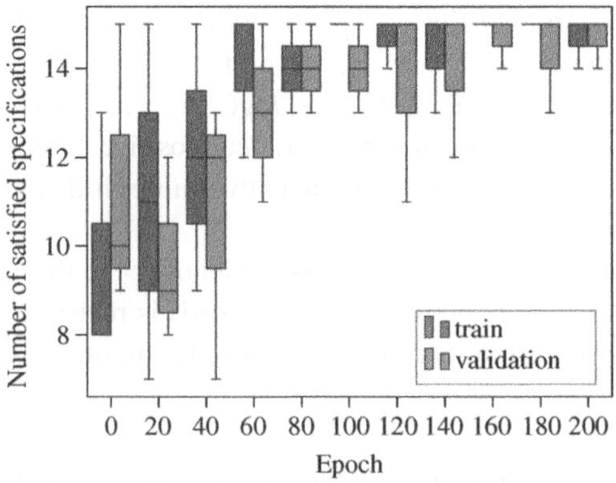

Figure 8.8 The number of specifications satisfied through formal verification vs. the epoch of DPO training.

Empirical Evaluation in a Simulated System: We have presented another approach to obtain feedback via empirical evaluation in Section 8.2.3. We will show consistency between feedback from empirical evaluation and formal verification.

As we obtain the controllers through the proposed method, we operate the controllers in the Carla simulator to collect operation data. Carla is a simulator for the autonomous driving system. During each operation of each controller, we obtain a sequence of propositions and actions – in the form of $(2^P \times 2^{P_A})^N$. The propositions come from the information returned by the autonomous system, and the actions come from the controller. The Carla simulator allows for the extraction of system information. We present visual demonstrations of extracting the propositions from the system in Figure 8.9. Then, we verify the sequence against the provided specifications, as we described in Section 8.2.3 under Empirical Evaluation. We operate the controllers multiple times in the system and verify the sequences against the specifications. For each specification, we get a percentage of the number of sequences satisfying this specification.

Figure 8.10 compares these percentages obtained before fine-tuning and after fine-tuning. Note that we run multiple controllers and collect multiple sequences for each controller. We show the results for the first five specifications as presented in Section 8.2.4.

We observe that the percentages after fine-tuning are consistently higher than before fine-tuning among all five specifications, which means all the specifications have a higher probability of being satisfied for a given execution after fine-tuning. In Figure 8.8, we show that outputs from the fine-tuned model (at epoch 200) satisfy more specifications compared to the pre-trained model (at epoch 0).

Figure 8.9 Visual demonstration of obtaining system information while operating the controllers. We use Carla to simulate the autonomous driving system.

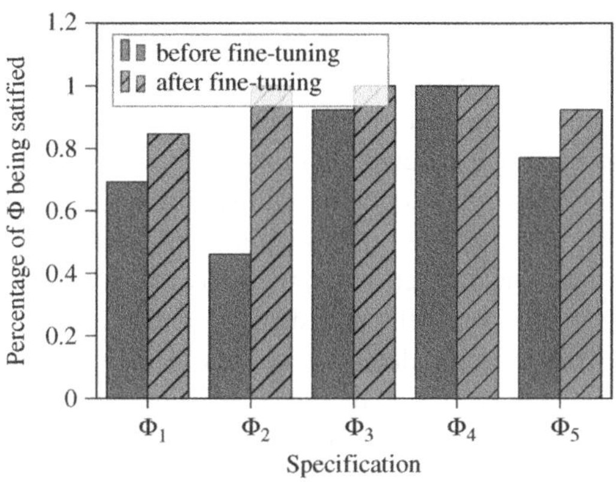

Figure 8.10 Percentage $\mathbb{P}_\Phi$ of each specification Φ being satisfied during actual operations in the system.

Hence, we obtain consistent feedback from the formal verification and empirical evaluation. Therefore, if we are unable to obtain automaton-based models for the system, empirical evaluation is a substitute for formal verification and is able to provide feedback consistent with formal verification.

From another perspective, this result provides additional evidence to show the effectiveness of the method DPO-AF, as it improves the probability of all the specifications being satisfied during operation.

We have the verified controllers constructed from the language model's outputs. In this section, we will show the real-world applicability of the generated controllers.

Note that the controllers make decisions solely based on the input symbols, which are composed of atomic propositions that describe environment observations. Furthermore, our models of the autonomous driving system enforce these propositions to be visual observations of the driving environment. The following statements hold true:

1. The controller's decisions are solely based on visual observations collected from the environment.
2. Suppose we have a vision model to perceive the environment. Consider a scenario wherein the vision model performs consistently in simulation and reality, e.g. object detection accuracies are approximately equal. The controllers behave consistently in simulation and reality in such a scenario.
3. If Statement 2 holds and if the controllers satisfy the critical specifications in simulation, then the controllers also satisfy the specifications in reality.

From the three statements, we know that if we show the vision model performs consistently in the simulation and reality, we can directly transfer the controllers to the real-world system with the same degree of formal guarantee (e.g. safety). To do so, we select a current state-of-the-art object detection model – Grounded SAM [22, 23] – to examine whether it performs consistently in both settings.

We extract images from the Carla simulator to build a simulation dataset and use NuImage [24] as the real-world driving dataset. Then, we apply the Grounded SAM to detect objects within the images from the two datasets and record the detection accuracies. We present some sample detection results in Figure 8.11. Next, we group the detection accuracies by the vision model's confidence score and obtain the confidence-accuracy mapping. This step follows the confidence calibration method proposed in an existing paper [25]. We argue that if the vision model's detection accuracies in both settings are approximately the same under all the confidence levels, then we say it performs consistently. We show the confidence-accuracy mappings in Figure 8.12.

Through experimental results, we show that the vision model performs consistently in the simulation and reality. Therefore, we can directly transfer the controllers constructed from the language model to real-world driving systems. This real-world applicability emphasizes the necessity and importance of the proposed approach because DPO-AF can fine-tune the language model to satisfy safety specifications, which are critical in real-world driving systems.

8.2.5 Conclusion

The approach we presented here features a **verifiable** and **scalable** neurosymbolic framework for automated fine-tuning of language models via formal verification of their outputs providing specification compliant models. The method

Figure 8.11 Comparison between the vision-language model's performance on the Carla simulator (bottom row) and the real world (top row) under different weather or light conditions.

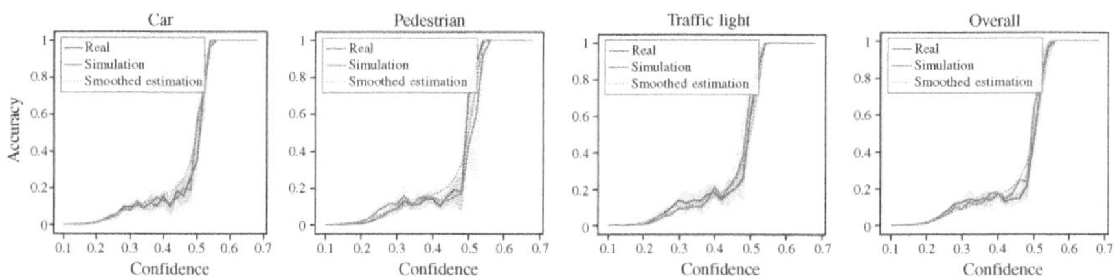

Figure 8.12 Quantitative comparison between the vision-language model's performance on detecting different objects within the Carla simulator and the real world.

converts the outputs from the pre-trained language model to automaton-based controllers and verifies how many of the externally provided specifications are satisfied by each controller. Subsequently, the verification results are used to obtain a rank for the pre-trained language model's outputs based on the number of satisfied specifications. We then utilize the ranked outputs within DPO for fine-tuning eliminating human feedback with automated feedback using formal methods.

We present empirical evidence to demonstrate the effectiveness of the automated neurosymbolic fine-tuning method using simulated autonomous driving scenarios. The fine-tuned language model is 30% specification compliant compared to the original model. Furthermore, we demonstrate the potential real-world applicability of the controllers highlighting the importance of using verifiable and scalable framework in producing controllers that satisfy safety-critical specifications.

8.3 Uncertainty-aware Fine-tuning and Inference for Multimodal Foundation Models

8.3.1 Introduction

Multimodal foundation models are a promising framework for robotic perception and planning as they readily process sensory inputs to generate actionable plans. However, a critical challenge to ensure task reliability is addressing uncertainty in both perception (sensory interpretation) and decision-making (plan generation). Emerging methods for quantifying uncertainty in the outcomes of pre-trained models [26–28] can inform their refinement with feedback signals richer than merely the binary signals from formal verification. For example, the theory of conformal prediction [29–31] provides confidence intervals or sets for predictions guaranteeing a specified error rate. We integrate such conformal prediction methods into a **scalable** reasoning workflow introduced above to construct an uncertainty score for language-based outcomes. This uncertainty score provides a probabilistic guarantee on the outcomes satisfying a given set of specifications. Moreover, when applied to multimodal foundation models, such as vision-language models, this aggregate uncertainty score provides merely a "black box" evaluation. Any assessment of task failure or risk afforded by this approach lacks insight into whether the uncertainty originates from perception limitations or decision-making flaws. This black box evaluation hinders targeted improvements as it obscures the root cause of performance issues. To address this limitation, we propose a neurosymbolic framework that (i) disentangles uncertainty in multimodal foundation models into perception (sensory interpretation) and decision (plan generation) components and subsequently perform quantification. This disentanglement enables (ii) performs automated and targeted refinement of foundation models utilizing feedback from **formal verification** to independently reduce each type of uncertainty. We demonstrate that this targeted refinement framework significantly reduces the output variability of multimodal foundational models and thereby enhances robustness, a key desired characteristic in an automated reasoning framework. Combined with formal verification and conformal prediction, this approach provides probabilistic assurances on task success rates within the target application.

8.3.2 Conformal Prediction

We can estimate the uncertainty of model predictions through the theory of conformal prediction and obtain statistical guarantees on the correctness of these predictions [29].

Formally, consider a space of (data, truth label) pairs $\mathcal{X} \times \mathcal{Y}$. We have a *calibration set* $S_C = \{(x_1, y_1), ..., (x_n, y_n)\}$ with n elements from the space $\mathcal{X} \times \mathcal{Y}$. These pairs are independent and identically distributed (i.i.d.). The goal is to find a *prediction band* $\hat{C} : \mathcal{X} \rightarrow \{\text{subsets of } \mathcal{Y}\}$. For example, $\hat{C}(x_i) = \{y_1, ..., y_i\} \subset \mathcal{Y}$.

Given a new test pair (x_{n+1}, y_{n+1}) sampled from $\mathcal{X} \times \mathcal{Y}$, we first make the following assumption:

Assumption 1: (x_{n+1}, y_{n+1}) is sampled from a distribution that is identically distributed with the distribution from which we sampled $S_C = \{(x_1, y_1), ..., (x_n, y_n)\}$.

Let $\epsilon \in [0, 1]$ be a score reflecting uncertainty. If assumption 1 holds, we expect the prediction band to meet the property

$$\mathbb{P}\left[y_{n+1} \in \hat{C}(x_{n+1})\right] \geq 1 - \epsilon. \tag{8.3}$$

The objective is to find $\hat{C}$ such that the probability of the ground truth label y_{n+1} belonging to the set $\hat{C}(x_{n+1})$ is bounded by $1 - \epsilon$. For instance, if $\hat{C}(x_{n+1})$ consists of two elements, then the probability of at least one of the elements matching the ground truth label is $1 - \epsilon$.

Table of Notations: For convenience, we present all notations used in the rest of the paper in Table 8.1.

Table 8.1 A summary of important notations.

Notation	Meaning	First Definition
M	foundation model	Section 8.3.3
$\mathcal{T}, \mathcal{I}$	text, image space	Section 8.3.3
I or I_i	a single image	Section 8.3.3
T or T_i	generated text instruction	Section 8.3.3
V	vision encoder	Section 8.3.3
H	projection head	Section 8.3.3
c	softmax confidence score	Section 8.3.3
y or y_i	image object label	Section 8.3.3
u_p	percep. uncertainty score	Definition 8.1
t_p	percep. threshold	Section 8.3.6
P_T or P_{T_i}	textual task description	Section 8.3.4
Y or Y_i	a set of observed objects	Section 8.3.4
u_d	decision uncertainty score	Definition 8.2
t_d	decision threshold	Section 8.3.5

8.3.3 Perception Uncertainty

A multimodal foundation model, $M : \mathcal{I} \times \mathcal{T} \rightarrow \mathcal{T} \times [0, 1]$, takes an image observation I in the image space $\mathcal{I}$, and a task description $P_{\mathcal{T}}$ in the text space $\mathcal{T}$ as inputs. It then produces a textual instruction $T \in \mathcal{T}$ for the given task and a softmax confidence $c \in [0, 1]$. M consists of a vision encoder $V : \mathcal{I} \rightarrow \mathbb{R}^d$ that maps input images from the image space to a d-dimensional embedding space. The vision encoder outputs a d-dimensional vector, which is sent as an input to a text generator for producing textual instructions. We define *perception uncertainty* in the vision encoder's output as below:

Definition 8.1: Let I be an image containing multiple objects, a *perception uncertainty score* u_p for I is a theoretical lower bound on the probability of correctly identifying all objects in the image. A lower score implies higher uncertainty.

Problem 1: Given a foundation model M, a task description $P_{\mathcal{T}} \in \mathcal{T}$ with an image $I \in \mathcal{I}$, estimate the *perception uncertainty score* u_p for I.

Conformal Confidence – Uncertainty Calibration: As ad-hoc confidence scores returned by machine learning models, such as softmax, do not accurately reflect prediction accuracies [32], it is essential to calibrate confidence scores to prediction accuracies for uncertainty estimation. However, we ask for a theoretical lower bound on the accuracy according to Definition 8.1, which existing calibration methods cannot provide [32, 33]. Conformal prediction provides confidence intervals or sets for predictions guaranteeing a specified error rate [29]. We leverage the theory of conformal prediction for confidence – uncertainty calibration.

We first learn a *projection head* $H : \mathbb{R}^d \rightarrow \mathbb{R}^k$ that maps image embeddings to a k-dimensional space where vector $v \in \mathbb{R}^k$ represents the softmax confidence scores over k object classes. We denote the confidence score for class $l \in [0, k]$ by v_l. The class associated with the highest confidence score is the model's *prediction*.

Consider a calibration set $\{I_i, y_i\}_{i=1}^n$, where $I_i \in \mathcal{I}$ and $y_i \in [0, k]$ is the true class label for the object of interest in I_i, and assume the calibration set is i.i.d. with the images we from evaluation tasks. We connect the vision encoder to the projection head $H \circ V : \mathcal{I} \rightarrow \mathbb{R}^k$ and obtain a set of *nonconformity scores* $S_{nc} = \{1 - H(V(I_i))_{y_i}\}_{i=1}^n$. Intuitively, a nonconformity score is the sum of the softmax confidences of wrong predictions.

We empirically estimate a probability density function (PDF) f_{nc} from the nonconformity scores. For an image I_{n+1} from the test task (beyond the calibration set), given an error bound ϵ, we can find corresponding confidence c^* such that $\hat{C}(I_{n+1}) = \{l \ : \ H(V(I_{n+1}))_l > 1 - c^*\}$ satisfies $\mathbb{P}\left[y_{n+1} \in \hat{C}(I_{n+1})\right] \geq 1 - \epsilon$ [29].

Conversely, given a c^*, we can compute the corresponding error bound $\epsilon = 1 - \int_0^{c^*} f_{nc}(x)dx$. Given a confidence vector $v \in \mathbb{R}^k$ of image I_{n+1}, let $c^* = 1 - sort(v)_{-2}$, where $sort(v)_{-2}$ is the second-greatest value in v. The prediction band becomes

$$\begin{aligned}\hat{C}(I_{n+1}) &= \{l \ : \ H(V(I_{n+1}))_l > 1 - c^*\} \\ &= \{l \ : \ H(V(I_{n+1}))_l > sort(v)_{-2}\} \\ &= \{argmax(H(V(I_{n+1})))\}.\end{aligned} \tag{8.4}$$

The prediction band contains a single element, which is the prediction with the maximum confidence. Let $y_{n+1} \in [0, k]$ be the ground truth object label. By the theory of conformal prediction, there exists an $\epsilon \in [0, 1]$ such that

$$\mathbb{P}\left[y_{n+1} \in \hat{C}(I_{n+1})\right] = \mathbb{P}\left[y_{n+1} = argmax(H(V(I_{n+1}))\right] \geq 1 - \epsilon, \tag{8.5}$$

where $1 - \epsilon$ is the perception uncertainty score per Definition 8.1.

We know that c^* is the $1 - \epsilon$ quantile of S_{nc}. Thus, $1 - \epsilon = \int_0^{c^*} f_{nc}(x)dx$. Then,

$$\mathbb{P}\left[y_{n+1} = argmax(H(V(I_{n+1}))\right] \geq 1 - \epsilon = \int_0^{c^*} f_{nc}(x)dx. \tag{8.6}$$

Hence, we can calibrate a confidence vector v into a perception uncertainty score

$$u_p = \int_0^{c^*} f_{nc}(x)dx, \text{ where } c^* = 1 - sort(v)_{-2}. \tag{8.7}$$

8.3.4 Decision Uncertainty

Existing frameworks lack scalability as they depend on human-annotated datasets to assess alignment of generated plans with human annotations [34, 35]. These approaches are limited in their ability to adapt to specific task requirements, resulting in less effective uncertainty estimates when applied to diverse or specialized scenarios [28]. We use formal verification techniques alongside conformal prediction to eliminate the need for human annotations and improve adaptability to various task domains.

Recall that a foundation model $M : \mathcal{I} \times \mathcal{T} \rightarrow \mathcal{T} \times [0, 1]$ returns a text-based instruction to complete a task and a confidence score between 0 and 1. For example,

```
1 <Image> <Task description>
2 <Instruction>
3 Does the instruction satisfy the rules?
4 <Specifications>
5 Y/N
```

The inputs to M are in lines 1, 3, and 4 and the outputs are in line 2 and 5. The confidence refers to the softmax score of token 'Y' (Yes).

Given a set Φ of temporal logic specifications, we expect the text-based instructions generated by M to satisfy all specifications. However, due to the black-box nature of M, we cannot provide a guarantee. Thus, we aim to estimate a *decision uncertainty score* for each generated instruction.

Definition 8.2: Let Φ be a set of temporal logic specifications and T be a text-based instruction. A *decision uncertainty score* u_d for T is a numeric value estimating the probability that T satisfies all specifications $\phi \in \Phi$.

We formulate our problem as:

Problem 2: Given a foundation model M, a set Φ of specifications, a task description $P_T \in \mathcal{T}$, and an image $I \in \mathcal{I}$, estimate the *decision uncertainty score* u_d for instruction T, where $T, c = M(P_T, I)$.

Formal-methods-driven Prediction: We present **formal-methods-driven Prediction (FMDP)**, which uses formal verification techniques alongside conformal prediction, to solve Problem 2. For each task description P_T and input image I, FMDP aims to find a prediction band $\hat{C}(M, P_T, I) \subseteq \{T \mid T, c = M(P_T, I)\}$ such that

$$\mathbb{P}\left[T \in \hat{C}(M, P_T, I) : \forall_{\phi \in \Phi}\ \mathbf{pEnc}(T, AP, Y) \models \phi\right] \geq 1 - \epsilon \tag{8.8}$$

for a given error tolerance $\epsilon \in [0, 1]$. Y is the set of objects from I, **pEnc** is an algorithm converting text to automaton, defined in Algorithm 2. AP is the set of atomic propositions that are used to formulate every $\phi \in \Phi$. Equation (8.8) implies that the probability that "at least one of the instructions obtained using the prediction band $\hat{C}$ satisfies the constraints defined by Φ" is at least $1 - \epsilon$.

Text-based Instruction to Automaton: Problem 2 requires verifying the textual outputs from M against the specifications. As we cannot directly verify texts against a logical specification, we develop an algorithm that expresses text-based instruction in a formal representation. The algorithm takes a textual instruction T, a set AP of atomic propositions, and a set Y of objects observed from them as inputs. It returns a *Kripke structure* [36] to represent the instruction. We show the details in Algorithm 2.

Definition 8.3: A Kripke structure $\mathcal{A} = (Q, Q_0, \delta, \lambda)$ is a tuple consisting of a set Q of states, a set Q_0 of initial states, transitions $\delta \subseteq Q \times Q$, and a label function $\lambda : Q \rightarrow 2^{AP}$.

In particular, the algorithm first parses the textual instruction into a set of verb and noun phrases using semantic parsing [37]. Next, we create an initial state q_0 whose label is the intersection of the set of atomic propositions and the set of observed objects. Then, we create a set of states, where each state corresponds to a phrase, and connect them linearly. Finally, we create a "final" state indicating the completion of the task.

Then, we verify this structure against the specification through a model checker [38]. The model checker takes a logical specification and a Kripke structure as inputs and returns a binary signal indicating whether this structure satisfies the specification. We consider the textual instruction to satisfy the specification if and only if its corresponding Kripke structure passes the model-checking step.

Algorithm 2 Natural Language to Kripke Structures

Input textual instruction T, atomic proposition set AP, set Y of observed objects
Output $(Q, q_0, \delta, \lambda)$
$Ph = \{Ph_1, Ph_2, ...\} = \textbf{parse}(T)$
$Q, \delta = [q_0], []$ ▷ {Define a set of states and transitions. q_0 denotes initial states}
$\lambda(q_0) = Y \cap AP$ ▷ {The initial state's label is the observed objects from the image}
for Ph_i in Ph
  Q.append(q_i), δ.append((q_{i-1}, q_i)),
  $\lambda(q_i) = \{p \in AP : p \in Ph_i\}$
end for
Q.append(q_{done}), δ.append(($q_{|Ph|}, q_{done}$)),
δ.append(q_{done}, q_{done})), $\lambda(q_{done}) = \emptyset$

Calibration Set and Nonconformity Distribution: Once we enable the verification of the generated instructions, we can use the verification outcomes to formulate a calibration set for estimating a nonconformity distribution.

Given a set $\{I_j, Y_j\}_{j=1}^{n}$ of images with observed objects, e.g. the objects for the second image in Figure 8.16 are {truck, car}, we supply each image I_j with a task description $P_{T_j} \in \mathcal{T}$ to M and obtain an instruction T_j and a confidence score c_j: $T_j, c_j = M(P_{T_j}, I_j)$. By repeating this step for all images, we obtain our calibration set $\{(T_j, c_j, Y_j)\}_{j=1}^{n}$.

We then obtain a set S_{nc} of *nonconformity scores*

$$S_{nc} = \{1 - c_j \ : \ \exists_{\phi \in \Phi} \ \mathbf{pEnc}(T_j, AP, Y_j) \models \phi\}_{j=1}^{n}. \tag{8.9}$$

We use S_{nc} to estimate a PDF f_{nc} for the nonconformity distribution.

After we get the set of nonconformity distributions, for a given error bound $\epsilon \in [0, 1]$, we can find a prediction band $\hat{C}(M, P_T, I) = \{T \mid T, c = M(P_T, I)$ and $c \geq 1 - c^*\}$ that satisfies Eq. (8.8), where c^* is the $1 - \epsilon$ quantile of S_{nc}.

8.3.5 Estimating Decision Uncertainty Score

In this section, we use FMDP to estimate a decision uncertainty score for each output from the foundation model, i.e. solve Problem 2.

Given a new image I_{n+1} and a task description $P_{T_{n+1}}$, the foundation model outputs an instruction T_{n+1} and a confidence c_{n+1}. We disregard the instructions whose confidence in satisfying the specifications is below 0.5. Then, we compute the decision uncertainty score u_d using the nonconformity distribution f_{nc}:

$$u_d = \int_0^{c_{n+1}} f_{nc}(x)dx. \tag{8.10}$$

Proof. Consider a prediction band $\hat{C}(M, P_T, I) \subseteq \{T \mid T, c = M(P_T, I)$ and $c \geq 1 - c^*\}$ that satisfies Eq. (8.8). For each ϵ, there is a corresponding value of c^*. Let $c^* = c$, $\hat{C}(M, P_T, I)$ will contain only one element, which is the instruction T. By the theory of conformal prediction, there exists an ϵ such that

$$\mathbb{P}\left[T : \forall_{\phi \in \Phi} \ \mathbf{pEnc}(T, AP, Y) \models \phi\right] \geq 1 - \epsilon.$$

The left-hand side is our decision uncertainty score u_d according to Definition 8.2. Therefore, if we find the value of ϵ, we can get the lower bound u_d. In conformal prediction, c^* is the $1 - \epsilon$ quantile of S_{nc}. Inversely, $\epsilon = 1 - \int_0^{c^*} f_{nc}(x)dx$. Hence, u_d is bounded by $1 - \epsilon = \int_0^{c^*} f_{nc}(x)dx$. Conservatively, we consider $u_d = \int_0^{c_*} f_{nc}(x)dx$.

8.3.6 Targeted Interventions

Building on the uncertainty disentanglement, we next present two key interventions, *Active Sensing* and *Automated Refinement*, designed to reduce these uncertainties during model deployment. The active sensing mechanism leverages perception uncertainty scores to dynamically guide re-observations, ensuring propagation of high-confidence visual inputs for subsequent plan generation. Meanwhile, automated refinement systematically fine-tunes the model based on both perception and decision uncertainty, using high-certainty data to enhance the model's ability to generate task-compliant instructions.

Together, these approaches create an iterative cycle, where active sensing feeds high-quality data into the planning module, and automated refinement iteratively improves the model's overall reliability, ultimately leading to a robust planning pipeline that effectively minimizes uncertainty from the perception to the decision-making stage.

Active Sensing with Perception Uncertainty: We incorporate perception uncertainty scores into an active sensing process, using these scores as indicators to initiate re-observation when necessary. This approach allows assessment of whether the observed image meets a predefined certainty threshold, enhancing the reliability of perception outcomes and the subsequent text generation step.

Figure 8.13 illustrates the active sensing process. Given an image I and a text description P_T, the vision encoder V first extracts image embeddings. Following the steps in Section 8.3.3, we obtain a perception uncertainty score u_p. If u_p exceeds a specified *perception threshold* $t_p \in [0, 1]$, we proceed to text generation. Otherwise, the robot is instructed to re-observe the scene by collecting a new image through camera rotation, switching to an alternate camera view, or by recapturing another image after a short delay until the perception uncertainty score rises above t_p. This iterative process continues until the perception uncertainty score surpasses the threshold. This active sensing mechanism ensures that only images with low perception uncertainty are fed into the text generator, reducing the risk of generating plans that fail due to perceptual inaccuracies.

Automated Refinement Using Both Uncertainties: However, even with precise visual inputs, foundation models may still produce instructions that fail to meet task specifications due to a lack of domain knowledge. To address this, we introduce an automated refinement process aimed at minimizing the likelihood of generating such specification-violating instructions.

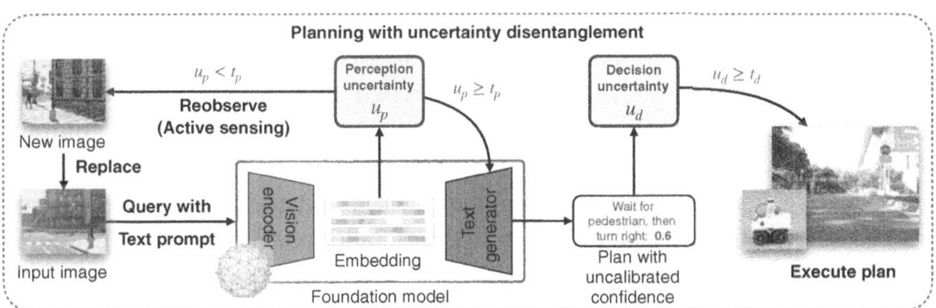

Figure 8.13 Our planning framework disentangles perception and decision uncertainty, triggering the active sensing intervention. The framework improves the robustness of generated plans by reducing the propagation of perceptual inaccuracies.

Algorithm 3 Procedure for Automated Refinement

```
Input task bank B_T, image set S_I, foundation model M, atomic propositions set
AP, specification set Φ, sample size N_S, perception threshold t_p
Output foundation model M
data = []                                ▷ {Initialize an empty fine-tuning data set}
while True
  I ~ S_I, P_T ~ B_T                                       ▷ {Sample I and P_T}
  Obtain perception uncertainty score u_p for I
  if u_p < t_p
    continue                                       ▷ {Skip high-uncertainty images}
  end if
  T, c = M(P_T, I)                                       ▷ {Query foundation model}
  Extract set of objects Y from I
  A = pEnc(T, AP, Y)
  if ∀_{φ∈Φ} pEnc(T, AP, Y) ⊨ φ
    data.add((I, P_T, T))
    if size(data) ≥ N_S
      break
    end if
  end if
end while
Fine-tune M with the collected data
```

Consider an *image set* containing task environment images and a *task bank* of text-based task descriptions. This data can be collected from high-fidelity simulations or real task executions. The proposed automated refinement procedure is outlined in Algorithm 3. In this process, we filter out images with high perception uncertainty, use the foundation model to generate instructions for each image-task description pair, verify the instructions against task specifications, and add only the valid instructions to the fine-tuning dataset.

The model is then fine-tuned in a supervised manner, where each image-task description pair serves as input, and the instruction is the expected output. If supervised fine-tuning is unavailable, we can generate positive and negative instruction pairs and apply direct preference optimization (DPO) [7]. Positive instructions are those whose automaton representations satisfy all specifications. Figure 8.14 visually demonstrates this fine-tuning framework. This approach eliminates the need for human annotations or labels, allowing the model to be refined with virtually unlimited data samples until it reaches the desired performance.

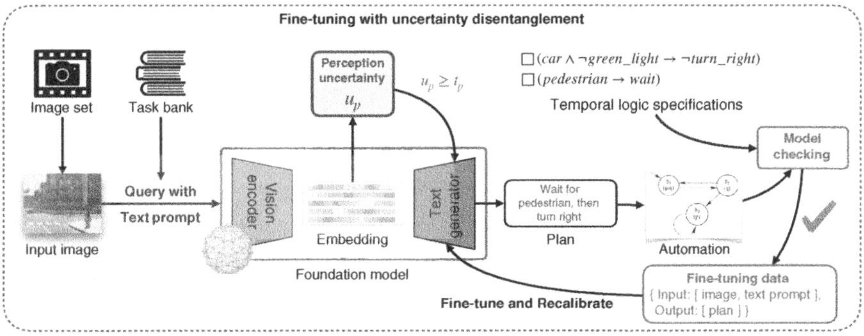

Figure 8.14 Our automated refinement framework generates high-certainty training data and fine-tunes the foundation model to improve its ability to generate plans that comply with task requirements.

Note: The refinement process occurs before grounding the planning pipeline in the task environment. Thus, we apply the FMDP described in Section 8.3.4 to obtain a nonconformity distribution after refinement, which is then used to estimate decision uncertainty scores during planning.

8.3.7 Experiments

We perform simulated and real-world autonomous driving experiments to demonstrate **(i)** how we disentangle and quantify perception and decision uncertainty in driving tasks; **(ii)** how the proposed active sensing mechanism enhances visual input quality and reduces perceptual errors; and **(iii)** how the proposed uncertainty-aware automated fine-tuning framework refines the model to improve its capability to meet task specifications. In our experiments, we use LLaVA-1.5-7B [39] for perception and plan generation; it consists of a CLIP-L-336px vision encoder [40] and a Vicuna-7B-v1.5 language generator [41].

Uncertainty Disentanglement and Quantification: **Perception Uncertainty:** We collect 542 images with ground truth labels from the Carla simulator forming a *calibration set*. Then, we apply CLIP with a pre-trained projection head to classify objects such as stop signs, cars, and pedestrians. We classify a total of 3000 objects within the 542 images and collect their confidence scores. Then, we obtain a nonconformity distribution, as shown in Figure 8.15, following the procedure outlined in Section 8.3.3.

Decision Uncertainty: We collect a *calibration set* containing 400 images from the Carla simulator – each associated with a task description – to obtain another nonconformity distribution (Figure 8.15) using the procedure in Sections. 8.3.4 and 8.3.5.

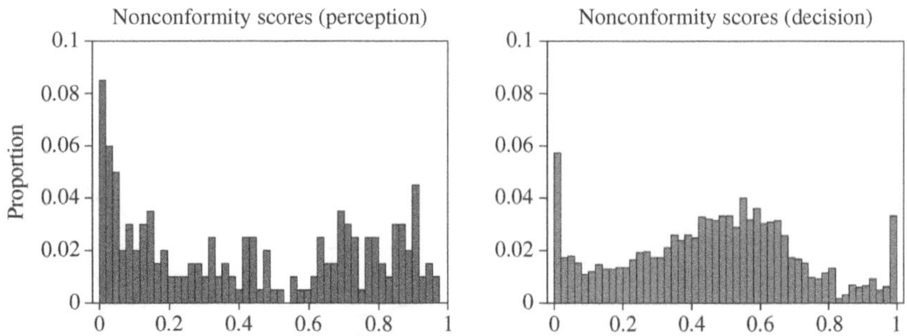

Figure 8.15 The first and second figures from left depict nonconformity distributions for perception and plan generation in simulated driving scenes (Carla) respectively.

For each image, we randomly select a task description from a set of tasks {*go straight, turn left, turn right, make a U-turn*} *at the* {*traffic light, stop sign*}. We define 10 safety-critical logical specifications for the driving tasks, some of which are listed below:

$\phi_1 = \Box(\text{red light} \rightarrow \neg\text{move forward}),$
$\phi_2 = \Box(\text{pedestrian} \rightarrow \text{wait}),$
$\phi_3 = \Box(\neg\text{stop sign} \wedge \neg \text{ traffic light } \rightarrow \text{move forward}),$
$\phi_4 = \Box(\text{green light} \wedge \neg\text{pedestrian} \rightarrow \circ\neg\text{wait}),$
$\phi_5 = \Box((\text{stop sign} \wedge \neg\text{car} \wedge \neg\text{pedestrian}) \rightarrow \circ\neg\text{wait}),$
where $\Box$, $\Diamond$, and $\circ$ refer to always, eventually, and next, respectively.

To avoid scenarios where the generated plans fail to meet the specifications due to language ambiguity or mismatching synonyms, we include in-context examples to constrain the sentence structure and vocabulary of the generated plans.

Quantification: Figure 8.15 shows the nonconformity distribution we obtained. We can estimate a probability density function for each distribution. For every object detection and corresponding confidence score, we use Eq. (8.7) to calibrate the confidence into perception uncertainty scores. We present examples of the calibrated scores in Figure 8.16 (next to the bounding boxes) for both types of uncertainty.

For every plan generated by the model, we follow the procedure to prompt the model at the beginning of Section 8.3.4 and obtain a confidence score and compute the decision uncertainty scores via Eq. (8.10). We present a scenario with high perception uncertainty and one with high decision uncertainty in Figure 8.16. After uncertainty disentanglement and quantification, we can pinpoint the source of high uncertainty and tailor targeted interventions for mitigation.

Targeted Intervention 1: Active Sensing: We deploy the active sensing mechanism to the planning pipeline that uses a raw foundation model without fine-tuning, as described in Section 8.3.6. We set the threshold $t_p = 0.7$, i.e. a 70% percent probability (and above) of correct visual interpretation is acceptable. On the simulated

Figure 8.16 The first figure shows a scenario with high perception uncertainty due to the shadow and occlusion (perception uncertainty scores next to bounding boxes). The second figure shows a scenario with low perception uncertainty but high decision uncertainty, due to the inconsistency between the image and task description (traffic light is absent).

Table 8.2 Real-world driving results show that active sensing (AS) and automated refinement improve average perception and decision uncertainty scores in addition to the average and standard deviation of the likelihood of specification compliance. The raw model refers to the pretrained foundation model without any fine-tuning.

Planning Pipeline	Avg. Percp. Unc. Score	Avg. Dec. Unc. Score	Prob. of Satisfying Spec. (Avg)	Prob. of Satisfying Spec. (SD)
Raw Model w/o AS	0.842	0.279	–	–
Raw Model with AS	**0.936**	0.306	0.316	0.180
Fine-tuned Model (Benchmark) with AS	**0.936**	0.931	0.933	0.048
Fine-tuned Model (Ours) with AS	**0.936**	**0.955**	**0.959**	**0.025**

data, we observe a 35% reduction in decision uncertainty. Across a *test set* of 50 driving scenes from our ground robot and NuScenes data [42], the active sensing mechanism reduces perception uncertainty by over 10% and subsequently reduces decision uncertainty by 10%. We present more results in Table 8.2.

We present qualitative results in Figure 8.17, illustrating successful plan executions with the active sensing mechanism in simulated and real-world autonomous driving scenes.

8.3.8 Automated Refinement

We cascade a complementary intervention on top of active sensing, building upon its benefits. To improve the foundation model's plan generation capability such that they satisfy task specifications, we apply our automated refinement framework to fine-tune the foundation model for autonomous driving tasks using a *train set* containing 800 images from the Carla simulator and the aforementioned 10 pre-defined logical specifications. We follow the steps outlined in Section 8.3.6 to

Figure 8.17 Illustration of autonomous driving tasks wherein our strategy presented in Figure 8.13 satisfies all task specifications during plan execution in both simulations and real-world environments.

automatically generate refinement data and fine-tune the foundation model's text generator.

Benchmark: To showcase the necessity of our uncertainty disentanglement framework, we select a refinement benchmark [43] that fine-tunes the same model using the dataset without uncertainty disentanglement.

This framework works as follows: (i) Create an empty set of fine-tuning data, (ii) select an image with a task description and query the foundation model for a plan, (iii) build automaton-based representation for the plan and verify it against the specifications, (iv) add the plan to the set of fine-tuning data (without uncertainty disentanglement) if it passes all the specifications, (v) repeat steps 1–5 until sufficient data is obtained, and (vi) freeze the vision encoder and fine-tune the model.

In contrast to the benchmark, our framework first quantifies perception uncertainty and filters out high-uncertainty data, hence enhancing data quality.

Experiment Setting: We fine-tune two identical LLaVA models using our framework and the benchmark and present the training losses in Figure 8.18. Our framework offers smoother convergence to a lower loss compared to the benchmark, indicating a higher potential for generating specification-compliant plans. During fine-tuning, we save a checkpoint every 80 steps. Next, we use the *test set* with 50 scenes (same as Section 8.3.7) to validate the fine-tuned models. We use each checkpoint to generate plans given those images with task descriptions and record the probability that the plans satisfy the specifications.

Result and Analysis: Figure 8.18 and Table 8.2 show the improvement in the model's ability to generate specification-compliant plans.

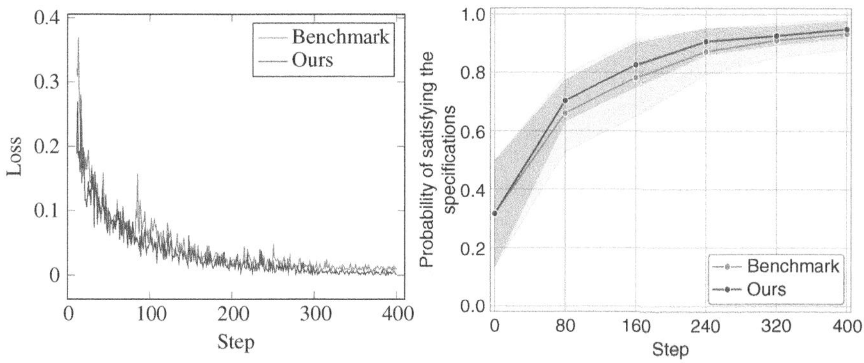

Figure 8.18 The left figure compares the fine-tuning cross-entropy loss obtained using our framework and the benchmark. The right figure shows the probability of specification compliance during fine-tuning (the color band shows the standard deviation (SD).

We observe over 50% improvement in the probability of generated plans satisfying the specifications after fine-tuning. Meanwhile, our framework outperforms the benchmark by improving this probability by up to **5%** while reducing the standard deviation by **40%**. The results indicate enhanced robustness and stability offered by our refinement framework, lowering uncertainty during planning. Uncertain visual observations increase the likelihood of generating plans that violate the specifications. For example, in the first image in Figure 8.16, uncertainty in observing the occluded pedestrian may result in a plan that overlooks the pedestrian, causing safety violations. Therefore, filtering out high-uncertainty images using our framework improves model performance consistency and scalability.

Sim2Real Transfer: Moreover, we fine-tune the model solely on simulated data and yet achieve over 95% probability of satisfying the specifications on real-world data, indicating an effective Sim2Real transfer of our uncertainty disentanglement framework and interventions.

Case Study: Figure 8.19 shows two examples indicating the superior performance of our refinement framework compared to the benchmark. In the first example, we feed the first image in Figure 8.19 along with a task description "turn right at the stop sign" to the foundation model and query for a plan. Note that this description is inconsistent with the image observation, as there is no stop sign in the image. We expect the foundation model to identify such inconsistency.

Prior to refinement, the raw model returns the following:

```
1. Pay attention to the stop sign.
2. Turn right onto the street.
```

The raw model completely ignores the inconsistency and instructs to turn right directly, which violates ϕ_2 in Section 8.3.7 (always wait for pedestrians). This can lead to severe consequences and is a dangerous action to execute.

Figure 8.19 Two examples where the foundation model fine-tuned via our refinement framework passes all the specifications while the benchmark fails. The first figure shows a scene with a red light and pedestrians crossing. The second figure shows a green light ahead.

The fine-tuned model using the benchmark returns:

```
1. There is no stop sign, move forward.
```

Compared to the raw model, it notices the image-description inconsistency. However, the decision to move forward violates ϕ_2 in Section 8.3.7. In contrast, the model fine-tuned using our framework successfully identifies the inconsistency and generates a plan that satisfies all the specifications:

```
1. Wait for the light to turn green.
2. Turn right.
```

In the second example, we feed the second image in Figure 8.19 with a task description "go straight at the traffic light" to the foundation model. The model fine-tuned using the benchmark framework returns the following:

```
1. Wait for the light to turn green.
2. Move straight ahead.
```

It does not consider that the light is already green and decides to wait, violating ϕ_4. In contrast, the model fine-tuned using our framework mitigates this issue:

```
1. The traffic light is green.
2. Move forward.
```

In both examples, we demonstrate how our refinement framework outperforms the benchmark.

Decision Uncertainty in Plan Execution: In the planning stage, the fine-tuned model attains an average decision uncertainty score of 0.955, whereas the raw model achieves a lower score of 0.852 (i.e. **10%** improvement). This improvement highlights the effectiveness of the refinement in substantially reducing decision uncertainty. The fine-tuned model does not achieve a 100% specification-satisfaction rate. We employ the decision uncertainty score to determine whether to execute the generated plans, as described at the end of Section 8.3.5. In the

50 scenes, 4 of the generated pans violate the specifications, and all of these plans have decision uncertainty scores below the pre-defined threshold $t_d = 0.7$. Consequently, restricting the execution of plans with uncertainty scores above t_d reduces the probability of specification violation from **8** to **0%**, underscoring the importance of decision uncertainty during planning.

8.3.9 Conclusion

The neurosymbolic framework presented in this section enables **scalable** uncertainty quantification and targeted interventions for uncertainty reduction in multimodal foundation models in robotic planning. Our framework isolates perception uncertainty arising from limitations in visual understanding and decision uncertainty relating to the robustness of generated plans. The proposed quantification methods, leverage conformal prediction for perception and FMDP for decision-making providing theoretical assurances for compliance with the provided task specifications or rules using feedback from formal **verification**. The targeted interventions improve model robustness by employing active sensing and automated refinement. Empirical studies demonstrate that our framework reduces variability by up to 40% and enhances task success rates by 5% compared to baselines, highlighting the importance of uncertainty disentanglement, which facilitates targeted interventions.

8.4 Toward a Hybrid Architecture: Dynamic Interleaving of Neural and Symbolic Reasoning

Unified neurosymbolic frameworks have achieved significant gains in accuracy, data efficiency, and explainability across various domains [43]. Instead of a static fusion, the key is a principled design that adapts its mode of reasoning – leaning on neural pattern recognition when faced with high-dimensional data and shifting to symbolic logic for tasks requiring precise, rule-based reasoning. The path forward for neurosymbolic AI would lie in a dynamic, adaptive hybrid architecture that intelligently switches between neural and symbolic reasoning based on the task at hand. Such a unified framework would feature a more adaptive process including:

- **Adaptive Feature Extraction:** Neural networks initially extract high-dimensional features from raw data, harnessing their strength in capturing complex, non-linear patterns that are challenging to encode manually. However, this phase need not necessarily be purely neural; adaptive mechanisms can already detect when the extracted features hit a bottleneck (e.g. ambiguity or noise) and signal a transition to a more structured, symbolic interpretation. Techniques such as self-attention can also be adaptively tuned to emphasize symbolic priors when the input data aligns with known rules or domain-specific constraints.

- **Dynamic Symbolic Lifting:** In this stage, we move beyond a fixed symbolic transformation. The system adaptively decides which aspects of the neural features are most suitable for symbolic reasoning. For example, if the extracted features suggest strong logical dependencies or known structural patterns (e.g. causal relationships or geometric invariants), they are lifted into a symbolic space using probabilistic circuits or geometry-inspired encoders – and we can perform exact symbolic reasoning on the lifted representation. However, the lifting process itself is dynamic, modulating the degree of symbolic abstraction based on task complexity. When the problem requires high precision and logical consistency, more aggressive lifting is applied; when flexibility and generalization are needed, the system retains more neural representation.
- **Adaptive Feedback Loop–Guided Learning with Dynamic Interleaving:** The real power of this architecture comes from a flexible, adaptive feedback loop. The symbolic reasoning component refines and informs the neural network's learning process, but the depth of this guidance varies dynamically. For straightforward, rule-based tasks, symbolic reasoning takes a stronger role, guiding the neural updates with strict logical constraints. For more ambiguous or data-driven tasks, the system scales back the symbolic influence, allowing the neural network to explore the solution space freely.

This adaptive interplay mirrors the dual-process nature of human cognition, where fast, intuitive (neural) thinking is balanced with slower, deliberate (symbolic) reasoning. However, the crucial innovation here is the system's ability to switch modes dynamically, deciding when to lean more on neural intuition versus when to enforce symbolic rigor based on real-time signals such as uncertainty estimation, task difficulty, or feedback from the environment.

While numerical fine-tuning excels at injecting new factual knowledge, symbolic updates offer flexible control of style and alignment without retraining. We envision a hybrid neurosymbolic framework that dynamically combines these two complementary strategies. Specifically, a unified monitoring signal can be utilized to dynamically employ neural updates for deeper factual reconstruction and apply symbolic updates for token-level edits. Additionally, the refined prompts produced during symbolic editing serve as high-quality, reusable training data, an important benefit in data-scarce domains like mathematical reasoning. This monitoring signal could serve as a means for the dynamic interleaving of numerical and symbolic updates to unlock a new level of versatility in language model fine-tuning.

A unified monitoring signal derived from key performance indicators such as training loss change ratio or gradient norm can provide a continuous assessment of model performance at each epoch. By tracking when this monitoring signal saturates while performing numerical updates, a trigger to a symbolic update phase can be initiated to refine style or re-route internal representations, echoing the concept of "knowledge displacement" by allowing latent knowledge to be reclaimed or redirected efficiently.

An ideal selection of the monitoring signal should ultimately inform whether it is worthwhile for new factual knowledge to be injected (via numerical updates) using the input sample or if contextual redirection for style alignment (via symbolic updates) is required.

At the start of model training, we can nominally initiate the numerical update phase in an attempt to learn new factual knowledge from the training dataset $\mathcal{D}$. Consider a question and answer problem setting that involves a textual description of the system prompt P, a question Q that the model f_θ attempts to answer, a ground truth answer A^*, and the model's prediction A. We want to identify a signal $C(x)$ such that the saturation in the signal serves as a trigger to a sparse symbolic update phase. Aligned with our problem setting, we perform symbolic updates until the model predicts the correct answer or if the number of allowable symbolic update iterations have been reached. Subsequently, we alternate back to the numerical update phase as this is our nominal and preferred update mode.

The first unified signal we may utilize to track saturation due to numerical updates is the loss change ratio across consecutive epochs, defined as $C(x)_1 = \frac{\mathcal{L}_t - \mathcal{L}_{t-1}}{\mathcal{L}_{t-1}}$, where $\mathcal{L}_t$ represents the training loss at epoch t. To facilitate a fair comparison of loss across consecutive epochs, we mark the data points sampled in a batch during the initial epoch and then use these same data points for numerical updates in the following epoch. Subsequently, we compare the model's predictions A with the ground truth answers A^* and identify instances in which the model's predictions are incorrect. Among these misclassified examples, we further isolate those whose loss change ratio lies within a pre-specified threshold k from zero. Such samples derive minimal benefit from the training data, presumably due to the absence of novel factual information. However, the pool of these samples can still benefit from contextual redirection via symbolic updates. Consequently, we apply symbolic updates specifically to a fraction p of these samples to update the question Q and indirectly refine internal representations and guide the model out of the local minima.

Another signal to monitor the saturation of numerical updates is the magnitude of the gradient norm of the training loss $C(x)_2 = ||\nabla \mathcal{L}_t||$. The intuition behind its selection as a monitoring signal is centered at the correlation between the magnitude of the gradient norm and the effective learning of new factual knowledge. In particular, a high magnitude of the gradient norm implies significant changes in the model weights, indicating that the training sample or batch of samples potentially contained new factual knowledge that the model was otherwise not trained on. Thus, the criteria to identify saturation during numerical updates would be to monitor the magnitude of the gradient norm until it plummets below a pre-specified threshold, acting as a trigger to initiate symbolic updates in an attempt to perform context redirection given limited knowledge gain.

8.5 Conclusion and Future Directions

While contemporary approaches relying on scaling laws have produced impressive results in vision and language, this process of developing increasingly large and assurance-deprived models is unsustainable and introduces a gate-keeping of the development of new AI approaches. The "Bitter Lesson" by Sutton [44] argues that progress in AI comes from leveraging scalable methods such as search and learning, rather than relying on human-crafted features. While this lesson warns against brittle, hand-engineered features, it does not preclude the integration of structured symbolic knowledge. As demonstrated by the automated fine-tuning framework that utilizes uncertainty quantification and formal verification feedback in Sections 8.2 and 8.3, such neurosymbolic AI frameworks offer a verifiable and scalable framework that aligns with these principles by using symbolic knowledge as a form of inductive bias that accelerates learning without constraining it.

As we start to confront the limitations of scaling laws in AI, it is time to explore a wider range of approaches. Neurosymbolic AI is one such path, combining the strengths of neural learning with the structured reasoning of symbolic methods. This shift isn't about discarding contemporary developments, but about expanding to other orthogonal approaches to better address the challenges faced by today's large-scale models, while moving closer to a vision of AI that mirrors human reasoning and discovery.

The era of pure scaling might be winding down, but a new phase of exploration and creativity is on the horizon. By thoughtfully integrating neural and symbolic approaches, we can build AI systems that are not just powerful, but also efficient, interpretable, and aligned with human-type think and solve problems. This direction aims to go beyond scaling, seeking a deeper synthesis of learning and reasoning that could mark the next big step forward in AI.

A key research challenge in this direction lies in developing effective heuristics and algorithms that determine the optimal balance between neural and symbolic reasoning. Some guiding principles could include:

- **Data Complexity and Structure:** When the data is high-dimensional, noisy, or unstructured, neural networks excel. However, as the system starts detecting clear patterns, relationships, or domain-specific rules, we can gradually transition to a more symbolic approach.

- **Uncertainty and Confidence Estimation:** High uncertainty in neural predictions may indicate that purely data-driven learning has reached its limit, triggering a switch to symbolic reasoning for added structure and guidance. An initial attempt in neurosymbolic uncertainty quantification was presented in Section 8.3.
- **Task Requirements:** Symbolic reasoning is preferred for tasks that require explicit logical constraints, consistency checks, or precise reasoning (e.g. legal text analysis or safety-critical decision-making). Neural methods are better suited for pattern recognition, generalization, and handling ambiguity. A recent cognitive science paper offers excellent insights here.
- **Feedback from the Environment:** Adaptive systems can use feedback signals (e.g. task performance metrics, error analysis) to adjust the neural-symbolic balance on-the-fly, ensuring the system remains responsive and efficient across varying tasks and conditions.

This dynamic, adaptive hybrid approach will represent a shift from static, monolithic models to flexible, context-sensitive systems. By interleaving neural and symbolic reasoning in a principled, adaptive manner, we can build AI systems that are not only more efficient and generalizable but also more aligned with human cognitive processes. This evolution mirrors the human ability to switch seamlessly between intuitive thinking and deliberate reasoning.

8.5.1 Extending the Scope: Symbolic Tool Use for Mathematical Reasoning

As we reimagine AI beyond the era of pure scaling, one promising avenue lies in augmenting neural models with the ability to leverage external symbolic tools for enhanced reasoning capabilities. This approach extends the neurosymbolic paradigm to encompass not only human crafted symbolic logic but also a diverse set of mathematical and probabilistic tools, effectively broadening the AI's scope of reasoning.

For instance, the recent interest in formal proof languages such as Lean highlights a compelling example [45]. Lean's foundational rigor in domains such as measure theory offers a pathway for deep, verifiable reasoning. However, its current practical utility in AI is limited by the overhead of constructing proofs from the ground up each time. This mismatch in development speed between Lean's rigorous approach and AI's demand for scalable, rapid reasoning is a significant gap, however, it also an opportunity worth taking advantage. Efficient abstractions or specialized libraries tailored to common AI needs could bridge this divide, making formal tools more accessible and practical for AI systems.

Similarly, languages such as Pyro, Stan, and Edward – designed for probabilistic modeling and Bayesian inference – will be invaluable in new generations of neurosymbolic frameworks [46–48]. They can serve as the symbolic backbone, where the neural component learns flexible data representations, and the symbolic component handles reasoning about uncertainties and dependencies explicitly. This interplay between neural learning and probabilistic reasoning aligns well with the hybrid architectures outlined earlier, enabling a dynamic transition between data-driven pattern recognition and precise, rule-based inference.

Graph-based reasoning tools, such as Neo4j for knowledge graphs, offer another layer of symbolic reasoning [49]. By structuring information as interconnected entities and relationships, these tools provide a framework for explicit logical reasoning, complementing the neural model's capacity for learning from unstructured data. The broader vision here is not merely integrating neural and symbolic components but empowering AI to dynamically utilize a suite of reasoning tools based on task requirements – a new form of symbolic reasoning that transcends traditional boundaries.

In this light, we can view tool use itself as an extension of the symbolic reasoning paradigm. Just as humans use different tools for different tasks, a truly adaptive AI system would seamlessly incorporate mathematical, probabilistic, and graph-based reasoning tools as part of its cognitive toolkit. This evolution in AI thinking – toward a modular, tool-augmented neurosymbolic system – represents a natural progression beyond the scaling limits we are encountering today.

References

1 Honghua Zhang, Liunian Harold Li, Tao Meng, Kai-Wei Chang, and Guy Van den Broeck. On the paradox of learning to reason from data. *arXiv preprint arXiv:2205.11502*, 2022.

2 Yunhao Yang, Neel P Bhatt, Tyler Ingebrand, William Ward, Steven Carr, Zhangyang Wang, and Ufuk Topcu. Fine-tuning language models using formal methods feedback. *arXiv preprint arXiv:2310.18239*, 2023a.

3 Neel P Bhatt, Yunhao Yang, Rohan Siva, Daniel Milan, Ufuk Topcu, and Zhangyang Wang. Know where you're uncertain when planning with multimodal foundation models: a formal framework. *arXiv preprint arXiv:2411.01639*, 2024.

4 Yingqiang Ge, Wenyue Hua, Kai Mei, Jianchao Ji, Juntao Tan, Shuyuan Xu, Zelong Li, Yongfeng Zhang. OpenAGI: when LLM meets domain experts. *Advances in Neural Information Processing Systems*, 36: 5539–5568, 2023.

5 Cunxiang Wang, Xiaoze Liu, Yuanhao Yue, Xiangru Tang, Tianhang Zhang, Cheng Jiayang, Yunzhi Yao, Wenyang Gao, Xuming Hu, Zehan Qi, et al. Survey on factuality in large language models: knowledge, retrieval and domain-specificity. *arXiv preprint arXiv:2310.07521*, 2023.

6 Paul F Christiano, Jan Leike, Tom Brown, Miljan Martic, Shane Legg, and Dario Amodei. Deep reinforcement learning from human preferences. *Advances in Neural Information Processing Systems 30*, 2017.

7 Rafael Rafailov, Archit Sharma, Eric Mitchell, Christopher D Manning, Stefano Ermon, and Chelsea Finn. Direct preference optimization: your language model is secretly a reward model. *Advances in Neural Information Processing Systems 36*, 2024.

8 Nisan Stiennon, Long Ouyang, Jeffrey Wu, Daniel Ziegler, Ryan Lowe, Chelsea Voss, Alec Radford, Dario Amodei, and Paul F Christiano. Learning to summarize with human feedback. *Advances in Neural Information Processing Systems*, 33: 3008–3021, 2020.

9 Chitta Baral, Juraj Dzifcak, Marcos Alvarez Gonzalez, and Jiayu Zhou. Using inverse lambda and generalization to translate English to formal languages. In Johan Bos and Stephen Pulman, editors, *International Conference on Computational Semantics*, pages 35–44, Oxford, UK, 2011. The Association for Computer Linguistics.

10 Driss Sadoun, Catherine Dubois, Yacine Ghamri-Doudane, and Brigitte Grau. From natural language requirements to formal specification using an ontology. In *International Conference on Tools with Artificial Intelligence*, pages 755–760, Herndon, VA, USA, 2013. IEEE Computer Society.

11 Shalini Ghosh, Daniel Elenius, Wenchao Li, Patrick Lincoln, Natarajan Shankar, and Wilfried Steiner. ARSENAL: automatic requirements specification extraction from natural language. In Sanjai Rayadurgam and Oksana Tkachuk, editors, *NASA Formal Methods, volume 9690 of Lecture Notes in Computer Science*, pages 41–46, Springer, Minneapolis, MN, USA, 2016.

12 Christopher Hahn, Frederik Schmitt, Julia J. Tillman, Niklas Metzger, Julian Siber, and Bernd Finkbeiner. Formal specifications from natural language. *arXiv preprint arXiv.2206.01962*, 2022.

13 Yuhuai Wu, Albert Qiaochu Jiang, Wenda Li, Markus N Rabe, Charles Staats, Mateja Jamnik, and Christian Szegedy. Autoformalization with large language models. In *Advances in Neural Information Processing Systems*, New Orleans, LA, USA, 2022.

14 Emily First, Markus N Rabe, Talia Ringer, and Yuriy Brun. Baldur: whole-proof generation and repair with large language models. *arXiv preprint arXiv.2303.04910*, 2023.

15 Zezhong Chen, Yuxin Deng, and Wenjie Du. Trusta: Reasoning about assurance cases with formal methods and large language models. *arXiv preprint arXiv:2309.12941*, 2023.

16 Susmit Jha, Sumit Kumar Jha, Patrick Lincoln, Nathaniel D Bastian, Alvaro Velasquez, and Sandeep Neema. Dehallucinating large language models using formal methods guided iterative prompting. In *IEEE International Conference on Assured Autonomy*, pages 149–152, Laurel, MD, USA, 2023. IEEE.

17 Yunhao Yang, Jean-Raphael Gaglione, Cyrus Neary, and Ufuk Topcu. Automaton-based representations of task knowledge from generative language models. *arXiv preprint arXiv:2212.01944*, 2022.

18 Amir Pnueli. The temporal logic of programs. In *Symposium on Foundations of Computer Science*, pages 46–57, Providence, Rhode Island, USA, 1977. IEEE Computer Society.

19 Alessandro Cimatti, Edmund M. Clarke, Enrico Giunchiglia, Fausto Giunchiglia, Marco Pistore, Marco Roveri, Roberto Sebastiani, and Armando Tacchella. NuSMV 2: An opensource tool for symbolic model checking. In Ed Brinksma and Kim Guldstrand Larsen, editors, *Computer Aided Verification, volume 2404 of Lecture Notes in Computer Science*, pages 359–364, Springer, Copenhagen, Denmark, 2002.

20 Edward J Hu, Yelong Shen, Phillip Wallis, Zeyuan Allen-Zhu, Yuanzhi Li, Shean Wang, and Weizhu Chen. Lora: low-rank adaptation of large language models. *arXiv preprint arXiv:2106.09685*, 2021.

21 Alexey Dosovitskiy, German Ros, Felipe Codevilla, Antonio Lopez, and Vladlen Koltun. CARLA: An open urban driving simulator. In *Conference on Robot Learning*, pages 1–16, 2017.

22 Alexander Kirillov, Eric Mintun, Nikhila Ravi, Hanzi Mao, Chloe Rolland, Laura Gustafson, Tete Xiao, Spencer Whitehead, Alexander C Berg, Wan-Yen Lo, et al. Segment anything. *arXiv preprint arXiv:2304.02643*, 2023.

23 Shilong Liu, Zhaoyang Zeng, Tianhe Ren, Feng Li, Hao Zhang, Jie Yang, Chunyuan Li, Jianwei Yang, Hang Su, Jun Zhu, et al. Grounding DINO: marrying DINO with grounded pre-training for open-set object detection. *arXiv preprint arXiv:2303.05499*, 2023.

24 Holger Caesar, Varun Bankiti, Alex H Lang, Sourabh Vora, Venice Erin Liong, Qiang Xu, Anush Krishnan, Yu Pan, Giancarlo Baldan, and Oscar Beijbom. Nuscenes: A multimodal dataset for autonomous driving. In *IEEE/CVF Conference on Computer Vision and Pattern Recognition*, pages 11618–11628. Computer Vision Foundation / IEEE, 2020.

25 Yunhao Yang, Jean-Raphaël Gaglione, Sandeep Chinchali, and Ufuk Topcu. Specification-driven video search via foundation models and formal verification. *arXiv preprint arXiv:2309.10171*, 2023b.

26 Wenqian Ye, Yunsheng Ma, and Xu Cao. Uncertainty estimation in deterministic vision transformer. In *Association for the Advancement of Artificial Intelligence*, 2023.

27 Artem Vazhentsev, Gleb Kuzmin, Artem Shelmanov, Akim Tsvigun, Evgenii Tsymbalov, Kirill Fedyanin, Maxim Panov, Alexander Panchenko, Gleb Gusev, Mikhail Burtsev, et al. Uncertainty estimation of transformer predictions for misclassification detection. In *Proceedings of the 60th Annual Meeting of the Association for Computational Linguistics* (Volume 1: *Long Papers*), pages 8237–8252, 2022.

28 Allen Z Ren, Anushri Dixit, Alexandra Bodrova, Sumeet Singh, Stephen Tu, Noah Brown, Peng Xu, Leila Takayama, Fei Xia, Jake Varley, et al. Robots that ask for help: uncertainty alignment for large language model planners. *arXiv preprint arXiv:2307.01928*, 2023.

29 Vladimir Vovk, Alexander Gammerman, and Glenn Shafer. *Algorithmic Learning in a Random World*, volume 29. Springer, 2005.

30 Anastasios N Angelopoulos and Stephen Bates. Conformal prediction: a gentle introduction. *Foundations and Trends® in Machine Learning*, 16(4): 494–591, 2023.

31 Vineeth Balasubramanian, Shen-Shyang Ho, and Vladimir Vovk. *Conformal Prediction for Reliable Machine Learning: Theory, Adaptations and Applications*. Newnes, 2014.

32 Chuan Guo, Geoff Pleiss, Yu Sun, and Kilian Q Weinberger. On calibration of modern neural networks. In *International Conference on Machine Learning*, pages 1321–1330. PMLR, 2017.

33 Zhipeng Ding, Xu Han, Peirong Liu, and Marc Niethammer. Local temperature scaling for probability calibration. In *IEEE/CVF International Conference on Computer Vision*, pages 6869–6879, Montreal, QC, Canada, 2021. IEEE. https://doi.org/10.1109/ICCV48922.2021.00681.

34 Andrey Malinin, Anton Ragni, Kate Knill, and Mark Gales. Incorporating uncertainty into deep learning for spoken language assessment. In *Proceedings of the 55th Annual Meeting of the Association for Computational Linguistics* (Volume 2: *Short Papers*), pages 45–50, 2017.

35 Zhengbao Jiang, Jun Araki, Haibo Ding, and Graham Neubig. How can we know when language models know? On the calibration of language models for question answering. *Transactions of the Association for Computational Linguistics*, 9: 962–977, 2021.

36 Michael C Browne, Edmund M Clarke, and Orna Grümberg. Characterizing finite Kripke structures in propositional temporal logic. *Theoretical Computer Science*, 59(1–2): 115–131, 1988.

37 Aishwarya Kamath and Rajarshi Das. A survey on semantic parsing. *arXiv preprint arXiv:1812.00978*, 2018.

38 Christel Baier and Joost-Pieter Katoen. *Principles of Model Checking*. MIT Press, 2008.

39 Haotian Liu, Chunyuan Li, Yuheng Li, and Yong Jae Lee. Improved baselines with visual instruction tuning. In *IEEE/CVF Conference on Computer Vision and Pattern Recognition*, pages 26296–26306. Computer Vision Foundation / IEEE, 2024.

40 Alec Radford, Jong Wook Kim, Chris Hallacy, Aditya Ramesh, Gabriel Goh, Sandhini Agarwal, Girish Sastry, Amanda Askell, Pamela Mishkin, Jack Clark, et al. Learning transferable visual models from natural language supervision. In *International Conference on Machine Learning*, pages 8748–8763. PMLR, 2021.

41 Lianmin Zheng, Wei-Lin Chiang, Ying Sheng, Siyuan Zhuang, Zhanghao Wu, Yonghao Zhuang, Zi Lin, Zhuohan Li, Dacheng Li, Eric Xing, et al. Judging

llm-as-a-judge with mt-bench and chatbot arena. *Advances in Neural Information Processing Systems*, 36: 46595–46623, 2023.

42 Yunhao Yang, Neel P Bhatt, Tyler Ingebrand, William Ward, Steven Carr, Atlas Wang, and Ufuk Topcu. Fine-tuning language models using formal methods feedback: a use case in autonomous systems. In Phillip B. Gibbons, Gennady Pekhimenko, and Christopher De Sa, editors, *Proceedings of the Seventh Annual Conference on Machine Learning and Systems*, Santa Clara, CA, USA, 2024. mlsys.org.

43 Jonathan Feldstein, Paulius Dilkas, Vaishak Belle, and Efthymia Tsamoura. Mapping the neuro-symbolic AI landscape by architectures: a handbook on augmenting deep learning through symbolic reasoning. *arXiv preprint arXiv:2410.22077*, 2024.

44 Richard Sutton. The bitter lesson. *Incomplete Ideas (blog)*, 13(1): 38, 2019.

45 Adarsh Kumarappan, Mo Tiwari, Peiyang Song, Robert Joseph George, Chaowei Xiao, and Anima Anandkumar. Leanagent: lifelong learning for formal theorem proving. *arXiv preprint arXiv:2410.06209*, 2024.

46 Eli Bingham, Jonathan P Chen, Martin Jankowiak, Fritz Obermeyer, Neeraj Pradhan, Theofanis Karaletsos, Rohit Singh, Paul Szerlip, Paul Horsfall, and Noah D Goodman. Pyro: Deep universal probabilistic programming. *Journal of Machine Learning Research*, 20(28): 1–6, 2019.

47 Bob Carpenter, Andrew Gelman, Matthew D Hoffman, Daniel Lee, Ben Goodrich, Michael Betancourt, Marcus Brubaker, Jiqiang Guo, Peter Li, and Allen Riddell. Stan: a probabilistic programming language. *Journal of Statistical Software*, 76: 1–32, 2017.

48 Dustin Tran, Matthew D Hoffman, Rif A Saurous, Eugene Brevdo, Kevin Murphy, and David M Blei. Deep probabilistic programming. *arXiv preprint arXiv:1701.03757*, 2017.

49 Mahesh Lal. *Neo4j Graph Data Modeling*. Packt Publishing, 2015.

Part II

Advanced Topics

9

Physics-informed Deep Learning

*Nithin Chalapathi, Yiheng Du, Sanjeev Raja, and Aditi S. Krishnapriyan**

EECS and Chemical Engineering, University of California, Berkeley, California, USA

*All authors contributed equally.
*Corresponding Author: aditik1@berkeley.edu

9.1 Introduction

Physics-informed machine learning (PIML) represents an area that bridges the gap between traditional scientific modeling and modern data-driven techniques. By combining the strengths of both physics and machine learning, PIML aims to improve our ability to understand and predict complex systems across various scientific and engineering domains.

Traditional machine learning methods, developed for areas such as natural language processing and computer vision, have proven to be powerful tools for identifying patterns and making predictions based on large datasets. In scientific domains, machine learning methods are appealing because they can give solutions to problems that are difficult for current physics models (e.g., convergence issues with numerical methods). They also allow for very fast inference of the solution, holding the promise of capturing the time and length scales needed to study scientific phenomena that are currently intractable with current mechanistic models. However, these methods often operate independently of the underlying physical principles that govern the systems being studied. On the other hand, physical models, which are based on well-established theories, offer a high level of interpretability and reliability but can be limited in their ability to handle the complexity and variability of real-world data.

Neurosymbolic AI: Foundations and Applications, First Edition. Edited by Alvaro Velasquez et al.

Given these considerations, PIML seeks to harness the power of machine learning while maintaining a connection to the physical principles that describe the natural world. This approach can lead to methods that are not only data-driven but also informed by scientific understanding, resulting in improved accuracy and generalization capabilities.

This chapter will introduce the key concepts and motivations behind physics-informed machine learning. In particular, we will focus on *deep learning*, as it has become a dominant part of PIML. To provide a general context within which to understand many current PIML methods, we will frame problems in terms of forward and inverse problems.

Forward and inverse problems are two types of problems related to solving partial differential equations (PDEs). A forward PDE problem involves predicting the behavior of a system based on a given set of initial and boundary conditions. For example, given a heat equation and the initial temperature distribution and boundary conditions, solving the forward problem would mean predicting the temperature distribution in a metal over time.

Formally, consider a parameterized PDE, $\mathcal{F}_\phi(u) = 0$. $\mathcal{F}_\phi$ is a differential operator, and the PDE parameters ϕ and solution u are functions defined over a spatial domain $\Omega \subset \mathbb{R}^d$. The boundary of this domain is denoted by $\partial\Omega$. If time is involved, we consider $\Omega \times [0, T]$ with boundary $\partial\Omega \times [0, T]$ for $t \in [0, T]$. Let Φ be a distribution of PDE-parameter functions ϕ. The goal is to solve the following feasibility problem by training a NN with parameters $\theta \in \mathbb{R}^p$, i.e., find θ such that, for all functions ϕ sampled from Φ, the NN solves the feasibility problem,

$$\mathcal{F}_\phi(u_\theta(\phi)) = 0. \tag{9.1}$$

An inverse PDE problem involves determining the unknown parameters of a system, given observed behavior of the system. For example, given the temperature distribution in a metal at a particular time, one could use it to determine the initial temperature distribution or parameters (e.g., thermal diffusivity) that would have led to this behavior. Framing this in terms of Eq. (9.1), given measurements corresponding to the solution field u, the goal would be to infer parameters ϕ.

Forward and inverse problems are fundamental in the modeling of spatiotemporal systems, such as fluid dynamics, material deformation, and climate phenomena. Using this framework of general forward and inverse problems, the rest of this chapter will be structured as follows: Section 9.1.1 will discuss standard data generation procedures for PIML, with a focus on generating data from numerical solvers. Section 9.1.2 will cover common architectures used in PIML. We introduce convolutional neural networks from computer vision and discuss their applications to PIML. Afterwards, we formulate the neural operator setting and the operator learning problem while examining instantiations of the framework. Given the success of transformers in other ML fields, we describe developments in transformers for PIML. The final class of architecture we cover are graph neural networks (GNNs). The section closes with deep learning methods integrated within numerical solvers, and we end on a discussion of model scaling, which is increasingly being exploited as a driving factor in performance. Section 9.1.3 will discuss common training objectives in PIML. We will discuss data-fitting and physics-constrained objectives for solving forward and inverse problems, as well as generative modeling objectives. Section 9.1.4 will survey open problems and challenges in the field that are yet to be tackled. While the majority of this chapter focuses on continuum problems, there are analogous problems in atomistic modeling. Section 9.1.5 discusses a brief overview of these problems, tying these connections into the rest of our broader chapter on PIML.

9.1.1 Data Generation in Physics-informed Machine Learning

PIML combines machine learning techniques with physical principles, often encoded in the form of PDEs. A fundamental component of PIML is data generation, which provides the foundation for training, validating, and evaluating models. This chapter explores various methods and strategies used for data generation in PIML, emphasizing their importance in ensuring that models align with physical laws while maintaining computational efficiency. A visual overview of data generation strategies in PIML is provided in Figure 9.1. We discuss and primarily focus on data generated from numerical simulations in Section 9.1.1.1, and briefly discuss experimental data generation in Section 9.1.1.2.

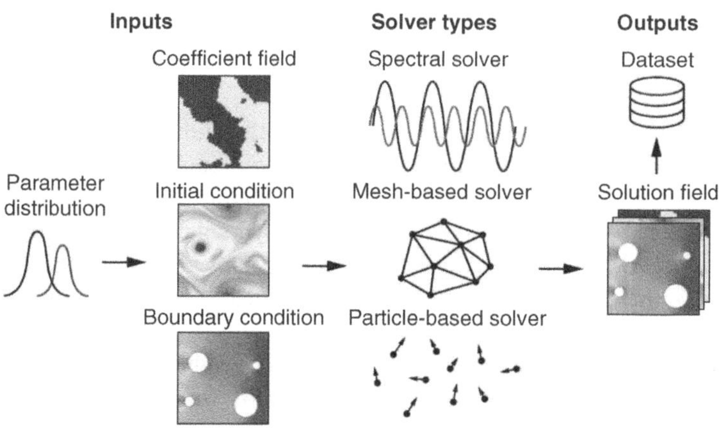

Figure 9.1 Data generation strategies to provide training data for physics-informed machine learning approaches.

9.1.1.1 Simulation-based Data

When the explicit form of the governing physics and corresponding numerical solvers are available, datasets in PIML are typically generated from numerical simulations that provide accurate representations of the system. A set of equation parameters, initial conditions, or boundary conditions θ is first sampled from a prior distribution $\theta \sim \mathcal{P}$.

Subsequently, a numerical solver is applied to these parameters, producing the numerical solution u_θ needed to train the ML model. The model's performance is then validated by comparing its outputs to the results from the numerical solver. We describe the key components of data generation via numerical solvers.

Parameter Sampling: Coefficient fields, initial conditions, and boundary conditions are often modeled as realizations of stochastic processes $\mathcal{P}$. These processes represent random fields or distributions with specific statistical properties, such as Gaussian processes with mean $\mu(x)$ and covariance $C(x_1, x_2)$. By introducing variability in the generated data, parameter sampling ensures robust model training and testing.

For inverse problems, parametric sampling defines the prior distribution of the unknown parameter or fields from observed data. It encapsulates assumptions about the parameter space, such as smoothness and length scales. For example, the width of a radical kernel $C(x_1, x_2) = k(\| x_1 - x_2 \|)$ is usually used to encode the prior knowledge of the typical length scale of the parameter field.

Numerical Solvers: Numerical solvers are essential for data generation in PIML. These solvers provide varying levels of accuracy and computational efficiency, depending on the problem domain and desired data format. Some commonly used solvers include:

1. Spectral solvers [1]: Ideal for problems with smooth solutions and regular domains, spectral solvers expand the solution using basis functions $u(x) = \sum_m c_m \phi_m(x)$, where c_m are spectral coefficients. Common choices of basis functions include Fourier series or Chebyshev polynomials [2]. The exponential convergence of these methods makes them highly accurate. Data can be recorded either as spectral coefficients or evaluated values at collocation points.
2. Mesh-based solvers [3]: For problems with complex geometries or solution singularities, mesh-based solvers like finite element or finite volume methods are necessary. These solvers approximate the solution $u(x_i)$ on (possibly unstructured) mesh grids or cells $\{x_i\}$. The gradients $\nabla u(x_i)$ are numerically evaluated on the mesh, and the PDE is discretized into an algebraic system.

The linear system is then solved by sparse solvers, including iterative methods [4] and multigrid methods [5]. For time-dependent problems, the dynamics are advanced to the next time step and solved iteratively.

When recording the solution, large meshes are often downsampled, using interpolation schemes to reduce data size while preserving fidelity.

3. Particle-based solvers [6]: For fluid problems involving free surfaces or multiphase flows, particle-based solvers are preferred. These solvers reformulate the governing equations in a Lagrangian framework, modeling physical quantities such as pressure and velocity through particle distributions. The resulting datasets consist of particle positions and their associated attributes.

Spatial Resolution: Spatial resolution pertains to the density of data points in the spatial domain. High resolution is important for reducing numerical dispersion and interpolation error, as well as capturing fine-grained details of physical fields. The smallest resolvable length scale must be fine enough to capture critical physical features; however, datasets are often downsampled when only large-scale dynamics are of interest. Downsampling reduces computational and storage burdens but must be done carefully to ensure fidelity, preserving the essential characteristics of the physical phenomena being modeled.

Adaptive meshing dynamically refines or coarsens the mesh based on error indicators, such as the magnitude of gradients or residuals. A common approach involves initially solving the system on a coarse mesh and computing an a posteriori error estimate $\eta(x_i)$, which quantifies the local discretization error at each mesh point x_i. Regions where $\eta(x_i)$ exceeds a predefined threshold trigger mesh refinement. For example, in problems involving shocks or boundary layers, areas with large $\nabla u(x_i)$ – steep solution gradients – are automatically refined to capture the critical dynamics. The refinement process is iterative: after mesh adjustment, the PDE is resolved on the updated mesh, and further refinement or coarsening is performed as necessary.

Temporal Resolution: For time-dependent problems, the task is to generate a sequence of solutions $u(t_1), u(t_2), \dots, u(t_n)$ given the initial condition $u(t_0)$. Higher temporal resolution provides finer details about dynamic processes but increases computational and storage requirements. Systems with slow or periodic dynamics can use coarse temporal sampling to reduce cost without losing accuracy. Numerical solvers usually approximate the solution by subdividing the interval $[t_i, t_{i+1}]$ and iteratively solving for $u(t_i) \rightarrow u(t_i + \Delta t) \rightarrow \dots \rightarrow u(t_{i+1})$. For each time step Δt, explicit/implicit stepping is usually used. For convergence, the time step Δt is usually chosen small enough, such that the corresponding spatial features are resolved.

Dataset Validation: Dataset validation ensures the reliability of data used in PIML by verifying its consistency with physical laws and system behaviors. For simulation data, validation involves either bounding the numerical residual of the solution or comparing it against the results of a higher-resolution solver. Robust validation is essential for building accurate and generalizable models that learn the underlying physical laws.

9.1.1.2 Experimental Data

Experimental data is another source for training PIML models, when the characterizing principle of the underlying system is unknown, or the parameters cannot be fully determined. Collected from physical systems using sensors, imaging tools, or other measurement devices, this data reflects real-world phenomena and can help address the limitations of simulation datasets. However, raw experimental data often contains noise and inconsistencies, necessitating preprocessing steps such as filtering, normalization, and data fusion. These steps ensure that the data is clean, reliable, and compatible with the requirements of machine learning models. While experimental data may lack the controlled variability of simulation data, its empirical nature makes it invaluable for assessing model performance under real-world conditions and identifying gaps between simulated predictions and observed behavior.

9.1.2 Architectures

Next, we survey common architectures that have been used in PIML. For forward problems where the goal is to roll out a dynamics trajectory given some initial state, multiple approaches have been proposed. The differentiating characteristic between approaches is the amount of physical information they incorporate and the extent to which they interface with numerical solvers. In Figure 9.2, we present a visual taxonomy of various architectures used in PIML.

Convolutional Neural Networks: Some of the first approaches in PIML leveraged deep learning techniques from computer vision. In many forward problem settings, the input domain is assumed to be a regular grid. The rolled-out dynamical trajectories bear a strong resemblance to images and can be formulated as computer vision tasks. For example, solving 2D Navier–Stokes from an initial condition maps onto image-to-video generation. Convolutional Neural Networks (CNNs) form the backbone for this class of approaches [7]. CNNs learn a set of filters that are convolved against the input image. The resulting feature maps contain local feature information while being translationally equivariant. As the depth of the CNN increases, the receptive field of each convolution progressively grows, capturing more complex features [8, 9]. Early filters detect colors, patterns, and edges,

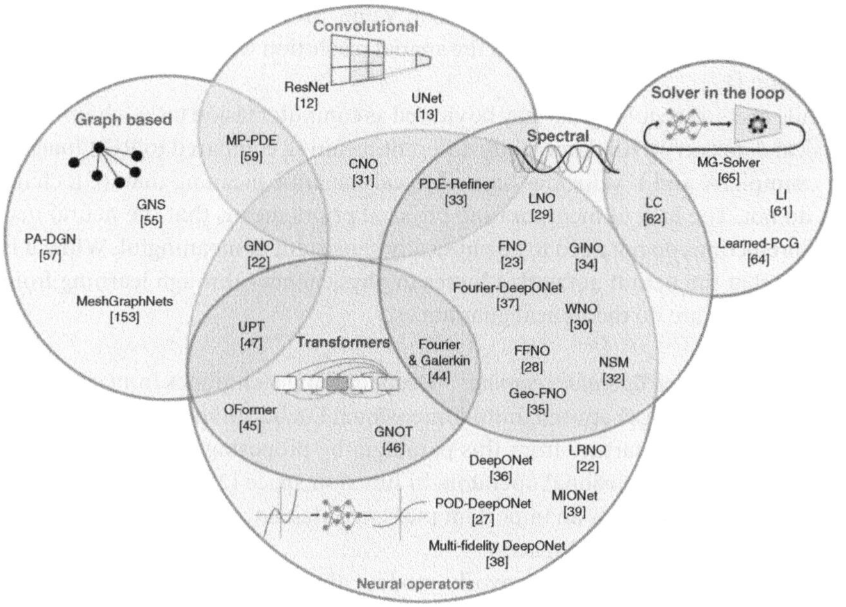

Figure 9.2 A broad classification of the different types of architectures in physics-informed machine learning.

while latter filters discern higher-order features (e.g., eyes, outlines, hair). As with fully connected networks, directly increasing the depth of CNNs encounters the vanishing gradient problem [10, 11]. Residual layers solve this issue by viewing each layer as a residual [12]:

$$x^{l+1} = x^l + f^{l+1}(x^l), \tag{9.2}$$

where x^l represents the activations from the l-th layer and f^{l+1} is the $l+1$-th layer.

In the forward problem, a common choice of architecture is a U-Net [13–17]. U-Net, originally introduced as an architecture for biomedical semantic segmentation, features a symmetric "U" shaped architecture with two parts: contraction (encoder) and expansion (decoder). Both the encoder and decoder use residual layers. The encoder progressively downsamples spatial resolution with increasing feature depth while the decoder expands spatial resolution with decreasing feature depth. Skip connections between the encoder and decoder help preserve spatial details lost during downsampling.

CNNs have also found use in inverse problems that map from a regular grid solution to some physical parameters ϕ [18–20]. Most common are Residual Networks (ResNets) consisting of a series of convolutional residual layers followed by a task-specific decision head, usually a multilayer perceptron, which outputs a final classification or regression value. Similar to the U-Net encoder, ResNet progressively downsamples the spatial resolution while increasing feature dimension [12].

While tasks on regular grids may be viewed as computer vision tasks, channels in physical data carry a fundamentally different meaning compared to RGB images. For example, X and Y velocities have physical semantic meaning that RGB channels do not. The lack of incorporating physical priors means that the neural network predictions do not need to be physically consistent or meaningful. While it is possible that the neural network adheres to physical laws through learning from the data, there are no theoretical guarantees.

Neural Operators and Operator Learning: Deep learning techniques from computer vision learn mappings between finite-dimensional Euclidean spaces. Neural Operators represent a departure from this paradigm by proposing to learn mappings between infinite-dimensional operators in function space [21, 22]. For modeling dynamical systems, this is an important inductive bias since the solutions to PDEs live in infinite-dimensional spaces.

The operator learning framework models the relationship between $\mathcal{A} = \mathcal{A}(D; \mathbb{R}^{d_a})$ and $\mathcal{U} = \mathcal{U}(D; \mathbb{R}^{d_u})$ where $D \subset \mathbb{R}^d$ is a bounded open set. Both $\mathcal{A}$ and $\mathcal{U}$ are separable Banach spaces of functions, which take values in $\mathbb{R}^{d_a}$ and $\mathbb{R}^{d_u}$, respectively. We want to learn the mapping $\mathcal{G} : \mathcal{A} \to \mathcal{U}$, typically a non linear map. Given probability measure μ over $\mathcal{A}$ and cost function $C : \mathcal{U} \times \mathcal{U} \to \mathbb{R}$, the objective is:

$$\min_{\theta} \mathbb{E}_{a \sim \mu}[C(\mathcal{G}_\theta(a), \mathcal{G}(a))] \tag{9.3}$$

Within the operator learning framework, $\mathcal{G}_\theta$ may be represented as a neural operator, an iterative architecture that maps function $v_i \mapsto v_{i+1}$. $v_0 = \mathcal{P}(a)$, a point-wise affine transformation that lifts $a \in \mathcal{A}$ to a function that takes values in d_v. Each iterative update takes the form:

$$v_{i+1} := \sigma\,(\mathcal{W}(v_i) + \mathcal{K}(v_i)), \tag{9.4}$$

where σ represents a nonlinear activation function (e.g., ReLU, GeLU). The entire parameterized network can be written in terms of function compositions performing the mapping in Eq. (9.4):

$$\mathcal{G}_\theta := \mathcal{Q} \circ \sigma(\mathcal{W}^{(L)} + \mathcal{L}^{(L)}) \circ \ldots \circ (\mathcal{W}^{(1)} + \mathcal{K}^{(1)}) \circ \mathcal{P} \tag{9.5}$$

$\mathcal{Q}$, like $\mathcal{P}$, is a point-wise feedforward layer. The affine operator $\mathcal{W}^{(l)}$ and kernel integral operator $\mathcal{K}^{(l)}$ are defined as:

$$(\mathcal{W}^{(l)}(v))(x) = W^l v(x) + b^l, \qquad (\mathcal{K}^{(l)}(v))(x) = \int_\Omega \kappa(x, y) v(y) dy. \tag{9.6}$$

A well-known and studied architecture in this space is the Fourier Neural Operator (FNO) [23]. In FNO, W^l is a linear transform and $\mathcal{K}^{(l)}$ is parameterized by a Fourier transform. By imposing that $\kappa(x, y) = \kappa(x - y)$, κ may be viewed as a convolutional operator. κ, using the convolution theorem, is equivalent to the point-wise multiplication of Fourier coefficients, which are learned through gradient descent. A popular class of numerical methods for solving PDEs include spectral solvers that solve the dynamics in Fourier space [1]. FNO mimics this process by learning in Fourier space, encoding a similar inductive bias to numerical solvers. It is learning something akin to a global, kernel-based transformation in the frequency domain, similar to how spectral solvers compute PDE solutions by transforming to the Fourier domain, applying operations, then transforming back. Using the Fourier representation enables the use of the Fast Fourier Transform (FFT) to compute the Fourier representation in $O(n \log_2 n)$ time, reducing the computational requirements [24]. In many cases, Fourier-based representations assume periodic boundary conditions. To accommodate other types of boundary conditions, either the basis functions must be changed or the solution field must be modified. By changing the basis function to either a sine series or cosine series, Dirichlet or Neumann boundary conditions may be represented. Chebyshev polynomials are another basis series to represent Dirchlet boundary conditions [25]. Instead of changing the basis functions, windowing or Fourier extension can be applied. Windowing transforms the solution field by multiplying by a smoothing function (e.g., Hann window, Tukey window, Gaussian window), while Fourier extension, also known as Fourier continuation, extends the solution domain with padding [23, 26, 27].

Many alternative characterizations and extensions have been formulated to FNO. Some of the most successful include Factorized Fourier Neural Operators (FFNO) [28], Low rank Neural Operators (LrNO) [22], Laplace Neural Operators (LNO) [29], Wavelet Neural Operators (WNO) [30], Convolutional Neural Operators (CNO) [31], and generalized Neural Spectral Methods (NSM) [32]. FFNO proposes to factorize the dimensions of the Fourier transform to create a separable Fourier representation. In order to handle nonperiodic domains, LNO uses the Laplace transform instead of the Fourier transform, replacing the Fourier layers. WNO replaces the Fourier representation with wavelets, and CNO extends CNNs to the neural operator setting. Finally, NSM provides a generalized framework for learning in spectral space with orthogonal basis functions. In contrast to the previous works, PDE-Refiner [33] feeds to predictions from an FNO into a diffusion model to stabilize longer autoregressive rollouts. Extensions to nonregular grids have also been proposed in the form of geometry-informed neural operators (GINO) [34] and geometry-aware neural operators (Geo-FNO) [35]. Neural operators promise a more general approach for solving PDEs across a range of geometries and tasks while encoding inductive biases derived from numerical methods.

Alongside FNO, deep operator networks (DeepONets) also learn in continuous function space [36]. DeepONets consist of two learnable components: a branch network and a trunk network. The branch network takes as input observations from a fixed number of sensors. In the forward problem, this is the initial condition and any physical parameters. The trunk network encodes the locations for the output function, typically spatial-temporal points. The outputs of both networks are merged via a dot product to produce a final prediction value. More formally, let $\mathcal{G}$ be an operator acting on the known input function ϕ (initial condition) that attempts to approximate function u (the solution to a PDE). Due to discretization, let $\{x_1, x_2, \dots x_m\}$ be locations where ϕ is known and y a point in the domain of u. The trunk network takes as input y and produces a set of outputs $[t_1, t_2, \dots t_p] \in \mathbb{R}^p$. The branch network takes as input $[\phi(x_1), \phi(x_2), \dots \phi(x_m)] \in \mathbb{R}^m$ and outputs $[b_1, b_2, \dots b_p] \in \mathbb{R}^p$. The two outputs are merged:

$$G(\phi)(y) = \sum_{k=1}^{p} b_k t_k. \tag{9.7}$$

Variations on DeepONets have been proposed including POD-DeepONet [27], Fourier-DeepONet [37], multi-fidelity DeepONet [38], and MIONet [39]. POD-DeepONet performs a proper orthogonal decomposition [40] of trunk information and extends the DeepONet method to multiple output functions. Similar to FNO, Fourier-DeepONet integrates Fourier information by applying FNO layers to the output of a DeepONet for full waveform inversion, the task of inferring structural information from seismic waveform data. Lu et al. [38] apply DeepONets to datasets of multiple resolutions and to inverse problems. Finally, MIONet replaces the branch-trunk dot product with a tensor product to accommodate multiple branch functions and approximates solutions that arise as a result of the product of many functional spaces. Lanthaler et al. [41] perform a theoretical analysis of DeepONets, providing lower and upper bounds on approximation error.

Transformer Architectures: Within the broader machine learning community, transformers have seen great success especially in natural language processing and computer vision. Transformers are models that use a combination of attention and feedforward layers to process sequences of tokens [42]. In natural language processing, tokens consist of words while in computer vision tokens are image patches [43]. Attention maps a query and a set of key-value inputs to an output where the query Q, key K, value V, and output are all vectors. Typically, a feedforward layer is used to project the query, key, and values into dimensions d_q, d_k, and d_v, respectively. A common formulation is the scaled dot-product attention:

$$\text{Attention}(Q, K, V) = \text{softmax}\left(\frac{QK^T}{\sqrt{d_k}}\right) V. \tag{9.8}$$

When the query, key, and values are the same sequence of tokens, then the attention mechanism becomes self-attention.

Transformers have not had the same performance gains when learning from dynamical systems. One major roadblock is the large memory requirement of a self-attention block, with each attention mechanism necessitating $O(n^2)$ memory where n is the number of grid points. Self-attention quickly becomes intractable, especially as n grows exponentially in the number of spatial-temporal dimensions. Most applications of transformers for the forward problem aim to solve this issue. One of the first proposed methods is the Fourier and Galerkin Transformer [44], which removes the softmax normalization and introduces a linear time attention mechanism with parallels to a Petrov–Galerkin projection. Li et al. [45] introduce OFormer, a transformer-based architecture that uses self-attention over the spatial domain and time marching using recurrent MLPs. The generalized neural operator transformer (GNOT) [46] uses a linear mechanism that also removes the softmax operation and normalizes the input sequence instead. GNOT combines the normalized attention with a geometric gating mechanism, which acts as a fuzzy mixture of experts.

While the former architectures design new attention mechanisms to deal with memory bottlenecks, the Universal Physics Transformer (UPT) [47] builds off of the Perceiver architecture [48], a generalized multi-modal attention mechanism. In contrast to self-attention, Perceiver utilizes cross-attention between a set of latent codes and inputs. The latent codes then go through a series of self-attention blocks, reducing the overall memory consumption of the network to linear in input dimensionality. UPT uses an encoder-transform-decoder architecture. The encoder uses a GNN [49] while the transform and decoder blocks use transformers. These transformer-based models have shown great promise in tackling dynamical systems, but simulating multi-scale systems remains a significant challenge. This includes turbulence, which involves both interacting eddies across a wide range of length scales. EddyFormer [50] introduced a Transformer-based spectral-element (SEM) architecture that combines the accuracy of spectral methods with the scalability of attention mechanisms. A key innovation is its SEM tokenization, which decomposes the flow into grid-scale and subgrid-scale components. This decomposition reduces the sequence length for attention calculations, enabling the model to focus on relevant scales more efficiently. By capturing both local fine-scale dynamics and global large-scale features, EddyFormer provides an effective solution to the scale-separation problem while significantly improving computational efficiency.

Graph Neural Networks: Many problems, forward and inverse, require simulation over irregular meshes. GNNs are a promising approach that represents the solution domain as a graph where neighboring domain locations are connected via edges. Unlike traditional neural networks that assume grid-like structures (e.g., images or sequences), GNNs leverage the relational information encoded in graphs to learn node, edge, or graph-level representations. Let graph $G = (V, E)$ be comprised of a set of vertices $V = \{v_1, v_2, \dots v_N\}$ and edges $E \subseteq V \times V$. Edges are represented with an adjacency matrix $A \in \mathbb{R}^{N \times N}$ where $A_{ij} = 1$ if there is an edge between v_i and v_j. Additionally, each node is represented with a feature vector, compactly expressed as a node feature matrix $X \in \mathbb{R}^{N \times d}$. GNNs learn a node representation h_v that captures both local structure and node features. The core mechanism of GNNs is message passing, where each node aggregates information from its neighbors. A general message passing step for node v at layer l is given by

$$h_v^{l+1} = \sigma\left(\sum_{u \in \mathcal{N}(v)} M_l(h_v^l, h_u^l, e_{uv})\right). \tag{9.9}$$

M_l is the message function that computes the message from neighbors $\mathcal{N}$ of u. Optionally, an edge feature e_{uv} is included. A common formulation of M_l is the graph convolution network (GCN) [51–53]:

$$h_v^{l+1} = \sigma\left(W_l \sum_{u \in \mathcal{N}(v)} \frac{h_u^l}{|\mathcal{N}(u)|}\right) \tag{9.10}$$

Graph convolution computes a weighted sum of node v's neighbors where W_l is a learnable weight matrix. There are multiple alternative proposed message passing algorithms, including graph attention [54].

Within the regime of the forward problem, Sanchez-Gonzalez et al. [55] and Pfaff et al. [56] both apply GNNs to predict dynamics. Sanchez-Gonzalez et al. [55] introduce Graph Network-based Simulators (GNS) that view the system as a volume of particles over which a GNN is applied. MeshGraphNets [56] apply GNNs over meshed based data and include the ability to adaptively refine mesh resolution. In a similar vein, Physics-Aware Difference Graph Networks (PA-DGA) [57] formulate message passing to resemble a finite difference scheme while operating on sparse irregular meshes. De Avila Belbute-Peres et al. [58] embed a GNN directly within a fluid flow simulator. The simulator runs on a coarse mesh while the GNN performs message passing over the fine mesh. Alongside the introduction of the neural operator formulation, [21, 22] use a GNN as the first neural operator (GNO). Finally, Brandstetter et al. [59] introduce a general purpose message passing PDE solver (MP-PDE) using GNNs alongside multiple methodological improvements including temporal bundling and unrolled training to improve the stability of autoregressive rollouts. GNNs have also seen usage in inverse problems. Zhao et al. [60], leveraging a GNN a surrogate model for a PDE solver, use a coordinate network to recover initial conditions by matching the predictions from the GNN to a ground truth solution.

Integration with Numerical Solvers: Another class of deep learning methods aims to directly interface with numerical solvers by replacing computational expensive steps with neural networks. By differentiating through the numerical solver, neural networks may be directly embedded within a finite elements or spectral solver. This class of approaches promises the guarantees given by numerical solvers with the computational speedups offered by neural networks. One representative approach is Kochkov et al. [61], which looks at numerical solvers for fluid dynamics. In finite volume methods for fluids, computing convective flux $u \otimes u$ is necessary and requires interpolating u. This is typically done via polynomial interpolation. One approach is to replace the interpolation step with a neural network that outputs the polynomial coefficients, called a learned interpolation (LI). A less interpretable method (LC), learned correction, learns a correction factor based on the numerical solver's prediction. If u^* is the uncorrected velocity field from a numerical solver and f is a neural network, then the learned correction takes the form:

$$u_{t+1} = u^*_{t+1} + f(u^*_{t+1}) \tag{9.11}$$

Follow-up work extends this framework to spectral solvers [62]. If $\hat{u}$ denotes the spectral representation of u and h a weighting factor, the spectral variant learns the correction:

$$\hat{u}_{t+1} = \text{Numerical-Solver}(\hat{u}_t) + h \cdot f(\hat{u}_t) \tag{9.12}$$

While the aforementioned methods are specific to fluid dynamics, similar approaches have been proposed for other systems. At the heart of many numerical solvers, a linear solve is performed to resolve the dynamics of the system. A common choice of algorithm is the preconditioned conjugate gradient algorithm (PCG) [63]. However, the choice of preconditioner is nontrivial and often problem-dependent, requiring domain knowledge. Li et al. [64] propose to learn the preconditioning using GNNs that optimize the number of iterations to convergence of PCG (Learned-PCG). Similarly, the prolongation matrix used in multiscale methods is also highly problem-dependent. Multiscale methods solve the PDE at multiple resolutions that are related by the prolongation matrix.

$$u^k = P\hat{u}^k \tag{9.13}$$

The superscript k denotes the solver iteration, $\hat{u}$ the coarse solution, and P the prolongation matrix. Greenfeld et al. [65] use a fully connected network that takes as input a 3×3 stencil of the fine solution and outputs a subset of P. After obtaining a full P matrix, the information is used to update the fine solution representation as usual in multi-scale methods using Eq. (9.14) (MG-Solver).

$$u^k_c = u^k + Pe^k, \tag{9.14}$$

where e is the error correction factor on the coarse grid solution $\hat{u}^k$ and the subscript c denotes a correct fine grid solution.

Model Scaling: Much of the success deep learning has had within the last decade can be attributed to significant increases in both compute and data. Computer vision and natural language processing have seen improvements in model performance due to pretraining objectives on large amounts of data, articulated by Kaplan et al. [66] for transformers. Within the broader field of scientific machine learning, large-scale training and datasets have been successful for many applications including atomistic modeling [67–69] and climate modeling [70, 71–73]. Similar efforts have been attempted in PIML. McCabe et al. [74] introduce multiple-physics pretraining (MPP) as a method for learning across physical systems. MPP uses an Axial vision transformer [75] and show that training on advection and diffusion systems individually helps performance on advection-diffusion systems. Poseidon [76], a Swin transformer [77] based approach, moves toward this regime by training across a variety of time-dependent dynamical systems including incompressible Navier-Stokes and compressible Euler equations for gas dynamics. In a similar vein, Subramanian et al. [78] examine transfer learning when pretraining on the Poisson, advection-diffusion, and Helmholtz equations. They find improved performance when compared to models trained only on the evaluation task data, hinting that it is possible to learn and transfer physical knowledge learned by the model. Recent scaling results point to the ability of deep learning methods to learn and enforce physics in a fully data-driven manner indicating that certain design choices or inductive biases may not be necessary in the presence of sufficiently large data. Large-scale model training and transfer learning is still a developing topic within the PIML research community with a lack of established foundation models. Nonetheless, it is a promising direction of particular interest to the community in order to learn the governing physical phenomena from large amounts of data.

9.1.3 Training Objectives

In this section, we will explore training objectives that can be used to train Physics-informed Neural Networks (PINN), a visual overview of which is shown in Figure 9.3. We will primarily discuss objectives that can be used to train neural networks (NNs) to learn the solution of PDEs given the parameters of the PDE. This is known as the forward problem. In Sections 9.1.3.1 and 9.1.3.2, we will explore data-fitting objectives and physics-constrained objectives to solve the forward problem. Then in Section 9.1.3.3, we will cover objectives relating to the inverse problem, which involves predicting underlying PDE parameters or governing equations

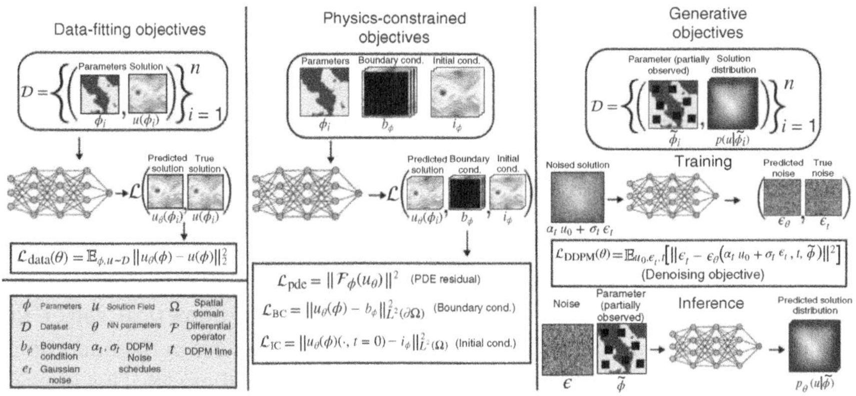

Figure 9.3 Overarching training strategies for physics-informed machine learning.

from solution or trajectory observations. Finally, in Section 9.1.3.4, we discuss generative objectives, which are particularly useful when the PDE parameters or solutions are sparsely observed, or if uncertainty/error quantification is desired over simple point estimates.

Forward Problem Formulation: Forward problems aim to solve the feasibility problem described in Eq. (9.15), i.e.,

$$\mathcal{F}_{\phi}(u_{\theta}(\phi)) = 0, \tag{9.15}$$

where Φ is a distribution of PDE-parameter functions ϕ, and a NN is trained with parameters θ. There are two broad classes of objective functions used to solve this feasibility problem with NNs, namely those that primarily rely on data and those that incorporate physical laws or constraints. We describe these two classes of methods, which we respectively denote as "data-fitting" and "physics-constrained" objectives, in more detail in Sections 9.1.3.1 and 9.1.3.2.

9.1.3.1 Data-fitting Objectives

Data-fitting objectives assume access to a dataset $\mathcal{D}$ containing pairs of PDE parameters and the corresponding PDE solution $u(\phi)$): $\mathcal{D} = \{(\phi, u(\phi)\}_{\phi\sim\Phi}$. The PDE solution data is typically obtained by running a numerical or analytical solver. The data-fitting objective function $\mathcal{L}_{\text{data}}(\theta)$ is a simple regression loss over the dataset:

$$\min_{\theta} \mathcal{L}_{\text{data}}(\theta) = \min_{\theta} \mathbb{E}_{\phi,u\sim\mathcal{D}} || u_{\theta}(\phi) - u(\phi) ||_2^2. \tag{9.16}$$

Data-fitting objectives are straightforward to implement and have favorable convergence properties in the limit of large, accurate datasets and expressive NNs.

Such objectives, when scaled to datasets with $\sim 10^9 - 10^{12}$ training examples, are the basis for many of the recent, high-profile advances in large language models (LLMs) [79] and generative image models [80, 81]. However, in the context of PIML, data-fitting objectives may require large quantities of paired parameter-solution data to achieve convergence of the optimization objective (9.15). As discussed in Section 9.1.1, large-scale data generation can also be highly computationally expensive. Furthermore, the implicit assumption of data-fitting objectives is that the ground truth data $u(\phi)$ is high-quality; that is, it satisfies the feasibility problem $\mathcal{F}_\phi(u(\phi)) = 0$. In practice, however, the data only approximately satisfy this relation due to finite discretization, numerical solver ill-conditioning, and a variety of other factors. These inaccuracies in the underlying dataset can ultimately affect the quality of the final, trained model. This is exacerbated by the fact that no explicit physical constraints are encoded in pure data-fitting objectives. As a result, there are essentially no physical guarantees on the output of the model, particularly in parameter regimes not explicitly encountered in the training data [82].

9.1.3.2 Physics-constrained Objectives

An alternative to pure data-fitting objectives for solving PDEs with NNs is the class of **physics-constrained objectives**. Broadly, physics-constrained objectives contain terms that exploit a certain mathematical or physical property of the underlying PDE, independent of external training data. They can be further divided into two subclasses, which we denote soft and hard physics-constrained objectives.

Soft-constrained Objectives: Soft physics-constrained objectives are those that encourage satisfaction of a physical constraint (or conversely, penalize violations of the constraint), but do not explicitly guarantee exact enforcement. Among the most popular soft constraints is known as the PDE residual loss, $\mathcal{L}_{\text{pde}}(\theta)$, defined as

$$\min_\theta \mathcal{L}_{\text{pde}} = \min_\theta \mathbb{E}_{\phi\sim\Phi} \|\mathcal{F}_\phi(u_\theta(\phi))\|_2^2. \tag{9.17}$$

In words, Eq. (9.17) encourages learned NN parameters θ that predict solutions $u_\theta(\phi)$ with low-norm PDE residuals. The differential operator $\mathcal{F}$ is typically computed via a finite-difference scheme or automatic differentiation software [83]. While $\mathcal{L}_{\text{pde}}$ exploits the known form of the PDE differential operator, it is inherently underconstrained. For instance, a zero-solution field trivially achieves a loss of zero. To combat this, the PDE residual loss is often combined with additional loss terms enforcing initial and boundary conditions of the PDE. For instance, if we assume Dirichlet boundary conditions of the form $u_\theta(\phi)\big|_{x\in\partial\Omega} = b_\phi(x)$, and an initial condition of the form $u_\theta(\phi)(x, 0) = i_\phi(x),\ x \in \Omega$, the combined loss $\mathcal{L}_{\text{combined}}$ is given as

$$\begin{aligned}\min_\theta \mathcal{L}_{\text{combined}} = \min_\theta \mathbb{E}_{\phi\sim\Phi} \Big[\left\|\mathcal{F}_\phi(u_\theta(\phi))\right\|_2^2 + \lambda_{\text{BC}} \left\|u_\theta(\phi) - b_\phi\right\|_{L^2(\partial\Omega)}^2 \\ + \lambda_{\text{IC}} \left\|u_\theta(\phi)(\cdot, 0) - i_\phi(\cdot)\right\|_{L^2(\Omega)}^2 \Big],\end{aligned} \tag{9.18}$$

where λ_{BC} and λ_{IC} are weights controlling the strengths of the boundary and initial condition terms, respectively.

It is also common to combine soft physics-constrained objectives with data-fitting objectives [84], resulting in a composite loss often referred to as a PINN loss:

$$\min_\theta \mathcal{L}_{\text{PINN}} = \min_\theta \mathbb{E}_{\phi\sim\Phi} \left[\mathcal{L}_{\text{data}} + \lambda_{\text{PINN}} \mathcal{L}_{\text{combined}}\right], \tag{9.19}$$

where λ_{PINN} is a weight controlling the strength of the physics-constrained term.

Soft physics-constrained objectives such as the PINN loss generally do *not* guarantee that the learned NN satisfies the physical constraints exactly, since (i) zero loss, even on training data, is generally not achievable in practice, and (ii) the behavior of the trained model on input parameters ϕ not seen during training or outside the training distribution Φ is generally unpredictable. Additionally, while the PINN loss can constrain the solution space of NN parameters to a more physically consistent region, there are numerous challenges that affect practical adoption. Chiefly, if the underlying training data (e.g., from a numerical solver) is inaccurate or itself has nonzero PDE residual, then the data-fitting term can conflict with the physics-constrained term, complicating gradient-based optimization schemes. Prior work has shown that combining soft-constrained physics losses with data-fitting objectives can lead to complex, ill-posed loss landscapes [85] that are difficult to optimize with NNs. To combat this issue, some works have proposed test-time refinement of NN-predicted solutions with the PDE residual loss [86], meta-learning over the space of auxiliary constraints that improve a primary objective [87], or learning from data in which physical constraints are only approximately satisfed [88].

Beyond the PDE differential operator and boundary/initial condition terms, various other approaches have been explored to incorporate physically relevant soft constraints into neural networks, including Lipschitz continuity [89], Bellman optimality [90], turbulence [91], numerical surrogates [92], prolongation matrices [93], solver iterations [94], spectral methods [32], and convexity over derivatives [95].

Hard-constrained Objectives: Hard physics-constrained objectives aim to exactly enforce physical constraints in the predicted solutions of NNs at both train and test time. The primary technique by which this is achieved is known as **differentiable optimization**, which embeds an auxiliary optimization problem into the forward pass of a neural network and uses the implicit function theorem (IFT) [96] to efficiently compute gradients through the optimization procedure. This "optimization-as-a-layer" approach was pioneered by OptNet [97], which integrated quadratic programs into neural network training. In the context of neural network PDE solving, Négiar et al. [98] framed PDE-constrained optimization as a linear least squares problem over a learned dictionary of basis functions, an approach that was subsequently scaled up in Chalapathi et al. [99] via a Mixture-of-Experts [100] approach. Hard constraints have also been enforced in multiple other PDE contexts, including neural conservation laws [101], constrained neural fields [102], boundary constraints and representations [103, 104], constitutive laws [105], boundary conditions [106], characteristic layers [107], and inverse modeling and design [108, 109].

9.1.3.3 Inverse Problem Objectives

Broadly, the goal of the inverse problem setting is to identify underlying parameters or governing laws from observations of a system. In the PDE context, this can be done by learning a function ϕ_θ that, given a solution u, predicts the parameters $\phi_\theta(u)$. One approach is a *data-fitting* objective, which uses available pairs (a, u) to directly minimize,

$$\min_{\theta} \quad \mathbb{E}_{(\phi,u)\sim\mathcal{D}}\big[||\phi_\theta(u) - \phi||_2^2\big], \tag{9.20}$$

relying on explicit parameter-solution training data. A complementary approach is a *PDE residual* objective, where one learns parameters so that the operator $\mathcal{F}_{\phi_\theta(u)}$ is close to zero when acting on u, i.e.,

$$\min_{\theta} \quad \mathbb{E}_{(u)\sim\mathcal{D}}\big[||\mathcal{F}_{\phi_\theta(u)}(u)||_2^2\big]. \tag{9.21}$$

These approaches are explored in the context of neural operators in [86].

A generalization of the above setting (inferring PDE parameters from solutions) is to infer governing dynamical equations from observed trajectories. There has been a rich line of work using machine learning techniques to achieve this. Early works used dictionary learning to identify a sparse set of basis functions explaining the dynamics [110, 111], while more recent approaches use more expressive, deep neural networks to infer underlying dynamics [112–116].

9.1.3.4 Generative Objectives

The objectives considered thus far assume a *deterministic* mapping between PDE parameters and solutions in both directions. However, in many physical and engineering applications, we encounter partial or noisy observations of either a *parameter* field ϕ driving a PDE or of its *solution* field u. This leads to scenarios where (i) we have partial observations of ϕ and seek the conditional distribution $p(u \mid \phi)$ (partially observed forward problem) or (ii) we observe some subset of the solution

u and aim to infer the posterior distribution $p(\phi \mid u)$ (partially observed inverse problem). In both cases, *learning the full conditional distribution* is preferable to simply finding a single-point estimate. Generative modeling frameworks are capable of addressing this challenge by learning conditional and/or joint *distributions* over PDE parameters and solutions. This is particularly useful for generating ensembles of predictions, from which uncertainty quantification can be done.

Forward Problem with Partial Parameter Observations: We define a prior distribution over parameter fields, $\phi \sim \Phi$. However, in a realistic setting, we might only have partial or noisy observations of ϕ, denoted by $\widetilde{\phi}$. Hence, we seek to learn the *conditional posterior* distribution of the solution u given these partial observations:

$$p(u \mid \widetilde{\phi}). \tag{9.22}$$

Inverse Problem with Partial Solution Observations: Conversely, in an *inverse* or *Bayesian inference* setting, one often has direct observations (possibly noisy) of the solution u at a sparse set of locations or times, denoted by $\widetilde{u}$. The aim is to infer the posterior distribution:

$$p(\phi \mid \widetilde{u}), \tag{9.23}$$

which describes all parameter fields ϕ consistent (up to noise or modeling error) with the observed data $\widetilde{u}$. In this inverse scenario, the forward map is $\phi \mapsto u$, but we only see partial data of u.

Denoising Diffusion Probabilistic Models: Generative models can learn to *sample* plausible instances of ϕ or u conditioned on partial observations. Denoising diffusion probabilistic models (DDPM) [117] are a popular class of generative models that have achieved state-of-the-art performance on many generative modeling tasks [81, 118, 119]. The central idea of DDPM is to define a *forward noising process* that gradually corrupts the data (u or ϕ) by adding Gaussian noise over a fixed number of steps T. A neural network with parameters θ is then trained to predict the noise that was added, using the following training objective:

$$\mathcal{L}_{\text{DDPM}}(\theta) = \mathbb{E}_{x_0, \epsilon_t, t}\Big[||\epsilon_t - \epsilon_\theta\Big(\alpha_t\, x_0 + \sigma_t\, \epsilon_t, t, \widetilde{z}\Big)||^2\Big], \tag{9.24}$$

where x_0 is a sample from the true (or training) distribution (e.g., PDE solution u or parameter ϕ), $\epsilon_t \sim \mathcal{N}(0, I)$ is the random noise added at step t, α_t, σ_t are noise schedule variables that combine to produce a noisy version of x_0, $\epsilon_\theta(\cdot)$ is the neural network that predicts the noise from the current corrupted sample, and $\widetilde{z}$ is the *conditioning* inputs (e.g., partial observations $\widetilde{u}$ or $\widetilde{\phi}$). The expectation is taken over all training samples x_0, noise samples ϵ_t, and timesteps t. By minimizing (9.24), the model $\epsilon_\theta(\cdot)$ learns an accurate denoising step for each t. At inference time, it can be used as a "de-noiser" to transform noise samples into realistic data samples. By composing the learned denoising steps from $t = T$ down to $t = 0$, we can start with a pure Gaussian noise sample $x_T \sim \mathcal{N}(0, I)$ and iteratively *sample* from the learned distribution, ultimately obtaining a sample $\hat{x}_0$ that (ideally) matches the true data distribution. In the PDE context, this procedure yields a plausible full solution u (or parameter ϕ) conditioned on the partial observations.

Recent works have demonstrated the broad practicality of diffusion-based generative models for PDEs and related physics-informed tasks. For instance, the approaches in [120–122] use diffusion models combined with PDE constraints to learn solution manifolds under uncertain or varying parameters. Similarly, diffusion models have been successfully employed for synthetic PDE data generation [123, 124], which is valuable for scenarios where numerical simulations are expensive. Recent fluid dynamics [125, 126] and climate/weather forecasting [127–129] applications employ diffusion models to capture spatiotemporal dependencies.

9.1.4 Open Challenges

Open challenges in PIML are particularly pronounced in handling large-scale problems on complex geometries, especially fluid problems involving turbulence.

Turbulence: Turbulent flows [130] are notoriously difficult to characterize due to their chaotic, multiscale, and highly nonlinear nature. Fully characterizing a turbulent flow requires resolving flow features down to dissipative length-scales. The capacity of existing machine learning models often falls short when it comes to representing the full spectrum of flow features, particularly in systems with high Reynolds number. Current PIML approaches struggle to generalize across multiple scales and flow regimes. In addition, current loss functions primarily focus on pointwise accuracy or cumulative errors, ignoring critical aspects like the preservation of energy spectra, vorticity transport, or long-term stability of flow predictions

Complex Geometries: Unlike simple domains, where uniform grids or structured meshes suffice, complex geometries often require unstructured or adaptive meshing techniques to accurately capture physical features near boundaries or within intricate regions. These geometries make it difficult to enforce boundary conditions accurately, leading to errors that propagate through the solution. Traditional solvers also face difficulties balancing resolution and computational efficiency in near-boundary regions. In the context of PIML, irregular mesh prevents the direct use of powerful spectral models, such as FNO. As discussed in Section 9.1.2 covering architectures, geometry-aware models have been proposed. Yet, challenges in generalizing across different geometric configurations still exist.

3D Systems: Most current PIML methods evaluate and focus on 2D dynamical systems, but many practical engineering tasks require solving 3D dynamics across time. 3D systems pose challenges on two fronts: computational complexity and modeling complexity. In grid-based methods, the number of points on the domain increases exponentially with spatial-temporal dimensionality, exacerbating both compute and memory requirements. For 3D systems, numerical solvers also necessitate increasing compute, which is reflected in the amount of data available for learning 3D systems, with few large-scale datasets or benchmarks. Beyond computational requirements, 3D systems often have high-dimensional state spaces where the number of variables and interactions can grow exponentially with complex dependencies across time and space. New methods will need to be developed to handle both increasing computational demands and task complexity.

9.1.5 Connections to Atomistic Modeling

In this review, we have largely focused on the use of machine learning to tackle physical modeling problems at the *continuum* scale, including fluid and climate modeling. However, machine learning approaches are also increasingly being used to tackle problems at considerably smaller length scales, notably atomistic and molecular systems. We provide a brief overview of ML approaches for atomistic modeling, as well as the connections to the methods discussed in this review for PDEs and continuum-scale modeling.

9.1.5.1 Molecular Simulation

Molecular dynamics (MD) simulation is a cornerstone of computational chemistry, physics, and materials science, where one integrates Newton's equations of motion for a collection of atoms interacting under a potential energy function [131]. MD simulations are invaluable for sampling the phase space of complex molecular systems – capturing thermodynamic properties, dynamical events such as rare conformational changes, and key physical or chemical processes at atomistic resolution. Although *ab initio* methods like density functional theory (DFT) can compute the interatomic forces needed to evolve MD simulations *on the fly* with quantum-mechanical accuracy [132], their computational cost grows rapidly with system size, making them impractical for extensive simulations [133]. Hence, empirical or semi-empirical force fields [134, 135] are often used in practice, sacrificing some accuracy to access larger time and length scales. Another challenge is the presence of large barriers in the potential energy surface of high-dimensional atomistic systems, which create a substantial difference in timescales between the fastest dynamical motions of the system (e.g., bond vibrations), and relevant scientific phenomena such as chemical reactions and protein folding [136, 137]

9.1.5.2 Machine Learning Techniques

Machine learning is increasingly being used to address these challenges and accelerate various aspects of molecular simulation [138]. An active area of research is Machine Learning Force Fields (MLFFs) [139, 140], which are neural network-parameterized surrogate models that learn the underlying quantum mechanical energy landscape of atomistic systems from large quantities of data labeled with electronic structure methods. ML-based approaches are also being used to learn bias potentials for enhanced sampling of rare events [141–144]. Generative models are also being used to directly sample from high-dimensional molecular distributions, with applications in the study and design of proteins [119, 145–147], small molecules [148, 149, 150], and materials [146, 151]. While appearing unrelated to neural PDE solvers, research in ML for molecular simulation centers on many similar design choices and concepts as discussed in this review, of which we highlight a select few.

Role of Constraints: Similar to PDEs for continuum systems, physics-constrained architectures and training objectives are a key consideration at the atomistic scale. Of particular interest has been the development of *equivariant* neural networks [152], which guarantee that predicted vector quantities, such as forces and possibly internal features, rotate consistently when the positions of the input rotate. While equivariant neural networks have demonstrated benefits in data efficiency and accuracy [67, 153], several recent approaches have called into the question the utility of this inductive bias, particularly in the presence of large-scale datasets, scalable model architectures, and techniques such as data augmentation [154–156]. Another core physical constraint is that predicted forces should be *conservative*, i.e., have zero curl. In practice, this is achieved by using automatic differentiation to compute the forces as the gradient of a predicted scalar potential energy. While some works have attempted to efficiently predict forces without this intermediate differentiation step, this has problematic consequences for the stability and accuracy of downstream simulations [157]. However, combining these approaches with model distillation techniques [158] can help incorporate energy conservation into the final distilled model. Paralleling the use of ML for PDEs and continuum problems, the role of constraints in molecular simulation tasks thus remains an open question.

Data Generation: Similar to the challenges associated with PDE data generation discussed in Section 9.1.1, generation of high-quality data for training ML models is a challenge in the molecular domain. For instance, MLFFs require data labeled with high-fidelity electronic structure methods, such as Density Functional Theory (DFT). These computations can be expensive and scale poorly with system size, making it difficult to gather sufficiently large datasets for ML training. Second, achieving good predictive performance requires sampling a broad distribution of structures and configurations, further increasing the computational burden. Finally, multiple levels of theory (e.g., different DFT functionals, post-Hartree-Fock methods) each come with trade-offs in accuracy and cost, making it nontrivial to combine or compare datasets derived under differing assumptions.

Differentiable Simulations: Recent ML approaches formulate end-to-end optimization procedures through the steps of a molecular simulation [141, 159, 160], using techniques such as implicit differentiation and the adjoint method [161] to enable efficient differentiation. This is closely related to differentiable optimization approaches for enforcing hard constraints in PDEs, which were discussed in Section 9.1.3.2.

References

1 C. Canuto. *Spectral Methods: Evolution to Complex Geometries and Applications to Fluid Dynamics*. Springer-Verlag, 2007.

2 John C Mason and David C Handscomb. *Chebyshev Polynomials*. Chapman and Hall/CRC, 2002.

3 Timothy Barth, Raphaèle Herbin, and Mario Ohlberger. Finite volume methods: foundation and analysis. In *Encyclopedia of Computational Mechanics, second edition*, pages 1–60, 2018.

4 Yousef Saad. *Iterative Methods for Sparse Linear Systems*. SIAM, 2003.

5 Jinchao Xu and Ludmil Zikatanov. Algebraic multigrid methods. *Acta Numerica*, 26: 591–721, 2017.

6 MB Liu and GR2593940 Liu. Smoothed particle hydrodynamics (sph): an overview and recent developments. *Archives of Computational Methods in Engineering*, 17: 25–76, 2010.

7 Yann LeCun, Bernhard Boser, John Denker, Donnie Henderson, R. Howard, Wayne Hubbard, and Lawrence Jackel. Handwritten digit recognition with a back-propagation network. In D. Touretzky, editor, *Advances in Neural Information Processing Systems*, volume 2. Morgan-Kaufmann, 1989. https://proceedings.neurips.cc/paper_files/paper/1989/file/53c3bce66e43be4f209556518c2fcb54-Paper.pdf.

8 Ramprasaath R. Selvaraju, Michael Cogswell, Abhishek Das, Ramakrishna Vedantam, Devi Parikh, and Dhruv Batra. Grad-CAM: visual explanations from deep networks via gradient-based localization. In *2017 IEEE International Conference on Computer Vision (ICCV)*, pages 618–626, 2017. https://doi.org/10.1109/ICCV.2017.74.

9 Matthew D. Zeiler and Rob Fergus. Visualizing and understanding convolutional networks. In David Fleet, Tomas Pajdla, Bernt Schiele, and Tinne Tuytelaars, editors, *Computer Vision – ECCV 2014*, pages 818–833, Springer International Publishing, Cham, 2014.

10 Y. Bengio, P. Simard, and P. Frasconi. Learning long-term dependencies with gradient descent is difficult. *IEEE Transactions on Neural Networks*, 5(2): 157–166, 1994. https://doi.org/10.1109/72.279181.

11 Xavier Glorot and Yoshua Bengio. Understanding the difficulty of training deep feedforward neural networks. In Yee Whye Teh and Mike Titterington, editors, *Proceedings of the Thirteenth International Conference on Artificial Intelligence and Statistics, volume 9 of Proceedings of Machine Learning Research*, pages 249–256, Chia Laguna Resort, Sardinia, Italy, 2010. PMLR. https://proceedings.mlr.press/v9/glorot10a.html.

12 Kaiming He, Xiangyu Zhang, Shaoqing Ren, and Jian Sun. Deep residual learning for image recognition. In *Proceedings of the IEEE Conference on Computer Vision and Pattern Recognition (CVPR)*, 2016.

13 Olaf Ronneberger, Philipp Fischer, and Thomas Brox. U-Net: convolutional networks for biomedical image segmentation. In Nassir Navab, Joachim Hornegger, William M. Wells, and Alejandro F. Frangi, editors, *Medical Image Computing and Computer-Assisted Intervention – MICCAI 2015*, pages 234–241, Springer International Publishing, Cham, 2015.

14 Jayesh K. Gupta and Johannes Brandstetter. Towards multi-spatiotemporal-scale generalized PDE modeling. *Transactions on Machine Learning Research*, 2023. https://openreview.net/forum?id=dPSTDbGtBY.

15 Nils Thuerey, Konstantin Weißenow, Lukas Prantl, and Xiangyu Hu. Deep learning methods for Reynolds-averaged Navier-Stokes simulations of airfoil flows. *AIAA Journal*, 58(1): 25–36, 2020. https://doi.org/10.2514/1.J058291.

16 Nils Wandel, Michael Weinmann, and Reinhard Klein. Learning incompressible fluid dynamics from scratch - towards fast, differentiable fluid models that generalize. In *International Conference on Learning Representations*, 2021. https://openreview.net/forum?id=KUDUoRsEphu.

17 Philipp Holl, Nils Thuerey, and Vladlen Koltun. Learning to control PDEs with differentiable physics. In *International Conference on Learning Representations*, 2020. https://openreview.net/forum?id=HyeSin4FPB.

18 Samira Pakravan, Pouria A. Mistani, Miguel A. Aragon-Calvo, and Frederic Gibou. Solving inverse-PDE problems with physics-aware neural networks.

Journal of Computational Physics, 440: 110414, 2021. https://doi.org/10.1016/j.jcp.2021.110414.

19 Pouria A. Mistani, Samira Pakravan, Rajesh Ilango, and Frederic Gibou. JAX-DIPS: neural bootstrapping of finite discretization methods and application to elliptic problems with discontinuities. *Journal of Computational Physics*, 493: 112480, 2023. https://doi.org/10.1016/j.jcp.2023.112480.

20 Jaydeep Rade, Aditya Balu, Ethan Herron, Jay Pathak, Rishikesh Ranade, Soumik Sarkar, and Adarsh Krishnamurthy. Algorithmically-consistent deep learning frameworks for structural topology optimization. *Engineering Applications of Artificial Intelligence*, 106: 104483, 2021. https://doi.org/10.1016/j.engappai.2021.104483.

21 Zongyi Li, Nikola Kovachki, Kamyar Azizzadenesheli, Burigede Liu, Andrew Stuart, Kaushik Bhattacharya, and Anima Anandkumar. Multipole graph neural operator for parametric partial differential equations. In H. Larochelle, M. Ranzato, R. Hadsell, M. F. Balcan, and H. Lin, editors, *Advances in Neural Information Processing Systems*, volume 33, pages 6755–6766, Curran Associates, Inc., 2020. https://proceedings.neurips.cc/paper_files/paper/2020/file/4b21cf96d4cf612f239a6c322b10c8fe-Paper.pdf.

22 Nikola Kovachki, Zongyi Li, Burigede Liu, Kamyar Azizzadenesheli, Kaushik Bhattacharya, Andrew Stuart, and Anima Anandkumar. Neural operator: learning maps between function spaces with applications to PDEs. *Journal of Machine Learning Research*, 24(89):1–97, 2023.

23 Zongyi Li, Nikola Borislavov Kovachki, Kamyar Azizzadenesheli, Burigede liu, Kaushik Bhattacharya, Andrew Stuart, and Anima Anandkumar. Fourier neural operator for parametric partial differential equations. In *International Conference on Learning Representations*, 2021. https://openreview.net/forum?id=c8P9NQVtmnO.

24 M. Frigo and S. G. Johnson. The Fastest Fourier Transform in the West. Technical report, Massachusetts Institute of Technology, USA, 1997.

25 John Boyd. *Chebyshev & Fourier Spectral Methods, first edition*. Lecture Notes in Engineering. Springer, Berlin, Heidelberg, 1998.

26 Oscar P. Bruno, Youngae Han, and Matthew M. Pohlman. Accurate, high-order representation of complex three-dimensional surfaces via Fourier continuation analysis. *Journal of Computational Physics*, 227(2): 1094–1125, 2007. https://doi.org/10.1016/j.jcp.2007.08.029.

27 Lu Lu, Xuhui Meng, Shengze Cai, Zhiping Mao, Somdatta Goswami, Zhongqiang Zhang, and George Em Karniadakis. A comprehensive and fair comparison of two neural operators (with practical extensions) based on FAIR data. *Computer Methods in Applied Mechanics and Engineering*, 393: 114778, 2022. https://doi.org/10.1016/j.cma.2022.114778.

28 Alasdair Tran, Alexander Mathews, Lexing Xie, and Cheng Soon Ong. Factorized Fourier neural operators. In *The Eleventh International Conference on Learning Representations*, 2023. https://openreview.net/forum?id=tmIiMPl4IPa.

29 Qianying Cao, Somdatta Goswami, and George Em Karniadakis. Laplace neural operator for solving differential equations. *Nature Machine Intelligence*, 6(6): 631–640, 2024. https://doi.org/10.1038/s42256-024-00844-4.

30 Tapas Tripura and Souvik Chakraborty. Wavelet Neural Operator for solving parametric partial differential equations in computational mechanics problems. *Computer Methods in Applied Mechanics and Engineering*, 404: 115783, 2023. https://doi.org/10.1016/j.cma.2022.115783.

31 Bogdan Raonic, Roberto Molinaro, Tim De Ryck, Tobias Rohner, Francesca Bartolucci, Rima Alaifari, Siddhartha Mishra, and Emmanuel de Bézenac. Convolutional Neural Operators for robust and accurate learning of PDEs. In A. Oh, T. Naumann, A. Globerson, K. Saenko, M. Hardt, and S. Levine, editors, *Advances in Neural Information Processing Systems*, volume 36, pages 77187–77200, Curran Associates, Inc., 2023. https://proceedings.neurips.cc/paper_files/paper/2023/file/f3c1951b34f7f55ffaecada7fde6bd5a-Paper-Conference.pdf.

32 Yiheng Du, Nithin Chalapathi, and Aditi Krishnapriyan. Neural spectral methods: self-supervised learning in the spectral domain. *The Twelfth International Conference on Learning Representations*, 2024.

33 Phillip Lippe, Bastiaan S. Veeling, Paris Perdikaris, Richard E. Turner, and Johannes Brandstetter. PDE-Refiner: achieving accurate long rollouts with neural PDE solvers. In *Thirty-seventh Conference on Neural Information Processing Systems*, 2023. https://openreview.net/forum?id=Qv6468llWS.

34 Zongyi Li, Nikola Borislavov Kovachki, Chris Choy, Boyi Li, Jean Kossaifi, Shourya Prakash Otta, Mohammad Amin Nabian, Maximilian Stadler, Christian Hundt, Kamyar Azizzadenesheli, and Anima Anandkumar. Geometry-informed neural operator for large-scale 3D PDEs. In *Thirty-seventh Conference on Neural Information Processing Systems*, 2023. https://openreview.net/forum?id=86dXbqT5Ua.

35 Zongyi Li, Daniel Zhengyu Huang, Burigede Liu, and Anima Anandkumar. Fourier neural operator with learned deformations for PDEs on general geometries. *Journal of Machine Learning Research*, 24(388): 1–26, 2023. http://jmlr.org/papers/v24/23-0064.html.

36 Lu Lu, Pengzhan Jin, Guofei Pang, Zhongqiang Zhang, and George Karniadakis. Learning nonlinear operators via DeepONet based on the universal approximation theorem of operators. In *Nature Machine Intelligence*, volume 3, pages 218–229, 2021. https://doi.org/10.1038/s42256-021-00302-5.

37 Min Zhu, Shihang Feng, Youzuo Lin, and Lu Lu. Fourier-DeepONet: Fourier-enhanced deep operator networks for full waveform inversion with improved accuracy, generalizability, and robustness. *Computer Methods in*

Applied Mechanics and Engineering, 416: 116300, 2023. https://doi.org/10.1016/j.cma.2023.116300.

38 Lu Lu, Raphaël Pestourie, Steven G. Johnson, and Giuseppe Romano. Multifidelity deep neural operators for efficient learning of partial differential equations with application to fast inverse design of nanoscale heat transport. *Physical Review Letters*, 4(2): 023210, 2022. https://doi.org/10.1103/PhysRevResearch.4.023210.

39 Pengzhan Jin, Shuai Meng, and Lu Lu. MIONet: learning multiple-input operators via tensor product. *SIAM Journal on Scientific Computing*, 44(6):A3490–A3514, 2022.

40 G. Berkooz, P. Holmes, and J. L. Lumley. The proper orthogonal decomposition in the analysis of turbulent flows. *Annual Review of Fluid Mechanics*, 25: 539–575, 1993. https://doi.org/10.1146/annurev.fl.25.010193.002543.

41 Samuel Lanthaler, Siddhartha Mishra, and George E. Karniadakis. Error estimates for DeepONets: a deep learning framework in infinite dimensions. *Transactions of Mathematics and Its Applications*, 6(1): tnac001, 2022. https://doi.org/10.1093/imatrm/tnac001.

42 Ashish Vaswani, Noam Shazeer, Niki Parmar, Jakob Uszkoreit, Llion Jones, Aidan N. Gomez, Łukasz Kaiser, and Illia Polosukhin. Attention is all you need. In I. Guyon, U. Von Luxburg, S. Bengio, H. Wallach, R. Fergus, S. Vishwanathan, and R. Garnett, editors, *Advances in Neural Information Processing Systems*, volume 30. Curran Associates, Inc., 2017. https://proceedings.neurips.cc/paper_files/paper/2017/file/3f5ee243547dee91fbd053c1c4a845aa-Paper.pdf.

43 Alexey Dosovitskiy, Lucas Beyer, Alexander Kolesnikov, Dirk Weissenborn, Xiaohua Zhai, Thomas Unterthiner, Mostafa Dehghani, Matthias Minderer, Georg Heigold, Sylvain Gelly, et al. An Image is Worth 16x16 Words: Transformers for Image Recognition at Scale. In *International Conference on Learning Representations*, 2021. https://openreview.net/forum?id=YicbFdNTTy.

44 Shuhao Cao. Choose a transformer: Fourier or Galerkin. In A. Beygelzimer, Y. Dauphin, P. Liang, and J. Wortman Vaughan, editors, *Advances in Neural Information Processing Systems*, 2021. https://openreview.net/forum?id=ssohLcmn4-r.

45 Zijie Li, Kazem Meidani, and Amir Barati Farimani. Transformer for partial differential equations' operator learning. *Transactions on Machine Learning Research*, 2023. https://openreview.net/forum?id=EPPqt3uERT.

46 Zhongkai Hao, Zhengyi Wang, Hang Su, Chengyang Ying, Yinpeng Dong, Songming Liu, Ze Cheng, Jian Song, and Jun Zhu. GNOT: a general neural operator transformer for operator learning. In *Proceedings of the 40th International Conference on Machine Learning*, ICML'23. JMLR.org, Honolulu, Hawaii, USA, 2023.

47 Benedikt Alkin, Andreas Fürst, Simon Lucas Schmid, Lukas Gruber, Markus Holzleitner, and Johannes Brandstetter. Universal physics transformers: a framework for efficiently scaling neural operators. In *The Thirty-eighth Annual Conference on Neural Information Processing Systems*, 2024. https://openreview.net/forum?id=oUXiNX5KRm.

48 Andrew Jaegle, Felix Gimeno, Andy Brock, Oriol Vinyals, Andrew Zisserman, and Joao Carreira. Perceiver: general perception with iterative attention. In Marina Meila and Tong Zhang, editors, *Proceedings of the 38th International Conference on Machine Learning, volume 139 of Proceedings of Machine Learning Research*, pages 4651–4664, PMLR, 2021. https://proceedings.mlr.press/v139/jaegle21a.html.

49 Jie Zhou, Ganqu Cui, Shengding Hu, Zhengyan Zhang, Cheng Yang, Zhiyuan Liu, Lifeng Wang, Changcheng Li, and Maosong Sun. Graph neural networks: a review of methods and applications. *AI Open*, 1: 57–81, 2020. https://doi.org/10.1016/j.aiopen.2021.01.001.

50 Yiheng Du and Aditi S. Krishnapriyan. The Thirty-Ninth Annual Conference on Neural Information Processing Systems, 2025. https://arxiv.org/abs/2510.24173.

51 Franco Scarselli, Marco Gori, Ah Chung Tsoi, Markus Hagenbuchner, and Gabriele Monfardini. The Graph Neural Network Model. *IEEE Transactions on Neural Networks*, 20(1): 61–80, 2009. https://doi.org/10.1109/TNN.2008.2005605.

52 Thomas N. Kipf and Max Welling. Semi-supervised classification with graph convolutional networks. In *International Conference on Learning Representations*, 2017. https://openreview.net/forum?id=SJU4ayYgl.

53 William L. Hamilton, Rex Ying, and Jure Leskovec. Inductive representation learning on large graphs. In *Proceedings of the 31st International Conference on Neural Information Processing Systems*, NIPS'17, pages 1025–1035, Red Hook, NY, USA, 2017. Curran Associates Inc. event-place: Long Beach, California, USA.

54 Petar Veličković, Guillem Cucurull, Arantxa Casanova, Adriana Romero, Pietro Liò, and Yoshua Bengio. Graph attention networks. In *International Conference on Learning Representations*, 2018. https://openreview.net/forum?id=rJXMpikCZ.

55 Alvaro Sanchez-Gonzalez, Jonathan Godwin, Tobias Pfaff, Rex Ying, Jure Leskovec, and Peter Battaglia. Learning to simulate complex physics with graph networks. In Hal Daumé III and Aarti Singh, editors, *Proceedings of the 37th International Conference on Machine Learning, volume 119 of Proceedings of Machine Learning Research*, pages 8459–8468, PMLR, 2020. https://proceedings.mlr.press/v119/sanchez-gonzalez20a.html.

56 Tobias Pfaff, Meire Fortunato, Alvaro Sanchez-Gonzalez, and Peter Battaglia. Learning mesh-based simulation with graph networks. In *International Conference on Learning Representations*, 2021. https://openreview.net/forum?id=roNqYL0_XP.

57 Sungyong Seo, Chuizheng Meng, and Yan Liu. Physics-aware difference graph networks for sparsely-observed dynamics. In *International Conference on Learning Representations*, 2020. https://openreview.net/forum?id=r1gelyrtwH.

58 Filipe De Avila Belbute-Peres, Thomas Economon, and Zico Kolter. Combining differentiable PDE solvers and graph neural networks for fluid flow prediction. In Hal Daumé III and Aarti Singh, editors, *Proceedings of the 37th International Conference on Machine Learning, volume 119 of Proceedings of Machine Learning Research*, pages 2402–2411, PMLR, 2020. https://proceedings.mlr.press/v119/de-avila-belbute-peres20a.html.

59 Johannes Brandstetter, Daniel E. Worrall, and Max Welling. Message passing neural PDE solvers. In *International Conference on Learning Representations*, 2022. https://openreview.net/forum?id=vSix3HPYKSU.

60 Qingqing Zhao, David B Lindell, and Gordon Wetzstein. Learning to solve PDE-constrained inverse problems with graph networks. In Kamalika Chaudhuri, Stefanie Jegelka, Le Song, Csaba Szepesvari, Gang Niu, and Sivan Sabato, editors, *Proceedings of the 39th International Conference on Machine Learning, volume 162 of Proceedings of Machine Learning Research*, pages 26895–26910. PMLR, 2022. https://proceedings.mlr.press/v162/zhao22d.html.

61 Dmitrii Kochkov, Jamie A. Smith, Ayya Alieva, Qing Wang, Michael P. Brenner, and Stephan Hoyer. Machine learning–accelerated computational fluid dynamics. *Proceedings of the National Academy of Sciences*, 118(21): e2101784118, 2021. https://doi.org/10.1073/pnas.2101784118.

62 Gideon Dresdner, Dmitrii Kochkov, Peter Christian Norgaard, Leonardo Zepeda-Nunez, Jamie Smith, Michael Brenner, and Stephan Hoyer. Learning to correct spectral methods for simulating turbulent flows. *Transactions on Machine Learning Research*, 2023. https://openreview.net/forum?id=wNBARGxoJn.

63 Málek Josef and Strakoš Zdeněk. *Preconditioning and the Conjugate Gradient Method in the Context of Solving PDEs*. Society for Industrial and Applied Mathematics, 2014.

64 Yichen Li, Peter Yichen Chen, Tao Du, and Wojciech Matusik. Learning preconditioners for conjugate gradient PDE solvers. In *Proceedings of the 40th International Conference on Machine Learning*, ICML'23. JMLR.org, Honolulu, Hawaii, USA, 2023.

65 Daniel Greenfeld, Meirav Galun, Ronen Basri, Irad Yavneh, and Ron Kimmel. Learning to optimize multigrid PDE solvers. In Kamalika Chaudhuri and Ruslan Salakhutdinov, editors, *Proceedings of the 36th International Conference on Machine Learning, volume 97 of Proceedings of Machine Learning Research*, pages 2415–2423, PMLR, 2019. https://proceedings.mlr.press/v97/greenfeld19a.html.

66 Jared Kaplan, Sam McCandlish, Tom Henighan, Tom B. Brown, Benjamin Chess, Rewon Child, Scott Gray, Alec Radford, Jeffrey Wu, and Dario Amodei. Scaling laws for neural language models. *CoRR*, 2020. https://arxiv.org/abs/2001.08361.

67 Ilyes Batatia, David P. Kovacs, Gregor Simm, Christoph Ortner, and Gabor Csanyi. Mace: Higher order equivariant message passing neural networks for fast and accurate force fields. In *Neural Information Processing Systems (NeurIPS)*, 2022.

68 Richard Tran, Janice Lan, Muhammed Shuaibi, Brandon M. Wood, Siddharth Goyal, Abhishek Das, Javier Heras-Domingo, Adeesh Kolluru, Ammar Rizvi, Nima Shoghi, et al. The Open Catalyst 2022 (OC22) dataset and challenges for oxide electrocatalysts. *ACS Catalysis*, 13(5): 3066–3084, 2023. http://dx.doi.org/10.1021/acscatal.2c05426.

69 Nima Shoghi, Adeesh Kolluru, John R. Kitchin, Zachary Ward Ulissi, C. Lawrence Zitnick, and Brandon M. Wood. From molecules to materials: pre-training large generalizable models for atomic property prediction. In *The Twelfth International Conference on Learning Representations*, 2024. https://openreview.net/forum?id=PfPnugdxup.

70 Thorsten Kurth, Shashank Subramanian, Peter Harrington, Jaideep Pathak, Morteza Mardani, David Hall, Andrea Miele, Karthik Kashinath, and Anima Anandkumar. FourCastNet: accelerating global high-resolution weather forecasting using adaptive Fourier neural operators. In *Proceedings of the Platform for Advanced Scientific Computing Conference*, PASC '23, Davos, Switzerland. Association for Computing Machinery, New York, NY, USA, 2023. https://doi-org.libproxy.berkeley.edu/10.1145/3592979.3593412.

71 Kaifeng Bi, Lingxi Xie, Hengheng Zhang, Xin Chen, Xiaotao Gu, and Qi Tian. Accurate medium-range global weather forecasting with 3D neural networks. *Nature*, 619(7970): 533–538, 2023. https://doi.org/10.1038/s41586-023-06185-3.

72 Cristian Bodnar, Wessel Bruinsma, Ana Lucic, Megan Stanley, Johannes Brandstetter, Patrick Garvan, Maik Riechert, Jonathan Weyn, Haiyu Dong, Anna Vaughan, et al. Aurora: a foundation model of the atmosphere Technical Report MSR-TR-2024-16, Microsoft Research AI for Science, 2024. https://www.microsoft.com/en-us/research/publication/aurora-a-foundation-model-of-the-atmosphere/.

73 Ilan Price, Alvaro Sanchez-Gonzalez, Ferran Alet, Tom R., Andersson, Andrew El-Kadi, Dominic Masters, Timo Ewalds, Jacklynn Stott, Shakir Mohamed, Peter Battaglia, Remi Lam, and Matthew Willson. Probabilistic weather forecasting with machine learning. *Nature*, 637(8044): 84–90, 2025. https://doi.org/10.1038/s41586-024-08252-9.

74 Michael McCabe, Bruno Régaldo-Saint Blancard, Liam Holden Parker, Ruben Ohana, Miles Cranmer, Alberto Bietti, Michael Eickenberg, Siavash Golkar, Geraud Krawezik, Francois Lanusse, Mariel Pettee, Tiberiu Tesileanu, Kyunghyun Cho, and Shirley Ho. Multiple physics pretraining for spatiotemporal surrogate models. In *The Thirty-eighth Annual Conference on Neural Information Processing Systems*, 2024. https://openreview.net/forum?id=DKSI3bULiZ.

75 Jonathan Ho, Nal Kalchbrenner, Dirk Weissenborn, and Tim Salimans. Axial attention in multidimensional transformers, 2020. https://openreview.net/forum?id=H1e5GJBtDr.

76 Maximilian Herde, Bogdan Raonic, Tobias Rohner, Roger Käppeli, Roberto Molinaro, Emmanuel de Bezenac, and Siddhartha Mishra. Poseidon: efficient foundation models for PDEs. In *The Thirty-eighth Annual Conference on Neural Information Processing Systems*, 2024. https://openreview.net/forum?id=JC1VKK3UXk.

77 Ze Liu, Han Hu, Yutong Lin, Zhuliang Yao, Zhenda Xie, Yixuan Wei, Jia Ning, Yue Cao, Zheng Zhang, Li Dong, Furu Wei, and Baining Guo. Swin transformer V2: scaling up capacity and resolution. In *2022 IEEE/CVF Conference on Computer Vision and Pattern Recognition (CVPR)*, pages 11999–12009, 2022. https://doi.org/10.1109/CVPR52688.2022.01170.

78 Shashank Subramanian, Peter Harrington, Kurt Keutzer, Wahid Bhimji, Dmitriy Morozov, Michael W. Mahoney, and Amir Gholami. Towards foundation models for scientific machine learning: characterizing scaling and transfer behavior. In *Thirty-seventh Conference on Neural Information Processing Systems*, 2023. https://openreview.net/forum?id=zANxvzflMl.

79 OpenAI, Josh Achiam, Steven Adler, Sandhini Agarwal, Lama Ahmad, Ilge Akkaya, Florencia Leoni Aleman, Diogo Almeida, Janko Altenschmidt, Sam Altman, et al. Gpt-4 Technical Report, 2024. https://arxiv.org/abs/2303.08774.

80 Adam Polyak, Amit Zohar, Andrew Brown, Andros Tjandra, Animesh Sinha, Ann Lee, Apoorv Vyas, Bowen Shi, Chih-Yao Ma, Ching-Yao Chuang, et al. Movie gen: a cast of media foundation models, 2024. https://arxiv.org/abs/2410.13720.

81 Jason Baldridge, Jakob Bauer, Mukul Bhutani, Nicole Brichtova, Andrew Bunner, Kelvin Chan, Yichang Chen, Sander Dieleman, Yuqing Du, Zach Eaton-Rosen, et al. Imagen 3. *arXiv preprint arXiv:2408.07009*, 2024.

82 Joaquin Quiñonero-Candela, Masashi Sugiyama, Anton Schwaighofer, and Neil D Lawrence. *Dataset Shift in Machine Learning*. MIT Press, 2022.

83 Adam Paszke, Sam Gross, Francisco Massa, Adam Lerer, James Bradbury, Gregory Chanan, Trevor Killeen, Zeming Lin, Natalia Gimelshein, Luca Antiga, et al. Pytorch: an imperative style, high-performance deep learning library, 2019. https://arxiv.org/abs/1912.01703.

84 Maziar Raissi, Paris Perdikaris, and George E Karniadakis. Physics-informed neural networks: a deep learning framework for solving forward and inverse problems involving nonlinear partial differential equations. *Journal of Computational physics*, 378: 686–707, 2019.

85 Aditi Krishnapriyan, Amir Gholami, Shandian Zhe, Robert Kirby, and Michael W Mahoney. Characterizing possible failure modes in physics-informed neural networks. *Advances in Neural Information Processing Systems*, 34: 26548–26560, 2021.

86 Zongyi Li, Hongkai Zheng, Nikola Kovachki, David Jin, Haoxuan Chen, Burigede Liu, Kamyar Azizzadenesheli, and Anima Anandkumar. Physics-informed neural operator for learning partial differential equations. *ACM/JMS Journal of Data Science*, 1(3): 1–27, 2024.

87 Ferran Alet, Dylan Doblar, Allan Zhou, Josh Tenenbaum, Kenji Kawaguchi, and Chelsea Finn. Noether networks: meta-learning useful conserved quantities. *Advances in Neural Information Processing Systems*, 34: 16384–16397, 2021.

88 Rui Wang, Robin Walters, and Rose Yu. Approximately equivariant networks for imperfectly symmetric dynamics. In *International Conference on Machine Learning*, pages 23078–23091, PMLR, 2022.

89 Takeru Miyato, Toshiki Kataoka, Masanori Koyama, and Yuichi Yoshida. Spectral normalization for generative adversarial networks. *arXiv preprint arXiv:1802.05957*, 2018.

90 Evgenii Nikishin, Romina Abachi, Rishabh Agarwal, and Pierre-Luc Bacon. Control-oriented model-based reinforcement learning with implicit differentiation. In *Proceedings of the AAAI Conference on Artificial Intelligence*, volume 36, pages 7886–7894, 2022.

91 Björn List, Li-Wei Chen, and Nils Thuerey. Learned turbulence modelling with differentiable fluid solvers. *arXiv preprint arXiv:2202.06988*, 2022.

92 Raphaël Pestourie, Youssef Mroueh, Chris Rackauckas, Payel Das, and Steven G. Johnson. Physics-enhanced deep surrogates for partial differential equations. *Nature Machine Intelligence*, 5(12): 1458–1465, 2023.

93 Zhichun Huang, Shaojie Bai, and J. Zico Kolter. (Implicit)^2: Implicit layers for implicit representations. *Advances in Neural Information Processing Systems*, 34: 9639–9650, 2021.

94 Jacob Kelly, Jesse Bettencourt, Matthew J Johnson, and David K Duvenaud. Learning differential equations that are easy to solve. *Advances in Neural Information Processing Systems*, 33: 4370–4380, 2020.

95 Brandon Amos, Lei Xu, and J Zico Kolter. Input convex neural networks. In *International Conference on Machine Learning*, pages 146–155. PMLR, 2017.

96 Mathieu Blondel, Quentin Berthet, Marco Cuturi, Roy Frostig, Stephan Hoyer, Felipe Llinares-López, Fabian Pedregosa, and Jean-Philippe Vert. Efficient and modular implicit differentiation. *Advances in Neural Information Processing Systems*, 35: 5230–5242, 2022.

97 Brandon Amos and J. Zico Kolter. Optnet: Differentiable optimization as a layer in neural networks. In *International Conference on Machine Learning*, pages 136–145. PMLR, 2017.

98 Geoffrey Négiar, Michael W. Mahoney, and Aditi Krishnapriyan. Learning differentiable solvers for systems with hard constraints. In *The Eleventh International Conference on Learning Representations*, 2023. https://openreview.net/forum?id=vdv6CmGksr0.

99 Nithin Chalapathi, Yiheng Du, and Aditi S. Krishnapriyan. Scaling physics-informed hard constraints with mixture-of-experts. In *The Twelfth International Conference on Learning Representations*, 2024. https://openreview.net/forum?id=u3dX2CEIZb.

100 Noam Shazeer, Azalia Mirhoseini, Krzysztof Maziarz, Andy Davis, Quoc Le, Geoffrey Hinton, and Jeff Dean. Outrageously large neural networks: the sparsely-gated mixture-of-experts layer. *arXiv preprint arXiv:1701.06538*, 2017.

101 Jack Richter-Powell, Yaron Lipman, and Ricky TQ Chen. Neural conservation laws: a divergence-free perspective. *Advances in Neural Information Processing Systems*, 35: 38075–38088, 2022.

102 Fangcheng Zhong, Kyle Fogarty, Param Hanji, Tianhao Wu, Alejandro Sztrajman, Andrew Spielberg, Andrea Tagliasacchi, Petra Bosilj, and Cengiz Oztireli. Neural fields with hard constraints of arbitrary differential order. *arXiv preprint arXiv:2306.08943*, 2023.

103 Nadim Saad, Gaurav Gupta, Shima Alizadeh, and Danielle C Maddix. Guiding continuous operator learning through physics-based boundary constraints. *arXiv preprint arXiv:2212.07477*, 2022.

104 Andreas Mayr, Sebastian Lehner, Arno Mayrhofer, Christoph Kloss, Sepp Hochreiter, and Johannes Brandstetter. Boundary graph neural networks for 3D simulations. In *Proceedings of the AAAI Conference on Artificial Intelligence*, volume *37*, pages 9099–9107, 2023.

105 Pingchuan Ma, Peter Yichen Chen, Bolei Deng, Joshua B. Tenenbaum, Tao Du, Chuang Gan, and Wojciech Matusik. Learning neural constitutive laws from motion observations for generalizable PDE dynamics. In *International Conference on Machine Learning*, pages 23279–23300, PMLR, 2023.

106 Natarajan Sukumar and Ankit Srivastava. Exact imposition of boundary conditions with distance functions in physics-informed deep neural networks. *Computer Methods in Applied Mechanics and Engineering*, 389: 114333, 2022.

107 U. Braga-Neto. Characteristics-informed neural networks for forward and inverse hyperbolic problems. *arXiv preprint arXiv:2212.14012.*

108 Lu Lu, Raphael Pestourie, Wenjie Yao, Zhicheng Wang, Francesc Verdugo, and Steven G. Johnson. Physics-informed neural networks with hard constraints for inverse design. *SIAM Journal on Scientific Computing*, 43(6):B1105–B1132, 2021.

109 Kailai Xu and Eric Darve. Physics constrained learning for data-driven inverse modeling from sparse observations. *Journal of Computational Physics*, 453: 110938, 2022.

110 Steven L. Brunton, Joshua L. Proctor, and J. Nathan Kutz. Discovering governing equations from data by sparse identification of nonlinear dynamical systems. *Proceedings of the National Academy of Sciences*, 113(15): 3932–3937, 2016.

111 Steven L. Brunton, Joshua L. Proctor, and J. Nathan Kutz. Sparse identification of nonlinear dynamics with control (sindyc). *IFAC-PapersOnLine*, 49(18): 710–715, 2016.

112 Seungwoong Ha and Hawoong Jeong. Discovering conservation laws from trajectories via machine learning. *arXiv preprint arXiv:2102.04008*, 2021.

113 Antonii Belyshev, Alexander Kovrigin, and Andrey Ustyuzhanin. Beyond dynamics: learning to discover conservation principles. *Machine Learning: Science and Technology*, 5(2): 025055, 2024.

114 Fernando Chirigati. From data to conservation laws. *Nature Computational Science*, 3(9): 733–733, 2023.

115 Ziming Liu and Max Tegmark. Machine learning conservation laws from trajectories. *Physical Review Letters*, 126(18): 180604, 2021.

116 Eurika Kaiser, J Nathan Kutz, and Steven L Brunton. Discovering conservation laws from data for control. In *2018 IEEE Conference on Decision and Control (CDC)*, pages 6415–6421, IEEE, 2018.

117 Jonathan Ho, Ajay Jain, and Pieter Abbeel. Denoising diffusion probabilistic models. *Advances in Neural Information Processing Systems*, 33: 6840–6851, 2020.

118 Prafulla Dhariwal and Alexander Nichol. Diffusion models beat GANs on image synthesis. *Advances in Neural Information Processing Systems*, 34: 8780–8794, 2021.

119 Sarah Lewis, Tim Hempel, José Jiménez Luna, Michael Gastegger, Yu Xie, Andrew YK Foong, Victor García Satorras, Osama Abdin, Bastiaan S Veeling, Iryna Zaporozhets, et al. Scalable emulation of protein equilibrium ensembles with generative deep learning. *bioRxiv*, 2024. https://www.biorxiv.org/content/10.1101/2024.12.05.626885v1

120 Han Gao, Sebastian Kaltenbach, and Petros Koumoutsakos. Generative learning of the solution of parametric partial differential equations using guided diffusion models and virtual observations. *Computer Methods in Applied Mechanics and Engineering*, 435: 117654, 2025.

121 Jiahe Huang, Guandao Yang, Zichen Wang, and Jeong Joon Park. Diffusionpde: generative pde-solving under partial observation. *arXiv preprint arXiv:2406.17763*, 2024.

122 Ting Wang, Petr Plechac, and Jaroslaw Knap. Generative diffusion learning for parametric partial differential equations, 2023. https://arxiv.org/abs/2305.14703.

123 Rucha Apte, Sheel Nidhan, Rishikesh Ranade, and Jay Pathak. Diffusion model based data generation for partial differential equations. *arXiv preprint arXiv:2306.11075*, 2023.

124 Marten Lienen, David Lüdke, Jan Hansen-Palmus, and Stephan Günnemann. From zero to turbulence: generative modeling for 3D flow simulation. *arXiv preprint arXiv:2306.01776*, 2023.

125 Dule Shu, Zijie Li, and Amir Barati Farimani. A physics-informed diffusion model for high-fidelity flow field reconstruction. *Journal of Computational Physics*, 478: 111972, 2023.

126 Gefan Yang and Stefan Sommer. A denoising diffusion model for fluid field prediction. *arXiv preprint arXiv:2301.11661*, 2023.

127 Salva Rühling Cachay, Bo Zhao, Hailey Joren, and Rose Yu. Dyffusion: a dynamics-informed diffusion model for spatiotemporal forecasting. *Advances in Neural Information Processing Systems*, 36: 45259–45287, 2023.

128 Seth Bassetti, Brian Hutchinson, Claudia Tebaldi, and Ben Kravitz. Diffesm: conditional emulation of temperature and precipitation in Earth system models with 3D diffusion models. *Journal of Advances in Modeling Earth Systems*, 16(10): e2023MS004194, 2024.

129 Lizao Li, Robert Carver, Ignacio Lopez-Gomez, Fei Sha, and John, Anderson. Generative emulation of weather forecast ensembles with diffusion models. *Science Advances*, 10(13): eadk4489, 2024.

130 Stephen B. Pope. Turbulent flows. *Measurement Science and Technology*, 12(11): 2020–2021, 2001.

131 Daan Frenkel and Berend Smit. *Understanding Molecular Simulation: From Algorithms to Applications, second edition*. Academic Press, 2001.

132 R. Car and M. Parrinello. Unified approach for molecular dynamics and density-functional theory. *Physical Review Letters*, 55: 2471, 1985. https://doi.org/10.1103/PhysRevLett.55.2471.

133 Richard A. Friesner. Ab initio quantum chemistry: methodology and applications. *Proceedings of the National Academy of Sciences*, 102(19): 6648–6653, 5 2005. https://doi.org/10.1073/pnas.0408036102.

134 Junmei Wang, Romain M. Wolf, James W Caldwell, Peter A. Kollman, and David A. Case. Development and testing of a general amber force field. *Journal of Computational Chemistry*, 25(9): 1157–1174, 2004.

135 Kenno Vanommeslaeghe, Elizabeth Hatcher, Chayan Acharya, Sibsankar Kundu, Shijun Zhong, Jihyun Shim, Eva Darian, Olgun Guvench, P. Lopes, Igor Vorobyov, et al. Charmm general force field: a force field for drug-like molecules compatible with the charmm all-atom additive biological force fields. *Journal of Computational Chemistry*, 31(4): 671–690, 2010.

136 Peter G Bolhuis, David Chandler, Christoph Dellago, and Phillip L Geissler. Transition path sampling: throwing ropes over rough mountain passes, in the dark. *Annual Review of Physical Chemistry*, 53(1): 291–318, 2002.

137 Christoph Dellago, Peter G. Bolhuis, and Phillip L. Geissler. Transition path sampling. *Advances in Chemical Physics*, 123: 1–78, 2002.

138 Frank Noé, Alexandre Tkatchenko, Klaus-Robert Müller, and Cecilia Clementi. Machine learning for molecular simulation. *Annual Review of Physical Chemistry*, 71(1): 361–390, 2020.

139 Volker L. Deringer, Miguel A. Caro, and Gábor Csányi. Machine learning interatomic potentials as emerging tools for materials science. *Advanced Materials*, 31(46): 1902765, 2019.

140 Tsz Wai Ko and Shyue Ping Ong. Recent advances and outstanding challenges for machine learning interatomic potentials. *Nature Computational Science*, 3(12): 998–1000, 2023.

141 Martin Sipka, Johannes C. B. Dietschreit, Lukáš Grajciar, and Rafael Gómez-Bombarelli. Differentiable simulations for enhanced sampling of rare events. In *International Conference on Machine Learning*, pages 31990–32007, PMLR, 2023.

142 Lars Holdijk, Yuanqi Du, Ferry Hooft, Priyank Jaini, Berend Ensing, and Max Welling. Stochastic optimal control for collective variable free sampling of molecular transition paths. *Advances in Neural Information Processing Systems 36*, 2024.

143 Yuanqi Du, Michael Plainer, Rob Brekelmans, Chenru Duan, Frank Noé, Carla P Gomes, Alán Aspuru-Guzik, and Kirill Neklyudov. Doob's lagrangian: a sample-efficient variational approach to transition path sampling. *arXiv preprint arXiv:2410.07974*, 2024.

144 Kiyoung Seong, Seonghyun Park, Seonghwan Kim, Woo Youn Kim, and Sungsoo Ahn. Transition path sampling with improved off-policy training of diffusion path samplers, International Conference on Learning Representations, 2025. https://arxiv.org/abs/2405.19961.

145 Marloes Arts, Victor Garcia Satorras, Chin-Wei Huang, Daniel Zugner, Marco Federici, Cecilia Clementi, Frank Noé, Robert Pinsler, and Rianne van den Berg. Two for one: diffusion models and force fields for coarse-grained molecular dynamics. *Journal of Chemical Theory and Computation*, 19(18): 6151–6159, 2023.

146 Shuxin Zheng, Jiyan He, Chang Liu, Yu Shi, Ziheng Lu, Weitao Feng, Fusong Ju, Jiaxi Wang, Jianwei Zhu, Yaosen Min, et al. Predicting equilibrium distributions for molecular systems with deep learning. *Nature Machine Intelligence*, 6:1–10, 2024.

147 Bowen Jing, Bonnie Berger, and Tommi Jaakkola. Alphafold meets flow matching for generating protein ensembles, 2024. https://arxiv.org/abs/2402.04845.

148 Lei Huang, Tingyang Xu, Yang Yu, Peilin Zhao, Xingjian Chen, Jing Han, Zhi Xie, Hailong Li, Wenge Zhong, Ka-Chun Wong, et al. A dual diffusion model enables 3D molecule generation and lead optimization based on target pockets. *Nature Communications*, 15(1): 2657, 2024.

149 Arne Schneuing, Charles Harris, Yuanqi Du, Kieran Didi, Arian Jamasb, Ilia Igashov, Weitao Du, Carla Gomes, Tom L. Blundell, Pietro Lio, et al. Structure-based drug design with equivariant diffusion models. *Nature Computational Science*, 4(12): 899–909, 2024.

150 Ilia Igashov, Hannes Stärk, Clément Vignac, Arne Schneuing, Victor Garcia Satorras, Pascal Frossard, Max Welling, Michael Bronstein, and Bruno Correia. Equivariant 3D-conditional diffusion model for molecular linker design. *Nature Machine Intelligence*, 1–11, 2024. Nature Publishing Group UK.

151 Claudio Zeni, Robert Pinsler, Daniel Zügner, Andrew Fowler, Matthew Horton, Xiang Fu, Sasha Shysheya, Jonathan Crabbé, Lixin Sun, Jake Smith, et al. Mattergen: a generative model for inorganic materials design. *arXiv preprint arXiv:2312.03687*, 2023.

152 Mario Geiger and Tess Smidt. e3nn: Euclidean neural networks, 2022. https://arxiv.org/abs/2207.09453.

153 Simon Batzner, Albert Musaelian, Lixin Sun, Mario Geiger, Jonathan P. Mailoa, Mordechai Kornbluth, Nicola Molinari, Tess E. Smidt, and Boris Kozinsky. E(3)-equivariant graph neural networks for data-efficient and accurate interatomic potentials. *Nature Communications*, 13(1):2453, 2022. https://doi.org/10.1038/s41467-022-29939-5.

154 Eric Qu and Aditi S Krishnapriyan. The importance of being scalable: improving the speed and accuracy of neural network interatomic potentials across chemical domains. *arXiv preprint arXiv:2410.24169*, 2024.

155 Mark Neumann, James Gin, Benjamin Rhodes, Steven Bennett, Zhiyi Li, Hitarth Choubisa, Arthur Hussey, and Jonathan Godwin. Orb: a fast, scalable neural network potential, 2024. https://arxiv.org/abs/2410.22570.

156 Sergey Pozdnyakov and Michele Ceriotti. Smooth, exact rotational symmetrization for deep learning on point clouds. *Advances in Neural Information Processing Systems 36*, 2024.

157 Filippo Bigi, Marcel Langer, and Michele Ceriotti. The dark side of the forces: assessing non-conservative force models for atomistic machine learning, 2024. https://arxiv.org/abs/2412.11569.

158 Ishan Amin, Sanjeev Raja, and Aditi S. Krishnapriyan. Towards fast, specialized machine learning force fields: distilling foundation models via energy hessians. In *The Thirteenth International Conference on Learning Representations*, 2025. https://openreview.net/forum?id=1durmugh3I.

159 Wujie Wang, Simon Axelrod, and Rafael Gómez-Bombarelli. Differentiable molecular simulations for control and learning, 2020. https://arxiv.org/abs/2003.00868.

160 Sanjeev Raja, Ishan Amin, Fabian Pedregosa, and Aditi S Krishnapriyan. Stability-aware training of neural network interatomic potentials with differentiable boltzmann estimators. *arXiv preprint arXiv:2402.13984*, 2024.

161 Ricky T. Q. Chen, Yulia Rubanova, Jesse Bettencourt, and David K. Duvenaud. Neural ordinary differential equations. *Advances in Neural Information Processing Systems 31*, 2018.

10

Causal Representation Learning

*Burak Varıcı, Chandler Squires, and Pradeep Ravikumar**

Machine Learning Department, Carnegie Mellon University, Pittsburgh, Pennsylvania, USA

*Corresponding Author: pradeepr@.cs.cmu.edu

10.1 Introduction

Modern AI approaches in computer vision and natural language processing are built on the idea of learning novel representations from raw, unstructured inputs. Concretely, neural models parameterize and learn mappings Φ that transform raw inputs $\mathbf{X}$ into higher-level features $\mathbf{Z} = \Phi(\mathbf{X})$. Core properties of the map Φ that is learned depend on various design choices, including neural architectures, dataset curation, and training objectives. A key question naturally arises: What makes certain representations "good" and others "bad"? Often, "good" representations are characterized as those that generalize to downstream tasks in new settings. This property can be formalized in terms of guarantees such as *out-of-distribution (OOD) generalization* [1–3] or *compositional generalization* [4, 5], which assure that models trained on data from one or more *source* domains will perform well on a set of distinct *target* domains. Beyond these formal guarantees, good characterizations are often those that reflect *structurally rich, higher-level factors* that align with the semantics of the domain [6]. Such representations enable the integration of domain knowledge (e.g., via supervision) into the representation space and enhance interpretability, making them more suitable for critical applications.

In practice, representations are generally learned using deep neural networks, which have enjoyed significant empirical success in recent years, owing to their

Neurosymbolic AI: Foundations and Applications, First Edition. Edited by Alvaro Velasquez et al.

great capacity for preserving relevant statistical properties. However, with such black-box neural models, we are typically not able to answer the key question of whether "good" features are learned. For example, it is often impossible to interpret the semantic meaning (or lack thereof) or to assess the robustness of the learned representation space with respect to various design choices (e.g., hyperparameters). This lack of conceptual understanding hampers the adoption of representation learning in critical domains such as medicine and healthcare. In this chapter, we address these issues from two intertwined angles: *identifiability* and *causal graphical models*. Specifically, we draw on the *causal representation learning* (CRL) framework to put representation learning on a principled foundation while meeting the desiderata of good representations.

First, in this chapter, we consider representation learning as a form of *model selection*. From this perspective, "learning a representation" corresponds to selecting a model M from some model class $\mathcal{M}$, and "using the representation for a downstream task" corresponds to generating a prediction from M through some form of reasoning (i.e., predictive inference). For simplicity, we focus on model selection in the *population* setting, i.e., we consider model selection algorithms that take distributions as inputs. This setup corresponds to taking the infinite-data limit; in practice, algorithms in this setting can often be adapted to the finite-sample scenario, with corresponding sample complexity guarantees [7]. Focusing on this setting allows us to temporarily put aside the questions of sample efficiency, instead highlighting two other objectives: *identifiability* and *feasibility*.

Mathematically, model selection can be viewed as a form of inverse problem. We work in the *well-specified* setting, that is, we assume a solution exists, and we focus on the issue of *identifiability* – whether solutions are unique (up to a prespecified notion of equivalence). In particular, suppose two models M and M' perform equally well for all tasks in the source domain (e.g., they make identical predictions there), but they make vastly different predictions in novel settings. How should a model selection algorithm pick between M and M'? In traditional machine learning, this issue is interpretability, as highlighted in seminal works [8, 9]. To resolve this ambiguity, as we describe in Section 10.2.1, one may consider either incorporating appropriate *inductive biases* (e.g., restricting the model class) or looking at *richer* data distribution(s) to distinguish between such models. We also focus on the *feasibility* aspect of this problem, that is whether there exists efficient algorithms that can learn identifiable representations in a scalable way. To this end, we present algorithms whose steps serve as *constructive* proofs of theoretical guarantees.

With these general considerations in mind, one must also consider which model classes are appropriate for specific tasks and goals. In particular, for modeling conceptually high-level features, what "symbols" can represent semantically meaningful yet possibly complex representations in the latent space? In this chapter, we focus on *causal graphical models* as the latent model classes. Causal models are used across a wide range of fields, including healthcare, epidemiology, econometrics, and the natural sciences – where causal reasoning and robustness are crucial. Causal models formalize causal reasoning [10] and thus can be used to generate predictions about the effects of novel actions in new contexts (e.g., the effect of a new drug combination on a new patient population). Furthermore, learning causal models is a step toward well-structured representation spaces that support intervention, planning, and reasoning [11]. While identifiability is a core concept in the foundations of causal inference, it typically addresses causal relationships among *observed* variables $\mathbf{X}$. In contrast, in CRL, the causal model is over the latent variables $\mathbf{Z}$.

So far, we have positioned CRL as a compelling framework for learning good representations. However, CRL is severely ill-posed due to the nonidentifiability results in both causal discovery and representation learning [8, 12]. For instance, even setting aside representation learning, identifying the causal graph is generally not possible [13]. When we add the challenge that causal variables are not given but must be *learned*, it becomes evident that the realization of CRL requires additional information. Ideally, this information should come from a realistic combination of model assumptions and the "richer" observations of $\mathbf{X}$. As a realistic choice of problem setting, this chapter focuses on *interventional CRL*.

An intervention over variables in a causal model alters the functional mechanisms that generate those variables. Such interventions create variations in the observed data that significantly narrow the solution set of the inverse problem of model selection. Notably, interventional CRL framework only requires *distribution-level* data access, e.g., observing samples from distributions before and after an intervention, rather than observing changes to each individual sample before and after an intervention. While such an interventional formulation was classically used to model the effects of designed experiments (e.g., in single-cell genomics [14]), in our context, it is particularly well-suited to capturing distribution shifts in practical settings, enabling the use of multiple datasets and leading to richer data. This chapter presents recent advancements in interventional CRL, including identifiability theorems with constructive proofs and associated algorithms that achieve these identifiability guarantees.

Outline of Chapter: Section 10.2 introduces the necessary background for the CRL framework with self-contained material on causal models, interventions, and identifiability notions. Section 10.3 formalizes the interventional CRL setting, for which the following sections will establish results. Specifically, Section 10.4 considers CRL with linear latent causal models, and Section 10.5 focuses on CRL with general latent causal models under various interventional settings. Section 10.6 demonstrates a small set of representative experimental results, and Section 10.7

provides a brief overview of related work on CRL. Finally, Section 10.8 summarizes the chapter and proposes directions for future work.

10.2 Background

Probability Notation: For simplicity, we assume continuous-valued random variables[1]. Random variables are denoted by capital letters, and random vectors are denoted by bold capital letters. We use calligraphic font to denote the sample spaces of random variables/vectors, and lowercase letters to denote elements of these spaces. For example, given random variables $V_1, \dots, V_n$ with sample spaces $\mathcal{V}_1, \dots, \mathcal{V}_n$, $\mathbf{V} = (V_1, \dots, V_n)$ is a random vector with sample space $\mathcal{V} := \times_{i=1}^{n} \mathcal{V}_i$, $\mathbf{v} \in \mathcal{V}$ denotes a possible value of $\mathbf{V}$, and v_i denotes the i-th component of $\mathbf{v}$. We also use sequences in our subscripts, e.g., we let $\mathbf{V}_{(2,4,5)} = (V_2, V_4, V_5)$ and $\mathcal{V}_{(2,4,5)} = \mathcal{V}_2 \times \mathcal{V}_4 \times \mathcal{V}_5$. We denote the set of continuous probability distributions on $\mathcal{V}$ as $\mathcal{P}(\mathcal{V})$, with $\mathbb{P}(\mathbf{V})$ denoting a specific probability distribution. Whenever we have a function $f : \mathcal{V}_1 \to \mathcal{V}_2$ for two measurable spaces $\mathcal{V}_1$ and $\mathcal{V}_2$, we assume f is measurable. Given $f : \mathcal{V}_1 \to \mathcal{V}_2$, we let $f_{\#} : \mathcal{P}(\mathcal{V}_1) \to \mathcal{P}(\mathcal{V}_2)$ denote the *pushforward* operator, which maps a distribution $\mathbb{P}(\mathbf{V}_1)$ over $\mathcal{V}_1$ to the distribution $\mathbb{P}(\mathbf{V}_2)$ over $\mathcal{V}_2$ induced by f, i.e., the distribution of $\mathbf{V}_2 = f(\mathbf{V}_1)$ when $\mathbf{V}_1 \sim \mathbb{P}(\mathbf{V}_1)$.

Linear Algebra: Given a set of vectors $\mathcal{A}$, we let $\text{span}\{\mathbf{a} : \mathbf{a} \in \mathcal{A}\}$ denote their span. Let W be a subspace of $\mathbb{R}^n$. We let proj_W denote the *projection operator* onto W, $W^\perp$ denote its orthogonal complement, and $\dim(W)$ denote its dimension. We let $[n] := \{1, \dots, n\}$ for $n \in \mathbb{N}$. Let σ be a permutation on a symmetric group (e.g., $[n]$) and $\mathbf{P}_\sigma \in \{0,1\}^{n \times n}$ denote the permutation matrix of σ. Let $\mathbf{A} \in \mathbb{R}^{d \times n}$ be a matrix. We let $\mathbf{A}_i$ denote the i-th row of $\mathbf{A}$ and $\mathbf{A}_{:,j}$ denote the j-th column of $\mathbf{A}$. We let $\text{row}(\mathbf{A}) := \text{span}\{\mathbf{A}_i : i \in [d]\}$ denote the rowspan of $\mathbf{A}$, and $\text{col}(\mathbf{A}) := \text{span}\{\mathbf{A}_{:,j} : j \in [n]\}$ denote the column span of $\mathbf{A}$. We denote the indicator function by $\mathbb{1}$ and use the convention that $\mathbb{1}\{\mathbf{A}\} \in \{0,1\}^{d \times n}$ with entries $\left(\mathbb{1}\{\mathbf{A}\}\right)_{i,j} = \mathbb{1}\{\mathbf{A}_{i,j} \neq 0\}$. Finally, we let $\mathbf{A}^\dagger$ denote the Moore-Penrose inverse (pseudoinverse) of $\mathbf{A}$.

Score Functions: Given a continuous probability distribution $\mathbb{P}(\mathbf{V})$, we associate a probability density function (pdf) $p(\mathbf{V})$. *Score function* of a density is defined as the gradient of its logarithm, denoted as $s(\mathbf{v}) := \nabla_{\mathbf{v}} \log p(\mathbf{v})$[2].

---

1 Our definitions can be straightforwardly generalized to more general settings; see Forré and Mooij [15] for a general measure-theoretic treatment.

2 Note that if $\mathcal{V}$ is an n-dimensional manifold embedded in $\mathbb{R}^d$ $(n < d)$, then the score function of $p(\mathcal{V})$ needs to be defined only for the points within the manifold. This can be done using the tangent space $T_{\mathbf{v}}\mathcal{V}$ of each point $\mathbf{v} \in \mathcal{V}$ and generalizing the gradient to differential operators [16, Section 3.2].

Given a function $f : \mathbb{R}^n \to \mathbb{R}^d$ that has first-order partial derivatives on $\mathbb{R}^d$, we denote the Jacobian matrix of f at $\mathbf{v} \in \mathbb{R}^n$ by $J_f(\mathbf{v}) \in \mathbb{R}^{d \times n}$ with entries $\left(J_f(\mathbf{v})\right)_{i,j} = \partial f(\mathbf{v})_i / \partial v_j$.

Equivalence Relations: Given an equivalence relation $\approx_a$ over a set $\mathcal{A}$ we denote the *equivalence class* of $A \in \mathcal{A}$ under $\approx_a$ as $[A]_a \triangleq \{A' \in \mathcal{A} : A' \approx_a A\}$. The set of equivalence classes of $\mathcal{A}$ under $\approx_a$ is denoted as $\mathcal{A}/\approx_a$. Given two equivalence relations $\approx_a$ and $\approx_b$, we say that $\approx_a$ is *coarser* than $\approx_b$ if $A \approx_b A'$ implies $A \approx_a A'$.

10.2.1 Model Classes and Identifiability

Throughout this chapter, we will discuss several classes of probabilistic models. To emphasize the common structure across these models, we define a few abstract notions that pervade identifiability theory.

Abstractly, we can specify a data-generating process in terms of two objects: a class $\mathcal{M}$ of mathematical models, and a fixed mapping ρ, which takes each model $M \in \mathcal{M}$ to an observable object $\rho(M)$. The pair $(\mathcal{M}, \rho)$ specifies a candidate set of forward, "data-generating" processes, one for each model $M \in \mathcal{M}$. Identifiability theory studies the associated *inverse problem* of determining M from $\rho(M)$. Formally, we define a problem setting as follows.

Definition 10.1: A *problem setting* $\mathcal{S}$ consists of a tuple $(\mathcal{M}, \rho)$, where $\mathcal{M}$ is an arbitrary set called the *model class*, and $\rho : \mathcal{M} \to \mathcal{R}$ is a mapping, called the *observation functional*, from $\mathcal{M}$ to some arbitrary set $\mathcal{R}$.

Typically in the study of probabilistic models, ρ maps each model to a probability distribution or an indexed family of probability distributions; this will become more clear by example in the following sections. For observation functionals $\rho_1 : \mathcal{M} \to \mathcal{R}_1$ and $\rho_2 : \mathcal{M} \to \mathcal{R}_2$, we say that ρ_1 is *richer* than ρ_2 if there exists a function r such that $\rho_2 = r \circ \rho_1$; this relation defines a preorder over observation functionals.

Definition 10.2 *(Identifiability)*: Consider the problem setting $\mathcal{S} = (\mathcal{M}, \rho)$. We define an equivalence relation $\approx_\rho$, with $M \approx_\rho M'$ for $M, M' \in \mathcal{M}$ such that $\rho(M) = \rho(M')$. Given an equivalence relation $\approx_e$ over $\mathcal{M}$, we say that $M \in \mathcal{M}$ is *identifiable up to* $\approx_e$ if $M \approx_\rho M'$ implies $M \approx_e M'$. If $[M]_\rho = \{M\}$, then we say that M is *fully identifiable*.

Given two related model classes $\mathcal{M}_1$ and $\mathcal{M}_2$, we often have a canonical way of translating models in $\mathcal{M}_1$ into the language of $\mathcal{M}_2$, which can be summarized as a *translation* mapping $\sigma : \mathcal{M}_1 \to \mathcal{M}_2$. Given such a mapping, we can relate model classes and problem settings as follows:

Definition 10.3: Let $\sigma : \mathcal{M}_1 \to \mathcal{M}_2$ be fixed. For problem settings $\mathcal{S}_1 = (\mathcal{M}_1, \rho_1)$ and $\mathcal{S}_2 = (\mathcal{M}_2, \rho_2)$, we say that $\mathcal{S}_1$ is *id-weaker* than $\mathcal{S}_2$ if $\mathcal{M}_1/\approx_{\rho_1}$ is coarser than $\sigma^{-1}(\mathcal{M}_2)/\approx_{\rho_2 \circ \sigma}$.

Note that the expressivity relation defines a preorder over model classes, and the id-weaker relation defines a preorder over problem settings. As an immediate application of this definition, if $\mathcal{M}_2 \subseteq \mathcal{M}_1$, then $\mathcal{M}_1$ is more expressive than $\mathcal{M}_2$, and $(\mathcal{M}_1, \rho)$ is id-weaker than $(\mathcal{M}_2, \rho)$; this captures the fact that adding restrictions to a model class can improve identifiability.

We now make our discussion more concrete by discussing some particular model classes that are foundational in the graphical study of causality.

10.2.2 Causal Graphical Models and Interventions

The basic models in graphical causality are built upon directed acyclic graphs (DAGs). A *directed acyclic graph (DAG)* $\mathcal{G}$ over a set of nodes $[n]$ is a graph consisting of directed edges (edges of the form $i \to j$, for $i, j \in [n]$), with no directed cycles, i.e., no directed paths of the form $i \to j \to \dots \to i$.

We adopt basic familial definitions and notation from graph theory, e.g., $\mathbf{pa}_{\mathcal{G}}(i) = \{j \in [n] : j \to i \text{ in } \mathcal{G}\}$ denotes the *parents* and $\mathbf{an}_{\mathcal{G}}(i) = \{j \in [n] : \exists \text{ directed path } j \to \dots \to i \text{ in } \mathcal{G}\}$ denotes the *ancestors* of node i in $\mathcal{G}$. We use overlines to denote inclusive versions of these definitions, e.g., $\overline{\mathbf{pa}}_{\mathcal{G}}(i) = \mathbf{pa}_{\mathcal{G}}(i) \cup \{i\}$. A node i is called a *source* node if it has no parents, i.e., $\mathbf{pa}_{\mathcal{G}}(i) = \emptyset$. We associate each node i in $\mathcal{G}$ with a random variable V_i; for convenience, we extend familial notation to random variables, e.g., $\mathbf{pa}_{\mathcal{G}}(V_i) = \{V_j \in \mathbf{V} : j \in \mathbf{pa}_{\mathcal{G}}(i)\}$. We also use $\mathrm{trc}(\mathcal{G})$ to denote the transitive closure of $\mathcal{G}$, which is defined with parent sets $\mathbf{pa}_{\mathrm{trc}(\mathcal{G})}(i) = \mathbf{an}_{\mathcal{G}}(i)$.

Definition 10.4 *(Structural causal model)*: Let $\mathcal{G}$ be a DAG over $[n]$. For $i = 1, \dots, n$, let $(\mathcal{E}_i)_{i\in[n]}$ be measurable spaces. A *structural causal model (SCM) M* with *causal graph* $\mathcal{G}$ consists of an indexed family of *exogenous noise distributions*

$$\left(\mathbb{P}_i^M(\varepsilon_i) \in \mathcal{P}(\mathcal{E}_i)\right)_{i\in[n]}$$

and an indexed family of *causal mechanisms*

$$\left(f_i^M : \mathcal{V}_{\mathbf{pa}_{\mathcal{G}}(i)} \times \mathcal{E}_i \to \mathcal{V}_i\right)_{i\in[n]}.$$

We denote by $\mathcal{M}_{\mathrm{scm}}(\mathbf{V}; \mathcal{G})$ the set of all SCMs on $\mathcal{G}$, and we denote by $\mathcal{M}_{\mathrm{scm}}(\mathbf{V})$ the set of all SCMs on any DAG over $[n]$. Given $M \in \mathcal{M}_{\mathrm{scm}}(\mathbf{V})$, we let $\mathcal{G}^M$ denote its causal graph.

Given an SCM M, we can derive for each node $i \in [n]$ a *causal kernel* by taking the pushforward of $\mathbb{P}_i^M(\varepsilon_i)$ through the causal mechanism f_i^M at every value $\mathbf{pa}_{\mathcal{G}}(V_i) \in \mathcal{V}_{\mathbf{pa}_{\mathcal{G}}(i)}$, i.e.,

$$\mathbb{P}_i^M(V_i \mid \mathbf{pa}_{\mathcal{G}}(V_i)) := \left(\varepsilon_i \mapsto f_i^M(\mathbf{pa}_{\mathcal{G}}(V_i), \varepsilon_i)\right)_{\#} \left(\mathbb{P}_i^M(\varepsilon_i)\right)$$

Formally, the family of causal kernels for $i \in [n]$ defines a *causal Bayesian network (CBN)*, which can be used for reasoning about interventions, but not counterfactuals [17]. Hence, the results in this chapter could be given directly in terms of CBNs, but we choose to use SCMs as they allow us to more conveniently state some assumptions and are necessary for connecting to results using counterfactuals. The causal kernels of an SCM are used to define its entailed distribution as follows.

Definition 10.5 *(Entailed distribution of an SCM)*: Let $M \in \mathcal{M}_{\mathrm{scm}}(\mathbf{V})$. The *entailed distribution* of M is

$$\mathbb{P}^M(\mathbf{V}) := \prod_{i=1}^{n} \mathbb{P}_i^M(V_i \mid \mathbf{pa}_{\mathcal{G}}(V_i)).$$

Now, we come to the truly *causal* aspects of SCMs by defining an intervention as a modular way of changing one SCM into a related one.

Definition 10.6 *(Intervention)*: Let $\mathcal{G}$ be a DAG over $[n]$. An *intervention* I on $\mathcal{G}$, with targets $\boldsymbol{T}(I) \subseteq [n]$ consists of an indexed family

$$\left(\mathbb{P}_i^I(\varepsilon_i) \in \mathcal{P}(\mathcal{E}_i)\right)_{i \in \boldsymbol{T}(I)}$$

and an indexed family of *interventional mechanisms*

$$\left(f_i^I : \mathcal{V}_{\mathbf{pa}_{\mathcal{G}}(i)} \times \mathcal{E}_i \to \mathcal{V}_i\right)_{i \in \boldsymbol{T}(I)}.$$

We denote by $\mathcal{I}(\mathcal{G})$ the set of all interventions on $\mathcal{G}$.

Given $M \in \mathcal{M}_{\mathrm{scm}}(\mathcal{G})$ and $I \in \mathcal{I}(\mathcal{G})$, we define the *interventional SCM* $M_I \in \mathcal{M}_{\mathrm{scm}}(\mathcal{G})$ as the structural causal model with exogenous noise distributions

$$\mathbb{P}_i^{M_I}(\varepsilon_i) := \begin{cases} \mathbb{P}_i^I(\varepsilon_i) & i \in \boldsymbol{T}(I) \\ \mathbb{P}_i^M(\varepsilon_i) & i \notin \boldsymbol{T}(I) \end{cases},$$

and causal mechanisms

$$f_i^{M_I} := \begin{cases} f_i^I & i \in \boldsymbol{T}(I) \\ f_i^M & i \notin \boldsymbol{T}(I) \end{cases}.$$

Often, the entailed distribution $\mathbb{P}^{M_I}(\mathbf{V})$ is called the *interventional distribution* of M under intervention I. We say that I is a stochastic *hard* (or *perfect*) intervention if for all $i \in T(I)$, $f_i^I(\mathbf{pa}_\mathcal{G}(V_i), \varepsilon_i) = f_i^I(\varepsilon_i)$, i.e., the interventional mechanism of V_i does not depend on its parents.[3] As the most general case, if f_i^I can maintain its dependence on $\mathbf{pa}_\mathcal{G}(V_i)$, I is called a *soft (or imperfect) intervention.*

10.2.3 Causal Representation Models

Thus far, the notions that we have defined on SCMs are the objects of study in more traditional subfields of causality, such as causal effect estimation and causal structure learning. Now, we introduce the model class that is the main object of study in CRL.

Definition 10.7 *(Causal representation model)*: Let $\mathbf{Z}$ and $\mathbf{X}$ be random vectors. A *causal representation model* M on $\mathbf{X}$ consists of a pair (S^M, g^M), where $S^M \in \mathcal{M}_{\text{scm}}(\mathbf{Z})$ is called the *latent SCM*, and $g^M : \mathcal{Z} \to \mathcal{X}$ is called the *mixing function*. We assume that g^M is a diffeomorphism onto its image, with inverse $h^M := (g^M)^{-1}$. We denote by $\mathcal{M}_{\text{crm}}(\mathbf{X})$ the set of all causal representation models on $\mathbf{X}$. See Figure 10.1 for an illustration.

Causal representation models are meant to capture the idea that one may not observe the "true" or "underlying" causal variables $\mathbf{Z}$ (those that obey traditional causal semantics), but instead one only observes a "mixed" version of these variables.[4] Thus, thinking of $\mathbf{X}$ as the observed variables, we define the entailed distribution of $\mathbf{X}$ as follows:

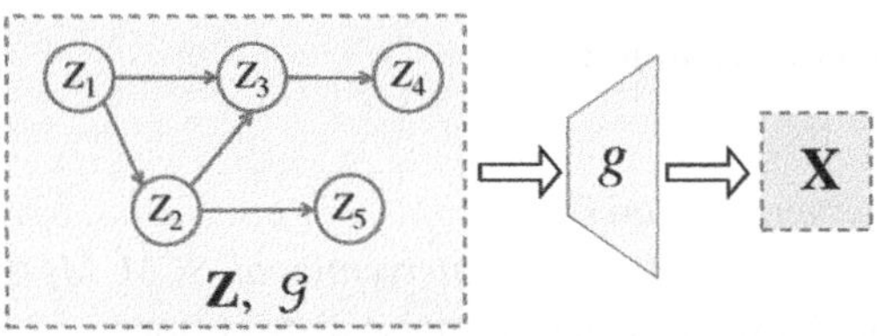

Figure 10.1 An example of CRM with latent causal variables $\mathbf{Z}$, the latent causal graph $\mathcal{G}$, unknown mixing function g, and observed variables $\mathbf{X}$.

---

3 *do* interventions, which deterministically set $f_i^I(\varepsilon_i) = c_i$ for a fixed value c_i, denoted by $do(V_i = c_i)$, are also referred to as hard interventions in the literature. We make the distinction by noting that we consider *stochastic* hard interventions.

4 More generally, causal representation models can be defined without the diffeomorphism requirement on g^M; indeed, g^M might even be a stochastic mapping. For this chapter, we always assume that g^M is a diffeomorphism, so we have incorporated that requirement into the definition. There exist other studies without this requirement, albeit under different data generation settings, e.g., [18, 19].

Definition 10.8 *(Entailed distribution of a CRM)*: The *entailed distribution* of a causal representation model is

$$\mathbb{P}^M(\mathbf{X}) := (g^M)_{\#}\left(\mathbb{P}^{S^M}(\mathbf{Z})\right).$$

Intuitively, this definition defines a two-step data-generating process, where $\mathbf{Z}$ is sampled from the distribution $\mathbb{P}^{S^M}(\mathbf{Z})$, then $\mathbf{X}$ is generated by taking $\mathbf{X} = g^M(\mathbf{Z})$. We extend the effect of interventions to CRMs as follows:

Definition 10.9 *(Interventional CRM)*: Let $M = (S^M, g^M) \in \mathcal{M}_{\text{crm}}(\mathbf{X})$ be a causal representation model with causal graph $\mathcal{G}^M$, and let $I \in \mathcal{I}(\mathcal{G})$ be an intervention. The *interventional CRM* $M_I \in \mathcal{M}_{\text{crm}}(\mathbf{X})$ is defined as $M_I := ((S^M)_I, g^M)$.

In particular, interventions act on the latent SCM and leave the mixing function g^M unchanged.

10.2.4 CRL Identifiability and Equivalence Classes

Our results will feature varying levels of identifiability, i.e., identifiability up to different equivalent classes. In this subsection, we define these different levels of identifiability. To achieve these results, we take a constructive approach in our treatment of CRL. Specifically, we aim to establish identifiability guarantees for causal representation models by designing algorithms, the steps of which serve as constructive proofs of identifiability. Accordingly, we first discuss the function classes and estimates that a CRL algorithm can produce.

Consider a causal representation model M with causal graph $\mathcal{G}$. We refer to the inverse mixing function $h := g^{-1}$ as the *true encoder*. Let $n = |\mathbf{Z}|$ and $d = |\mathbf{X}|$. In the algorithmic sense, identifying the latent representation $\mathbf{Z} = h(\mathbf{X})$ involves forming an estimate $\widehat{\mathcal{G}}$ of $\mathcal{G}$, and an estimate $\widehat{h}$ of h, so that we can generate $\widehat{\mathbf{Z}} = \widehat{h}(\mathbf{X})$, and use $\widehat{\mathcal{G}}$ to perform causal reasoning over $\widehat{\mathbf{Z}}$. To formalize the procedures for estimating true encoder h, we define $\mathcal{H}$ as the set of invertible functions defined on $\mathcal{X}$,

$$\mathcal{H} := \{\widehat{h} : \mathcal{X} \to \mathbb{R}^n : \exists \widehat{h}^{-1} : \mathbb{R}^n \to \mathbb{R}^d \text{ s.t. } (\widehat{h}^{-1} \circ \widehat{h})(\mathbf{x}) = \mathbf{x}, \forall \mathbf{x} \in \mathcal{X}\}. \quad (10.1)$$

Next, for any candidate $\widehat{h} \in \mathcal{H}$, we define

$$\widehat{\mathbf{Z}}(\mathbf{X}; \widehat{h}) := \widehat{h}(\mathbf{X}) = (\widehat{h} \circ g)(\mathbf{Z}). \quad (10.2)$$

The estimate $\widehat{\mathbf{Z}}(\mathbf{X}; \widehat{h})$ inherits its randomness from $\mathbf{X}$, and its causal behavior is governed by that of $\mathbf{Z}$ under the chosen $\widehat{h}$. Finally, note that there may be different algorithmic approaches to forming estimates for h and $\mathcal{G}$, such as jointly, separately, or sequentially estimating them. To assess the fidelity of the estimates $\widehat{h}$ and $\widehat{\mathcal{G}}$ with respect to h and $\mathcal{G}$, we define the following identifiability measures.

Definition 10.10 ***(Latent variable identifiability)*****:** Consider two encoders (unmixing functions) $h_1, h_2 \in \mathcal{H}$.

- **Componentwise transform:** h_1 and h_2 are equivalent up to componentwise transform, denoted by $h_1 \approx_{\text{cmp}} h_2$ if

$$\widehat{\mathbf{Z}}(\mathbf{X}; h_1) = \mathbf{P}_\sigma \cdot \phi(\widehat{\mathbf{Z}}(\mathbf{X}; h_2)) \tag{10.3}$$

  for a componentwise diffeomorphism $\phi(\mathbf{Z}) := (\phi_1(Z_1), \dots, \phi_n(Z_n))$ and permutation matrix $\mathbf{P}_\sigma$.
- **Scaling:** h_1 and h_2 are equivalent up to scaling, denoted by $h_1 \approx_{\text{scale}} h_2$ if

$$\widehat{\mathbf{Z}}(\mathbf{X}; h_1) = \mathbf{P}_\sigma \cdot \mathbf{C}_{\text{scale}} \cdot \widehat{\mathbf{Z}}(\mathbf{X}; h_2) \tag{10.4}$$

  for a diagonal matrix $\mathbf{C}_{\text{scale}} \in \mathbb{R}^{n \times n}$ and permutation matrix $\mathbf{P}_\sigma$.
- **Mixing with parents:** h_1 and h_2 are equivalent up to mixing with parents, denoted by $h_1 \approx_{\text{pa}} h_2$ if

$$\widehat{\mathbf{Z}}(\mathbf{X}; h_1) = \mathbf{P}_\sigma \cdot \mathbf{C}_{\text{pa}} \cdot \widehat{\mathbf{Z}}(\mathbf{X}; h_2) \tag{10.5}$$

  for a constant matrix $\mathbf{C}_{\text{pa}} \in \mathbb{R}^{n \times n}$ that has nonzero diagonal entries and $(\mathbf{C}_{\text{pa}})_{i,j} = 0$ for $Z_j \notin \overline{\mathbf{pa}}_{\mathcal{G}}(Z_i)$, and permutation matrix $\mathbf{P}_\sigma$.
- **Mixing with ancestors:** h_1 and h_2 are equivalent up to mixing with ancestors, denoted by $h_1 \approx_{\text{an}} h_2$ if

$$\widehat{\mathbf{Z}}(\mathbf{X}; h_1) = \mathbf{P}_\sigma \cdot \mathbf{C}_{\text{an}} \cdot \widehat{\mathbf{Z}}(\mathbf{X}; h_2) \tag{10.6}$$

  for a constant matrix $\mathbf{C}_{\text{an}} \in \mathbb{R}^{n \times n}$ that has nonzero diagonal entries and $(\mathbf{C}_{\text{an}})_{i,j} = 0$ for $Z_j \notin \overline{\mathbf{an}}_{\mathcal{G}}(Z_i)$, and permutation matrix $\mathbf{P}_\sigma$.

We note that $\approx_{\text{scale}}$ is a special case of $\approx_{\text{cmp}}$, in which the componentwise transform is restricted to be a scaling factor. Furthermore, $\approx_{\text{an}} \rightarrow \approx_{\text{pa}} \rightarrow \approx_{\text{scale}}$ transition reflects going from coarser equivalence classes (e.g., partial identifiability) to more refined identifiability levels.[5]

Definition 10.11 ***(Latent graph identifiability)*****:** Consider two graphs $\mathcal{G}_1$ and $\mathcal{G}_2$ with n nodes. We denote

- **Isormorphism:** $\mathcal{G}_1$ and $\mathcal{G}_2$ are isomorphic, denoted by $\mathcal{G}_1 \approx_{\text{iso}} \mathcal{G}_2$ if $\mathcal{G}_1 = \sigma(\mathcal{G}_2)$ for a permutation σ.

5 These identifiability levels are slightly modified versions of standard notions in the literature. Note that there exist other similar notions, including block-identifiability [20], identifiability up to surrounding parents [21], or affine identifiability [22]. For the scope of this chapter, we only define granularity levels relevant to the results we discuss.

- **Transitive closure:** $\mathcal{G}_1$ and $\mathcal{G}_2$ are equivalent up to transitive closure, denoted by $\mathcal{G}_1 \approx_{\text{an}} \mathcal{G}_2$ if $\text{trc}(\mathcal{G}_1) = \sigma(\text{trc}(\mathcal{G}_2))$ for a permutation σ.

Technical Note: Here, we have defined identifiability levels in terms of equivalence relations that are defined on the set of latent graphs or on the set of (un)mixing functions, rather than on $\mathcal{M}_{\text{crm}}$, the set of CRMs. Formally, we can "lift" such equivalence relations to $\mathcal{M}_{\text{crm}}$ by defining further equivalence relations, e.g., for $M, M' \in \mathcal{M}_{\text{crm}}$, we could define $M \approx_{\text{graph}} M'$ if S^M and $S^{M'}$ have the same causal graph, and similarly for (un)mixing functions. However, such meticulousness is unnecessary for our purposes, so we speak directly in terms of latent graphs and equivalence relations.

10.3 Interventional CRL

Consider a single data set of samples drawn from the distribution $\mathbb{P}^M(\mathbf{X})$. In general, achieving the levels of identifiability described in Section 10.2.4 is impossible when using only $\mathbb{P}^M(\mathbf{X})$. For instance, consider the classical causal discovery problem with observed variables, which corresponds to identifying the causal graph $\mathcal{G}^M$ under an identity mapping $\mathbf{X} = \mathbf{Z}$. It is well-known that $\mathcal{G}^M$ can only be identified up to its Markov equivalence class [13]. Under an unknown mixing function g^M, insufficiency of $\mathbb{P}^M(\mathbf{X})$ alone becomes more evident.

To address this, we consider problem settings $\mathcal{S}$ that contain data from multiple *environments*. Specifically, we focus on leveraging interventional data. We describe the generic *interventional CRL* problem setting as follows.

Problem setting (*$\mathcal{S}_{\text{int}}$ – Interventional CRL*): Let $M^0 \in \mathcal{M}_{\text{crm}}(\mathbf{X})$ with causal graph $\mathcal{G}$, and let $\mathcal{E}^0$ denote this observational environment. Consider K interventional environments where $I^k \in \mathcal{I}(\mathcal{G})$ denotes the intervention in the k-th environment. For $k = 1, \dots, K$, we let $M^k := M_{I^k} \in \mathcal{M}_{\text{crm}}(\mathbf{X})$. Thus, formally, the model class for this problem setting is

$$\mathcal{M}_{\text{int}} := \mathcal{M}_{\text{crm}}(\mathbf{X}) \times \underbrace{\mathcal{I}(\mathcal{G}) \times \mathcal{I}(\mathcal{G}) \dots \times \mathcal{I}(\mathcal{G})}_{K \text{times}},$$

where $\mathcal{G}$ is the causal graph of M^0. Finally, the observation functional for this problem setting is

$$\rho_{\text{int}}(M^0, I^1, \dots, I^K) := \left(\mathbb{P}^0(\mathbf{X}), \mathbb{P}^1(\mathbf{X}), \dots, \mathbb{P}^K(\mathbf{X})\right),$$

where $\mathbb{P}^k(\mathbf{X})$ denotes the entailed distribution of M^k, i.e., $\mathbb{P}^k(\mathbf{X}) := \mathbb{P}^{M^k}(\mathbf{X})$.

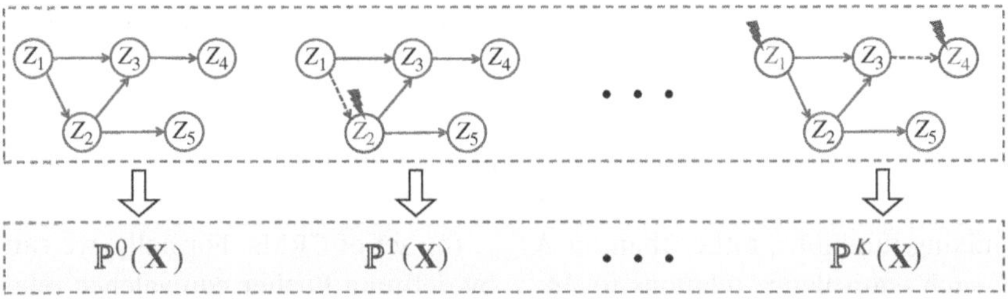

Figure 10.2 Illustration of $\mathcal{S}_{\text{int}}$ interventional CRL setting.

For brevity, we will explain our later adaptations of this problem setting in words; knowing that it can always be translated into our more formal notation. We note the following assumptions and explanations on the interventional CRL problem setting that will be relevant to our discussion in the sequel. See Figure 10.2 for an illustration.

Notations: We use the following notation for brevity. First, we use the superscript k instead of M^k; e.g., $S^k := S^{M^k}$ denotes the latent SCM in the k-th environment, $p^k_{\mathbf{Z}}$ denotes the density of $\mathbb{P}^k(\mathbf{Z}) := \mathbb{P}^{S^k}(\mathbf{Z})$, and $p^k_{\mathbf{X}}$ denotes the density of $\mathbb{P}^k(\mathbf{X}) := \mathbb{P}^{S^k}(\mathbf{X})$. Second, we drop the subscript $\mathcal{G}$ when the corresponding graph is clear from the context. Third, we use $g := g^{M^0}$ since the mixing function is the same between all environments. Without loss of generality, we assume that $1, \ldots, n$ is a topological order of the causal graph $\mathcal{G}$.

Probability: We assume that each probability distribution $\mathbb{P}^k(\mathbf{V})$ has full support over $\mathbb{R}^n$ and that each conditional density $p^k_i(V_i \mid \mathbf{pa}(V_i))$ is continuously differentiable. Throughout the chapter, all expectations denoted by $\mathbb{E}$ are under the probability measure of the observational environment.

Intervention Properties: Note that the problem setting is given for the most general case of soft (imperfect) interventions. In the sequel, we will consider different model classes under various intervention scenarios, e.g., soft versus hard interventions or single-node versus multi-node interventions. Throughout, we assume *successful* interventions, i.e., if $i \in \boldsymbol{T}(I^k)$, then we have $\mathbb{P}^k_i(V_i \mid \mathbf{pa}(V_i)) \neq \mathbb{P}^0_i(V_i \mid \mathbf{pa}(V_i))$. Note that $\boldsymbol{T}(I^k) = \boldsymbol{T}(I^j)$ *does not* imply $I^k = I^j$, e.g., for $i \in \boldsymbol{T}(I^k) = \boldsymbol{T}(I^j)$, the interventions I^k and I^j can impose different causal mechanisms on V_i, that is $p^k_i(V_i \mid \mathbf{pa}(V_i)) \neq p^j_i(V_i \mid \mathbf{pa}(V_i))$. This distinction will be important when considering multiple interventions on the same variable.

Before we discuss CRL identifiability results and algorithms, it is helpful to understand the limits of identifiability under interventional data.

1. To guarantee componentwise identifiability in all cases, the union of intervention sets must cover all latent variables. In other words, there exist models $M \in \mathcal{M}_{\text{crm}}(\mathbf{X})$ and interventions $I_1, \ldots, I_K$ that cannot be identified under $\mathcal{S}_{\text{int}}$ if $\bigcup_{k \in [K]} \boldsymbol{T}(I^k) \neq [n]$ [23, Proposition 4]. Therefore, we will consider instances of $\mathcal{S}_{\text{int}}$ in which all latent variables are intervened at least once.
2. Identifiability up to component diffeomorphisms is the best one can achieve using interventional data without additional assumptions on the setting $\mathcal{S}_{\text{int}}$ [27, Proposition 3.1].

We will consider various instances of $\mathcal{S}_{\text{int}}$ (see Table 10.1 for a summary). First, we define the single-node intervention setting that will be repeatedly used.

Problem setting ($\mathcal{S}_{\text{single}}$ – *One single-node intervention per node*): Consider interventional CRL problem setting $\mathcal{S}_{\text{int}}$. Suppose that we have one single-node intervention per node, that is, $K = n$ and $\boldsymbol{T}(I^k) = \{\tau_k\}$ for all $k \in [n]$ where τ is a permutation of $\{1, \ldots, n\}$.

Remark 10.1: Having *exactly* one intervention per node in $\mathcal{S}_{\text{single}}$ is not required for any of the results in this chapter and can be readily extended to having *at least* one intervention per node. The simplification is merely made for presenting the results more clearly.

Table 10.1 Summary of the interventional CRL results presented in this chapter. Equivalence classes are specified in Definition 10.2. For brevity, the main identifiability results for latent variables $\mathbf{Z}$ are listed.

	Mixing function	Latent SCM	$\mathcal{S}_{\text{int}}$ setting	Main result
Theorem 10.1	Linear	Linear	$\mathcal{S}_{\text{single}}$-hard	$\approx_{\text{scale}}$
[23]	Linear	Linear	$\mathcal{S}_{\text{single}}$-soft	$\approx_{\text{an}}$
Theorem 10.2	General	Lin. Gaussian	$\mathcal{S}_{\text{single}}$-hard	$\approx_{\text{scale}}$
[24]	General	Lin. Gaussian	$\mathcal{S}_{\text{single}}$-soft	$\approx_{\text{an}}$
Theorem 10.3	Linear	General	$\mathcal{S}_{\text{single}}$-hard	$\approx_{\text{scale}}$
[16]	Linear	General	$\mathcal{S}_{\text{single}}$-soft	$\approx_{\text{pa}}$
Theorem 10.4	Linear	General	$\mathcal{S}_{\text{single}}$-hard	$\approx_{\text{scale}}$
[25]	Linear	General	$\mathcal{S}_{\text{single}}$-soft	$\approx_{\text{an}}$
Theorem 10.5	General	General	$\mathcal{S}_{2\text{-single}}$-hard	$\approx_{\text{cmp}}$
[26]				

10.4 CRL with Linear SCMs

In this section, we consider the special case of causal representation models with *linear* latent SCMs. Furthermore, we specialize to the case of *single-node* interventions; we drop both of these assumptions in the next section.

Additive Noise SCMs: Let $S \in \mathcal{M}_{\text{scm}}(\mathbf{Z})$. We say that S is an *additive noise* SCM if, for all $i \in [n]$, there exists $\widetilde{f}_i^S : \mathcal{Z}_{\mathbf{pa}(i)} \to \mathcal{Z}_i$ such that

$$f_i^S(\mathbf{pa}(Z_i), \varepsilon_i) = \widetilde{f}_i^S(\mathbf{pa}(Z_i)) + \varepsilon_i.$$

Furthermore, we say that an additive noise SCM S is *Gaussian* if, for all $i \in [n]$, $\mathbb{P}_i^S(\varepsilon_i)$ is a Gaussian distribution.

Linear SCMs: Let $S \in \mathcal{M}_{\text{scm}}(\mathbf{Z})$. We say that S is a *linear SCM* if, for all $i \in [n]$, f_i^S is linear; note that this is a special case of an additive noise SCM. In this case, we can compactly write S in matrix-vector form as

$$\mathbf{Z} = \mathbf{W}\mathbf{Z} + \Omega^{1/2}\varepsilon, \tag{10.7}$$

where $\mathbf{W} \in \mathbb{R}^{n \times n}$ is a matrix with $\mathbf{W}_{ij} = 0$ if $Z_j \to Z_i$ is not in $\mathcal{G}$, Ω is a positive diagonal matrix, and ε is a random vector with components ε_i for $Z_i \in \mathbf{Z}$ such that $\text{Cov}(\varepsilon) = \mathbf{I}_n$. Note that, for convenience and without loss of generality, we have here picked to re-scale ε so that the variance of these exogenous noise is made explicit. By simple linear algebra, we can re-write S as follows:

$$\mathbf{Z} = \mathbf{B}\varepsilon, \qquad \mathbf{B} := \Omega^{-1/2}(\mathbf{I}_n - \mathbf{W}), \tag{10.8}$$

where we call $\mathbf{B}$ the *causal matrix* of S. For convenience, we assume that $\mathbb{E}[\varepsilon] = \mathbf{0}$; though this is not necessary [24].

Technical Note: Many of our identifiability results require some form of *genericity* (or nondegeneracy) assumption on the model parameters. In particular, denoting the model parameters as $\theta \in \mathbb{R}^p$ (for some p), the statement may be violated on a set $\Theta_{\text{degen}} \subseteq \mathbb{R}^p$, which has Lebesgue measure zero. For specific settings, the exact characterization of Θ_{degen} may be of great interest.[6] However, such results are often fairly involved and do not offer much conceptual insight, so we omit them here.

---

6 For example, exact characterizations of Θ_{degen} are relevant to the finite sample setting; see Uhler et al. [28].

10.4.1 Linear Mixing on Linear Latent SCMs

The first theorem, adapted from Theorem 1 and Proposition 3 of Squires et al. [23], establishes that, in the case of single-node interventions, interventional coverage is in fact *sufficient* for identifiability of a CRM with both a linear latent SCM and a linear mixing function. Note that Gaussianity is *not* assumed for this result. For the linear mixing function, we denote

$$\mathbf{X} = \mathbf{G} \cdot \mathbf{Z}, \tag{10.9}$$

where $\mathbf{G} \in \mathbb{R}^{d \times n}$ is the *unknown* full-rank matrix mapping the latent variables to the observed ones, and let $\mathbf{H} := \mathbf{G}^{\dagger}$.

Theorem 10.1: *Assume the problem setting $\mathcal{S}_{\text{single}}$. Furthermore, assume that the latent SCM S and the mixing function g are linear. Then, there exists an algorithm which returns $\mathcal{G}^*$, $\mathbf{H}^*$ such that*

i. ***Soft interventions:*** *$\mathcal{G}^* \approx_{\text{an}} \mathcal{G}$ and $\mathbf{H}^* \approx_{\text{an}} \mathbf{H}$, i.e., we recover the latent graph up to transitive closure and the latent variables up to mixing with ancestors.*
ii. ***Hard interventions:*** *$\mathcal{G}^* \approx_{\text{iso}} \mathcal{G}$ and $\mathbf{H}^* \approx_{\text{scale}} \mathbf{H}$, i.e., we recover the graph perfectly and the latent variables up to componentwise scaling.*

The double linearity assumption in this theorem (on both the SCM and the mixing function) allows the proof to be given using purely linear algebraic concepts.

Deriving a Key Relation: First, we can relate the observable moments of $\mathbb{P}^k(\mathbf{X})$ to model parameters. In particular, let the $\Theta^k := \text{Cov}^k(\mathbf{X})^{\dagger}$ be the pseudoinverse of the covariance matrix over $\mathbf{X}$ in the k-th environment; we call this the *precision* matrix of $\mathbb{P}^k(\mathbf{X})$. Letting $\mathbf{B}^k$ be the causal matrix of M^k, it is straightforward to show that $\Theta^k = \mathbf{H}^{\top}(\mathbf{B}^k)^{\top}\mathbf{B}^k\mathbf{H}$, where we recall that $\mathbf{H} = \mathbf{G}^{\dagger}$.

Using this equation, we can characterize *differences* between interventional and observational precision matrices, leading to one of the key equalities of the proof:

$$\Delta^k := \Theta^k - \Theta^0 = \mathbf{H}^{\top}\left((\mathbf{B}^k_{\tau_k})^{\otimes 2} - (\mathbf{B}^0_{\tau_k})^{\otimes 2}\right)\mathbf{H}, \tag{10.10}$$

where $\mathbf{v}^{\otimes 2} := \mathbf{v}\mathbf{v}^{\top}$ for any vector $\mathbf{v}$. Usefully, this equality implies the relation

$$\text{row}(\Delta^k) \subseteq \text{span}\{\mathbf{H}_i : i \in \overline{\mathbf{pa}}(\tau_k)\}, \tag{10.11}$$

which is the core tool for identifying the model in iterative fashion.

Finding the Transitive Closure: As a warm-up, we consider distinguishing between source nodes and non-source nodes. If τ_k is a non-source node, then under genericity conditions, $\text{rank}(\Delta^k) = 2$, since Δ^k is, up to conjugation, equal to the difference between two rank-one matrices. On the other hand, if τ_k is a source node, we have by (10.11) that $\text{row}(\Delta^k) \subseteq \text{span}\{\mathbf{H}_{\tau_k}\}$, so $\text{rank}(\Delta^k) \leq 1$. Thus, we can distinguish source nodes based on these ranks. In fact, when τ_k is a source node, we have $\text{row}(\Delta^k) = \text{span}\{\mathbf{H}_{\tau_k}\}$, so we can recover the row $\mathbf{H}_{\tau_k}$ up to a constant.

This case can be extended into a more general inductive argument to find a topological order of $\mathcal{G}$. For convenience, we shift to working fully in terms of subspaces instead of matrices. Suppose that, for $\mathcal{A} \subseteq [n]$, we know the subspace $W_{\mathcal{A}} := \text{span}\{\mathbf{H}_i : i \in \mathcal{A}\}$. We start with $\mathcal{A} = \emptyset$, so $W_{\mathcal{A}} = \{\mathbf{0}\}$. We can then in the base case recover the distinguishing source nodes as already discussed, adding these to $\mathcal{A}$.

For $k \in [n]$, let $V^k := \text{proj}_{W_{\mathcal{A}}^{\perp}}(\text{row}(\Delta^k))$. For k such that $\mathbf{pa}(\tau_k) \nsubseteq \mathcal{A}$, we generically have $\dim(V^k) = 2$, for reasons similar to those in the base case. On the other hand, for any k such that $\mathbf{pa}(\tau_k) \subseteq \mathcal{A}$, we have by (10.11) that $V^k \subseteq \text{span}\{\mathbf{H}_{\tau_k}\}$; hence, $\dim(V^k) \leq 1$. We can use this to distinguish a new "layer" of source nodes based on these subspace dimensions. To expand on how, when $\mathbf{pa}(\tau_k) \subseteq \mathcal{A}$, we actually have $V^k = \text{span}\{\mathbf{q}^k\}$ for $\mathbf{q}^k = \text{proj}_{W_{\mathcal{A}}^{\perp}}(\mathbf{H}_{\tau_k})$. By taking $\mathcal{A}' = \mathcal{A} \cup \{\tau_k\}$, we have the equality $W_{\mathcal{A}'} = W_{\mathcal{A}} \oplus V^k$, so we now know $W_{\mathcal{A}'}$.

Through this process, elements can be added to $\mathcal{A}$ if and only if all of their ancestors have been added to $\mathcal{A}$. Hence, this process recovers the transitive closure of $\mathcal{G}$. In terms of the unmixing function, the process performs a *partial order RQ decomposition* [23, Definition 1] of $\mathbf{H}$, a generalization of the classical RQ decomposition. In particular, by stacking the recovered $\mathbf{q}^k$ vectors in topological order, we obtain a matrix $\widehat{\mathbf{Q}}$ such that $\widehat{\mathbf{Q}} \approx_{\text{an}} \mathbf{H}$. This fact is not mentioned in Theorem 1 of [23], but is a direct corollary of their Proposition 3. In the case of soft interventions, the algorithm stops here and returns $\mathbf{H}^* = \widehat{\mathbf{Q}}$.

Finding the Graph for Hard Interventions: Meanwhile, in the case of hard interventions, the algorithm continues. Take the Cholesky factor $\mathbf{U}^k$ of $(\widehat{\mathbf{Q}}^{\dagger})^{\mathsf{T}} \Theta^k (\widehat{\mathbf{Q}}^{\dagger})$, i.e., the unique upper triangular matrix with positive diagonal such that $(\mathbf{U}^k)^{\mathsf{T}} \mathbf{U}^k = (\widehat{\mathbf{Q}}^{\dagger})^{\mathsf{T}} \Theta^k (\widehat{\mathbf{Q}}^{\dagger})$. Then, since $\widehat{\mathbf{Q}} \approx_{\text{an}} \mathbf{H}$, it also holds that $\mathbf{U}^k \approx_{\text{an}} \mathbf{B}^k$, in particular, $\mathbf{U}^k \approx_{\text{scale}} \mathbf{B}^k \mathbf{C}_{\text{an}}$ for some $\mathbf{C}_{\text{an}} \in \mathbb{R}^{n \times n}$ whose sparsity pattern matches the transitive closure of $\mathcal{G}$. In the setting of hard interventions, we can use the expected form of $\mathbf{B}^k - \mathbf{B}^0$ to find $\mathbf{C}_{\text{an}}$. Essentially, the final step decomposes $(\mathbf{U}^0, \mathbf{U}^1, \dots, \mathbf{U}^K)$ into $(\widehat{\mathbf{B}}^0, \widehat{\mathbf{B}}^1, \dots, \widehat{\mathbf{B}}^K)$ and $\mathbf{C}_{\text{an}}$ such that each $\widehat{\mathbf{B}}^k - \widehat{\mathbf{B}}^0$ has only one nonzero row and so that $\widehat{\mathbf{B}}^0$ is as sparse as possible.

10.4.2 General Mixing on Linear Latent SCMs

The second theorem, adapted from Buchholz et al. [24], establishes that the same interventional coverage condition suffices for linear latent SCMs under general mixing functions, under the additional assumption of Gaussianity.

Theorem 10.2: *Assume the problem setting $\mathcal{S}_{\text{single}}$. Furthermore, assume that S^k is linear Gaussian for all $k = 0, 1, \ldots, K$. Then we can recover $\mathcal{G}^*$ and h^* such that:*

i. ***Soft interventions:*** *$\mathcal{G}^* \approx_{\text{an}} \mathcal{G}$ and $h^* \approx_{\text{an}} h$, i.e., we recover the latent graph up to transitive closure and the latent variables up to mixing with ancestors.*
ii. ***Hard interventions:*** *$\mathcal{G}^* \approx_{\text{iso}} \mathcal{G}$ and $h^* \approx_{\text{scale}} h$, i.e., we recover the graph perfectly and the latent variables up to componentwise scaling.*

Reduction to Linear Mixing: The Gaussianity assumption makes it possible to reduce the problem to the linear mixing case of Theorem 10.1. In Buchholz et al. [24], the authors gave an inductive proof of this result leveraging interventions. Alternatively, we provide a more direct approach that uses only the entailed distribution (under no interventions).

Consider two causal representation models $M = (S, g)$ and $\widehat{M} = (\widehat{S}, \widehat{g})$, with entailed latent distributions $\mathbb{P}^0(\mathbf{Z})$ and $\widehat{\mathbb{P}}^0(\mathbf{Z})$, respectively. Suppose that M and $\widehat{M}$ entail the same *observed* distribution, i.e., $\mathbb{P}^0(\mathbf{X}) = \widehat{\mathbb{P}}^0(\mathbf{X})$. Then, under injectivity of $\widehat{g}$, we can define $q := \widehat{g}^{-1} \circ g$, and it is straightforward to show that $\widehat{\mathbb{P}}^0(\mathbf{Z}) = q_{\#}\left(\mathbb{P}^0(\mathbf{Z})\right)$. Furthermore, if g is injective, then q is bijective. Then, assuming that $\widehat{\mathbb{P}}^0(\widehat{\mathbf{Z}})$ and $\mathbb{P}^0(\mathbf{Z})$ are multivariate Gaussian, Nabeya and Kariya [29, Theorem 1] establishes that q must be affine. Under our simplifying assumptions, $\mathbb{E}[\mathbf{Z}] = 0$ under both distributions, so q must be linear. Thus, $g = \widehat{g} \circ q$, i.e., g and $\widehat{g}$ are related by an invertible linear transformation.

Contrastive Learning Methodology: In the linear mixing setting, we could learn $\mathbf{H} := \mathbf{G}^{\dagger}$ in a row-wise fashion. To learn $h := g^{-1}$ in the general mixing setting, we use a quite different approach based on *contrastive learning*, establishing a novel connection between CRL and other areas of representation learning. This approach once more relies on the Gaussianity assumption for $\mathbb{P}^k(\mathbf{Z})$ for each environment $k = 0, 1, \ldots, K$. As shown in Lemma 1 of Buchholz et al. [24], we have

$$\ln p_{\mathbf{X}}^k(\mathbf{x}) - \ln p_{\mathbf{X}}^0(\mathbf{x}) = c_k - \frac{1}{2}\lambda_k^2 \cdot h_{\tau_k}^2(\mathbf{x}) + \eta_k \cdot \lambda_k \cdot h_{\tau_k}(\mathbf{x}) + \frac{1}{2}\langle h(\mathbf{x}), \mathbf{B}_{\tau_k}^0 \rangle^2 \tag{10.12}$$

for constants c_k, λ_k, and η_k that depend on $\mathbf{B}_{\tau_k}^k$ and $\mathbf{B}_{\tau_k}^0$, but not on $\mathbf{x}$. To learn this log-odds function, we consider a semiparametric function class of the same form. In particular, for vectors $\alpha, \beta, \gamma \in \mathbb{R}^K$, an upper-triangular matrix $\widehat{\mathbf{B}} \in \mathbb{R}^{n \times n}$, and a function $\widehat{h} : \mathbb{R}^d \to \mathbb{R}^n$, let $\ell(\cdot; \alpha, \beta, \gamma, \widehat{\mathbf{B}}, \widehat{h}) : \mathbb{R}^d \to \mathbb{R}^K$ have the following components:

$$\ell_k(\mathbf{x}; \alpha, \beta, \gamma, \widehat{\mathbf{B}}, \widehat{h}) := \alpha_k - \beta_k \cdot \widehat{h}_k^2(\mathbf{x}) + \gamma_k \cdot \beta_k \cdot \widehat{h}_k^2(\mathbf{x}) + \frac{1}{2}\langle \widehat{h}(\mathbf{x}), \widehat{\mathbf{B}}_k \rangle. \tag{10.13}$$

Finally, define a cross entropy-based loss function

$$\mathcal{L}_{\text{CE}}(\ell) := \sum_{k=1}^{K} \mathcal{L}_{\text{CE}}^k(\ell_k), \quad \text{where}$$
$$\mathcal{L}_{\text{CE}}^k(\ell_k) := -\frac{1}{2}\mathbb{E}_{\mathbf{X}\sim\mathbb{P}^0(\mathbf{X})}\left[\ln\left(\frac{1}{e^{\ell_k(\mathbf{X})}+1}\right)\right] - \frac{1}{2}\mathbb{E}_{\mathbf{X}\sim\mathbb{P}^k(\mathbf{X})}\left[\ln\left(\frac{e^{\ell_k(\mathbf{X})}}{e^{\ell_k(\mathbf{X})}+1}\right)\right].$$

If $\widehat{h}$ is parameterized as a neural network, then $\mathcal{L}_{\text{CE}}$ can be minimized using standard gradient-based techniques. Let $(\alpha^*, \beta^*, \gamma^*, \mathbf{B}^*, h^*)$ be a minimizer of $\mathcal{L}_{\text{CE}}$, and let $\mathcal{G}^*$ be the DAG associated with the sparsity pattern of $\mathbf{B}^*$; then we can return $(\mathcal{G}^*, h^*)$ as the final estimate. By the identifiability guarantee (Theorem 10.2), if this estimate matches the data-generating assumptions (e.g., latent Gaussianity), then it satisfies the associated equivalence relations.

10.5 CRL with General SCMs

In the previous section, we have shown that single-node interventions are sufficient to identify the latent model M if the underlying SCM S^M is a linear model. In this section, we consider *general* causal models where the underlying SCM S^M can be parametric or nonparametric. We present the results for three different settings: (i) linear mixing function with single-node interventions, (ii) linear mixing function with multi-node interventions, and (iii) general mixing function with two single-node interventions. Note that the last case represents the most general causal representation model since it does not impose any parametric assumptions on either the latent SCM or the mixing function.

Specifically, we develop a constructive *score-based* methodology using the score functions. First, for $k \in \{0, 1, \dots, K\}$, we denote the score functions associated with latent variables $\mathbf{Z}$ and observed variables $\mathbf{X}$ for the k-th environment by

$$s_{\mathbf{Z}}^k(\mathbf{z}) := \nabla_{\mathbf{z}} \log p_{\mathbf{Z}}^k(\mathbf{z}), \quad \text{and} \quad s_{\mathbf{X}}^k(\mathbf{x}) := \nabla_{\mathbf{x}} \log p_{\mathbf{X}}^k(\mathbf{x}), \tag{10.14}$$

where $k = 0$ denotes the observational environment with $\boldsymbol{T}(I^0) = \emptyset$. Note that changes across different latent $s_{\mathbf{Z}}^k$ functions are induced by the interventions on $\mathbf{Z}$. Using the factorization in Definition 10.5, we have

$$s_{\mathbf{Z}}^k(\mathbf{z}) = \sum_{i \in T(I^k)} \nabla_{\mathbf{z}} \log p_i^k(z_i \mid \mathbf{pa}(z_i)) + \sum_{i \in [n] \setminus T(I^k)} \nabla_{\mathbf{z}} \log p_j(z_j \mid \mathbf{pa}(z_j)). \tag{10.15}$$

Hence, $s_{\mathbf{Z}}^{0}$ and $s_{\mathbf{Z}}^{k}$ differ in only the causal mechanisms of the intervened nodes in $\boldsymbol{T}(I^k)$. These invariances will play a pivotal role in our algorithmic approaches, so we define the score difference functions as

$$d_{\mathbf{Z}}^{k}(\mathbf{z}) := s_{\mathbf{Z}}^{k}(\mathbf{z}) - s_{\mathbf{Z}}^{0}(\mathbf{z}), \quad \text{and} \quad d_{\mathbf{X}}^{k}(\mathbf{x}) := s_{\mathbf{X}}^{k}(\mathbf{x}) - s_{\mathbf{X}}^{0}(\mathbf{x}). \tag{10.16}$$

For a single-node intervention I^k with $\boldsymbol{T}(I^k) = \{i\}$, j-th coordinate of the score difference $d_{\mathbf{Z}}^{k}(\mathbf{z})$ becomes

$$\left(d_{\mathbf{Z}}^{k}(\mathbf{z})\right)_j = \frac{\partial}{\partial z_j} \log p_i^k(z_i \mid \mathbf{pa}(z_i)) - \frac{\partial}{\partial z_j} \log p_i(z_i \mid \mathbf{pa}(z_i)), \tag{10.17}$$

which is zero if $Z_j \notin \overline{\mathbf{pa}}(Z_i)$. The following lemma formalizes this sparsity property.

Lemma 10.1 ***(Score changes with respect to observational environment)***: *Consider k-th environment with unknown target $\mathbf{T}(I^k) = \{i\}$. If I^k is*

1. *a hard (perfect) intervention on any SCM or*
2. *a soft (imperfect) intervention on an additive noise model,*

then score difference function $d_{\mathbf{Z}}^{k}(\mathbf{Z})$ satisfies

$$\mathbb{E}\left[\left|d_{\mathbf{Z}}^{k}(\mathbf{Z})\right|_j\right] \neq 0 \quad \iff \quad j \in \overline{\mathbf{pa}}(i). \tag{10.18}$$

We note that $\Rightarrow$ direction is true for any SCM and the additive noise model assumption is used only for $\Leftarrow$ direction of soft interventions.

Lemma 10.1 provides the necessary and sufficient conditions for the invariance of the coordinates of the score functions of latent variables. The core idea of the score-based approach is that tracing these sparse changes guides finding reliable estimates for the inverse mixing function $h := g^{-1}$, which in turn facilitates estimating $\mathbf{Z}$. At a high level, we will search for the encoders $\widehat{h}$ such that the variations between the score functions of $\widehat{\mathbf{Z}}(\mathbf{X}; \widehat{h}) = \widehat{h}(\mathbf{X})$ will be similar to the true score variations given by Lemma 10.1. To emphasize the dependence on h, we denote the score functions associated with the pdfs of $\widehat{\mathbf{Z}}(\mathbf{X}; \widehat{h})$ under k-th environment by $s_{\widehat{\mathbf{Z}}}^{k}(\widehat{\mathbf{Z}}; \widehat{h})$ and define estimated latent score differences

$$d_{\widehat{\mathbf{Z}}}^{k}(\widehat{\mathbf{z}}; \widehat{h}) := s_{\widehat{\mathbf{Z}}}^{k}(\widehat{\mathbf{z}}; \widehat{h}) - s_{\widehat{\mathbf{Z}}}^{0}(\widehat{\mathbf{z}}; \widehat{h}), \qquad \forall k \in [n]. \tag{10.19}$$

However, the scores of the latent variables are not directly accessible since we only observe the variables $\mathbf{X}$. To circumvent this, we will leverage the connection between score functions of $\mathbf{X}$ and $\mathbf{Z}$. The next lemma establishes the relationship for *any* injective mapping f from latent to observed space, which we will customize to special use cases.

Lemma 10.2 (*Score Difference Transformation*): *Consider random vectors* $\mathbf{Y}, \mathbf{Y}' \in \mathbb{R}^r$ *and* $\mathbf{V}, \mathbf{V}' \in \mathbb{R}^n$ *that are related through* $\mathbf{Y} = f(\mathbf{V})$ *and* $\mathbf{Y}' = f(\mathbf{V}')$ *where* $r \geq n$ *and* $f : \mathbb{R}^n \to \mathbb{R}^r$ *is an injective and continuously differentiable function. Then, for* $\mathbf{y} = f(\mathbf{v})$, *the score functions are related as*

$$s_{\mathbf{V}}(\mathbf{v}) - s_{\mathbf{V}'}(\mathbf{v}) = \left(J_f(\mathbf{v})\right)^{\top} \cdot \left[s_{\mathbf{Y}}(\mathbf{y}) - s_{\mathbf{Y}'}(\mathbf{y})\right], \tag{10.20}$$

$$\text{and} \quad s_{\mathbf{Y}}(\mathbf{y}) - s_{\mathbf{Y}'}(\mathbf{y}) = \left(J_f(\mathbf{v})^{\dagger}\right)^{\top} \cdot \left[s_{\mathbf{V}}(\mathbf{v}) - s_{\mathbf{V}'}(\mathbf{v})\right]. \tag{10.21}$$

Equipped with these properties, we continue with our first setting for general latent SCMs.

10.5.1 Linear Mixing on General Latent SCMs

In this setting, we consider general (unconstrained) SCMs under a linear mixing function.[7] Recalling (10.9), we have $\mathbf{X} = \mathbf{G} \cdot \mathbf{Z}$, where $\mathbf{G} \in \mathbb{R}^{d \times n}$ is the *unknown* full-rank matrix mapping the latent variables to the observed ones, and $\mathbf{H} = \mathbf{G}^{\dagger}$. We consider one single-node intervention per node, formalized as $\mathcal{S}_{\text{single}}$ in Section 10.3.

We will present steps of leveraging the properties of the score functions to design **L**inear **S**core-based **Ca**usal **L**atent **E**stimation via **I**nterventions (LSCALE-I) algorithm to learn the latent variables **Z** and graph $\mathcal{G}$ up to identifiability classes introduced in Section 10.2.4.

First, to ensure that a single-node intervention sufficiently differentiates the target variable and its parents in the score function, we adopt the following regularity condition, which holds for a large class of models, including additive noise models under hard interventions [16, Lemma 2].

Assumption 1: For a single-node intervention I^k with $T(I^k) = \{i\}$, for all $j \in \mathbf{pa}(i)$, the term $\left(d_{\mathbf{z}}^k\right)_j / \left(d_{\mathbf{z}}^k\right)_i$ is not a constant function of **z**.

Theorem 10.3: *Assume the problem setting* $\mathcal{S}_{\text{single}}$ *and the mixing function g is linear. Then, there exists an algorithm that returns* $\mathcal{G}^*$ *and* $\mathbf{H}^*$ *such that*

i. ***Soft interventions:*** $\mathcal{G}^* \approx_{\text{an}} \mathcal{G}$ *and* $\mathbf{H}^* \approx_{\text{pa}} \mathbf{H}$, *i.e., we recover the latent graph up to transitive closure and the latent variables up to mixing with parents.*[8]
ii. ***Hard interventions:*** $\mathcal{G}^* \approx_{\text{iso}} \mathcal{G}$ *and* $\mathbf{H}^* \approx_{\text{scale}} \mathbf{H}$, *i.e., we recover the latent graph perfectly and the latent variables up to componentwise scaling.*

Furthermore, Algorithm 1 achieves these guarantees.

---

7 The results in this section are established in Varıcı et al. [16] and Acartürk et al. [7]. For brevity, here we focus on the methodology and the proof sketches.

8 This result holds without constraints on the latent SCM. For sufficiently nonlinear SCMs, soft interventions suffice to perfectly recover $\mathcal{G}^* \approx_{\text{iso}} \mathcal{G}$ [16, Theorem 2].

Summary: The rest of this section builds a constructive proof for Theorem 10.3. First, we scrutinize the properties of score functions under linear mixing. Using the column spaces of score difference correlations, we form an estimate of $\mathbf{H}$ that recovers each Z_i up to mixing with $\mathbf{pa}(Z_i)$. Then, using this estimate, we form a graph estimate $\mathcal{G}^*$ that recovers the transitive closure of $\mathcal{G}$. Finally, for hard interventions, we use Markov property to refine these results and achieve component-wise scaling and perfect graph recovery.

Score Differences for Linear Transformation: For the linear mixing function $\mathbf{G}$, Jacobian $J_{\mathbf{G}}(\mathbf{z})$ is independent of $\mathbf{z}$ and equal to matrix $\mathbf{G}$. Hence, for linear transformation $\mathbf{X} = \mathbf{G} \cdot \mathbf{Z}$, using Lemma 10.2 we have

$$d^k_{\mathbf{X}}(\mathbf{x}) = \mathbf{H}^\top \cdot d^k_{\mathbf{Z}}(\mathbf{z}) \,. \tag{10.22}$$

Denote the correlation matrices for $d^k_{\mathbf{X}}$ and $d^k_{\mathbf{Z}}$ by

$$\mathbf{R}^k_{\mathbf{X}} := \mathbb{E}\big[d^k_{\mathbf{X}}(\mathbf{x}) \cdot (d^k_{\mathbf{X}}(\mathbf{x}))^\top\big] \quad \text{and} \quad \mathbf{R}^k_{\mathbf{Z}} := \mathbb{E}\big[d^k_{\mathbf{Z}}(\mathbf{z}) \cdot (d^k_{\mathbf{Z}}(\mathbf{z}))^\top\big]. \tag{10.23}$$

This implies $\mathbf{R}^k_{\mathbf{X}} = \mathbf{H}^\top \cdot \mathbf{R}^k_{\mathbf{Z}} \cdot \mathbf{H}$. The next lemma specifies that the structure of the column space of correlation matrix $\mathbf{R}^k_{\mathbf{X}}$ is heavily constrained by the true encoder $\mathbf{H}$, the graph $\mathcal{G}$, and the intervention target τ_k in k-th environment.

Lemma 10.3: *For any $k \in [n]$, $\text{col}(\mathbf{R}^k_{\mathbf{X}}) \subseteq \text{span}\{(\mathbf{H}_i)^\top \ : \ i \in \overline{\mathbf{pa}}(\tau_k)\}$.*

Proof. Using (10.17), we know that $(d^k_{\mathbf{Z}}(\mathbf{z}))_i = 0$ for $i \notin \overline{\mathbf{pa}}(\tau_k)$. Then, using (10.22), we have $d^k_{\mathbf{X}}(\mathbf{x}) = \sum_{i \in \overline{\mathbf{pa}}(\tau_k)} (\mathbf{H}_i)^\top \cdot (d^k_{\mathbf{Z}}(\mathbf{z}))_i \in \text{span}\{(\mathbf{H}_i)^\top \ : \ i \in \overline{\mathbf{pa}}(\tau_k)\}$. Since this holds for any $\mathbf{x} \in \text{col}(\mathbf{G})$, we have

$$\text{span}\{\, d^k_{\mathbf{X}}(\mathbf{x}) \ : \ \mathbf{x} \in \text{col}(\mathbf{G}) \,\} \subseteq \text{span}\{\, (\mathbf{H}_i)^\top \ : \ i \in \overline{\mathbf{pa}}(\tau_k) \,\}. \tag{10.24}$$

Noting that $\text{span}\{d^k_{\mathbf{X}}(\mathbf{x}) \ : \ \mathbf{x} \in \text{col}(\mathbf{G})\} = \text{col}(\mathbf{R}^k_{\mathbf{X}})$ concludes the proof. □

Encoder Estimation: In Step 1 of Algorithm 1, we estimate rows of the encoder using column spaces of $(\mathbf{R}^k_{\mathbf{X}})_{k \in [n]}$. Using Lemma 10.3, for any $\mathbf{h} \in \text{col}(\mathbf{R}^k_{\mathbf{X}})$, we have $\mathbf{h} \in \text{span}\{(\mathbf{H}_i)^\top \ : \ i \in \overline{\mathbf{pa}}(\tau_k)\}$. This means any $\mathbf{h} \in \text{col}(\mathbf{R}^k_{\mathbf{X}})$ can be expressed as

$$\mathbf{h} = \sum_{i \in \overline{\mathbf{pa}}(\tau_k)} c_i \cdot (\mathbf{H}_i)^\top, \tag{10.25}$$

for some constants $\{c_i \ : \ i \in \overline{\mathbf{pa}}(\tau_k)\}$. Then, using $\mathbf{H}_i \cdot \mathbf{G} = \mathbf{e}_i$, i-th standard basis vector, we have $(\mathbf{h}^\top \cdot \mathbf{G})_i = c_i$ for $i \in \overline{\mathbf{pa}}(\tau_k)$, and 0 otherwise. Also note that by picking $\mathbf{y}$ uniformly at random from unit sphere $\mathbb{S}^{d-1} \subset \mathbb{R}^d$ and letting $\mathbf{h} = \mathbf{R}^k_{\mathbf{X}} \cdot \mathbf{y}$, the coefficient $c_{\tau_k} \neq 0$ almost surely. Therefore, for the output $\mathbf{H}^*$ of Step 1 in Algorithm 1, we have

$$\hat{\mathbf{Z}}(\mathbf{X}; \mathbf{H}^*) = \mathbf{P}_\tau \cdot \mathbf{C}_{\text{pa}} \cdot \mathbf{Z} \tag{10.26}$$

for some $\mathbf{C}_{\text{pa}} \in \mathbb{R}^{n \times n}$ with nonzero diagonal entries and $(\mathbf{C}_{\text{pa}})_{i,j} = 0$ for all $j \notin \overline{\text{pa}}(i)$. Hence, we have identified $\mathbf{Z}$ up to mixing with parents.

Algorithm 1 Linear Score-based Causal Latent Estimation via Interventions (LSCALE-I)

Input: $\mathbf{R}_{\mathbf{X}}^k$ for all $m \in [n]$ ▷ compute using (10.23)

Step 1: Encoder estimation

$\mathbf{H}^* \leftarrow \mathbf{0}_{n \times d}$

for $k \in (1, \dots, n)$ **do**

  Pick $\mathbf{y} \in \mathbb{S}^{d-1}$ uniformly at random, set $\mathbf{h} \leftarrow \mathbf{R}_{\mathbf{X}}^k \cdot \mathbf{y}$

  $\mathbf{H}_k^* \leftarrow \mathbf{h}^\top$

Step 2: Latent graph estimation

Construct latent DAG estimate $\mathcal{G}^*$ according to

$$\mathbf{pa}_{\mathcal{G}^*}(k) := \left\{ i \neq k : \mathbb{E}\left[\left| d_{\hat{\mathbf{Z}}}^k(\hat{\mathbf{Z}}; \mathbf{H}^*) \right|_i \right] \neq 0 \right\}, \quad \forall k \in [n]$$

$\mathcal{G}^* \leftarrow \text{trc}(\mathcal{G}^*)$

---

if the interventions are hard **then**

  Step 3: Unmixing procedure

  $\pi \leftarrow$ a topological order of $\mathcal{G}^*$

  for $k \in (1, \dots, n)$ **do** ▷ refine rows of $\mathbf{H}^*$ sequentially

    $\hat{\mathbf{Z}} \leftarrow \hat{\mathbf{Z}}^{\pi_k}(\mathbf{X}; \mathbf{H}^*)$

    $\mathbf{u} \leftarrow -\text{Cov}(\hat{\mathbf{Z}}_k, \hat{\mathbf{Z}}_{\mathbf{pa}_{\mathcal{G}^*}(k)}) \cdot \left(\text{Cov}(\hat{\mathbf{Z}}_{\mathbf{pa}_{\mathcal{G}^*}(k)})\right)^{-1}$

    $\mathbf{H}_{\pi_k}^* \leftarrow \mathbf{H}_{\pi_k}^* + \mathbf{u} \cdot \mathbf{H}_{\mathbf{pa}_{\mathcal{G}^*}(k)}^*$

  Refine $\mathcal{G}^*$ according to

$$\mathbf{pa}_{\mathcal{G}^*}(k) := \left\{ i \neq k : \mathbb{E}\left[\left| d_{\hat{\mathbf{Z}}}^k(\hat{\mathbf{Z}}; \mathbf{H}^*) \right|_i \right] \neq 0 \right\}, \quad \forall k \in [n]$$

Return $\mathcal{G}^*$, $\mathbf{H}^*$, and $\hat{\mathbf{Z}}$

Latent Graph Estimation: Next, we use the encoder estimate $\mathbf{H}^*$ for recovering the transitive closure of latent graph $\mathcal{G}$. Since we are interested in recovering $\mathcal{G}$ up to isomorphism, for simplicity, let $T(I^k) = k$ and also let $d^k_{\hat{\mathbf{Z}}}$ denote $d^k_{\hat{\mathbf{Z}}}(\hat{\mathbf{Z}}; \mathbf{H}^*)$. Motivated by Lemma 10.1, we form $\mathcal{G}^*$ with parent sets

$$\mathbf{pa}_{\mathcal{G}^*}(k) := \left\{ i \neq k : \mathbb{E}\left[\left| d^k_{\hat{\mathbf{Z}}} \right|_i \right] \neq 0 \right\}. \tag{10.27}$$

Note that $\left(\mathbf{C}_{\text{pa}}\right)_{i,j} = 0$ for all $j \notin \overline{\mathbf{pa}}(i)$ implies that $\left(\mathbf{C}_{\text{pa}}^{-\top}\right)_{i,j} = 0$ for all $j \notin \overline{\mathbf{de}}(i)$. Then, using Lemma 10.2 and (10.26), we have

$$\left(d^k_{\hat{\mathbf{Z}}}\right)_i = \left(\mathbf{C}_{\text{pa}}^{-\top}\right)_i \cdot d^k_{\mathbf{Z}} = \sum_{j \in \overline{\mathbf{de}}(i) \cap \overline{\mathbf{pa}}(k)} \left(\mathbf{C}_{\text{pa}}^{-\top}\right)_{i,j} \cdot \left(d^k_{\mathbf{Z}}\right)_j. \tag{10.28}$$

Subsequently, $\mathbb{E}\left[\left| d^k_{\hat{\mathbf{Z}}} \right|_i \right] \neq 0$ implies that $\overline{\mathbf{de}}(i) \cap \overline{\mathbf{pa}}(k) \neq \emptyset$, and $i \in \overline{\mathbf{an}}(k)$. Therefore, we have $\mathbf{pa}_{\mathcal{G}^*}(k) \subseteq \overline{\mathbf{an}}(k)$, and $\text{trc}(\mathcal{G})$ is a supergraph of $\mathcal{G}^*$. Next, let $i \rightarrow k$ be an edge in the transitive reduction of $\mathcal{G}$, i.e., there is no other directed path between i and k in $\mathcal{G}$. This implies that $\overline{\mathbf{de}}(i) \cap \overline{\mathbf{pa}}(k) = \{i, k\}$, and (10.28) becomes $\left(d^k_{\hat{\mathbf{Z}}}\right)_i = \left(\mathbf{C}_{\text{pa}}^{-\top}\right)_{i,i} \cdot \left(d^k_{\mathbf{Z}}\right)_i + \left(\mathbf{C}_{\text{pa}}^{-\top}\right)_{i,k} \cdot \left(d^k_{\mathbf{Z}}\right)_k$. Assumption 1 ensures that $\left(d^k_{\hat{\mathbf{Z}}}\right)_i$ is not constantly zero. Then, $\mathcal{G}^*$ preserves all the edges in the transitive reduction of $\mathcal{G}$, and taking the transitive closure of $\mathcal{G}^*$ gives us the transitive closure of $\mathcal{G}$, up to relabeling of the nodes.

Unmixing Procedure for Hard Interventions: Hard interventions can be leveraged to establish stronger identifiability guarantees. This is because a hard intervention I^k with $T(I^k) = \{i\}$ ensures that the Z_i loses its functional dependence on $\mathbf{pa}(Z_i)$. Then, for the k-th environment,

$$Z^k_i \perp\!\!\!\perp Z^k_j, \quad \forall j \notin \overline{\mathbf{de}}(i). \tag{10.29}$$

This is due to the Markov property, which states that each variable in a DAG is independent of its nondescendants given its parents. Motivated by this observation, we aim to update rows of the encoder estimate $\mathbf{H}^*$ to remove effects of $\mathbf{pa}(Z_i)$ on $\hat{Z}_i$.

Note that (10.29) provides us with random variable pairs that are supposed to be independent in k-th environment. In Step 3 of Algorithm 1, for each row of $\mathbf{H}^*$, we use covariance as a surrogate of independence and compute an unmixing vector $\mathbf{u}$ by making covariances of those random variables pairs zero. Finally, for the perfect DAG recovery, we compute the latent score differences under the final encoder estimate and construct the graph $\mathcal{G}^*$ with parent sets

$$\mathbf{pa}_{\mathcal{G}^*}(k) := \left\{ i \neq k : \mathbb{E}\left[\left| d^k_{\hat{\mathbf{Z}}}(\hat{\mathbf{Z}}; \mathbf{H}^*) \right|_i \right] \neq 0 \right\}, \quad \forall k \in [n]. \tag{10.30}$$

10.5.2 Multi-node Interventions

In this section, we extend the results for linear mixing functions on general latent SCMs to the setting of unknown multi-node interventions [25]. Despite strong identifiability and algorithmic results, single-node interventions $\mathcal{S}_{\text{single}}$ can be restrictive in certain CRL applications, such as biology and robotics, where the subset of nodes intervened in an intervention environment can be *unknown*. For instance, biological perturbations in genomics often result in imperfect interventions with off-target effects on other genes [14, 30], or interventions in robotics applications typically affect multiple causal variables [31]. Thus, fulfilling the potential of CRL requires moving beyond the assumption of single-node interventions. In this section, we address this challenge by considering the $\mathcal{S}_{\text{int}}$ setting under additional minor assumptions and define the multi-node interventional CRL setting as follows.

Problem setting *($\mathcal{S}_{\text{multi}}$ – Multi-node interventions)*: Consider interventional CRL problem setting $\mathcal{S}_{\text{int}}$ with unknown intervention targets. Suppose that interventions with overlapping targets share the same interventional mechanisms for the intervened nodes, i.e., for $i \in \boldsymbol{T}(I^k) \cap \boldsymbol{T}(I^j)$, we have $p_i^k(z_i \mid \mathbf{pa}(z_i)) = p_i^j(z_i \mid \mathbf{pa}(z_i))$, which we denote by $p_i^*(z_i \mid \mathbf{pa}(z_i))$.

We define the *intervention signature matrix* $\mathbf{E}_{\text{int}} \in \{0, 1\}^{n \times K}$ to compactly represent the intervention targets in each environment as

$$(\mathbf{E}_{\text{int}})_{i,k} = \mathbb{1}\{i \in \boldsymbol{T}(I^k)\}, \quad \forall i \in [n], \quad \forall k \in [K]. \tag{10.31}$$

The k-th column of $\mathbf{E}_{\text{int}}$ lists the indices of the intervention targets $\boldsymbol{T}(I^k)$, which we refer to as the *intervention vector* of k-th environment. Ensuring identifiability inevitably imposes restrictions on the structure of $\mathbf{E}_{\text{int}}$. We impose the mild condition that $\mathbf{E}_{\text{int}}$ has sufficiently diverse columns.

Assumption 2 *(Diverse multi-node interventions)*: Intervention signature matrix $\mathbf{E}_{\text{int}}$ has full row rank, i.e., it contains n linearly independent intervention vectors.

Assumption 3 *(Intervention regularity)*: We say that an interventions are *regular* if for every possible triplet (i, j, c) where $i \in [n]$, $j \in \mathbf{pa}(i)$ and $c \in \mathbb{Q}$, the following ratio cannot be a constant function in $\mathbf{z}$

$$\frac{\partial}{\partial z_j}\left(\log \frac{p_i(z_i \mid \mathbf{pa}(z_i))}{p_i^*(z_i \mid \mathbf{pa}(z_i))} + c \cdot \log \frac{p_j(z_j \mid \mathbf{pa}(z_j))}{p_j^*(z_j \mid \mathbf{pa}(z_j))}\right)\left(\frac{\partial}{\partial z_i} \log \frac{p_i(z_i \mid \mathbf{pa}(z_i))}{p_i^*(z_i \mid \mathbf{pa}(z_i))}\right)^{-1}. \tag{10.32}$$

Assumption 3 is the extension of Assumption 1 in $\mathcal{S}_{\text{single}}$ setting to $\mathcal{S}_{\text{multi}}$. Essentially, $\frac{\partial}{\partial z_j} \log \frac{p_i}{p_i^*}(z_i \mid \mathbf{pa}(z_i))$ captures the effect of intervening on Z_i on the *score* associated with Z_j. Hence, Assumption 3 ensures that the effect of a multi-node intervention is not the same on the scores associated with different variables. Under these conditions, we present our main result.[9]

Theorem 10.4: *Assume the problem setting $\mathcal{S}_{\text{multi}}$, mixing function g is linear, and $\mathcal{S}_{\text{multi}}$ satisfies Assumptions 2 and 3. Then, there exists an algorithm that returns $\mathcal{G}^*$ and $\mathbf{H}^*$ such that*

i. ***Soft interventions:*** *$\mathcal{G}^* \approx_{\text{an}} \mathcal{G}$ and $\mathbf{H}^* \approx_{\text{an}} \mathbf{H}$, i.e., we recover the latent graph up to transitive closure and the latent variables up to mixing with ancestors.*
ii. ***Hard interventions:*** *$\mathcal{G}^* \approx_{\text{iso}} \mathcal{G}$ and $\mathbf{H}^* \approx_{\text{scale}} \mathbf{H}$, i.e., we recover the latent graph perfectly and the latent variables up to componentwise scaling.*

Key Idea: To solve CRL in $\mathcal{S}_{\text{multi}}$ setting and prove Theorem 10.4, our central algorithmic idea is to aggregate multi-node interventional environments (with *unknown* targets) in a way that creates new distinct environments, making the inherent sparsity properties more accessible. Intuitively, if we can reconstruct the score differences for any desired hypothetical set of intervention targets, then $\mathcal{S}_{\text{multi}}$ setting becomes similar to $\mathcal{S}_{\text{single}}$, allowing us to adopt the proof techniques from Section 10.5.1. To achieve this, we first obtain *basis score difference functions* that we will use to create sparser interventions.

Basis Score Differences: Note that $\mathbf{E}_{\text{int}}$ has K columns, n of which are linearly independent. We can show that linearly independent columns of $\mathbf{E}_{\text{int}}$ exactly correspond to the linearly independent score differences $d^k_{\mathbf{X}}$, which can be identified among all $(d^k_{\mathbf{X}})_{k\in[K]}$. Without loss of generality, we assume that the first n columns of $\mathbf{E}_{\text{int}}$ are linearly independent and define *basis intervention matrix* $\mathbf{E} \in \{0, 1\}^{n\times n}$ using these columns as $\mathbf{E}_{:,k} := (\mathbf{E}_{\text{int}})_{:,k}$ for all $k \in [n]$. As such, $(d^k_{\mathbf{X}})_{k\in[n]}$ are linearly independent and serve as *basis score difference* functions. In other words, these score differences are sufficient to reconstruct the remaining unavailable score difference functions, e.g., those of single-node interventions. We stack these basis score differences to construct the matrix-valued function $\Delta\mathbf{S}_X := \left[d^1_{\mathbf{X}}, \dots, d^n_{\mathbf{X}}\right]$. Using the fact that $d^k_{\mathbf{X}}(\mathbf{x}) = \mathbf{H}^\top \cdot d^k_{\mathbf{Z}}(\mathbf{z})$ for score differences $d^k_{\mathbf{X}}(\mathbf{x})$ and $d^k_{\mathbf{Z}}(\mathbf{z})$ defined in (10.16), we have

$$d^k_{\mathbf{X}}(\mathbf{x}) = \mathbf{H}^\top \cdot \sum_{i\in T(I^k)} \nabla \log \frac{p^*_i(z_i \mid \mathbf{pa}(z_i))}{p_i(z_i \mid \mathbf{pa}(z_i))} . \tag{10.33}$$

Quest for Sparse Interventions: We describe the preliminary step of creating new interventional environments with desired sparsity properties. Note that $\Delta\mathbf{S}_X \cdot \mathbf{w}$ is essentially a combination of score differences of single-node interventions via

9 Adapted from Varıcı et al. [25, Theorem 3, 6, and Algorithm 1].

(10.33). Also, the image of $\nabla \log \frac{p_i}{p_i^*}(z_i \mid \mathbf{pa}(z_i))$ is a one-dimensional subspace if and only if the intervened variable Z_i has no parents. Hence, by searching for an integer-valued $\mathbf{w}$ that makes $\mathrm{im}(\Delta \mathbf{S}_\mathbf{X} \cdot \mathbf{w})$ a one-dimensional subspace, we can create a *single source node* intervention, without knowing the intervention matrix $\mathbf{E}$. Also note that using Lemma 10.3 and (10.33), any column vector $\mathbf{h}$ chosen from the image of $\Delta \mathbf{S}_\mathbf{X} \cdot \mathbf{w}$ is a scalar factor of $(\mathbf{H}_i)^\top$.

Motivated by this observation, step $t = 1$ of Algorithm 2 exactly performs this operation. For each subsequent step, we search for $\mathbf{w}$ such that the projection of $\Delta \mathbf{S}_\mathbf{X} \cdot \mathbf{w}$ onto the nullspace of previously recovered subspaces is a one-dimensional subspace. This projection is required to ensure that the subspace of the newly created $\mathrm{im}(\Delta \mathbf{S}_\mathbf{X})$ will be different from the previous ones. The final question is how to construct a finite search space for $\mathbf{w}$? By investigating the range of entries of $\mathbf{E}^{-1}$, we can show that the set $\mathcal{W} := \{-\kappa, \dots, +\kappa\}^n$ is guaranteed to contain such $\mathbf{w}$ vectors, where κ denotes the maximum determinant of a matrix in $\{0,1\}^{(n-1)\times(n-1)}$.

After performing Algorithm 2, we effectively obtain a new intervention matrix $\mathbf{E}^* := \mathbf{E} \cdot \mathbf{W}$, which is upper triangular. Specifically, we know the support of $\mathbf{E}^*$ (but not its specific entries). Having these structured interventions instead of a fully unknown case, we can continue our search to create sparser interventions and further refine $\mathbf{E}^*$ to reflect ancestral relationships in $\mathcal{G}$, that is $\mathbb{1}(\mathbf{E}^*_{i,j} \neq 0) = \mathbb{1}(i \in \overline{\mathbf{an}}(j))$. Once we have this property, we can modify the steps of Algorithm 1 to achieve the identifiability results in Theorem 10.4 Varıcı et al. [16, Algorithm 1].

Algorithm 2 Unknown Multi-node Interventional CRL – Preliminary step

---

Input: Samples of $\mathbf{X}$ under $\mathcal{S}_{\text{multi}}$ setting.
Choose basis score differences and construct $\Delta \mathbf{S}_\mathbf{X}$
for $t \in (1, \dots, n)$ **do**
    for $\mathbf{w} \in \mathcal{W}$ **do**
        $\mathcal{V} \leftarrow \mathrm{proj}_{\mathrm{null}(\{\mathbf{H}_i^* \,:\, i \in [t-1]\})} \mathrm{im}(\Delta \mathbf{S}_X \cdot \mathbf{w})$
        if $\dim(\mathcal{V}) = 1$ **then**
            pick $\mathbf{v} \in \mathrm{im}(\Delta \mathbf{S}_X \cdot \mathbf{w}) \setminus \mathrm{span}(\{(\mathbf{H}_i^*)^\top : i \in [t-1]\})$
            $(\mathbf{W})_{:,t} \leftarrow \mathbf{w}$ and $\mathbf{H}_t^* \leftarrow \mathbf{v}^\top / \| \mathbf{v}^\top \|_2$
            break
Return mixing matrix $\mathbf{W}$

10.5.3 General Mixing on General Latent SCMs

In this setting, we consider general mixing functions without any parametric assumption.[10] In the previous sections, we exploited the linear parameterization

10 The results in this section are established in Varıcı et al. [26] and Varıcı et al. [16].

of g and sequentially recovered the parameters of the inverse mixing function h using *one* intervention per node. However, for *general* mixing functions (parametric or nonparametric), this parametric approach is no longer applicable. To address this and design the general CRL algorithm, we incorporate additional information by using *two* interventions per node, formalized as follows.

Problem setting (*$\mathcal{S}_{2-\text{single}}$ – Two single-node interventions per node*): Consider interventional CRL problem setting $\mathcal{S}_{\text{int}}$. Suppose that we have two single-node interventions per node. Specifically, for every $k \in [n]$, we have environments k and $\widetilde{k}$ with interventions I^k and $\widetilde{I}^k$, respectively, where $\boldsymbol{T}(I^k) = \boldsymbol{T}(\widetilde{I}^k) = \{\tau_k\}$ and τ is a permutation of $\{1, \dots, n\}$.

Remark 10.2: In $\mathcal{S}_{2-\text{single}}$, for the sake of presentation, we know which two environments target the same node (without knowing the actual target). However, this assumption is not necessary for the results presented in this chapter. The alternative case, where the matching of interventional environments is unknown, is referred to as the *uncoupled* setting. The coupling problem can be solved concurrently with the CRL problem [26, Theorem 1].

For $\mathcal{S}_{2-\text{single}}$ being more informative than $\mathcal{S}_{\text{single}}$, we assume that the effects of the I^k and $\widetilde{I}^k$ on the target variable are sufficiently distinct. This is formalized by *interventional discrepancy* between the two causal mechanisms.

Assumption 4 (*Interventional Discrepancy*): Consider hard interventions I^k and $\widetilde{I}^k$ such that $\boldsymbol{T}(I^k) = \boldsymbol{T}(\widetilde{I}^k) = \{i\}$. These two interventions satisfy interventional discrepancy if $\frac{\partial}{\partial z_i} \frac{p_i^k(z_i)}{\widetilde{p}_i^k(z_i)} \neq 0$ almost everywhere.

We note that Assumption 4 is a mild condition. For instance, two univariate distinct Gaussians trivially satisfy this condition.[11] Under this mild assumption, we give our main result.

Theorem 10.5: *Assume the problem setting $\mathcal{S}_{2-\text{single}}$ and interventions satisfy Assumption 4. Then, there exists an algorithm that returns $\mathcal{G}^*$ and h^* such that $\mathcal{G}^* \approx_{\text{iso}} \mathcal{G}$ and $h^* \approx_{\text{cmp}} h$, i.e., we recover the latent graph perfectly and the latent variables up to componentwise diffeomorphisms. Furthermore, Algorithm 3 achieves these guarantees.*

The rest of this section presents the constructive proof sketch for Theorem 10.5, steps of which are summarized in Algorithm 3.

11 Liang et al. [32] also show that, even when the latent graph $\mathcal{G}$ is known, interventional discrepancy is necessary for identifiability in $\mathcal{S}_{\text{single}}$.

Sparsity Structure: In contrast to the linear mixing case, the estimated and true latent score differences are *not* always related by a constant matrix for general mixing functions. To circumvent this issue using the power of two interventions per node, we refine Lemma 10.1 to compare two single-node interventions.

Lemma 10.4: *Consider two environments with single-node hard interventions such that $\boldsymbol{T}(I^k) = \boldsymbol{T}(\tilde{I}^k) = \{i\}$. If I^k and $\tilde{I}^k$ are different intervention mechanisms, that is $p_i^k(Z_i) \neq \tilde{p}_i^k(Z_i)$, then $\mathbb{E}\left[\left|s_{\mathbf{Z}}^k(\mathbf{Z}) - \tilde{s}_{\mathbf{Z}}^k(\mathbf{Z})\right|_j\right] \neq 0 \iff j = i$.*

Lemma 10.4 shows that the score difference between coupled interventions is one-sparse. Subsequently, the key idea for identifying the encoder is that the changes between the score $s_{\hat{\mathbf{Z}}}^k(\hat{\mathbf{z}}; \hat{h})$ and $\tilde{s}_{\hat{\mathbf{Z}}}^k(\hat{\mathbf{z}}; \hat{h})$ should match the sparsity structure for those under the true encoder h. To formalize, we define score change matrix $\mathbf{D}(\hat{h})$ for each encoder $\hat{h} \in \mathcal{H}$ with entries

$$\left(\mathbf{D}(\hat{h})\right)_{i,k} := \mathbb{E}\left[\,\left|s_{\hat{\mathbf{Z}}}^k(\hat{\mathbf{Z}}; \hat{h}) - \tilde{s}_{\hat{\mathbf{Z}}}^k(\hat{\mathbf{Z}}; \hat{h})\right|_i\,\right]. \tag{10.34}$$

Since the only varying causal mechanism between k-th and $\tilde{k}$-th environments is the intervened node $\boldsymbol{T}(I^k) = \boldsymbol{T}(\tilde{I}^k) = \{\tau_k\}$, Lemma 10.4 gives that $\left(\mathbf{D}(h)\right)_{i,k} \neq 0$ if and only if $i = \tau_k$. Therefore, $\mathbb{1}\{\mathbf{D}(h)\}$ is a permutation matrix $\mathbb{1}\{\mathbf{D}(h)\} = \mathbf{P}_\tau^\top$. We leverage this property to identify the encoder.

Identifying the Encoder: At the first step of Algorithm 3, we select $h^* \in \mathcal{H}$ such that $\mathbf{D}(h^*)$ is a diagonal matrix. We show that such h^* achieves the identifiability guarantees in Theorem 10.5 as follows. First, using Lemma 10.2 for $f = (h^* \circ g)^{-1}$ and Lemma 10.4, the entries of $\mathbf{D}(h^*)$ can be written as

$$\begin{aligned}
\left(\mathbf{D}(h^*)\right)_{i,k} &= \mathbb{E}\left[\left|\left(J_f^\top(\mathbf{Z})\right)_i \cdot \left(s_{\mathbf{Z}}^k(\mathbf{Z}) - \tilde{s}_{\mathbf{Z}}^k(\mathbf{Z})\right)\right|\right] &(10.35)\\
&= \mathbb{E}\left[\left|\left(J_f(\mathbf{Z})\right)_{\tau_k,i} \cdot \left(s_{\mathbf{Z}}^k(\mathbf{Z}) - \tilde{s}_{\mathbf{Z}}^k(\mathbf{Z})\right)_{\tau_k}\right|\right], \quad \forall \quad i,k \in [n]. &(10.36)
\end{aligned}$$

Next, using the Assumption 4, we know that $(s_{\mathbf{Z}}^k(\mathbf{z}))_{\tau_k} \neq (\tilde{s}_{\mathbf{Z}}^k(\mathbf{z}))_{\tau_k}$ almost everywhere. This implies that, if $\left(J_f(\mathbf{z})\right)_{\tau_k,i}$ is nonzero over a nonzero-measure set within $\mathbb{R}^n$, then we have $\left(\mathbf{D}(h^*)\right)_{i,k} \neq 0$. Therefore, since $\mathbf{D}(h^*)$ is a diagonal matrix, for all $i \neq k$ we have that $\left(J_f(\mathbf{z})\right)_{\tau_k,i} = 0$ on a set of measure 1. Since J_f is a continuous function, this implies that $\left(J_f(\mathbf{z})\right)_{\tau_k,i} = 0$ for all $i \neq k$, and $\mathbf{z} \in \mathbb{R}^n$. Finally, since $f = (h^* \circ g)^{-1}$ is a diffeomorphism, $J_f(\mathbf{z})$ is full-rank for all $\mathbf{z} \in \mathbb{R}^n$, which implies $\left(J_f(\mathbf{z})\right)_{\tau_k,k} \neq 0$ for all $k \in [n]$ and $\mathbf{z} \in \mathbb{R}^n$. This implies that each $\hat{\mathbf{Z}}_k$ is a function of only $\mathbf{Z}_{\tau_k}$, and $\hat{\mathbf{Z}} = h^*(\mathbf{X}) = f^{-1}(\mathbf{Z})$ satisfies componentwise identifiability specified in Definition 10.2.

Algorithm 3 Generalized Score-based Causal Latent Estimation via Interventions (GSCALE-I)

Input: $\mathcal{H}$, samples of $\mathbf{X}$ under $\mathcal{S}_{2-\text{single}}$
Compute score functions: $s_{\mathbf{X}}$, $s^k_{\mathbf{X}}$, and $\tilde{s}^k_{\mathbf{X}}$ for all $k \in [n]$.

Stage 1: Identifying the encoder
Select a solution $h^* \in \mathcal{H}$ such that $\mathbf{D}(h^*)$ is diagonal.
Latent estimates: $\hat{\mathbf{Z}} = h^*(\mathbf{X})$.

Stage 2: Latent DAG recovery: Construct $\mathcal{G}^*$ according to

$$\mathbf{pa}_{\mathcal{G}^*}(k) := \left\{ i \neq k : \mathbb{E}\left[\left| d^k_{\hat{\mathbf{Z}}}(\hat{\mathbf{Z}}; h^*) \right|_i \right] \neq 0 \right\}, \quad \forall k \in [n] .$$

return $h^*, \mathcal{G}^*$, and $\hat{\mathbf{Z}}$.

Latent DAG Recovery: The latent graph recovery for general transformations is similar to that for linear transformations. In particular, using Lemma 10.1 for all $i, k \in [n]$ we have $\mathbb{E}\left[\left| d^k_{\mathbf{Z}}(\mathbf{Z}) \right|_i \right] \neq 0$ if and only if $i \in \overline{\mathbf{pa}}(\tau_k)$. Hence, after finding an encoder h^* that makes $\mathbf{D}(h^*)$ a diagonal matrix, we compute the score differences $d^k_{\hat{\mathbf{Z}}}(\hat{\mathbf{Z}}; h^*)$, and construct $\mathcal{G}^*$ with the following the parent sets

$$\mathbf{pa}_{\mathcal{G}^*}(k) := \left\{ i \neq k : \mathbb{E}\left[\left| d^k_{\hat{\mathbf{Z}}}(\hat{\mathbf{Z}}; h^*) \right|_i \right] \neq 0 \right\}, \quad \forall k \in [n]. \tag{10.37}$$

Since $\hat{\mathbf{Z}}_k$ is a function of $\mathbf{Z}_{\tau_k}$, $\mathcal{G}^*$ is related to the true latent graph $\mathcal{G}$ by a graph isomorphism with permutation τ.

10.6 Experiments

Throughout the chapter, we often emphasized the algorithmic aspect of the presented results, that is our identifiability results come with feasible algorithms. In this section, we provide a brief demonstration of the provided CRL algorithms. In particular, we present two cases: (i) $\mathcal{S}_{\text{single}}$ on linear mixing functions and (ii) $\mathcal{S}_{2-\text{single}}$ on high-dimensional image data.

Evaluation Metrics: We use the following metrics to evaluate the accuracy of the CRL algorithms to recover the latent graph $\mathcal{G}$ and latent variables $\mathbf{Z}$. For each metric, we will report the mean and standard error over multiple runs.

- **Structural Hamming distance** (SHD) captures the number of edge operations (add, delete, flip) needed to transform the estimate $\mathcal{G}^*$ to true $\mathcal{G}$.

- **Mean correlation coefficient** (MCC) measures the linear correlations between $\widehat{\mathbf{Z}}$ and $\mathbf{Z}$, which is a standard metric for CRL [33]. Since the recovery of latent variables is up to permutations, it is reported for the best-matching permutation of components,

$$\mathrm{MCC}(\mathbf{Z}, \widehat{\mathbf{Z}}) \triangleq \max_{\pi} \frac{1}{n} \sum_{i \in [n]} \mathrm{corr}(Z_i, \widehat{Z}_{\pi_i}). \tag{10.38}$$

10.6.1 Linear Mixing with Synthetic Data

We adopt single-node intervention setting $\mathcal{S}_{\text{single}}$ under a linear mixing function and evaluate the performance of Algorithm 1.

Data Generation: We generate $\mathcal{G}$ using Erdős-Rényi model with density 0.5 and $|\mathbf{Z}| = n = 5$ nodes, consider target dimension values $|\mathbf{X}| = d \in \{5, 25, 100\}$, and generate 100 latent graphs for each d value. For causal mechanisms, we adopt a linear Gaussian SCM with $\mathbf{Z} = \mathbf{W}\mathbf{Z} + \Omega^{1/2}\varepsilon$, where the nonzero edge weights of $\mathbf{W}$ are sampled from Unif($\pm$[0.5, 1.5]) and diagonal entries of Ω are sampled from Unif([0.5, 1.5]) and $\mathrm{Cov}(\varepsilon) = \mathbf{I}_n$. A hard intervention on Z_i sets $Z_i = N_i$ and a soft intervention sets $Z_i = \frac{\mathbf{W}_i}{2}\mathbf{Z} + N_i$, where $N_i \sim \mathcal{N}(0, \frac{\Omega_{i,i}}{4})$. For each graph, we sample $n_s \in \{5000, 10,000, 50,000\}$ i.i.d. samples of $\mathbf{Z}$ from each environment. The observed variables $\mathbf{X}$ are generated according to $\mathbf{X} = \mathbf{G} \cdot \mathbf{Z}$, in which $\mathbf{G} \in \mathbb{R}^{d \times n}$ is a randomly sampled full-rank matrix.

Algorithm: For the data generating setting mentioned earlier, we use LSCALE-I (Algorithm 1) presented in Section 10.5.1 to learn $\mathcal{G}$ and $\mathbf{Z}$. Note that $\mathbf{X}$ is a multivariate Gaussian in this setting. Hence, we have the closed-form score function $s_{\mathbf{X}}(\mathbf{x}) = -\Theta \cdot \mathbf{x}$, in which Θ is the precision matrix of $\mathbf{X}$ and can be estimated from observed samples. Next, we report a representative subset of results from Varıcı et al. [16, Section 7.1].

Observations: Table 10.2 shows that Algorithm 1 has near excellent performance under hard interventions, demonstrated by a perfect MCC score of 1 and rapidly decreasing SHD between the estimated and true latent graphs, which becomes approximately 0.2 when using 50, 000 samples. Similarly, increasing the number of samples significantly improves the performance under soft interventions. For instance, given 50, 000 samples, the average SHD between the transitive closures $\mathrm{trc}(\mathcal{G}^*)$ and $\mathrm{trc}(\mathcal{G})$ is approximately 0.2. Finally, we note that an MCC of 0.90 under soft interventions signifies a very strong performance since we only have guarantees for identifiability up to mixing with parents. The final key observation is that the results remain consistent while the dimension of $\mathbf{X}$ increases from $d = 5$ to

Table 10.2 Algorithm 1's performance for a linear causal model with $\mathcal{S}_{\text{single}}$ (mean ± std error).

			Hard intervention		Soft intervention	
$\|\mathbf{Z}\|$	$\|\mathbf{X}\|$	n_{samples}	MCC	$\text{SHD}_{\text{iso}}(\mathcal{G}^*, \mathcal{G})$	MCC	$\text{SHD}_{\text{trc}}(\mathcal{G}^*, \mathcal{G})$
5	5	5000	1.00 ± 0.00	1.55 ± 0.13	0.82 ± 0.01	2.16 ± 0.18
5	25	5000	1.00 ± 0.00	1.58 ± 0.12	0.82 ± 0.01	1.90 ± 0.18
5	100	5000	1.00 ± 0.00	1.61 ± 0.12	0.80 ± 0.01	2.09 ± 0.17
5	5	10, 000	1.00 ± 0.00	0.74 ± 0.10	0.82 ± 0.01	1.51 ± 0.15
5	25	10, 000	1.00 ± 0.00	1.02 ± 0.11	0.82 ± 0.01	1.30 ± 0.14
5	100	10, 000	1.00 ± 0.00	0.74 ± 0.10	0.81 ± 0.01	1.70 ± 0.17
5	5	50, 000	1.00 ± 0.00	0.11 ± 0.03	0.88 ± 0.01	0.15 ± 0.06
5	25	50, 000	1.00 ± 0.00	0.08 ± 0.03	0.88 ± 0.01	0.22 ± 0.08
5	100	50, 000	1.00 ± 0.00	0.23 ± 0.05	0.90 ± 0.01	0.10 ± 0.06

$d = 100$, which confirms our theoretical analysis that dimensionality of $\mathbf{X}$ does not play a role in identifiability.

10.6.2 Experiments on Image Data

In this section, we perform experiments on CRL where the general transformation is image rendering, a highly nonlinear transformation, by applying the GSCALE-I (Algorithm 3) on synthetic image data. We adopt $\mathcal{S}_{2-\text{single}}$ setting and report the results from Varıcı et al. [16].

Image Data Generation: We consider images of the form in Figure 10.3, which are generated as follows. The pairs of latent variables (Z_{2i-1}, Z_{2i}) describe the coordinates of the i-th ball's center in a $64 \times 64 \times 3$ RGB image. We use three balls and $n = 6$ latent variables. We sample $\mathcal{G}$ from Erdős–Rényi model with an expected number of 12 edges. Given $\mathcal{G}$, we use a *truncated* linear Gaussian model and generate interventions similarly to Section 10.6.1. We generate 5 graphs and 10, 000 samples from each graph in each environment.

Algorithm: For computing the score difference functions in Algorithm 3, we adopt a binary classifier-based log density ratio (LDR) estimator and use the gradients of these learned LDRs as our score difference functions. We train one LDR model for each pair of hard interventions on the same node.

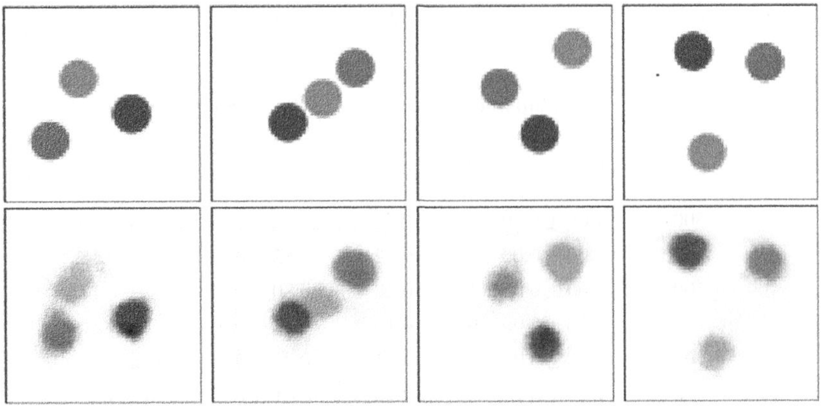

Figure 10.3 Sample images (top row) versus their reconstructions (bottom row).

Recall that we need to find $h^* \in \mathcal{H}$ such that $\mathbf{D}(h^*)$ is a diagonal matrix. To this end, we parameterize $(\hat{h}, \hat{h}^{-1})$ in an autoencoder structure and solve

$$\min_{\hat{h}} \| \mathbf{D}(\hat{h}) - \mathbf{I}_n \|_{1,1} + \lambda \mathbb{E}\left[\| \hat{h}^{-1}(\hat{h}(\mathbf{X})) - \mathbf{X} \|_2^2 \right]. \tag{10.39}$$

We note that constraining $\mathbf{D}(h^*)$ to be the identity matrix instead of a general diagonal matrix is a practical choice to stabilize the optimization procedure. To see this, note that if we componentwise scale the output of $\hat{h}$ by a diagonal matrix $\mathbf{S}$, the score difference matrix scales via $\mathbf{D}(\mathbf{S} \cdot \hat{h}) = \mathbf{S}^{-1} \cdot \mathbf{D}(\hat{h})$. Thus, recalling that $\mathbf{D}(h) = \mathbf{P}_\tau^\top$, $\mathbf{D}(h^*) = \mathbf{I}_n$ is only achieved by $h^* = \mathbf{S} \cdot \mathbf{P}_\tau \cdot h$ where $\mathbf{S} = \mathbf{D}(\mathbf{P}_\tau \cdot h)$. Hence, enforcing $\mathbf{D}(h^*) = \mathbf{I}_n$ prevents h^* from becoming arbitrarily close to zero. Finally, the second term being zero ensures that the minimizer h^* belongs to $\mathcal{H}$, i.e., it is invertible.

Results: We report MCC between $\hat{\mathbf{Z}}$ and $\mathbf{Z}$ as a metric of latent variables recovery. Over five different image datasets, we observe MCC values of

#1: 0.98 #2: 0.49 #3: 0.65 #4: 0.87 #5: 0.81 | mean: 0.76 std: 0.17

During training, we observed that MCC highly correlates with the reconstruction performance, i.e., when reconstruction loss converges to small values, latent variable recovery is also successful (e.g., MCC is 0.98 in run #1). We note that this is a simplified scenario, so high MCC does not guarantee a perfect reconstruction (see the samples in Figure 10.3). We emphasize that our results on five *different image datasets* demonstrate the dependence of the performance on the specific dataset, indicated by a standard deviation of 0.17 in MCC. Our goal in this setting is to showcase the potential of our framework on complex nonlinear transforms, e.g., image rendering, and we achieve this goal by demonstrating a competitive performance at latent variable recovery.

10.7 Other Approaches

We emphasize that this chapter is not intended to provide a comprehensive overview of the rapidly growing literature on CRL. Apart from the materials directly used in this chapter [7, 16, 23–26], we only briefly mention other relevant studies and refer interested readers to the cited references for further details.

Interventional CRL: The $\mathcal{S}_{\text{single}}$ setting has been studied under various assumptions and methods: by Ahuja et al. [22] with polynomial mixing and *do* interventions on general SCMs, by Zhang et al. [34] with polynomial mixing and soft interventions on nonlinear latent SCMs, by Liang et al. [32] with a general mixing and a *known* latent causal graph (of a general SCM), and by Jiang and Aragam [35] with general mixing function while focusing on learning only the latent graph (of a general SCM). The $\mathcal{S}_{2-\text{single}}$ setting has been explored by von Kügelgen et al. [27] with general mixing and general SCMs under additional assumptions such as faithfulness. Jin and Syrgkanis [36] consider $\mathcal{S}_{\text{int}}$ with multiple interventional mechanisms with linear mixing and soft interventions on linear non-Gaussian SCMs. The $\mathcal{S}_{\text{multi}}$ setting has also been addressed by Bing et al. [37] with linear mixing and *do* interventions on general SCMs.

Alternatives: There are several alternative approaches to CRL with different data generation settings that, while not directly comparable to $\mathcal{S}_{\text{int}}$, are nonetheless interesting in their own right. Counterfactual data samples arising from interventions on general SCMs and general mixing functions are leveraged for self-supervised learning [20] and for learning implicit latent SCMs over exogenous noise variables [38]. Multi-view CRL investigates scenarios where a causal representation model is partially observed under multiple views (or domains) with distinct mixing functions. This setting is studied for linear mixing functions and linear SCMs [18] and nonlinear mixing functions and general SCMs [39]. In contrast to the static data setting $\mathcal{S}_{\text{int}}$, temporal data for CRL represents another widely studied direction: Lippe et al. [40] consider a general mixing function and latent dynamical Bayesian networks with known interventions on temporal sequences, Lachapelle et al. [41] consider general mixing functions and unknown interventions on temporal sequences while imposing sparsity constraints, though restricted to learning temporal causal relationships, and Lippe et al. [42] investigate a related setting, albeit with binary interventions on latent SCMs with instantaneous causal effects. In some other approaches, Zhang et al. [43] consider general mixing functions and general SCMs under sparsity constraints,

Liu et al. [44] leverage nonlinear ICA principles to work with nonlinear mixing functions and polynomial latent SCMs, Morioka and Hyvärinen [45] consider disjoint groups of observational variables, with general mixing function and pairwise latent causal relationships, and Welch et al. [46] use score functions for linear mixing functions and nonlinear Gaussian SCMs to derive coarser identifiability results.

Finally, as a special case of CRL, there is extensive literature on identifying latent representations with independent variables. For instance, nonlinear ICA leverages side information such as structured time series to exploit temporal patterns [47], or auxiliary variables that render latent variables conditionally independent [33, 48, 49]. Kivva et al. [50] examine the identifiability of deep generative models without auxiliary information.

10.8 Summary

In this chapter, we provided a general overview of the problem of *CRL*, starting from its key motivations (e.g., robustness and generalization) and concluding with some recent state-of-the-art results in this domain.

Throughout the chapter, we emphasized the importance of rigorous *identifiability* guarantees, the conditions of which involve an interplay between *model expressivity* on the one hand and *observation richness* on the other (see Section 10.2.1). We devoted particular attention to a form of observation richness unique to causal models: learning from *interventional* data.

Many of the core insights into CRL are likely to generalize to other settings. The problem of learning *causal* variables can be thought of as a special case of learning *symbolic* variables, related by a specific structure (i.e., a causal graph) that supports a specific form of reasoning (i.e., causal reasoning). The framework described in this chapter provides a first step toward applying the principles of CRL to other problems in *neurosymbolic* representation learning.

Extensions to Neurosymbolic Representation Learning: Our definition of a causal representation model M (Definition 10.7) can be readily adapted by replacing the latent SCM S^M with a different type of mathematical structure, such as a dynamical system, a logical circuit, or a computer program. Similarly, the general notions of identifiability discussed in Section 10.2.1 can be extended to define structure-specific equivalence relations, analogous to those outlined in Section 10.2.4. In many cases, given only a single "observational" dataset, such equivalence classes tend to be quite large (i.e., the models are often quite weakly identified), resulting in poor robustness, limited generalization, and reduced interpretability. Thus far, such nonidentifiability issues have often been overlooked or addressed in an ad hoc manner.

This chapter draws more attention to these issues, and the ideas presented here may help to pave the way forward. To generalize the concept of an "intervention" to other structures, it is essential to consider what kinds of *local* or *modular* changes are realistic to those structures. The interventional perspective has already been applied to structures such as linear time-invariant systems [51], and it may be quite naturally applied to modularly defined structures such as logical circuits or computer programs.

Future Directions: We conclude with a brief summary of future directions for CRL, many of which can be easily adapted to other areas of neurosymbolic representation learning. First, as discussed in Section 10.7, several other problem settings have been studied in CRL, e.g., the multi-view setting, and it would be quite interesting to combine such settings into a *hybrid* setting, with datasets indexed both by view and by (interventional) environment. Second, we have focused on the identifiability of *latent variables* and *latent graph*, without going substantially into detail about how the identified representation could be used for downstream tasks. An interesting direction for future research is to address *targeted* identifiability, where the goal is to identify only those components of the model that are directly relevant to specific downstream tasks. A relevant question in this direction can be to investigate how to learn causal "concepts," e.g., instead of explicitly learning causal variables, we can learn more general representations of concepts that possess further substructures amenable for causal reasoning [52].

Acknowledgments: We thank our collaborators for their contributions to the papers that formed the foundation of the technical results presented in this chapter. In particular, we thank Anna Seigal, Salil Bhate, and Caroline Uhler for their contributions to Section 10.4.1; Simon Buchholz, Goutham Rajendran, Elan Rosenfeld, Bryon Aragam, and Bernhard Schölkopf for Section 10.4.2; and Emre Acartürk, Karthikeyan Shanmugam, and Ali Tajer for Section 10.5.

References

1 Dan Hendrycks, Steven Basart, Norman Mu, Saurav Kadavath, Frank Wang, Evan Dorundo, Rahul Desai, Tyler Zhu, Samyak Parajuli, Mike Guo, et al. The many faces of robustness: a critical analysis of out-of-distribution generalization. In *Proceedings IEEE/CVF International Conference on Computer Vision*, pages 8340–8349, 2021.

2 Pang Wei Koh, Shiori Sagawa, Henrik Marklund, Sang Michael Xie, Marvin Zhang, Akshay Balsubramani, Weihua Hu, Michihiro Yasunaga, Richard Lanas Phillips, Irena Gao, et al. Wilds: a benchmark of in-the-wild distribution shifts. In *Proceedings International Conference on Machine Learning*, 2021.

3 Joaquin Quiñonero-Candela, Masashi Sugiyama, Anton Schwaighofer, and Neil D Lawrence. *Dataset Shift in Machine Learning*. MIT Press, 2022.

4 Pan Lu, Baolin Peng, Hao Cheng, Michel Galley, Kai-Wei Chang, Ying Nian Wu, Song-Chun Zhu, and Jianfeng Gao. Chameleon: Plug-and-play compositional reasoning with large language models. In *Proceedings Advances in Neural Information Processing Systems*, New Orleans, LA, 2023.

5 Thaddäus Wiedemer, Prasanna Mayilvahanan, Matthias Bethge, and Wieland Brendel. Compositional generalization from first principles. In *Proceedings Advances in Neural Information Processing Systems*, New Orleans, LA, 2023.

6 Yoshua Bengio, Aaron Courville, and Pascal Vincent. Representation learning: a review and new perspectives. *IEEE Transactions on Pattern Analysis and Machine Intelligence*, 35(8): 1798–1828, 2013.

7 Emre Acartürk, Burak Varıcı, Karthikeyan Shanmugam, and Ali Tajer. Sample complexity of interventional causal representation learning. In *Proceedings Advances in Neural Information Processing Systems*, Vancouver, Canada, 2024.

8 Francesco Locatello, Stefan Bauer, Mario Lucic, Gunnar Raetsch, Sylvain Gelly, Bernhard Schölkopf, and Olivier Bachem. Challenging common assumptions in the unsupervised learning of disentangled representations. In *Proceedings International Conference on Machine Learning*, Long Beach, CA, 2019.

9 Alexander D'Amour, Katherine Heller, Dan Moldovan, Ben Adlam, Babak Alipanahi, Alex Beutel, Christina Chen, Jonathan Deaton, Jacob Eisenstein, Matthew D Hoffman, et al. Underspecification presents challenges for credibility in modern machine learning. *Journal of Machine Learning Research*, 23(226): 1–61, 2022.

10 Judea Pearl. *Causality*. Cambridge University Press, Cambridge, UK, 2009.

11 Bernhard Schölkopf, Francesco Locatello, Stefan Bauer, Nan Rosemary Ke, Nal Kalchbrenner, Anirudh Goyal, and Yoshua Bengio. Toward causal representation learning. *Proceedings of the IEEE*, 109(5): 612–634, 2021.

12 Aapo Hyvärinen and Petteri Pajunen. Nonlinear independent component analysis: Existence and uniqueness results. *Neural Networks*, 12(3): 429–439, 1999.

13 Peter Spirtes, Clark Glymour, and Richard Scheines. *Causation, Prediction, and Search*. MIT press, 2001.

14 Alejandro Tejada-Lapuerta, Paul Bertin, Stefan Bauer, Hananeh Aliee, Yoshua Bengio, and Fabian J. Theis. Causal machine learning for single-cell genomics. arXiv preprint *Nature Genetics, 1–12, 2025. Nature Publishing Group US New York.*

15 Elias Bareinboim, Juan D. Correa, Duligur Ibeling, and Thomas Icard. On pearl's hierarchy and the foundations of causal inference. In *Probabilistic and Causal Inference: The Works of Judea Pearl*, volume 36 of *ACM Books*, pages 507–556, ACM, 2022.

16 Chandler Squires, Anna Seigal, Salil S. Bhate, and Caroline Uhler. Linear causal disentanglement via interventions. In *International Conference on Machine Learning*, pages 32540–32560, PMLR, 2023.

17 Julius von Kügelgen, Michel Besserve, Wendong Liang, Luigi Gresele, Armin Kekić, Elias Bareinboim, David M. Blei, and Bernhard Schölkopf. Nonparametric identifiability of causal representations from unknown interventions. In *Proceedings Advances in Neural Information Processing Systems*, New Orleans, LA, 2023.

18 Simon Buchholz, Goutham Rajendran, Elan Rosenfeld, Bryon Aragam, Bernhard Schölkopf, and Pradeep Ravikumar. Learning linear causal representations from interventions under general nonlinear mixing. In *Proceedings Advances in Neural Information Processing Systems*, New Orleans, LA, 2023.

19 Burak Varıcı, Emre Acartürk, Karthikeyan Shanmugam, Abhishek Kumar, and Ali Tajer. Score-based causal representation learning: Linear and general transformations, 26(112):1–90, 2025.

20 Burak Varıcı, Emre Acartürk, Karthikeyan Shanmugam, and Ali Tajer. Linear causal representation learning from unknown multi-node interventions. In *Proceedings Advances in Neural Information Processing Systems*, Vancouver, Canada, 2024.

21 Burak Varıcı, Emre Acartürk, Karthikeyan Shanmugam, and Ali Tajer. General identifiability and achievability for causal representation learning. In *Proceedings International Conference on Artificial Intelligence and Statistics*, Valencia, Spain, 2024.

22 Seiji Nabeya and Takeaki Kariya. Transformations preserving normality and wishart-ness. *Journal of Multivariate Analysis*, 20(2): 251–264, 1986.

23 Chandler Squires, Yuhao Wang, and Caroline Uhler. Permutation-based causal structure learning with unknown intervention targets. In *Proceedings Conference in Uncertainty in Artificial Intelligence*, 2020.

24 Tabitha Edith Lee, Shivam Vats, Siddharth Girdhar, and Oliver Kroemer. Scale: Causal learning and discovery of robot manipulation skills using simulation. In *CoRL 2023 Workshop on Learning Effective Abstractions for Planning*, Atlanta, GA, 2023.

25 Ilyes Khemakhem, Ricardo Monti, Diederik Kingma, and Aapo Hyvärinen. Ice-beem: Identifiable conditional energy-based deep models based on nonlinear ICA. In *Proceedings Advances in Neural Information Processing Systems*, 2020.

26 Kartik Ahuja, Divyat Mahajan, Yixin Wang, and Yoshua Bengio. Interventional causal representation learning. In *Proceedings International Conference on Machine Learning*, Honolulu, Hawaii, 2023.

27 Jiaqi Zhang, Chandler Squires, Kristjan Greenewald, Akash Srivastava, Karthikeyan Shanmugam, and Caroline Uhler. Identifiability guarantees for causal disentanglement from soft interventions. In *Proceedings Advances in Neural Information Processing Systems*, New Orleans, LA, 2023.

28 Wendong Liang, Armin Kekić, Julius von Kügelgen, Simon Buchholz, Michel Besserve, Luigi Gresele, and Bernhard Schölkopf. Causal component analysis. In *Proceedings Advances in Neural Information Processing Systems*, New Orleans, LA, 2023.

29 Yibo Jiang and Bryon Aragam. Learning nonparametric latent causal graphs with unknown interventions. In *Proceedings Advances in Neural Information Processing Systems*, New Orleans, LA, 2023.

30 Jikai Jin and Vasilis Syrgkanis. Learning causal representations from general environments: Identifiability and intrinsic ambiguity. In *Proceedings Advances in Neural Information Processing Systems*, Vancouver, Canada, 2024.

31 Simon Bing, Urmi Ninad, Jonas Wahl, and Jakob Runge. Identifying linearly-mixed causal representations from multi-node interventions. In *Proceedings Causal Learning and Reasoning*, Los Angeles, CA, 2024.

32 Julius von Kügelgen, Yash Sharma, Luigi Gresele, Wieland Brendel, Bernhard Schölkopf, Michel Besserve, and Francesco Locatello. Self-supervised learning with data augmentations provably isolates content from style. In *Proceedings Advances in Neural Information Processing Systems*, 2021.

33 Johann Brehmer, Pim De Haan, Phillip Lippe, and Taco S. Cohen. Weakly supervised causal representation learning. In *Proceedings Advances in Neural Information Processing Systems*, New Orleans, LA, 2022.

34 Nils Sturma, Chandler Squires, Mathias Drton, and Caroline Uhler. Unpaired multi-domain causal representation learning. In *Proceedings Advances in Neural Information Processing Systems*, New Orleans, LA, 2023.

35 Dingling Yao, Danru Xu, Sebastien Lachapelle, Sara Magliacane, Perouz Taslakian, Georg Martius, Julius von Kügelgen, and Francesco Locatello. Multi-view causal representation learning with partial observability. In *Proceedings International Conference on Learning Representations*, Vienna, Austria, 2024.

36 Phillip Lippe, Sara Magliacane, Sindy Löwe, Yuki M. Asano, Taco Cohen, and Efstratios Gavves. Causal representation learning for instantaneous and temporal effects in interactive systems. In *Proceedings International Conference on Learning Representations*, Kigali, Rwanda, 2023.

37 Sébastien Lachapelle, Pau Rodríguez López, Yash Sharma, Katie Everett, Rémi Le Priol, Alexandre Lacoste, and Simon Lacoste-Julien. Nonparametric partial disentanglement via mechanism sparsity: sparse actions, interventions and sparse temporal dependencies. *arXiv preprint arXiv:2401.04890*, 2024.

38 Phillip Lippe, Sara Magliacane, Sindy Löwe, Yuki M. Asano, Taco Cohen, and Efstratios Gavves. BISCUIT: Causal representation learning from binary interactions. In *Proceedings Uncertainty in Artificial Intelligence*, Pittsburgh, PA, 2023.

39 Kun Zhang, Shaoan Xie, Ignavier Ng, and Yujia Zheng. Causal representation learning from multiple distributions: A general setting. In *Proceedings International Conference on Machine Learning*, Vienna, Austria, 2024.

40 Yuhang Liu, Zhen Zhang, Dong Gong, Mingming Gong, Biwei Huang, Anton van den Hengel, Kun Zhang, and Javen Qinfeng Shi. Identifiable latent polynomial causal models through the lens of change. In *Proceedings International Conference on Learning Representations*, Vienna, Austria, 2024.

41 Hiroshi Morioka and Aapo Hyvärinen. Causal representation learning made identifiable by grouping of observational variables. In *Proceedings International Conference on Machine Learning*, Vienna, Austria, 2024.

42 Ryan Welch, Jiaqi Zhang, and Caroline Uhler. Identifiability guarantees for causal disentanglement from purely observational data. In *Proceedings Advances in Neural Information Processing Systems*, Vancouver, Canada, 2024.

43 Hermanni Hälvä and Aapo Hyvärinen. Hidden Markov nonlinear ICA: Unsupervised learning from nonstationary time series. In *Proceedings Conference on Uncertainty in Artificial Intelligence*, 2020.

44 Ilyes Khemakhem, Diederik Kingma, Ricardo Monti, and Aapo Hyvärinen. Variational autoencoders and nonlinear ICA: a unifying framework. In *Proceedings International Conference on Artificial Intelligence and Statistics*, 2020.

45 Aapo Hyvärinen, Hiroaki Sasaki, and Richard Turner. Nonlinear ICA using auxiliary variables and generalized contrastive learning. In *Proceedings International Conference on Artificial Intelligence and Statistics*, Naha, Japan, 2019.

46 Bohdan Kivva, Goutham Rajendran, Pradeep Ravikumar, and Bryon Aragam. Identifiability of deep generative models under mixture priors without auxiliary information. In *Proceedings Advances in Neural Information Processing Systems*, New Orleans, LA, 2022.

47 Goutham Rajendran, Patrik Reizinger, Wieland Brendel, and Pradeep Kumar Ravikumar. An interventional perspective on identifiability in gaussian lti systems with independent component analysis. In *Proceedings Causal Learning and Reasoning*, Los Angeles, CA, 2024.

48 Goutham Rajendran, Simon Buchholz, Bryon Aragam, Bernhard Schölkopf, and Pradeep Kumar Ravikumar. From causal to concept-based representation learning. In *Proceedings Advances in Neural Information Processing Systems*, Vancouver, Canada, 2024.

49 Caroline Uhler, Garvesh Raskutti, Peter Bühlmann, and Bin Yu. Geometry of the faithfulness assumption in causal inference. *The Annals of Statistics*, 41(2): 436–463, 2013.

50 Guangyi Chen, Yifan Shen, Zhenhao Chen, Xiangchen Song, Yuewen Sun, Weiran Yao, Xiao Liu, and Kun Zhang. CaRiNG: Learning temporal causal representation under non-invertible generation process. In *Proceedings International Conference on Machine Learning*, Vienna, Austria, 2024.

51 Patrick Forré and Joris M. Mooij. A mathematical introduction to causality. *Lecture Notes*, 2023. https://staff.fnwi.uva.nl/j.m.mooij/articles/causality_lecture_notes_2023.pdf.

52 Burak Varıcı, Emre Acartürk, Karthikeyan Shanmugam, Abhishek Kumar, and Ali Tajer. Score-based causal representation learning with interventions. *arXiv preprint arXiv:2301.08230*, 2023.

11

Neurosymbolic Computing: Hardware–Software Co-design

Xiaoxuan Yang,[1] *Zhangyang Wang,*[2] *Miroslav Pajic,*[3] *Hai "Helen" Li,*[3*] *Yiran Chen,*[3] *X. Sharon Hu,*[4] *Chris H. Kim,*[5] *Shimeng Yu,*[6] *and Rajit Manohar*[7]

[1] *University of Virginia, Charlottesville, Virginia, USA*
[2] *Oden Institute of Computational Sciences and Engineering, University of Texas at Austin, Austin, Texas, USA*
[3] *Duke University, Durham, North Carolina, USA*
[4] *University of Nortre Dame, Notre Dame, Indiana, USA*
[5] *University of Minnesota, Minneapolis, Minnesota, USA*
[6] *Georgia Institute of Technology, Atlanta, Georgia, USA*
[7] *Yale University, New Haven, Connecticut, USA*

*Corresponding Author: hai.li@duke.com

11.1 Introduction

The rapid growth of artificial intelligence (AI) has reshaped nearly every dimension of modern life. From digital assistants and health diagnostics to autonomous vehicles, AI technologies continue to expand their impact. A closer look at their progression shows remarkable advances in areas such as speech processing, image understanding, and object recognition [1]. Over time, AI systems have grown from models with only thousands of parameters [2] to large-scale language models (LLMs) containing billions [3–5]. This explosive increase in scale has enabled performance levels that, in many domains, now rival or exceed human capabilities.

Despite these accomplishments, much of today's AI development has focused on maximizing benchmark performance, often with narrow task-specific goals. This pursuit has come at the expense of broader reasoning abilities. For example, deep neural networks (DNNs) typically struggle to generalize when confronted with unseen distributions or new problem settings [6]. Likewise, LLMs still

Neurosymbolic AI: Foundations and Applications, First Edition. Edited by Alvaro Velasquez et al.

face difficulties with uncertainty estimation and precise mathematical reasoning [7], limiting their adaptability. These gaps highlight the importance of integrating symbolic reasoning with data-driven learning, motivating research in neurosymbolic (NeSy) computing [8, 9].

Neural models rely on end-to-end training and global optimization, where parameter interdependence prevents modular recombination of layers into new, high-performing networks. Their lack of inherent compositionality also makes them difficult to interpret. Addressing these challenges has led researchers to explore compositional and interpretable approaches within NeSy frameworks [10–12].

On the hardware side, neural networks are often deployed using accelerators tailored for specific workloads – for instance, systolic arrays optimized for convolutional neural networks [13] or memristor-based crossbars for vector–matrix multiplications (VMMs) [14]. However, such architectures are tightly coupled to the computational patterns of particular models. As a result, optimization in one setting rarely transfers directly to others [15]. Solving the compositionality challenge could therefore open pathways to more flexible and reusable hardware solutions across diverse applications.

Because NeSy methods combine dense neural computation with symbolic reasoning, they demand significant compute power. Hardware acceleration can help mitigate this cost, underscoring the need for close hardware–software co-design. In this chapter, we present a comprehensive examination of contemporary co-design strategies for NeSy AI and analyze the challenges of boosting efficiency in heterogeneous computing environments. Our discussion highlights emerging directions in enabling generalization and reasoning (especially compositional generalization), addressing uncertainty, improving system efficiency, and advancing toward full-stack NeSy implementations.

11.2 Background

11.2.1 Neurosymbolic Artificial Intelligence

Based on Henry Kautz's classification [16], neurosymbolic (NeSy) computing can be organized into six distinct design categories, each reflecting a different degree of interaction between neural and symbolic components.

The first design, termed Symbolic Neuro Symbolic, employs neural models as intermediaries between symbolic inputs and outputs. A clear example is the Transformer architecture [17]. Here, a document input is first processed by an embedding layer, then passed through multi-head self-attention and feedforward blocks, before a softmax layer maps the results to symbolic tokens or categories.

This design benefits from extensive prior work on neural hardware acceleration, enabling improvements in energy efficiency and chip area through custom architectures [18, 19] and co-design strategies [20, 21]. Nonetheless, because neural components dominate in this integration, such systems often sacrifice transparency and compositional reasoning.

The second category, Symbolic[Neuro], treats the neural module as a subroutine embedded within a symbolic reasoning process. AlphaGo is a representative example [22]: to keep inference latency under five seconds, the system employed 1,202 CPUs and 176 GPUs to evaluate policy and value networks in tandem with Monte Carlo tree search. A closely related third type, Neuro;Symbolic, instead uses neural models as coroutines. This allows the system to accept raw, non-symbolic data, which the neural component transforms into symbolic representations before further processing. For both of these cases, effective task allocation and scheduling between symbolic and neural modules become critical challenges in architectural design.

The fourth variant, Neuro;Symbolic→Neuro, focuses on compiling symbolic knowledge into data used for neural training. Examples include encoding expression trees [23], logic programs [24], or graph structures [25] as inputs to improve reasoning capacity. A fifth category, Neuro_Symbolic, applies neural methods directly to tensorized versions of first-order logic statements [26]. Both categories lend themselves to exploring combinatorial reasoning strategies [16], and their implementation benefits from heterogeneous architectures that can efficiently support flexible dataflow and memory access patterns [27].

The sixth and final design, Neuro[Symbolic], can be seen as a structural inversion of Symbolic[Neuro]. Here, a symbolic reasoning engine is embedded inside a neural framework, enabling high-performance neural computation while retaining symbolic-level inference. In this design, the neural component identifies the problem domain, while the symbolic module performs combinatorial reasoning, after which results are mapped back into neural representations for execution. The symbolic engine may act as a callable subroutine or be combined with other symbolic units to tackle more complex reasoning tasks. This design is particularly promising for advancing cognitive, interpretable NeSy systems.

In conclusion, two defining characteristics emerge across NeSy approaches. First, they emphasize compositionality – a property not unique to NeSy but also present in compositional neural networks [28–30]. Second, they rely on the interleaving and hierarchical stacking of symbolic and neural modules, as illustrated in Figure 11.1.

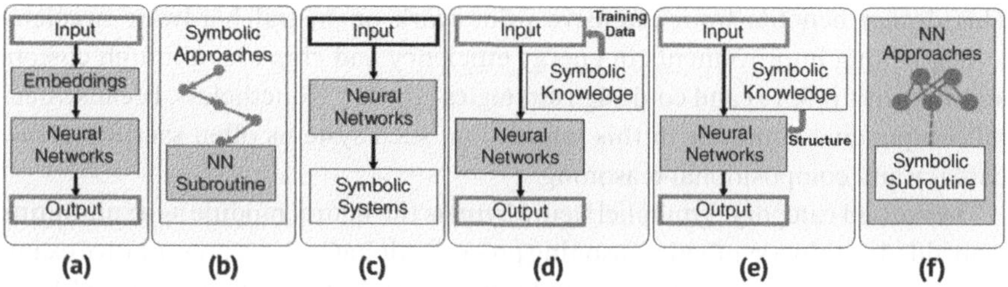

Figure 11.1 Six representative Neurosymbolic designs.

11.2.2 Emerging Hardware Computing Platforms

We investigate multiple hardware platforms suitable for implementing NeSy systems, ranging from conventional architectures to recently developed device technologies. This section highlights several emerging computing substrates, including resistive random-access memory (ReRAM), ferroelectric field-effect transistors (FeFETs), and coupled oscillators. We also examine their potential to accelerate NeSy workloads.

Resistive Random-Access Memory (ReRAM): A ReRAM device consists of a thin metal-oxide layer placed between two metal electrodes. When arranged in crossbar arrays, ReRAM can directly execute VMMs, substantially lowering the overhead of data transfer between memory and processors [31]. As VMM operations are central to many neural computations, in-memory computing with ReRAM provides a compelling route toward highly energy-efficient NeSy implementations.

Ferroelectric Field-Effect Transistor (FeFET): FeFETs are realized by integrating a ferroelectric layer onto the gate of a MOSFET. One practical use is FeFET-based ternary content-addressable memory (CAM), which enables fast, parallel searches across memory blocks for a given query – making it effective for associative memory, databases, and in-memory processing tasks [32, 33]. In addition, multi-level FeFETs have been employed in hyperdimensional computing [34], offering area-efficient and composition-friendly deployment pathways for NeSy workloads.

Coupled Oscillator: In oscillator-based systems, information is represented by the phase of oscillations. When nonlinearities are introduced, an oscillator tuned to a given frequency can synchronize with a pump at double that frequency, yielding two stable phase states, 0 and π, which correspond to digital bits. This property enables massively parallel and inherently efficient computation [36]. Coupled oscillator networks, in particular, have shown promise in solving combinatorial optimization problems (COPs) [35, 37]. As shown in Figure 11.2, a large COP can be divided into smaller subproblems, each solved by an all-to-all connected oscillator array [38]. Such architectures are attractive for NeSy for two reasons: (i) many reasoning applications, including robotic design [39], rely on efficient COP solvers,

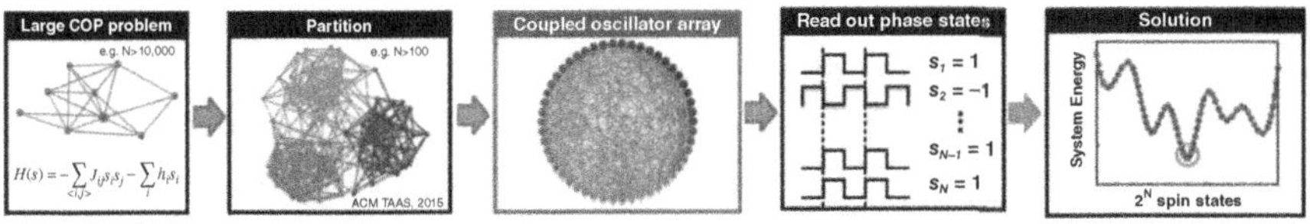

Figure 11.2 General workflow of Ising computers, including applications, problem partition, and obtaining solutions. *Source*: Adapted from [35].

and (ii) NeSy systems themselves are complex and benefit from hardware capable of optimizing large-scale design configurations.

11.3 Trends and Challenges

NeSy models have already shown encouraging outcomes on targeted tasks, making them highly appealing for future research directions. For example, symbolic regression produces analytic expressions with efficiency advantages and achieves up to 13× lower latency than a three-layer neural network on physics-related benchmarks [40]. Another instance is the symbolic branching algorithm, which transforms a reinforcement learning agent into a symbolic decision tree, yielding a 23× acceleration [41]. These efforts primarily address simpler NeSy workloads and represent initial steps in evaluating the performance–resource tradeoff of such systems. In this section, we move toward more advanced NeSy architectures, learning paradigms, and system-level considerations. We also highlight emerging opportunities and open challenges for hardware–software co-design in NeSy.

11.3.1 Enhance Reasoning and Generalization

Significant progress has been made in combining the data-driven efficiency of neural networks with the structured reasoning of symbolic methods, yielding advanced hybrid architectures capable of handling challenging tasks [42]. In visual question answering, embedding symbolic priors provides a transparent reasoning pipeline while reducing memory requirements for intensive workloads [43]. Similarly, the visual concept–metaconcept framework jointly trains both the concept (embedding-based) and the metaconcept (a predictor over concept relations), which improves sample efficiency and boosts generalization to unseen examples [44].

For abstract reasoning, neurosymbolic probabilistic abduction with execution learning leverages probabilistic scene representations to mimic cognitive manipulation of objects. This enables not only more robust generalization across task configurations but also the ability to autonomously generate candidate answers rather than merely selecting from a set [45].

To realize such reasoning-driven NeSy architectures, careful orchestration of submodules is essential. Consider the neurosymbolic dynamic reasoning model [46], where the dynamic predictor emerges as the main computational bottleneck [47]. Based on PropNet [48], this predictor acts as a learned physics engine, composed of compact neural networks with fully connected and convolutional layers. In practice, multiple executions are needed per frame to propagate force information to the symbolic layer, creating substantial data traffic between symbolic and neural parts. More broadly, NeSy architectures consist of symbolic executors and neural modules working in tandem, constrained by rules and domain knowledge to achieve reasoning and generalization [43, 49, 50]. However, when symbolic logic and neural inference are mapped separately to CPUs and GPUs, the resulting data movement overhead becomes a barrier to efficiency. This motivates exploration into emerging hardware platforms that can alleviate communication costs.

11.3.2 Enable Compositionality

Vector symbolic architectures (VSAs), also known as hyperdimensional computing (HDC), rely on high-dimensional distributed vectors and the algebraic operations defined over them [51]. These operations naturally support compositional reasoning. For example, attribute vectors can be combined into object vectors, and multiple object vectors can be bound into a composite vector. Even within these composites, attributes can be retrieved using distance-based decoding.

Such representations are particularly useful for compositional reasoning, paving the way for the integration of HDC with neural networks into neuro-vector-symbolic architectures (NVSAs). These architectures offer both efficient probabilistic reasoning and low-latency performance [52]. At the same time, storing and manipulating large collections of hyperdimensional vectors raises efficiency concerns. Dedicated accelerators for VSAs/HDC [34, 53] can be combined with NeSy accelerators to improve performance.

Compositionality also provides efficiency at the hardware level through modular design. Tree-like symbolic models, for instance, can be implemented with reusable blocks to reduce redundancy [54]. This modularity further supports higher-level abstraction, customization, and flexible system packaging. Recent work [55] demonstrates this principle by proposing a CAM-based platform optimized for sparse tree-model learning and efficient CAM array utilization.

11.3.3 Handle Uncertainty

Uncertainty is intrinsic to many reasoning and control problems, either due to incomplete observations or stochastic environmental dynamics. For safety-critical domains, probabilistic inference becomes indispensable [56]. Extending deterministic reasoning primitives to their probabilistic counterparts allows systematic modeling of uncertainty.

In this paradigm, a deterministic relation is generalized into a conditional probability distribution. With the connectionist probabilistic program (CPP) framework [57], large probabilistic networks can be composed from a small set of atomic probabilistic functions, as illustrated in Figure 11.3. While atomic functions permit direct evaluation, inference over composite functions involves costly summations that scale exponentially. Thus, approximate inference techniques are essential [58].

From a hardware perspective, uncertainty introduces additional design challenges. Probabilistic computation may require either true random number generators or pseudo-random sources [59, 60]. Interestingly, intrinsic randomness in devices can also be exploited: for example, variations in ReRAM cell currents can

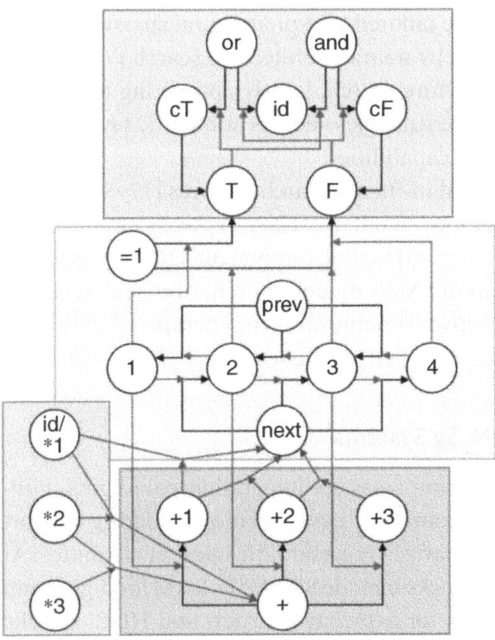

Figure 11.3 A connection probabilistic program example of Boolean logic and basic arithmetic [57]. Top region: Boolean logic; Middle region: Counting logic; Bottom region: Integer addition; Bottom-left region: Integer multiplication.

be used to generate distributions [61], while amplified spontaneous emission noise can provide sampling for Bayesian neural networks [62]. Such mechanisms enable efficient stochastic inference and broaden support for uncertainty handling.

11.3.4 Improve System Efficiency

As discussed in Section 11.2, both symbolic and neural modules contribute to NeSy systems, though their resource profiles differ. Software-level optimizations such as pruning and quantization [63, 64] reduce memory traffic and improve efficiency, but hardware–software co-design remains necessary for optimal deployment. Symbolic components, being relatively lightweight [43], consume fewer resources while also enabling smaller, more generalizable neural models [65–70]. Consequently, symbolic integration indirectly enhances efficiency by reducing neural computation requirements.

Nevertheless, heavy operations such as GEMM, convolution (CONV), and attention dominate overall costs [47]. GEMM for reasoning often involves irregular sparse matrices, calling for flexible accelerators to maintain utilization [71]. In-memory computing accelerators for convolution demand high parallelism, including inter- and intra-layer parallelism, to improve energy efficiency [72]. Sparse computation designs can also be tailored to exploit neural sparsity for efficiency gains [73]. Approaches inspired by neural architecture search [74, 75] can be extended to neurosymbolic architecture search, jointly optimizing reasoning, generalization, and efficiency. Adaptive strategies such as automatic layer expansion [76] may further strengthen NeSy capabilities.

Recent advances in near-memory and in-memory architectures [77–84] further illustrate strategies to minimize data movement overhead. As NeSy architectures allow flexible combinations of symbolic and neural components, there is substantial room for optimization. Furthermore, NeSy models with hardware-associative memory can further boost the speedup and energy efficiency compared with CPU and GPU baselines [85].

11.3.5 Demonstrate Full-stack NeSy Systems

As outlined in Section 11.2, NeSy encompasses six integration paradigms. Full-stack system design must therefore account for these variations, offering support for diverse dataflows. Table 11.1 summarizes representative design attributes. At the platform level, potential building blocks include SRAM/ReRAM for digital and analog in-memory computing, FeFETs for associative search and HDC, systolic arrays for GEMM, and coupled oscillators or logic substrates for reasoning.

A practical full-stack system should be paired with comprehensive modeling frameworks, akin to those developed for DNN accelerators [86, 87]. Moreover,

Table 11.1 Design space of NeSy systems.

Attribute	Details
NeSy Type	Type I - VI as described in Section 11.2
Computation	GEMM, CONV, FC, Sparse MM
Technology	SRAM, DRAM, Flash, ReRAM, FeFET
Specifics	Technology Node, Integration, Interconnect
Evaluation	Area, Power
Target	Latency, Throughput, Energy, Capability

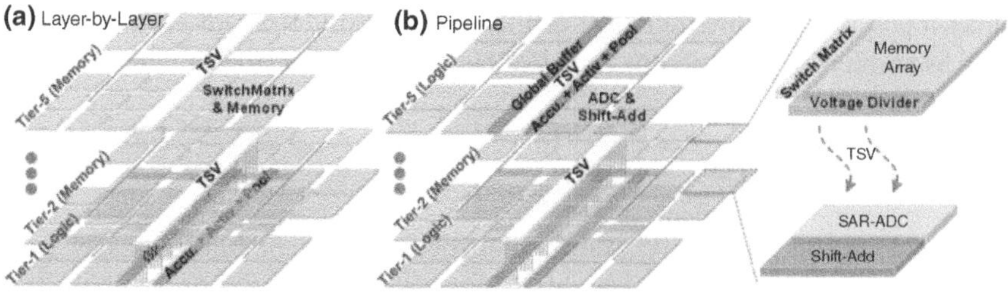

Figure 11.4 Floorplan of heterogeneous 3D multitier CIM accelerator [88].

advanced packaging strategies such as heterogeneous 3D integration are essential. This enables multiple chiplets specialized for different NeSy primitives to be stacked into a cohesive architecture [88], as depicted in Figure 11.4.

Given the diversity of attributes, NeSy system design naturally forms a multi-objective optimization problem. Coupled-oscillator platforms, already effective at solving combinatorial optimization tasks, could be directly leveraged to search this design space, enabling more agile co-design of future full-stack cognitive NeSy architectures.

11.4 Applications and Future Topics

One rapidly growing NeSy application lies in natural language processing (NLP), where it is being applied to tasks such as context interpretation, extractive summarization, and semantic-level reasoning [89, 90]. By merging statistical learning with structured symbolic knowledge, NeSy architectures can improve both comprehension and response generation. Looking forward, NeSy techniques are likely to extend to spoken dialogue systems, offering improvements in the responsiveness and reliability of digital assistants.

In robotics, NeSy methods have proven valuable for strengthening perception, planning, and decision-making pipelines. Through the integration of neural perception models with logical reasoning mechanisms, robotic platforms are better equipped to interpret and maneuver within complex environments. A critical requirement is the ability of robots to generalize to novel or unseen scenarios [91], and NeSy designs provide a pathway to achieving this adaptability.

For autonomous driving, incorporating NeSy principles may enable safer and more reliable self-driving frameworks that are robust, context-sensitive, and resilient to adversarial disturbances. Since autonomous vehicles must operate with strong guarantees of reliability in contested and potentially adversarial settings, the NeSy paradigm provides opportunities to embed higher assurance levels. This makes it possible to strengthen user confidence and build trust in self-driving systems, as emphasized in a recent survey of NeSy approaches [92].

11.5 Conclusions

We provide a comprehensive examination of the inherent limitations of conventional neural networks and highlight the pivotal role of neurosymbolic AI. Furthermore, this work outlines the spectrum of available NeSy architectures and sheds light on current research directions, particularly emphasizing hardware–software co-design strategies. Looking ahead, our subsequent efforts aim to construct a heterogeneous computing framework that integrates both CPUs and GPUs as execution units, tailored to the specific task requirements, thereby unlocking the full potential of compositional NeSy systems.

References

1 Douwe Kiela, Max Bartolo, Yixin Nie, Divyansh Kaushik, Atticus Geiger, Zhengxuan Wu, Bertie Vidgen, Grusha Prasad, Amanpreet Singh, Pratik Ringshia, et al. Dynabench: rethinking benchmarking in nlp. In *Proceedings of the 2021 Conference of the North American Chapter of the Association for Computational Linguistics: Human Language Technologies, NAACL-HLT 2021*, pages 4110–4124, ACL, 2021.

2 Simone Bianco, Remi Cadene, Luigi Celona, and Paolo Napoletano. Benchmark analysis of representative deep neural network architectures. *IEEE Access*, 6: 64270–64277, 2018.

3 Tom Brown, Benjamin Mann, Nick Ryder, Melanie Subbiah, Jared D Kaplan, Prafulla Dhariwal, Arvind Neelakantan, Pranav Shyam, Girish Sastry, Amanda Askell, et al. Language models are few-shot learners. *Advances in Neural Information Processing Systems*, 33: 1877–1901, 2020.

4 Haopeng Zhang, Philip S. Yu, and Jiawei Zhang. A systematic survey of text summarization: from statistical methods to large language models. *ACM Computing Surveys*, 57(11): 1–41, 2025.

5 Shan Haoxuan, Wei Chiyue, Yang Xiaoxuan, Guo Cong, Li Hai, and Chen Yiran. Neuromorphic computing in the era of large models. *Artificial Intelligence Science and Engineering*, 1(1): 17–30, 2025.

6 Jingkang Yang, Kaiyang Zhou, Yixuan Li, and Ziwei Liu. Generalized out-of-distribution detection: a survey. *arXiv preprint arXiv:2110.11334*, 2021.

7 Luciano Floridi and Massimo Chiriatti. Gpt-3: its nature, scope, limits, and consequences. *Minds and Machines*, 30: 681–694, 2020.

8 Sebastian Bader and Pascal Hitzler. Dimensions of neural-symbolic integration-a structured survey. In *We Will Show Them! Essays in Honour of Dov Gabbay, Volume 1*, pages 167–194. College Publications, 2005.

9 Artur d'Avila Garcez, Marco Gori, Luis C. Lamb, Luciano Serafini, Michael Spranger, and Son N. Tran. Neural-symbolic computing: an effective methodology for principled integration of machine learning and reasoning. *FLAP*, 6(4): 611–632, 2019.

10 Efthymia Tsamoura, Timothy Hospedales, and Loizos Michael. Neural-symbolic integration: a compositional perspective. In *Proceedings of the AAAI Conference On Artificial Intelligence*, volume 35, pages 5051–5060, 2021.

11 Xinyun Chen, Chen Liang, Adams Wei Yu, Dawn Song, and Denny Zhou. Compositional generalization via neural-symbolic stack machines. *Advances in Neural Information Processing Systems*, 33: 1690–1701, 2020.

12 Luís C. Lamb, Artur Garcez, Marco Gori, Marcelo Prates, Pedro Avelar, and Moshe Vardi. Graph neural networks meet neural-symbolic computing: a survey and perspective. In *Proceedings of the Twenty-Ninth International Joint Conference on Artificial Intelligence, IJCAI 2020*, pages 4877–4884. ijcai.org, 2020.

13 Yu-Hsin Chen, Tushar Krishna, Joel S. Emer, and Vivienne Sze. Eyeriss: an energy-efficient reconfigurable accelerator for deep convolutional neural networks. *IEEE Journal of Solid-State Circuits*, 52(1): 127–138, 2016.

14 Miao Hu, Hai Li, Qing Wu, Garrett S. Rose, and Yiran Chen. Memristor crossbar based hardware realization of bsb recall function. In *The 2012 International Joint Conference on Neural Networks (IJCNN)*, pages 1–7, IEEE, 2012.

15 Xiaoxuan Yang, Syrine Belakaria, Biresh Kumar Joardar, Huanrui Yang, Janardhan Rao Doppa, Partha Pratim Pande, Krishnendu Chakrabarty, and Hai Helen Li. Multi-objective optimization of reram crossbars for robust dnn inferencing under stochastic noise. In *2021 IEEE/ACM International Conference On Computer Aided Design (ICCAD)*, pages 1–9, IEEE, 2021.

16 Henry Kautz. The third ai summer: aaai robert s. engelmore memorial lecture. *AI Magazine*, 43(1): 105–125, 2022.

17 Ashish Vaswani, Noam Shazeer, Niki Parmar, Jakob Uszkoreit, Llion Jones, Aidan N Gomez, Łukasz Kaiser, and Illia Polosukhin. Attention is all you need. *Advances in Neural Information Processing Systems*, 30: 6000–6010, 2017.

18 Xiaoxuan Yang, Bonan Yan, Hai Li, and Yiran Chen. Retransformer: Reram-based processing-in-memory architecture for transformer acceleration. In *Proceedings of the 39th International Conference on Computer-Aided Design*, pages 1–9, 2020.

19 Myeonggu Kang, Hyein Shin, Junkyum Kim, and Lee-Sup Kim. Mgen: a framework for energy-efficient in-reram acceleration of multi-task bert. *IEEE Transactions on Computers*, 72(11): 3140–3152, 2023.

20 Panjie Qi, Edwin Hsing-Mean Sha, Qingfeng Zhuge, Hongwu Peng, Shaoyi Huang, Zhenglun Kong, Yuhong Song, and Bingbing Li. Accelerating framework of transformer by hardware design and model compression co-optimization. In *2021 IEEE/ACM International Conference On Computer Aided Design (ICCAD)*, pages 1–9, IEEE, 2021.

21 Shikhar Tuli and Niraj K. Jha. Transcode: co-design of transformers and accelerators for efficient training and inference. *IEEE Transactions on Computer-Aided Design of Integrated Circuits and Systems*, 2023.

22 David Silver, Aja Huang, Chris J. Maddison, Arthur Guez, Laurent Sifre, George Van Den Driessche, Julian Schrittwieser, Ioannis Antonoglou, Veda Panneershelvam, Marc Lanctot, et al. Mastering the game of go with deep neural networks and tree search. *Nature*, 529(7587): 484–489, 2016.

23 Forough Arabshahi, Zhichu Lu, Sameer Singh, and Animashree Anandkumar. Memory augmented recursive neural networks. *arXiv*, 2019.

24 Artur S. d'Avila Garcez, Tarek R. Besold, Luc De Raedt, Peter Földiak, Pascal Hitzler, Thomas Icard, Kai-Uwe Kühnberger, Luis C. Lamb, Risto Miikkulainen, and Daniel L. Silver. Neural-symbolic learning and reasoning: contributions and challenges. In *2015 AAAI Spring Symposium Series*, 2015.

25 Jiawei Zhang. Graph-toolformer: to empower llms with graph reasoning ability via prompt augmented by chatgpt. *arXiv preprint arXiv:2304.11116*, 2023.

26 Luciano Serafini and Artur d'Avila Garcez. Logic tensor networks: deep learning and logical reasoning from data and knowledge. In *Proceedings of the 11th International Workshop on Neural-Symbolic Learning and Reasoning (NeSy'16)*, volume 1768. CEUR-WS.org, 2016.

27 Ioannis Karageorgos, Karthik Sriram, Ján Veselý, Michael Wu, Marc Powell, David Borton, Rajit Manohar, and Abhisheks Bhattacharjee. Hardware-software co-design for brain-computer interfaces. In *2020 ACM/IEEE 47th Annual International Symposium on Computer Architecture (ISCA)*, pages 391–404, IEEE, 2020.

28 Adam Kortylewski, Ju He, Qing Liu, and Alan L Yuille. Compositional convolutional neural networks: a deep architecture with innate robustness to partial occlusion. In *Proceedings of the IEEE/CVF Conference on Computer Vision and Pattern Recognition*, pages 8940–8949, 2020.

29 Wen Shen, Zhihua Wei, Shikun Huang, Binbin Zhang, Jiaqi Fan, Ping Zhao, and Quanshi Zhang. Interpretable compositional convolutional neural networks. In *Proceedings of the Thirtieth International Joint Conference on Artificial Intelligence, IJCAI 2021*, pages 2971–2978, ijcai.org, 2021.

30 Wanjun Zhong, Tingting Ma, Jiahai Wang, Jian Yin, Tiejun Zhao, Chin-Yew Lin, and Nan Duan. Disentangling reasoning capabilities from language models with compositional reasoning transformers. In *Findings of the Association for Computational Linguistics: ACL 2023*, pages 7587–7600, ACL, 2023.

31 Xiaoxuan Yang, Brady Taylor, Ailong Wu, Yiran Chen, and Leon O Chua. Research progress on memristor: from synapses to computing systems. *IEEE Transactions on Circuits and Systems I: Regular Papers*, 69(5): 1845–1857, 2022.

32 Xunzhao Yin, Michael Niemier, and X Sharon Hu. Design and benchmarking of ferroelectric fet based tcam. In *Design, Automation & Test in Europe Conference & Exhibition (DATE), 2017*, pages 1444–1449, IEEE, 2017.

33 Tergel Molom-Ochir, Brady Taylor, Hai Li, and Yiran Chen. Advancements in content-addressable memory (cam) circuits: State-of-the-art, applications, and future directions in the ai domain. *IEEE Transactions on Circuits and Systems I: Regular Papers*, 72(8): 3971–3982, 2025.

34 Arman Kazemi, Mohammad Mehdi Sharifi, Zhuowen Zou, Michael Niemier, X Sharon Hu, and Mohsen Imani. Mimhd: Accurate and efficient hyperdimensional inference using multi-bit in-memory computing. In *2021 IEEE/ACM International Symposium on Low Power Electronics and Design (ISLPED)*, pages 1–6, IEEE, 2021.

35 Ibrahim Ahmed, Po-Wei Chiu, William Moy, and Chris H Kim. A probabilistic compute fabric based on coupled ring oscillators for solving combinatorial optimization problems. *IEEE Journal of Solid-State Circuits*, 56(9): 2870–2880, 2021.

36 Gyorgy Csaba and Wolfgang Porod. Coupled oscillators for computing: a review and perspective. *Applied Physics Reviews*, 7(1): 011302, 2020.

37 William Moy, Ibrahim Ahmed, Po-wei Chiu, John Moy, Sachin S. Sapatnekar, and Chris H. Kim. A 1,968-node coupled ring oscillator circuit for combinatorial optimization problem solving. *Nature Electronics*, 5(5): 310–317, 2022.

38 Hao Lo, William Moy, Hanzhao Yu, Sachin Sapatnekar, and Chris H. Kim. An ising solver chip based on coupled ring oscillators with a 48-node all-to-all connected array architecture. *Nature Electronics*, 6: 771–778, 2023.

39 Niklas Funk, Georgia Chalvatzaki, Boris Belousov, and Jan Peters. Learn2assemble with structured representations and search for robotic architectural construction. In *Conference on Robot Learning*, pages 1401–1411, PMLR, 2022.

40 Ho Fung Tsoi, Adrian Alan Pol, Vladimir Loncar, Ekaterina Govorkova, Miles Cranmer, Sridhara Dasu, Peter Elmer, Philip Harris, Isobel Ojalvo, and Maurizio Pierini. Symbolic regression on fpgas for fast machine learning inference. *arXiv preprint arXiv:2305.04099*, 2023.

41 SP Sharan, Wenqing Zheng, Kuo-Feng Hsu, Jiarong Xing, Ang Chen, and Zhangyang Wang. Symbolic distillation for learned tcp congestion control. *Advances in Neural Information Processing Systems*, 35: 10684–10695, 2022.

42 Xiaoxuan Yang, Zhangyang Wang, X Sharon Hu, Chris H. Kim, Shimeng Yu, Miroslav Pajic, Rajit Manohar, Yiran Chen, and Hai Helen Li. Neuro-symbolic computing: advancements and challenges in hardware-software co-design. *IEEE Transactions on Circuits and Systems II: Express Briefs*, 71(3): 1683–1689, 2023.

43 Kexin Yi, Jiajun Wu, Chuang Gan, Antonio Torralba, Pushmeet Kohli, and Josh Tenenbaum. Neural-symbolic vqa: disentangling reasoning from vision and language understanding. *Advances in Neural Information Processing Systems*, 31: 1039–1050, 2018.

44 Chi Han, Jiayuan Mao, Chuang Gan, Josh Tenenbaum, and Jiajun Wu. Visual concept-metaconcept learning. *Advances in Neural Information Processing Systems*, 32: 5001–5012, 2019.

45 Chi Zhang, Baoxiong Jia, Song-Chun Zhu, and Yixin Zhu. Abstract spatial-temporal reasoning via probabilistic abduction and execution. In *Proceedings of the IEEE/CVF Conference on Computer Vision and Pattern Recognition*, pages 9736–9746, 2021.

46 Kexin Yi, Chuang Gan, Yunzhu Li, Pushmeet Kohli, Jiajun Wu, Antonio Torralba, and Joshua B. Tenenbaum. Clevrer: collision events for video representation and reasoning. In *8th International Conference on Learning Representations, ICLR 2020*. OpenReview.net, 2020.

47 Zachary Susskind, Bryce Arden, Lizy K. John, Patrick Stockton, and Eugene B. John. Neuro-symbolic ai: an emerging class of ai workloads and their characterization. *arXiv preprint arXiv:2109.06133*, 2021.

48 Yunzhu Li, Jiajun Wu, Jun-Yan Zhu, Joshua B. Tenenbaum, Antonio Torralba, and Russ Tedrake. Propagation networks for model-based control under partial observation. In *2019 International Conference on Robotics and Automation (ICRA)*, pages 1205–1211, IEEE, 2019.

49 Xinyun Chen, Chen Liang, Adams Wei Yu, Denny Zhou, Dawn Song, and Quoc V Le. Neural symbolic reader: scalable integration of distributed and symbolic representations for reading comprehension. In *International Conference on Learning Representations*, 2019.

50 Natalia Díaz-Rodríguez, Alberto Lamas, Jules Sanchez, Gianni Franchi, Ivan Donadello, Siham Tabik, David Filliat, Policarpo Cruz, Rosana Montes, and Francisco Herrera. Explainable neural-symbolic learning (x-nesyl) methodology to fuse deep learning representations with expert knowledge graphs: the monumai cultural heritage use case. *Information Fusion*, 79: 58–83, 2022.

51 Denis Kleyko, Mike Davies, Edward Paxon Frady, Pentti Kanerva, Spencer J. Kent, Bruno A. Olshausen, Evgeny Osipov, Jan M. Rabaey, Dmitri A. Rachkovskij, Abbas Rahimi, et al. Vector symbolic architectures as a computing framework for emerging hardware. *Proceedings of the IEEE*, 110(10): 1538–1571, 2022.

52 Michael Hersche, Mustafa Zeqiri, Luca Benini, Abu Sebastian, and Abbas Rahimi. A neuro-vector-symbolic architecture for solving raven's progressive matrices. *Nature Machine Intelligence*, 5(4): 363–375, 2023.

53 Yeseong Kim, Mohsen Imani, Niema Moshiri, and Tajana Rosing. Geniehd: efficient dna pattern matching accelerator using hyperdimensional computing. In *2020 Design, Automation & Test in Europe Conference & Exhibition (DATE)*, pages 115–120, IEEE, 2020.

54 Adam Kortylewski, Aleksander Wieczorek, Mario Wieser, Clemens Blumer, Sonali Parbhoo, Andreas Morel-Forster, Volker Roth, and Thomas Vetter. Greedy structure learning of hierarchical compositional models. In *Proceedings of the IEEE/CVF Conference on Computer Vision and Pattern Recognition*, pages 11612–11621, 2019.

55 Tergel Molom-Ochir, Brady Taylor, Hai Li, and Yiran Chen. Monosparse-cam: Harnessing monotonicity and sparsity for enhanced tree model processing on cams. *arXiv preprint arXiv:2407.11071*, 2024.

56 Xu Yang, Hanwang Zhang, Guojun Qi, and Jianfei Cai. Causal attention for vision-language tasks. In *Proceedings of the IEEE/CVF Conference on Computer Vision and Pattern Recognition*, pages 9847–9857, 2021.

57 Ximing Qiao and Hai Li. On a new type of neural computation for probabilistic symbolic reasoning. In *International Joint Conference on Neural Networks, IJCNN 2023*, pages 1–9, IEEE, 2023.

58 Frank Wood, Jan Willem Meent, and Vikash Mansinghka. A new approach to probabilistic programming inference. In *Artificial intelligence and statistics*, pages 1024–1032, PMLR, 2014.

59 Yandan Wang, Wei Wen, Hai Li, and Miao Hu. A novel true random number generator design leveraging emerging memristor technology. In *Proceedings of the 25th edition on Great Lakes Symposium on VLSI*, pages 271–276, 2015.

60 Xiaoxuan Yang, Huanrui Yang, Janardhan Rao Doppa, Partha Pratim Pande, Krishnendu Chakrabarty, and Hai Li. Essence: exploiting structured stochastic gradient pruning for endurance-aware reram-based in-memory training systems. *IEEE Transactions on Computer-Aided Design of Integrated Circuits and Systems*, 2022.

61 Thomas Dalgaty, Elisa Vianello, and Damien Querlioz. Harnessing intrinsic memristor randomness with bayesian neural networks. In *2021 International Conference on IC Design and Technology (ICICDT)*, pages 1–4, IEEE, 2021.

62 Changming Wu, Xiaoxuan Yang, Yiran Chen, and Mo Li. Photonic bayesian neural network using programmed optical noises. *IEEE Journal of Selected Topics in Quantum Electronics*, 29(2: Optical Computing):1–6, 2022.

63 Huanrui Yang, Xiaoxuan Yang, Neil Zhenqiang Gong, and Yiran Chen. Hero: hessian-enhanced robust optimization for unifying and improving generalization and quantization performance. In *Proceedings of the 59th ACM/IEEE Design Automation Conference*, pages 25–30, 2022.

64 Huanrui Yang, Lin Duan, Yiran Chen, and Hai Li. Bsq: exploring bit-level sparsity for mixed-precision neural network quantization. *arXiv preprint arXiv:2102.10462*, 2021.

65 Peter West, Chandra Bhagavatula, Jack Hessel, Jena D. Hwang, Liwei Jiang, Ronan Le Bras, Ximing Lu, Sean Welleck, and Yejin Choi. Symbolic knowledge distillation: from general language models to commonsense models. In *Proceedings of the 2022 Conference of the North American Chapter of the Association for Computational Linguistics: Human Language Technologies, NAACL 2022*, pages 4602–4625, ACL, 2022.

66 Chandra Bhagavatula, Jena D. Hwang, Doug Downey, Ronan Le Bras, Ximing Lu, Lianhui Qin, Keisuke Sakaguchi, Swabha Swayamdipta, Peter West, and Yejin Choi. I2d2: Inductive knowledge distillation with neurologic and self-imitation. In *Proceedings of the 61st Annual Meeting of the Association for Computational Linguistics* (Volume 1: *Long Papers)*, pages 9614–9630, ACL, 2023.

67 Phillip Howard, Junlin Wang, Vasudev Lal, Gadi Singer, Yejin Choi, and Swabha Swayamdipta. Neurocomparatives: neuro-symbolic distillation of comparative knowledge. *arXiv preprint arXiv:2305.04978*, 2023.

68 Jaehun Jung, Peter West, Liwei Jiang, Faeze Brahman, Ximing Lu, Jillian Fisher, Taylor Sorensen, and Yejin Choi. Impossible distillation: from low-quality model to high-quality dataset & model for summarization and paraphrasing. *arXiv preprint arXiv:2305.16635*, 2023.

69 Wangchunshu Zhou, Ronan Le Bras, and Yejin Choi. Commonsense knowledge transfer for pre-trained language models. In *Findings of the Association for Computational Linguistics: ACL 2023*, pages 5946–5960, ACL, 2023.

70 Liunian Harold Li, Jack Hessel, Youngjae Yu, Xiang Ren, Kai-Wei Chang, and Yejin Choi. Symbolic chain-of-thought distillation: Small models can also “think” step-by-step. In *Proceedings of the 61st Annual Meeting of the Association for Computational Linguistics (Volume 1: Long Papers), ACL 2023*, pages 2665–2679, ACL, 2023.

71 Eric Qin, Ananda Samajdar, Hyoukjun Kwon, Vineet Nadella, Sudarshan Srinivasan, Dipankar Das, Bharat Kaul, and Tushar Krishna. Sigma: a sparse and irregular gemm accelerator with flexible interconnects for dnn training. In *2020 IEEE International Symposium on High Performance Computer Architecture (HPCA)*, pages 58–70, IEEE, 2020.

72 Linghao Song, Xuehai Qian, Hai Li, and Yiran Chen. Pipelayer: a pipelined reram-based accelerator for deep learning. In *2017 IEEE International Symposium on High Performance Computer Architecture (HPCA)*, pages 541–552, IEEE, 2017.

73 Shiyu Li, Edward Hanson, Xuehai Qian, Hai "Helen" Li, and Yiran Chen. Escalate: boosting the efficiency of sparse cnn accelerator with kernel decomposition. In *MICRO-54: 54th Annual IEEE/ACM International Symposium on Microarchitecture*, pages 992–1004, 2021.

74 Tunhou Zhang, Wei Wen, Igor Fedorov, Xi Liu, Buyun Zhang, Fangqiu Han, Wen-Yen Chen, Yiping Han, Feng Yan, Hai Li, et al. Distdnas: search efficient feature interactions within 2 hours. In *2024 IEEE International Conference on Big Data (BigData)*, pages 1492–1499, IEEE, 2024.

75 Wei Wen, Hanxiao Liu, Yiran Chen, Hai Li, Gabriel Bender, and Pieter-Jan Kindermans. Neural predictor for neural architecture search. In *European Conference on Computer Vision*, pages 660–676, Springer, 2020.

76 Wei Wen, Feng Yan, Yiran Chen, and Hai Li. Autogrow: automatic layer growing in deep convolutional networks. In *Proceedings of the 26th ACM SIGKDD International Conference on Knowledge Discovery & Data Mining*, pages 833–841, 2020.

77 Fan Chen, Linghao Song, and Yiran Chen. Regan: a pipelined reram-based accelerator for generative adversarial networks. In *2018 23rd Asia and South Pacific Design Automation Conference (ASP-DAC)*, pages 178–183, IEEE, 2018.

78 Ximing Qiao, Xiong Cao, Huanrui Yang, Linghao Song, and Hai Li. Atomlayer: a universal reram-based cnn accelerator with atomic layer computation. In *Proceedings of the 55th Annual Design Automation Conference*, pages 1–6, 2018.

79 Onur Mutlu. Processing data where it makes sense in modern computing systems: Enabling in-memory computation. In *Proceedings of the 2019 on Great Lakes Symposium on VLSI*, pages 5–6, 2019.

80 Bonan Yan, Bing Li, Ximing Qiao, Cheng-Xin Xue, Meng-Fan Chang, Yiran Chen, and Hai Li. Resistive memory-based in-memory computing: from device and large-scale integration system perspectives. *Advanced Intelligent Systems*, 1(7): 1900068, 2019.

81 Qilin Zheng, Xingchen Li, Zongwei Wang, Guangyu Sun, Yimao Cai, Ru Huang, Yiran Chen, and Hai Li. Mobilatice: a depth-wise dcnn accelerator with hybrid digital/analog nonvolatile processing-in-memory block. In *Proceedings of the 39th International Conference on Computer-Aided Design*, pages 1–9, 2020.

82 Shimeng Yu, Hongwu Jiang, Shanshi Huang, Xiaochen Peng, and Anni Lu. Compute-in-memory chips for deep learning: recent trends and prospects. *IEEE Circuits and Systems Magazine*, 21(3): 31–56, 2021.

83 Arman Kazemi, Franz Müller, Mohammad Mehdi Sharifi, Hamza Errahmouni, Gerald Gerlach, Thomas Kämpfe, Mohsen Imani, Xiaobo Sharon Hu, and Michael Niemier. Achieving software-equivalent accuracy for hyperdimensional computing with ferroelectric-based in-memory computing. *Scientific Reports*, 12(1): 19201, 2022.

84 Peilin Chen and Xiaoxuan Yang. Optimizing and exploring system performance in compact processing-in-memory-based chips. *arXiv preprint arXiv:2502.21259*, 2025.

85 Tergel Molom-Ochir, Naman Saxena, Jiwoo Kim, Yiran Chen, Zhangyang Wang, Miroslav Pajic, and Hai Li. Efficient neuro-symbolic policy using in-memory computing. In *International Conference on Neuro-symbolic Systems*, pages 384–395, PMLR, 2025.

86 Xiaochen Peng, Shanshi Huang, Yandong Luo, Xiaoyu Sun, and Shimeng Yu. Dnn+ neurosim: an end-to-end benchmarking framework for compute-in-memory accelerators with versatile device technologies. In *2019 IEEE International Electron Devices Meeting (IEDM)*, pages 32–5, IEEE, 2019.

87 Xiaochen Peng, Wriddhi Chakraborty, Ankit Kaul, Wonbo Shim, Muhannad S. Bakir, Suman Datta, and Shimeng Yu. Benchmarking monolithic 3d integration for compute-in-memory accelerators: overcoming adc bottlenecks and maintaining scalability to 7nm or beyond. In *2020 IEEE International Electron Devices Meeting (IEDM)*, pages 30–4, IEEE, 2020.

88 Xiaochen Peng, Ankit Kaul, Muhannad S. Bakir, and Shimeng Yu. Heterogeneous 3-d integration of multitier compute-in-memory accelerators: an electrical-thermal co-design. *IEEE Transactions on Electron Devices*, 68(11): 5598–5605, 2021.

89 Haopeng Zhang, Xiao Liu, and Jiawei Zhang. Extractive summarization via chatgpt for faithful summary generation. *arXiv preprint arXiv:2304.04193*, 2023.

90 Abhiramon Rajasekharan, Yankai Zeng, Parth Padalkar, and Gopal Gupta. Reliable natural language understanding with large language models and answer set programming. *arXiv preprint arXiv:2302.03780*, 2023.

91 Alper Kamil Bozkurt, Yu Wang, and Miroslav Pajic. Secure planning against stealthy attacks via model-free reinforcement learning. In *2021 IEEE International Conference on Robotics and Automation (ICRA)*, pages 10656–10662, IEEE, 2021.

92 Amit Sheth, Kaushik Roy, and Manas Gaur. Neurosymbolic artificial intelligence (why, what, and how). *IEEE Intelligent Systems*, 38(3): 56–62, 2023.

12

Programmatic Reinforcement Learning

Swarat Chaudhuri

Department of Computer Science, The University of Texas at Austin, Austin, Texas, USA

Corresponding Author: swarat@cs.utexas.edu

12.1 Introduction

Reinforcement learning (RL) [1], in which an agent learns via the exploration of an unknown environment, is a fundamental paradigm in machine learning. Typically, the learning problem in this setting is framed as the discovery of a policy – a map from environment states to agent actions – for a Markov Decision Process (MDP). In state-of-the-art *deep RL* approaches, one represents policies as neural networks. The algorithmic objective is to learn, from data on the effects of various actions at various states, a policy that maximizes the agent's expected long-term *reward*.

The deep RL approach has seen impressive successes, solving learning tasks far beyond the ability of traditional RL approaches, which represented policies using tables or simple function approximations. For example, deep RL is the workhorse of Alphago, which beat the reigning world champion at Go [2]; the Alphachip [3] agent for automated chip design; Spot, a mobile robot shown to function in a range of unstructured environments; and Alphaproof, which recently achieved silver-medal-level performance at the International Mathematics Olympiad.

However, there are at least two impediments to the broad deployment of deep RL in real-world settings. The first is that, as opaque, nonmodular black boxes, deep neural networks are hard to trust and interpret. A second issue is learning efficiency. While human programmers can naturally exploit commonsense and

Neurosymbolic AI: Foundations and Applications, First Edition. Edited by Alvaro Velasquez et al.

expert knowledge, deep RL does not offer a natural way of utilizing such prior knowledge as an inductive bias. As such, deep RL training can be unacceptably sample-inefficient, and the learned neural controllers often behave unreliably on out-of-distribution inputs [4, 5].

RL as Program Sythesis: Motivated to overcome these problems, a recent body of work [6–8] has approached RL using the tools of *neurosymbolic learning* [9, 10]. In neurosymbolic learning, one injects human-provided symbolic knowledge into a deep learning process, for example, into the structure of the models, the loss function, or the learning and inference algorithms. This symbolic knowledge can be seen as a *regularizer* that improves the reliability and transparency of learning and the quality of outputs during inference.

In particular, this paper focuses on programmatic RL(PRL), an approach where RL is cast as *program synthesis* [10, 11]. The goal in program synthesis is to automatically discover programs that satisfy a given task specification. These programs can be in a domain-specific language (DSL) or a general-purpose language like Python; the task specification can be a statement in formal logic or a natural-language expression of intent. Historically, the synthesis problem was solved using symbolic methods such as discrete search and logic-based pruning. More recently, neural and *neurosymbolic* methods – from token-by-token code generation using large language models (LLMs) [12, 13] to more sophisticated search guided by neural models [14, 15] – have emerged as the standard approach to the problem.

To adapt the program synthesis perspective to RL, one sets up a class of learnable policies as programs in a DSL, then uses program synthesis techniques to generate a program in this class. The goal is to find a program that minimizes a standard long-term cost objective.

An important benefit of PRL is that it allows fine-grained control over the structure of learnable policies. In particular, the class of policies can be restricted to what a user may consider "interpretable." Also, the policy DSL can be used to implicitly encode the learner's inductive bias that is used for generalization. Third, the language can allow effective pruning of undesired policies to make the search for a good policy more efficient. Finally, it allows us to use symbolic program verification techniques to formally reason about the learned policies and check consistency with correctness properties. At the same time, policies in PRL can have rich semantics, for example, allowing actions to depend on events far back in history.

From a research perspective, the PRL setting opens up an exciting new space of algorithm design. Because the space of learnable programs is large and non-smooth, traditional gradient-based approaches to deep RL no longer suffice. At the same time, the problem is not a straightforward application of LLM-based code generation [12]. While LLMs excel at translating high-level (e.g., natural-language) intent into code that follows well-known idioms, the goal in PRL is to discover *novel* programmatic solutions to complex optimization problems. While these programs may very well reuse certain insights available in popular program corpora, ultimately, we do not just want to generate policies that a human control engineer could write relatively easily. For these reasons, desirable solutions to the PRL problem commonly involve nontrivial integrations of deep RL and symbolic and neural program synthesis.

In particular, in this paper, we spell out a specific *neurosymbolic* approach to the PRL problem – *Imitation-projected Policy Gradients* – that was originally introduced in a simplified form in Verma et al. [6], became fully developed in Verma et al. [7], and then extended further in Anderson et al. [8]. Here, PRL is viewed as a constrained policy optimization problem in which the desired policies are constrained to be those that have a programmatic representation. This insight motivates an iterative method in which one takes a gradient step into the unconstrained policy space, then repeatedly *projects* back onto the constrained space. We allow the unconstrained policy space to be neurosymbolic – specifically, a weighted sum of a neural and a symbolic policy – which allows the use of standard deep policy gradient approaches [16–19] to compute the unconstrained gradient step. The projection operator can be viewed as the *distillation* of a neurosymbolic policy into a purely symbolic one and can be implemented using classical program synthesis. In Anderson et al. [8], the same framework was used in the setting of formally verified RL.

The rest of the paper is organized as follows. In Section 12.2, we formalize the PRL problem. In Section 12.3, we describe the imitation-projected RL framework. We connect the PRL space to related work in RL and program synthesis in Section 12.4. We conclude with some discussion in Section 12.5.

12.2 Programmatic RL

Now we spell out the PRL framework in more detail. Like other RL frameworks, PRL is formalized using an MDP, $\mathcal{M}$. The definition of $\mathcal{M} = (\mathcal{S}, \mathcal{A}, P, c, p_0, \gamma)$ is standard [1], with $\mathcal{S}$ being a state space, $\mathcal{A}$ the action space, $P(s'|s, a)$ the probability density function of transitioning from a state-action pair to a new state, $c(s, a)$ the state-action cost function, $p_0(s)$ the distribution over starting states, and $\gamma \in (0, 1)$ the discount factor. The state space $\mathcal{S}$ and action space $\mathcal{A}$ can be either discrete or continuous. A policy $\pi : \mathcal{S} \to \Pr[\mathcal{A}]$ stochastically maps states to actions.

A distinctive feature of PRL is the availability of a *programmatic policy class* Π as an additional input. Such a class consists of policies that can be represented parsimoniously in a DSL. For example, Figure 12.1 shows the syntax of a modular, high-level DSL from Verma et al. [7]. This language assumes a library of parameterized functions $\oplus_\theta$ representing standard controllers, for instance, Proportional-Integral-Derivative (PID) [20] or bang-bang controllers [21]. Programs in the language take states s as inputs, produce actions a as outputs, and can invoke fully instantiated library controllers along with predefined arithmetic, boolean, and relational operators.

The learning goal in PRL is to find a programmatic policy $\pi^* \in \Pi$ such that:

$$\pi^* = \arg\min_{\pi \in \Pi} J(\pi), \qquad \text{where: } J(\pi) = \mathbf{E}\left[\sum_{i=0}^{\infty} \gamma^i c(s_i, a_i \sim \pi(s_i))\right] \tag{12.1}$$

with the expectation taken over the initial state distribution $s_0 \sim p_0$, the policy decisions, and the transition dynamics P. One can also use rewards, in which case Equation (12.1) becomes a maximization problem.

Example: Consider the problem of learning a programmatic policy, in the language of Figure 12.1, that controls a car's accelerator in the TORCS car-racing environment [22]. Figure 12.2 shows a program in our language for this task. The program invokes PID controllers $\mathrm{PID}_{j,\theta_P,\theta_I,\theta_D}$, where j identifies the sensor (out of 29) that provides inputs to the controller, and θ_P, θ_I, and θ_D are respectively the real-valued coefficients of the proportional, integral, and derivative terms in the controller. Note that the program only uses the sensors `TrackPos` and `RPM`. While `TrackPos` (for the position of the car relative to the track axis) is used to decide which controller to use, only the `RPM` sensor is needed to calculate the acceleration.

$$\pi(s) ::= a \mid Op(\pi_1(s), \ldots, \pi_k(s)) \mid \textbf{if } b \textbf{ then } \pi_1(s) \textbf{ else } \pi_2(s) \mid \oplus_\theta(\pi_1(s), \ldots, \pi_k(s))$$
$$b ::= \phi(s) \mid BOp(b_1, \ldots, b_k)$$

Figure 12.1 A high-level syntax for programmatic policies. A policy $\pi(s)$ takes a state s as input and produces an action a as output. b represents boolean expressions; ϕ is a boolean-valued operator on states; *Op* is an operator that combines multiple policies into one policy; *BOp* is a standard boolean operator; and $\oplus_\theta$ is a "library function" parameterized by θ. *Source*: [7]. NeurIPS.

$$\textbf{if } (s[\texttt{TrackPos}] < 0.011 \textbf{ and } s[\texttt{TrackPos}] > -0.011)$$
$$\textbf{then } \mathrm{PID}_{\mathrm{RPM},0.45,3.54,0.03,53.39}(s) \textbf{ else } \mathrm{PID}_{\mathrm{RPM},0.39,3.54,0.03,53.39}(s)$$

Figure 12.2 A programmatic policy for acceleration in TORCS, automatically discovered by IPPG. s[`TrackPos`] represents the most recent reading from sensor `TrackPos`. *Source*: Adapted from [22].

12.3 Imitation-projected Policy Gradients

Now we elaborate on a specific approach to PRL – imitation-projected policy gradients – originally developed in Verma et al. [6] and Verma et al. [7]. At the highest level, this method maintains two representations of policies: a programmatic representation in the DSL provided as input to the PRL problem, and a highly expressive neurosymbolic representation. The key intuition is that the class of neurosymbolic policies has learning-friendly gradients, even though the class Π of programmatic policies does not. As the algorithm learns better policies in the neurosymbolic representation, it *projects* these policies into the more restricted programmatic space, leading to the discovery of higher-performance programs.

The projection step in this method is naturally interpreted as the distillation of a high-capacity, neurosymbolic *teacher model* into a lower-capacity *student model*. This idea has a long history in machine learning. The traditional reason for distillation was to execute learning models on platforms with limited computational resources. Distillation-based program synthesis leverages this idea to more general ends.

In more detail, suppose we have a neurosymbolic teacher policy h that is learned using gradient-based optimization. The core projection operation involves the synthesis of a program from the function class Π expressible in the policy DSL, with the same domain and range as h, that maximally imitates the input-output behavior of h. In versions of the problem that arise in safe or verified learning, the symbolic program is additionally required to satisfy a correctness constraint.

Formally, let us assume, in addition to the class Π of DSL programs, a statistically estimable distribution D over function inputs and a distance function δ over the space of function outputs. The problem of *projecting into the programmatic space* can be can be stated as

$$\pi^* = \arg\min_{\pi \in \Pi} \mathbf{E}_{x \in D}\, \delta(\pi(x), h(x)) \tag{12.2}$$

For projection to be profitable, the aforementioned problem must be easier than the end-to-end program synthesis problem, and the teacher g should be easy to construct. These assumptions hold in the RL setting, where direct search for optimal programmatic policies is simply intractable and the teacher can be learned using deep RL.

Now we elaborate on three versions of this approach. While we describe the methods in some detail, we omit any discussion of experimental results. Those details are available in the original papers.

One-shot Projection: PIRL [6] was an early projection-based approach to PRL. This method solves the PRL spelled out in Equation (12.1) through a two-step process. The first step learns a neural policy that performs well in the task objective using a standard deep RL algorithm. This neural network is then distilled into a symbolic program using *online imitation learning*, a family of methods for learning policies that behaviorally mimic a given oracle policy. Specifically, PIRLuses a variant of DAGGER [23], an imitation learning algorithm that grows a dataset of input-output pairs through repeated queries to the oracle. Projection amounts to finding a program that fits this dataset, which is an instance of program synthesis from examples [11].

Algorithm 1 shows the pseudocode of the PIRLapproach. The algorithm iterates over a series of programmatic student policies and maintains a dataset of MDP states labeled with teacher-suggested actions at those states. In each iteration, the current student policy is rolled out in the environment, and the dataset is augmented with states observed in the rollouts and actions that the teacher would take at those states. The algorithm then synthesizes a new student policy – using standard supervised methods for program synthesis [11, 24] – from this dataset.

Mirror Descent with Imitation Projection: The subsequent PROPEL approach [7] incorporates the projection procedure inside an iterative training loop. The idea here is to consider neurosymbolic policies $h(x)$ of the form $h(x) = f(x) + \pi(x)$, where $f(x)$ is a neural policy and $\pi(x)$ is a programmatic policy. The set of programmatic policies is viewed as forming a proper subset Π of the set $\mathcal{H}$ of neurosymbolic policies, and the discovery of an optimal programmatic policy is framed as a constrained optimization task. The learning process, an instance

Algorithm 1 *Project*$_{\Pi}$: Program Synthesis via Imitation Learning

Input: Programmatic Policy Class: Π.
Input: Teacher policy: h
Roll-out h on environment, get trajectory: $\tau_0 = (s^0, h(s^0), s^1, h(s^1), \ldots)$
Create supervised demonstration set: $\Gamma_0 = \{(s, h(s))\}$ from τ_0
Derive π_0 from Γ_0 via program synthesis
for $k = 1, \ldots, M$ **do**
    Roll-out π_{k-1}, creating trajectory: τ_k
    Collect demonstration data: $\Gamma' = \{(s, h(s)) | s \in \tau_k\}$
    $\Gamma_k \leftarrow \Gamma' \cup \Gamma_{k-1}$
    Derive π_k from Γ_k via program synthesis
end for
Return: π_M

of *approximate functional mirror descent*, starts with an initial, suboptimal neurosymbolic policy. In each learning step, it iterates between the following steps:

1. Applying a series of gradient updates ($Update_{\mathcal{F}}$) to the current neurosymbolic policy. Importantly, these updates are based on the gradient of the neural component of the policy and are thus an *approximation* to the true gradient in the $\mathcal{H}$-space.
2. Using an operation $Project_{\Pi}$ to distill this neurosymbolic policy into a programmatic policy.
3. Lifting this programmatic policy back into the neurosymbolic space $\mathcal{H}$ by adding a (randomly initialized or warm-started) neural component.

Thus, both the neural and the symbolic components of the program are learned from data through a synergistic process. Pseudocode of the method, sourced from Verma et al. [7], appears in Algorithm 2. Figure 12.3 illustrates the process visually.

Imitation-projected Learning with Formal Verification: A key benefit of programmatic policies is that unlike neural network, they can be audited and debugged like traditional software. In particular, there has been work on the automated formal verification of policies synthesized through PRL. In these efforts, the PRL problem has a formal correctness, robustness, or safety requirement as an additional input. For example, such properties could assert that the TORCS car-racing agent mentioned earlier avoids a set of bad states or reaches a set of good states under certain

---

Algorithm 2 Imitation-projected Policy Gradients (IPPG)

Input: Programmatic & Neural Policy Classes: Π & $\mathcal{F}$.
Input: Either initial π_0 or initial f_0
Define joint policy class: $\mathcal{H} \equiv \Pi \oplus \mathcal{F}$ // $h \equiv \pi + f$ defined as $h(s) = \pi(s) + f(s)$
if given initial f_0 **then**
    $\pi_0 \leftarrow Project(f_0)$ // projection operation
end if
for $t = 1, \ldots, T$ **do**
    $h_t \leftarrow Update_{\mathcal{F}}(\pi_{t-1}, \eta)$ // policy gradient in neural space with learning rate η
    $\pi_t \leftarrow Project_{\Pi}(h_t)$ // projection operation
end for
Return: Policy π_T

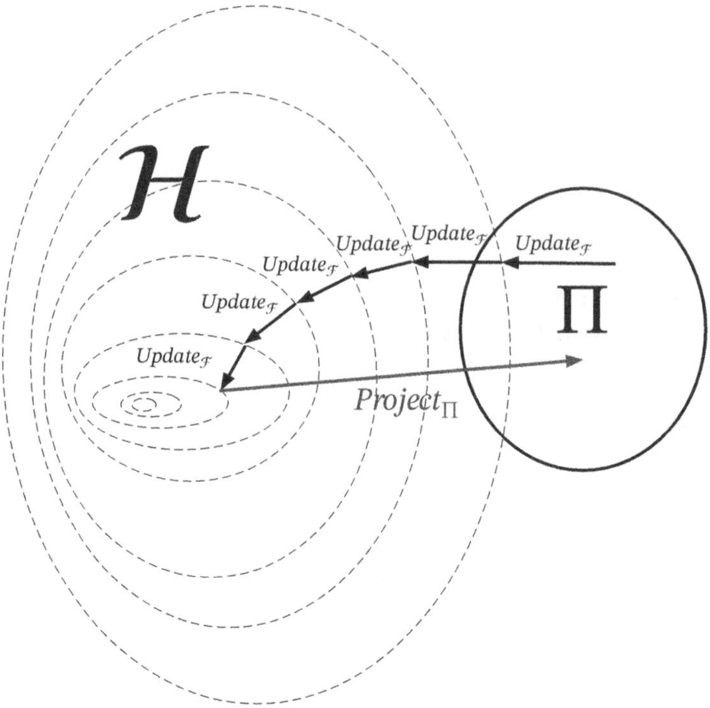

Figure 12.3 The Propel algorithm. *Source*: [7]. NeurIPS.

assumptions on the environment dynamics, or that the policy is not overly sensitive to perturbations to the system state. The goal is to learn a programmatic policy that minimizes a cost function while satisfying (ideally, in a provable manner) the requirements.

In particular, Zhu et al. [25] study the problem of computing, given a neural teacher policy, a provably safe programmatic policy that imitates the teacher as closely as possible. To solve this problem, the method complements imitation learning with *counterexample-guide inductive synthesis* [26], where a solver is used to generate inputs on which π violates the safety constraint. A key benefit of the method is that it does not require verification of neural networks. The only artifact that needs formal verification is the programmatic student policy into which the teacher is distilled.

The REVEL approach [8] takes on the stronger requirement of *formally verified exploration*. This means that the programmatic policy that the learning process converges on is required to be provably safe, as is *every intermediate policy encountered during learning*. The approach extends PROPEL by considering neurosymbolic policies of the form

$$h(x) = \textbf{if } (\psi(x, f(x))\ \textbf{then } f(x)\ \textbf{else } g(x).$$

where $g(x)$ is a shield (a safe programmatic policy), $f(x)$ is a potentially unsafe neural policy, and ψ is a programmatic *monitor predicate.*

Each learning iteration consists of an update to the neural component of the current neurosymbolic policy, a projection step that produces a new monitor and shield, and a lifting operation that constructs a new neurosymbolic policy. The main difference from PROPEL is that each of these steps maintains the invariant of provable safety.

Specifically, the provably safe projection step in REVEL synthesizes a function $h(x)$ that provably satisfies the safety requirement and imitates the teacher $h(x)$ as closely as possible. The proof that $g(x)$ is safe takes the form of an *adequate inductive invariant* $\mathcal{I}$: a set of states that (i) includes all of the system's initial states, (ii) overapproximates all states reachable with $g(x)$ as the policy, and (iii) does not violate the requirement.

Once constructed, the invariant $\mathcal{I}$ (represented symbolically as a formula) can be used to construct a monitor predicate ψ. Consider an action $f(x)$ taken by the neural component f at a state x. If $\psi(x, f(x))$ takes the system out of the state set $\mathcal{I}$, then the action is not provably safe. Instead, we use the *shield* g, which has the property that the action $g(x)$ keeps the system state within $\mathcal{I}$, i.e., preserves safety. This means that the overall neurosymbolic policy behaves safely no matter what its neural component is.

This observation implies that the neural component may be updated using gradients without compromising provable safety. It also means that a symbolic shield may be safely lifted into the neurosymbolic form with a randomly initialized neural component.

12.4 Related Work

Program Synthesis: Work on PRL draws on a large body of work on program synthesis [11], the discovery of programs from task specifications expressed as, for example, tests, natural-language expressions of intent, and formal constraints. Pre-deep-learning approaches to the problem were based on symbolic methods [27–29]; a few numerical optimization approaches [30, 31] had been proposed, but these methods were not mainstream. The field underwent a paradigm shift in the mid-2010s with the rise of neural and neurosymbolic program synthesis [24, 32–35]. In the recent past, LLMs [12, 14, 36] have emerged as the state-of-the-art approach to program synthesis. While much of the work here is on generating code that follows popular idioms, there is also recent work [14, 15] on the LLM-based synthesis of *novel* programs.

The idea of learning a student model that incorporates the knowledge stored in a teacher or oracle is well established in the deep learning [37–39] and program synthesis [29] communities. The projection step in methods like PIRL and PROPEL was built on this prior work. While these approaches preceded the rise of LLMs, one can imagine using LLM-based search [14, 15] for this kind of program synthesis.

Constrained Policy Learning: There is a sizeable body of work on constrained policy learning, motivated by the goal of imposing side guarantees such as stability and safety on the policy's behavior. Broadly, there are two approaches to imposing constraints: specifying constraints as an additional cost function [40, 41], and explicitly encoding constraints into the policy class [19, 42–45]. In some cases, these two approaches can be viewed as duals of each other. For instance, work that uses control-theoretic policies as a functional regularizer [19, 43] can be viewed from the perspective of both regularization (additional cost) and an explicitly constrained policy class (a specific mix of neural and control-theoretic policies). The PRL literature builds on this perspective by interpreting the DSL and additional behavioral specifications as constraints.

RL Using Imitation Learning: There are two ways to utilize imitation learning subroutines within RL. First, one can leverage limited-access or sub-optimal experts to speed up learning [46–49]. Second, one can learn over two policy classes (or one policy and one model class) to achieve accelerated learning compared to using only one policy class [50–53]. The imitation-projected approach has some stylistic similarities to previous efforts [50, 52] that use a richer policy space to search for improvements before re-training the primary policy to imitate the richer policy.

RL with Mirror Descent: The mirror descent framework has been used to analyze and design RL algorithms. For example, Thomas et al. [54] and Mahadevan and Liu [55] use composite objective mirror descent, or COMID [56], which allows incorporating adaptive regularizers into gradient updates, thus offering connections to either natural gradient RL [54] or sparsity inducing RL algorithms [55]. However, the PROPEL approach was the first to connect mirror descent to program synthesis.

12.5 Conclusion

We have given an overview of PRL, a recently proposed dialect or RL in which policies are represented as neurosymbolic programs. We sketched a formal definition of the problem and described a mirror descent approach [7, 8] to solving it.

Limitations: Some of the limitations of PRL are shared with other RL approaches. For example, a general issue in RL methods is that they typically need high-quality simulators. While such simulators are available in settings like game-playing, they are often hard to find in real-world tasks. This challenge has often impeded the deployment of RL, and PRL methods also face this challenge.

However, PRL faces a new set of challenges as well. An important one is *scalability*. Deep RL is already known to be hard to scale because of sample-inefficiency, and by using human-provided priors, PRL can potentially improve the scalability of deep RL. But on the other hand, searching over programs is a combinatorially hard problem. When the program structures follow broadly known idioms, one can use LLMs to generate the code step-by-step. However, research on using LLMs to generate entirely novel programs, a key objective in PRL, is in its infancy.

A second challenge, unique to the PRL setting, is *specification*. PRL assumes that humans can specify domain knowledge effectively via DSLs and behavioral constraints. However, constructing the "right" specification for a domain is nontrivial, and unnecessarily restrictive specifications can impede learning performance.

The Future: We are excited about the future prospects of PRL. RL is frequently motivated by applications where data efficiency, safety, and interpretability are salient issues. PRL offers a fresh set of principles for this setting. In terms of practicality, the field of AI-based code generation has seen tremendous progress in the recent past [12, 14, 57]. We are optimistic that these gains will also transfer to the field of PRL.

In particular, we believe that modern LLMs can help with the scalability and specification challenges that we mentioned earlier. Recent methods such as Funsearch [14] and LaSR [15] illustrate that the priors and abstraction capabilities of LLMs can prove useful even when one wants to generate novel programs. As for specification, LLMs have been successfully used in the *autoformalization* of informal mathematical statements [58]. One can imagine such autoformalization techniques being more generally used to construct specifications for PRL.

Among other priorities for research in this area is the design of software frameworks that simplify the deployment of PRL in new domains. Standardized benchmarks and competitions that showcase the value of PRL and are also of interest to the broader community would also be of great value. Researchers in this area should also prioritize the development of infrastructures that enable their methods to scale. Of particular interest are new methods for parallelizing large-scale LLM-guided search over programs. Finally, finding new real-world tasks where one can showcase the unique capabilities of PRL remains a high priority. Safety-critical or regulated domains like robotics, finance, and healthcare seem like promising sources for such tasks.

References

1 Richard S. Sutton and Andrew G. Barto. *Reinforcement learning: an introduction.* MIT press, 2018.

2 David Silver, Aja Huang, Chris J. Maddison, Arthur Guez, Laurent Sifre, George van den Driessche, Julian Schrittwieser, Ioannis Antonoglou, Vedavyas Panneershelvam, Marc Lanctot, et al. Mastering the game of Go with deep neural networks and tree search. *Nature*, 529(7587): 484–489, 2016.

3 Azalia Mirhoseini, Anna Goldie, Mustafa Yazgan, Joe Wenjie Jiang, Ebrahim Songhori, Shen Wang, Young-Joon Lee, Eric Johnson, Omkar Pathak, Azade Nazi, et al. A graph placement methodology for fast chip design. *Nature*, 594(7862): 207–212, 2021.

4 Christian Szegedy, Wojciech Zaremba, Ilya Sutskever, Joan Bruna, Dumitru Erhan, Ian J. Goodfellow, and Rob Fergus. Intriguing properties of neural networks. *CoRR*, abs/1312.6199, 2013.

5 Alexey Kurakin, Ian J. Goodfellow, and Samy Bengio. Adversarial examples in the physical world. *CoRR*, abs/1607.02533, 2016.

6 Abhinav Verma, Vijayaraghavan Murali, Rishabh Singh, Pushmeet Kohli, and Swarat Chaudhuri. Programmatically interpretable reinforcement learning. In *ICML*, pages 5052–5061, 2018.

7 Abhinav Verma, Hoang M. Le, Yisong Yue, and Swarat Chaudhuri. Imitation-projected programmatic reinforcement learning. In *Neural Information Processing Systems (NeurIPS)*, 2019.

8 Greg, Anderson, Abhinav Verma, Isil Dillig, and Swarat Chaudhuri. Neurosymbolic reinforcement learning with formally verified exploration. In *Neural Information Processesing Systems (NeurIPS)*, 2020.

9 Artur d'Avila Garcez and Luis C Lamb. Neurosymbolic AI: the 3rd wave. *arXiv preprint arXiv:2012.05876*, 2020.

10 Swarat Chaudhuri, Kevin Ellis, Oleksandr Polozov, Rishabh Singh, Armando Solar-Lezama, and Yisong Yue. Neurosymbolic programming. *Foundations and Trends® in Programming Languages*, 7(3): 158–243, 2021.

11 Sumit Gulwani, Oleksandr Polozov, and Rishabh Singh. Program synthesis. *Foundations and Trends in Programming Languages*, 4(1–2): 1–119, 2017.

12 Mark Chen, Jerry Tworek, Heewoo Jun, Qiming Yuan, Henrique Ponde De Oliveira Pinto, Jared Kaplan, Harri Edwards, Yuri Burda, Nicholas Joseph, Greg Brockman, et al. Evaluating large language models trained on code. *arXiv preprint arXiv:2107.03374*, 2021.

13 Jiawei Liu, Chunqiu Steven Xia, Yuyao Wang, and Lingming Zhang. Is your code generated by chatgpt really correct? Rigorous evaluation of large language models for code generation. *Advances in Neural Information Processing Systems*, 36:21558–21572, 2024.

14 Bernardino Romera-Paredes, Mohammadamin Barekatain, Alexander Novikov, Matej Balog, M. Pawan Kumar, Emilien Dupont, Francisco J. R. Ruiz, Jordan S. Ellenberg, Pengming Wang, Omar Fawzi, et al. Mathematical discoveries from program search with large language models. *Nature*, 625(7995): 468–475, 2024.

15 Arya Grayeli, Atharva Sehgal, Omar Costilla-Reyes, Miles Cranmer, and Swarat Chaudhuri. Symbolic regression with a learned concept library. In *Neural Information Processing Systems*, 2024.

16 Timothy P. Lillicrap, Jonathan J. Hunt, Alexander Pritzel, Nicolas Heess, Tom Erez, Yuval Tassa, David Silver, and Daan Wierstra. Continuous control with deep reinforcement learning. *arXiv preprint arXiv:1509.02971*, 2015.

17 John Schulman, Sergey Levine, Pieter Abbeel, Michael Jordan, and Philipp Moritz. Trust region policy optimization. In *International Conference on Machine Learning*, pages 1889–1897, 2015.

18 John Schulman, Filip Wolski, Prafulla Dhariwal, Alec Radford, and Oleg Klimov. Proximal policy optimization algorithms. *arXiv preprint arXiv:1707.06347*, 2017.

19 Richard Cheng, Abhinav Verma, Gabor Orosz, Swarat Chaudhuri, Yisong Yue, and Joel W. Burdick. Control regularization for reduced variance reinforcement learning. In *International Conference on Machine Learning (ICML)*, 2019.

20 Karl Johan Åström and Tore Hägglund. Automatic tuning of simple regulators with specifications on phase and amplitude margins. *Automatica*, 20(5): 645–651, 1984.

21 Richard Bellman, Irving Glicksberg, and Oliver Gross. On the "bang-bang" control problem. *Quarterly of Applied Mathematics*, 14(1): 11–18, 1956.

22 Bernhard Wymann, Eric Espié, Christophe Guionneau, Christos Dimitrakakis, Rémi Coulom, and Andrew Sumner. TORCS, The Open Racing Car Simulator, 2014. http://www.torcs.org.

23 Stéphane Ross and Drew Bagnell. Efficient reductions for imitation learning. In *Proceedings of the Thirteenth International Conference on Artificial Intelligence and Statistics, AISTATS 2010*, Chia Laguna Resort, Sardinia, Italy, *May 13-15, 2010*, pages 661–668, 2010.

24 Ameesh Shah, Eric Zhan, Jennifer J. Sun, Abhinav Verma, Yisong Yue, and Swarat Chaudhuri. Learning differentiable programs with admissible neural heuristics. In *Advances in Neural Information Processing Systems*, 2020.

25 He Zhu, Zikang Xiong, Stephen Magill, and Suresh Jagannathan. An inductive synthesis framework for verifiable reinforcement learning. In *PLDI*, 2019.

26 Rajeev Alur, Rastislav Bodík, Eric Dallal, Dana Fisman, Pranav Garg, Garvit Juniwal, Hadas Kress-Gazit, P. Madhusudan, Milo M. K. Martin, Mukund Raghothaman et al. In *Dependable Software Systems Engineering*, pages 1–25. 2015. https://doi.org/10.3233/978-1-61499-495-4-1.

27 John K. Feser, Swarat Chaudhuri, and Isil Dillig. Synthesizing data structure transformations from input-output examples. In *Proceedings of the 36th ACM*

SIGPLAN Conference on Programming Language Design and Implementation, Portland, OR, USA, *June 15-17, 2015*, pages 229–239, 2015.

28 Armando Solar-Lezama, Liviu Tancau, Rastislav Bodík, Sanjit A. Seshia, and Vijay A. Saraswat. Combinatorial sketching for finite programs. In *ASPLOS*, pages 404–415, 2006.

29 Susmit Jha, Sumit Gulwani, Sanjit A. Seshia, and Ashish Tiwari. Oracle-guided component-based program synthesis. In *Proceedings of the 32nd ACM/IEEE International Conference on Software Engineering – Volume 1*, ICSE '10, pages 215–224, New York, NY, USA, 2010. ACM.

30 Swarat Chaudhuri and Armando Solar-Lezama. Smooth interpretation. In *PLDI*, pages 279–291, 2010.

31 Swarat Chaudhuri and Armando Solar-Lezama. Smoothing a program soundly and robustly. In *CAV*, pages 277–292, 2011.

32 Matej Balog, Alexander L. Gaunt, Marc Brockschmidt, Sebastian Nowozin, and Daniel Tarlow. Deepcoder: learning to write programs. *CoRR*, abs/1611.01989, 2016.

33 Emilio Parisotto, Abdel-rahman Mohamed, Rishabh Singh, Lihong Li, Dengyong Zhou, and Pushmeet Kohli. Neuro-symbolic program synthesis. In *5th International Conference on Learning Representations, ICLR 2017*, Toulon, France, April 24-26, 2017, *Conference Track Proceedings*. OpenReview.net, 2017. https://openreview.net/forum?id=rJ0JwFcex.

34 Jacob Devlin, Jonathan Uesato, Surya Bhupatiraju, Rishabh Singh, Abdel-rahman Mohamed, and Pushmeet Kohli. Robustfill: neural program learning under noisy I/O. In *ICML*, 2017.

35 Kevin Ellis, Daniel Ritchie, Armando Solar-Lezama, and Josh Tenenbaum. Learning to infer graphics programs from hand-drawn images. In *NeurIPS*, pages 6059–6068, 2018.

36 Xinyi Hou, Yanjie Zhao, Yue Liu, Zhou Yang, Kailong Wang, Li Li, Xiapu Luo, David Lo, John Grundy, and Haoyu Wang. Large language models for software engineering: a systematic literature review. *ACM Transactions on Software Engineering and Methodology*, 33(8): 1–79, 2024.

37 Geoffrey Hinton. Distilling the knowledge in a neural network. *arXiv preprint arXiv:1503.02531*, 2015.

38 Nicholas Frosst and Geoffrey E. Hinton. Distilling a neural network into a soft decision tree. *CoRR*, abs/1711.09784, 2017.

39 Nicolas Papernot, Patrick D. McDaniel, Xi Wu, Somesh Jha, and Ananthram Swami. Distillation as a defense to adversarial perturbations against deep neural networks. *CoRR*, abs/1511.04508, 2015.

40 Joshua Achiam, David Held, Aviv Tamar, and Pieter Abbeel. Constrained policy optimization. In Proceedings of the 34th International Conference on Machine Learning-Volume 70, pages 22–31. JMLR.org, 2017.

41 Hoang M. Le, Cameron Voloshin, and Yisong Yue. Batch policy learning under constraints. In *International Conference on Machine Learning (ICML)*, 2019.

42 Mohammed Alshiekh, Roderick Bloem, Rüdiger Ehlers, Bettina Könighofer, Scott Niekum, and Ufuk Topcu. Safe reinforcement learning via shielding. In Sheila A. McIlraith and Kilian Q. Weinberger, editors, *Proceedings of the Thirty-Second AAAI Conference on Artificial Intelligence, (AAAI-18)*, pages 2669–2678. AAAI Press, 2018.

43 Hoang M. Le, Andrew Kang, Yisong Yue, and Peter Carr. Smooth imitation learning for online sequence prediction. In *International Conference on Machine Learning (ICML)*, 2016.

44 Gal Dalal, Krishnamurthy Dvijotham, Matej Vecerik, Todd Hester, Cosmin Paduraru, and Yuval Tassa. Safe exploration in continuous action spaces. *arXiv preprint arXiv:1801.08757*, 2018.

45 Felix Berkenkamp, Matteo Turchetta, Angela Schoellig, and Andreas Krause. Safe model-based reinforcement learning with stability guarantees. In *Advances in Neural Information Processing Systems*, pages 908–918, 2017.

46 Stephane Ross and J. Andrew Bagnell. Reinforcement and imitation learning via interactive no-regret learning. *arXiv preprint arXiv:1406.5979*, 2014.

47 Ching-An Cheng, Xinyan Yan, Nolan Wagener, and Byron Boots. Fast policy learning through imitation and reinforcement. In *Uncertainty in Artificial Intelligence*, 2019.

48 Kai-Wei Chang, Akshay Krishnamurthy, Alekh Agarwal, Hal Daumé III, and John Langford. Learning to search better than your teacher. In *International Conference on Machine Learning (ICML)*, 2015.

49 Wen Sun, J. Andrew Bagnell, and Byron Boots. Truncated horizon policy search: combining reinforcement learning & imitation learning. *arXiv preprint arXiv:1805.11240*, 2018.

50 William H. Montgomery and Sergey Levine. Guided policy search via approximate mirror descent. In *Advances in Neural Information Processing Systems*, pages 4008–4016, 2016.

51 Ching-An Cheng, Xinyan Yan, Evangelos Theodorou, and Byron Boots. Accelerating imitation learning with predictive models. In *International Conference on Artificial Intelligence and Statistics (AISTATS)*, 2019.

52 Wen Sun, Geoffrey J. Gordon, Byron Boots, and J. Bagnell. Dual policy iteration. In *Advances in Neural Information Processing Systems*, pages 7059–7069, 2018.

53 Ching-An Cheng, Xinyan Yan, Nathan Ratliff, and Byron Boots. Predictor-corrector policy optimization. In *International Conference on Machine Learning (ICML)*, 2019.

54 Philip S. Thomas, William C. Dabney, Stephen Giguere, and Sridhar Mahadevan. Projected natural actor-critic. In *Advances in Neural Information Processing Systems*, pages 2337–2345, 2013.

55 Sridhar Mahadevan and Bo Liu. Sparse q-learning with mirror descent. In *Proceedings of the Twenty-Eighth Conference on Uncertainty in Artificial Intelligence*, pages 564–573. AUAI Press, 2012.

56 John C. Duchi, Shai Shalev-Shwartz, Yoram Singer, and Ambuj Tewari. Composite objective mirror descent. In *COLT*, pages 14–26, 2010.

57 John Yang, Carlos E. Jimenez, Alexander Wettig, Kilian Lieret, Shunyu Yao, Karthik Narasimhan, and Ofir Press. Swe-agent: agent-computer interfaces enable automated software engineering. *arXiv preprint arXiv:2405.15793*, 2024.

58 Yuhuai Wu, Albert Qiaochu Jiang, Wenda Li, Markus Rabe, Charles Staats, Mateja Jamnik, and Christian Szegedy. Autoformalization with large language models. *Advances in Neural Information Processing Systems*, 35: 32353–32368, 2022.

Part III

Applications

13

From Symbolic to Neurosymbolic Information Extraction

Mihai Surdeanu,[1] Marco A. Valenzuela-Escárcega,[2] Gus Hahn-Powell,[1] Robert Vacareanu,[1] Gwendolen Herongrove,[3] Enrique Noriega-Atala,[1] Özgün Babur,[4] Emek Demir,[5] and Clayton T. Morrison[1]*

[1] *University of Arizona, Tucson, Arizona, USA*
[2] *Lex Machina, Menlo Park, California, USA*
[3] *RiverStone Resources, Manchester, New Hampshire, USA*
[4] *University of Massachusetts Boston, Boston, Massachusetts, USA*
[5] *Oregon Health & Science University, Portland, Oregon, USA*

*Corresponding Author: msurdeanu@arizona.edu

13.1 Motivation and Overview

Information extraction (IE), a subfield of natural language processing (NLP), works on the problem of automating the extraction of structured information from unstructured text. IE has many important real-world applications, especially those that are overwhelmed by data, such as biomedicine, the legal fields, finance, and intelligence. For example, for more than 10 years now, over one million publications have been added to PubMed *each year* [1] (see Figure 13.1). At the same time, one of several large-scale patient profiling efforts currently generates petabytes of data, and this is expected to grow to exabytes in the near future [2]. These large datasets can be combined with mechanistic biological information to produce causal and predictive models of cellular processes, which can in turn enable important downstream applications in biology and medicine. Unfortunately, most of this mechanistic knowledge is not available in the literature in a form computers can make use of; instead, this knowledge is largely buried in the sheer scale of available data. Existing human-driven biocuration projects are making extremely

Neurosymbolic AI: Foundations and Applications, First Edition. Edited by Alvaro Velasquez et al.

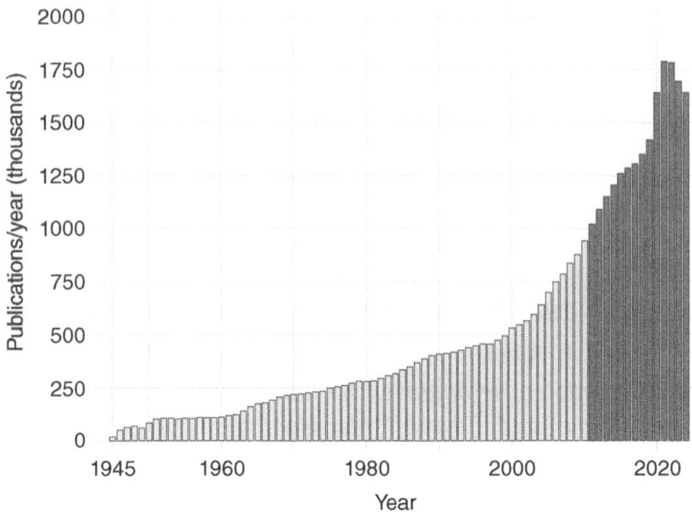

Figure 13.1 This figure plots the number of PubMed publications per year. The darker gray columns to the right highlight that since 2011, the quantity of publications has exceeded one million per year.

valuable contributions toward addressing this problem, but they are outpaced and overwhelmed by rate at which the literature is growing, and the situation is rapidly getting worse. For example, it is estimated that public pathway databases such as Pathway Commons[1] capture only 1–3% of the literature, and the gap is widening every day.[2] IE provides a set of tools to help to reduce this gap.

Since the onset of the "deep learning tsunami" [3], neural network approaches to IE have played a central role in extending the state of the art in many NLP tasks [4–8]. All of these advances, however, come at a cost, including (i) low explainability [9] and (ii) fragility [10]. The advent of large language models (LLMs) has advanced the field even further but has also introduced additional reliability challenges, such as LLM "hallucinations" [11]. Explainability and reliability are critical requirements in many domains, including intelligence and healthcare [12–14]. There are efforts to incorporate explainability into neural network models [15–17], but unfortunately most of the resulting explanations are restricted to being *local* and *post-hoc*, and this has two important consequences. First, local and post-hoc explanations are not guaranteed to be *faithful* [18]; that is, they may not accurately represent the actual reasoning process that produced the model's prediction. Second, they are not *actionable*, meaning that we may not be able to use the insights from the explanation to modify the underlying model

1 www.pathwaycommons.org.
2 Internal analysis of the Pathway Commons team.

Table 13.1 An example of an IE rule together with one sentence that the rule matches. The rule captures the org:founder relation, which extracts founders of an organization. The rule implements a syntactic pattern where the predicate *founded* serves as an anchor that, in turn, has a subject that is a person named entity and a direct object that is an organization named entity.

Rule	[ne=per]+ <nsubj founded >dobj [ne=org]+
Sentence	Daniel Dines founded UiPath

without risking introducing new, unexpected behavior. On the other hand, symbolic IE systems, such as those based on rules,[3] are explainable and *pliable*.[4] However, these systems currently lack the generalization power of state-of-the-art deep learning systems [17]. Consider the simple example shown in Table 13.1. The example rule can be understood with minimal training; it is pliable, i.e., it can be modified simply by adjusting the underlying pattern, and its matches are explainable, i.e., we can trace back which parts of the retrieved text were matched by components of the rule pattern. While this example demonstrates the desired properties of explainability and pliability, it also exposes a key shortcoming: this rule does not match semantically equivalent sentences that use different lexical or syntactic forms, e.g., *Daniel Dines is the founder of UiPath* clearly has an equivalent meaning but fails to match the rule.

In this chapter, we advocate for methods that combine the two directions – symbolic and neural – into hybrid approaches that preserve the advantages of both. To set the stage, we begin in the next section with a description of a symbolic IE system and its applications to the biomedical domain (Section 13.2). We show that this system holds its own against systems based on neural networks in an IE evaluation in the biomedical domain. Moreover, the system is shown to be capable of hypothesis generating, as it discovers previously unreported causal explanations for seven different cancers. Building on this, we next discuss the challenges faced by symbolic systems (Section 13.3), such as the high cost of writing rules manually and their limited capacity for generalization. In the following sections, we propose neurosymbolic approaches to address these issues. In Section 13.4, we present a novel strategy for rule acquisition that works with minimal human supervision. Then, in Section 13.5, we introduce a new neurosymbolic method that enhances the generalization power of rules by semantically matching rules to text, rather than relying on the encoded lexical-syntactic patterns. We show that these hybrid directions outperform neural state-of-the-art methods on several IE datasets.

---

3 We refer to surface and syntactic patterns as rules, for example, [ne=per]+ <nsubj founded >dobj [ne=org]+.

4 We use this term "pliable" as it was introduced by Dayne Freitag during the panel discussion at the PaN-DL workshop [19] to indicate that rules can be modified to improve the corresponding local behavior while minimizing the impact on the rest of the model.

13.2 An Example of Symbolic IE

13.2.1 Introduction

A vast reservoir of published findings remains outside machine-readable form (see Section 13.1), and this conversion shortfall sharply limits how far large-scale data methods can be pushed in biology. For instance, take the identification of "driver" mutations in cancer. A repeatedly observed phenomenon is that, across a cohort, specific driver alterations rarely co-occur – fewer patients harbor both than random expectation would predict. This pattern typically reflects convergence on the same oncogenic pathway: after one alteration confers the growth advantage, an additional one adds little; in effect, "one suffices." Injecting prior pathway structure concentrates the search, conserving statistical power that broad multiple-hypothesis correction would otherwise erode. Additionally, it helps provide mechanistic explanations for the observed associations [20]. However, recall rates can remain low due to limitations in database coverage. As a result, researchers must choose between high-coverage, no-prior methods that lack mechanistic insight and prior-based, low-coverage approaches that risk missing important events.

To address these complex biological questions, we present a symbolic IE approach[5] designed to achieve a system-level, mechanistic understanding of cellular processes by automatically and comprehensively reading scientific literature. We demonstrate that this method enables the generation of novel biological hypotheses across multiple cancer types. We refer to our method as Reach (*RE*ading and *A*ssembling *C*ontextual and *H*olistic mechanisms from text).

This research makes two key contributions. The first is the machine reading framework itself. At its core, Reach employs a cascade of automata driven by *compact*, *interpretable*, and *adaptable* grammars designed to extract relevant entities (e.g., proteins) and events (e.g., biochemical interactions). Taken together, these properties keep the model's inner logic inspectable and readily adjustable or extensible by knowledgeable practitioners. The efficiency of this compact grammar enables rapid runtime performance – on average, a single paper is processed in just 4.5 seconds – while the system can also be parallelized to leverage cluster computing and multicore architectures for large-scale deployments. Furthermore, Reach handles complex linguistic structures such as coreference and can accurately determine event polarity even in statements involving nested contrasts (e.g., "a *reduction* of *increased* phosphorylation led to ..."). In addition, Reach resolves intricate linguistic phenomena (e.g., coreference) and correctly infers event polarity even under layered reversals (e.g., "a *reduction* of *increased* phosphorylation ..."). Independent assessment confirmed that Reach sustains strong

---

5 Originally introduced and developed in [21–23].

precision on cancer signaling extractions while operating fast enough to cover the full open-access corpus within days.

The second major contribution lies in demonstrating that combining machine-generated "big data" with manually curated "big mechanisms" yields novel insights that would otherwise remain undiscovered. The second principal contribution shows that fusing machine-read "big data" with expert-curated "big mechanisms" uncovers mechanistic insights that manual curation alone would miss. Specifically, we show that Reach significantly enhances the inference capabilities of existing biological data analysis algorithms, which traditionally relied only on manually curated pathway resources such as Pathway Commons (PC). In this work, we augmented the Pathway Commons database with over one million biochemical interactions automatically extracted by Reach from all papers in the PubMed Open Access subset (as of June 2015). Using this expanded prior graph, the Mutex algorithm [20] surfaced many formerly unreported yet strongly significant mutually exclusive signaling modules across TCGA cohorts. A manual review of these modules revealed that between 65 and 80% of the pathway fragments discovered by Reach are accurate, and importantly, these findings facilitate the generation of novel biological hypotheses within the relevant cancer contexts.

13.2.2 Approach

At a high level, Reach employs a cascade of rule-based and statistical methods to process scientific papers and detect mentions of molecular events that represent fragments of signaling pathways. As illustrated in Figure 13.2, these steps progress

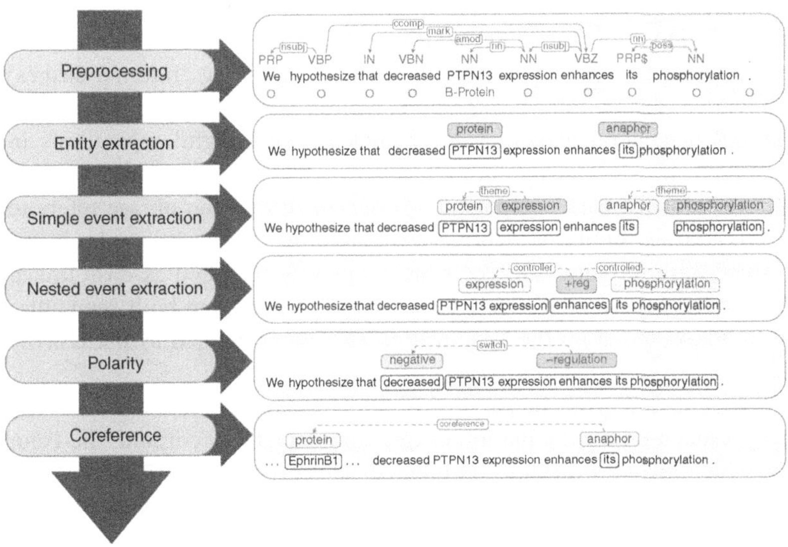

Figure 13.2 The Reach system architecture illustrated with a demonstration example.

from simpler to increasingly complex representations, with each stage building upon the outputs generated by the preceding ones.

The internal representation of these mentions is modeled using a format inspired by the BioPAX standard language [24]. Importantly, Reach can capture detailed biochemical conversions in which entities undergo "state" changes, such as phosphorylation or relocation within the cell. When the text specifies controllers or catalysts driving these conversions, Reach represents them as well. Similar to BioPAX, these mentions are encoded using a *composite* structure in which events can include other events as participants, enabling the representation of arbitrarily complex biological processes. A key extension beyond BioPAX is Reach's ability to extract higher-level control relationships between entities (e.g., "KRAS activates p53"). While such relations are biologically less specific than mechanistic representations (e.g., the statement "KRAS promotes phosphorylation of p53 on Ser37" provides a more detailed mechanism), they nevertheless convey valuable insights to domain experts.

In the following sections, we provide a detailed description of the Reach architecture components shown in Figure 13.2, focusing on the modules responsible for extracting these mechanistic pathway fragments.

13.2.2.1 Preprocessing

Reach begins by preprocessing the text using NLP tools adapted specifically for the biomedical domain. This preprocessing stage involves sentence and word segmentation, part-of-speech (POS) tagging, and syntactic parsing to prepare the text for downstream extraction tasks.

The sentence and word segmentation stage identifies boundaries between sentences and individual tokens in the input text. Biomedical tokenization departs from open-domain practice because domain conventions (e.g., internal dashes) encode functional distinctions. For example, while dashes within words are typically ignored in general text, they often indicate meaningful separations in biomedical contexts. Correctly splitting terms like "GAP-mediated" at the dash is essential for downstream components to recognize that the phrase refers to GAP-driven catalysis. Similarly, incorrect dash handling can mask complex membership, since multi-protein constructs are frequently rendered as dash-linked strings. To address these challenges, Reach employs a custom-built segmenter designed in-house, based on the tokenization guidelines defined by the GENIA corpus [25].

For POS tagging and syntactic parsing, Reach leverages the Stanford CoreNLP toolkit [26], trained on a combination of two complementary corpora: the Penn Treebank, which includes various non-biomedical genres such as IBM computer manuals and Wall Street Journal articles [27, 28], and the GENIA corpus, a manually annotated collection of 2,000 MEDLINE abstracts [25]. Augmenting training with GENIA material equips the parser to manage the dense, specialized syntactic constructions prevalent in biomedical prose.

13.2.2.2 Entity Extraction

Next, Reach employs a custom named entity recognizer (NER) specifically designed to identify mentions of relevant biological entities and classify them by type. These include categories such as protein families, cellular components, simple chemicals, sites, and genes or gene products (the latter encompassing both genes and proteins). The full set of entity types recognized by Reach, along with the biochemical events extracted later, is detailed in the taxonomy shown in Figure 13.3.

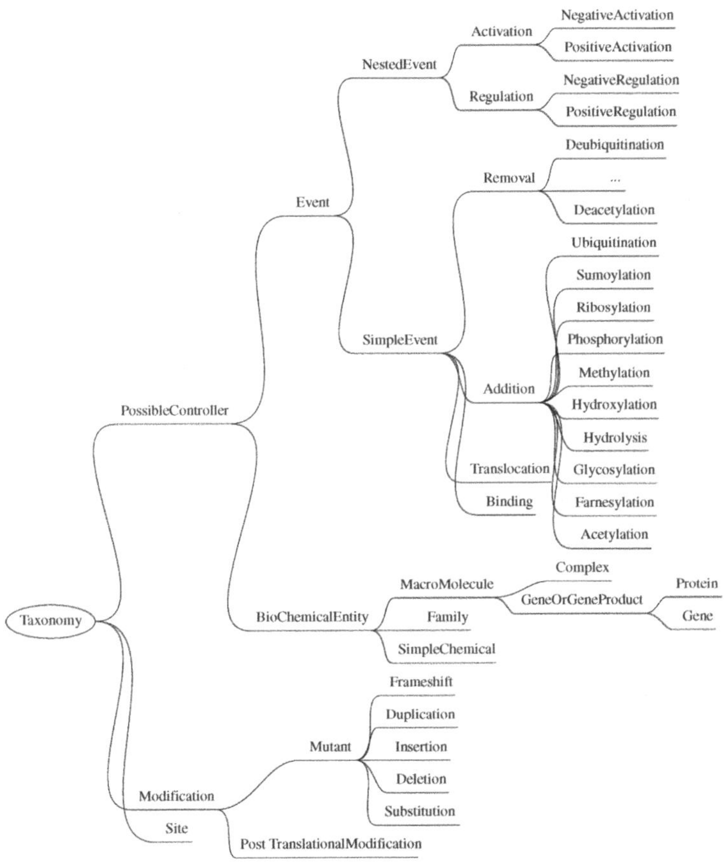

Figure 13.3 Complete taxonomy of entities and events that Reach can recognize. While condensed for space, the `Removal` events correspond to those shown under `Addition`.

Table 13.2 Knowledge bases utilized by the rule-based named entity recognizer and for entity grounding.

Entity type	Database	URL
Protein	UniProt	www.uniprot.org/
Protein families	InterPro	www.ebi.ac.uk/interpro/
Simple chemicals	HMDB	www.hmdb.ca/
Simple chemicals	ChEBI	www.ebi.ac.uk/chebi/
Sites	InterPro	www.ebi.ac.uk/interpro/

The custom NER in Reach adopts a hybrid strategy that integrates both rule-based and statistical methods. The rule-based component identifies mentions of known entity names and their synonyms using the knowledge bases (KBs) listed in Table 13.2. To broaden recall, bespoke grammars target under-represented classes (e.g., subcellular structures, modification sites) absent or sparse in the listed KBs. The statistical component leverages CoreNLP's conditional random field (CRF) sequence classifier, trained on the BioCreative corpus [29], which focuses specifically on mentions of genes and gene products. The final hybrid NER combines the outputs from both components, giving precedence to the rule-based results in cases where overlapping predictions occur.

Next, Reach performs entity grounding by linking the identified biochemical entities to their corresponding unique identifiers in the KBs listed in Table 13.2. For example, the text span "MEK1" grounds to UniProt `Q02750`, harmonizing references for subsequent analytical pipelines.

Finally, Reach identifies mentions of gene mutations and protein post-translational modifications (PTMs) and associates them with the corresponding biochemical entity mentions extracted earlier. This is achieved using an additional grammar specifically designed to detect state changes in entities. For example, from the phrase "wild type EHR," Reach extracts the state wild type (i.e., non-mutated) and links it directly to the previously identified entity mention "EHR."

13.2.2.3 Event Extraction

After Reach identifies the entities mentioned in the text, it proceeds to extract the biochemical processes in which they are involved. This is done using a two-step, bottom-up event extraction strategy, guided by biochemical semantics inspired by BioPAX. In the first step, Reach detects biochemical reactions that act directly on entities, such as the phosphorylation of a protein, while temporarily ignoring catalysts and other controlling factors. In NLP terminology, these are referred to as "simple" events. In the second step, Reach identifies processes that regulate or control these conversions, such as a kinase catalyzing the phosphorylation.

These are referred to as "nested" events because they involve other events as their targets – for example, the catalysis event operates on the simple phosphorylation event.

A key contribution of this work is the use of a relatively small set of rules for event extraction. This efficiency is achieved by first identifying common syntactic patterns that are shared across different event mentions – such as subject–verb–object (S–V–O) constructions in both active and passive voice – and then reusing these generalized syntactic structures for all event types. Efficiency arises by abstracting recurrent syntactic skeletons (e.g., active/passive S–V–O frames) and instantiating them across event inventories.

We implement this approach using templates defined in the Odin IE rule language [21, 22]. Odin templates allow us to express rules as parameterized patterns that can be reused across multiple event types. For instance, a single template can capture the active-voice S–V–O syntactic structure, leaving the verb itself as a parameter to be filled in later. At runtime, this parameter is instantiated with event-specific verbs, such as "phosphorylate" for phosphorylation events, enabling a flexible yet compact rule set.

Overall, Reach supports 12 types of simple events, as shown in Figure 13.3. Nine of these correspond to biochemical reactions: phosphorylation, ubiquitination, hydroxylation, sumoylation, glycosylation, acetylation, farnesylation, ribosylation, and methylation. Each of these reactions involves the covalent modification of a protein by attaching a specific functional group. The key distinction between these events and the PTMs extracted in the earlier step is that these events describe the process of modifying the protein, whereas the previously extracted PTMs indicate proteins that are already in a modified state, potentially as the result of such simple events described elsewhere in the text.

The other three simple events are translocation (relocating an entity between cellular compartments), binding (assembling multi-protein complexes), and hydrolysis (water-mediated bond cleavage, covering degradation-like processes).

Nested events are processes that regulate other events, such as catalysis or inhibition. Reach identifies both positive controls (e.g., "promotes") and negative controls (e.g., "inhibits"). Moreover, the control logic can be chained, allowing the representation of more complex relationships, such as the co-modulation of a catalytic process. Following BioNLP terminology [30], we group all these regulatory processes under the general category of "regulations" for simplicity.

Reach also detects mentions of "activations," which represent higher-level interactions describing the direct control of an entity's activity (e.g., "A activates B," where A and B are proteins). Structurally, activations are similar to regulations, with the key distinction being that the "controlled" participant refers to an implied downstream activity of a biochemical entity rather than an explicitly defined event. Unlike regulations, these are not supported in BioPAX due to the semantic ambiguity introduced by the fact that proteins can possess multiple, overlapping activities. However, Reach includes activations because they are commonly used in the literature as abstractions summarizing the outcome of a sequence of signaling steps. While activations provide less detail than full regulations when viewed in isolation, they offer valuable insights, including the author's high-level interpretation of the mechanism and indirect relationships between proteins.

Like simple events, nested events follow the same underlying syntactic patterns, such as S–V–O constructions, described earlier. Leveraging these recurring patterns, the extraction system was implemented in Odin using 154 unique rule templates, as summarized in Table 13.3.

13.2.2.4 Complex Natural Language Phenomena

In addition to the previously described event and entity extraction grammars, Reach also handles more complex linguistic phenomena that are challenging to capture with rules alone – specifically, polarity, and coreference.

Polarity: Special handling is required for statements involving nested controls with differing polarities. For instance, in the example from Figure 13.2, "decreased PTPN13 expression enhances EphrinB1 phosphorylation," the verb "enhances" might initially suggest that PTPN13 positively regulates EphrinB1 phosphorylation. However, closer examination of the context shows that it is actually the decrease in PTPN13 expression that leads to increased phosphorylation. Reach correctly interprets this as a polarity flip, changing the inferred regulation from positive to negative.

Table 13.3 Count of rule templates in Reach's extraction grammars.

Type	Syntax	Surface	Total
Entities	0	15	15
Generic entities	0	2	2
Modifications	0	6	6
Mutants	0	9	9
Total	0	32	32
Simple events	15	11	26
Binding	30	7	37
Hydrolysis	8	2	10
Translocation	12	0	12
Positive regulation/activation	16	4	20
Negative regulation/activation	14	3	17
Total events	95	27	122
Total	95	59	154

Polarity correction is managed by traversing the syntactic dependency path that links the event trigger to all its associated arguments within the dependency graph, while tracking any words that indicate a reversal of polarity. Additionally, adjectival modifiers attached to any part of this path are also taken into account. For example, in the regulation event shown in Figure 13.2, the modifier "decreased" serves as a key signal for the polarity flip.

Coreference Resolution: Coreference – the phenomenon where different mentions in text refer to the same real-world entity or event – is particularly common in the biomedical domain. Resolving these links significantly improves recall in IE; however, it is rarely addressed in biomedical NLP systems. Coreference can involve both entities and events and often spans across sentence boundaries. For example, in the following cases, the bold text refers back to the italicized text. Correctly resolving these references enables Reach to extract additional events that would otherwise be missed.

- "In the current study, we describe the phosphorylation, localization, and genome-wide regulatory functions of *HP1γ* in gonadal tissue, gametes, and the preimplantation embryo. We demonstrate that phosphorylation of **this protein** at S83, which occurs in response to Aurora A, is necessary for supporting proper mitotic cell division in cells from the sperm lineage."
- "When Wnt signaling or Cdc42 activity was blocked, the induced, but not the basal level of this interaction, was lost, suggesting both Wnt and Cdc42 activities are required to promote a *Dvl2/aPKC interaction* after scratching. In contrast, aPKC inhibitors did not block **this interaction**, suggesting aPKC activity was not required for Dvl2/aPKC complex formation."

Inspired by Lee et al. [31], we adopt a sieve-based architecture for coreference resolution, where deterministic resolution rules ("sieves") are applied in order from highest to lowest precision and lowest to highest recall. This design offers similar benefits to the previously described rule-based framework for entity and event extraction, including stability, human interpretability, and strong overall performance.

However, direct transplantation of Lee et al. [31]'s system degraded precision in this domain, chiefly from aggressive cluster merging. We mitigated this by pruning redundant or overly liberal sieves and inserting domain-aware passes that exploit biomedical signals to sharpen linking.

For example, the ability to recognize mutants – even when the word "mutant" is not explicitly mentioned – enables Reach to correctly resolve references in sentences like: "... We prepared recombinant H2AX-K134A ... The intensity of the band corresponding to histone H2AX methylation was significantly diminished in the K134A mutant compared with that of wild-type H2AX (H2AX-WT) ...". Similarly, identifying specific protein reactions facilitates resolving otherwise challenging cases, such as linking two distinct mentions of the same binding event in: "LL-37 forms a complex together with the IGF-1R ... and this binding results in IGF-1R activation ...". A detailed description of this approach can be found in [32].

13.2.3 Intrinsic Evaluation: Machine Reading Performance

In an independently administered evaluation [33],[6] Reach demonstrated the ability to extract signaling pathways with relatively high precision while achieving a throughput sufficient to process the entire open-access biomedical literature within just a few days. During the evaluation, participating systems analyzed 1000 papers on the Ras signaling pathway over the course of a week.

Two metrics were used to assess performance: (i) *Precision* – defined as the proportion of interactions judged "largely correct," which required that (a) the extracted interaction matched the supporting text evidence, (b) both participants (if applicable) and the interaction type were correctly identified, and (c) the system accurately determined whether the interaction was negated in the text. (ii) *Throughput* – the estimated number of "largely correct" interactions extracted per day from the 1,000 publications.

Importantly, entity grounding correctness – linking textual mentions of interaction participants to their corresponding KB identifiers – was not considered when computing precision. Additionally, throughput was used as a proxy for recall, since calculating true recall would have been prohibitively expensive at this scale.

Four other teams participated in the evaluation, each employing distinct strategies. For anonymity, the participating consortia are not named, but their approaches are summarized here. Group A developed a pipeline composed of multiple machine learning components, each addressing different subtasks, such as detecting interaction types and identifying interaction participants. Teams 2 and 3 adopted a hybrid approach, combining machine learning techniques to construct semantic representations of text [34, 35] with a rule-based system to extract domain-specific information from these open-domain representations. Group D relied on a fully rule-based approach, using rules designed specifically to capture surface-level patterns in the text.

In this evaluation, Reach and Group D were part of the same consortium and were evaluated jointly. The final results of the assessment are summarized in Table 13.4.[7]

---

6 Conducted by MITRE as part of the DARPA Big Mechanism program (www.darpa.mil/program/big-mechanism).

7 Please note that the precision scores in the table are based on slightly different paper selections for each team. This adjustment was necessary because the number of extracted

Table 13.4 Performance results from the big mechanism machine reading evaluation.

Team	Throughput	Precision (%)
Group A	62	59
Group B	342	23
Group C	110	**63**
Reach + group D	**695**	49
Reach	486	62

The results in Table 13.4 show that the Reach + Group D consortium achieved the optimal balance between precision and throughput, obtaining the highest throughput while maintaining relatively high precision. Group B recorded the second-highest throughput, but both its throughput and precision were less than half of those achieved by Reach + Group D. While Groups A and C attained higher precision scores, their throughputs were significantly lower – specifically, 11.2 times smaller for Group A and 6.3 times smaller for Group C compared to Reach + Group D's throughput.

Although the evaluation reports combined results for Reach and Group D, we conducted a post hoc internal analysis to isolate Reach's individual contribution within the consortium. In this analysis, we separated the extractions produced by Reach from those generated by Group D. The results revealed that Reach alone achieved a precision of 62% and accounted for approximately 70% of the consortium's total throughput. As shown in the last row of Table 13.4, these findings reinforce the earlier conclusion: Reach delivers substantially higher throughput than all other participating teams while maintaining precision close to the highest levels observed in the evaluation.

The high throughput achieved by Reach can be attributed to two main factors. First, the system's design – built on Odin grammars that integrate syntactic and surface-pattern rules, along with coreference resolution, polarity handling, and other mechanisms (see Section 13.2.2) – ensures broad coverage of the diverse linguistic phenomena present in the dataset. Second, the Reach grammar runtime is highly efficient, processing a single publication in under five seconds on average. This speed enabled the team to process the entire set of 1000 papers well within

interactions varied widely among submissions. To ensure statistical reliability, MITRE evaluated additional papers for systems producing fewer extractions. All teams were assessed on the same eight papers; however, Group A, Group C, and Reach + Group D were scored on two additional publications, while Group C was further evaluated on three more.

the evaluation timeframe. In fact, the Reach submission was completed within the first few hours of the seven-day evaluation period.

Overall, this analysis demonstrates that Reach achieves comparatively high precision while maintaining exceptionally high throughput. As we illustrate in the next subsection, this high throughput can be further leveraged to improve precision by exploiting redundancy – that is, the more frequently an interaction is extracted across different papers, the greater the likelihood that the extraction is correct.

13.2.4 Extrinsic Evaluation: Discovery of Biological Hypotheses

Next, we demonstrate how Reach enables the discovery of previously unknown biological hypotheses, focusing on the identification of mutually exclusive alterations among "driver" mutations in cancer. We observe that, across a cohort of cancer patients, certain mutations co-occur less frequently than expected by chance. This pattern often arises because these alterations activate the same cancer-driving pathways, meaning that once one mutation occurs, the selective advantage of the other is greatly reduced. A simple analogy helps illustrate this concept: imagine a burglar attempting to enter a building to steal valuable property. The burglar can gain access either by breaking a window or forcing a door, but typically not both – one entry point is sufficient. Similarly, across a large enough set of burglary cases, broken windows and doors would overlap less frequently than random chance would predict. In the context of cancer mutations, the same principle applies: for many pathways, "one is enough."

A straightforward, no-prior approach to identifying mutually exclusive (*mutex*) relationships is to test all possible pairs of genes using a hypergeometric test. However, in practice, we often observe cases where three or more genes within the same pathway display mutually exclusive patterns. In these scenarios, this brute-force approach becomes less effective because the number of hypotheses grows exponentially with the size of the module,[8] which leads to a significant loss of statistical power due to multiple-comparison corrections.

For larger modules, it also becomes increasingly important to provide a mechanistic explanation for why a given set of alterations exhibits mutual exclusivity, as additional confounding factors come into play. To address these limitations, the Mutex algorithm [20] integrates large-scale omic profiles with prior knowledge of pathway mechanisms. Given a set of omic profiles, Mutex performs a graph search over prior networks constructed from pathway information, testing at each step whether a network module is mutually exclusively altered and whether the underlying pathway structure can explain the observed pattern.

---

8 Here, a module refers to a group of signaling pathways that converge on the same downstream protein.

By leveraging prior pathway knowledge, Mutex achieves higher accuracy by reducing the search space and preserving statistical power. Additionally, it provides mechanistic explanations for the observed correlations. However, relying only on curated sources (e.g., Pathway Commons) caps recall because their coverage footprint is inherently limited.

In this chapter, we investigate whether the performance of the "vanilla" Mutex algorithm can be improved by augmenting its prior pathway knowledge with information extracted by Reach. Specifically, we enhanced the Pathway Commons[9] human-curated pathways, which were used in the original implementation of Mutex, by incorporating pathway fragments automatically extracted by Reach from 1, 046, 662 papers in the PubMed Open Access subset (as of June 2015), as illustrated in Figure 13.4.

Using this combined prior network, we identified previously undiscovered, yet highly statistically significant, mutually exclusively altered signaling modules in the TCGA cancer datasets by applying the Mutex algorithm described earlier. Figures 13.5 and 13.6 illustrate the identified Mutex groups for TCGA breast cancer, while Table 13.5 provides a summary of the findings across all enhanced TCGA cancer studies. In this table, ***R*** denotes the Mutex configuration that uses the combined Reach + Pathway Commons network, *P* represents the configuration using only the Pathway Commons network, and *W* corresponds to the

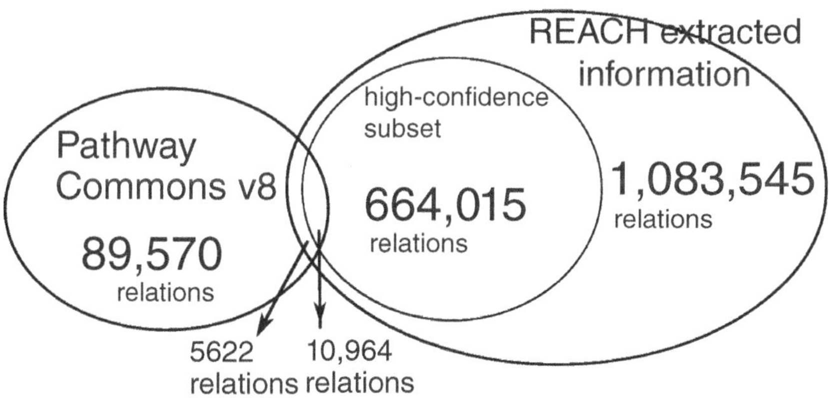

Figure 13.4 Comparison showing Reach output is approximately 12 times larger than Pathway Commons. The limited overlap likely stems from Reach interactions being extracted from open-access publications, while Pathway Commons pathways derive primarily from paywalled publications. High-confidence subset represents relations found in multiple papers.

9 http://www.pathwaycommons.org/.

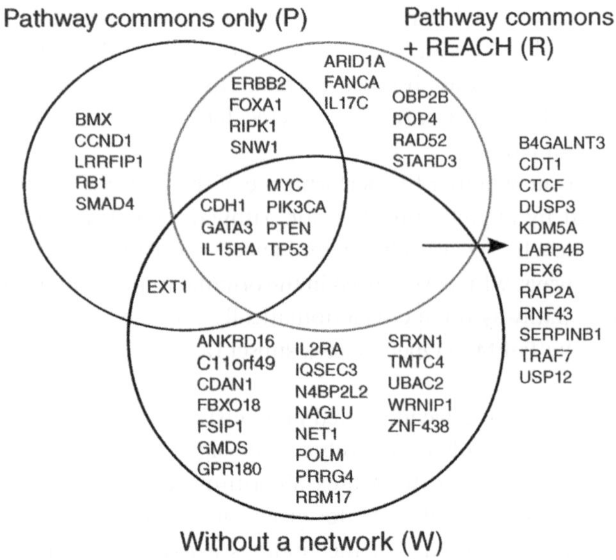

Figure 13.5 Reach enables Mutex to identify seven novel candidate "driver" genes for breast cancer that remain undetected when using Pathway Commons alone or no network at all. Similar patterns were observed across six additional cancers in the TCGA dataset.

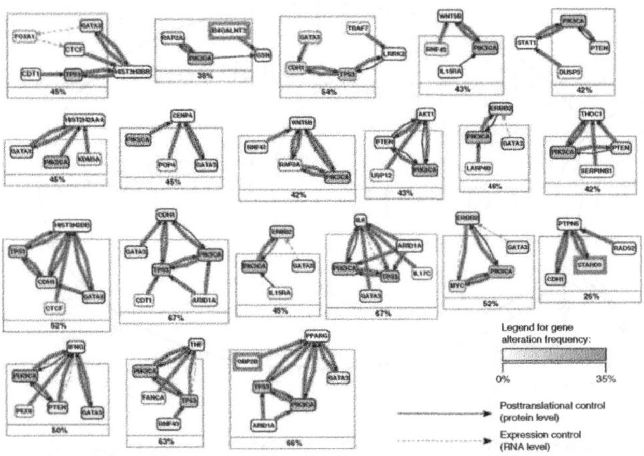

Figure 13.6 Identified Mutex groups in TCGA breast cancer data. The graph displays interactions between genes in each Mutex group and their downstream targets. Emphasized relations exist in Reach data but are absent from Pathway Commons. Emphasized genes cannot be detected without Reach data.

Table 13.5 TCGA analysis results using Mutex enhanced with Reach. The **R**-P-W and **R**W-P ablation studies demonstrate that Reach extractions enable new hypothesis discovery across seven cancer types.

Cancer study	R	P	W	R-P-W	RW-P
BLCA	2	2	6	0	0
BRCA	30	17	40	7	12
CESC	5	6	7	0	0
DLBC	0	5	0	0	0
GBM	23	14	40	3	7
HNSC	26	23	25	3	2
KICH	0	0	6	0	0
LAML	2	2	2	0	0
LGG	26	12	51	0	14
LIHC	12	17	16	0	0
LUAD	14	16	11	1	0
OV	7	11	7	2	0
PAAD	22	7	17	10	5
SARC	15	22	25	0	0
THCA	9	11	12	0	0
UVM	2	3	34	0	0

configuration that runs without any supporting prior network. In Table 13.5, we also present ablation results to isolate the contribution of machine reading. For example, ***R**-P-W* represents the output of the ***R*** configuration after removing all hypotheses that were also discovered by either the *P* (Pathway Commons only) or *W* (no-prior network) approaches. Overall, Table 13.5 demonstrates that machine reading via Reach directly contributes to the discovery of novel biological hypotheses in seven different cancers.

A manual evaluation of these modules conducted by an external cancer researcher (Table 13.6) shows that, despite the inherent noise in machine reading, 65% of the hypotheses generated by the Mutex algorithm – when enhanced with signaling pathways extracted by Reach – are correct according to the literature. Moreover, applying a simple redundancy filter that retains Reach extractions only if they are observed at least twice in the literature increases accuracy to 80%.

These results demonstrate that our approach systematically and incrementally expands the coverage of existing curated pathway networks using NLP-driven machine reading. We believe this strategy is particularly valuable for molecular tumor boards and other scenarios where integrating system-scale omics data with

Table 13.6 Accuracy assessment of hypotheses produced by Mutex enhanced with Reach. The "With direction" column evaluates strict, directional hypotheses, e.g., *GATA3 activates PTEN*. The "Ignoring direction" column evaluates non-directional hypotheses, e.g., either *GATA3 activates PTEN* or *PTEN activates GATA3*.

	Hypotheses generated	With direction (%)	Ignoring direction (%)
Seen at least once	51	65	71
Seen at least twice	21	80	80

Table 13.7 Analysis of errors in incorrect hypotheses produced by Mutex + Reach.

Error type	Frequency (%)	Example input and incorrect output
Complex syntax	39 (7)	*Input:* "In mouse models of leukemia and melanoma, IDH mutants accelerated cell cycle transition by activation of the MAPK and ERK pathway and repression of tumor suppressors CDKN2A and CDKN2B (Chaturvedi et al., Shibata et al.)" *Incorrect output:* CDKN2A controls IDH. The correct interaction to be extracted from this statement is: IDH controls CDKN2A
NER	22 (4)	*Input:* "At PND100, BPA significantly increased expression of EGFR ($p = 0.0132$), phospho-IGF-1R ($p = 0.007$), ..." *Incorrect output:* BPA is a protein. In this paper, BPA refers to the corresponding chemical not the protein with the same name
Hedging	22 (4)	"Therefore, we next investigated whether CIC promotes mutant p53 GOF" *Incorrect output:* CIC activates p53, which is unsupported by the hedged statement
Other	17 (3)	—

literature-derived knowledge is essential for generating biologically meaningful insights.

However, a post hoc error analysis of the incorrect hypotheses generated by this approach (Table 13.7) reveals that machine reading with symbolic systems remains an open challenge. Specifically, 39% of the errors stem from incorrect syntactic analyses, 22% arise from errors in entity recognition or grounding (e.g., in the example from the table, "BPA" refers to the chemical Bisphenol A, not the protein with the same acronym), and another 22% result from hedged statements – claims made in the literature that are not actually supported by experimental evidence.

13.2.5 Conclusion

This section introduced Reach, a symbolic IE system designed to convert statements from biomedical literature into mechanistic knowledge. An independently administered evaluation showed that Reach outperforms other systems when considering a metric that balances both precision and throughput. Overall, Reach demonstrated relatively high precision – comparable to human-level annotation in some cases – while maintaining very high throughput, processing a single paper in just 4.5 seconds. The system is released as open-source software and is available at github.com/clulab/reach.

This study shows that scaling automated literature reading bridges "big data" (machine-harvested mechanistic statements) with "big mechanisms" (expert pathway schemata) to surface new oncogenic hypotheses. Using Reach, we processed a vast collection of PubMed Central articles containing mechanistic information and showed that incorporating this knowledge enhances the performance of biological data analysis algorithms. By combining information extracted by Reach with the curated pathways from Pathway Commons, we identified previously unknown cancer-driving mechanisms across seven cancers in the TCGA dataset. Furthermore, an external biologist's evaluation of the hypotheses generated by the algorithm revealed that 65% were supported by the literature, and when considering only interactions observed at least twice in the literature, the accuracy increased to 80%.

13.3 Problems of Symbolic IE Systems

Section 13.2 demonstrated the clear value of symbolic IE systems: they perform well and can be developed relatively fast using only human expertise, without the need for training data, due to their explainability and pliability. However, these advantages are accompanied by a series of disadvantages:

- The rule matching algorithm can be slow. Theoretically, the rule matching system is an instance of the subgraph isomorphism problem, where the rule encodes the subgraph of interest (typically capturing patterns over syntactic dependencies or semantic roles) and the syntactic/semantic representation of the text constitutes the larger graph. Subgraph isomorphism is an NP-complete problem [36], which means that the rule matching engine can have a significant runtime overhead. Due to space constraints, we will not discuss solutions to this limitation here. Instead, we refer the interested readers to Valenzuela-Escárcega et al. [37], where we show that the rule matching engine can be significantly sped up by indexing the graphs representing the syntactic/semantic representations of sentences ahead of time. This optimization results in a rule matching engine that is nearly 150,000 times faster than the system described in Section 13.2.

- Writing rules can be labor-intensive. For instance, in the effort described in Section 13.2, the team developed a grammar consisting of approximately 150 rules over the course of two person-months. In many scenarios – such as when an intelligence analyst must rapidly assess a new threat – this amount of time is simply not feasible. In the next section, we describe an alternative to the manual creation of rules: an algorithm that synthesizes rules from a few provided examples using methods inspired by the field of program synthesis.
- Traditionally, rules match exactly the encoded pattern and nothing more. As mentioned in Section 13.1, this limits their capacity for generalization. To overcome this limitation, in Section 13.5, we present a neurosymbolic approach to rule matching that combines the strengths of both paradigms: the precision and transparency of rule-based systems with the generalization power of neural networks. Our proposed approach consists of two components: a rule-based component that transparently applies rules over text and a neural component that enhances rule generalizability through semantic text matching.

13.4 Generating Rules

13.4.1 Introduction

In Section 13.2, we presented evidence that rule-based IE is precise, and that its coverage can be improved by composing patterns that reference syntactic and semantic regularities. While powerful and interpretable, such rules require linguistic expertise to craft. This limits the portability of the approach: a subject matter expert (SME) must either devote time to mastering an otherwise esoteric language or partner with someone who already possesses this knowledge. None of these options is ideal. The former proposes an unrealistic solution in which an already-busy SME must dedicate time to learn a complex topic entirely disconnected from their own field of expertise. The latter involves building an interdisciplinary team composed of experts who may not share a common technical "language," e.g., biomedical researchers and computer scientists. In the effort described in Section 13.3, we adopted the interdisciplinary team approach. However, it took us several months of learning each other's "language" before we became truly productive.

In this section, we propose a third option: an interdisciplinary team composed of *human* SMEs, who bring domain expertise, and *machine* computer scientists, who know how to write code. With the advent of LLMs trained to generate code, this collaboration is becoming increasingly common. However, there is one significant difference between our approach and how code-generating LLMs are typically used today: instead of providing formal technical descriptions of the desired code, our approach allows users to simply supply examples of inputs and expected outputs. This strategy facilitates interaction between the SME, who understands the task to be implemented, and the code-generating algorithm. As a simple example, imagine a biomedical researcher who wants to train a computer to extract protein names from research publications. The only information the SME needs to provide is a small number of input sentences and the protein names to be extracted from them, such as *"In response to DNA damage, p53 is phosphorylated, leading to its stabilization and activation as a transcription factor,"* from which the protein name *p53* should be extracted. Using such examples, the computer can generate patterns (or rules) that consistently extract protein names, e.g., patterns such as *X is phosphorylated*, where *X* represents the protein name.

More formally, here we describe a technique[10] for neural program synthesis to learn rules for a new domain. We bring two self-imposed constraints to our method: (i) the end user needn't have any knowledge of linguistics or machine learning in order to use the system, and (ii) to reduce the barrier of entry to new domains, the method for rule generation should rely on domain-agnostic data for its development. Despite these constraints, we show that our method outperforms other strong baselines that have the same level of supervision. We present two types of evaluations that demonstrate the benefits of the proposed approach. The first evaluation focuses on interactive sessions where users generate rules that extract mentions of named entity classes, e.g., `CITY` or `ACADEMIC INSTITUTION`, from a *single example extraction*. Using six different users, we show that, despite the minimal supervision, the tool produces named entities in the corresponding classes with high precision, e.g., precision at 20 (P@20) at over 75% for the `CITY` class. This suggests that the proposed method is useful to domain scientists that need to perform IE quickly, without understanding the underlying technology. We also include a non-interactive evaluation, on the TACRED dataset [5], through which we show that the rules synthesized by our approach outperform the manually written rules by over four F1 points, even though our synthesis component is *not* retrained on the TACRED data.

13.4.2 Approach

Program synthesis is a well-established area of study in computer science focused on methods for deriving programs that satisfy some predefined goal. Approaches to program synthesis require three components: (i) a program space defined by a language (e.g., a DSL), (ii) a user intent (the program *specification*), and (iii) an algorithm that guides program creation via search or constraint satisfaction. One popular paradigm in program synthesis is *program by example* [41–43], where the

10 This technique was first introduced and developed in Vacareanu et al. [38, 39], Noriega-Atala et al. [40].

specification is defined as a series of (input, output) pairs. We adapt the *program by example* paradigm to the task of IE, where (input, output) pairs are defined as natural language sentences as the input with targeted spans as the output. We call our method OdinSynth because we *synth*esize rules in the *Odin*son IE language [37].

Thus, in our take on program synthesis, we use the Odinson IE language as our program space. User intent or *specification* is collected as one or more highlighted text spans in a given sentence. Prior work in program synthesis uses a deductive search to discover valid solutions in the program space; however, as the depth of the search increases, this approach becomes intractable. For even simple programs, possible states can number in the billions. To navigate the search space efficiently, we use a series of heuristics in tandem with an encoder-only transformer neural network trained to score all legal transitions or next states in the program derivation process for prioritized exploration of the program space [40].

To train our scoring function, we select random spans of text in a corpus to serve as program *specifications*, and use these target spans to automatically derive a non-exhaustive sample of Odinson queries that meet each specification through a random rule generation process. For details, see Algorithm 3 in Noriega-Atala et al. [40]. For each specification in this dataset, we also retain the intermediary forms of the derived rule (referred to as a partial rule), as well as a sample of snapshots for failed derivations. In total, this dataset includes over 1.5 million randomly generated rules.

Each program search (rule generation) begins with a placeholder, □, which can be replaced or expanded with any element deemed valid in our DSL's abstract syntax tree given our sentence (input). Each step or expansion of a placeholder constitutes a single state in the program synthesis process.

We use this collection of specifications to train a transformer neural network to rank possible next states in the program creation process to ensure that all derived programs are valid Odinson queries that also satisfy the specification. The scoring function is trained in two stages. First, to familiarize the transformer with the structure of our DSL, we take each randomly generated Odinson query in our dataset and concatenate its corresponding sentence, and learn to predict the rule's matching span. In this way, the network learns both the syntax of the DSL, as well as something of its semantics [40]. Next, the network is trained to score possible program transitions using the set of intermediate or "partial" rules and their corresponding target matches (see Figure 13.7). Our goal is to teach the scoring network how to efficiently navigate the search space by learning to estimate how likely a partial rule (intermediate step) is to lead to a solution. Partial rules in our dataset that led to successful derivations are treated as positive examples and take a ground truth score of 1. Our sample of partial rules for *failed* derivations serves as negative examples and receives a ground truth score of 0.

```
[CLS] [tag = JJR] [lemma = bizarre] □ [SEP]
The <MATCH\> more bizarre the example </MATCH> ,
the more memorable . [SEP]
```

Figure 13.7 A partial rule matching the span "more bizarre" where the rule's final form will match "more bizarre the example" in the sentence *The more bizarre the example, the more memorable.* Special tokens are used to wrap the targeted span. Encodings of successful and unsuccessful partial rules are used to train the scoring network with a mean squared error loss.

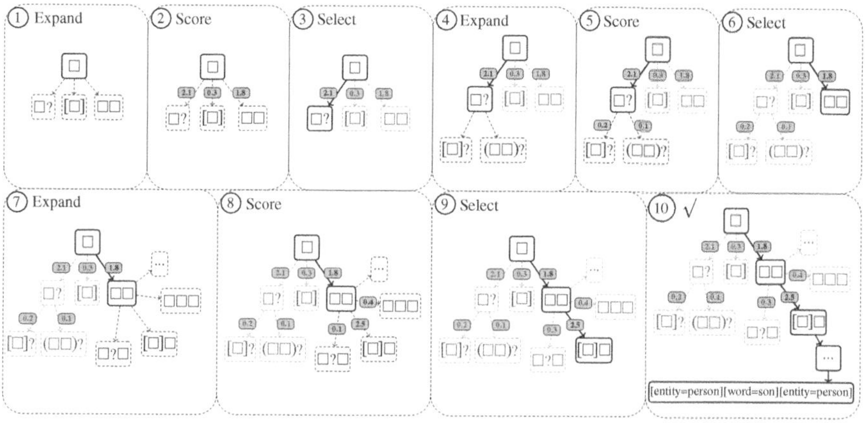

Figure 13.8 Our algorithm follows three main steps: **expand** the current state, **score** the possible next states, and **select** the state with the highest score. The process begins from the placeholder (□) and expands it (1). Each possible expansion is then scored (2), and the state with the highest score is selected (3). The system then repeats the expansion and scoring steps (4, 5). At this stage, note that the highest-scoring state is □ □, located in a different subtree than the current state (□?). The enumerative searcher, which uses Branch & Bound as its underlying algorithm, transitions to the highest-scoring state regardless of that state's position in the tree (6). This procedure continues (7–9) until a valid rule is reached (10) or the maximum number of steps is exceeded.

Given a user's specification, we begin deriving a rule by expanding possible transitions from a start state, scoring these transitions using our trained network for prioritized exploration, and then repeating this process until we arrive at a solution (complete program that satisfies the specification). Figure 13.8 illustrates this process.

13.4.3 Evaluation

To demonstrate the value of the proposed method, we describe two evaluations below. The first evaluation focuses on interactive sessions where users generate rules to extract information of interest. This evaluation shows that such interactive sessions combined with the pliability of rules yield extractions of high quality despite the fact that the users do not have to understand the underlying technology. In the second evaluation, we evaluate our approach on the TACRED dataset [5] and show that the rules synthesized by our approach outperform the manually written rules by over four F1 points, even though our synthesis component is *not* retrained on the TACRED data.

13.4.3.1 Interactive Evaluation

We evaluated the system's performance in an interactive, human-in-the-loop setting. The goal of this interactive evaluation was to measure how effectively rules generated through the interface could extract specific entity types using only a limited number of examples. In this setup, the user's task was to employ the system to synthesize a rule for extracting a given named entity type, and then manually verify that the extracted entities corresponded to the intended type. For each entity type, the user queried an index of the UMBC corpus to locate and select a sentence containing a representative pattern. This pattern served as the user's specification, consisting of the *context* and an *entity* of the target type. In Figure 13.9, we show an example of this pattern selection process.

Once the specification is chosen, it is used to generate a candidate rule and retrieve matching sample sentences. To simulate a one-shot learning scenario, the evaluation was restricted to a single specification per task – forcing the model to generate rules from minimal input. The user then examined both the generated rule and its corresponding matches to assess whether the rule accurately reflected the original intent. If not, the next candidate rule is generated and the process is repeated. Users were encouraged to iterate up to three times, with the option of a fourth attempt at their discretion.

The interactive evaluation used the following entity pairs: `CITY/CAPITAL`, `PERSON/ACTOR`, and `ORGANIZATION/ACADEMIC INSTITUTION`. Each pair captures two different levels of granularity for a single concept.

Each entity pair was assigned to one or two users, who used the interface to create three rules per entity type. For every rule, users manually assessed precision at 10 (P@10) and precision at 20 (P@20) using the most frequent entities retrieved from the UMBC corpus.

Table 13.8 reports the precision at 10 (P@10) and precision at 20 (P@20) for each entity type. The results show that, with minimal supervision – specifically, using

Figure 13.9 Example of a specification annotated by a user in the interactive evaluation. The entity is highlighted in dark gray and its context in gray.

Table 13.8 P@10 and P@20 of our rule synthesis on six different named entity types. `CAPITAL`, `ACTOR`, and `ACADEMIC INSTITUTION` are finer-grained entity types. `CITY`, `PERSON`, and `ORGANIZATION` are entity types that are more coarse.

Entity type	P@10	P@20
`Capital`	0.83	0.75
`City`	0.85	0.85
`Actor`	0.71	0.72
`Person`	0.78	0.77
`Academic Institution`	0.70	0.63
`Organization`	0.93	0.85

a single specification to synthesize a rule for each named entity type – the system produces high-precision rules (P@20 $\geq$ 0.77) for coarse-grained entities and comparable, though slightly lower, precision (P@20 $\geq$ 0.63) for fine-grained entities. This is achieved within three to four iterations, demonstrating that domain experts can effectively leverage our approach with minimal effort.

13.4.3.2 Non-interactive Evaluation

To enable comparison with existing methods, we also evaluate our approach on the TACRED dataset, a widely used benchmark for relation classification [5]. In this setting, we generate specifications by clustering the training sentences. Specifically, for each sentence, we compute an embedding by averaging the embeddings of the words located between the two target entities.[11] Sentence similarity is then measured using cosine similarity, where sentences with high similarity are grouped into clusters, each representing a single specification. For each cluster, we run our system to generate a rule, treating the words between the two entities as the highlighted segment.

We compare our method against several state-of-the-art approaches and three baselines. Our first baseline is a traditional transformer-based [44] sequence-to-sequence model [45], trained to decode a rule from a specification – analogous to a standard machine translation task.

Our second baseline (*Patterns*) is a rule-based system that uses the *hand-crafted* rules compiled for TACRED [5]. Our third baseline, *No Learning*, directly returns a rule for trivial cases – such as when no words or only a single word occur between the two entities. In the former case, the resulting rule is empty; in the latter, the rule consists of a word, lemma, or tag constraint, whichever yields the shortest form. The results are summarized in Table 13.9.

11 We use GloVe embeddings [46].

Table 13.9 Results of our rule synthesis on the TACRED test partition, reported in terms of precision (P), recall (R), and F1 score. We compare our approach against three baselines and prior supervised methods. Variants of our contextualized model with different transformer backbones are also included.

Model	P	R	F1
	Baselines		
Seq2Seq with transformers	53.0	19.0	28.0
Patterns	86.9	23.2	36.6
No learning	53.0	19.0	28.0
	Supervised approaches		
Joshi et al. [49]	70.8	70.9	70.8
Zhou and Chen [50]	—	—	74.6
Cohen et al. [51]	74.6	75.2	74.8
	Our approach		
Static weights	54.9	24.6	34.0
Contextual weights (BERT-Tiny)	57.6	29.6	39.1
Contextual weights (BERT-Mini)	57.2	32.5	41.4
Contextual weights (BERT-Small)	57.3	32.2	41.2
Contextual weights (BERT-Medium)	55.0	31.8	40.3
Contextual weights (BERT-Base)	55.6	32.4	41.0

All variants of our approach with contextualized embeddings outperform the baselines. Notably, our contextualized weights model achieves a higher F1 score (41.4 F1 vs. 36.6 F1) than the hand-crafted pattern baseline, trading some precision for substantially higher recall. This suggests that it might be possible to replace the human expert with a neural expert.

When comparing our contextualized-scoring approach to the supervised baselines, we note that while we do not match their performance, there are two important factors to consider. First, our method is trained on *domain-agnostic* data that is automatically generated and applied to TACRED *without fine-tuning*, whereas the supervised models are explicitly trained or fine-tuned on the TACRED splits.

Second, our system produces *human-interpretable rules*, while supervised models yield only a label prediction. Consequently, prior work tends to be more opaque – making it harder to interpret, debug, adapt, maintain, or safeguard against latent biases in the training data [47, 48].

13.4.4 Conclusion

This section outlines a pliable and precise method for neural program synthesis of IE rules that only requires end users to specify their information need in terms of one or more example sentences.

Our neural program synthesis method offers a guarantee that all derived programs are executable, but this guarantee comes at a high computational cost. Though not discussed here, preliminary work indicates that LLM-based rule generation is a promising alternative. While rule generation using LLMs provides no guarantees around program validity, instruction tuning of LLMs has the advantage of *soft* rule matching (a concept discussed in more detail in Section 13.5). Through prompting, one can even use the LLM to extend the IE query language with new features that may have no concrete implementation. Finally, LLM preference tuning methods provide a way to bias rule generation to favor precision, recall, or another preferred metric.

13.5 Matching Rules

13.5.1 Introduction

As discussed in Section 13.3, another critical limitation of traditional rule-based engines is within their matching algorithm. That is, traditional rule-based engines enforce a strict match of all lexical and syntactic constraints encoded within a given rule. While precise, this does not capture semantically equivalent sentences that use different lexical or syntactic forms. We provide in Table 13.10 an example in which a given rule misses semantically equivalent variations of a given sentence.

Table 13.10 We extend the example from Table 13.1 to highlight the need for a matching algorithm capable of disregarding superficial variations. In this case, the rule successfully matches *Sentence 1* but fails to match *Sentences 2* and *3*. Notably, although *Sentence 1* and *Sentence 2* are semantically equivalent, conventional rule engines do not recognize the match in the second sentence. As a result, they assign the same non-matching outcome to both *Sentences 2* and *3*, even though the latter is clearly less similar to the intended match.

Rule	`[ne=per]+ <nsubj founded >dobj [ne=org]+`
Sentence 1	Daniel Dines founded UiPath
Sentence 2	Daniel Dines is the founder of UiPath
Sentence 3	Bob moved to London

Continuing the analogy from Section 13.4, in which we paired a human SME with a rule-generating algorithm, the potential lack of generalization in the resulting rules is caused by the disconnect between the human SME and the task-agnostic rule-generating machine. That is, if the only interaction between the human SME and the rule-generating machine is a set of input/output examples, the algorithm may err on the side of generating rules that are correct but overly specific. For example, building on the scenario shown in Table 13.10, consider the sentence *Daniel Dines founded UiPath*, which contains a `founder` relation between *Daniel Dines* and *UiPath*. The method introduced in Section 13.4 would generate a syntactic pattern that contains the verb *founded* with a person's name as the nominal subject and an organization name as its direct object to extract this relation. While this rule is accurate for the given example, it fails to generalize to semantically equivalent sentences such as *Daniel Dines is the founder of UiPath*. To mitigate this limitation, we ideally want a rule matching algorithm that can align rules with sentences based on language and task semantics, rather than relying solely on strict syntactic structure.

More formally, to mitigate this potential limitation in generalization, we introduce a neurosymbolic method[12] for rule matching that incorporates "soft-matching," enabling more nuanced, semantic outcomes rather than the binary match/no-match decisions of conventional rule-based systems. To realize this objective, we design a new hybrid architecture for relation classification (RC) that retains the strengths of both paradigms, i.e., the generalization capacity of neural techniques and the flexibility of rule-based strategies. Our architecture follows a modular design, consisting of two key parts: a declarative rule-based model and a neural module. The rule-based module performs relation classification through a collection of interpretable rules. The neural module enhances the generalization of rules by semantically aligning them with textual input.

The contributions of this research are summarized as follows:

1. We introduce a modular neurosymbolic framework for relation classification that unifies the strengths of symbolic and neural approaches. The symbolic, rule-driven module employs syntactic or surface rules that are automatically extracted from example sentences, defined as the minimal syntactic paths connecting two entities in a sentence. The neural module, responsible for semantically aligning these rules with textual input, is trained entirely without human annotations. Its training relies on a distinctive procedure: sentences are sampled at random from a large corpus, and rules are automatically constructed between randomly chosen entities within them. The model is subsequently optimized using a contrastive learning setup,

12 This method was first introduced in [52].

where it assigns high scores to the correct (rule, sentence) pair (or to a paraphrase of the sentence) and low scores to incorrect pairs. Finally, the semantic matcher is integrated with the rule-based model within a two-stage sieve framework that gives precedence to the more precise component.

2. We achieve state-of-the-art results in three out of four evaluation settings across two challenging few-shot relation classification datasets – Few-Shot TACRED [5, 53] and a few-shot adaptation of the NYT29 dataset [54–56] – all without relying on the background training data. On TACRED, for instance, our approach surpasses prior neural supervised methods by more than 12 F1 points, reaching scores of 24.19 in the 1-shot setting and 39.38 in the 5-shot setting, despite the model never being trained on annotated examples from this dataset. Moreover, the model remains relatively compact, consisting of roughly 350 million parameters.
3. We demonstrate the flexibility of our approach through a user study where two domain experts manually refined the rules for the `org:parents` relation in TACRED. Remarkably, without retraining the semantic-matching neural module, performance on this relation improved across all settings for both experts, while the results for other relations remained unaffected. To the best of our knowledge, this is the first work to establish that pliability can be maintained within neural approaches to IE.

13.5.2 Approach

We introduce a modular neurosymbolic framework that integrates the strengths of both symbolic and neural models. The framework is structured as a two-stage sieve: in the first stage, a conventional rule-based engine attempts to exactly match a rule to the input sentence. When no such match is identified, the process shifts to the neural module in the second stage, which computes a matching score between the rule and the sentence. This fallback strategy enables the system to capture semantically equivalent sentences that may not fully conform to the strict constraints of an individual rule.

The first component, the traditional rule-based engine, is implemented using Odinson [37].

The second component is a semantic rule matcher (SRM), built on the encoder of a transformer architecture [44, 57]. In this setup, the encoder generates two vector-based representations (or *embeddings*), one for the rule and one for the sentence. The model is trained to increase the cosine similarity of these embeddings for true matches while decreasing it for non-matches. During inference, the cosine similarity between the rule and sentence embeddings is used as the *matching score*.

At this stage, the careful reader may ask: why not use a LLM to perform the semantic matching between sentences and rules? Especially since, as we will see later in this section, we *do* use an LLM to generate paraphrases of the example sentences to increase the semantic variation in the training data. The answer is simple: we choose encoders for efficiency. For example, the encoder used in the experiments reported in this section has approximately 350 million parameters. In recent experiments (not detailed here), we replaced this encoder with a decoder-based LLM. However, to achieve comparable performance, we had to use an LLM with 14 billion parameters – almost 50 times larger than our encoder. The reason for this is that LLMs are designed as general-purpose tools, encapsulating significantly more knowledge (e.g., much of the Web) than encoders. In contrast, encoders are pretrained on much smaller datasets and are intended to be fine-tuned for task-specific data.

We outline the training process for our semantic rule matching component, beginning with the construction of the training dataset.

13.5.2.1 Training Dataset

An important challenge lies in constructing training data for the semantic rule matching component, that is, data that pairs rules with sentences they should match, since no such dataset exists by default. Our approach removes the need for gold-labeled relation classification data by leveraging a key insight: for any entity pair in a sentence, it is possible to automatically generate a representative rule. For example, consider the following sentence:

Bob traveled to London.

Using the following two entities, *Bob* and *London*, and the underlying syntactic structure of the sentence, we can derive the following rule:

```
[ne=per]+ <nsubj traveled >nmod_ to [ne=loc]+
```

Such a rule naturally reflects the relationship between the entities, regardless of its specific type. Building on this idea, we train the model to assign a high matching score to the pair formed by the rule and the original entities in context, while giving low scores to all other pairings. In this way, we can automatically generate a training dataset and eliminate the need for pre-labeled relation classification data. The only prerequisites are a dependency parser and a named entity recognition system, both of which benefit from larger datasets (and broader language coverage) compared to relation classification.

To further encourage the SRM to move beyond syntactic or surface-level patterns, we augment the extracted sentences with paraphrases. For instance, *Bob traveled to London* can be paraphrased as *Bob visited London* without altering its meaning. We apply this principle to expand the dataset with paraphrased sentences containing the entities of interest.[13]

13 We use OpenAI's ChatGPT for this purpose (`gpt-3.5-turbo-1106`).

We begin with UMBC, a large collection of English paragraphs comprising of roughly three billion words [58]. Importantly, the use of this external corpus does not compromise the comparability between our approach and other recent methods for relation classification [39, 53]. For context, RoBERTa was trained on 160 GB of text [57], effectively encoding much of this data into its model weights [59, 60].

We preprocess UMBC using standard NLP tools [26] to perform named entity recognition and dependency parsing. From there, we randomly select a sentence s_i containing two randomly chosen entities (e_1, e_2) and automatically generate a rule r_i designed to match it, forming the tuple (r_i, s_i), which is then added to our dataset. This procedure yielded an initial collection of about 140 million sentence–rule pairs, which we subsequently refined through the additional preprocessing steps below:

(1) Filtering: We further refine the dataset by removing duplicates and downsampling overly frequent rules and entities to reduce the risk of the model overfitting to common patterns. For instance, the entity pair (ORG, COUNTRY) appears nearly two orders of magnitude more often than (ORG, EMAIL). Similarly, simple syntactic rules such as [ne=title]+ <compound [ne=person]+ dominate the rule distribution. Our filtering strategy proceeds in several stages.

First, we remove exact duplicates, which may arise when the rule generation process is repeated with different random seeds. Next, we downsample frequent rules and entities – for example, ([ne=title]+ <compound [ne=person]+, Dr, Bob) – retaining only a number of instances proportional to the square root of their frequency. We then apply the same square-root-based subsampling directly to rules themselves, followed by a similar adjustment for frequent entity types such as (ORG, COUNTRY). To avoid further shrinking the representation of rare pairs, we normalize the final counts using the minimum observed frequency. After this filtering stage, the dataset is reduced to approximately four million data points.

(2) Augmentation: We expand the set of entity types with synonyms to encourage the SRM component to generalize beyond surface-level cues associated with entity labels. Additionally, these augmentations might allow the model to work with named entities previously unseen. For instance, the entity type per may be randomly replaced with alternatives such as human or individual. An illustration of this rule augmentation process, achieved through entity type substitution, is presented in Table 13.11.

Table 13.11 Example of rule augmentation through entity type substitution: converting `per` to `human` and `org` to `company`.

Original rule	[ne=per]+ <nsubj founder >nmod_of [ne=org]+
Modified rule	[ne=human]+ <nsubj founder >nmod_of [ne=company]+

Table 13.12 Examples of paraphrases created by the LLM. We underline the two entities that participate in the relation in focus.

Original	One year I served as research assistant to Wendell Bennett, a brilliant young anthropologist and the next year was the research assistant to Tom McCormick, an excellent, but inarticulate statistician
Paraphrase	After assisting anthropologist Wendell Bennett, I worked as a research assistant to Tom McCormick, a talented statistician who was not very articulate
Original	In April 1915, Sir John Nixon took command of British forces in Iraq and received orders to draw up plans for an advance on Baghdad
Paraphrase	In April 1915, Sir John Nixon was assigned to lead the British military in Iraq and was instructed to make plans for an assault on Baghdad

(3) Paraphrases: We create paraphrases of the original sentences while ensuring that the two target entities remain present. For this, we employ OpenAI's ChatGPT (`gpt-3.5-turbo-1106`) with a straightforward prompt instructing the model to produce paraphrases that preserve the original meaning. From the generated outputs, we retain only those paraphrases that include both entities, providing an initial safeguard for quality. In addition, we manually reviewed 50 randomly selected paraphrases and found all to be of high quality. Examples of these paraphrases are shown in Table 13.12.

The final dataset contains roughly 5.6 million (rule, sentence) pairs, of which about 1.6 million were produced through paraphrasing. For learning sentence representations, we adopt the common practice in relation extraction [5, 49, 50] of wrapping entities with special tokens alongside their named entity type. This step is essential to explicitly indicate which entity pairs are being evaluated. For example, in the sentence *Bob traveled to London and Jane to Paris*, it would otherwise be ambiguous whether the model should test the pairs (*Bob, London*), (*Jane, Paris*), (*Bob, Paris*), etc.

An illustration of this entity-aware encoding is shown in Table 13.13. For instance, given the entities *Daniel Dines* and *UiPath*, the sentence *Daniel Dines founded UiPath* is transformed into *# * per * Daniel Dines # founded # * org * UiPath #*. Because our pretraining dataset does not specify which entity is the subject and which is the object, both are enclosed with the same type of markers; however, previous work distinguishes explicitly between subject and object roles [50].

Table 13.13 Example of a modified sentence after wrapping the entities with special tokens. In addition, we provide an example where we distinguish between the subject and the object, wrapping them with different special tokens.

Original sentence	Daniel Dines founded UiPath
Sentence with wrapped entities	# * per * Daniel Dines # founded # * org * UiPath #
Sentence with wrapped entities (subj/obj aware)	# * per * Daniel Dines # founded ^ @ org @ UiPath ^

13.5.2.2 Training Procedure

We use the constructed dataset to train the semantic rule matching (SRM) component with a CLIP-style objective. Specifically, the dataset contains pairs of the form (r, s), such as (`[ne=per]+ nmod_in [ne=org]+`, *# * per * Daniel Dines # founded # * org * UiPath #*). The SRM is trained to produce high cosine similarity between the embeddings of r and s, while treating the remaining in-batch examples as negatives [61]. Importantly, this process does not rely on human annotations or relation-specific labels. Figure 13.10 illustrates the training procedure: the SRM encodes both rules and sentences from the batch, cosine similarities are computed for every rule–sentence combination, and the objective is to maximize similarity for matching pairs (on the diagonal of the matrix) while minimizing it for non-matches (off-diagonal entries).

At the end of the training, the resulting model will be able to assign a matching score to (rule, sentence) pairs. We provide a qualitative example in Table 13.14, where the SRM component is capable of assigning a high matching score between the following two semantically equivalent constructions: (i) *got his degree from* and (ii) *graduated from.*

After training, the model is able to assign a matching score to any (rule, sentence) pair. We show a qualitative example in Table 13.14, where the SRM successfully assigns a high score to two semantically equivalent expressions: (i) *got his degree from* and (ii) *graduated from.*

13.5.3 Evaluation

13.5.3.1 Experimental Setup

We evaluate our approach on Few-Shot TACRED, a few-shot adaptation of the TACRED relation classification dataset.

For the semantic-matching component, we use `RoBERTa-large` [57], together with a CLIP-like setup [61] with one model encoding the rules and another encoding the sentences. Rules are generated from the support sentences in each dataset, using `CoreNLP` [26] to extract the syntactic structures required for rule construction.

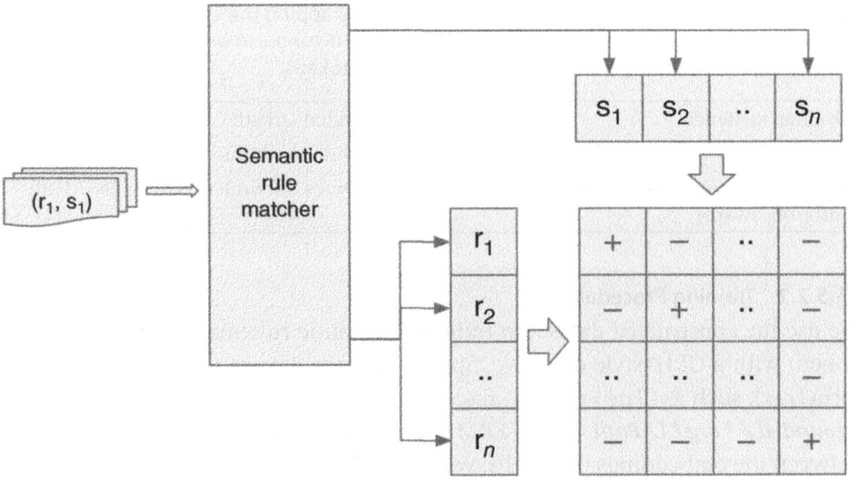

Figure 13.10 During training of the semantic rule matcher (SRM), we encode both rules and sentences and compute cosine similarity for every possible pair. The objective is to increase similarity for true matches, represented by the diagonal entries of the matrix, while reducing similarity for non-matching pairs, corresponding to the off-diagonal elements.

Table 13.14 We present a qualitative example showing that the soft matcher assigns a high score to two semantically equivalent expressions: (i) *got his degree from* and (ii) *graduated from*. In contrast, traditional rule-based engines would not output a match between the rule and the sentence, even though their meanings clearly align.

Sentence	Steve got his degree from Oxford
Rule	[ne=per]+ graduated from [ne=org]+
Matching score	0.82

At test time, we evaluate our method in three configurations: (i) applying the rules in a binary, match-or-no-match fashion without the SRM (**Hard-matching Rules**); (ii) using the SRM module to calculate a similarity score between each rule and sentence, with matches considered over a threshold t[14] (**Soft-matching Rules**); and (iii) a hybrid approach where rules are first applied in the hard-matching manner, and if no match is found, the semantic matcher is used as a fallback (**Hybrid**).

14 The threshold is tuned on the development set; no training is performed on the datasets themselves.

13.5.3.2 Few-Shot TACRED

Table 13.15 presents the performance of our proposed method on Few-Shot TACRED for the standard 1-shot and 5-shot settings. We also distinguish between approaches that use background training data and those that do not (i.e., zero-shot[15]).

Our discussion focuses on comparisons with contemporary rule-based methods – particularly OdinSynth, which synthesizes Odinson rules as described previously – and strong neural-based approaches such as MNAV. Notably, our method outperforms MNAV, the state-of-the-art neural-based model on Few-Shot TACRED, in both settings; for instance, in the 1-shot scenario, it improves F1 by over 12 points, representing roughly a 100% relative gain, despite not using any human-annotated or TACRED-specific data. Furthermore, our hybrid approach significantly surpasses OdinSynth, the leading rule-based method, in both 1-shot and 5-shot settings, confirming that integrating neural networks with traditional rule-based strategies yields superior results compared to rule-only methods. Importantly, this performance boost does not compromise precision, as our method achieves higher precision and recall than OdinSynth. These observations also extend to the few-shot variant of NYT29, though results are not shown here due to space constraints. Overall, our approach obtains state-of-the-art performance *without relying on any human-annotated examples from the respective training datasets.*

13.5.3.3 Ablation Study

Next, we examine the contributions of each major component in our proposed method, with ablation results presented in Table 13.16. The three components we analyze are as follows:

- **i.** The preprocessing of the training dataset, which removes duplicates and subsamples overly frequent rules and entities;
- **ii.** Data augmentation, where entities in rules and sentences are randomly replaced with synonyms – for example, a rule like:

  ```
  [ne=per]+ <nsubj founded >nmod_ in [ne=org]+
  ```

  is transformed into:

  ```
  [ne=human]+ <nsubj founded >nmod_ in [ne=company]+
  ```

  Similar substitutions are applied to sentences by changing the named entity in the marker [39]; and
- **iii.** The inclusion of paraphrases, such as automatically converting *Daniel Dines founded UiPath* to *Daniel Dines is the founder of UiPath* using an LLM, without altering the underlying semantic meaning.

---

15 Zero-shot refers to methods that do not rely on human-annotated examples for training.

Table 13.15 Results for the 5-way 1-shot and 5-way 5-shot settings on the test set of the Few-Shot TACRED dataset. The results are grouped into four sections: (i) a strong unsupervised baseline that classifies based on entity types, (ii) state-of-the-art neural approaches, (iii) rule synthesis using transformer networks, and (iv) our proposed method. Across both the 1- and 5-shot splits, our approach surpasses all previous state-of-the-art methods.

	5-way 1-shot			5-way 5-shot			
Model	**P**	**R**	**F1**	**P**	**R**	**F1**	**Background data**
Unsupervised baseline	5.70 ± 0.10	91.02 ± 0.65	10.73 ± 0.18	5.65 ± 0.11	95.56 ± 0.70	10.67 ± 0.20	No
Sentence-pair (not fine-tuned)	3.9 ± 0.21	5.21 ± 0.31	4.45 ± 0.24	2.76 ± 0.16	8.79 ± 0.58	4.2 ± 0.25	No
Sentence-pair (fine-tuned)	6.89 ± 0.33	28.56 ± 1.67	11.10 ± 0.55	14.94 ± 0.26	24.03 ± 0.32	18.42 ± 0.16	Yes
MNAV (reported)	-	-	12.39 ± 1.01	-	-	30.04 ± 1.92	Yes
MNAV (re-run by us)	15.11 ± 0.46	8.47 ± 0.31	10.85 ± 0.29	24.48 ± 1.02	32.00 ± 1.07	27.73 ± 0.94	Yes
OdinSynth	23.48 ± 1.46	11.46 ± 1.02	15.40 ± 1.21	29.77 ± 0.83	20.34 ± 0.53	24.16 ± 0.44	No
Hard-matching rules (ours)	51.35 ± 6.53	2.94 ± 0.48	5.56 ± 0.90	45.94 ± 5.31	10.81 ± 1.23	17.50 ± 1.98	No
Soft-matching rules (ours)	37.22 ± 1.04	18.21 ± 0.62	**24.45 ± 0.72**	47.73 ± 2.23	35.52 ± 1.88	**40.71 ± 1.83**	No
Hybrid (ours)	35.91 ± 0.97	18.24 ± 0.62	24.19 ± 0.73	42.77 ± 1.88	36.53 ± 1.83	39.38 ± 1.57	No

Table 13.16 The ablation results for the 5-way 1-shot and 5-way 5-shot settings, reported on the few-shot development partition of TACRED. Each ablation scenario is evaluated independently, with only a single change applied relative to the Original model.

		5-way 1-shot			5-way 5-shots		
Model type	**Ablation**	**P**	**R**	**F1**	**P**	**R**	**F1**
Hybrid	Original	55.67 ± 3.75	32.19 ± 1.26	40.78 ± 1.99	55.04 ± 1.47	50.93 ± 1.94	52.90 ± 1.67
	No paraphrases	42.88 ± 3.70	27.53 ± 1.38	33.52 ± 2.10	43.84 ± 2.14	51.28 ± 2.63	47.25 ± 2.21
	No data preprocessing	43.00 ± 3.21	22.38 ± 1.82	29.43 ± 2.25	48.16 ± 2.09	44.44 ± 2.89	46.22 ± 2.49
	No rule/Sentence augmentation	49.13 ± 3.55	32.77 ± 1.37	39.31 ± 2.11	47.63 ± 1.85	53.36 ± 2.16	50.33 ± 1.96
SoftRules	Original	56.81 ± 3.94	31.70 ± 1.43	40.68 ± 2.17	58.94 ± 1.79	49.60 ± 2.08	53.87 ± 1.96
	No paraphrases	43.39 ± 3.96	27.10 ± 1.53	33.35 ± 2.29	45.93 ± 2.18	50.59 ± 2.88	48.14 ± 2.40
	No data preprocessing	43.50 ± 3.77	21.92 ± 2.06	29.14 ± 2.62	51.20 ± 1.85	43.15 ± 2.72	46.83 ± 2.37
	No rule/sentence augmentation	49.95 ± 3.71	32.34 ± 1.54	39.25 ± 2.27	50.14 ± 1.94	51.98 ± 2.42	51.04 ± 2.16

The analysis in the table indicates that all three components contribute to the overall performance to varying degrees. Our findings suggest that dataset pre-processing has the largest impact, highlighting the importance of high-quality, well-structured input data for handling the complexities of relation classification. The performance drop in the "No paraphrases" setting indicates that the usage of paraphrases helps the model learn less obvious semantic variations. Finally, rule and sentence augmentation shows the smallest effect, likely because the common named entities in TACRED, such as `person` and `organization`, are already prevalent in the training data. We hypothesize that augmentation would be more beneficial for entities not seen during training, an investigation we leave for future work.

13.5.3.4 Are Soft-matching Rules Pliable?

A major advantage of rules is their flexibility and modularity, allowing domain experts to adjust the model without the risk of introducing unexpected or undesirable behavior [10].

We investigate how interventions on the generated rules can improve overall performance. We focus on the `org:parents` relation from the development set, which is relatively well represented but where our model achieves a lower F1 score. In our experiment, two experts are given access to the syntactic rules derived from the support sentences in the Few-Shot TACRED development partition and are allowed up to two hours to improve the rule set using the following operations:

ADD Rule, which introduces a new rule available in all the episodes. This operation simulates the scenario of incorporating new knowledge at inference time;
DELETE Rule, which removes a rule for a specific support sentence containing the `org:parents` relation for a particular episode; and
MODIFY Rule, which alters an existing rule. The modification affects only the episodes in which that rule appears.

Table 13.17 presents our results, highlighting two sets of experiments that demonstrate the adaptability and effectiveness of our method in relation classification. The first set involves expert rule modifications without changing the classification threshold, while the second set increases the threshold specifically for the `org:parents` rules. This increase is motivated by the higher average similarity observed with more general rules created by human annotators compared to the lower alignment of highly specific rules automatically generated from support sentences. For example, rules synthesized from support sentences often produce highly specific constructs, such as [ne=org]+ <nmod_from taken >conj_and operating >nmod_under brandname >compound [ne=org]+, which typically match poorly with most sentences and yield lower similarity scores. In contrast, more general rules, like [ne=org]+ >appos subsidiary >nmod_of [ne=org]+, improve rule-to-sentence similarity.

Table 13.17 F1 scores for the `org:parents` relation after two domain experts independently adjusted the corresponding rules. We compare the results before and after these modifications under two conditions: (i) using the original threshold and (ii) applying a stricter threshold.

Model	Original threshold	Stricter threshold
Original	15.57 ± 1.39	15.57 ± 1.39
Expert 1	19.42 ± 0.65	31.78 ± 2.18
Expert 2	19.77 ± 1.08	34.03 ± 1.91

Since this increase in average similarity was not reflected under the original classification threshold, we conducted a second set of experiments, raising the threshold by 0.1 only for the `org:parents` relation.

Across both expert interventions and threshold scenarios, performance consistently improved: with the threshold unchanged, expert modifications increased F1 by roughly four points (about 25% relative gain); raising the threshold for `org:parents` produced gains exceeding 15 F1 points, or roughly 100% relative improvement. Importantly, these enhancements did not negatively impact performance on other relations.

13.5.4 Conclusion

This section presented a novel neurosymbolic architecture for relation classification. Traditional rule-based systems often suffer from low recall because they cannot distinguish between near matches and exact matches. To overcome this limitation, we introduce a model that first tries to match rules using a conventional rule-based system; if no match is found, a neural network predicts a *semantic* matching score ranging from 0 to 1. Notably, the neural network is trained in a zero-shot setting, without relying on any human-annotated data. Our results demonstrate that this approach achieves state-of-the-art performance in relation classification, surpassing both purely rule-based and neural methods, while retaining key properties of rules, such as their modularity and pliability.

13.6 Take Away

To quote Chiticariu et al. [62], despite the seemingly common belief that "rule-based information extraction is dead!," this chapter instead proclaims: "Long live rule-based information extraction systems!" More formally, this chapter demonstrates that symbolic IE systems retain advantages that are highly relevant today: they are both explainable and pliable. These qualities are particularly valuable in important real-world domains such as law and healthcare. However, traditional symbolic IE methods often lack the generalization capabilities of modern deep learning systems. Additionally, developing rule-based models can be labor-intensive. In this chapter, we introduced several neurosymbolic strategies to address these two limitations. We showed that these neurosymbolic approaches outperform purely neural methods while retaining the explainability and pliability of symbolic directions. All in all, this chapter argues that, at least for IE domains where explainability and reliability are crucial, neurosymbolic strategies are a strong contender.

References

1 Konstantinos Z Vardakas, Grigorios Tsopanakis, Alexandra Poulopoulou, and Mathew E Falagas. An analysis of factors contributing to pubmed's growth. *Journal of Informetrics*, 9(3): 592–617, 2015.

2 Zachary D Stephens, Skylar Y Lee, Faraz Faghri, Roy H Campbell, Chengxiang Zhai, Miles J Efron, Ravishankar Iyer, Michael C Schatz, Saurabh Sinha, and Gene E Robinson. Big data: astronomical or genomical? *PLoS Biology*, 13(7): e1002195, 2015.

3 Christopher D Manning. Computational linguistics and deep learning. *Computational Linguistics*, 41: 701–707, 2015.

4 Zichao Yang, Diyi Yang, Chris Dyer, Xiaodong He, Alex Smola, and Eduard H Hovy. Hierarchical attention networks for document classification. In *North American Chapter of the Association for Computational Linguistics*, 2016.

5 Yuhao Zhang, Victor Zhong, Danqi Chen, Gabor Angeli, and Christopher D Manning. Position-aware attention and supervised data improve slot filling. In *Proceedings of the 2017 Conference on Empirical Methods in Natural Language Processing (EMNLP 2017)*, pages 35–45, 2017. https://nlp.stanford.edu/pubs/zhang2017tacred.pdf.

6 Zhijiang Guo, Yan Zhang, and Wei Lu. Attention guided graph convolutional networks for relation extraction. In *Proceedings of the 57th Annual Meeting of the Association for Computational Linguistics*, pages 241–251, Association for Computational Linguistics, Florence, Italy, 2019. https://doi.org/10.18653/v1/P19-1024.

7 Ikuya Yamada, Akari Asai, Hiroyuki Shindo, Hideaki Takeda, and Yuji Matsumoto. Luke: deep contextualized entity representations with entity-aware self-attention. In *Conference on Empirical Methods in Natural Language Processing*, 2020.

8 Zexuan Zhong and Danqi Chen. A frustratingly easy approach for entity and relation extraction. *arXiv*, 2020. https://arxiv.org/abs/2010.12812.

9 Marina Danilevsky, Shipi Dhanorkar, Yunyao Li, Lucian Popa, Kun Qian, and Anbang Xu. Explainability for natural language processing. In *Proceedings of the 27th ACM SIGKDD Conference on Knowledge Discovery & Data Mining*, KDD '21, pages 4033–4034, Association for Computing Machinery, New York, NY, USA, 2021. https://doi.org/10.1145/3447548.3470808.

10 D. Sculley, Gary Holt, Daniel Golovin, Eugene Davydov, Todd Phillips, Dietmar Ebner, Vinay Chaudhary, Michael Young, Jean-François Crespo, and Dan Dennison. Hidden technical debt in machine learning systems. In *Proceedings of Advances in Neural Information Processing Systems 28 (NIPS 2015)*, pages 1–9, 2015.

11 OpenAI. Gpt-4 Technical Report, 2023. https://cdn.openai.com/papers/gpt-4.pdf.

12 Amina Adadi and Mohammed Berrada. Peeking inside the black-box: a survey on explainable artificial intelligence (XAI). *IEEE Access*, 6: 52138–52160, 2018.

13 Bryce Goodman and Seth Flaxman. European union regulations on algorithmic decision-making and a "right to explanation". *AI Magazine*, 38: 50–57, 2016.

14 Erico Tjoa and Cuntai Guan. A survey on explainable artificial intelligence (XAI): toward medical XAI. *IEEE Transactions on Neural Networks and Learning Systems*, 32: 4793–4813, 2019.

15 Marco Tulio Ribeiro, Sameer Singh, and Carlos Guestrin. "Why should I trust you?": explaining the predictions of any classifier. In *Proceedings of the 22nd ACM SIGKDD International Conference on Knowledge Discovery and Data Mining*, KDD '16, pages 1135–1144, New York, NY, USA, 2016. Association for Computing Machinery. https://doi.org/10.1145/2939672.2939778.

16 Scott M Lundberg and Su-In Lee. A unified approach to interpreting model predictions. In I. Guyon, U. V. Luxburg, S. Bengio, H. Wallach, R. Fergus, S. Vishwanathan, and R. Garnett, editors, *Advances in Neural Information Processing Systems 30*, pages 4765–4774, Curran Associates, Inc., 2017. http://papers.nips.cc/paper/7062-a-unified-approach-to-interpreting-model-predictions.pdf.

17 Zheng Tang and Mihai Surdeanu. It takes two flints to make a fire: multitask learning of neural relation and explanation classifiers. *Computational Linguistics*, 2023. https://arxiv.org/pdf/2204.11424.pdf.

18 Alon Jacovi and Yoav Goldberg. Towards faithfully interpretable NLP systems: how should we define and evaluate faithfulness? *arXiv*, 2020. https://arxiv.org/abs/2004.03685.

19 Laura Chiticariu, Yoav Goldberg, Gus Hahn-Powell, Clayton T Morrison, Aakanksha Naik, Rebecca Sharp, Mihai Surdeanu, Marco Valenzuela-Escárcega, and Enrique Noriega-Atala, editors. In *Proceedings of the First Workshop on Pattern-based Approaches to NLP in the Age of Deep Learning*, International Conference on Computational Linguistics, Gyeongju, Republic of Korea, 2022. https://aclanthology.org/2022.pandl-1.0.

20 Özgün Babur, Mithat Gönen, Bülent Arman Aksoy, Nikolaus Schultz, Giovanni Ciriello, Chris Sander, and Emek Demir. Systematic identification of cancer driving signaling pathways based on mutual exclusivity of genomic alterations. *Genome Biology*, 16(1): 45, 2015.

21 Marco A Valenzuela-Escárcega, Gus Hahn-Powell, and Mihai Surdeanu. Description of the Odin event extraction framework and rule language. *ArXiv*, 2015. http://arxiv.org/abs/1509.07513.

22 Marco A Valenzuela-Escárcega, Gus Hahn-Powell, and Mihai Surdeanu. Odin's runes: a rule language for information extraction. In *Proceedings of the Tenth International Conference on Language Resources and Evaluation (LREC 2016)*, pages 322–329, 2016.

23 Marco A Valenzuela-Escárcega, Ozgun Babur, Gus Hahn-Powell, Dane Bell, Thomas Hicks, Enrique Noriega-Atala, Xia Wang, Mihai Surdeanu, Emek Demir, and Clayton T Morrison. Large-scale automated machine reading discovers new cancer driving mechanisms. *Database: The Journal of Biological Databases and Curation*, 2018. https://doi.org/10.1093/database/bay098.

24 Emek Demir, Michael P Cary, Suzanne Paley, Ken Fukuda, Christian Lemer, Imre Vastrik, Guanming Wu, Peter D'Eustachio, Carl Schaefer, Joanne Luciano, et al. The biopax community standard for pathway data sharing. *Nature Biotechnology*, 28(9): 935–942, 2010.

25 Jin-Dong Kim, Tomoko Ohta, Yuka Tateisi, and Jun'ichi Tsujii. GENIA corpus—a semantically annotated corpus for bio-textmining. *Bioinformatics*, 19(suppl 1): i180–i182, 2003.

26 Christopher D Manning, Mihai Surdeanu, John Bauer, Jenny Rose Finkel, Steven Bethard, and David McClosky. The Stanford CoreNLP natural language processing toolkit. In *Proceedings of 52nd Annual Meeting of the Association for Computational Linguistics: System Demonstrations*, pages 55–60, 2014.

27 Mitchell P Marcus, Mary Ann Marcinkiewicz, and Beatrice Santorini. Building a large annotated corpus of English: the Penn Treebank. *Computational Linguistics*, 19(2): 313–330, 1993.

28 Ann Taylor, Mitchell Marcus, and Beatrice Santorini. The Penn Treebank: an overview. In *Treebanks*, pages 5–22. Springer, 2003.

29 Lynette Hirschman, Alexander Yeh, Christian Blaschke, and Alfonso Valencia. Overview of BioCreAtIvE: critical assessment of information extraction for biology. *BMC Bioinformatics*, 6(Suppl 1): S1, 2005.

30 Jin-Dong Kim, Tomoko Ohta, Sampo Pyysalo, Yoshinobu Kano, and Jun'ichi Tsujii. Overview of BioNLP'09 shared task on event extraction. In *Proceedings of the Workshop on Current Trends in Biomedical Natural Language Processing: Shared Task*, pages 1–9, Association for Computational Linguistics, 2009.

31 Heeyoung Lee, Angel Chang, Yves Peirsman, Nathanael Chambers, Mihai Surdeanu, and Dan Jurafsky. Deterministic coreference resolution based on entity-centric, precision-ranked rules. *Computational Linguistics*, 39(4): 885–916, 2013.

32 Dane Bell, Gus Hahn-Powell, Marco A Valenzuela-Escárcega, and Mihai Surdeanu. Sieve-based coreference resolution in the biomedical domain. In *Proceedings of the Tenth International Conference on Language Resources and Evaluation (LREC 2016)*, pages 177–183, 2016.

33 Matthew W Peterson, Tonia Korves, Christopher D Garay, Robyn Kozierok, and Lynette Hirschman. Guiding the development of human-machine systems for complex mechanistic modeling: the role of evaluation. *MITRE Technical Report, Document No: MTR180273*, 2018.

34 James F Allen, Mary Swift, and Will De Beaumont. Deep semantic analysis of text. In *Proceedings of the 2008 Conference on Semantics in Text Processing*, pages 343–354. Association for Computational Linguistics, 2008.

35 Laura Banarescu, Claire Bonial, Shu Cai, Madalina Georgescu, Kira Griffitt, Ulf Hermjakob, Kevin Knight, Philipp Koehn, Martha Palmer, and Nathan Schneider. Abstract Meaning Representation (AMR) 1.0 specification. In *Parsing on Freebase from Question-Answer Pairs." In Proceedings of the 2013 Conference on Empirical Methods in Natural Language Processing. Seattle: ACL*, pages 1533–1544, 2012.

36 Stephen A Cook. The complexity of theorem-proving procedures. In *Logic, Automata, and Computational Complexity: The Works of Stephen A. Cook*, pages 143–152. 2023. Morgan & Claypool.

37 Marco A Valenzuela-Escárcega, Gus Hahn-Powell, and Dane Bell. Odinson: a fast rule-based information extraction framework. In *Proceedings of the 12th Language Resources and Evaluation Conference*, pages 2183–2191, 2020.

38 Robert Vacareanu, George CG Barbosa, Enrique Noriega-Atala, Gus Hahn-Powell, Rebecca Sharp, Marco A Valenzuela-Escárcega, and Mihai Surdeanu. A human-machine interface for few-shot rule synthesis for information extraction. In *Proceedings of the 2022 Conference of the North American Chapter of the Association for Computational Linguistics: Human Language Technologies: System Demonstrations*, pages 64–70, Association for Computational Linguistics, Hybrid: Seattle, Washington + Online, 2022. https://aclanthology.org/2022.naacl-demo.8.

39 Robert Vacareanu, Marco A Valenzuela-Escárcega, George Barbosa, Rebecca Sharp, Gus Hahn-Powell, and Mihai Surdeanu. From examples to rules: neural guided rule synthesis for information extraction. In *Proceedings of the 13th Language Resources and Evaluation Conference (LREC)*, 2022. http://www.lrec-conf.org/proceedings/lrec2022/pdf/2022.lrec-1.665.pdf.

40 Enrique Noriega-Atala, Robert Vacareanu, Gus Hahn-Powell, and Marco A Valenzuela-Escárcega. Neural-guided program synthesis of information extraction rules using self-supervision. In *Proceedings of the First Workshop on Pattern-based Approaches to NLP in the Age of Deep Learning*, pages 85–93,

International Conference on Computational Linguistics, Gyeongju, Republic of Korea, 2022. https://aclanthology.org/2022.pandl-1.10.

41 Allen Cypher and Daniel Conrad Halbert. *Watch What I Do: Programming by Demonstration*. MIT press, 1993.

42 Henry Lieberman. *Your Wish Is My Command: Programming by Example*. Morgan Kaufmann, 2001.

43 Sumit Gulwani. Synthesis from examples: interaction models and algorithms. In *2012 14th International Symposium on Symbolic and Numeric Algorithms for Scientific Computing*, pages 8–14, 2012. https://doi.org/10.1109/SYNASC.2012.69.

44 Ashish Vaswani, Noam Shazeer, Niki Parmar, Jakob Uszkoreit, Llion Jones, Aidan N Gomez, undefinedukasz Kaiser, and Illia Polosukhin. Attention is all you need. In *Proceedings of the 31st International Conference on Neural Information Processing Systems*, NIPS'17, page 6000–6010, Curran Associates Inc., Red Hook, NY, USA, 2017.

45 Ilya Sutskever, Oriol Vinyals, and Quoc V Le. Sequence to sequence learning with neural networks. In *Proceedings of the 27th International Conference on Neural Information Processing Systems – Volume 2*, NIPS'14, page 3104–3112, MIT Press, Cambridge, MA, USA, 2014.

46 Jeffrey Pennington, Richard Socher, and Christopher Manning. GloVe: global vectors for word representation. In *Proceedings of the 2014 Conference on Empirical Methods in Natural Language Processing (EMNLP)*, pages 1532–1543, Association for Computational Linguistics, Doha, Qatar, 2014. https://doi.org/10.3115/v1/D14-1162.

47 Keita Kurita, Nidhi Vyas, Ayush Pareek, Alan W Black, and Yulia Tsvetkov. Measuring bias in contextualized word representations. *arXiv preprint arXiv:1906.07337*, 2019.

48 Emily Sheng, Kai-Wei Chang, Prem Natarajan, and Nanyun Peng. The woman worked as a babysitter: on biases in language generation. In *Proceedings of the 2019 Conference on Empirical Methods in Natural Language Processing and the 9th International Joint Conference on Natural Language Processing (EMNLP-IJCNLP)*, pages 3398–3403, 2019.

49 Mandar Joshi, Danqi Chen, Yinhan Liu, Daniel S Weld, Luke Zettlemoyer, and Omer Levy. SpanBERT: improving pre-training by representing and predicting spans. *Transactions of the Association for Computational Linguistics*, 8: 64–77, 2020. https://doi.org/10.1162/tacl_a_00300.

50 Wenxuan Zhou and Muhao Chen. An improved baseline for sentence-level relation extraction. *arXiv preprint arXiv:2102.01373*, 2021.

51 Amir DN Cohen, Shachar Rosenman, and Yoav Goldberg. Relation classification as two-way span-prediction. *arXiv preprint arXiv:2010.04829*, 2020.

52 Robert Vacareanu, Fahmida Alam, Md Asiful Islam, Haris Riaz, and Mihai Surdeanu. Best of both worlds: a pliable and generalizable neuro-symbolic approach for relation classification. In *Findings of the Association for Computational Linguistics: NAACL 2024*, Association for Computational Linguistics, Mexico City, Mexico, 2024. https://arxiv.org/pdf/2403.03305.pdf.

53 O. Mahamane Sani Sabo, Yanai Elazar, Yoav Goldberg, and Ido Dagan. Revisiting few-shot relation classification: evaluation data and classification schemes. *Transactions of the Association for Computational Linguistics*, 9: 691–706, 2021.

54 Sebastian Riedel, Limin Yao, and Andrew McCallum. Modeling relations and their mentions without labeled text. In *Joint European Conference on Machine Learning and Knowledge Discovery in Databases*, pages 148–163. Springer, 2010.

55 Ryuichi Takanobu, Tianyang Zhang, Jiexi Liu, and Minlie Huang. A hierarchical framework for relation extraction with reinforcement learning. In *Proceedings of the AAAI Conference on Artificial Intelligence*, 33(01): 7072–7079, 2019.

56 Fahmida Alam, Md Asiful Islam, Robert Vacareanu, and Mihai Surdeanu. Towards realistic few-shot relation extraction: a new meta dataset and evaluation. In *Proceedings of the 2024 Joint International Conference on Computational Linguistics, Language Resources and Evaluation*, 2024.

57 Yinhan Liu, Myle Ott, Naman Goyal, Jingfei Du, Mandar Joshi, Danqi Chen, Omer Levy, Mike Lewis, Luke Zettlemoyer, and Veselin Stoyanov. Roberta: a robustly optimized bert pretraining approach. *arXiv*, 2019. https://arxiv.org/abs/1907.11692.

58 Lushan Han, Abhay Lokesh Kashyap, Timothy W Finin, James Mayfield, and Jonathan Weese. Umbc_ebiquity-core: semantic textual similarity systems. In *Second Joint Conference on Lexical and Computational Semantics (*SEM), Volume 1: Proceedings of the Main Conferenceand the Shared Task*, pages 44–52, 2013.

59 Ruisi Zhang, Seira Hidano, and Farinaz Koushanfar. Text revealer: private text reconstruction via model inversion attacks against transformers. *arXiv*, 2022. https://arxiv.org/abs/2209.10505.

60 John Abascal, Stanley Wu, Alina Oprea, and Jonathan Ullman. TMI! Finetuned models leak private information from their pretraining data. *arXiv*, 2023. https://arxiv.org/abs/2306.01181.

61 Alec Radford, Jong Wook Kim, Chris Hallacy, Aditya Ramesh, Gabriel Goh, Sandhini Agarwal, Girish Sastry, Amanda Askell, Pamela Mishkin, Jack Clark, et al. Learning transferable visual models from natural language supervision. In *International Conference on Machine Learning*, 2021. https://api.semanticscholar.org/CorpusID:231591445.

62 Laura Chiticariu, Yunyao Li, and Frederick Reiss. Rule-based information extraction is dead! Long live rule-based information extraction systems! In *Proceedings of the 2013 Conference on Empirical Methods in Natural Language Processing*, pages 827–832, 2013.

14

Neurosymbolic AI for Legal AI-TRISM: Trustworthy, Reliable, Interpretable, Safe Models

Deepa Tilwani,[1] Yash Saxena,[2] Ankur Padia,[2] Srinivasan Parthasarathy,[3] and Manas Gaur[2]*

[1] *Department of Computer Science, AI Institute, University of South Carolina, Columbia, South Carolina, USA*
[2] *Department of Computer Science, University of Maryland, Baltimore, Maryland, USA*
[3] *Department of Computer Science, Ohio State University, Columbus, Ohio, USA*

*Corresponding Author: dtilwani@mailbox.sc.edu

14.1 Introduction

Generative AI is beginning to impact the legal profession, with emerging applications in document analysis, legal research, and draft preparation [1, 2]. Large Language Models (LLMs) show promise in processing legal documents, identifying key information, and assisting with preliminary drafts of contracts, briefs, and memoranda [3, 4, 5].

While LLM-based AI systems can recognize legal terminology and suggest relevant precedents, their capabilities remain limited and require careful human oversight to ensure accuracy and consistency [6, 7]. Moreover, such systems face significant challenges in downstream legal applications, particularly in understanding complex legal principles and their contextual application [8]. To better understand the problem, consider a dispute between the landlord and the tenant over an emergency repair; an LLM in zero-shot setting can correctly identify that tenants generally have the right to withhold rent for severe habitability issues, such as a broken heating system during winter. However, the off-the-shelf model might fail to consider specific state laws and side information, which require tenants to first notify the landlord in writing and provide a reasonable repair period

Neurosymbolic AI: Foundations and Applications, First Edition. Edited by Alvaro Velasquez et al.

before withholding rent. Furthermore, while suggesting relevant cases about rent withholding, the LLM might miss critical local housing court decisions that require tenants to deposit the withheld rent into an escrow account. This illustrates how LLMs can simulate understanding of basic legal principles but struggle with the nuance requirements and procedural steps based on jurisdiction – the knowledge that experienced lawyers use daily to properly advise clients.

While LLMs can identify common legal rules, they often struggle to integrate multiple sources of law and recognize priorities between local regulations and general principles where local regulations might override general principles [3]. Such limitations in understanding legal hierarchies and jurisdictional nuances highlight current capabilities of LLM and the need for human legal expertise for accurate legal analysis and advice.

Neurosymbolic AI represents a novel approach that integrates neural networks with symbolic reasoning (e.g., KG, legal precedents, guidelines) to help build trustworthy artificial intelligence systems [9]. At its foundation, this hybrid approach combines the pattern recognition capabilities of neural networks with the logical inference abilities of symbolic systems, addressing the limitations of each method when used in isolation. The neural component processes raw data and learns patterns, which it does very well; however, a symbolic component is required to understand the explicit and implicit entities and relationships in the data. The symbolic component handles logical reasoning and rule-based operations, allowing a neural network to either follow expert-defined instructions, understand domain definitions or structured knowledge (e.g., guidelines, protocols, precedents in the case of the legal domain), in some scenarios, memorize it, and perform generation that is understandable to subject matter experts.

Despite advances through human feedback and training, current AI models like ChatGPT still struggle to produce information that is both domain-safe and traceable in its reasoning [10]. Neurosymbolic AI addresses these limitations by incorporating structured symbolic knowledge alongside neural patterns, leading to reduced hallucinations, improved explainability, and enhanced reasoning capabilities. The CREST framework proposed by Gaur and Sheth [11] demonstrates how neurosymbolic methods can ensure consistency, reliability, and safety in critical applications. In this chapter we make cover following topics:

- Current limitations of using Generative AI as legal assistant as potential opportunities to support further research on using AI in legal domain
- We survey recent approaches using Neural and Neurosymbolic-based approaches in the legal domain.
- We formalize the process of creating symbolic knowledge from legal textual documents along with role of using Retrieval Augmented Generation in legal domain.

14.1.1 Neurosymbolic RAG

Neurosymbolic Retrieval Augmented Generation (RAG) offers an innovative architecture that integrates neural retrieval mechanisms, typically powered by LLMs, with symbolic reasoning frameworks. This architecture, as shown in Figure 14.1, is particularly well-suited to the legal domain, where precision, compliance, and explainability are critical, yet the domain is characterized by complex, evolving jurisprudence and inherently ambiguous language. By combining the interpretive capabilities of neural models with the logical rigor of symbolic systems, neurosymbolic RAG facilitates advanced legal knowledge retrieval, reasoning, and text generation for diverse legal tasks.

Architecture: The architecture of a neurosymbolic RAG system is centered on the interplay between its neural and symbolic components. Neural retrieval employs LLMs to process unstructured legal texts, such as case law, statutes, and procedural documentation, and extract semantically relevant information. These models, trained on vast legal corpora, leverage contextual embeddings to identify connections between concepts even when terminology varies. For instance, the system can match a query concerning "duty of care" with cases discussing "reasonable care" due to the neural model's ability to generalize across related terms. This retrieval process ensures that the system captures the breadth of relevant information while accommodating the linguistic variability inherent in legal texts.

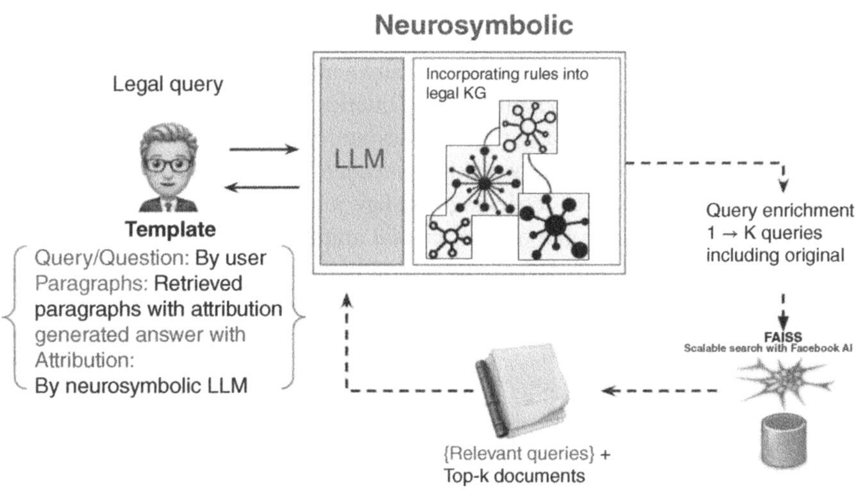

Figure 14.1 Neurosymbolic RAG Pipeline integrating TRISM principles. The framework combines a Large Language Model (LLM) with a Legal Knowledge Graph (KG), leveraging query enrichment and retrieval techniques (e.g., FAISS) for scalable and secure document retrieval. It incorporates trust, responsibility, and security through enriched rule-based reasoning in the KG, ensuring robust query-answering in legal contexts.

Validation: Once information is retrieved, the symbolic reasoning layer validates and refines the results using formal legal ontologies and rule-based logic. The symbolic component encodes domain-specific knowledge in structured formats, such as hierarchical taxonomies and procedural rules, enabling the system to enforce compliance with jurisdictional, temporal, and procedural constraints. For example, the symbolic reasoning module can filter retrieved case law to exclude precedents that fall outside the relevant jurisdiction or statutory timeframe, ensuring the validity of the results. Additionally, deductive reasoning techniques are applied to infer implicit relationships and validate logical consistency within the retrieved data.

Generation: The generation phase synthesizes outputs by combining the contextual richness of neural models with the structured reasoning of symbolic systems. Neural generation produces fluent and comprehensive responses, while symbolic reasoning constrains these outputs to align with legal norms and procedural requirements. This synthesis is particularly valuable for generating legal arguments, drafting procedural documents, or summarizing case law. For example, when drafting a legal brief, the system incorporates retrieved case law and procedural rules, presenting them in a manner that adheres to jurisdictional and argumentative standards. This dual-layered approach ensures that the outputs are both semantically rich and procedurally sound.

14.1.2 Advantages of Using Neurosymbolic RAG

Capabilities: One of the key strengths of neurosymbolic RAG in the legal domain is its ability to handle complex, multifaceted queries. Legal questions often require the synthesis of diverse information sources and the application of procedural constraints. For example, a query seeking precedents for admissible evidence in a specific jurisdiction involves retrieving case law, interpreting procedural statutes, and ensuring relevance to the query's factual and temporal context. Neurosymbolic RAG addresses this by leveraging neural retrieval to access broad, semantically relevant data and symbolic reasoning to refine and contextualize the results. This ensures that the system delivers precise and actionable insights tailored to the user's specific needs.

Adaptability: The adaptability of neurosymbolic RAG is another critical advantage in the dynamic legal environment. Laws, precedents, and procedural standards evolve, and the system is designed to accommodate such changes. Neural models can be fine-tuned with updated corpora to reflect shifts in legal language and interpretive trends, while symbolic ontologies can be revised to incorporate new rules and statutory interpretations. This continuous updating process ensures that the system remains aligned with current legal standards, enabling practitioners to rely on it for accurate and timely guidance.

Transparency: Transparency is a defining feature of neurosymbolic RAG, particularly in legal contexts where trust and accountability are paramount. Unlike purely neural systems, which often function as black boxes, the symbolic reasoning layer provides traceable and explainable decision-making paths. For example, when the system suggests a particular case as a precedent, it can articulate the reasoning process, citing the specific principles, jurisdictional rules, and procedural constraints that informed its decision. This transparency not only builds trust in the system's recommendations but also ensures that legal professionals can confidently use its outputs in their work.

14.2 Limitation of Using LLM as Legal Assistant

LLMs are trained on massive datasets with billions of tokens and often simulate the understanding of the real world. Such capabilities have provided performance gain in summarization [12], boundary detection [13], information extraction [14], legal judgment prediction [15], named entity recognition [16], and text segmentation [17]. However, several challenges exist as described below:

- *Complex Family Law Cases*: In child custody arrangements, AI struggles to understand the nuanced family dynamics, emotional considerations, and child well-being that require a level of understanding beyond AI's current capabilities [18]. Human lawyers can factor in empathy, consequences, and lived experiences to make judgments that AI cannot replicate.
- *Ethical Dilemmas*: Navigating ethical dilemmas in the legal context requires a deep understanding of professional responsibilities, moral principles, and the potential consequences of one's actions. The case of "E.F. Hutton & Co. v. Brown" (1986) illustrates the complexities of conflicts of interest in corporate law, highlighting the importance of rigorous conflict checks and transparent communication [19].
- *Causal Reasoning in Law*: Legal reasoning often involves understanding cause-and-effect relationships, which LLMs struggle to grasp. This limitation becomes evident when analyzing complex chains of events or determining liability in intricate legal cases [20].
- *Analogical Reasoning*: While Generative AI can identify similar cases (e.g., LegalRAG), it struggles with the nuanced task of determining which cases are truly analogous and why. This requires a deeper understanding of legal principles and their underlying rationales, which current AI systems lack [21].
- *Contextual Interpretation*: AI often processes information in a fragmented manner, focusing on specific words or phrases without grasping the overall context (e.g., LegalBERT [22]). This can lead to misinterpretations of legal concepts. *Legal language* often requires nuanced interpretation based on context. AI may struggle to differentiate between subtle variations in meaning

that are clear to human legal experts. *Legal reasoning* often relies on implicit understanding and unwritten principles. AI systems may miss these crucial elements, leading to incomplete or inaccurate analyses.

- *Hallucinations and Temporal Mismatch*: A Stanford-Yale study challenged claims by major legal AI providers about eliminating hallucinations through retrieval augmented generation (RAG) [23]. Although Casetext, Thomson Reuters, and LexisNexis marketed their tools as hallucination-free, the research found that their products still hallucinated 33% of the time, compared to the rate of GPT-4 43%. In addition, outdated legal databases and suboptimal text fragmentation methods in LegalRAG systems can compromise the precision of the response by retrieving obsolete information and fragmenting critical legal context.

The path forward lies in developing neurosymbolic systems that combine the pattern recognition strengths of neural networks with symbolic reasoning capabilities. Such hybrid systems could better represent and manipulate legal concepts, rules, and precedents while maintaining the flexibility to handle natural language. By incorporating explicit knowledge representation and logical inference mechanisms, next-generation legal AI assistants could provide more reliable analysis, better handle edge cases, and offer clearer explanations of their reasoning.

14.3 Neurosymbolic AI for Legal Domain

The application of Neurosymbolic AI in the legal domain introduces an innovative synthesis of neural learning and symbolic reasoning, essential for handling the intricate and interpretative nature of legal knowledge. Legal processes demand not just textual comprehension but also logical consistency, rule-based validation, and the ability to support nuanced decision-making under jurisdictional constraints [24, 25]. Neurosymbolic systems are exceptionally suited to address these challenges by combining the neural networks' ability to recognize patterns with the structured logical reasoning provided by symbolic frameworks.

Legal reasoning is uniquely challenging because it requires aligning textual and contextual information with codified rules and precedence hierarchies. The duality of neural and symbolic approaches is uniquely positioned to meet these demands. Neural models, such as LLMs, excel in processing and generating textual data, often capturing subtleties in legal language that would otherwise require significant human expertise. However, these models fall short in tasks requiring logical consistency and explainability, such as validating precedents or resolving jurisdictional conflicts. Symbolic systems, on the other hand, are inherently rule-based and operate within a framework of well-defined logic, making them ideal for encoding legal principles, procedural norms, and hierarchical relationships.

Neurosymbolic AI synergizes these two approaches by utilizing the interpretative power of neural networks alongside the structured rigor of symbolic reasoning.

The potential of this integration can be fully realized through the incorporation of Knowledge Graphs (KGs), which act as structured repositories of legal knowledge. By organizing legal entities such as statutes, cases, and principles into graph-based relationships, KGs provide the foundational structure for reasoning. Retrieval Augmented Generation (RAG) architectures further enhance this framework by leveraging the KG to ground generative tasks in precise, context-specific legal knowledge. For instance, when tasked with generating a legal brief, a Neurosymbolic AI system retrieves relevant precedents and statutes from the KG, synthesizing them into a coherent, procedurally sound argument. This process not only improves the accuracy of legal outputs but also ensures that every element is traceable to its source, a feature critical for maintaining trustworthiness in legal contexts.

A hallmark of legal reasoning is its reliance on precedential hierarchies and jurisdictional rules. Neurosymbolic AI addresses this by embedding legal ontologies within its symbolic reasoning layer. These ontologies encode the structural relationships and hierarchies among legal concepts, such as the interplay between state and federal laws or the precedence of constitutional rulings over statutory interpretations. This structured representation enables the system to reconcile conflicts, such as determining, which law prevails in cases of jurisdictional overlap. For example, when analyzing a dispute involving both state and federal regulations, the system retrieves and ranks relevant statutes and cases. The neural component contextualizes the retrieved data, while the symbolic layer applies jurisdictional precedence rules, ensuring that the resulting analysis adheres to legal norms and standards.

Neurosymbolic AI's ability to generate explainable outputs further underscores its relevance to the legal domain. Unlike traditional neural systems, which often operate as opaque black boxes, Neurosymbolic AI systems provide reasoning paths for their outputs. Each recommendation or decision, whether it involves citing a statute or resolving a conflict, is accompanied by a detailed explanation derived from the symbolic reasoning process and the KG. This transparency is particularly valuable in high-stakes applications, such as judicial decision-making or legislative drafting, where every assertion must withstand scrutiny. By enabling traceability and accountability, Neurosymbolic AI aligns itself with the stringent demands of the legal profession.

The significance of Neurosymbolic AI extends beyond practical applications to advancing legal domain. By automating the retrieval, reasoning, and synthesis of legal knowledge, it accelerates research and enables scholars to tackle complex legal questions with greater depth and efficiency. Its ability to model abstract legal concepts also paves the way for developing new legal theories and frameworks. For example, in analyzing the evolving concept of "reasonable care" in tort law, the system could integrate historical precedents with contemporary interpretations, offering scholars a comprehensive perspective.

Drawing inspiration from REASONS [26], Neurosymbolic AI aligns with the benchmark's emphasis on generating precise, context-aware, and explainable responses. Like REASONS, which integrates retrieval and reasoning to provide faithful and grounded outputs, Neurosymbolic AI ensures that every conclusion is anchored in validated knowledge. This alignment reinforces its suitability for domains where accuracy, interpretability, and compliance are paramount.

14.4 AI-TRISM with Neurosymbolic AI

In order to use a neurosymbolic AI-based system, domain knowledge needs to be encoded in machine-processible form. One of the methods to explicitly encode the legal domain is to construct a legal knowledge graph (KG).

14.4.1 KG Construction

KG is a graph with entities as nodes and relations between the entities as edges [27]. Compared to neural network learning patterns from the data, KG explicitly makes complex relationships among the entities, thereby offering a structured and semantically enriched framework to address these challenges.

In the legal domain, a KG can significantly enhance decision-making, information retrieval, and case analysis with legal data in an interconnected framework. Legal KG provides relationships between the entities, such as cases, laws, legal principles, and stakeholders, to enable comprehensive analysis and support the roles of prosecutors, defenders, and judges, by representing legal entities (e.g., statutes, cases, legal principles) as nodes and their relationships as edges, KGs enable advanced reasoning and querying capabilities. We present a formal methodology for constructing KGs, highlighting the integration of legal ontologies, graph construction techniques, and reasoning mechanisms to enhance legal research and support decision-making.

Formal Framework for KG Construction: A KG G is formally defined as a directed labeled graph:

$$G = (V, E, \mathcal{L}),$$

where: V is the set of nodes representing legal entities such as statutes, cases, or legal principles, $E \subseteq V \times V$ is the set of relationships between nodes. $\mathcal{L}$ is the set of labels that annotate nodes and edges with semantic meaning. Each node $v \in V$ is associated with an attribute set $\mathcal{A}(v)$, containing metadata such as jurisdiction, date, and legal domain:

$$\mathcal{A}(v) = \{\text{Vedict: Defense Won, Date: 11-Jan-2002, ... , Domain: Criminal Law}\}.$$

A KG can be constructed using `Closed Information Extraction` (Closed IE) or `Open Information Extraction` (Open IE) [28] based approaches. Closed Information Extraction assumes that the system has access to a predefined set of information to be extracted, such as the name of the defendant. In contrast, in an Open IE setup, the system does not have access to specific information to extract but instead aims to extract all possible information from the text.

Ontology Integration: For an information extraction system to extract information, a Closed IE system needs access to an ontology. An ontology $\mathcal{O}$ provides a schema for the KG, defining the structure and semantics of the graph:

$$\mathcal{O} = (C, R, H, \mathcal{P}),$$

where C is the set of concepts (e.g., "Statute", "Court Decision"). R is the set of relations (e.g., "cites", "interprets"). $H \subseteq C \times C$ is a hierarchical structure, where $(c_1, c_2) \in H$ indicates c_2 is a subclass of c_1. $\mathcal{P}$ is the set of properties for concepts, such as "Effective Date" or "Jurisdiction".

Formal Representation of Relationships: In a KG each relationships between entities are modeled as triples:

$$t = (s, p, o),$$

where $s \in V$: the subject (e.g., a case), $p \in R$: the predicate (e.g., "cites"), $o \in V$: the object (e.g., a statute). For example, if a case c_1 cites a statute s_1, this relationship is represented as:

$$(c_1, \texttt{cites}, s_1) \in E.$$

14.4.2 Graph Construction Methodology

An example of a legal KG is shown in Figure 14.2. One of the necessary steps to create a KG is to extract entities (including events) from the text to represent nodes and relations as edges. Constructed KGs can be refined with Ontology alignment and graph augmentation and can be catered to the public with enabled reasoning and querying support. Each of the phases is described below:

Entity Extraction: Given a corpus of legal documents $D = \{d_1, d_2, \dots, d_n\}$, entities V are extracted using Named Entity Recognition (NER). For example, entities include:

$$V = \{s_1, s_2, c_1, c_2, p_1, p_2\},$$

where s_i are statutes, c_i are cases, and p_i are legal principles.

Relation Extraction: Relations E are extracted using dependency parsing and semantic role labeling. For a sentence S, dependency parsing identifies syntactic structures $\mathcal{D}(S)$, while semantic role labeling assigns relationships. For example: S: "Case c_1 cites Statute s_1," yields: $(c_1$, cites, $s_1)$.

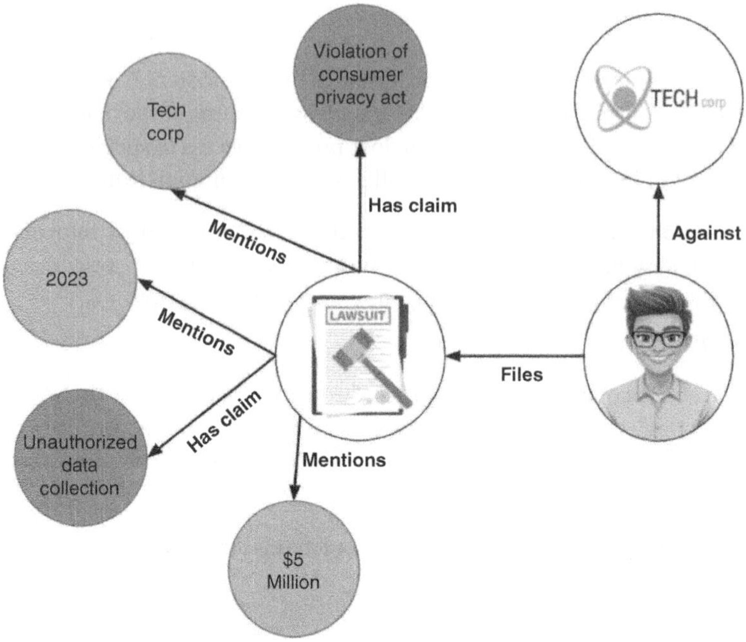

Figure 14.2 A representation of a Legal Knowledge Graph (KG) showcasing the relationships in a legal case, including entities such as a lawsuit, claims of violation of the Consumer Privacy Act and unauthorized data collection, the involved parties (an individual and Tech Corp), the year (2023), and the associated claim of $5 million in damages.

Ontology Alignment: Extracted entities and relations are aligned with the ontology $\mathcal{O}$, ensuring semantic consistency. For example:

$$c_1 \in C_{\text{Court Decision}}, \quad s_1 \in C_{\text{Statute}}.$$

Graph Augmentation: The graph G is enriched with metadata $\mathcal{M}$. For instance, a case c_1 is augmented as:

$$\mathcal{M}(c_1) = \{\text{"Date: 2023-06-30," "Jurisdiction: U.S. Supreme Court"}\}.$$

Reasoning and Querying: Reasoning enables advanced inferences over the KG. Transitive reasoning applies to relations such as "cites":

$$\text{If } (c_1, \text{cites}, s_1) \text{ and } (s_1, \text{cites}, s_2), \text{ then infer } (c_1, \text{cites}, s_2).$$

Querying is facilitated using SPARQL-like expressions. For example, to find all statutes cited by a case:

$$\text{MATCH } (c) - [: \text{cites}] -> (s) \text{ RETURN } s.$$

Together, the algorithm for building KG is provided in the representation shown in Algorithm 1.

Algorithm 1 KG Construction for Legal Domain

Input: Legal corpus $D = \{d_1, d_2, \dots, d_n\}$, Ontology $\mathcal{O} = (C, R, H, \mathcal{P})$
Output: KG $G = (V, E, \mathcal{L})$
Step 1: Ontology Development
Define concepts C, relationships R, hierarchy H, and properties $\mathcal{P}$.
Step 2: Entity Extraction
for each document $d_i \in D$ **do**
    Extract entities $V = \{s_i, c_i, p_i\}$ using Named Entity Recognition (NER).
end for
Step 3: Relation Extraction
for each sentence S in D **do**
    Use dependency parsing and semantic role labeling to identify relations E.
    Map relations to triples $t = (s, p, o)$.
end for
Step 4: Ontology Alignment
for each entity $v \in V$ and relation $e \in E$ **do**
    Align v and e with concepts and relationships in $\mathcal{O}$.
end for
Step 5: Graph Augmentation
for each node $v \in V$ **do**
    Annotate with metadata $\mathcal{A}(v) = \{\text{Jurisdiction, Date, Domain}\}$.
end for
Step 6: Reasoning and Inference
for each relation $(c_1, \text{cites}, s_1) \in E$ **do**
    if $(s_1, \text{cites}, s_2) \in E$ **then**
        Add (c_1, cites, s_2) to E.
    end if
end for
Step 7: Querying
Provide SPARQL-like interface for querying G.
Return KG $G = (V, E, \mathcal{L})$

14.5 Symbiosis of LLM and KG for Neurosymbolic RAG in Legal Domain

One challenge with KGs is the need for their continuous updating to reflect new information and changing relationships within the domain they represent, as static knowledge quickly becomes outdated and less valuable. Manual updates to knowledge graphs (KGs) are not feasible at scale, particularly within the legal domain, where legislative bodies and courts continuously enact new statutes, implement regulatory amendments, establish precedential decisions, and create exceptions to existing rules – all of which require thorough validation and careful integration into KG.

KG scalability can be enhanced while maintaining its expressive capabilities by combining two key elements: (a) leveraging LLMs generative capabilities and extensive world knowledge and (b) integrating this with KG through KG embedding techniques. The process of enriching KGs with information from LLMs is guided by a metric known as the Knowledge Gap. This gap represents areas where KG embedding methods can perform basic tasks like classification, recommendation, or attribute assignment but do so with low confidence levels, indicating incomplete or uncertain knowledge in those areas.

The overall process of automatic updating of legal KG is shown as a 10-step process in Figure 14.3.

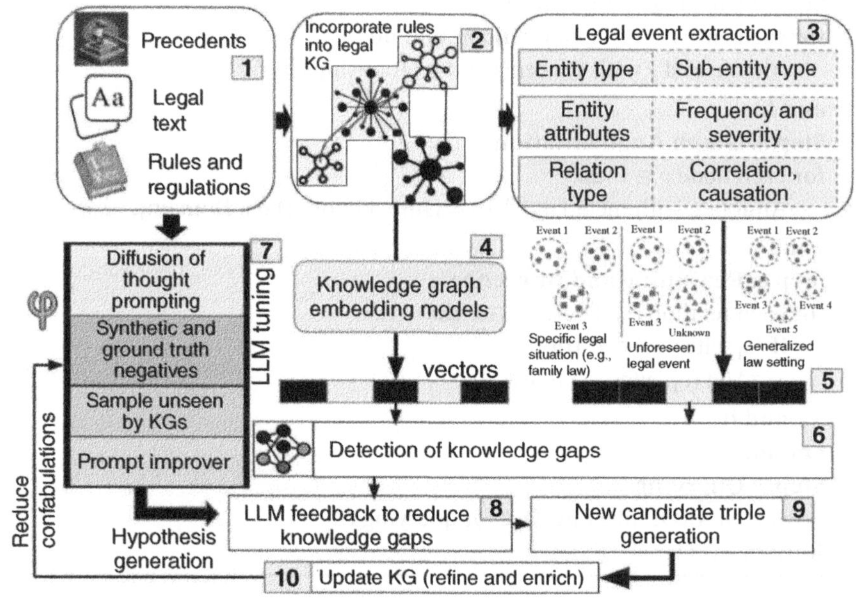

Figure 14.3 A 10 step process to automate the process of updating Legal KG using LLMs. The architecture highlights transformation of legal KG to embedding, identification of new legal events, detection of knowledge gaps, and addressing the knowledge gaps with new candidate triples. These major phases are powered by a pre-trained LLM through three key mechanisms: tuning with synthetic negative samples to establish clear decision boundaries and validate existing knowledge in the KG, identification of unseen instances to explore and fill gaps in the current legal knowledge representation, and dynamic prompt improvement to optimize hypothesis generation. The updated legal KG is then used to refine the LLM and even reduce hallucinations

Steps 1 and 2 Legal KG construction: We have described the process for carrying out the Steps 1 and 2 in Section 14.1.1.

Step 3 Legal Event Extraction: This process involves instantiating the process of verb phrase extraction over the legal KG to extract triples containing information about a legal event. A legal event is manifested in the form of formal documentation (contracts, court orders, legislative acts), significant actions (violations, compliance, fulfillment of obligations), procedural events (filing of lawsuits, administrative decisions, regulatory approvals), or status changes (bankruptcy declarations, corporate formations, property transfers). Triples in KG that belong to such events are extracted and formed into clusters. For clustering we recommend soft clustering techniques, such as locality sensitive hashing for creating event clusters.

Step 4 Knowledge Graph Embedding Models: These are word embedding models trained over open source KGs. The three popular KG embedding models we recommend to use for creating embedding of legal KG is TransE (distance based, which can be modified to similarity based; [29]), HolE [30], and ANALOGY [31].

Step 5 Vectorization : A simple process of vectorizing the event clusters using KGE models and vectorizing legal KG models.

Step 6 Detection of Knowledge Gaps in KGE models: The suggested Knowledge Graph Embedding (KGE) models are off the shelf and might not correctly represent rare or unseen legal events. To quantify the knowledge gaps in KGE, we compute divergence between knowledge representation of event clusters and their associated entity embeddings using multiple metrics. This divergence is calculated through a combination of (1) embedding space distance measures such as cosine similarity and Euclidean distance, (2) probability distribution divergence using Kullback-Leibler (KL) divergence or Jensen-Shannon divergence, and (3) structural entropy measures that capture the uncertainty in the graph topology. A high divergence score, coupled with low confidence in link prediction or entity classification tasks, indicates potential knowledge gaps. These gaps are particularly prevalent in areas where the KGE model encounters rare legal events, complex multi-hop relationships, or novel combinations of entities that weren't well-represented in the training data.

Step 7 Hypothesis generation: With the use of legal benchmarks, we fine-tune LLMs into generating hypothesis through role-playing strategy, where LLMs are provided with cases to act on as defender and then subsequently as prosecutor. By understanding both sides of the coin in a legal argument, LLMs attain finesse in identifying gaps in knowledge in legal KG.

Steps 8 and 9 Reduction of Knowledge Gaps and Identification of New Candidate Triples: The Hypothesis generated by LLMs is carefully compared with the existing knowledge in the legal KG. This comparison process identifies three key aspects: exact matches (where the LLM's output perfectly aligns with existing knowledge), similarities (where there's partial overlap or close alignment), and differences (where the LLM suggests entirely new information). By evaluating these aspects and using specialized algorithms to predict possible connections in the legal knowledge graph, we can identify new, reliable pieces of information that could be added to enrich the knowledge graph while maintaining legal accuracy and relevance.

Step 10 Update KG: The process of updating the legal KG comprises of two static functions: (a) Refine: If existing triple is outdated or is incorrect, new candidate triple replace such triples. This ensures the accuracy and currency of the knowledge graph by removing obsolete or erroneous information and replacing it with validated, up-to-date knowledge. (b) Enrich: This is the process of expanding the knowledge graph by adding new, validated triples that represent previously uncaptured legal relationships, events, or entities. This function helps fill knowledge gaps and increases the coverage of the legal domain without compromising the integrity of existing, accurate information. The enrichment process carefully validates new triples through confidence scoring and legal consistency checks before integration.

Figure 14.3 present an illustration to achieve an up-to-date legal KG and a stable legal LLM, which can be used to power neurosymbolic RAG, shown in Figure 14.1.

14.6 Related Work

The use of LLMs in the legal domain is an active field of research. Even though LLMs are proficient in downstream NLP tasks, legal texts present subtle nuances and specific legal terms. These terms pose a challenge to LLMs when generating text for downstream tasks. This paper covers work related to the use and construction of KGs, work around legal citation and recommendation, and legal tasks that rely solely on neural-based approaches. Table 14.1 shows organization of the neural network approaches with and without using graph to encode knowledge. Because of the diversity of tasks in legal domain, we limit ourself to the task listed hereby. However, this is not an exhaustive list of tasks and more information can be found in Lai et al. [32].

14.6.1 KG Construction

There are multiple techniques used to construct a KG in the legal domain, ranging from human-in-the-loop approaches to fully automated methods.

Kondo et al. [33] presents a human-in-the-loop approach for creating a legal KG by combining LLMs and legal experts to model complex relationships using a hierarchical tree structure. The hierarchical tree is constructed by aggregating legal

Table 14.1 Neural-based approaches, with and without the use of graphs, for various downstream legal tasks. Here, ' – ' indicates "not applicable," "Explicit" denotes that knowledge is represented in the form of a graph, and "Implicit" signifies that knowledge encoded in a neural network is used, either by pre-training a language model on legal data or by relying on the knowledge present in an off-the-shelf language model.

Task	Category	Knowledge Encoding	Reference
KG Construction	Construction	–	Kondo et al. [33], Hlyzov et al. [34], Filtz [35], Tang et al. [36], Song and de la Clergerie [37]
Charge/Judgement Prediction	Classification	Explicit Implict	Bi et al. [38], Gan et al. [39] He et al. [40], Wang et al. [41]
Legal Statute Identification		Explicit	Nguyen et al. [42]
Question Answer	Question Answer	Explicit Implicit	Jiang et al. [43] Louis et al. [44], McElvain et al. [45]
Law Article/Case Retrieval	Information Retreival	Explicit Implicit	Tang et al. [46] Li et al. [47], Deng et al. [48], Ma et al. [49]
Citation Recommendation	Information Retreival	Explicit Implicit	Dhani et al. [50] [51], Wang et al. [41]
Citation Interoperability		Explicit Implicit	Sadeghian et al. [52] Luo et al. [53]

information from the bottom up, with fine-tuned LLMs capturing the tree structure. Since the output may be imperfect, human feedback is employed to refine the final results and ensure accuracy.

In contrast, Filtz [35] adopts a more manual approach to building a KG schema. This iterative process begins with existing publicly available KGs, which are used for downstream tasks to evaluate quality. If the results are unsatisfactory, the KG is modified to meet specific requirements, and the process is repeated until satisfactory results are achieved.

Song and de la Clergerie [37] employs an automatic method to rapidly create a KG of legal entities, enabling tasks such as contract verification, contract generation, and contract analysis. This method uses a clustering-based approach applied to a predetermined set of contracts without requiring supplemental references and is robust against typos.

Tang et al. [36] proposes a semi-automatic method leveraging NLP-based techniques to extract entities from text. These entities are then annotated by humans with specific relationships to generate final triples. The resulting graph is consumed using tools like Neo4j.

14.6.2 Legal Classification

The legal classification task aims to predict one or more labels from a set of predetermined labels.

Bi et al. [38] introduces a novel legal schematic knowledge-aware model designed for challenging legal cases, leveraging a transformer-based model and Graph Convolution Network. The authors create structural and semantic graphs using fact descriptions, integrating legal knowledge of groups, charges, and elements to derive final representations for classification.

Gan et al. [39] employs declarative language to represent legal knowledge. Using first-order logic rules, Gan et al. [39] captures interactions between different entities and integrates these rules into neural networks via co-attention mechanisms. By explicitly modeling interactions, the use of logic rules enhances the interpretability of the model.

He et al. [40] models legal knowledge of charges as a set of tuples, where each charge is associated with its definition, subjectivity, subject, object, objectivity, and legal basis. This graph is encoded using a neural model and then integrated with fact descriptions to generate charge-level representations for classification.

Wang et al. [41] introduces LegalReasoner, a system that combines LLMs with infused legal knowledge. The process involves pretraining an off-the-shelf model on a large legal corpus using a contrastive learning method. Subsequently, a graph neural network retrieves relevant cases, which are then provided as input to a transformer-based model and a generative network to deliver sound judgments with explanations.

Nguyen et al. [42] presents an approach aimed at assisting users with clarifications on Land Law matters. The authors construct a KG of questions and articles to capture intricate connections and associations among various legal entities and concepts, employing graph-based representation to determine the status of legal cases.

14.6.3 Legal Question Answering

Several approaches have been developed to perform question-answering tasks in legal contexts by combining information retrieval and language models.

Jiang et al. [43] propose an approach to perform question answering on a legal knowledge base, where the question is a user query, and the answer is generated using a LLM with legal knowledge infused from a database of law articles. First, articles related to the query are retrieved and de-duplicated before generating the answer using the LLM.

Similarly, Louis et al. [44] present a "retrieve-then-read" pipeline approach to support interpretability for legal documents written in French. For a given question, their approach first retrieves relevant articles using a bi-encoder model. Based on the retrieved documents, an answer is then generated.

Finally, and similar to the above approaches, McElvain et al. [45] propose a method that uses an information retriever and natural language processing (NLP) models to obtain concise, single-sentence answers to basic non-factoid questions about the law.

14.6.4 Legal Article and Case Retrieval

Innovative approaches have been developed to enhance legal case retrieval and analysis by leveraging graph-based methods, pre-trained language models, and LLMs.

Tang et al. [46] propose a graph-based approach, CaseLink, to retrieve legal cases. They create a graph that connects query cases, candidate cases, and ground truth references between the query and candidates. During the testing phase, a given query case is converted into a representation and used to identify neighboring cases. To achieve this, Tang et al. [46] employs a graph neural network to transform textual queries into a representable format.

Li et al. [47] utilize pre-trained language models to retrieve legal cases. However, since off-the-shelf language models lack inherent legal knowledge, they incorporate domain-specific structures into the model. These structures are categorized as procedure, fact, reasoning, decision, and tail. Ma et al. [49] constructed a fine-grained corpus of articles from the original dataset to encode legal cases better. Deng et al. [48] prompt a LLM to extract crimes and corresponding law articles from legal cases. They leverage encoded knowledge from a legal expert database to map crimes accurately to the relevant law articles. Subsequently, the LLM is prompted with the extracted "crime-article" pairs to summarize the sub-facts of the crime from the legal case. The rationale behind using law articles is to provide high-level abstractions of criminal events, making it easier to identify critical sub-facts.

14.6.5 Citation Recommendation and Interoperability

Dhani et al. [50] use a KG to recommend similar cases. They first construct a KG from Indian court judgments and select features to train a graph neural network. The trained model generates representations of the judgments, which are then used to identify similar cases.

Huang et al. [51] highlight that lawyers and judges spend significant time researching appropriate legal authorities to cite when drafting decisions. They propose a citation recommendation tool to improve the efficiency of opinion drafting. Four machine learning models are trained: a citation-list-based method (collaborative filtering) and three context-based methods (text similarity, BiLSTM, and RoBERTa classifiers). Their experiments demonstrate that leveraging local textual context improves recommendations and that deep neural models perform well. They observe that non-deep, text-based methods benefit from structured case metadata, while deep models only gain from such metadata when the context length is insufficient. Despite RoBERTa's pretraining advantages, it does not outperform a recurrent neural model after extensive training. A behavior analysis of the RoBERTa model reveals stable predictive performance across time and citation classes.

Wang et al. [54] address the limitations of collaborative filtering (CF)-based legal recommendation methods by introducing a model based on the Instruction GPT with Low-Rank Adaptation (IGPT-LoRA) architecture. This approach enhances legal citation recommendations by fine-tuning pre-trained language models (PLMs), improving performance while reducing computational demands. Additionally, Wang et al. [54] incorporate domain-specific instruction templates to guide the adaptation of PLMs.

Luo et al. [53] address the legal citation prediction (LCP) requirements by designing the task to reflect the thought process of lawyers, incorporating both precedents and legislative provisions. They introduce a prototype-based architecture that enhances interpretability, delivering strong performance while aligning with the decision-making parameters used by lawyers. This approach refines citation predictions through feedback from legal experts.

Sadeghian et al. [52] propose an algorithm that uses citing text along with its surrounding context to construct a citation graph from a text document. Once the graph is built, each edge is automatically labeled based on a predetermined set of labels.

14.6.6 Other Related Work

Other distinctly related works include developing alert systems for users and assessing the quality of patents.

Hannah et al. [55] propose a prompt engineering-based approach to generate alerts by combining the capabilities of LLMs with structured outputs. The system processes a user query to generate a response that identifies legal issues and retrieves relevant law citations for each issue. It then provides a concise, user-friendly summary of the applicable laws. These outputs populate an alert card, offering users a clear overview of legal concerns and corresponding references.

Wang et al. [56] evaluate the value of patents using a probabilistic mixture approach that incorporates both technological and legal citations through citation network-based methods. This approach includes an iterative learning process that integrates a temporal decay function to enhance the analysis.

Acknowledgement

We acknowledge the support from UMBC Cybersecurity Leadership – Exploratory Grant Program. Any opinions, conclusions, or recommendations expressed in this material are those of the authors and do not necessarily reflect the views of UMBC.

References

1 The Impact of Generative AI on the Legal Profession—usiaffinity.com. https://www.usiaffinity.com/news-center/news-center-articles/risk-management/2024-q4/the-impact-of-generative-ai-on-the-legal-profession/, 2024. [Accessed 25-12-2024].

2 Benjamin Liu. How is generative artificial intelligence changing the legal profession? - Economics Observatory—economicsobservatory.com. https://www.economicsobservatory.com/how-is-generative-artificial-intelligence-changing-the-legal-profession, 2024. [Accessed 25-12-2024].

3 Weicong Qin and Zhongxiang Sun. Exploring the nexus of large language models and legal systems: a short survey. *arXiv*, https://arxiv.org/abs/2404.00990, 2024.

4 Axel Constant, Hannes Westermann, Bryan Wilson, Alex Kiefer, Ines Hipolito, Sylvain Pronovost, Steven Swanson, Mahault Albarracin, and Maxwell J. D. D Ramstead. A path towards legal autonomy: an interoperable and explainable approach to extracting, transforming, loading and computing legal information using large language models, expert systems and bayesian networks. *arXiv preprint arXiv:2403.18537*, 2024.

5 Jakub Drápal, Hannes Westermann, and Jaromír Savelka. Using large language models to support thematic analysis in empirical legal studies. *CoRR*, abs/2310.18729, 2023. https://doi.org/10.48550/ARXIV.2310.18729. https://doi.org/10.48550/arXiv.2310.18729.

6 Olga and Kassi. Legal Tech: 5 Use Cases for Large Language Models in Legal Departments—docket.acc.com. https://docket.acc.com/legal-tech-5-use-cases-large-language-models-legal-departments, 2024. [Accessed 25-12-2024].

7 Kyryl. Harnessing the power of Large Language Models forlegal document review - LegalTechTalk—legaltech-talk.com. https://www.legaltech-talk.com/harnessing-the-power-of-large-language-models-forlegal-document-review/, 2024. [Accessed 25-12-2024].

8 Jinqi Lai, Wensheng Gan, Jiayang Wu, Zhenlian Qi, and Philip S Yu. Large language models in law: a survey, 2023. https://arxiv.org/abs/2312.03718

9 Amit Sheth, Kaushik Roy, and Manas Gaur. Neurosymbolic ai – why, what, and how, 2023. https://arxiv.org/abs/2305.00813.

10 Marçal Mora-Cantallops, Salvador Sánchez-Alonso, Elena García-Barriocanal, and Miguel-Angel Sicilia. Traceability for trustworthy ai: a review of models and tools. *Big Data and Cognitive Computing*, 5(2), 2021. ISSN 2504-2289. https://doi.org/10.3390/bdcc5020020. 2289/5/2/20.

11 Manas Gaur and Amit Sheth. Building trustworthy neurosymbolic ai systems: Consistency, reliability, explainability, and safety, 2023. https://arxiv.org/abs/2312.06798.

12 Daniele Licari, Praveen Bushipaka, Gabriele Marino, Giovanni Comandè, and Tommaso Cucinotta. Legal holding extraction from italian case documents using italian-legal-bert text summarization. In Matthias Grabmair, Francisco, Andrade, and Paulo Novais, editors, *Proceedings of the Nineteenth International Conference on Artificial Intelligence and Law, ICAIL 2023, Braga, Portugal, June 19-23, 2023*, pages 148–156. ACM, 2023. https://doi.org/10.1145/3594536.3595177.

13 Xiaoyan Qu and Xiangfeng Meng. TM-TREK at SemEval-2024 task 8: towards LLM-based automatic boundary detection for human-machine mixed text. In Atul Kr. Ojha, A. Seza Dog˘ruöz, Harish Tayyar Madabushi, Giovanni Da San Martino, Sara Rosenthal, and Aiala Rosá, editors, *Proceedings of the 18th International Workshop on Semantic Evaluation (SemEval-2024)*, pages 710–715, Mexico City, Mexico, 2024. Association for Computational Linguistics. https://doi.org/10.18653/v1/2024.semeval-1.102.

14 Randy Goebel, Yoshinobu Kano, Mi-Young Kim, Juliano Rabelo, Ken Satoh, and Masaharu Yoshioka. Summary of the competition on legal information, extraction/entailment (COLIEE) 2023. In Matthias Grabmair, Francisco, Andrade, and Paulo Novais, editors, *Proceedings of the Nineteenth International Conference on Artificial Intelligence and Law, ICAIL 2023, Braga, Portugal, June 19-23, 2023*, pages 472–480. ACM, 2023. https://doi.org/10.1145/3594536.3595176.

15 Cong Jiang and Xiaolei Yang. Legal syllogism prompting: Teaching large language models for legal judgment prediction. In Matthias Grabmair, Francisco, Andrade, and Paulo Novais, editors, *Proceedings of the Nineteenth International Conference on Artificial Intelligence and Law, ICAIL 2023, Braga, Portugal, June 19-23, 2023*, pages 417–421. ACM, 2023. https://doi.org/10.1145/3594536.3595170.

16 Shao-Man Lee, Yu-Hsiang Tan, and Han-Ting Yu. Learner: few-shot legal argument named entity recognition. In Matthias Grabmair, Francisco, Andrade, and Paulo Novais, editors, *Proceedings of the Nineteenth International Conference on Artificial Intelligence and Law, ICAIL 2023, Braga, Portugal, June 19-23, 2023*, pages 422–426. ACM, 2023. https://doi.org/10.1145/3594536.3595144.

17 Dennis Aumiller, Satya Almasian, Sebastian Lackner, and Michael Gertz. Structural text segmentation of legal documents. In Juliano Maranhão and Adam Zachary Wyner, editors, *ICAIL '21: Eighteenth International Conference for Artificial Intelligence and Law*, São Paulo Brazil pages 2–11. ACM, 2021. https://doi.org/10.1145/3462757.3466085.

18 Limitations of AI in Law Firm Marketing—hennessey.com. https://hennessey.com/ai-for-law-firms/limitations/. [Accessed 06-01-2025].

19 Jessa. Legal ethics: common dilemmas and how to handle them. https://www.lawyersofdistinction.com/legal-ethics-common-dilemmas-and-how-to-, 2024. Accessed: 2025-1-6.

20 Anthony Autore. Why ai can't replace lawyers just yet: the limits of generative ai in legal reasoning. https://www.linkedin.com/pulse/why-ai-cant-replace-lawyers-just-yet-limits-legal-reasoning-autore-4emxc, 2024. [Accessed 06-01-2025].

21 Cass R Sunstein. Of artificial intelligence and legal reasoning. *U. Chi. L. Sch. Roundtable*, 8: 29, 2001.

22 Ilias Chalkidis, Manos Fergadiotis, Prodromos Malakasiotis, Nikolaos Aletras, and Ion, Androutsopoulos. Legal-bert: the muppets straight out of law school. In *Findings of the Association for Computational Linguistics: EMNLP 2020*, pages 2898–2904, 2020.

23 Varun Magesh, Faiz Surani, Matthew Dahl, Mirac Suzgun, Christopher D Manning, and Daniel E Ho. Hallucination-free? assessing the reliability of leading ai legal research tools. *arXiv preprint arXiv:2405.20362*, 2024.

24 Joseph A Wszalek. Cognitive communication and the law: a model for systemic risks and systemic interventions. *Journal of Law and the Biosciences*, 8(1):lsab005, 2021.

25 Ni Zhang and Zixuan Zhang. The application of cognitive neuroscience to judicial models: recent progress and trends. *Frontiers in Neuroscience*, 17: 1257004, 2023.

26 Deepa Tilwani, Yash Saxena, Ali Mohammadi, Edward Raff, Amit Sheth, Srinivasan Parthasarathy, and Manas Gaur. Reasons: a benchmark for retrieval and automated citations of scientific sentences using public and proprietary llms. *arXiv preprint arXiv:2405.02228*, 2024.

27 Xin Dong, Evgeniy Gabrilovich, Geremy Heitz, Wilko Horn, Ni Lao, Kevin Murphy, Thomas Strohmann, Shaohua Sun, and Wei Zhang. Knowledge vault: A web-scale approach to probabilistic knowledge fusion. In *Proceedings of the 20th ACM SIGKDD International Conference on Knowledge Discovery and Data Mining*, pages 601–610, 2014.

28 Oren Etzioni, Michele Banko, Stephen Soderland, and Daniel S Weld. Open information extraction from the web. *Communications of the ACM*, 51(12): 68–74, 2008.

29 Antoine Bordes, Nicolas Usunier, Alberto Garcia-Duran, Jason Weston, and Oksana Yakhnenko. Translating embeddings for modeling multi-relational data. *Advances in Neural Information Processing Systems*, 26, 2013.

30 Maximilian Nickel, Lorenzo Rosasco, and Tomaso Poggio. Holographic embeddings of knowledge graphs. In *Proceedings of the AAAI Conference on Artificial Intelligence*, volume 30, 2016.

31 Hanxiao Liu, Yuexin Wu, and Yiming Yang. Analogical inference for multi-relational embeddings. In *International Conference on Machine Learning*, pages 2168–2178. PMLR, 2017.

32 Jinqi Lai, Wensheng Gan, Jiayang Wu, Zhenlian Qi, and S Yu Philip. Large language models in law: a survey. *AI Open*, 5:181–196, 2024.

33 Ryoma Kondo, Tomohiro Watanabe, Takahiro Yoshida, Kazuyuki Yamasawa, and Ryohei Hisano. Collaborative system synergizing human expertise and large-scale language models for legal knowledge graph construction. In *Proceedings of the 23rd International Semantic Web Conference: Posters, Demos, and Industry Tracks*, 2024.

34 Eugene Hlyzov, Sergey Isaev, Yury Emelyanov, Dmitry Pavlov, Olga Belyaeva, Dmitry Mouromtsev, Olga Parkhimovich, and Maxim Kolchin. Business analytics using the knowledge graph built over the russian legal entities registry. In *CEUR Workshop Proceedings*, 2017.

35 Erwin Filtz. Building and processing a knowledge-graph for legal data. In *The Semantic Web: 14th International Conference, ESWC 2017, Portorož, Slovenia, May 28–June 1, 2017, Proceedings, Part II 14*, pages 184–194. Springer, 2017.

36 Mingwei Tang, Cui Su, Haihua Chen, Jingye Qu, and Junhua Ding. Salkg: a semantic annotation system for building a high-quality legal knowledge graph. In *2020 IEEE International Conference on Big Data (Big Data)*, pages 2153–2159. IEEE, 2020.

37 Fuqi Song and Éric de la Clergerie. Clustering-based automatic construction of legal entity knowledge base from contracts. In Xintao Wu, Chris Jermaine, Li Xiong, Xiaohua Hu, Olivera Kotevska, Siyuan Lu, Weija Xu, Srinivas Aluru, Chengxiang Zhai, Eyhab Al-Masri, Zhiyuan Chen, and Jeff Saltz, editors, *2020 IEEE International Conference on Big Data (IEEE BigData 2020)*, Atlanta, GA, USA, *December 10-13, 2020*, pages 2149–2152. IEEE, 2020. https://doi.org/10.1109/BIGDATA50022.2020.9378166.

38 Sheng Bi, Zafar Ali, Tianxing Wu, and Guilin Qi. Knowledge-enhanced model with dual-graph interaction for confusing legal charge prediction. *Expert Systems with Applications*, 249: 123626, 2024.

39 Leilei Gan, Kun Kuang, Yi Yang, and Fei Wu. Judgment prediction via injecting legal knowledge into neural networks. In *Thirty-Fifth AAAI Conference on Artificial Intelligence, AAAI 2021, Thirty-Third Conference on Innovative Applications of Artificial Intelligence, IAAI 2021, The Eleventh Symposium on*

Educational Advances in Artificial Intelligence, EAAI 2021, Virtual Event, February 2–9, 2021, pages 12866–12874. AAAI Press, 2021. https://doi.org/10.1609/AAAI.V35I14.17522.

40 Congqing He, Tien-Ping Tan, Xiaobo Zhang, and Sheng Xue. Knowledge-enriched multi-cross attention network for legal judgment prediction. *IEEE Access*, 11: 87571–87582, 2023. https://doi.org/10.1109/ACCESS.2023.3305259.

41 Xuran Wang, Xinguang Zhang, Vanessa Hoo, Zhouhang Shao, and Xuguang Zhang. Legalreasoner: a multi-stage framework for legal judgment prediction via large language models and knowledge integration. *IEEE Access*, 12: 166843–166854, 2024. https://doi.org/10.1109/ACCESS.2024.3496666.

42 Duc Nguyen, Thien Huynh, Thang Phung, Thu Bui, Phuong Thai, Long Huynh, Ty Nguyen, An Nguyen, Huu Pham, and Tho Quan. Vn-legal-kg: Vietnam legal knowledge graph for legal statute identification on land law matters. In *International Conference on Computational Data and Social Networks*, pages 102–110. Springer, 2023.

43 Yue Jiang, Ziyu Guan, Jie Zhao, Wei Zhao, and Jiaqi Yang. H-legalki: a hierarchical legal knowledge integration framework for legal community question answering. In Yaser Al-Onaizan, Mohit Bansal, and Yun-Nung Chen, editors, *Findings of the Association for Computational Linguistics: EMNLP 2024*, Miami, Florida, USA, *November 12-16, 2024*, pages 14614–14625. Association for Computational Linguistics, 2024. https://aclanthology.org/2024.findings-emnlp.856.

44 Antoine Louis, Gijs van Dijck, and Gerasimos Spanakis. Interpretable long-form legal question answering with retrieval-augmented large language models. In Michael J. Wooldridge, Jennifer G. Dy, and Sriraam Natarajan, editors, *Thirty-Eighth AAAI Conference on Artificial Intelligence, AAAI 2024, Thirty-Sixth Conference on Innovative Applications of Artificial Intelligence, IAAI 2024, Fourteenth Symposium on Educational Advances in Artificial Intelligence, EAAI 2014*, February 20-27, 2024, *Vancouver, Canada*, pages 22266–22275. AAAI Press, 2024. https://doi.org/10.1609/AAAI.V38I20.30232.

45 Gayle McElvain, George Sanchez, Seán Matthews, Don Teo, Filippo Pompili, and Tonya Custis. Westsearch plus: a non-factoid question-answering system for the legal domain. In Benjamin Piwowarski, Max Chevalier, Éric Gaussier, Yoelle Maarek, Jian-Yun Nie, and Falk Scholer, editors, *Proceedings of the 42nd International ACM SIGIR Conference on Research and Development in Information Retrieval, SIGIR 2019*, Paris, France, *July 21–25, 2019*, pages 1361–1364. ACM, 2019. https://doi.org/10.1145/3331184.3331397.

46 Yanran Tang, Ruihong Qiu, Hongzhi Yin, Xue Li, and Zi Huang. Caselink: Inductive graph learning for legal case retrieval. In Grace Hui Yang, Hongning Wang, Sam Han, Claudia Hauff, Guido Zuccon, and Yi Zhang, editors, *Proceedings of the 47th International ACM SIGIR Conference on Research and Development in*

Information Retrieval, SIGIR 2024, Washington DC, USA, *July 14-18, 2024*, pages 2199–2209. ACM, 2024. https://doi.org/10.1145/3626772.3657693.

47 Haitao Li, Qingyao Ai, Jia Chen, Qian Dong, Yueyue Wu, Yiqun Liu, Chong Chen, and Qi Tian. SAILER: structure-aware pre-trained language model for legal case retrieval. In Hsin-Hsi Chen, Wei-Jou (Edward) Duh, Hen-Hsen Huang, Makoto P Kato, Josiane Mothe, and Barbara Poblete, editors, *Proceedings of the 46th International ACM SIGIR Conference on Research and Development in Information Retrieval, SIGIR 2023*, Taipei, Taiwan, *July 23-27, 2023*, pages 1035–1044. ACM, 2023. https://doi.org/10.1145/3539618.3591761.

48 Chenlong Deng, Kelong Mao, and Zhicheng Dou. Learning interpretable legal case retrieval via knowledge-guided case reformulation. *arXiv preprint arXiv:2406.19760*, 2024.

49 Yixiao Ma, Yueyue Wu, Weihang Su, Qingyao Ai, and Yiqun Liu. Caseencoder: a knowledge-enhanced pre-trained model for legal case encoding. In Houda Bouamor, Juan Pino, and Kalika Bali, editors, *Proceedings of the 2023 Conference on Empirical Methods in Natural Language Processing, EMNLP 2023*, Singapore, *December 6–10, 2023*, pages 7134–7143. Association for Computational Linguistics, 2023. https://doi.org/10.18653/V1/2023.EMNLP-MAIN.441.

50 Jaspreet Singh Dhani, Ruchika Bhatt, Balaji Ganesan, Parikshet Sirohi, and Vasudha Bhatnagar. Similar cases recommendation using legal knowledge graphs. *arXiv preprint arXiv:2107.04771*, 2021.

51 Zihan Huang, Charles Low, Mengqiu Teng, Hongyi Zhang, Daniel E Ho, Mark S Krass, and Matthias Grabmair. Context-aware legal citation recommendation using deep learning. In *Proceedings of the Eighteenth InterNational Conference on Artificial Intelligence and Law*, pages 79–88, 2021.

52 Ali Sadeghian, Laksshman Sundaram, Daisy Zhe Wang, William F Hamilton, Karl Branting, and Craig Pfeifer. Automatic semantic edge labeling over legal citation graphs. *Artificial Intelligence and Law*, 26: 127–144, 2018.

53 Chu Fei Luo, Rohan Bhambhoria, Samuel Dahan, and Xiaodan Zhu. Prototype-based interpretability for legal citation prediction, 2023. https://arxiv.org/abs/2305.16490.

54 Jie Wang, Kanha Bansal, Ioannis Arapakis, Xuri Ge, and Joemon M. Jose. Empowering legal citation recommendation via efficient instruction-tuning of pre-trained language models. In Nazli Goharian, Nicola Tonellotto, Yulan He, Aldo Lipani, Graham McDonald, Craig Macdonald, and Iadh Ounis, editors, *Advances in Information Retrieval - 46th European Conference on Information Retrieval, ECIR 2024*, Glasgow, UK, March 24-28, 2024, *Proceedings, Part I*, volume 14608 of *Lecture Notes in Computer Science*, pages 310–324. Springer, 2024. https://doi.org/10.1007/978-3-031-56027-9_19.

55 George Hannah, Rita T Sousa, Ioannis Dasoulas, and Claudia d'Amato. A prompt engineering approach and a knowledge graph based framework for tackling legal implications of large language model answers. *arXiv preprint arXiv:2410.15064*, 2024.

56 Shuting Wang, Zhen Lei, and Wang-Chien Lee. Exploring legal patent citations for patent valuation. In *Proceedings of the 23rd ACM International Conference on Conference on Information and Knowledge Management*, pages 1379–1388, 2014.

Index

Note: Page numbers in *italics* and **bold** refers to figures and tables respectively.

Neurosymbolic AI: Foundations and Applications, First Edition. Edited by Alvaro Velasquez et al.

Printed and bound by CPI Group (UK) Ltd, Croydon, CR0 4YY
04/08/2026
14935743-0002